ENGLAND IN 1819

ENGLAND IN 1819

*The Politics of
Literary Culture and the
Case of Romantic Historicism*

JAMES CHANDLER

THE UNIVERSITY OF CHICAGO PRESS

CHICAGO AND LONDON

JAMES CHANDLER is professor of English language and literature
at the University of Chicago

The University of Chicago Press, Chicago 60637
The University of Chicago Press, Ltd., London
© 1998 by The University of Chicago
All rights reserved. Published 1998
Printed in the United States of America
07 06 05 04 03 02 01 00 99 98   1 2 3 4 5
ISBN: 0-226-10108-8 (cloth)

Library of Congress Cataloging-in-Publication Data

Chandler, James.
    England in 1819 : the politics of literary culture and the case of
romantic historicism / James Chandler.
        p.   cm.
    Includes bibliographical references and index.
    ISBN 0-226-10108-8 (alk. paper)
    1. English literature—19th century—History and criticism.
    2. Politics and literature—Great Britain—History—19th century.
    3. Literature and history—England—History—19th century.
    4. Peterloo Massacre, Manchester, England, 1819.   5. England—
Civilization—19th century.   6. Great Britain—History—1789–1820.
    7. Historicism in literature.   8. Romanticism—Great Britain.
    I. Title.
    PR457.C39   1998
    820.9'358—dc21   97-24564
                                                                              CIP

⊗ The paper used in this publication meets the minimum requirements of the
American National Standard for Information Sciences—Permanence of Paper for
Printed Library Materials, ANSI Z39.48—1984.

For Becky

Contents

PART ONE
The "Historical Situation" of Romanticism

Section One   Writing Historicism, Then and Now

Illustrations

Preface

This project began, more or less straightforwardly, as a commentary on a moment in the history of a literary culture. My aim was to explain historically the quantity and quality of extraordinary writings produced in a relatively brief epoch by a number of British writers we call "Romantic." Over time, I grew more concerned with an analysis of what it means, in the context of current critical practice, to identify "a moment in the history of a literary culture" as one's object of study. I found myself asking questions, no doubt like many of my contemporaries, about what we do when we "date" a literary work. What exactly do we think we learn in establishing its time and place? What happens as one mediates the act of reading with the knowledge of such specifics? Has does such mediation affect our understanding of what a literary work "represents"? Under what circumstances do we consider literary texts representative of specific cultures (as opposed to, say, "life," "the world," or "human nature")? If there is a politics of literary culture, or a sense of public stakes in literary representation, then what political consequences follow, if any do, from various ways of taking a work's specific time and place into account when we read it?

In the end, the book became an attempt to understand the relation of the epoch with which I began, let us call it "England in 1819," to the categories of analysis implicit in the questions I brought to it. It became a study in the cultural history of our cultural-historical literary practices, a retrospective on the politics of literary representation in a regime of historicism. This, in turn, meant that its questions also changed in kind and scope. One that stands out is the very large question of the point of studying the writings of British Romanticism in the first place: what makes such a pursuit worthwhile? Part of my answer is that we should study the these writings, and study them in relation to the conditions in which they were produced, precisely to discover the historical formation, the "datedness," of some of our now-familiar categories of analysis. Another part

of it is that we should study them so that we can avail ourselves more deliberately of their conceptual resources, their literary-historical possibilities, their
sentimental reflexivity, and their capacity to give pleasure.

In recent decades, British Romanticism has more often been understood as
a critical object of historical analysis than as an enabling framework for it. Its
achievements have been understood as poetical, and its poetry chiefly transcendental—or self-deceived (depending on one's point of view). Meanwhile, historicism itself—or one brand of it—has generally been traced to developments
on the Continent, and especially to German thinkers such as Hegel. In arguing
for the peculiar relevance of literature in Britain's post-Waterloo period to
present-day critical and pedagogical practices, therefore, I am working doubly
against the grain. That is, I argue that the writings of England in 1819 are in important instances distinctively historicist—but also that they are, in their historicism, distinctively British, in the sense that they arise from a distinctively
British position in then-contemporary world culture. This is a position from
which it was possible, for example, to register the historical and geographical
peculiarity of "manners" in different stages and stations around the world. Even
a writer like Keats, who did not much travel until after his major work, could
read descriptive accounts of other ways of life in hundreds of narratives of
"travels," "journeys," and "residences" in foreign places.

Of course, except in their sheer volume, travel accounts were themselves
nothing new in English culture. The Earl of Shaftesbury had warned young
British readers of the deleterious effects of such writings more than a hundred
years before, but informed British readers of Keats's time found themselves in
quite novel relations to manners and to the issue of how manners were to be understood. This was so because such readers would have had to come to terms
not only with what Burke famously called the revolution in manners in France
but also, as I emphasize here, with the new constitution of manners in American society and the new theorization of manners in the work of the Scottish
Enlightenment. To think through these new developments, astute and literate
observers of the current scene such as Keats or Byron or Anna Barbauld or
William Cobbett had to attend to the question of how manners are meaning-
fully coded into "systems of manners" or cultures. They also had to attend to the
further question of how we give meaning to such cultures—and to the texts
that mediate or "represent" them—in the act of assigning such cultures or such
texts a date of place.

Overall, then, I aim to show how our undertheorized concept of the "historical situation" can be situated in a history of Romanticism. Questions about
the scale on which we conceive of a historical situation's assigned date of place

are much exercised in what follows. *England in 1819,* the title of the famous sonnet by Shelley from which I have borrowed my own title, is obviously the cultural assignment with which I am most concerned, though I date situations on other scales as well. What I claim to read in *England in 1819,* in effect, are historiographical preconditions that make our own (my own) historicism practicable. In arguing that claim, I show how a new and urgent sense of contemporaneity was implicated in writings for the "reform of representation," a campaign that was thought to lead Britain to the brink of revolution in 1819. I explain how this new sense of period—involved with what might be called "comparative contemporaneities"—quickly took shape in the rash of literary invention on the theme of "the spirit of the age." I pay careful attention to the writings on this topic, explicit discussions of the post-Waterloo period and less explicit discussions of decades prior, for I contend that they tell us much about the periodizing and contextualizing practices of our contemporary "return to history" in literary studies.

As a way of suggesting the book's various forms of reflexivity, one might make a rough distinction—following R. G. Collingwood, Dominick LaCapra, and others—between two modes of thinking about history and textuality. In one mode, the text has a "documentary" function; it refers and informs the historian about some state of affairs in the past. In the other mode, the text has an effective or what LaCapra calls a "worklike" function, critically constructing or reconstructing the given in history and foregrounding the historian's "transferential" relation in the dialogue with the past. To begin with, I attempt to read the texts of England in 1819 (beginning with Shelley's sonnet) in both documentary and "worklike" terms. The failure to recognize the documentary aspect of these texts on the part of some close readers has resulted in a failure to understand how they participate in a self-consciously historicist literary culture, a culture dominated by a massively influential new literary form, Scott's historical novel, which began to sweep across Britain, America, and the Continent in the years just before 1819. By the same token, the failure to recognize the "worklike" aspects of these texts on the part of some historicists has resulted in the loss of a resource for understanding literary culture in terms that resist both a pre-Enlightenment paradigm of historical exemplification (where examples need not respect historical epochs) and its Hegelian revision (where examples must respect historical epochs). Scott's innovative form of historical representation, for example, finally does not, contrary to Georg Lukács's influential account, reduce to Hegel's theoretical categories. That is partly because, like others who made Romantic historicism what it was in Britain (few of them proper historians), Scott was so self-consciously "literary" in his historiographical practice.

Beyond this twofold argument, however, I press for a way of historicizing the very distinction between the documentary and the worklike aspects of texts. That is, I try to show that some such distinction is already operating in the politicized literary culture of England in 1819—as in the instance of Shelley's profoundly difficult argument that contemporary poets were determined by the spirit of the age to become the unacknowledged legislators of the world. The emergence of this distinction—between writings as marking and making history—is a crucial part of what *defines* the new concept of culture and what now, as then, underwrites historicist interpretation. The paradoxes and possibilities of that distinction, and thus the practicalities of what I call the "historiographical-ethnographical correlation," are very much what is coming into being in the account I have to offer.

That account has been a long time in the writing and will not be brief in the reading. Although part 1 of the book attempts to sustain a continuous analysis of the relation between our notion of the "historical situation" and its emergence in the historical situation of Romanticism, the argument of these four chapters remains an extended prolegomenon to the cases I take up in part 2. Conversely, while the case studies that form the chapters of part 2 all attempt to produce a reading of England in 1819, whatever force they have as an ensemble depends very much on the capacity of the arguments of part 1 to, as it were, encase them. Part 2 is a book-within-a-book, but not a book-in-itself.

Within part 1, the first section, "Writing Historicism, Then and Now," tries to establish a way of talking about "dated specificity" in literary-cultural studies that makes patent the repetition between the "spirit of the age" discourse of British Romanticism and the contemporary discourse of the "return to history" in the Anglo-American academy. The second section, "Romanticism in the Representative State," moves from the notion of historical culture implicit in that "dated specificity" to consider the representation practices that such a notion of culture presupposes or demands. Representative anecdote, literary specimen, "text of culture," and historical "case": all these notions, crucial to contemporary criticism, undergo a decisive transformation, well registered in certain works of 1819, in the period of Britain's self-conscious literary struggles over how to represent itself. I try both to outline a conceptual structure in the ambitious public writings of Bentham and Shelley that I call a "casuistry of the general will" and to show how such a formation emerges from the historicization of the ethical and juridical "case." Then, having established how one might understand England in 1819 as a historical case, its literature as a historicizing casuistry, I turn in part 2's first section "Cases, Causes, Casuistries," to explicate a series of works, all produced or consumed in that year, as cases in respect to that larger frame of reference. The last section takes the case of Shelley, and his own ostentatiously prophetic way of taking historical cases, as an occasion for raising further questions about the entire scene of Romantic historicism as I have depicted it. All five of the cases I review in part 2 as I present them—those of Scott's fiction, Byron's *Don Juan,* Keats's "psychological" poetry, the U.S. culture of Irving's "English Writers," and, most explicitly, Shelley's casuistical work of 1819—share not only a self-consciously historical sense of their constitution as cases and casuistries, but also an uncanny capacity to anticipate late-twentieth century attempts to historicize them.

The introduction to the book as a whole sets out the vocabulary that will serve as both apparatus and object of study, including especially such terms as "situation," "case," and "casuistry." It also outlines the reasons for needing to re-visit the intellectual history of new historicism itself in order to understand how the newly dated specificity of literary studies came to be what it is. Having argued for a more avowed relationship between the forms of historical representation we deploy and those we unwittingly imitate, I introduce the figure of the Irish poet, Thomas Moore, as a kind of "mediocre hero" of the sort that we find in the new historical novels of the post-Waterloo period, an Edward Waverley or Natty Bummpo. Moore was simply everywhere one looked in the literary scene here called "England in 1819." I present him not exactly as a "case" but rather as a character whose interaction with the texts and authors addressed in part 2 helps to organize them within the daily life of a historical situation.

While I hope, naturally, that every reader who picks it up will read this book in its entirety—still better, at one sitting—I recognize that such a hope might be a little unrealistic. Not only is the book long by conventional standards, it also addresses several kinds of readers, in view of several kinds of uses. Readers with critical and literary-historical interests in the study of Anna Barbauld, Byron, Cobbett, Hazlitt, Irving, Keats, Thomas Moore, Scott, Percy Shelley, and Mary Tighe will find sustained—and, in some cases, multiple—discussions and analyses of their works here. Such readers will gain a reasonably clear sense of the frameworks I have developed for any of these authors if they read the introduction and chapters 2 through 4. Readers interested more generally, but still primarily, in Romanticism or in British literary culture of the late- eighteenth and early-nineteenth centuries should find most of the book germane, but they too may choose to skip or skim chapter 1, which takes its starting point in contemporary American cultural criticism and theory. It will be clear that this is by no means a book intended solely for Romanticists, however, and the argument I am making about Romantic historicism is also for students of poetry, fiction, and drama more generally—and indeed of literary history more broadly. Beyond the larger field of literary studies, indeed, I also aspire to reach readers with interests primarily in other disciplines—some historians, certainly, and perhaps a few anthropologists as well. Such readers further afield will find, I hope, that the way I have broached the inaugurating questions of chapter 1 will provide some means of access into the later discussions, even as those later discussions become more particularized.

I have been emboldened to offer an argument so large in scope, and so at large in its movement among the Humanities, in good part on the strength of those on whom I have relied for help in writing it. It is a badge of honor to be indebted to the likes of them. My students in "England in 1819" and related courses have been patient in helping me to develop lines of argument in class discussions that not only often began with hard questions but sometimes ended with the posing of others. The faculty at Chicago are known for their relish of interdisciplinary conversation, and I have profited much from this great resource both inside and outside the English Department—especially from those members of the Committee on Critical Practice on whom I once tried to pass off a brief and half-cooked version of the argument of chapters 1–3. Jean and John Comaroff, Norma Field, Michael Geyer, Miriam Hansen, Rashid Khalidi, Tom Mitchell, Moishe Postone, and Bill Sewell were among those who gave specific advice about what further cooking it needed. Away from Chicago, sometimes far away, I have delivered versions of other chapters at various venues over the decade from 1986 to 1996: parts of chapter 2 at Amman, Canberra, Melbourne, Exeter, and Northwestern; part of chapter 3 at Harvard; part of chapter 4 at Cambridge and Caltech; parts of chapter 5 at Johns Hopkins and Edinburgh; a part of chapter 6 at Hofstra; a part of chapter 7 at Texas; parts of chapter 8 at Indiana, Dartmouth, and Strathclyde; and an early version of chapter 10 at UCLA. On these occasions, I have relied not only on the kindness of strangers but also on the hospitality of friends and the intellectual generosity of all: of Marilyn Butler, for example, whose knowledge of Romantic literary history is matched by her great willingness to share it.

The book benefitted enormously from superb and speedy readers reports by Alan Liu and Mary Poovey. Prior to that late stage, a number of colleagues and friends whom I have burdened with requests to read work-in-progress came back with searching criticisms and sage counsel. Robert Ferguson, Kevin Gilmartin, Beth Helsinger, Paul Hunter, Alice Levine, Saree Makdisi, Richard Maxwell, Iain McCalman, Jerry McGann, Robert Pippin, Laura Rigal, Fiona Robertson, Marshall Sahlins, Jay Schleusener, Stuart Tave, and Katie Trumpener made telling critical contributions to individual chapters. Others took on larger portions of this book and responded in ways that helped me wrestle the whole of it into shape. From their diverse angles of approach, Homi Bhabha, Julie Carlson, Harry Harootunian, Janel Mueller, Larry Rothfield, Terry Turner, and Alison Winter spelled out numerous suggestions that improved the chances that my argument could stand up to their kinds of strenuous reading. Celeste Langan managed a revelatory scanning of the whole manuscript that saved me from numerous errors, especially of omission, at the eleventh hour. My largest intellectual debt, unquestionably, is to Bill Brown, whose faith in this project was exceeded only by the strength of his commitment, and by the depth of his capacity, to help me realize its possibilities. Scarcely a page of this book stands unimproved by his work and wisdom. I first heard the term "historicism" from my wife, Elizabeth O'Connor Chandler, long before it became a fashionable topic, though that is not why this book is lovingly dedicated to her. Nor could I begin to explain my gratitude here. As for Catherine and Michael (whose day will come), it must have felt to them at times that this book was *begun* in 1819. Their patience was a boon to its eventual completion—then again, so was their impatience.

An NEH Fellowship helped to launch this book by supporting a year's work at the British Library. I am grateful to the Institute of Historical Research of the University of London for affiliating me that year and to Philip Gossett, Dean of Humanities at Chicago, for an additional quarter's research time to finish some of the writing. For help with myriad day-to-day library tasks, I thank my successive work-study student assistants, all of whom worked hard and skillfully feigned interest when I tried out new arguments with them: Karen Neumer, Deborah Weiss, John Chaimov, Karen DiNal, and Gina Di Giovanni. Noel Jackson responded ably to a late call for extra help. For the last two years, Mary Lass Stewart not only assumed diverse research tasks but also remained steadfast in the push against each deadline for manuscript revision and preparation. Kathleen Chandler Roszell and Jasmina Brankovic patiently combed the page-proofs for errors. At the University of Chicago Press, I thank Alan Thomas for his willingness to read and discuss my work, since it made his support for it the more meaningful, Randy Petillos (once a student in "England in 1819") for his care with details, and Joe Parsons for his heroic efforts in the face of so much copy editing.

A note on texts and citations. Where clearly standard editions exist for repeatedly cited works, I have tried to use them. Shelley continues to pose a problem, and I have solved it by the usual combination of older and more recent editions. A major new edition of Scott's Waverley novels is in progress from the Edinburgh University Press, based on first editions rather than on the Magnum edition of 1830. Where the new edition exists, I have cited it; where not, I have cited by chapter reference to the first edition.

Parts of chapter 3 appeared in somewhat different form in my "Representative Men, Spirits of the Age, and Other Romantic Types," in *Romantic Revolutions: Criticism and Theory,* ed. Kenneth R. Johnston, Gilbert Chaitin, Karen Hanson, and Herbert Marks (Bloomington: Indiana University Press, 1990), pp. 104–32. Chapter 5 included material from "Scott and the Scene of Explanation: Framing Contextuality in *The Bride of Lammermoor,*" *Studies in the Novel* 26, no. 2 (Summer 1994): 69–98 (© 1994 The University of North Texas). Chapter 6 includes material from "Man Fell with Apples: The Moral Mechanics of *Don Juan,*" in *Rereading Byron,* ed. Alice Levine and Robert N. Keane (New York: Garland Publishing, 1993), pp. 67–86. All are reprinted by permission of the publisher. A substantially similar version of chapter 8 is scheduled to appear in *American Literary History* 10 (Winter 1998). I reworked some material from chapter 2 for my contribution on "Romantic Historicism" to the *Oxford Companion to British Romanticism* ed. Iain McCalman (Oxford: Oxford University Press, forthcoming).

Abbreviations

BLJ   *Byron's Letters and Journals.* Edited by Leslie A. Marchand, 12 vols. Cambridge, Mass.: Harvard University Press, 1973–1982.

CPWB   George Gordon, Lord Byron, *The Complete Poetical Works.* Edited by Jerome J. McGann, 7 vols. Oxford: Clarendon Press, 1980–1993.

CWWH   *The Collected Works of William Hazlitt.* Edited by P. P. Howe, 21 vols. London and Toronto: J. M. Dent & Sons, 1931.

GM   Kenneth Burke, *A Grammar of Motives.* Berkeley and Los Angeles: University of California Press, 1969.

Iv   Walter Scott, *Ivanhoe; a Romance,* 1st ed. Edinburgh: Archibald Constable, 1819.

LJK   *Letters of John Keats, 1814–1821.* Edited by Hyder E. Rollins, 2 vols. Cambridge, Mass.: Harvard University Press, 1958.

LPBS   Percy Bysshe Shelley, *Letters.* Edited by Frederick L. Jones, 2 vols. Oxford: Clarendon Press, 1964.

JTM   *Journal of Thomas Moore.* Edited by Wilfred S. Dowden, 6 vols. (Newark, Del.: University of Delaware Press, 1983–91.

LYL   Anna Laetitia Barbauld, *A Legacy for Young Ladies.* London: Longman, 1826.

PJK   John Keats, *Complete Poems.* Edited by Jack Stillinger. Cambridge, Mass.: Harvard University Press, 1982.

Redg   Walter Scott, *Redgauntlet,* 1st ed. Edinburgh: Constable, 1824.

SPP   *Shelley's Poetry and Prose: Authoritative Texts, Criticism.* Edited by D. H. Reiman and Sharon B. Powers. New York: W. W. Norton, 1977.

TML1   Walter Scott, "Tales of My Landlord", 1st ed., 4 vols. Edinburgh: Constable, 1816.

TML2   Scott, "Tales of My Landlord", 2d ser., 1st ed., 4 vols. Edinburgh: Constable, 1818.

TML3   Scott, "Tales of My Landlord", 3d ser., 1st ed., 4 vols. Edinburgh: Constable, 1819.

Wav   Walter Scott, *Waverly; or, 'Tis Sixty Years Since,* 1st ed. Edinburgh: Consta-
             ble, 1814.
WPBS   *The Complete Works of Percy Bysshe Shelley.* Edited by Roger Ingpen and
             Walter E. Peck, 10 vols. London: Ernest Benn, 1926–30.

ENGLAND IN 1819

Introduction: Works and Days

This is a book about a somewhat remote period in the history of British literary culture but also, less directly, about the current period in Anglo-American literary criticism. The remote period, the one we call "Romantic," is an age for which literary historians have produced what Claude Lévi-Strauss terms a "hot chronology," an age that, because of what we take to be its peculiar eventfulness, we use many dates to record.[1] A simple index of the Romantic period's chronological temperature appears in those standard anthologies and textbooks in which Romanticism has been granted an amplitude of materials and references far out of proportion to its nominal duration: in spite of the relatively brief span of years to which it is usually assigned (say, 1790–1830), it has not been uncommon to see Romanticism given more pages for its representative writings, closer attention to its literary activity, than the nominally longer literary-historical periods that tend to appear on either side of it. Within the momentous period of Romanticism, this book pays especially close attention to the extraordinary array of literary work from a particularly momentous year. This is the year of "Peterloo," a name given by journalists to what took place on August 16 in St. Peter's Field, Manchester, four years after the defeat of Napoleon at Waterloo began to shift national attention from military to domestic crises. Peterloo was a massacre, widely represented in the public press, of unarmed women, men, and children taking part in a peaceable assembly, 60,000 strong, to protest the present state of Parliamentary representation. The literary coverage of this event was a challenging representation of a challenge to representation, and therein lay its contagious intensity.

England in 1819 thus might be said to frame the events of one hot chronol-

---

1. Claude Lévi-Strauss, *The Savage Mind* (Chicago: University of Chicago Press, 1966) p. 259. This is the standard English translation of *La Pensée Sauvage* (Paris: Librairie Plon, 1962).

Figure 1. A "representation" of the great Manchester meeting for the reform of representation, August 16, 1819, J. Slack, Central Library, Manchester, Local Studies Unit

ogy within those of another. In a fashion that I mean to make explicit, however, this book also dramatizes its participation in the recent "return to history" in literary studies, an effort to read texts in representative relation to the dated historical situation in which they were produced and once consumed.[2] The relation between contemporary critical historicism and the literature of Romanticism has been presented variously in the commentaries, but many historicist arguments of the last decade and a half, including some of my own, have offered themselves as critical renunciations of a Romanticism they deem dehistoricizing. In the present study, that relation will tend to appear more as repetition than renunciation. I will argue that it is precisely by our work of situating Romantic writings historically that we share their blindness, their ideology. Thus, our critical renunciations of Romanticism must be understood as a repetition of a cer-

2. In this preliminary definition of the historicism of the recent "return to history," I am preparing for the way in which I want to trace its contemporary emergence beyond the work of Louis Althusser and Michel Foucault to the prior debate between Lévi-Strauss and Sartre, which seems to me largely to have set the terms for what has followed.

tain kind. Indeed, it is a kind of repetition that might be said to involve a change in kind itself, as in Marx's suggestion that history indeed repeats itself but undergoes a change of genres from tragedy to farce when it does so.

In Marx's celebrated account of the 1848 revolution in France, *The Eighteenth Brumaire of Louis Bonaparte,* the central conceit depends on the repeatability of specific dated events (including the Napoleonic coup of 1799 named by Marx's title) in the form of a text that changes generic mode from tragedy to farce.[3] My concern here is with a repetition of the discourse of dated specificity as such—the discourse, that is, to which the "return to history" itself unwittingly returns. To recognize this repetition—between the writings of the post–French Revolution period in Britain and the critical categories of our own moment—we must acknowledge some of the precise and characteristic ways in which what we now call "British Romanticism" was itself constituted as a practice of specifying the dated state of historical cultures in and as literary texts: the "England in 1819" of my title names both a poem and its contemporary site. Such a specifying practice was indeed an enabling condition for Marx's virtuoso analysis of the meaning of the great "days" of 1848–51. In its turn, however, Marx's account of 1848 became an absolutely seminal text for the two great theorists of the date in our own time, Lévi-Strauss and his rival, Sartre. Their early 1960s controversy about "history" figures crucially in my meditations on method in what follows. And it must do so, I argue, because it figures so formatively—if, again, often unwittingly—in the critical practice of my academic generation.

To a far greater degree than 1848 in France, the year of Peterloo in British history was exceptional for the recorded volume, value, and topical vicinity of the body of literary work it produced in a range of genres and forms. Many of these writings tend to be self-conscious about the collective mobilization of literary talent and energy in which they participated; some make it an explicit topic of their own work. Like the literature of the larger period we call Romanticism, but with a particular intensity, English writing from 1819 is aware of its place in and as history. Much literary work *of* England in 1819, in other words, seems concerned with its place *in* England in 1819—concerned, that is, with a national operation of self-dating, or -redating, that is meant to count as a national self-making, or -remaking. It is concerned with historical specificity

3. Marx's celebrated opening words at once explicate his title and announce his analytic theme: "Hegel remarks somewhere that all facts and personages of great importance in world history occur, as it were, twice. He forgot to add: the first time as tragedy, the second as farce." *The Eighteenth Brumaire of Louis Bonaparte* (New York: International Publishers, 1977), p. 15.

understood as the product of a political activity and with that activity of specifying as it takes place in literary representation itself. Rephrasing the point in
terms I will subsequently develop, one might say my concern is with writings
that seek to state *the case of the nation*—and to do so in such a way as to alter its
case. One might even say that such writings shift the case of the nation from
the nominative (the case of the name) to the accusative (the case of the cause):
they take on the national cause. However we phrase it, the political motive of
such writing was sufficiently clear to members of the British Parliament that
by year's end they would pass legislation to curb severely the capacity of public writing to affect what was called, suggestively, "the state of the representation."

I try to address the literary activity of England in 1819 at least partly by way
of examining that activity's own historical self-representation. To this end I
eventually set forth a series of cases in Romantic cultural historiography—that
is, cases in what I will describe as a newly historicized mode of Romantic casuistry. The terms of this discussion—*history, culture, period, movement, repetition,
situation, specificity, state, date, text, kind, case,* and *casuistry*—might be said to form
both a mode and target of analysis, a part at once of my subject and apparatus,
and thus to sustain a certain reflexivity throughout. Among the various justifi-
cations I will give for this reflexivity, one of the crudest and yet most important
will have to do with the renewed importance attached in contemporary Anglo-
American public commentary to the politics and pedagogy of literary culture.
Why, in a moment self-conscious of its proliferating media of cultural dissemination, political controversy should develop around the issue of *literary* culture
is a question that is difficult to answer.[4] At the heart of these debates, it seems
fair to say, are two questions of representation: which persons speak for whom
in the classroom, and which texts speak for whom in the canon?

The implied relationship between them—between the politics of representation in the conduct of literary discussion and the politics of representativeness in the choice of literary texts—becomes more intelligible when it is
historicized in a Romantic-period discourse where political and literary representation are innovatively articulated together.[5] In the years around 1800,

---

4. For three recent accounts of these debates, see Gerald Graff, *Beyond the Culture Wars* (New
York: Norton, 1992); John Guillory, *Cultural Capital: The Politics of Literary Canon Formation*
(Chicago: University of Chicago Press, 1993); and Michael Berube, *Public Access: Literary Theory
and American Cultural Politics* (London: Verso, 1994).

5. As Judith Butler puts the point in the context of contemporary debates within feminism,
if the "critical point of departure is *the historical present,*" we must understand that "the task is not
to refuse representational politics." "The juridical structures of language and politics constitute

British writers and publishers institutionalize the literary-cultural "specimen," a piece of work whose representative status could be contested in the most heated political terms.[6] A recurrent juxtaposition of literary and political representational practices, more generally, is one of the distinctive novelties of the Romantic era, the period Hannah Arendt saw dominated by the "pathos of novelty" itself.[7] I should add that the most important novelty of that time for Arendt is the invention of the American political system, for, within the hot chronology of the period, this figures prominently in much of the British writing about representation, political and literary, that I review here. According to Marx's logic, the repetition of the public discourse of Romantic humanism within the contemporary academic discourse of the Humanities must involve a shift from one genre to another. Whether we must regard writings of the so-called age of revolution as "tragic" or our own academic practice as "farcical" are questions I take to be related but still, both of them, unresolved.

As one way of sketching the contexts in which the topics of this book are kept reflexively in play, let me describe in some detail the teaching experiment from the early 1980s in which this book had its genesis. The experiment was an effort to heighten the sense of historical specificity in a graduate course on Romantic Poetry, while at the same time preserving the widely acknowledged gains of a residual New-Critical discussion pedagogy, by clustering course readings around the years 1798 and 1819. At the time—for convenience we can call it 1981—I was only partly aware of the intellectual culture that conditioned such a revision. I knew that literary pedagogy was changing rapidly. In a paper he gave at Chicago that year for example, Edward Said was already worrying the question of how, in the face of changing critical paradigms, to save what might

---

the contemporary field of power; hence, there is no position outside this field, but only a critical genealogy of its own legitimating practices." *Gender Trouble* (New York: Routledge, 1990), p. 5. Putting the question this way helps make it possible to recognize the repetition between the identity politics implicit in academic cultural studies and the identity politics implicit in writings of the Romantic period, despite the obvious difference in disposition toward, say, "nationalism"—not that what counts as a "nation" or a "society" in the period of literary culture's consolidation is itself an easy matter to settle. See, for example, Partha Chatterjee's complication of such questions, especially in respect to the role of literature and education, in *The Nation and Its Fragments. Colonial and Postcolonial Histories* (Princeton, N.J.: Princeton University Press, 1993).

6. Such was the case with the notorious controversy (over Alexander Pope's place in the national pantheon) touched off in 1819 with the publication of Thomas Campbell's *Specimens of the English Poets: With Biographical Notices, and Essay on English Poetry* (London: John Murray, 1819), which is itself an interesting specimen of the discourse of cultural specimens in this culture. I have analyzed that famous episode elsewhere, in "The Pope Controversy: Romantic Poetics and the English Canon," *Critical Inquiry* 10 (spring 1984): 481–509.

7. Hannah Arendt, *On Revolution* (Harmondsworth: Penguin, 1965), p. 34.

be thought of as democratic about the New-Critical classroom.[8] I understood that my interest in historicizing literary and cultural studies was part of a wider transformation of the field but was not yet aware that this development was about to have its own name, its own "ism." I was relatively ignorant of the extent of the more general cultural, even mass-cultural, thematization of "history" just then intensifying.[9] Nor had I gotten far in either theorizing or historicizing the notion of "specificity"—in establishing the specificity of the "specificity"—that guided my teaching efforts. Then again, the experiment itself was not exactly earthshaking, any more than its format was constraining. Part of the modest point, after all, and part of the pleasure, was to show that the narrowed temporal frame accommodated almost all of the authors and many of the texts typically included in the standard version of such a course.

The programmatic writings of Wordsworth and Coleridge, then the focus of my own research, tended to dominate the first half of the new syllabus. The second half proved both more complicated and more rewarding, and when it came time to teach Romantic poetry again, I made it stand on its own as a course entitled "England in 1819." The year 1819 witnessed both the production and publication of an extraordinary wealth of texts from the modern canon of Romantic poetry. Students of Keats and Shelley, for example, have long regarded it as the personal annus mirabilis for each of them.[10] From October 1818 to September 1819, and mostly after mid-January, Keats wrote virtually all of the poetry on which his rep-

---

8. Said's paper was later collected in W. J. T. Mitchell, ed., *The Politics of Interpretation* (Chicago: University of Chicago Press, 1983). "Leaving aside the questionable value of the New Criticism's ultimate social and moral message," Said nonetheless felt compelled to concede that "the school deliberately and perhaps incongruously tried to create a wide community of responsive readers out of a very large, potentially unlimited, constituency of students and teachers of literature" (p. 11).

9. Fredric Jameson has produced a series of valuable essays on the problem of "history" since the 1970s, and in each he links events in academic and nonacademic public spheres. See, for example, "Nostalgia for the Present," *South Atlantic Quarterly* 88 (spring 1989): 519–37. This and other related pieces have been collected in Jameson's *Signatures of the Visible* (New York: Routledge, 1994). Similar connections are made in Marlon Ross's essay "Contingent Predilections: The Newest Historicism and the Question of Method," *Centennial Review* 34 (1990): 485–538. Speculating on what it would mean to write "a new historicist history of new historicism," Ross suggests that his history "would stress 1980, the year *Renaissance Self-Fashioning* was published and the year Ronald Reagan won the presidency" (p. 509), and produces a serio-comic pastiche narrative to situate this mode of narrative situation. For a counterpart study of the state of the "past-and-present" question in Britain, see Patrick Wright, *On Living in an Old Country*. (London: Verso, 1985), and Raphael Samuels, *Theatres of Memory*. Vol. 1: *Past and Present in Contemporary Culture* (London: Verso, 1994).

10. See, for example, Robert Gittings, *John Keats: The Living Year* (Cambridge, Mass.: Harvard University Press, 1954), and Stuart Curran, *Shelley's Annus Mirabilis* (San Marino, Calif.: Huntington Library, 1975).

utation has come to stand, including the two Hyperions, all the Great Odes, *The Eve of St. Agnes, Lamia, La Belle Dame Sans Merci,* and the late sonnets. For Shelley, we can include a similarly impressive range of writing: his two mutually supplementary dramatic masterpieces, *Prometheus Unbound* and *The Cenci,* as well as the great *Ode to the West Wind.* It was in 1819, too, that Shelley produced most of the radical poetry that would later inspire English labor movements from the Chartists onward: *The Mask of Anarchy* and a number of lyrics for "a little volume of *popular songs* wholly political."[11] Before the end of the year, Shelley had also begun his extraordinary tract, *A Philosophical View of Reform,* in which he first made and explained the memorable claim, later repeated in *A Defence of Poetry,* that poets are the unacknowledged legislators of the world. Byron's high critical standing and massive popularity were well established before 1819, but even among contemporary estimates his recognized chef d'oeuvre is *Don Juan,* the poem in which, as Leigh Hunt wrote, his "real genius is to be found."[12] Byron published the first two cantos of *Don Juan* in 1819, and, before the year was out, he began a third, perhaps after having worked out a scheme for subsequent cantos as well.

This was already a substantial body of work around which to build a course of study. Since questions of biography tend to arise in reading authors of this stature, the course also made it apparent that events of 1819 proved decisive for these literary careers. I suppose this goes without saying for Keats, who not only wrote his best work during this year but had also abandoned poetry altogether before it ended. For Shelley, 1819 marked his last round of attempts to achieve the recognition and influence of a wide readership in his own time. Most of the writings I have mentioned—including *The Cenci,* the political poems, and *A Philosophical View of Reform*—comprised an explicitly popularizing campaign, and all failed of their purpose. The importance of 1819 for Byron's career lies in two decisions about the fate of *Don Juan,* one made for him, the other by him. The first is the decision of Byron's publisher, John Murray, in nervous consultation with Thomas Moore and others, about whether to risk publishing the first two cantos, in spite of the threat of prosecution.[13] They appeared on July 15, unidentified by reference either to author or to publisher.[14] The second de-

---

11. To Leigh Hunt, May 1, 1820, in Frederick L. Jones, ed. *The Letters of Percy Bysshe Shelley,* 2 vols. (Oxford: Clarendon Press, 1964), 2:191 (italics original).

12. From an 1830 review by Hunt in *The Tatler.* Cited in Edmund Blunden, *Leigh Hunt: A Biography* (London: Cobden-Sanderson, 1930), p. 241.

13. Moore reports in his journal for January 31, 1819, that he "[w]ent to breakfast with Hobhouse, in order to read Lord Byron's Poem—a strange production," having learned the day before "that Byron had desired it might be referred to my decision." JTM, 1:141, 139.

14. See Jerome McGann's comments on the significance of the title page of *Don Juan* in "Some Forms of Critical Discourse," *Critical Inquiry* 11 (March 1985): 402–406.

cision, Byron's own, was about whether to extend the project beyond the initial two cantos. Byron warns at the end of canto 1 that the future of his poem will depend on the wishes of his readers. It is not clear what does decide the issue for him, since Byron had little immediate evidence of his poem's appeal, but we do know that by the end of the year he had begun in earnest with canto 3 and probably with a design for something roughly on the scale of the more than sixteen-canto epic that would become his great literary preoccupation until his death in 1824.

Although Wordsworth's most enduring poetic work was long since behind him by 1819, he did choose the spring of that year to publish *Peter Bell,* a manifesto poem from the time of his most intense work on *Lyrical Ballads* in the spring of 1798. *Peter Bell* in turn not only became the most widely reviewed of any work he published during his lifetime but also occasioned important responses by other poets: a notoriously preemptive parody by Keats's friend, John Hamilton Reynolds, which was actually composed and published before Wordsworth's own version appeared, and the extraordinary piece of Romantic satire by Shelley, *Peter Bell the Third,* which was written later in the year. Wordsworth also produced freshly composed work in 1819, including two lyrics of the autumn after the Peterloo Massacre of August 16, both titled *September 1819,* that make an interesting contrast to the more celebrated autumn poems by Keats (*To Autumn*) and Shelley (*Ode to the West Wind*) of that same year and season.

Thus, even from the point of view of a literary history that relied on author-centered perspectives and traditional genre distinctions—the history of poetry as opposed to the history of fiction or drama—the temporal restriction to 1819 still left a great deal to work with. But that point of view was itself under long-overdue challenge by 1981, when, for example, Marilyn Butler published *Romantics, Rebels, and Reactionaries,* a historical survey of Romantic literature that showed how much was lost in such a view and how much was gained in proceeding otherwise. Certainly the six-male-poets-in-two-generations course in Romantic poetry—the program that, under the powerful influence of Harold Bloom and others, had come to dominate the teaching of Romanticism in North American graduate schools by the early 1970s—was losing its status as standard procedure. By 1981, serious efforts were being made across many periods that would change the configuration of the canon for literary study—efforts to integrate the various genres of writing into a single course, to recuperate writings by women, to blur the major-minor distinction in selecting writers and texts, and indeed to historicize the very notion of "literature" in terms of which the modern study of English has been practiced.[15] It soon became clear that a course entitled "England in 1819" could provide a very different list of readings as well as a different way of reading.

The widening of focus to prose fiction made it possible, in the first place, to read (as post-Waterloo Britain did) Walter Scott's fiction alongside the contemporary productions of the poets. Restoring Scott's place in Romantic literary culture became one of the subordinate goals of the course and remains so in this book. Scott published three novels in 1819, including two of his best—*The Bride of Lammermoor,* which J. G. Lockhart claimed Scott had dictated on what was thought to be his deathbed that summer,[16] and *Ivanhoe,* his first novel not to take Scottish history for its subject matter. Scott completed *Ivanhoe* in time for him to devote some of December to a series of published attacks on critics of the government's handling of the Peterloo Massacre (and to the raising of a counterrevolutionary militia in the Scottish Borders). One commentator, Graham McMaster, has addressed Scott's response to Peterloo by analogy with Georg Lukács's more generalized argument that, in the face of the events of 1848, many European bourgeois writers "had to either recognise and accept the new epoch that was dawning, or else be doomed to the role of apologists of a declining era": Scott, argues McMaster, "experienced a similar crisis in 1819, the year of Peterloo."[17] Scott's biographers have also tended to regard his later decline in popular-

15. Each of these changes has been accompanied by theoretical developments: in genre theory (Alastair Fowler, *Kinds of Literature: An Introduction to the Theory of Genres and Modes* [Cambridge, Mass.: Harvard University Press, 1982], and Mary Jacobus, "Apostrophe and Lyric Voice in *The Prelude*" in *Lyric Poetry: Beyond New Criticism,* ed. Chaviva Hôsek and Patricia Parker [Ithaca, N.Y.: Cornell University Press, 1985], pp. 167–81.); in feminist literary history (Sandra M. Gilbert and Susan Gubar, *The Madwoman in the Attic: The Woman Writer and the Nineteenth-Century Literary Imagination* [New Haven: Yale University Press, 1979], Margaret Homans, *Bearing the Word: Language and Female Experience in Nineteenth-Century Women's Writing* [Chicago: University of Chicago Press, 1986], and Marlon B. Ross, *The Contours of Masculine Desire: Romanticism and the Rise of Women's Poetry* [New York: Oxford University Press, 1989]); in canon theory (Gilles Deleuze and Felix Guattari, *Kafka: Toward a Minor Literature,* trans. Dana Polan [Minneapolis: University of Minnesota Press, 1986], and David Lloyd, *Nationalism and Minor Literature: James Clarence Mangan and the Emergence of Irish Cultural Nationalism* [Berkeley: University of California Press, 1987]; and on the concept of "the literary" (Philippe Lacoue-Labarthe and Jean-Luc Nancy, *The Literary Absolute: The Theory of Literature in German Romanticism,* trans. with an introduction and additional notes by Philip Barnard and Cheryl Lester [Albany: State University of New York Press, 1988]).

16. John Gibson Lockhart, *Narrative of the Life of Sir Walter Scott* (London: J. M. Dent, 1906), pp. 361–64. But see Jane Millgate's dispelling of this deathbed myth, in *Walter Scott: The Making of a Novelist* (Toronto: University of Toronto Press, 1984), pp. 169–71.

17. Graham McMaster, *Scott and Society* (Cambridge: Cambridge University Press, 1981), p. 90.

ity and his descent toward bankruptcy as beginning with the decade of the 1820s.[18] From the point of view of the domestic celebrity and sales of his novels, 1819 often figures as a kind of zenith: the year of the first collected edition of the Waverley novels and probably the peak of the frenzied renown that accompanied the publication of each of his first dozen or so novels in Britain.

At its height, the craze for Scott in Britain rose to astonishing levels. Throughout 1819, Scott's recent novels, such as *The Heart of Mid-Lothian* (1818), were not only widely consumed in England and actively exported for sale abroad in America and on the Continent, they were also instantly adapted for the stage and often dominated the theatrical scene. Within weeks after the publication of *Ivanhoe*, it was possible, for a brief time, to attend dramatic adaptations of the novel at both of London's legitimate theaters: one, simply called *Ivanhoe*, at Covent Garden, and another, called *The Hebrew* (which focused more narrowly on the novel's Isaac and Rebecca subplot) at Drury Lane. This de facto monopoly occurred in theaters all over England and Scotland. As Hazlitt put it in early 1820: "Mr. Walter Scott no sooner conjures up the Muse of old romance, and brings us acquainted with her in ancient hall, cavern, or mossy dell, than Messrs. Harris and Ellston, with all their tribe, instantly set their tailors at work to take the pattern of the dresses, their artists to paint the wildwood scenery or some proud dungeon-keep, their musicians to compose the fragments of bewildered ditties, and their penmen to connect the author's scattered narrative and broken dialogue, into a sort of theatrical join-hand."[19] In December 1819, Sydney Smith declared that Scott's novels became, at the time

---

18. Edgar Johnson summarizes as follows: "[At the end of 1819] Scott's fortunes seemed unassailable. Within a single year of widespread adversity, he had written and published one short novel . . . and two full-length novels . . . , all three selling better than any of their seven predecessors." *Sir Walter Scott: The Great Unknown,* 2 vols. (New York: Macmillan, 1970), 1:691. And Scott's own contemporary Boswell, J. G. Lockhart (his son-in-law), closes off his account of Scott's eventful year in 1819 with the following: "I cannot conclude without observing that the publication of Ivanhoe marks the most brilliant epoch in Scott's history as the literary favorite of his contemporaries. With the novel which he next put forth [*The Monastery,* 1820], the immediate sale of these works began gradually to decline; and though, even when that had reached its lowest declension, it was still far above the most ambitious dreams of any other novelist, yet the publishers were afraid the announcement of anything like a falling off might cast a damp over the spirits of the author. He was allowed to remain for several years under the impression that whatever novel he threw off commanded at once the triumphant sale of ten or twelve thousand, and was afterwards, when included in the collective edition, to be circulated in that shape also as widely as Waverley or Ivanhoe [sic]." *Narrative of the Life of Sir Walter Scott,* p. 369. The best account of the bankruptcy is John Sutherland's recent biography, *The Life of Walter Scott* (London: Blackwell, 1995), pp. 272–98.

19. William Hazlitt, "General Reporter" feature on "The Drama," *The London Magazine* 1, no. 4, (April 1820), p. 437.

of their publication, "holidays for the whole kingdom."[20] The passion for Scott's fiction at the accession of George IV was a cultural force to be reckoned with, and not even Scott's fellow literary lions were immune to it. Byron, who made a practice of reading Scott for at least an hour every day, repeatedly wrote Murray, urging him to expedite the posting of Scott's latest novels to him in Venice. Coleridge, who held no particular critical brief for Scott's novels, admitted to a penchant for rereading them.[21]

Coleridge himself, after a period of relative invisibility, produced a spate of publications in a brief space of time. *Biographia Literaria,* the *Lay Sermons, Sybilline Leaves,* and the two volume-edition of *The Friend* were all published in 1817–18 and thus, his days of lyric composition mostly behind him, established his later reputation as the "Sage of Highgate." Every week from December 1818 through March of 1819, he descended from Highgate Hill to the celebrated Crown and Anchor Tavern in the Strand to deliver his *Philosophical Lectures.* These lectures not only "mark a decisive turn in the chronology of his thought"[22] but also address perhaps the most ambitious topics ever taken up by this most ambitious of critics: the history of human thought since the Greeks.[23] The *Philosophical Lectures* alternated at the Crown and Anchor with Coleridge's famous lectures on Shakespeare, but Hazlitt was offering a concurrent (and to some extent competing) lecture series at the same venue. Once Coleridge's disciple, now a rival advancing his own reputation with an increasing pace of publication, Hazlitt brought out his *Lectures on the English Poets* in 1818 and managed to publish *Lectures on the English Comic Writers* (from the series that rivaled Coleridge's) before the year 1819 had ended. Two other important books, moreover, were published by Hazlitt in between. In March, the "great hater" published what is perhaps his most trenchant single attack in the *Letter to William Gifford,* a polemic he introduced with the bold promise to expose the editor of the *Quarterly Review* as "the Government Critic, . . . the invisible link, that connects literature with the police" (CWWH, 9:13). By the end of the

20. Cited in Johnson, *Sir Walter Scott: The Great Unknown,* 1:691.

21. Coleridge wrote as follows to Thomas Allsop in a long and critical letter about Scott on April 8, 1820: "I have read the far greater part of his Novels twice, & several three times, over with undiminished pleasure and interest." *Collected Letters,* 6 vols. Edited by Earl Leslie Griggs (Oxford: Clarendon Press, 1971), 5:33.

22. Walter Jackson Bate, *Coleridge* (New York: Macmillan, 1963), p. 181.

23. Kathleen Coburn's edition of the *Philosophical Lectures* (New York: Philosophical Library, 1949) is full of useful information about Coleridge's obsession with chronology and history in these lectures of 1819. A good expository discussion can be found in Charles de Paolo, "Coleridge and the History of Western Civilization, ca. 4004 B.C.–500 A.D.," *Clio* 14 (winter 1985): 183–203.

year, Hazlitt would also have published his first major collection of contemporary commentaries, the *Political Essays,* a crucial forerunner to the essays later collected in *The Spirit of the Age* (which begin to appear in the early 1820s).

William Cobbett, a journalist probably unrivaled in English history for his impact on his own times, and a writer widely regarded by his contemporaries as the leading British authority on the United States, published his first book on America in 1819, part of a burgeoning survey literature on that subject. Cobbett also continued to publish his *Weekly Register* from exile on Long Island until his spectacular return in November, when he disembarked at Liverpool bearing what he claimed were the remains of Thomas Paine back to their native English soil. In this same year another writer on the England-America question, Washington Irving, published his most celebrated collection of stories and essays, *The Sketch-Book of Geoffrey Crayon, Esq.,* a book that appeared almost simultaneously in America and in Britain, where Irving had gained favor with Scott and his circle at *Blackwood's Edinburgh Magazine.*

The *Sketch-Book* not only includes the famous cross-cultural "legends" of Rip Van Winkle and Sleepy Hollow but also the essay called "English Writers on America," which addresses itself precisely to the journalistic polemics that engaged Cobbett, his friends, and their adversaries. These polemics were part of a major (if now largely forgotten) controversy over the state of the American republic, and the suitability of the rapidly developing part of America known as the "Western Country"—largely the land on either side of the Ohio River between Cincinnati and the Mississippi—as a site of emigration for Britons disaffected by high taxes and the British government's resistance to parliamentary reform. This controversy about North American emigration reached a crescendo in 1819 parallel to the rising volume of debate over what was called "the internal state of the country," and it ramified widely and variously. Keats's brother George, for example, emigrated to the Western Settlement in late 1818 after reading accounts by at least one of the "English Writers" alluded to by Irving, and Keats's letters to George and his wife Georgiana in Kentucky supply a valuable key—as they once offered a spur—to the work he did in his "living year" of extraordinary composition. Finally, as various historians have noted, the year's events in journalism and in the hyperactive sphere of popular satire were carried out at extraordinary levels of intensity across the political spectrum by the likes of T. J. Wooler, William Hone, Richard Carlyle, Leigh Hunt, Francis Jeffrey, J. G. Lockhart, William Gifford, and John Wilson Croker.[24]

24. Richard D. Altick, *The English Common Reader: A Social History of the Mass Reading Public, 1800–1900* (Chicago: University of Chicago Press, 1957); Kevin Gilmartin, *Print Politics: The*

My students and I were surprised to learn that the wealth of literary production for 1819 far exceeded the capacity of a graduate course to accommodate it.[25] Yet many of these writings, across this wide range of genres, eventually found their way into one or another version of the course I called "England in 1819" (as indeed they have into this book) along with even less "literary" texts as well: records of the emergency debates on representation in the Parliament called by the Prince Regent in November; the texts of the repressive Six Acts, which Parliament voted into law on December 30, 1819; documents on England's post-Waterloo economic condition; various journalistic reports of the reform movement, its specific legal struggles, and the Peterloo Massacre; and more recent histories that emphasized the crises of 1819, such as E. P. Thompson's *The Making of the English Working Class,* which in turn generated further readings such as the moving chapters on Peterloo in Samuel Bamford's autobiography, *Passages in the Life of a Radical.* With the help of such additional documents and histories, it became possible to sketch the place of Peterloo in the social and political history of 1819 and in the renewed movement for reform after the close of the Napoleonic Wars.[26]

The plan for the great assembly at St. Peter's Field in Manchester was to have been a key action in the campaign led by Henry "Orator" Hunt and others to organize working people in London, in the north of England, and in Scotland under what Hunt called "the watchwords of freemen: Annual Parliaments and Universal Suffrage."[27] The August 16 meeting had been in preparation since Hunt's visit to Manchester in January, and the people who attended it marched

---

Press and Radical Opposition in Early Nineteenth-Century England (Cambridge: Cambridge University Press, 1996); Jon P. Klancher, *The Making of English Reading Audiences, 1790–1832* (Madison: University of Wisconsin Press, 1987); R. K. Webb, *The British Working Class Reader 1790–1848: Literacy and Social Tension* (London: George Allen and Unwin, 1955); W. Hardy Wickwar, *The Struggle for the Freedom of the Press, 1819–1832* (London: George Allen and Unwin, 1928); and Marcus Wood, *Radical Satire and Print Culture* (Oxford: Oxford University Press, 1994). For important studies of radical culture more generally at this time, see Iain McCalman, *Radical Underworld, Revolutionaries, and Pornographers in London: 1795–1840* (Cambridge: Cambridge University Press, 1988); and James Epstein, *Radical Expression: Political Language, Ritual, and Symbol in England, 1790–1850* (New York: Oxford University Press, 1994).

25. This is not yet to speak of volumes of poetry produced by then-major, now-minor writers such as George Crabbe, Felicia Hemans, Leigh Hunt, Thomas Moore, and Samuel Rogers.

26. I discuss the cultural significance of 1815, including its occasioning of the resumed reform movement, in "'Wordsworth' after Waterloo," in *The Age of William Wordsworth,* ed. Kenneth Johnston and Gene Ruoff (New Brunswick, N.J.: Rutgers University Press, 1987), pp. 84–111, especially pp. 102–111.

27. Banners bearing these same slogans were carried at the great public demonstrations, including Peterloo. See Samuel Bamford, *Passages in the Life of a Radical* (Oxford: Oxford University Press, 1984), p. 146.

to the meeting grounds in disciplined phalanxes, subdivided into platoons according to their place of dwelling in or around Lancashire. They had rehearsed, drilled, for weeks. The explicit aim of the planners was to produce a spectacle unprecedented in its display of organization and strength, and the rhetoric of the "unexampled" incident became very much a part of the coverage of Peterloo and its aftermath.[28] The massive numbers and premeditated orderliness of the demonstrators assembled on this occasion and others like it in 1819 prompted government mistrust and would have gained widespread public recognition even in the absence of violence. This public recognition was in turn registered by Shelley (who was tracking events largely through newspaper accounts sent to him in Italy) in the slogan he made the refrain for *The Mask of Anarchy:* "Ye are many, they are few" (SPP, 301–10).

The terrible story of Peterloo is well known to students of nineteenth-century British history. Just as Hunt began to address the assembled multitude in St. Peter's field, they were attacked by the Manchester Yeomanry. This local militia was backed up in the course of the action by the Fifteenth Regiment of British Hussars, veterans of Waterloo, many of whom were wearing medals won in the campaign against Napoleon. Although the presence of the Hussars gave the massacre its notorious nickname, most of the damage was done by the Yeomanry itself, as Samuel Bamford, who had organized the Stockton platoon, movingly recalled in his blow-by-blow history of the first minutes of violence:

> "Stand fast," I said, "they are riding upon us, stand fast." And there was a general cry in our quarter of "Stand fast." The cavalry were in confusion: they evidently could not, with all the weight of man and horse, penetrate that compact mass of human beings; and their sabres were plied to hew a way through naked held-up hands, and defenceless heads; and then chopped limbs, and wound-gaping skulls were seen; and groans and cries were mingled with

---

28. Bamford wrote in his autobiography that, in the spring planning sessions for the demonstration at St. Peter's fields, it "was deemed expedient that this meeting should be as morally effective as possible, and, that it should exhibit a spectacle such as had never before been witnessed in England." *Passages in the Life of a Radical,* p. 131. Cf. coverage of Henry Hunt's triumphal entry into London the following month: "From the City-road, to the Crown and Anchor, never, we believe, was such a crowd seen." *The Triumphal Entry of Henry Hunt, Esq. into London, On Monday, September 13, 1819* (London: Thomas Dolby, 1819), p. 9. This rhetoric appears, as well, in Hunt's address: "I am overwhelmed with gratitude, for the unexampled honour you have this day shewn me. Unexampled, I say, for I challenge the enemies of Reform to name one instance where the public feeling has been so mightily, so powerfully, and so unequivocally expressed, not towards an individual, but in that sacred and overwhelming cause in which the people are engaged." *The Triumphal Entry of Henry Hunt,* p. 8. This is not, of course, to say that the rhetoric of "the unexampled moment" should itself simply be taken as entirely unexampled, but rather, as I argue below, that there is some serious warrant for it in this case.

the din of that horrid confusion. "Ah! ah!" "for shame! for shame!" was shouted. Then "Break! break! they are killing them in front, and they cannot get away"; and there was a general cry of "break! break." For a moment the crowd held back as in a pause; then was a rush, heavy and resistless as a headlong sea; and a sound like low thunder, with screams, prayers, and imprecations from the crowd-moiled, and sabre-doomed, who could not escape.

On the breaking of the crowd, the yeomanry wheeled; and dashing wherever there was an opening, they followed, pressing and wounding. Many females appeared as the crowd opened; and striplings or mere youths also were found. Their cries were piteous and heart-rending; and would, one might have supposed, have disarmed any human resentment; but here, their appeals were vain.[29]

Bamford writes after the passing of a quarter century, but he captures the sense of outrage that is clear in much of the more immediate public reaction to the event. His account, moreover, is largely corroborated by both contemporary reports and subsequent research. The facts and figures of Peterloo continue to be debated to this day, but civilian casualties probably ran to over three hundred, with perhaps a dozen fatalities among them.[30]

Writers present on the hustings that day included Richard Carlile (on whose behalf Shelley would write a long public letter, unpublished, to *The Examiner* in October), as well as reporters from the Liverpool *Mercury,* the Leeds *Mercury,* and (most unusually, given the distance of the meeting from the metropolis) *The Times* of London.[31] The incident was told and retold in the daily and weekly press and then reconstructed from the newspaper accounts in works like Shelley's *The Mask of Anarchy* and William Hone's *The Political House that Jack Built,* the latter alleged to have sold 100,000 copies by the end of the year (though this is almost certainly an inflated figure). The ripple effects of this incident on the British nation from the day it took place until the Gag Acts were passed in December were massive, but its proleptic impact on national life actually occurred well in advance of August 16. Indeed, it started to be felt at the beginning of the year, when the initial plans for an assembly at Manchester began to be laid, amid great public controversy. On January 18, Henry Hunt, who presided at the Peterloo assembly, had held a meeting of 8,000 "operatives" on

29. Bamford, *Passages in the Life of a Radical,* p. 152. For other eyewitness narratives of the massacre, see Francis Braton, ed., *Three Accounts of Peterloo by Eyewitnesses: Bishop Stanley, Lord Hylton, and John Benjamin Smith* (Manchester: Manchester University Press, 1921).

30. Much of the recent research on Peterloo was assembled, at least representatively, in the special issue devoted to the subject by the *Manchester Region History Review* 3, no. 1 (spring/summer 1989).

31. Joyce Marlow, *The Peterloo Massacre* (London: Rapp and Whiting, 1970), p. 130. A more recent popular history of the event is Robert Reid, *The Peterloo Massacre* (London: Heinemann, 1989).

the same site.[32] The plans for a second meeting were to be cleared with government officials, and these negotiations had not proven easy. More than one such project had to be scrapped before the August 16 meeting was replanned and eventually carried out. In the meantime, British laborers mobilized for reform in several other venues. A highly visible series of demonstrations preceded Peterloo, and, unintimidated by the event itself, reformers continued to meet through to the late autumn. Meanwhile, writers of all descriptions persisted through the year to keep the events of August 16 in the forefront of public attention, shaping and reshaping its implications, reconfiguring the very practices of literary and political representation in the bargain.

All this is to say that "Peterloo"—like "The French Revolution" on a higher scale or perhaps even "Romanticism," itself on a scale yet higher still—names an event of indeterminate duration that marks a major transformation in the practices of modern literary and political representation, one understood in its moment to have revolutionary potential.[33] It is in such a frame of reference that Peterloo can be seen, to invoke E. P. Thompson's emphatic description, as "without question a formative experience in British social and political history."[34] And it is in this sense that what Thompson calls "the sheer *size* of the event" constantly eludes definition. For it is not just, as Asa Briggs argues, that "1819 was one of the most troubled years of the nineteenth century," nor that "working-class 'distress' took the clearest political form it had ever taken, and

32. Hunt had a run-in with the Fifteenth Hussars on this early occasion. Robert Walmsley, a modern apologist for the actions of the Manchester Magistracy, alleges that Hunt was baiting Hussars on his January visit to Manchester, in his *Peterloo: The Case Reopened* (Manchester, England: Manchester University Press, 1969), p. 46. Walmsley also reprints a defiant poem by Bamford with the unwieldy title: "Touch Him! Or, Verses occasioned by the Outrage committed upon Mr Hunt, and His Friends, at the Theatre, Manchester, on the evening of Friday, January 22, 1819 . . . " (p. 47–49). The poem, which seems prophetic of events at the August 16 meeting, begins as follows:

> Touch him, aye! touch him, if you dare;
> Pluck from his head one single hair—
>   Ye sneaking, coward crew:
> Touch him—and blasted by the hand
> That graspeth not a vengeful brand,
> To rid our long oppressed land
>   Of reptiles such as you. (p. 47)

33. In the sonnet, "England in 1819" (SPP, p. 311), which I analyze in some detail below, the sense of possibility seems to be stressed by the use of "may" as the line-ending rhyme word with the last word in the poem, "day," in the poem's closing couplet.

34. Thompson, *The Making of the English Working Class* (New York: Vintage, 1966), p. 687. There have been at least two historical novels about this "formative experience" of Peterloo: Mrs. G. Linnaeus Banks, *The Manchester Man* (1886; rpt. London: Victor Gollancz, 1970); and Howard Spring, *Fame Is the Spur* (New York: Viking, 1940).

there was a consequent fierce struggle between the forces of 'movement' and the defenders of order."[35] It is also that the modes and means of national self-representation itself were contested in the most fundamental ways in these struggles over the rights of assembly and publication, "tongue" and "pen" (as Bentham put it in his *Plan of Reform* [1817]).

In coming to terms with Peterloo and its representations, therefore, we necessarily find ourselves addressing not only the "works" of 1819 but also its "days." I refer to "days" here in the new sense given that word during the mass movements of the French Revolution and reprised by Marx in his celebrated "day book," *The Eighteenth Brumaire of Louis Bonaparte*. Just as it is possible to list the momentous years in the Romantic period, so one can identify a number of such "days" of popular activity for England in 1819:

1. January 18: Henry Hunt presides at a meeting of 8,000 operatives on St. Peter's Field in Manchester.

2. February 15 (The "Sandy Brow Fight"): William Fitton presides at a public meeting at Sandy Brow in Stockport, number present not known, where a scuffle involving stones and brickbats occurs over an attempt by the military to seize the Cap of Liberty; the Riot Act is read three times.

3. June 14: Joseph Harrison presides at a meeting of 12,000–15,000 at Ashton-under-Lyne; this was typical of a spate of June meetings at Oldham, Bolton, Royton, Bury, Heywood, Stockport, Failsworth, Gee Cross, Lees, Middleton, Rochdale, Todmorden, Barnsley, Holmfirth, Leeds, and other towns that were unrepresented in Parliament.

4. June 16: 40,000 weavers meet at Glasgow to petition the Prince Regent for passage money to Canada for the unemployed.

5. June 28: At the great Stockport meeting, the largest of its kind besides Peterloo, upwards of 20,000 hear Sir Charles Wolseley speak on Parliamentary reform.

6. August 16 (Peterloo): 60,000 people assemble on St. Peter's field Manchester, with Henry Hunt presiding.

7. September 2: 15,000–50,000 people assemble in Westminster and are addressed by Francis Burdett and Major Cartwright. (Thompson dates this to September 5, but the *Examiner* for that date confirms September 2.) This follows a smaller protest meeting at Smithfield the week before.

8. November 1: simultaneous meetings held, by prior agreement, at Newcastle, Carlisle, Leeds, Halifax, Manchester, Bolton, Nottingham, Leicester, Coventry, and elsewhere in England and Scotland.

35. Asa Briggs, *The Age of Improvement* (London: Longmans, Green, 1959), p. 208.

9. November 15: simultaneous meetings at Paisley, Glasgow, and other lo-
cations across Scotland.[36]

Like the years 1798 or 1819 within the Romantic period, these days can be understood either as ordinally sequenced in some higher-order period or as classificatory categories for lower-order temporal units. To see this is to grasp the
logic of the date, as explicated in Lévi-Strauss's response to Sartre, which I will
consider in detail in chapter 1.

In gauging the new sense of historical movement felt in these days of 1819,
it should be conceded that these massive demonstrations of 1819 had been
somewhat anticipated within the post-Waterloo period by the assembly at Spa
Fields in London in late 1816 and the Pentridge Rebellion of 1817. E. P.
Thompson has indeed called the years from 1815 to 1819 "the heroic age of
popular Radicalism."[37] Further, this four-year period in turn could be seen as a
postwar renewal (though with many differences) of some of the mass scale activity of the 1780s and 1790s. In the popular activity of 1819, however, the
unprecedented or (in Henry Hunt's term) "unexampled" elements are the persistence of popular pressure and the recurrence of the assemblies on a mass
scale.[38] Thompson's own speculation is that Britain may have come as close to
a revolution at this moment as it had at any point since the English Revolution
itself in the 1640s and that, if the movement had better leadership from stump
and page than was provided by the likes of "Orator" Hunt and journalist Cobbett, some more radical outcome might actually have been attained.[39]

Thompson's history is now celebrated for having achieved a powerful sympathetic identification with the energies and hopes of the historical actors who
form its subject—and that identification seems to radiate backward and forward in his narrative from his imaginative reenactment of the radical possibili-

36. These later meetings are well documented in the reports collected by Parliament in November as "Papers Relevant to the Internal State of the Country," in *Hansard's Parliamentary Debates,* 1st ser., 41 (1820): cols. 230–301. See especially the final report, by Sir John Byng,
November 18, 1819, cols. 300–301; cf. the debate on H. G. Bennet's motion "on the state of the
manufacturing districts," cols. 924–26. This is only a partial list of the demonstrations, which in
fact continued into the early autumn. Joyce Marlow notes that in Paisley, Birmingham, Leeds,
and Newcastle the meetings were "attended by crowds of up to 50,000." *The Peterloo Massacre,*
p. 183. The Scottish meetings of November are mentioned in Elie Halévy, *The Liberal Awakening.*
Vol. 2 of *A History of the English People in the Nineteenth Century,* trans. E. I. Watkin (New York:
Barnes & Noble, 1961), p. 67.

37. Thompson, *The Making of the English Working Class,* p. 603.

38. "Not surprisingly," writes Asa Briggs, "some historians have chosen these tense years between Waterloo and Peterloo as the nearest point Britain ever reached to social revolution," but,
though he himself calls 1819 "the worst of all years," he is not persuaded that the probability of revolution was ever really so strong. *The Age of Improvement* (London: Longman, 1960), pp. 208, 210.

39. Thompson, *The Making of the English Working Class,* pp. 620–30.

ties of Peterloo in 1819. Some historians have doubted the validity of this counterfactual speculation on the grounds that it exaggerates the depth of the radical movement that stirred Britain in these months.[40] What is not a matter of speculation is the view of the crisis expressed by contemporary intellectuals. The more one reads in either public or private commentary by intellectuals across the political spectrum of England in 1819, the more one sees of revolutionary hopes and fears. Shelley's comment in a letter to Leigh Hunt on December 23—"I suppose we shall soon have to fight in England" (LPBS, 2:167)—is closely linked with his contemporary declaration in *A Philosophical View of Reform* that "we live among such philosophers and poets as surpass beyond comparison any who have appeared in our nation since its last struggle for liberty" (WPBS, 7:19). The imminence of revolution is explicit in Byron's more ambivalent political comments of these months: "To me [he wrote to Augusta Leigh from Venice on October 15] it appears you are on the eve of a revolution which won't be made with rose water however" (BLJ, 6:228). It is also alluded to in recorded statements by many other political observers who were closer to the unfolding events in Britain. In letters of December 1819, Scott both notes the nearby disturbances of November in Glasgow and Paisley and discusses his efforts to marshall a small corps to put down a possibly imminent insurrection—"We think we may raise 300 men."[41] Furthermore, in a scenario lifted straight from one of his historical novels, but which he justified in practical terms, Scott also mentions the possibility of an alliance with the "highland Chiefs" for the same purpose.[42] Certainly the situation was thought dire enough to warrant emergency measures in the session of Parliament that the Prince Regent convened on November 23.[43]

40. From the right and left, respectively, such critiques have been made by R. J. White, *From Waterloo to Peterloo* (London: William Heinemann, 1957), and Craig Calhoun, *The Question of Class Struggle* (Chicago: University of Chicago Press, 1982).

41. Sir Walter Scott, *The Letters of Sir Walter Scott*, 12 vols. Edited by H. J. C. Grierson (London: Constable, 1932), 6:54.

42. Scott writes to John B. S. Morritt in mid-December: "The highland Chiefs have offered their clans and I think they cannot do better than accept a regiment or two of them. They have no common sympathies with the insurgents and could be better trusted than any *new* forces that could be levied" (*Letters*, 6.58). According to John Sutherland, Scott had persuaded himself in December that "upwards of 50,000 blackguards are ready to rise between Tyne and Wear" (*Life of Walter Scott*, p. 233). Coleridge, for one, expressed skepticism of these dire forecasts.

43. "The Prince Regent's Speech on Opening the Session" includes his explanation of the emergency: "I regret to have been under the necessity of calling you together at this period of the year; but the seditious practices so long prevalent in some of the manufacturing districts of the country have . . . led to proceedings incompatible with the public tranquillity, and with the peaceful habits of the industrious classes of the community; and a spirit is now fully manifested, utterly hostile to the constitution of this kingdom. . . ." *Hansard's Parliamentary Debates*, 1st ser.,

From the perspective of the documents dating from 1819, what is perhaps most extraordinary is that in the space of a few weeks the growing agitation all came to so abrupt a halt. The timing of the political reversal of 1820 might be attributed to the combined effect of arrests of key leaders (Henry Hunt, Major Cartwright, Francis Burdett, Richard Carlile, Sir Charles Wolseley), government countermeasures (the Gag Acts, passed on December 30, 1819), historical accident (the death of George III, January 29, 1820), and desperate radical plots (the Cato Street Conspiracy, discovered on February 23, 1820).[44] By mid-1820, the movement that had been gaining force since 1815 was to undergo, as Thomas Laqueur has suggested, a full-scale public displacement, and subsequent aestheticization, in the affair over the newly crowned King's attempts to divorce his estranged wife Caroline in 1820.[45] The "triumphs" of Caroline through the streets of England seem in retrospect like so many parodic repetitions of the post-Waterloo "triumphs" of Henry Hunt and William Cobbett in late 1819. The sense of closure on the events around Peterloo, but also the sense of general historical acceleration in this intensely "hot" period of literary and political activity, are captured in a pamphlet of April 1820 containing a speech that the newly reelected George Canning made before his constituents at Liverpool on March 18. For Canning declared on that occasion that—in view of events of recent months—November 1819 and March 1820 effectively belonged to different "epochs" in the nation's history.[46]

These, then, were the kinds of materials and issues, the conjunctions of works and days, that made up the course entitled "England in 1819." Yet the question of whether such an array actually constituted a discrete subject matter was marked by a certain uncertainty from the start. Historians will recognize that the title I chose for this course obliquely echoes *England in 1815,* the initial volume of Elie Halévy's magisterial account of England in the nineteenth century. Methodologically, however, Halévy's book was not a close precedent,

---

41 (1820): cols. 1–2. Cf. Hunt's reference to the "spirit" working through the people assembled to greet him on his entry into London [n. 29], *Triumphal Entry of Henry Hunt,* pp. 8–9.

44. These, says Thompson, were "only a few of those imprisoned or awaiting prosecution by the end of 1819." *Making of the English Working Class,* p. 684.

45. Thomas Laqueur, "The Queen Caroline Affair: Politics as Art in the Reign of George IV," *Journal of Modern History* 54 (September 1982): 417–66. Cf. Anna Clark, "Queen Caroline and the Sexual Politics of Popular Culture in London, 1820" *Representations* 31 (summer 1990): 47–68. The interesting conjunction of what Laqueur calls the "aestheticization of public political life" with the Caroline affair and the new aestheticism that develops in a writer like Shelley between Peterloo and "A Defence of Poetry" (1821) is a matter that deserves more attention than it has received.

46. *Speech of the Right Hon. George Canning, to his Constituents at Liverpool, On Saturday, March 18, 1820* (London: John Murray, 1820), p. 7. I thank Kevin Gilmartin for the reference.

since it was less a study of that year in England's past than an effort to provide deep background for the subsequent volumes in that history—that is, an effort to outline how England got to where it was *by* 1815.[47] Indeed, notwithstanding Halévy's title, I might well not have thought to frame a course in these terms, much less a book, if it had not been for the sonnet—*England in 1819*— first published in Mary Shelley's 1839 edition of her deceased husband's works.

Literary history has ever found it notoriously difficult to define its object of study, and this vagueness can only become more troublesome when literary historicism itself is changing its protocols. I suppose that, according to a curious but familiar convention in the genre of literary commentary, the appropriation of Percy Shelley's title for my own project must have conferred a kind of propriety on what was, at some level, an arbitrarily framed subject matter.[48] Furthermore, as I reflected on the sonnet itself and refined an analysis of it in collaboration with my students, I began to see in its execution much that argued for its special relevance to the problematics of literary, political, and historical representation in the culture from and to which it is addressed:

England in 1819

An old, mad, blind, despised, and dying King;
Princes, the dregs of their dull race, who flow
Through public scorn,—mud from a muddy spring;
Rulers who neither see nor feel nor know,
But leechlike to their fainting country cling
Till they drop, blind in blood, without a blow,

47. Halévy, *England in 1815.* Vol. 2 of *The History of the English People in the Nineteenth Century,* trans. E. I. Watkin and D. A. Barker (1913; New York: Barnes & Noble, 1961). This is not to say that Halévy's choice was merely arbitrary. There were good reasons for Halévy to have settled on it in the first place, as he himself explains, reasons relevant to the intelligibility of the period that has been called "Waterloo to Peterloo." The year 1815 is a date of genuinely pan-European significance, the beginning of a self-conscious "restoration" in the great nation-states and of a retrospective stock-taking after the astounding era through which most of Europe had recently passed. It was also important for reopening cross-cultural influences, the year of renewed travel from England to the Continent. Byron, Shelley, Scott, and Wordsworth went to the Continent in the year after Waterloo. Much of this travel issued in literary works on European topics that (most especially in Byron's case) the reading public back in England was eager to receive. I might add that in view of Halévy's self-conscious emulation of the English Whig tradition, the title of his first volume, *England in 1815,* might well be understood as inspired by the starting-point chapter of Lord Macaulay's *History of England:* "The State of England in 1685." I take up Macaulay's relation to Scott, and Scott's development of this kind of formula, in chapter 2.

48. For a suggestive meditation on the relation between title and entitlement see John Fisher, "Entitling," *Critical Inquiry* 11 (December 1984): 286–88.

> A people starved and stabbed in th'untilled field;
> An army, whom liberticide and prey
> Makes as a two-edged sword to all who wield;
> Golden and sanguine laws which tempt and slay;
> Religion Christless, Godless—a book sealed;
> A senate, Time's worst statute, unrepealed—
> Are graves from which a glorious Phantom may
> Burst, to illumine our tempestuous day. (SPP, p. 311)

The sonnet began to appear as a refashioning of the millenarian political aspiration of English writers from the 1790s in a way that shows a distinctive historical self-consciousness—an awareness of conditions of movement from one historical epoch to the next. That is, as I will try to explain more fully below, where political debate in the 1790s tended to structure itself in terms of threshold distinctions—reason/passion, liberty/slavery, state of nature/state of civil society, nature/second nature—political debate after Waterloo tends to involve arguments about historical movements, historical necessities, epochs, and formations. The sonnet's particular way of encoding this self-consciousness offers a promising synecdoche for what I wanted to explore in a literary culture dominated by Scott's new historical novels. Many readers, it seemed, had not gotten beyond the sense of the poem as an empirical catalogue, some not beyond the famous first item in the catalogue, the opening line's Lear-like description of George the Third, which is often quoted ornamentally by political historians of the Regency.

Among literary historians and literary critics, certainly, the poem has never enjoyed much attention. For casual readers, as well as for readers who may know enough to associate it with Shelley's volume of popular songs, "England in 1819" has apparently been regarded as a very simple affair. It looks to be a poem of one trick, after all, and a rather obvious one at that. An unrelieved catalogue of contemporary social ills constitutes its first twelve lines, and then the poem makes use of perhaps the best known structural convention in English poetry, the thematic pivot in the closing couplet of the so-called Shakespearean sonnet, to suggest that these ills, and the deaths they involve, may somehow be transcended in an illuminating resurrection. The grammatical device by which this transformation is accomplished could scarcely be more overt: the sheer predication ("Are graves") that at once turns the catalogue into a compound subject and reduces its items to a common fate. The body of the sonnet might be said to reflect accurately the woes of English society; the couplet to express a hope of their being overcome. The sonnet would appear, on this reading, to confirm those commentators who would dismiss Shelley's politics as so much wishful thinking. After all, when this sort of resolution occurs in comedy we call it "deus ex machina" and label the work sentimental.

So little respect has this poem commanded that its sources in Shelley's own writings have rarely been commented on. About two years earlier, before his self-exile to Italy and while still living on the Thames at Marlow, Shelley wrote and published a political pamphet that first developed some of the material used in the sonnet. This journalistic tour de force, *An Address to the People on the Death of Princess Charlotte*, takes as its focus the conjunction of two events in late 1817. The first is the execution on November 6 of Brandreth, Ludlam, and Turner, the leaders of the Pentridge Rebellion staged by the weavers of Derbyshire. The second was the death of the Prince Regent's daughter the next day, November 7.[49] Shelley's concern, which he knew ran against the grain of the public lamentation for the Princess, is for the cause of the weavers. Although in the course of their trial it had emerged that the entire affair had been a government trap set by the agent provocateur known as "Oliver the Spy," the three leaders had nonetheless been found guilty and beheaded. In its rhetorical climax, Shelley's 1817 pamphlet represents this execution as a death blow dealt to English liberty, and represents this death in its turn as the demise of a well-loved princess:

> She loved the domestic affections, and cherished arts which adorn, and valour which defends. She was amiable and would have become wise, but she was young, and in the flower of youth the despoiler came. LIBERTY is dead. Slave! I charge thee disturb not the depth and solemnity of our grief by any meaner sorrow. If One has died who was like her that should have ruled over this land, like Liberty, young, innocent, and lovely, know that the power through which that one perished was God, and that it was a private grief. But *man* has murdered Liberty, and whilst the life was ebbing from its wound, there descended on the head and on the hearts of every human thing, the sympathy of an universal blast and curse.[50]

Here the atheist Shelley assumes the role of minister to the deceased, now preaching, now conducting the surviving public in a ritual service not unlike the funeral procession that figures several years later in *Adonais,* his great elegy for Keats. In 1817, his suggestion is this: "Let us follow the corpse of British Liberty slowly and reverentially to its tomb: and *if some glorious Phantom should appear,* and make its throne of broken swords and sceptres and royal crowns trampled in the dust, let us say that the Spirit of Liberty has arisen from its grave

49. For a full account of the death and the events surrounding her mourning, see Esther C. Schor, *Bearing the Dead: The British Culture of Mourning from the Enlightenment to Victoria* (Princeton, N.J.: Princeton University Press, 1994), pp. 196–229.

50. E. B. Murray, ed., *The Prose Works of Percy Bysshe Shelley* (Oxford: Clarendon Press, 1993), p. 239.

and left all that was gross and mortal there, and kneel down and worship it as our Queen."[51] Since the resurrection of this "glorious Phantom" clearly anticipates what we find in the closing couplet of the sonnet, it behooves us to consider how this earlier resurrection scene is framed.

The pamphlet actually supplies a reasonably clear (if inexplicit) answer to this question in an act of interpretation that redistributes symbolic value in the two scenes it juxtaposes. Shelley suggests that to look past the death of Charlotte to a proper understanding of the executions of Brandreth, Ludlam, and Turner is to see the spirit or meaning of that event, the metaphorical death of princess Liberty. To acknowledge the death is to be in a position to mourn it. To mourn the death of Liberty is to be in a position to revive it. Indeed, it is to take the first step in reviving it, for mourning respects the spirit of Liberty, and liberty survives precisely in virtue of the respect it is paid. The symbolic power once invested in the title of princess dwindles with the Hanoverian line itself and is now to be reinvested in Liberty as a philosophical abstraction. The capacities for fresh figurative conception, for sympathy, and for social change are on this account all mutually involved and are together involved in a notion of liberty that allies itself—just as Charlotte is remembered for having done—to the domestic affections, the ornamental arts, and valor in defense. To read the spirit symbolized by a given event, to respond to it in the appropriate spirit, and to generate the spirit of political hope all prove to be just so many dimensions of the same complex imaginative act, exactly the act Shelley performs in his pamphlet.[52]

In view of the complexity of this act of resurrecting the "glorious Phantom" in the pamphlet, we should probably expect nothing simpler from its extended resurrection two years later in the sonnet, and the sonnet's peculiar formal features should signal major complications. While the poem may involve some use of the Elizabethan pivot at line thirteen, for example, it also declares itself as something other than a conventional English sonnet, or indeed as a conventional sonnet of any kind. Reminiscent of Keats's experiments with the Great Odes earlier in the year, this scrambling of sonnet traditions—the rhyme scheme (ababab cdcd cc dd) may be unprecedented—discourages taking poetic convention at face value. The expectation of thematic reversal encoded in the closing couplet, for example, is complicated by the presence of *paired* closing couplets. The "sealed"/"repealed" rhyme lends thematic and formal closure without reversal: just two final items in the unrelieved catalogue of ills. But in

---

51. Ibid., 1:239.

52. Timothy Webb briefly notes the echo of "glorious Phantom" in the sonnet in his *Shelley: A Voice Not Understood* (Atlantic Highlands, N.J.: Humanities Press, 1977), p. 107.

the *final* couplet, all of the public ills catalogued in the first dozen lines are suddenly presented in a new light. For England, the present dark moment, let us call it 1819, holds out the possibility of a millenarian illumination that will mark its general rebirth.

In a way, therefore, that resonates with my larger interest in the new modes of historical representation in this moment of British culture, Shelley makes a historical turning point appear to coincide with the formal turning point of the poem. The case is not so easily stated, however, and the conspicuous fact that the formal turning point occurs in a scrambled sequence of rhymes should warn us against oversimplification. It is not quite accurate, for example, to say that the social ills of England are suddenly presented in a new light. The items in the twelve-line catalogue are not merely ills, the practices of an ancien régime that enlightenment will abolish. They are contradictory conditions that become a Miltonic "darkness visible." The poem that represents these conditions is governed, to borrow a phrase slightly out of context, by a "dialectic of enlightenment." Consider, for instance, the reference to religion as "Christless, Godless." Shelley was one of the most celebrated atheists of his day. English readers probably knew more about his atheism than about his poetry.[53] Shelley did, it is true, admire the life and teachings of Christ, but he thought that the name "Christ" had been deeply misused in ecclesiastical appropriation of what he took the historical Jesus to have represented. A "Christ"-less religion could no more be called an unequivocal evil in Shelley's terms than a Godless one could.[54] Or consider the interestingly self-canceling historical references convened in the figure of the "sealed book" in line 11. Taken as a proper noun, the phrase refers to the Book of Common Prayer, reinstitutionalized by the Anglican Church in 1662, soon after the Restoration of Charles II. Taken as a common idiom, the phrase means an obscure text, a sense tied to its most literal and obvious mean-

53. On hotel registers during a journey into the Alps in 1816, under the heading "Occupation," Shelley had written, in Greek, "Democrat, Philanthropist, Atheist." The entry was scornfully remarked by Thomas Raffles in his *Letters During a Tour,* of 1818, and by Robert Southey, who referred to it in an attack on Shelley in the *Quarterly Review* of January 1818. It was also mentioned in the conservative *London Chronicle* in June 1819. See Richard Holmes, *Shelley: The Pursuit* (New York: E. P. Dutton, 1975), p. 342; see also Webb, *Shelley: A Voice Not Understood,* pp. 140–42.

54. In *A Philosophical View of Reform,* which he was working on at just this time, Shelley spelled out his considered view of Jesus in relation to Christianity: "Berkeley and Hume, [and] Hartley . . . have clearly established the certainty of our ignorance with respect to those obscure questions which under the name of religious truths have been the watchwords of contention and the symbols of unjust power ever since they were distorted by the narrow passions of the immediate followers of Jesus from that meaning to which philosophers are even now restoring them" (p. 9).

ing as a book that is encased in such a way that it cannot be opened.[55] One plausible interpretation of how the phrase functions in the poem, therefore, would conclude the following: the High Church tyranny that censors and controls its books thereby withholds public access to them and thus restricts their influence.

As one looks more closely at these items, one sees that each is structured on some sort of contradiction. "Golden and sanguine laws," to move from the religious to the political sphere, surely implies a reference to money and blood, and thus to greed and vengeance. But the resonances of the do-unto-others imperative in "golden" law and of revolutionary legislative *espérance* in "sanguine" law reinforce each other in the destabilization of that reference. Moreover, this reading gains support from a passage in *The Mask of Anarchy,* written just weeks earlier, which harkens with radical nostalgia to the legal arrangements of a more just and hopeful age.[56] The most famous item in the catalogue, the notorious opening line, is itself a catalogue of epithets, and these inaugurate the poem with what is already a strange mix of meanings. For while George III's particularly loathsome qualities are at least partly a function of his agedness, of the fact that he is a "dying King," this fact is also a redeeming feature of the situation: this King who had held actual or nominal power for six decades was in fact within weeks of his death at the time Shelley would have been writing. Similarly, that the Princes are the dregs of their dull race seems an evil, until one stops to think that, being the dregs, their flow through public scorn is also nearing an end.[57] Their "muddiness" seems particularly fertilizing in the context of the untilled field of line 7. Shelley explained why the army becomes as a two-edged sword

55. The sealed book is also, of course, an image from the Christian apocalypse: Rev: 5:1, 2, 9 and 6:1.

56. The uncharacteristically (for Shelley) nostalgic passage in the *Mask* is as follows:

> Let the Laws of your own land,
> Good or ill, between ye stand
> Hand to hand, and foot to foot,
> Arbiters of the dispute,

> The old laws of England—they
> Whose reverend heads with age are grey,
> Children of a wiser day;
> And whose solemn voice must be
> Thine own echo—Liberty! (ll. 327–35)

So speaks the disembodied voice of the land, the voice of Liberty's spirit, to the English people in *The Mask of Anarchy.* It celebrates England's golden and sanguine laws, and it is a voice not obviously ironized. (SPP, p. 309.)

57. Thus the death of Charlotte made possible the eventual ascent to the throne by another woman, Victoria, in 1837. See Murray's comments in his edition of volume one of the *Prose Works,* pp. 447–51.

to all who wield it in his analysis of military psychology in *A Philosophical View of Reform*.[58] Perhaps the clearest example of the two-edgedness of the poem's (s)word(s) is the most fully elaborated figure in the list, that of the leechlike rulers, for this simile cannot possibly be read without recalling the medicinal uses to which leeches were put in this period. The application of harsh medicine, it might be argued, is just what a fainting country needs.

This pattern of ambiguity and paradox has obviously not figured in what little commentary we have on this poem. Thus, for example, a standard anthology of Romantic poetry sees fit to gloss only one line in the poem—"A senate, Time's worst statute, unrepealed"—identifying "Time's worst statute" straightforwardly as a reference to the question of Catholic emancipation.[59] Read this way, line 12 would be the only unproblematized verse in the poem and would therefore form a relatively flat conclusion to the list of social conditions itemized in the poem's first dozen lines. Such a reading, moreover, makes nothing of the sense of grammatical apposition between the two noun phrases in the line—"A senate, Time's worst statute unrepealed." Without the appositional relation, the internal logic of the line seems arbitrary in a way that is true of no other line in the poem. Donald Reiman properly takes the whole line for the object of his gloss—"Shelley details his objections to Parliament for being unrepresentative of the British people in his *Philosophical View of Reform*" (p. 311)—and his suggestion about "representation" points in a fruitful direction. It still leaves us to face the appositional grammar of the line, however, and therefore to address the irony that plays off the sense of "senate" not as a statute but as an institution in which statutes are made.

Just this irony, in the end, is what gives an otherwise dull figure vitality here. The argument of *A Philosophical View of Reform,* like many other reformist arguments made in the year of Peterloo, centered precisely on the question of the legitimacy of the English parliament as a lawmaking institution, questioning the legitimacy even of the American Congress with which the Parliament is invidiously compared. As a Godwinite, Shelley's philosophical (as opposed to his practical) position on this question is that as a form of government, the parliament should eventually be abolished entirely in favor of the internal rule of all people over themselves, a rule fostered by the work of poetry's unacknowledged legislators. This is the goal of philosophical anarchism, the triumph of love. The antithesis of this ideal is what Shelley later calls "the triumph

58. Shelley's comments on nonviolent resistance appear in chapter 3 of *A Philosophical View of Reform*, pp. 42–55.

59. William Heath, ed., *Major British Poets of the Romantic Period* (New York: Macmillan, 1973), p. 906.

of life."[60] The triumph of life is a triumph of external law over internal law in two senses: the subjugation of moral instinct to natural instinct and the concomitant subjugation of people to external rule.

The English senate is thus time's *worst* statute because, as reformers of the period suggested, the current Parliament was a form of tyranny posing as a form of self-rule. It is not an instrument of the self-legislation of the English people; it is only the instrument of base nature, a function of the laws of time. Its only "legitimate" legislative act, therefore, is the repeal of the form that Time has given it, the passing of what the Parliament of Oliver Cromwell's era, with more practical and local considerations in view, called a "self-denying ordinance." This is what most reformers were, in some fashion or degree, working to achieve. Taken as an allusion to the major issue of contemporary political debate, then, the figure in line 12 would appropriately stand as the last in the poem's catalogue of social conditions. Like the others, too, when thus construed, the line would figure an apparently unmitigated evil (the senate as statute) inscribed as a potentially regenerative act of self-annihilation (self-repeal): an act of self-annihilation that might be likened, say, to the work of certain self-destructive parasites which help to heal as they fall, blind in blood, but without a blow. How this revolution might be made to happen "without a blow," furthermore, is a question explicitly addressed in Shelley's discussion of passive resistance in the third section of *A Philosophical View of Reform*. Why it is more likely to happen in England than in America—because of England's poetic resources and in spite of America's institutional advantages—is also explained in the *View*, as we shall see in chapters 3 and 8.

We are now in a position to understand why the terms of the times in Shelley's catalogue—the conditions of his tempestuous day—are not simple evils and are not simply overcome by the arrival of an enlightening "deus ex machina." Rather, these conditions, these "terms" of social existence, are in each instance the source from which the illumination will spring, as the figurative spirit of the word springs from the dead letter, as a shared meaning springs from the juxtaposed events of November 1817 in the earlier pamphlet on the death of Charlotte and the Pentridge executions.[61] In the sonnet, the idea of

60. In *A Philosophical View of Reform,* Shelley wrote that the Long Parliament of the 1640s, unique among English senates, had become for a time "the organ of the will of all classes of people in England since it effected the complete revolution in a tyranny consecrated by time" (WPBS, 7:22).

61. It matters to what I shall be arguing below about the derivation of the new concept of the "spirit of the age" from the periodical public sphere that the temporal conjunction of the two events in Shelley's poem was probably suggested to him by a similar observation in the liberal press. See Murray, ed., *Prose Works,* 1:447.

"condition," the unstated term that haunts the poem, thus seems to reappear in its grammatical sense: like the concepts of the *explanandum* and the *explanans* in the theory of explanation, the condition must be understood as a *verbal* formulation, a "saying together," a *representation* of a state of affairs, a text. But representation does not here reduce to "reflection." Conditions must, that is, be *read*, like fine print, not merely seen. And it is in the instability of Shelley's fine formulations—with all their ambiguity, paradox, and paranomasia (as twentieth century practices of close reading have helped us to recognize)—that the conditions of his day become the occasion for the kind of illumination that the final couplet anticipates. The letter killeth only itself, and in so doing giveth life to the spirit *in terms of which* the letter can be called dead.

In his experiment with the form of the sonnet, Shelley thus produces an even more powerful and self-conscious tour de force than he had managed in the conclusion to his pamphlet on the death of Queen Charlotte. In the prose account of 1817 the imaginary procession that follows the corpse of British liberty to its tomb allows him to suggest the possibility of resurrecting its spirit as a glorious phantom. In the sonnet, by contrast, the act of reading the first twelve lines itself becomes the occasion of a resurrection. The "glorious phantom" of the closing couplet is, from this perspective, just the meaning of the terms that come before. In the sonnet, but not in the pamphlet, there is a strange undertone to the use of the idiom of "arising from the grave." The pivotal phrase at the start of line 13—"Are graves"—certainly makes prima facie sense in connection with the various deaths summed up in the synecdoche of the dying monarch. But there may also be a lexically unorthodox, quasi-Blakean suggestion of "things which are graven," i.e., printed type, graven words, even graven images, that open up into the day's illuminations.[62] I could never quite persuade my students of this last point, though I regard it as a way to test the limits of the poem's performative self-consciousness about historical representation—of its apparent commitment to the notion of changing history *by* interpreting it (to rephrase Marx's *Eleventh Thesis on Feuerbach*)—by pushing (as Blake might say) beyond "enough" in the analysis to "Too much."

With this reading of the sonnet as its opening set piece, therefore, the course on literature, history, and politics in England in 1819 seemed to assume a degree of plausibility, and so did the research project that followed from it. Nor was it difficult to translate the "phantom" that lends intelligibility to the sonnet's

---

62. This kind of textual self-reference certainly occurs elsewhere in Shelley. One thinks of the allusion to his own pages at the start of the last part of the *Ode to the West Wind*, composed just weeks before: "Make me thy lyre, even as the forest is: / What if my leaves are falling like its own!" (SPP, p. 223). See below, chapter 9.

terms of the times into the idiom that informs what Thomas Carlyle would soon be calling the "signs of the times" and what Shelley was already, pioneeringly, calling the "spirit of the age." This was an idiom that was, by common reckoning, gaining serious hegemony in the British public sphere at just this moment.[63] It was hard, under these circumstances, not to be struck by the sonnet's relation to the new discourse of the spirit of the age in Britain, and the resonance of both with the principle of intelligibility that organized the materials of my course and my developing research project.

However, in the process of work on that project I made two discoveries that dramatically altered my sense of its own historical bearings. The first, which dawned on me only gradually, was that the practice of framing the object of literary study in terms of a single year's writings—in essays, conferences, monographs, encyclopedic literary histories—had become quite prevalent just around the time when I had begun to offer the course on England in 1819. As I proceeded with research on the book, this new literary-cultural historiography on the scale of the year began to be more evident and the fact of it more insistent.[64] The second discovery I made, smaller in magnitude but more embarrassing in implication, was that the title of the sonnet, *England in 1819,* is in fact not Percy's but rather Mary Shelley's invention. It is a title she gave to the poem for purposes of the 1839 posthumous edition. To compound matters, Mary Shelley's fair copy manuscript for the posthumous poems indicates that the first title she assigned it was actually "England in 1820"![65]

Taken together, these discomfiting surprises seemed to pose a certain threat to the critical legitimacy of the planned clustering of literary case studies in late Romantic history making under the rubric "England in 1819." I seemed to have lost the use of poem's title as evidence for a claim that the culture of England in 1819 could name and frame itself as such, and I seemed to have gained reason to suspect that merely a local and temporary development in my own academic culture had prompted me to do so for it. Unseemly questions began to pose themselves. What was the basis of the kind of periodization I had adopted for this study? What normative status did it have? What could explain

63. There is much to come on these matters below, but I should note that both the phantom of the day in the "sonnet" and the "spirit of the age" of the new idiom might be profitably discussed in terms of those Marxian "specters" that Jacques Derrida has recently found haunting European economic modernity in *Specters of Marx* (London: Routledge, 1994). See also Emma J. Clery on "The Value of the Supernatural in Commercial Society," in *The Rise of Supernatural Fiction 1762–1800* (Cambridge: Cambridge University Press, 1995), pp. 80–91.

64. See chapter 1, for examples and analysis of this phenomenon in recent scholarship.

65. See Irving Massey, ed., *Posthumous Poems of Shelley: Mary Shelley's Fair Copy Book* (Montreal: McGill-Queen's University Press, 1969), pp. 114–15.

it, and what could it explain? Was my sense of the self-consciousness about historicity in England in 1819, and about annualized chronology more particularly, nothing more than an especially convoluted form of anachronism?

What seemed called for was an argument to vindicate Mary Shelley's title, *England in 1819,* together with an account of why my own project took the shape it did in the context of what might be called, in shorthand, "English in 1981." The argument for the propriety of Mary's title for Percy's sonnet would have to address not only its content but also its form—not only the settling on the date, 1819, rather than 1820, but also the notion of giving a title in the form of a national territory and a calendar year, as if such a title could *tell* something, as if a *date of the nation* could figure the *state of the nation.* The account of the turn to annualized models of literary history, by the same token, would have to address matters of content as well as form—not only the growing practice of titling critical projects by annual dates, but also the more general changes in conceptions of historical explanation and intelligibility that go along with it. Above all, it would suggest that the interest in cultural chronology, rather than being explained away as an anachronistic cultural projection from the present onto the late-Romantic period, could be understood instead, or in addition, as a suppressed residue from the earlier period still operative in the contemporary practice of literary and cultural history These are, in any event, the tasks I presently undertake (in part 1) before getting down to cases (in part 2). I seek, in effect, to historicize the question of historicism not only in the literary culture of England in 1819 but also, from this later moment in the 1990s, the literary-critical culture of what I am calling English in 1981.[66]

66. My task thus aligns itself variously with suggested connections between recent and earlier historicisms in a number of recent studies, especially Alan Liu's self-consciously eclectic meditations on the Romanticism of recent practice in two related essays: "The Power of Formalism: The New Historicism," *ELH* 56 (winter 1989): 745–46, and "Local Transcendence: Cultural Criticism, Postmodernism, and the Romanticism of Detail," *Representations* 32 (fall 1990): 83–96. See also (in reverse chronological order) Orrin N. C. Wang, *Fantastic Modernity: Dialectical Readings in Romanticism and Theory* (Baltimore: Johns Hopkins University Press, 1996); Jerome Christensen, "The Romantic Movement at the End of History," *Critical Inquiry* 20 (spring 1994): 452–76; David Simpson, *Romanticism, Nationalism, and the Revolt Against Theory* (Chicago: University of Chicago Press, 1993); the essays in Marjorie Levinson, ed. *Rethinking Historicism* (London: Basil Blackwell, 1989); Clifford Siskin, *The Historicity of Romantic Discourse* (New York: Oxford University Press, 1988); and the book with which all of this work is in dialogue, Jerome McGann, *The Romantic Ideology* (Chicago: University of Chicago Press, 1983). Also relevant here, especially for my discussion of Shelley, is the discussion of the relation between Romanticism and the "crisis of representation" in Steven Goldsmith, *Unbuilding Jerusalem: Apocalypse and Romantic Representation* (Ithaca, N.Y.: Cornell University Press, 1993), p. 191. The ways in which my discussion below agrees and disagrees with such arguments, or means to reframe or supplement them, should emerge in the course of its execution.

To explore these critical tasks in relation to the historical project of our recent historicisms, I will be turning relatively early in the discussion to those writers whose work has done most to shape the contemporary understanding of the relevant questions, including the question of the historical "project" as such. It was Sartre, of course, who most emphatically spelled out the concept of the project as part of the debate with Lévi-Strauss that ran through the 1950s and 1960s over the questions of history and structure, determination and agency, analytic and dialectical reason. The debate concerned the principles with which Sartre attempted to defend the theory and practice of the project, principles summed up in the "progressive-regressive method" that he announced in his *Question de Methode* (*Search for a Method*), published together with, and as kind of prolegomenon to, his *Critique of Dialectical Reason* in 1960. This method, suggested to Sartre by some remarks of Henri Lefebvre and touted as an effort to ground the project of "structural anthropology," can be taken as a revisiting of the argument of *What Is Literature?* (1948), where Sartre famously asked: "What is Writing?" "Why Write?" and "For Whom Does One Write?" before addressing "The Situation of the Writer in 1947." The announced purpose of Sartre's method was to offer a way of providing appropriate ethical and political thrust to literary projects in the present by determining the *sens d'histoire* (meaning/direction of history) implicit in literary projects of one's influential predecessors. It was a historical method for textual analysis, given and received as such.[67]

Sartre's program was promptly and trenchantly criticized by Lévi-Strauss in *The Savage Mind* (1962), where it formed the subtext of the entire book and the explicit target of the final chapter, "History and Dialectic." There Lévi-Strauss argued that Sartre had failed to grasp the extent to which his self-styled "method" for the historical orientation of political-intellectual-literary praxis was implicated in something Lévi-Strauss called "the historian's code," whereby the historical continuity on which Sartre's method is predicated appears as a ruse of time, a piece of chronological legerdemain, a trick played with the concept of the date. Where Sartre imagined a meaningful historicity that could be plotted in terms of a dated succession of human projects each helping to create the conditons for projects to come, Lévi-Strauss saw only the disjointed projections of historical partiality. This critique, Lévi-Strauss insisted, vitiated Sartre's project almost to the point of total incoherence.[68] The entire episode became in its

67. See Jean-Paul Sartre, *Search for a Method,* trans. Hazel Barnes (New York: Knopf, 1963), especially pp. 85–181. See also *Theory of Practical Ensembles.* Vol. 1. of *Critique of Dialectical Reason,* trans. Alan Sheridan-Smith (London: Verso, 1991).

68. Lévi-Strauss, *The Savage Mind,* p. 259.

turn the subject of a vigorous discussion by a host of commentators, including Lefebvre himself, who attacked Sartre's way of redeploying his earlier methodological proposals. The terms of the debate were eventually assimilated into Anglo-American critical practice, as I shall be suggesting, and became part of its framework of assumptions. This assimilation was partially effected through the influential intervention of Fredric Jameson, among others, who devoted long chapters of *Marxism and Form* (1971) to the genealogy, exposition, recommendation, and critique of the Sartrean method. There is, of course, a far more complicated story to tell about these developments, and it involves changes in the way in which *both* criticism and historiography (and indeed anthropology) have been conceptualized as fields. Only a part of this larger story comes into play in the chapters that immediately follow.

The terms elaborated in the debate on method between Sartre and Lévi-Strauss, which index the acute self-consciousness that developed around both "the progressive-regressive method" and "the historian's code," came to frame subsequent cultural criticism in ways that have not been properly accounted for or even widely acknowledged. In the context of Romantic studies, the progressive-regressive method has been explicitly reinvoked by Marjorie Levinson in her provocative and important study of Keats. In Levinson's account of Keats, however, the method serves, as it had served others in Romanticism less explicitly or deliberately, as a way of critiquing British Romanticism by historicizing it.[69] I will be arguing to very different effect. My claim will be that a number of British writers whom we call Romantic, not excluding Keats, but certainly including many others, such as Shelley, Hazlitt, Byron, Anna Barbauld, William Cobbett, and Walter Scott, can be read as already working within the conceptual framework made newly visible, freshly relevant, in Sartre and Lévi-Strauss's debate on historical method. The historicist framework of contemporary commentary does not afford the critical distance we sometimes tend to imagine. In this sense, a number of our current modes of historicism can be seen as so many forms of neoclassicism with Romanticism (paradoxically) as the *locus classicus* in question. The argument for a new understanding of the relationship between poststructuralist and Romantic historicisms may gain a certain additional frisson from the recognition that, whereas poststructuralist historicism most immediately derives from Continental intellectual traditions, the Romantic historicism in question, insofar as it can be nationalized, is associated primarily with Britain—especially, as I will argue, with unprecedented

---

69. Marjorie Levinson, *Keats's Life of Allegory: The Origins of a Style* (Oxford: Basil Blackwell, 1988), p. 34, n.34.

developments in the theory and practice of political economy in the century after the Union of England and Scotland in 1707.

As far as Romantic studies more narrowly are concerned, my claim is not (or not only) that, as our recent historicist critiques have it, we are often invoking the ahistorical terms of Romanticism to explain it ahistorically. It is that we most invoke the terms of a historicism that is emergent within Romanticism when we make the historicist critique. In my particular argument for such a claim, which has been suggested in different forms by different commentators, I attend closely to a number of mediational moments, stressing that the return to history in recent years returns to a much older conjunction of two discursive frameworks: a discourse of chronology, which Lévi-Strauss attempted to reveal as the "historian's code," and a discourse of culture, which presumes a sense of equivalence between historiographical and ethnographical operations. In the latter, this sense of equivalence is itself grounded in the practice of correlating the uneven development of societies in relation to a given "state of the world." I try to relate the focus on microhistory and cultural "states" in the contemporary study of texts to the literary representation of the "state" in eighteenth and early nineteenth-century public writing, especially in Britain. I also try to show the conceptual importance for subsequent cultural historiography of the peculiarly British articulation of "uneven development" (especially in Scottish-Enlightenment theory) with the increasingly regularized or "even" chronology established by the accelerated growth of periodicals in the British public sphere.

As I note below, in chapter 1, the book that Sartre and Lévi-Strauss both revered, their common point of departure, was *The Eighteenth Brumaire of Louis Bonaparte,* and the homiletic "text" on which each of them based their political sermons in the early 1960s is Marx's famous declaration on the very first page of that book (soon after the comment on Hegel and repetition): "Men make their own history, but they do not make it just as they please; they do not make it under circumstances chosen by themselves, but under circumstances directly encountered, given and transmitted from the past."[70] To see how this formulation sets the terms for the debate about the historian's code is to see how the question at issue relates to the vexed issue of determination. Calling attention to the ambiguity that developed historically around the idea of "being determined" to do something, Raymond Williams once wrote that "no problem in Marxist cultural theory is more difficult than that of 'determination.'"[71] One could do worse than read his entire theoretical oeuvre, like that of his American coun-

---

70. Marx, *The Eighteenth Brumaire of Louis Bonaparte,* p. 15.
71. Raymond Williams, *Marxism and Literature* (New York: Oxford, 1977), p. 83.

terpart, Kenneth Burke, as an effort to rethink issues of agency, motivation, movement, historicity, and context under what Lukács might have called the notion of a "specifically historical" determination.[72]

The crucial point, from the point of view of my discussion here, is that historicism posits the question of agency in relation to the concept of the "historical situation"—it employs narratives of action wherein motivation can be assigned to a social "scene" particularized in place and time. This concept has, of course, underwritten the way in which commentators across a variety of disciplines and critical orientations have recently gone about the business of discussing texts from the newly historicized point of view. We speak routinely and casually of the need to restore works to the "historical situation" in which they were produced, or of sketching "historical situations" for our own studies. The concept has turned slogan, and the inevitability with which it has accompanied efforts, especially programmatic efforts, to argue *against* certain kinds of formalism—New Criticism, Deconstruction—and *for* a certain kind of contextualism would be impossible to document exhaustively here: the practice has simply been too pervasive. The naturalized familiarity of the term is precisely, I think, what has kept us from stopping to consider how it might itself be, so to speak, situated historically.

Sketching in what he meant by the injunction always to historicize, Jameson himself explained that historicizing a text involved study of "the historicity of its forms and of its content, the historical moment of emergence of its linguistic possibilities, the situation-specific function of its aesthetic" and so forth. He also emphasized, however, that this was only half the work of historicization. The other part—indeed, the part with which he proposed to concern himself in *The Political Unconscious* (1981)—involved foregrounding "the interpretive categories or codes through which we read and receive the text in question."[73] To "historicize," to make the category of the historical situation central to one's analysis, is thus implicitly to produce two historical situations. The relation between these two "produced places" of the historiographical operation can vary greatly, with either receiving greater emphasis and either working as the projected image of the other.[74]

72. Georg Lukács, *The Historical Novel,* trans. Hannah and Stanley Mitchell (London: Merlin Press, 1962), p. 19.

73. Fredrick Jameson, *The Political Unconscious: Narrative as a Socially Symbolic Act* (Ithaca, N.Y.: Cornell University Press, 1981), p. 9.

74. On the "production of place" in the "historiographical operation," see Michel de Certeau, *The Writing of History,* trans. Tom Conley (New York: Columbia University Press, 1988), pp. 56–113; initially published as *L'Ecriture de l'Histoire* (Paris: Gallimard, 1975).

The recognition that the dialectic of historicism depends on this redoubling of the historical situation can be found in a number of theoretical discussions of history and criticism in recent years. Dominick LaCapra has insisted that the contexts in which we frame the texts for study are always themselves relevant, in turn, to the contexts of the framing activity, a variation on R. G. Collingwood's older argument that historical evidence is always generated in response to particular questions posed by a historian whose interrogation takes place at a later moment in time.[75] Such formulations are echoed in the double displacement—what de Certeau calls the "two reductions" that are not further reducible.[76] In addressing what he calls "the situation of history," de Certeau (working explicitly from, among others, Paul Veyne, whose contribution I recount below) suggests that "the fragile and necessary boundary between a past object and a current praxis begins to waver, as soon as the fictive postulate of a *given* that is to be understood is replaced by the study of an *operation* always affected by determinisms, always having to be taken up, always depending on the place where it occurs in a society, and specified, however, by a problem, methods, and a function which are its own."[77] De Certeau would call our attention to the historical specificity of our ways of specifying historically, and certainly, from where we stand now, it seems plausible to place Jameson's opening discussion of historicization in *The Political Unconscious* in this developing line of argument.

I will be looking, then, both at the historical situation of the texts of England in 1819 and at the hermeneutic conceptualization of this very work of historically situating texts as it has been recently practiced in English roughly since the time (1981) when *The Political Unconscious* was published. In this way, I try to heed the double aspect of Jameson's own dialectical injunction. If the effort to identify the relevant interpretive categories and codes of "English in 1981" has required a revisiting of the Sartre/Lévi-Strauss debate in the early 1960s, I have also tried to stress throughout how that controversy lends itself to analysis as a struggle over the intelligibility of historical situatedness. Certainly, the double aspect of the historical situation appears in both Sartre's and Lévi-Strauss's argu-

75. R. G. Collingwood, *The Idea of History* (Oxford: Oxford University Press, 1946). Behind Collingwood, to be sure, lies a long history of reflection on this subject, especially in the German tradition on which he was drawing. See H. G. Gadamer's helpful discussions in *Truth and Method* (New York: Seabury, 1975), especially the account of "Dilthey's entanglement in the impasses of historicism," pp. 192–214.

76. De Certeau, *The Writing of History*, p. 44.

77. Ibid., p. 37. De Certeau later reformulates the conundrum as follows: "Thus founded on the rupture between a past that is its object, and a present that is the place of its practice, history endlessly finds the present in its object and the past in its practice" (p. 36).

ments. In Sartre, it is the power of progressive-regressive praxis to reactivate the collective cultural deposit he calls the "practico-inert"—to animate the past's residue of humanly worked matter in such a way as to reveal it as, precisely, the work of prior human praxis and thus ultimately to reverse the logic of its alienation. In Lévi-Strauss, the fact that the historian makes choices about how to encode the past means that the situation in which those choices are made cannot itself be illuminated solely by the narrative in which they issue. As I suggest in chapter 1, some key aspects of the discussions of historical poetics in Veyne, Hayden White, de Certeau, and LaCapra were anticipated in that earlier exchange.

I hope to make it equally clear that, in addition to this work of contextualization, I am also trying to do something else: to address the historicity of this very framework, the one that Sartre and Lévi-Strauss assume, as evidenced in their common reliance on Marx's *Eighteenth Brumaire,* as the starting assumption for debate. In this respect, my concern is with the situation of what Henri Lefebvre indeed came to call "situationism." (And while I am not concerned with that movement as such, it is true that Sartre credited Lefebvre himself with prompting the notion of a "progressive-regressive method" in the first place.) To this end, therefore, I invoke, examine, and deploy a vocabulary that has long been associated with the problematics of the situation: the idiom of "the case." It is a concept whose history, as it happens, Lefebvre himself had investigated in the work he produced on seventeenth-century casuistry just prior to his formulation of the "progressive-regressive method" in the early 1950s.[78]

In recent years, the currency of "cases" has increased nearly as dramatically as has that of the term "historical situation" itself. And it has done so, I believe, for related reasons. The case might be initially defined as the genre in which we represent situations, and casuistry as the developed practice for making such representation, the discourse of the application of principle to circumstances. The word *case,* as its root suggests, has to do with falls and befallings, with the world of chance and contingency and with the positing of worlds—normative

78. I am not sure that critics interested in Lefebvre's work on the "production of social space" have fully registered its genealogy in the study of moral situations and cases of conscience. Not only does his earliest work from the 1930s address the issue of conscience, but the work he was doing around the time he invented the "progressive-regressive method" quite centrally concerned Pascal and jesuitical casuistry. Calling the casuistry of the Jesuits "an invention as genial as it is perfidious," Lefebvre credits the Jesuits with having had, in the early modern context, "the sense of the individual, and of the *case* of the individual." What this implies for Lefebvre is that the Jesuits must have known, "à leur maniere," that "to understand is to excuse," which in turn, for Lefebvre, has to do with a sense of how action is situated in a set of circumstances, how it is "the result of a sum of influences on isolated individual consciences." In *Pascal,* 2 vols. (Paris: Nagel, 1949, 1954), 1:85, 86 (my translation).

orders—against which chance and contingency might be established as such.[79] My aim is to consider the history of the situation by way of the history of casuistry. I consider both the transformation of casuistry in late-eighteenth-century western European writing and the peculiar resurfacing of casuistical topics and procedures in British public discourse after Waterloo: Scott's Waverley Novels, Bentham's *Plan of Reform*, Shelley's *The Cenci*. In *The Cenci*, for example, casuistry forms both part of the historical subject matter of the play—it is about the casuistry of Roman Catholicism in 1599—and part of its spectatorial form: Shelley insists that the dramatic character of the play actually "consists" in the "casuistry" enacted in its audience. It is in writings such as these, leading to and dealing with the events of 1819, that the altering of the case, not this or that case but the very concept of the case, becomes salient for the work of representation. And since the altering of the case goes hand in hand with changes in the concept of the "cause," tracing the problem of casuistry becomes another way of explaining changes in modes of explanation. "Case" and

---

79. Derrida calls attention to the etymological adventures of "case" in "My Chances/*Mes Chances:* A Rendezvous with Some Epicurean Stereophanies," collected, in English translation, in *Taking Chances: Derrida, Psychoanalysis, and Literature* (Baltimore: Johns Hopkins University Press, 1984):

> As you know, the words "chance" and "case" descend, as it were, according to the same Latin filiation, from *cadere,* which—to indicate the sense of the fall—still resounds in "cadence," "fall" (*choir*), "to fall due (*échoir*), "expiry date" (*écheance*), as well as "accident" and "incident." But, apart from this linguistic family, the same case can be made for *Zufall* or *Zufällingheit,* which in German means "chance," for *zufallen* (to fall due, *zufällig,* the accidental, fortuitous, contingent, occasional—and the word occasion belongs to the same Latin descent. A *Fall* is a case; *Einfall,* an idea that comes to mind in an apparently unforeseeable manner. Now, I would say that the unforeseeable is precisely the case, involving as it does that which falls and is not seen in advance. Is not what befalls us or descends upon us, as it comes from above, like destiny or thunder, taking our faces and hands by surprise—is this not exactly what thwarts our expectation and disappoints our *anticipation?* (p. 5)

The dual role of Blaise Pascal as, at once, leading critic of casuistry and early theorist of modern probability lends relevance to Derrida's meditation in respect to modern European intellectual history. As Ian Hacking writes in *The Emergence of Probability* (Cambridge: Cambridge University Press, 1975), "Pascal is called the founder of modern probability theory. He earns this title not only for the familiar correspondence with Fermat on games of chance, but also for his conception of decision theory, and because he was an instrument in the demolition of probabalism [the Jesuit casuistical doctrine, as Hacking explains, which is the butt of the sixth of Pascal's *Provincial Letters*], a doctrine which would have precluded rational probability theory" (p. 23). Mark Seltzer makes use of Derrida in his important account of the "passion for *cases,* in several senses, and for case histories" in "late nineteenth-century discourse generally" in *Bodies and Machines* (London: Routledge, 1992), p. 106. The agenda of chapter 4 below is at once to begin to fill in the neglected history of "the case" from the moment of Pascal to the "late nineteenth century" *and* to suggest the particular relevance of "Romantic-historical casuistry" for the recent "return to history" in literary and cultural studies.

"cause" are terms that share a grammatical intimacy we have scarcely begun to recognize.

The kind of connection I argue for, and try to illustrate, between the cases of Romantic and poststructuralist historicisms has been most explicitly recognized, I believe, on the history side of the disciplinary-administrative divide between the fields of literature and history. Carlo Ginzburg has provocatively maintained that the sort of "new history" associated with the work of Natalie Zemon Davis and himself, a historiography he discusses explicitly in terms of legal and historical cases, is best understood in terms of what he himself calls the "model" of early nineteenth-century historical fiction. Though I raise problems in chapter 4 for some of Ginzburg's particular claims, especially his refusal to extend his genealogy past Balzac and Manzoni to Scott and the Scottish Enlightenment, I think his general intuition is generous and well founded.

Behind the New History's appropriation of the historical novel, I suspect, and certainly behind my own appropriations of it here, lies Lukács's great critical study, *The Historical Novel*, introduced into Anglo-American academic circulation when it was translated into English in 1962. Lukács's book figures prominently in the argument of Jameson's *Marxism and Form* (1971), where it exemplifies for Jameson a salutary model of continental dialetic, and it has stimulated much of the increased critical attention to Scott over the last quarter century. Lukács plays a large role in the following accounts of England in 1819, and of the relationship of Romantic writing to recent critical practice. It is, however, a complex role. I take some trouble, for example, to outline a comparison between Lukács's Marxist-Hegelian history of Scott's place in post–French Revolution British culture, and M. H. Abrams's very differently situated, differently motivated, theological-Hegelian history of Wordsworth's place in post–French Revolution British culture. Both books, I argue, offer themselves as reperformances of a Hegelianism they find in their respective objects of study. While trying to resist this sort of assimilation of British Romanticism to Hegelianism here, I will nonetheless try to explore the implications of that form of critical repetition. I will also recast some of Lukács's particular claims about the genesis and "soul" of the new historical self-consciousness he saw Scott "embodying" in a new literary form.

In the course of thinking through these varied and complex topics since I first taught "England in 1819" back in 1981, I am sure I have raised more questions than I have settled. One relatively simple question that the course made unavoidable was how to explain the magnitude and quality of literary work produced in so brief a stretch of months in the late Regency around the time of Peterloo. A related question that emerged was why confine a cultural study of

England in 1819 to literary materials. I wish to offer just a concluding comment about each of these questions, but to do so I will route my remarks through Lukacs's argument about the role of new forms of "massification" in producing the phenomenon that was "the Waverley novels" in the years after Waterloo.

As students of *The Historical Novel* will recall, Lukács's opening explanation of the form's genesis argues that the practices of mass conscription and propagandization in the Napoleonic wars were crucial in the concrete shaping of the new historicity. On Lukács's account, what he calls the "inner life of the nation" is linked with the modern mass army in a way it could not have been with the absolutist armies, and in two ways: first, "recruitment propaganda for Europe's first mass wars" had, as Lukács puts it, to "reveal the social content, the historical presuppositions and circumstances of the struggle, to connect up the war with the entire life and possibilities of the nation's development"; and, second, in respect to the issue of access to travel, "[w]hat previously was experienced only by isolated and mostly adventurous-minded individuals, namely an acquaintance with Europe or at least certain parts of it, becomes in this period the mass experience of hundreds of thousands, of millions."[80] Hence arise what Lukács calls "the concrete possibilities for men to comprehend their own existence as something historically conditioned, for them to see in history something which deeply affects their daily lives and immediately concerns them."[81] It should be clear that in the context of a discussion of military history, Lukács's "men" cannot be taken as gender neutral, and the gendering of the historical domain is an issue that will arise in the case of Anna Barbauld, discussed in chapter 2. My point here, though, is that massification continued in Britain "by other means," as it were, after the conclusion of the war, and produced a sense of social life as *both* conditioned *and* made by working human beings.

The powerful mass demonstrations and mass media of England in 1819 fueled each other in a mutual challenge that aimed not only at the Liverpool Administration but at the very terms on which it conceived its legitimacy. The Six Acts, which were framed to counter this challenge, addressed both fronts at once. The texts of the Seditious Meetings Prevention Bill (number four of the

---

80. Lukács, *The Historical Novel,* p. 24.

81. Ibid., p. 24. Nor should my heuristic use of Lukács here and elsewhere in this account be understood as unaware of Katie Trumpener's critique in "National Character, Nationalist Plots: National Tale and Historical Novel in the Age of *Waverley,* 1806–1830," *ELH* 60 (fall 1993): 685–731, and in her groundbreaking study, *Bardic Nationalism* (Princeton, N.J.: Princeton University Press, forthcoming). Although Scott synthesized many more kinds of literary developments than Lukács allows, it remains true that the Waverley series became the historical node through which these synthesized materials interpreted and changed the world of history and fiction writing. Hence my focus on Scott here.

six) and the Newspaper Stamp Duties Bill (number six) give evidence of such mutual involvement in the politics of representation. The latter, for example, is aimed explicitly at "all pamphlets and printed papers containing observations upon public events and occurrences, tending to excite hatred and contempt of the government and constitution of these realms as by law established," the former at public events that could be staged for such published "observations."[82]

The fight over the Six Acts was a metadebate staged both in and out of Parliament and carried out with a sense of urgency that makes clear the magnitude of the stakes for both sides. The record of the Parliamentary arguments alone, from November 18 until the vote on December 30, fills almost sixteen hundred pages in Hansard's register.[83] It amounts to so much evidence of a widespread consensus about the power of public letters at this moment of English history. It is the consensus that Shelley wrote from when he pressed Leigh Hunt to write a paper on the "actual state of the country" in the final days of 1819: "Every word a man has to say is valuable to the public now" and might "awaken the minds of the people."[84] By 1819, England's fourth estate, like the third estate that the Abbé Sieyes announced to France in 1788, had achieved a new level of intensity. The eighteenth-century public sphere, one might say, had come of age.[85]

And yet, in doing so, it also reached a particular kind of crisis. As I have noted, it is almost certainly during the latter stages of the debate on Peterloo, which is to say precisely during the framing of the Six Acts, that Shelley not only composed the sonnet we call "England in 1819" but also first ventured his famous claim about the "unacknowledged legislators of the world."[86] Even as it testifies to the complexity of relations between the sphere of the state and the public sphere in the England of 1819, Shelley's remark also adumbrates a complicating development, for it is addressed as much to the prosaic literary public sphere of the Benthamite reformers as it is to the official state apparatuses that those reformers, and Shelley himself in his less exalted moods, sought to challenge. What we find signaled here with Shelley (though anticipated by

---

82. The citation is from Hansard's texts of the Six Acts, *Hansard Parliamentary Debates*, 1st ser., 41 (1820), col. 1678.

83. That is, most of volume 41 of Hansard's *Debates*.

84. Shelley to Leigh Hunt, December 23, 1819, LPBS, 2:166.

85. In addition to his *Making of English Reading Audiences,* see Jon Klancher's "Introduction" to the forum on "Romanticism and its Publics," in *Studies in Romanticism* 33, no. 4 (summer 1995): 523–25.

86. The remark survives in the manuscript of *A Philosophical View of Reform,* where it follows the discussion of the status of various representative systems both in the course of Western history and at the present moment of global development (WPBS, 7:20). The phrase itself, however, is not original with Shelley, as I explain below in chapter 2.

other writers) is the emergence within the literary public sphere of what might, with some qualification, be called a nineteenth-century "counter public sphere," one which was soon recognized as such. Contextualizing Tennyson's aestheticism in 1831, his friend Arthur Henry Hallam would look back on the moment of 1819, though he called it the moment of Shelley and Keats, to insist that it witnessed the establishment of a new kind of literary domain. This was, Hallam wrote, a domain of distinterested writing, imaginative poetry, what Hallam himself, uncannily echoing Keats's own letters of this period, called a "poetry of sensation." The fact that the world of English letters could develop this alternative world within itself, and that both could be assigned so powerful a social role, further attests to the press's power to dominate public culture in that historical moment.[87] The institutional forms forged by that power have been so far reaching in their effects as to leave neither means nor place of vantage for taking their measure.[88]

It is no doubt true that a full-dress "cultural studies" approach to "England in 1819" would want to go well beyond the spheres I have described here to address painting, theater, architecture, urban planning (the Regent's commissioning of Thomas Nash to reconfigure fashionable London), educational practices, and dress itself—this *was* still the Beau Brummell era.[89] My emphasis

87. For an overview of these developments, see Nancy Fraser, "Rethinking the Public Sphere: A Contribution to the Critique of Actually Existing Democracy," in *The Phantom Public Sphere,* ed. Bruce Robbins (Minneapolis: University of Minnesota Press, 1993), pp. 1–32. For a fuller account of its possible application to the late-Romantic assessment of the literary culture of England in 1819, see my "Hallam, Tennyson, and the Poetry of Sensation: Aesthetic Allegories of a Counter Public Sphere," *Studies in Romanticism* 33, no. 4 (winter 1994): 527–37.

88. In our century, however, cinema has begun to take on this task. One need only think of how central to the mode and matter of *Citizen Kane* is the print culture of the nineteenth-century, from its opening quotation of a poem of 1800—"In Xanadu did Kubla Khan / A stately pleasure dome decree"—to its interest in the apotheosis of print leverage in the role played by William Randolph Hearst's newspapers in U.S. foreign policy in the 1890s.

89. Much of the broader-gauged work on the rich material culture of this period of Regency England has yet to be written, but see, for example, Richard Altick's remarks on this period in *The Shows of London* (Cambridge, Mass.: Belknap Press, 1978) and some of the work on, for example, English fairs, in Peter Stallybrass and Allon White, *The Politics and Poetics of Transgression* (London: Methuen, 1986), pp. 118–24. See also Mark Judd, "The Oddest Combination of Town and Country: Popular Culture and the London Fairs, 1800–1860," in *Leisure in Britain 1780–1939,* ed. John K. Walton and James Walvin (Manchester: Manchester University Press, 1983), pp. 11–30. Certainly, it was a time when the material culture of the past was beginning to be seriously organized in museums, public antiquarian collections, and in the houses of private collectors, such as Walter Scott's Abbotsford, which Scott constructed from 1812–24 as a monument to the material culture of the past. See Sutherland, *Life of Walter Scott,* pp. 156–57. Moreover, as we shall see, there is reason to read Scott as creating strong analogies between his own novels and the nonliterary popular amusements of the past, such as the tournament depicted in *Ivanhoe.* For a remarkable study of literature in relation to popular amusement, and a methodological tour de

here has been on what I have from the start been calling *literary culture,* partly because of the special role of public letters in creating the kind of de facto contemporaneity that Sigfried Kracauer sees as established in the changing conditions of communicative exchange.[90] By the same token, however, in insisting on the special place of the "literary" in the contest over how and by whom England is to be represented in 1819, I nonetheless want to maintain a relatively broad sense of what constitutes the literary itself. Indeed, as Raymond Williams has argued, what we call the Romantic period marks a critical phase in the history of the very concept of "literature,"[91] and of course in the correlated concept of "criticism." All this is quite patent in English writing after Waterloo, especially in 1819, and I attend to such topics throughout.

It is in any event just this sense of the vital *political* power of national literary self-representation in 1819, and in England's post-Waterloo moment more generally, that helps to explain the extraordinary literary production of this period in virtually all forms.[92] Most of the writers, at least the male writers, who dominate English letters in 1819 earlier showed talent for and interest in some other professional field: Shelley in science, Scott in law, Keats in pharmacology. Byron seemed destined for politics (though he published poetry before his maiden address to the House of Lords); Hazlitt was a painter; Cobbett a soldier. They were

---

force, see Bill Brown, *The Material Unconscious: Stephen Crane and American Amusement* (Cambridge, Mass.: Harvard University Press, 1997).

90. Kracauer produces this notion of a de facto contemporaneity in his response to Walter Benjamin's and George Kubler's critiques of the "homogeneous empty time" posited in bourgeois historiography. Kracauer's account appears in the chapter called "The Riddle of Time," in *History: The Last Things before the Last,* (New York: Oxford University Press, 1969), pp. 139–63.

91. Raymond Williams, *Marxism and Literature* (New York: Oxford University Press, 1977), pp. 45–54. See also David Bromwich, "The Invention of Literature," in *A Choice of Inheritance: Self and Community from Edmund Burke to Robert Frost* (Cambridge, Mass.: Harvard University Press, 1989), pp. 1–19. See also Michel Foucault, *The Order of Things: An Archaeology of the Human Sciences* (New York: Random House, 1970), pp. 299–300; and Philippe Lacaue-Labarthe and Jean-Luc Nancy, *The Literary Absolute,* trans. Philip Barnard and Cheryl Lester (Albany, N.Y.: SUNY Press, 1988).

92. One of the most far-reaching contemporary accounts of the power of writing in society for this period, of course, was produced by Madame de Stael, in *De La Litterature Consideré dans ses Rapports Avecs Les Institutions Sociales* (1800), translated into English, with the suggestive title *The Influence of Literature Upon Society,* 2 vols. (Boston: Wells and Wait, 1813). This is not to suggest, needless to say, that women had no access to the literary public sphere in this period, though, as we shall see below in the case of Anna Barbauld, a stubborn misogyny in the reviewing establishment often sought to deny women writers the historically interventionist role more and more accorded to male writers. The groundbreaking discussion of writing, gender, and professionalism in this period is Mary Poovey's *The Proper Lady and the Woman Writer: Ideology and Style in the Works of Mary Wollstonecraft, Mary Shelley, and Jane Austen* (Chicago: University of Chicago Press,

all arguably, though in different degrees, drawn to letters out of sense that this is where (in every sense) the action was—where the work of cultural specification, historical determination, and national constitution seemed crucially to be going on. The motivations of literary scholars who have willy-nilly adopted the paradigms of this moment are probably murkier and more various. Certainly they cannot claim quite the same cultural leverage for their academic practices. But while new media and new forms of publicity have challenged the domain of literature and literary culture, the power of culture in that medium, residual as it may be, has clearly been thought worth the fight. The age of the world picture is not behind us yet.

1984). For a longer historical perspective on the same question, see Catherine Gallagher, *Nobody's Story: The Vanishing Acts of Women Writers in the Marketplace, 1670–1820* (Berkeley: University of California Press, 1994).

PART ONE

The "Historical Situation"
of Romanticism

Section One

WRITING
HISTORICISM,
THEN AND NOW

Chapter One

CULTURAL SPECIFICITY AFTER STRUCTURALISM: DATING THE "RETURN TO HISTORY"

$\mathcal{N}$ot even the briefest account of the way literary studies have been conducted in recent years, at least in England and America, could avoid coming to terms with the historicization of methods and objects of inquiry in the field. This new historicity in criticism has been fashioned by diverse hands that have not always let each other know what they are doing, or agreed about it when they do. The turn, or return, to history could not be described as entirely inadvertent, however, since it seems to have been made at least partly in response to an explicit call for a change in practice. "Always historicize," Fredric Jameson famously enjoined his readers in the very opening words of *The Political Unconscious* (1981), a book that would win an immense academic readership through the 1980s.[1] And though the terms of this advice were by no means self-explanatory, many readers evidently attempted to heed it. Not that *The Political Unconscious* was the only place readers would have found such an injunction at that particular moment in our recent critical history.[2] A number of books appeared between roughly 1977 and 1983, that issued a similar call, and the injunction would eventually be understood as having been implicit in criticism interested in the new "microhistory" brought into focus by the work of Michel

---

1. Fredric Jameson, *The Political Unconscious: Narrative as a Socially Symbolic Act* (Ithaca, N.Y.: Cornell University Press, 1981), p. 9.
2. They would have found it, or some variation, in Raymond Williams's *Marxism and Literature* (New York: Oxford University Press, 1977), Frank Lentricchia's *After the New Criticism* (Chicago: University of Chicago Press, 1980), Stephen Greenblatt's *Renaissance Self-Fashioning* (Chicago: University of Chicago Press, 1980), Marilyn Butler's *Romantics, Rebels, and Reactionaries* (New York: Oxford University Press, 1981), and Jerome McGann's *The Romantic Ideology* (Chicago: University of Chicago Press, 1983). Lentricchia's much-read, widely reviewed book bears two telling epigraphs: "Anti-historical method is nothing but metaphysics," from Gramsci, and, from Lukács, " . . . in the case of almost every insoluble problem we perceive that the search for a solution leads us to history."

Foucault and in the criticism of feminists who saw their cause advanced by closer attention to "history."[3]

The vagueness of the injunction to "historicize" meant, however, that it could mean different things to different people, and questions of motive, implication, and self-conception across the range of this new work have in fact been much debated. Almost as soon as the new wave of historical criticism began to form, it had become in turn an object of analysis.[4] Numerous metacommentaries now exist, and they most readily identify their object of criticism, problematically, by the term "new historicism," usually attributed to Stephen Greenblatt.[5] The term is problematic in part because of the parallel, and to some extent complementary, narrative that one could produce about developments in Anglo-American—or at least in American—departments of history over the same period. The very concept of context, never a stable one, came under direct and insistent scrutiny in the late 1970s by historians with interests in literary and aesthetic theory, and the challenge would continue to be pressed in the ensuing years. Books of 1978 by Hayden White and Dominick LaCapra explicitly problematized the question of historical contexts.[6] The issues raised in each have continued to remain very much in play.[7]

As I sketch some contexts for my own contextual studies of England in 1819, I will not, of course, be producing a systematic review of the complex and dy-

3. For an overview of Foucauldian historicism see Simon During, *Foucault and Literature: Towards a Genealogy of Writing* (London: Routledge, 1992); for an overview of feminist historicism, see Catherine Hall, *White, Male, and Middle Class* (London: Routledge, 1992), especially pp. 1–40.

4. There has been at least one book-length study of this issue—Brook Thomas, *The New Historicism and Other Old-Fashioned Topics* (Princeton, N.J.: Princeton University Press, 1991)—and two anthologies, both edited by H. Aram Veeser, *The New Historicism* (London: Routledge, 1989), and *The New Historicism Reader* (New York: Routledge, 1994). For a challenge to the novelty of the new historicism, see Carolyn Porter, "Are We Being Historical Yet?" *South Atlantic Quarterly* 87 (fall 1988): 743–86. For a defense of the practice and a suggestive genealogy, see Catherine Gallagher, "Marxism and the New Historicism," in *The New Historicism,* ed. Veeser, pp. 37–48.

5. Stephen Greenblatt uses the term to describe what he takes to be the new critical practice, in a special issue of *Genre* 15 (spring-summer 1982): 5. As has been often pointed out, however, there have been many similar coinages in the past, most relevantly, for example, James Harvey Robinson's *The New History* (New York: Macmillan, 1916), pp. 1–25.

6. Hayden White, *Tropics of Discourse* (Baltimore: Johns Hopkins University Press, 1978), and Dominick LaCapra, *A Preface to Sartre* (London: Methuen, 1978). White's book revisits questions raised by his earlier *Metahistory: The Historical Imagination in Nineteenth-Century Europe* (Baltimore: Johns Hopkins University Press, 1973), while LaCapra's book anticipates a series of later essays collected in *Rethinking Intellectual History: Texts, Contexts, Language* (Ithaca, N.Y.: Cornell University Press, 1983) and in *Soundings in Critical Theory* (Ithaca, N.Y.: Cornell University Press, 1989).

7. For a critique of the so-called linguistic turn in recent historiography, see Bryan D. Palmer, *Descent into Discourse: The Reification of Language and the Writing of Social History* (Philadelphia: Temple University Press, 1990).

namic relations between history and criticism in recent years. Nor will I try to survey the general reconfiguration of methods and practices among the disciplines of the humanities, let alone between those of the humanities and the social and natural sciences—though any claim about the relation of history and criticism must acknowledge changing relationships in those wider domains of recent institutional history.[8] Nor yet will I synopsize the growing body of commentary on the "return to history" in criticism—though I will begin by considering some issues raised by one of those commentaries in particular. Rather, I wish to examine, with some care, the concept of historical specificity that informs critical practice in literary and cultural studies of recent years. I want to consider both its own specificity and its own history. Tracing its genealogy to the Sartre/Lévi-Strauss debate of the late 1950s and early 1960s, I will attempt to move from a relatively broad view of how nominalism and structural "homology" inform recent criticism to a more particular understanding of cultural chronology, historical scale, and the status of what I call "dated specificity" in that same body of critical theory and practice. I will try to describe the features of the conceptual framework in which I see this dated specificity achieving its distinctive form of intelligibility and then suggest in a preliminary way how this framework relates to the British discourse on the spirit of the age in writers such as Shelley, Hazlitt, Carlyle, and Mill.

1. Exemplifying Nominalism

The commentary with which I would like to launch this discussion is an analysis offered by Jameson a decade or so after he urged his readers always to historicize, and it appears in the book—*Postmodernism, Or The Cultural Logic of Late Capitalism*—that has begun to achieve the same kind of status in the 1990s that *The Political Unconscious* enjoyed in the 1980s. One can fairly read the book's long central discussion, which appears under the simple rubric "Theory," as Jameson's effort to survey some of the ways in which his own injunction has or has not been heeded in the intervening decade. After a decade of historicisms in, for example, literature, literary criticism, and film, Jameson returns on this occasion for a new historicization of historicism itself.[9] Although Jameson dis-

8. Efforts to address these wider domains, but with "literature" and "history" very much in focus, can be found in the essays collected in *Questions of Evidence: Proof, Practice, and Persuasion Across the Disciplines*, ed. James Chandler, Arnold Davidson, and Harry Harootunian (Chicago: University of Chicago Press, 1994).

9. I am not forgetting Jameson's early essay, "Marxism and Historicism," *New Literary History* 11 (autumn 1979): 41–73; it is just that, in retrospect, this survey of various modes of historicism seems to be an exploratory warm-up for the methodological discussion in *The Political Unconscious* rather than a fully elaborated account of it before the fact.

cusses new historicism under the philosophical rubrics "immanence and nominalism," it becomes clear as he proceeds that the latter category subsumes the former: he considers new historicism as part of a "general movement toward immanence or what Theodore Adorno called nominalism."[10] Jameson thus borrows from Adorno a term that Adorno had taken from Benedetto Croce. In Croce, the nominalist claim that "classes" do not exist is pointedly inflected with an anti-Marxian critique that may provide some indication of what is politically at stake in this argument for both Adorno and Jameson.[11] Croce himself adopted the term from the history of medieval and post-medieval philosophy, where it stands in opposition to philosophical realism. Nominalism can be taken, for present purposes, to name the view that names themselves are imposed on the things they name, that individuals in the world may be real but not the classes, kinds, or concepts by which we organize them. Such categories, for nominalism, as it is traditionally distinguished from "realism," are best understood as heuristic frames, matters of convenience.[12]

One of the distinct advantages of Jameson's discussion of new historicism as a form of nominalism is that it gives him something to say in the first place about the problem of the very term, "new historicism," for the term has been, in a sense, just a name, a category imposed on a diverse array of academic work that has been produced over the last ten or fifteen years. Jameson's account of new historicism's status as a category term for "a shared writing practice" masquerading as a critical movement thus permits us to see it as practicing the nom-

10. Fredric Jameson, *Postmodernism, or, The Cultural Logic of Late Capitalism* (Durham, N.C.: Duke University Press, 1991), p. 191.

11. Croce articulates his nominalist refusal of the theory of social classes in "The Idea of Classes as Real Entities," in *My Philosophy* (London: George Allen & Unwin, 1949), pp. 79–83, which begins by lamenting that for the past century the world has been beset by "something like a medieval troop of hellequins or harlequins, or a ride of devils, called the 'social classes'" and ends by insisting that "the life of classes is a fiction." For a recent commentary on these issues, see the discussion of "Historicism, Radicalism, and Marxism," in David D. Roberts, *Benedetto Croce and the Uses of Historicism* (Berkeley: University of California Press, 1987), pp. 238–65. For a recent account that addresses historical nominalism in relation to political ideologies of class, see Jacques Rancière, *The Names of History: On the Poetics of Knowledge,* trans. Hassan Melehy (Minneapolis: University of Minnesota Press, 1994), where Rancière explains why, in the "royal-empiricist" mode of historians such as Alfred Cobban, the "words of history must be names": "A name identifies, it doesn't class. The evil is slight as long as kings—whose names, with the exception of a few impostors, guarantee their identity—make the history. It risks becoming irremediable when classes take the place of kings, precisely since these classes are not classes" (pp. 33–34).

12. For a recent, post-Kuhnian account of the nominalism-realism debate, see Ian Hacking, *Representing and Intervening* (Cambridge: Cambridge University Press, 1983), pp. 108–111. For a celebrated nominalist manifesto that includes an account of "the principle of nominalism," see Nelson Goodman, *Problems and Projects* (Indianapolis: Bobbs-Merrill, 1972), especially pp. 155–98.

inalism that, in effect, it preaches.[13] Because new historicism can be thought of in this way, as a movement that is not a movement, it becomes, for Jameson, paradoxically "typical" of Postmodernism itself, a condition which seems to prohibit the level of historical generality required to establish historical movements in the first place. Offered as a loose frame of reference for conceptualizing a range of practices and practitioners, it is refused by the very "individuals" it was meant to name: Jameson tellingly notes that almost no one whom anyone else thinks of as a new historicist tends to regard himself or herself in that way. New historicism can therefore be said to perform its nominalism on different levels—that is, not only in respect to its particularizing critical practice but also in respect to its own self-construction.

To turn from new historicism's "performance" to its "pedagogy," one may also take Jameson to be suggesting that, in its teaching about the past, new historicism retroactively seems to make earlier forms and outcomes of classification practices—genres, periods, "isms" themselves—seem nominalistically suspect, mere names in a discourse.[14] There is considerable independent corroboration for Jameson's argument here. One could point to the work of René Wellek, for example, who in his writings from the 1940s had strongly urged a realist position on the issue of the normative shape of periods in literary history.[15] Late in his career, for an early number of *New Literary History*, Wellek produced a more skeptical essay, "The Fall of Literary History," that anticipated with dismay the growing sense of arbitrariness about such categories and that dramatized his own inability to respond to it satisfactorily.[16] The spread of

13. Jameson, *Postmodernism*, p. 184. The second half of the central "theory" chapter of this book deals with deconstruction and the example of de Man's *Allegories of Reading*. The link between de Man and the nominalism of the new historicism, a connection that is self-consciously stretched, has to do for Jameson precisely with de Man's problematic relation to periods as categories: "[De Man's] repudiation of the periodizing categories of the manuals is a complicated and dialectical one, since they are also *retained* in de Man's work"; it is crucial for de Man, says Jameson, "to secure the historical specificity of the eighteenth century" for on Jameson's account the "uncertainties about the . . . historical specificity" of de Man's Rousseau, "project uncertainties about de Man's own project" (pp. 221, 220).

14. The performance-pedagogy distinction, which I return to in chapter 5, is developed by Homi K. Bhabha, "DissemiNation: Time, Narrative, and the Margins of the Modern Nation," in *Nation and Narration*, ed. Homi K. Bhabha (London: Routledge, 1990), pp. 295–99.

15. In the early Wellek, the period concept is worked out over the course of several pieces, "Periods and Movements in Literary History," *English Institute Annual 1940* (1941; rprt. New York: AMS Press, 1965), pp. 73–93; see also the closing chapter of Wellek and Austin Warren's influential manual, *Theory of Literature* (1942; rprt. New York: Harcourt Brace Jovanovich, 1984), pp. 252–69, and the two-part essay "The Concept of 'Romanticism' in Literary History," *Comparative Literature* 1 (winter 1949): 1–23 and 147–72.

16. Rene Wellek, *The Attack on Literature and Other Essays* (Chapel Hill: University of North Carolina Press, 1982), pp. 64–77. The larger problem at issue here, to which I shall be returning

nominalist suspicion could indeed be illustrated by reference to any number of critical works in the last ten or twenty years, especially in works that enforce a self-conscious commitment to the local and the particular.[17]

Jameson's point is precisely not, however, that this new nominalism comes out of nowhere. Looking outside the academy to survey various forms of cultural and intellectual activity since modernism, including filmic techniques of unresolved montage, Jameson insists that he has "every interest" in pursuing such practices to contextualize more broadly the nominalism he sees informing Postmodern critical practice.[18] In this respect, he follows Adorno's own representation of nominalism's gradual emergence in modernism. Nor does Jameson avow a nostalgia for the universals of a prior order, though his disavowal of nostalgia takes the oblique form of a report that *Adorno* suffers from no such nostalgia. What Jameson seems to be seeking, still following Adorno, is a mode of intellectual practice that will eschew mere localism and retain the totalizing impulses of antinominalist conceptualization, without at the same time lapsing into a nonmaterialist dialectic of "ideas." Jameson's effort produces a striking analysis of the way in which specificity is conceptualized in the cultural-historical work of his moment, though that is not quite the way in which he puts things.

When Jameson looks inside the academy to the intellectual genealogy of new historicist nominalism, he traces it to Lévi-Straussian structuralism and to the development and spread of "the method of the *homology*" in the study of culture (p. 187). This "method," Jameson reminds his readers, offered an analysis that breaks down a culture into interchangeable signs in a social system. By means of homology, one could extend the sense of "text" to identify a range of seemingly disparate cultural formations and thus study them in juxtaposition as cultural ensembles. It is not that this in itself is news. Rather, Jameson is keen to show how the method of homology enables such "texts" as "family, class, daily

---

again and again in what follows, is the assignment of normative power to the historical period or date, paradoxically, in conjunction with an arbitrary manner of determining dates in the new periodicalized public sphere of the chronological code.

17. See for example, Clifford Geertz's much-cited *Local Knowledge* (New York: Basic Books, 1983) and Naomi Schor's "story of the rise of detail" in *Reading in Detail* (New York: Methuen, 1987), p. 3. Alan Liu provides a rich survey of what he calls the commitment to such "detailism" in recent cultural history in his essay, "Local Transcendence: Cultural Criticism, Postmodernism, and the Romanticism of Detail," *Representations* 32 (fall 1990): 83–96. Jameson, for his part, remarks that "power" in recent criticism is "not a 'transcendental' theoretical object on which the text works and which it seeks to produce, but rather a reassurance that secures its immanence and allows the reader's attention to dwell and persist in the detail without guilt or discomfort." *Postmodernism*, p. 189.

18. Jameson, *Postmodernism*, p. 192. Further citations will appear in the text.

life, the visual, and narrative" (p. 186) to (if I may so put it) overcome their specificity. For in a structuralist analysis, he says, in spite of presenting what he terms "specific problems," such homological texts are nonetheless constructed so as to "combine into problems of a qualitatively heightened type when we try to read them side by side and incorporate them into a single, relatively unified discourse" (p. 187) The crucial point to notice in the homological method thus has to do with its curious double game: "Lévi-Strauss evades the establishment of some fictive totalizing entity such as Society itself, under which more local and heterogeneous entities of the type already enumerated used to be organically and hierarchically ordered. But he can do so only by inventing a different kind of fictive . . . entity [the category of 'structure'] in terms of which the various texts . . . can be read as somehow being 'the same': this is the method of the *homology*" (p. 187). Retrospectively viewed, homology becomes in Jameson's account the means of establishing the new relations of writing and culture—what Serge Eisenstein in another context called a "montage of historical attractions"—that would distinguish the new historicism from both the New Criticism and the literary historicism that had been practiced in preceding decades (p. 190).[19]

Jameson's own relation to this "method" is no simple matter, however, for the evidence of the homological construction of evidence is indeed conspicuous in Jameson's critique of it. For instance, while he allows, even contends, that the very idea of taking or making an example of new historicism is problematic in the extreme, he is immediately led to try doing both. In pursuit of this goal, he settles on Walter Benn Michaels's production of "yet another such montage" in a well-known study of American naturalism: "It is therefore as inappropriate as it is unavoidable to read *The Gold Standard* as a characteristic specimen of new historicism, an operation which . . . requires us to develop or to abstract some useful stereotype of this 'movement'" (p. 186). We can underestimate the extreme reflexivity of Jameson's procedure here if we fail to see, although Jameson does not make the point explicitly, that the status of the example is already markedly troubled in Michaels's own account of his project. When Michaels introduces the argument of *The Gold Standard* with a set-piece reading of Charlotte Perkins Gilman's *The Yellow Wallpaper,* he offers the story precisely as an "exemplary text" about an "exemplary disease" (hysteria). Aware of the pressure he puts on the story, Michaels makes a point of announcing that "the

19. In these invocations of Lévi-Strauss and Eisenstein, Jameson is describing or redescribing a feature of new-historicist practice that has also been noted by Liu, who calls this feature "paradigmatism" in "The Power of Formalism," p. 741, and by LaCapra, who calls it "weak montage" in *Soundings in Critical Theory,* pp. 193–94.

only relation that literature as such has to culture as such is that it is part of it."[20]

Despite the disclaimer, however, Michaels finds himself having to maintain that there is a way in which a "a certain literature" can be taken as "exemplary." Not surprisingly, the attempt to qualify the point runs afoul, most uncharacteristically for as clear a stylist as Michaels, of a quite blatant redundancy: "if 'The Yellow Wallpaper' is for me an exemplary text" for the culture of consumption, he says, it is because "it *exemplifies* that culture."[21] Though not a passage Jameson himself cites, Michaels's curious tautology might be taken as itself exemplifying, with particular force, Jameson's point about homology in New-Historicist practice. It illustrates how seemingly incomparable products of a culture may be juxtaposed in such a way as to suggest relationships of expressive similarity without having to articulate the basis of their fungibility. It is as if, to anticipate a vocabulary I will be developing below, the case of Michaels's book were being used to illustrate the "writing practice" wherein a range of cases are accepted and promoted as the same kind of case but with no indication of what it is that they are all supposed to be cases *of.*

The problem of cultural exemplification in historical criticism, or what Kenneth Burke long ago called the problem of the "representative anecdote," is inextricable from the problem of how to identify a historical culture in the first place (GM, pp. 59–61). Thus, Jameson's self-implicating pastiche of new historicist exemplification also implicates him in questionable practices for asserting the historical contemporaneity and cultural intelligibility of his field of objects. Through various forms of juxtaposition, the "Theory" chapter as a whole, and indeed the entire book, *Postmodernism,* constructs a reading of the culture of the 1980s, just as Jameson had done for an earlier decade in the predecessor essay of 1984, "Periodizing the '60s."[22] In this light, the Andy Warhol

20. Walter Benn Michaels, *The Gold Standard and the Logic of Naturalism: American Literature at the Turn of the Century* (Berkeley: University of California Press, 1987), p. 27.

21. The passage reads as follows:

[I]f "The Yellow Wallpaper" is for me an exemplary text, it is not because it criticizes or endorses the culture of consumption but precisely because, in a rigorous, not to say obsessive, way, it exemplifies that culture. The nervous breakdown of its narrator may well be, as I have suggested, a function of her involvement in a certain political economy of selfhood, but even if . . . that breakdown is not a gesture of resistance to the economy, it would surely be odd to construe it as an endorsement of the economy. After all, it is not as if the narrator *likes* thinking of the self as permanently under construction; she just thinks it is. And "The Yellow Wallpaper" shows us exactly what it would mean to think that. (ibid., p. 27.)

22. Jameson organizes the entire "theory" chapter as an analysis of juxtaposed texts, Walter Benn Michaels's in the first half and Paul de Man's in the second—books which were published just three years apart in the mid-1980s—and makes other local juxtapositions along the way. "Periodizing the '60s" collected in Jameson, *The Syntax of History,* Vol. 2 of *The Ideologies of Theory: Essays 1971–1986* (Minneapolis: University of Minnesota Press, 1988), pp. 178–208.

painting that adorns the cover of Jameson's book may be seen as establishing, by its title, the book's terminus a quo: "Diamond Dust Shoes, 1980." The ironized basis for this periodization of the 1980s, the claim for the intelligibility of the decade as a field of study, is precisely its status as a time without a movement. Only such deeply nondescript critical activities as are named by "the new historicism" could be accounted a critical movement in such a time. It is a time when structuralist homologies appear without the "structures" that warrant them, as if (Jameson suggests) this had been the whole point of the structuralist project in the first instance.

2. Specifying History

I have singled out these two related insights in Jameson's analysis—both the point about new historicism as a form of nominalism and the one about its genealogical relation to the structuralist methodology—because, taken together, they seem to open up a perspective on the question of the conceptual and intellectual-historical status of "specificity" in recent discussions of history and literature. I have in mind the kind of claims in which the commentator explicitly critiques a generalized or ahistorical approach in favor of a close examination of the "specific historical circumstances" of production or reception, or the "specific historical conditions" that made such and such a cultural outcome possible. With the help of French theorist and historian Paul Veyne, I would like to elaborate this question of "specificity" in a direction different from the one taken by Jameson himself.

In his provocative but often enigmatic methodological study, *Comment On Écrit L'Histoire* (1971), Veyne argued that "the interest specific to history" is precisely its interest in the specific as such.[23] When Veyne's discussion finally reaches its "definition of history," we find that, epistemologically, history is just "knowledge of the specific" (p. 60) and that, practically, it is just "the description of what is specific . . . in human events" (p. 59). This means that history is "not universal, and not singular" (p. 59), which is to say that it must be "generic" or, what amounts to the same thing for Veyne, "specific": "For it not to be universal, there must be a difference; for it not to be singular, it must be specific."[24] Long before it was translated into English as *Writing History* in 1984, Veyne's book had begun to affect the theory and practice of history in the Anglophone world by way of Hayden White's deployment of it in his work on "metahis-

---

23. Paul Veyne, *Writing History,* trans. Mina Moore-Rinvolucri (Middletown, Conn.: Wesleyan University Press, 1984), p. 55. Page references will hereafter appear in the text.

24. It seems plausible to take this as aimed at the "singularities" given pride of place in the historiography of Veyne's friend Foucault.

tory." Veyne's book has a twofold relevance, however, to the argument I have been sketching in Jameson. It lies partly in the fact that Veyne's avowal of historical nominalism is explicit: "nothing is more reasonable," writes Veyne, "than a nominalist conception of history" for coming to terms with what he calls "the paradox . . . of historical découpage" (pp. 46, 44). But it also lies partly in the fact that Veyne explicitly derives his account of this central paradox from perhaps Lévi-Strauss's most trenchantly polemical argument for structuralist analysis of cultures and their "logics," the argument worked out in the final chapter of *The Savage Mind* (1962).[25]

At some basic level, the problem of historical découpage turns on the double question of how to cut documents for citation and how to frame the context in which such cuttings signify as historical evidence. On Veyne's own account, the "paradox" of découpage lies in the assumption that one can, in the historiographical act, produce an objective account of events understood as in any degree the preconditions of that act. Veyne's skepticism, in other words, takes the form of a question about how it is possible to imagine that (to use Veyne's own abstract terms) "the constitution of the event as one will call it into being" (p. 44) can legitimate a constitution of the present in which this act is carried out.[26] Veyne's contention is that, while history is just the "relating of true events [or] of true facts" (pp. 11–12), the form in which such truths become historically intelligible and by which they are therefore "specified" (p. 31)

25. Although I argue for the importance of Lévi-Strauss's commentary to the recent development of this metaphor, LaCapra's remarks probably derive in part from still earlier accounts of historical practice, such as R. G. Collingwood's in *The Idea of History* (Oxford: Oxford University Press, 1945), where the phrase "scissors-and-paste history" is used to describe a set of common (and, for Collingwood, mistaken) assumptions about how the discipline is practiced (p. 260). The metaphor of *découpage* in historiography managed to achieve a peculiar kind of currency in Veyne's moment and to sustain it afterward. La Capra would soon be launching similarly oriented critiques against that sort of "cut-and-paste" historiography that relies on an exclusively "documentary" approach to reading texts, critiques made in behalf of an approach to texts as constitutive ("worklike") rather than reflective in their operation—in *Rethinking Intellectual History*, pp. 23–71, and in *Soundings in Critical Theory*, pp. 182–209. We might recall here a related notion in Foucault: what he promotes as "effective history" involves a Nietzschean knowledge that "is not made for understanding"; "it is made for cutting." See "Nietzsche, Genealogy, History," collected in *The Foucault Reader*, ed. Paul Rabinow (New York: Pantheon, 1984), p. 88. In 1971, Jameson refers to historicism's "coupures epistemologiques" in *Marxism and Form: Twentieth-Century Dialectical Theories of Literature* (Princeton, N.J.: Princeton University Press, 1971), p. 321, perhaps drawing on Louis Althusser's critique of historicism's epistemological "coupe d'essence"—or historical cross-cut—in the account of an "Outline of a Concept of Historical Time," from *Reading Capital*, trans. Ben Brewster (London: Verso, 1970), pp. 91–118.

26. Much the same kind of paradox, it seems clear, is elaborated at far greater length in a subsequent meditation on similar questions by Michel de Certeau, *The Writing of History*, trans. Tom Conley (New York: Columbia University Press, 1988), especially his discussion of "The Historiographical Operation," pp. 56–114.

is the historical plot. The choice of the kind of plot one wishes to deploy for the comprehension of one's facts is finally arbitrary. Veyne's historian indeed confronts many choices—choices in respect to point of view, scale, density, and scope. The field of history is completely undetermined, he says, except only that everything in it "must really have taken place" (pp. 11–12). If a piece of writing fulfills that one condition, it counts as a work of historiography, irrespective of the density or texture of the presentation. Although "everything is historic" on Veyne's account, there are nonetheless only "partial histories"—"partial" not only in the sense of less than total, but also in the sense of partisan. Indeed, in Veyne's more provocative reformulation of his central paradox, it is precisely *because* everything is historic that "history is what we will choose" (p. 42).

Like Jameson, Veyne refers his remarks to the theoretical framework established by Lévi-Strauss. Unlike Jameson, however, Veyne directs his readers not to Lévi-Straussian structuralism, broadly considered, but to a particular passage in a particular book: "History and Dialectic," the final chapter of *The Savage Mind*. Moreover, both in its explicit references to this chapter and in its way of echoing Lévi-Strauss's remarks, Veyne actually points to the particular context of debate in which that famous discussion appeared, for it was in "History and Dialectic" that Lévi-Strauss attempted to clinch his book-length critique of the historical method that Sartre had outlined two years earlier in *Search for a Method* and the *Critique of Dialectical Reason*. Indeed, the work of Sartre and Lévi-Strauss is so mutually defined and defining in the late 1950s and early 1960s (and arguably from much earlier) that it becomes well-nigh impossible to talk about the writings of one from that period without talking about the other, especially if "the historical" is the topic in question. The role of history in relation to anthropology—history as a process and a practice—was recognized as the fundamental question on both sides of this widely ramifying discussion. Certain echoes of this debate haunt Jameson's way of connecting structuralism and new historicism, and for good reason. Just recently this debate seems to have fallen into the penumbra of the historical middle distance—a distance like the one Sir Walter Scott tried to explain in the introduction to the first of his historical novels— where something that is neither so current as to be an object of fashion nor so ancient as to be an object of antiquarianism becomes historically invisible. Part of the burden of what follows will be to bring the terms and issues of the debate, and their survival in contemporary critical practice, more explicitly to the fore.[27]

27. Sartre, Lefebvre, the progressive-regressive method, and the Lévi-Straussian critique of it are all surprisingly neglected in the recent anthology of French and French historiographical thought in the postwar period: *Histories: French Constructions of the Past,* ed. Jacques Revel and Lynn Hunt. Vol. 1 of *Postwar French Thought,* ed. Ramona Naddaff (New York: New Press, 1995).

Sartre developed his new method on the urging of a magazine editor who asked for his views on the subject of how to think through Marxism and Existentialism after the Hungarian Revolution of 1956. Drawing on some methodological suggestions made in 1953 by Henri Lefebvre, Sartre (it is often noted) set himself the problem of how to conjoin, on the one hand, an existentialist emphasis on human agency, the stress on action in situation, and the centrality of the life-project with, on the other, a Marxian respect for historical-materialist determination.[28] Most readers familiar with Sartre's massive text of 1960, which included both the *Search* and the *Critique,* would agree, I suspect, in seeing it as extended phenomenological meditation on the maxim that appears in various forms throughout the oeuvre of Marx and Engels, most prominently at the beginning of *The Eighteenth Brumaire of Louis Bonaparte,* and that maxim is more than once cited by Sartre as summing up the central problem in his discussion: "Men make their own history, . . . but under conditions encountered, given, and transmitted from the past."[29] To offer a provisional simplification of a complex argument in a brief space, Sartre attacked this problem by way of the hypothesis that, in choosing how to frame one's course of action in the life-

---

28. At the beginning of his extended discussion of "Sartre and History" in *Marxism and Form: Twentieth-Century Dialectical Theories of Literature* (Princeton, N.J.: Princeton University Press, 1971), p. 206, however, Jameson identifies a characterization rather like this one of the project as "the customary description" and finds it inadequate.

29. Karl Marx, *The Eighteenth Brumaire of Louis Bonaparte* (first German publication 1852; rprt. New York: International Publishers, 1977), p. 15. Sartre (*Search for a Method,* trans. Hazel Barnes [New York: Knopf, 1963]) tends to attribute the slogan to Engels, as for example when he buttresses his critique of "Idealist Marxism" (p. 85) with the first such reference:

> To go further, we are also in full agreement with Engels when he wrote in that letter which furnished Plekhanov the occasion for a famous attack against Bernstein: "There does not exist, as one would like to imagine now and then, simply for convenience, any effect produced automatically by the economic situation. On the contrary, it is men themselves who make their history, but within a given environment which conditions them. . . ." (p. 31; cf. pp. 48, 87, 99)

This Marxian "text"—at once the sentence about men making history and the book for which it has come to stand as a synecdoche—seems to me to establish part of the common framework that brings Sartre and Lévi-Strauss into such fierce debate. Recounting his early intellectual development in *Tristes Tropiques,* trans. John and Doreen Weightman (Hammondsworth: Penguin, 1992; first French publication Paris: Librarie Plon, 1955), Lévi-Strauss recalls that he was introduced to Marxism when he was sixteen, that since then his "admiration for Marx has remained constant," and that he rarely broaches "a new sociological problem without first stimulating my thought by rereading a few pages of *The Eighteenth Brumaire of Louis Bonaparte* or the *Critique of Political Economy*" (p. 56). In the introduction to *Structural Anthropology,* [French ed. 1958] trans. Claire Jacobson and Brooke Schoepf (New York: Basic Books, 1963), Lévi-Strauss slightly misquotes the "famous statement by Marx, 'Men make their own history, but they do not know that they are making it,'" as indicative of his claim that the two approaches represented by history and anthropology "are inseparable" (p. 23).

project, one could be *guided* by the determining conditions of one's historical situation if one were able to see those conditions as themselves the result of earlier life-projects in earlier conditions. That is, by resort to the "regressive" analysis of the meaning or direction of history (*sens d'histoire*) generated in earlier encounters of human beings with their past (itself constituted by yet-prior encounters), one could make a better choice about the "progressive" possibilities for one's life-project.[30] Lévi-Strauss's basic response to this methodological proposal, the response echoed in Veyne's discussions, is that one cannot rely on a made history to guide the decision about a history-making project in a given situation because the history constructed for this purpose will already reflect one's choices.[31]

Noting the privileged place accorded to the epoch of the French Revolution in Sartre's (arguably prophetic) imagination of the situation facing France in the 1960s, Lévi-Strauss introduces his discussion of the historian's code by way of an analysis of the plurality of possible histories of the French Revolution and the function of decision making in historical representation—that is, by way of an argument that links historiographical "partiality" to the historian's choice:[32]

> A truly total history would cancel itself out—its product would be nought. What makes history possible is that a sub-set of events is found, for a given period, to have approximately the same significance for a contingent of individuals who have not necessarily experienced the events and may even consider them at an interval of several centuries. History is therefore never history, but history-for. It is partial in the sense of being biased even when it claims not to be, for it inevitably remains partial—that is, incomplete—and this is itself a form of partiality. When one proposes to write a history of the French Revolution one knows (or ought

30. The *Critique,* on my account, thus focuses on what LaCapra distinguishes as the "second sense of freedom" in Sartre: not the "sublime" sense of freedom as pertaining to "a desire totally to transcend a context in which existing institutions seem either empty and exhausted or overly rigid and oppressive" but, rather, a "situated freedom":

> Freedom in this second sense does not require an activist leap that defines *ab ovo* the meaning and value of the situation. However far back it goes in its reflection on itself, it finds itself already engaged in situations that are in part defined by more or less vital or exhausted traditions and institutions. Its ultimate origins are lost or continually displaced. And its task is to take up a situation whose creation it cannot claim fully as its own and to do something with it. (*Rethinking Intellectual History,* pp. 200–202).

31. I should note here that Jameson probably presupposes Sartre's work, rather than eliding it, in his analysis of structuralism and new historicism. As LaCapra observes, Sartre really is Jameson's "mentor in more than one sense"—*Rethinking Intellectual History,* p. 235.

32. One obvious precedent for seeing Marxist French-Revolution historiography as keyed to the needs of the present would be George Lefebvre's *Quatre-Vingt-Neuf* (Paris: Maison du Livre Français, 1939), in which Lefebvre concludes his account of the "men of 1789" with a rousing call, in the final paragraph of the history, to the "Jeunesse de 1939" to remember the principles of the Declaration of the Rights of Man and Citizen in their struggles against fascism (p. 246).

to know) that it cannot, simultaneously and under the same heading, be that of the Jacobin and that of the aristocrat. *Ex hypothesi,* their respective totalizations (each of which is antisymmetric to the other) are equally true.[33]

To attend to this logic, says Lévi-Strauss, is to see that one must choose between two alternative courses. One course means choosing (in turn) among the alternative partial histories and thus giving up the attempt to provide a totalizing account of them; the second course means recognizing that all these partial histories are "equally real, but only to discover that the French Revolution as commonly conceived never took place" (p. 258). Lévi-Strauss repeatedly underscores the sense that the dilemma is brought on in the first place by the Sartrean claim that one can find guidance for a project in a given historical situation in the act of consultation with the past—that one could, as Sartre insisted, establish the ground or intelligibility of a "structural anthropology" by resort to "history and dialectic."[34]

I have displaced Jameson's genealogical account of new historicism into these receding contexts in order to suggest that a fairly straightforward intellectual-historical linkage can be established between avowedly nominalist and structuralist accounts of historiography.[35] I think it is clear enough from the way in which Veyne echoes Lévi-Strauss's discussion of Sartre not only that his conceptual debt to Lévi-Strauss is considerable but also that he has chosen sides in the controversy. Indeed, while Veyne tends to link his own position on historiography to the self-identified historical nominalism of H. I. Marrou, many of the key claims of *Writing History* are implicit in Lévi-Strauss's argument.[36] To focus on this connection, then, is to begin to see something potentially revealing about how Jameson's account of new historicism and nominalism brings structuralism into play. For in Jameson, the relevance of Lévi-Strauss to new historicism is developed by way of reference to the general relationship between structure and homology in the Lévi-Straussian oeuvre rather than by

33. Lévi-Strauss, *The Savage Mind* (Chicago: University of Chicago Press, 1966), pp. 257–58. Page references will hereafter appear in the text.

34. On Sartre's claim to be carrying off this foundational project in the *Critique,* see *Search for a Method,* pp. 167–81. Lévi-Strauss's counterclaim is that the French Revolution is simply a "myth" in which "the contemporary Frenchman must believe . . . in order fully to play the part of an historical agent"—*Savage Mind,* p. 254.

35. "Nominalism" is a term that is featured in the work of both writers. Lévi-Strauss refers to the nominalism that appears in ethnological efforts to sustain a vacuous concept of "totemism." See "Australian Nominalism," chapter 2 of *Totemism,* trans. Rodney Needham (Boston: Beacon, 1963), pp. 33–55. Sartre refers to his own work as a "dialectical nominalism"—*Critique of Dialectical Reason,* vol. 1., p. 37.

36. Veyne aligns himself with Marrou's nominalism explicitly, for example, on pp. 42–43 of *Writing History.*

way of the particular analysis of historical method in *The Savage Mind*. Jameson's account of the double game in which specificity is overcome in the homological method is fair enough as a rough-and-ready sketch of what Derrida has described as "the structurality of structure" in Lévi-Strauss,[37] but it begins to stray from the topic of structuralism's relation precisely to the intellectual genealogy of new historicism, of the "history" in new historicism. It does not, in other words, address the way in which Lévi-Strauss brings his critical apparatus to bear on the problem of history as such. One can engage this question far more directly by way of the explicit analysis of "the historian's code" in the final chapter of *The Savage Mind*.

It is true that the moment when Lévi-Strauss turns to the historian's code can be read as confirming Jameson's general point about structuralism's displacement of a received form of totality—the *historical* form. But while the main body of the discussion in *The Savage Mind* addresses the specifying operations of mythical thought (what Lévi-Strauss calls "the logic of totemic classifications" [p. 35]), the point of the last chapter is to consider the specifying operations of *historical* thought (what might be called, in a parallel formulation, the logic of *chronological* classifications). Indeed, if Veyne's testimony points to Lévi-Strauss's explicit analysis of historicism in structuralist terms, rather than to the more general remarks on structure cited by Jameson, it is also true that one can find in Lévi-Strauss's own account the explicit claim that the historian's code already has its own distinctive features that set it apart from other codes, its own "particular nature" (*sa nature particulière* [p. 258]).[38] Coming to terms with that "particularity" ought, surely, to have particular relevance for thinking through Lévi-Strauss's relation to a putative neonominalism in the recent writing of history or, for that matter, in the recent historiography of literary cultures. The immediate question to be faced, therefore, is simply this: in what, for Lévi-Strauss, does the "particular nature" of historical coding consist?

Early on in his account, Lévi-Strauss supplies a reasonably straightforward answer to this question. The distinctive feature of the historian's code is that it "consists in chronology: there is no history without dates." Dates may not be all there is to history, but "they are its sine qua non, for history's entire originality and distinctive nature lie in apprehending the relation between before and af-

---

37. Jacques Derrida, "Structure, Sign, and Play," in *Writing and Difference*, trans. Alan Bass (Chicago: University of Chicago Press, 1978), p. 280.

38. To be sure, the moment when Lévi-Strauss turns to the historian's code is one that confirms Jameson's general point about structuralism's displacement of a received form of totality: here the historical form. One may nonetheless attend, as I try to do below, to the particularity of the historical code within the (totalizing) structuralist differentiation of codes.

ter, which would perforce dissolve if its terms could not, at least in principle, be dated" (p. 258). Nor, in singling out the practice of dating, is Lévi-Strauss producing a category that Sartre could call alien to the progressive-regressive method or its genealogy. The dating of events is polemically and repeatedly emphasized in Sartre's texts, both in his autobiographical claims—one must "recognize that a book written in 1956 does not resemble a book of the 1930s"—and in more remote historical claims. Against the idealizing sociology he found in much contemporary Marxism, Sartre inveighs: "A historian—even a Marxist—cannot forget that the political reality for the men of 1792 is an absolute, an irreducible. To be sure, they commit the error of ignoring the action of other forces, more muffled, less clearly discernible, infinitely more powerful. But that is exactly what defines these men as the bourgeois of 1792."[39]

Moreover, the essay by Henri Lefebvre from which Sartre says he is borrowing the very term "regressive" insists that the regressive analysis depends crucially on an exhaustive effort to date those events of the past that one seeks to investigate. In a passage that Sartre partially quotes in a footnote, Lefebvre describes one of the stages of his proposed historical-sociological method as follows: "*Analytico-régressif. Analyse de la réalite décrite. Effort pour la dater exactement (pour ne pas se contenter d'un constat portant sur des 'archaïsmes' non datés, non comparés les uns aux autres)*" [emphasis Lefebvre's].[40] What is more, in the work that Sartre so clearly made his "text" for the long sermon of the *Critique*, Marx's *Eighteenth Brumaire*, we have Marx's own most extended treatment of the problem of chronology, one which seems to involve something of a double game. On the one hand, Marx's narrative is, with the starkest possible insistence, minutely dated, and the particular dates have particular significance: "June 13[, 1849,] had still another meaning" is the sort of claim that recurs throughout Marx's analysis of the events of 1848–51 in France.[41] On the

39. *Search for a Method,* pp. 49, 41.

40. Henri Lefebvre, "Perspectives de la Sociologie Rurale," *Cahiers Internationaux de Sociologie* 14 (1953):134. It seems clear that Lefebvre's critique of "undated archaisms" is already at this point involved with Lévi-Strauss's work. In an earlier number of the *Cahiers,* Lévi-Strauss had published a famous essay, later collected in the volume *Structural Anthropology,* trans. Claire Jacobson and Brooke Grundfest Schoepf (New York: Basic Books, 1963), entitled "La Notion d'Archaïsme en Ethnologie," *Cahiers* 12 (1952):3–25, which extended the argument of a yet-earlier discussion, the chapter on the "Archaic Illusion," in *The Elementary Structures of Kinship* (*Les Structures élémentaires de la Parenté* [Paris: Presses Universitaires de France, 1949], pp. 108–25). I discuss the relation between dating practices and the historiographic-ethnographic notion of "archaism" in chapter 2. Further, to suggest the developing currency of a particular configuration of topics at this time, in the same volume of the *Cahiers* as Lefebvre's essay, one might note Claude Lefort's essay on a topic that would become crucial to the Sartre-Lévi-Strauss debate: "Societé 'sans histoire' et Historicité," *Cahiers* 14 (1953):91–114.

41. Marx, *Eighteenth Brumaire,* p. 57.

other hand, the notion of the repeatability of dates, albeit with different generic inflections, is no less central to Marx's text, where it is signaled by a joke in the book's title and explained in that famous punch line that Marx can't suppress beyond the book's celebrated second sentence: "Hegel remarks that all facts and personages of great importance in world history occur, as it were, twice. He forgot to add: the first time as tragedy, the second as farce."[42]

What I am suggesting, then, is that discussion of the structuralist preconditioning or prompting of the return to history in textual studies ought to take account not only of the general role of homology in reading the text(s) of culture but also of the particular issues involved in reading the text(s) of a *dated* culture. The problematic of the date, broadly understood as involving the whole conceptual framework for establishing chronology in historiography, has, it is now possible to see, been more central to the return to history than we might at first think. It is to come to terms more effectively with this problematic—and its attendant issues of historical explanation, contemporaneity, periodicity, anachronism, and indeed exemplification—that I revisit Lévi-Strauss's critique of Sartre's historical method.

3. Dating Cultures

In Lévi-Strauss's polemical exposition of the historian's code in "History and Dialectic," dating cultures proves to be something much more complicated than the assignment of temporal priority or posteriority to a given event. The matter of before and after does, as it were, come first, but to this "ordinal function" of dates, Lévi-Strauss adds what he calls a *cardinal* function, which indicates chronological distances and densities. Historians use fewer dates to code some periods than others, he explains, and this "variable quantity of dates applied to periods of equal duration" becomes "a gauge of what might be called the pressure of history": "there are 'hot chronologies' which are those of periods where in the eyes of the historian numerous events appear as differential elements; others, on the contrary, where for him (although not of course for the men who lived through them) very little or nothing took place" (*Savage Mind*, p. 259). So, from the point of view of studies in English literary culture, for example, the Romantic period has long been registered as a particularly hot chronology, a period given critical and editorial attention greatly disproportionate to its length because of its perceived literary intensity, and I have isolated 1819 as a hot chronology within the Romantic period for the same reasons.

42. Ibid., p. 15. For a brief commentary on Marx's meditation on the meanings of June 13 and on the problem of repetition in Marx, see Jeffrey Mehlman, *Revolution and Repetition: Marx/Hugo/Balzac* (Berkeley: University of California Press, 1977), pp. 9–17.

In Lévi-Strauss, the distinction between hot and cold chronologies follows the more famous distinction he had made in the *Conversations with Charles Charbonnier* (a broadcast on French radio in late 1959, the transcript of which was later published in French and in English translation), and then in his Inaugural Lecture for the Collège de France in 1960 (published as *The Scope of Anthropology*). He explained there that he did not recognize the common distinction made between societies that do not exist in history and those that do. In its place he puts a distinction between societies that do or do not resist "structural modification which would afford history a point of entry into their lives."[43] Cold, or "primitive," societies are machines that lack internal temperature deviation, like watches—and unlike steam engines, his preferred metaphor for "advanced societies." Cold societies have an internal environment that "neighbors on the zero of historical temperature."[44] Lévi-Strauss made several stabs at this temperature metaphor, no two exactly the same, and I offer an explanation of its recurrence for him at the end of this chapter.

For now let me point out that the historian's code described in the last chapter of *The Savage Mind* can be provisionally understood to operate entirely from within the domain of hot societies, societies in which time may be said to count, and to be counted.[45] To count or be counted for hot societies, however, time must go beyond the mere recording of temperature changes. Considered only in their ordinal and cardinal functions, dates do not by themselves constitute a basis for the historian's code, since these are not, as Lévi-Strauss says, "recurrent." To explain the point he reinvokes, under a different aspect, the thermometric metaphor:

> Changes of temperature can be coded with the help of figures, because the reading of a figure on the thermometer evokes the return of an earlier situation: whenever I read O'C., I know that it is freezing and put on my warmest coat. But a historical date, taken in itself, would have no meaning, for it has no reference outside itself: if I know nothing about modern history, the date 1643 makes me none the wiser. The code can therefore consist only of classes of dates, where each date has meaning in as much as it stands in complex relations of correlation and opposition with other dates. (p. 259)

It is not clear that Lévi-Strauss's distinction between the date and the temperature reading can stand: if I really "know *nothing*" about weather, then the thirty-degree reading does not help me much either. Nor is it clear exactly what this invocation of the thermometric metaphor implies for the distinction between

43. Lévi-Strauss, *The Scope of Anthropology*, trans. Sherry Ortner and Robert A. Paul (London: Jonathan Cape, 1967), pp. 46–47.
44. Ibid., p. 47.
45. See Marshall Sahlins, *Culture and Practical Reason* (Chicago: University of Chicago Press, 1976), pp. 50–51.

hot and cold societies. What is clear is that the third function served by dates, the function on which Lévi-Strauss dilates at some length, has to do with his claim that dates can be organized by different classes, levels, or orders of magnitude. This claim will become crucial to his exploration of the other side of his question about the historian's code: not what makes it peculiarly historical, but what makes it, for all its peculiarity, nonetheless a code.

To clarify this notion of chronological classes, Lévi-Strauss offers illustrations: "the date 1685 belongs to a class of which 1610, 1648, and 1715 are likewise members"; another class would be "1st, 2nd, 3rd, and 4th millennium"; another "January 23, 17 August, 30 September, etc" (p. 259). In this emphasis on classificatory organization lies an explanation for Lévi-Strauss's double claim that while the historian's code depends on dates it does not consist in them. The code, qua code, he says, "consists not in dates which can be ordered in a linear series but in classes of dates," i.e., in a structural principle in terms of which historical knowledge appears like myth, as "discontinuous and classificatory" in nature (p. 260). It follows that, insofar as it admits of this characterization, historical knowledge does not extend over a continuous line of time but forms instead a rectangular matrix or table composed of parallel rows of unconnected points. Each row in this matrix "represents classes of dates, which may be called hourly, daily, annual, secular, millennial for the purposes of schematization and which together make up a discontinuous set."[46] So conceived, therefore, although Lévi-Strauss does not make this connection himself, the historian's code thus obviously provides for the possibility of recognizing hot chronologies on different orders or levels, on the annual as well as the secular level: 1819 as well as the Romantic Period or the nineteenth century.

Lévi-Strauss's conception of what is involved in such a shift in levels cannot really be grasped without noting yet a further and more crucial step in his argument: each class of dates constitutes a domain that is always to be tacitly referred to the domain (the line or class of dates) just above it on the grid, of which the

---

46. Using Stephen Jay Gould's admittedly simplified binary opposition in *Time's Arrow, Time's Cycle* (Cambridge, Mass.: Harvard University Press, 1987), one might understand (1) the left to right axis of Lévi-Strauss's chart as defined by the ordinal directionality of time's arrow; (2) the vertical axis of the chart as involving ordered generalities of magnitude in the cyclical repetition; and (3) the relation between the two axes as given by the cardinal or "hinge" function of the number. Claudio Guillen's commentary on Lévi-Strauss's scheme reaches a similar conclusion, but without calling explicit attention to the cardinal dimension as the "hinge," when he explains how periods "form a series of discontinuous parts, as separate from one another as cardinal numbers are. Periods, existing somewhere between the order of chronology and that of an atemporal typology, between diachrony and synchrony, are thus a good example of 'le caractère discontinu et classificatoire de la connaissance historique.'" See *Literature as System* (Princeton, N.J.: Princton University Press, 1971) pp. 437–38.

latter class contains the principle of an intelligibility to which the former could not itself aspire. Thus, for example, the "history of the 17th century is 'annual' but the 17th century, as a domain of history belongs to another class, which codes it in relation to earlier and later centuries; and this domain of modern times in its turn becomes an element of a class where it appears correlated with and opposed to other 'times': the middle ages, antiquity, the present day, etc." (*Savage Mind*, p. 261). It follows from this description that these lines or classes or domains will correspond to histories of different "power," and thus, although Lévi-Strauss doesn't say so, this third numerical function of dates beyond the *ordinal* and *cardinal* might be called the *exponential* function. He does say that the sense of "power" conveyed in these exponential relations between dates has to do with *explanatory* power: this is what he means by a greater principle of "intelligibility." It is in this sense that he speaks of "biographical or anecdotal history," for example, as "low powered": it is "not intelligible in itself and only becomes so when it is transferred *en bloc* to a form of history of a higher power than itself; and the latter stands in the same relation to the class above it" (p. 261).[47] Losses, too, however, are incurred in the movement to the domain of higher power.

For, while lower-order forms of history such as the biographical and anecdotal are the "least explanatory," they are also "the richest in point of information." Such information is first backgrounded and then eliminated as one moves up through "histories of progressively greater power." Moving up and down the scale in this fashion, "the historian loses in information what he gains in comprehension or vice versa." The logic of this kind of trade-off is what Lévi-Strauss calls the "dilemma" of the historiographical operation. The full intelligibility that Sartre imagined he could locate in the historical process as a unity and could disclose in the dialectic comprehension of "singular universals," was all an illusion (p. 261).[48] What Sartre punningly calls the "sense of his-

47. Several years later, in *L'Archéologie du Savoir* (1969), Foucault made a similar point about the question of scale in the history of science but assigned credit for it elsewhere: "There is the distinction, which we also owe to Canguilhem, between the *microscopic* and the *macroscopic scales* of the history of the sciences, in which events and their consequences are not arranged in the same way." *The Archaeology of Knowledge,* trans. A. M. Sheridan Smith (New York: Harper & Row, 1972), p. 4.

48. This difficult Sartrean concept receives its most concise definition in "Kierkegaard: The Singular Universal," in *Sartre: Between Existentialism and Marxism,* trans. John Matthews (New York: Pantheon, 1974), where Sartre asserts, "[M]an is that being who transforms his being into meaning, and through whom meaning comes into the world. The singular universal is this meaning: through his *Self*—the practical assumption and supersession of being as it is—man restores to the universe its enveloping unity, by engraving it as a finite determination and a mortgage on future History in the being which envelops him" (pp. 160–61). Sartre also discusses the concept in

tory" (*sens d'histoire*) proves both senseless and directionless. Lévi-Strauss seeks to show that whatever sense history has is a sense it has been given. Its sense emerges not by virtue of any "direction" in its "movement" but by virtue of the scheme of logical (in this case, *chronological*) categories to which it is assigned. An account of what one did last Monday belongs to a different order of magnitude from a history of the last millennium, and the quantum distinctions of the dating code do not provide the means of effecting a bridge of continuity across that difference. For Lévi-Strauss, the singular universal is comprehensible neither "dialectically" nor any other way.

Thus, the intelligibility of the historian's code might be said to lie in its classificatory structure—that is, the exponential dimension of the number used to date an event—even though the "distinctive character" of the code lies in the ordinal dimension of the numbers involved, their capacity to assign to events the relation of before and after.[49] But in closing his discussion of Sartre's progressive-regressive method and its premise or promise of a specifically historical intelligibility for contemporary "anthropology," Lévi-Strauss cannot resist a parting shot. The field of history, he insists, can be only a point of departure, not a terminus, in the quest for intelligibility: "As we say of certain careers, history may lead to anything, provided you get out of it" (p. 262). It is a conclusion that raises again the question: how could Lévi-Strauss's brand of structural anthropology have the apparent effect, which I think Jameson is right in identifying, of getting scholars who had presumably been "out of" history "into" it?

One way of answering the question is to say that Lévi-Strauss has established the possibility of elaborating the anecdote into higher-order forms of general-

---

the preface to the study of Flaubert that he called the "sequel" to *Search for a Method: The Family Idiot,* vol. 1 (Chicago: University of Chicago Press, 1981), p. ix: "[M]an is never an individual; it would be more fitting to call him a universal singular. Summed up and for this reason universalized by his epoch, he in turn resumes it by reproducing himself in it as singularity. Universal by the singular universality of human history, singular by the universalizing singularity of his projects, he requires simultaneous examination from both ends." Anticipating, in effect, the later argument I want to make about the centrality of the notion of the case in this project, Sartre also says in this preface that his question in the book—"what, at this point in time, can we know about a man?"—can "only be answered by studying a specific case" (p. ix).

49. This notion of an intelligibility given to the historiographical operation by virtue of the vertical classificatory structure might be understood to bear indirectly on the arguments made on the Hempel side of the famous debate about "covering laws" for historical explanation in Anglo-American philosophy of history from the 1940s through the 1960s. See Alan Donagan and Barbara Donagan, eds., *Philosophy of History* (New York: Macmillan, 1965), and Patrick Gardiner, ed., *The Philosophy of History* (Oxford: Oxford University Press, 1974), for a representative sampling of essays from this debate. See Maurice Mandelbaum, *The Anatomy of Historical Knowledge* (Baltimore: Johns Hopkins University Press, 1977), for a summary of it and a late effort to resolve it.

ity at the expense, primarily, of foregoing the narrative unity of the *sens de l'his-toire*. This is an answer consistent, as we shall see, with various accounts of what the so-called new historicists have actually done. Still, we must not fail to note how much depends here on Lévi-Strauss's defamiliarizing account of the function of the specific date and of dated specificity in the historiographical operation. Lévi-Strauss argues that, as the historian moves up or down the levels of the chronological code, the level of specificity will change. It will change as the mix of information and explanation shifts. This is not to say that the mix will be "more specific" at the lower levels or less so at the higher ones. "Specificity" here, as in Veyne, is itself a term of mediation.[50] No matter what the level, it will always involve incoherence and information, intelligibility and ignorance. On the other hand, the shift of level may make the distinctive specificity of the code itself, with its various operations, more apparent.

To specialize in a roughly secular period, as historically oriented academics in our own century have long tended to do, is already to have achieved—or to imagine having achieved—a particular equilibrium between the demands of comprehension and those of information. The equilibrium is normalized in institutional practices such as departmental fields and job categories—seventeenth-century, eighteenth-century, nineteenth-century literature—and, unchallenged, comes to seem natural to practitioners.[51] The distinctive specificity of the practice tends to be invisible to itself. In the field of history proper, an important challenge to this normative practice had been mounted in the work of the *Annales* school—Braudel, Febvre, Bloch, and Ladurie. Fernand Braudel's famous theorization of the Annaliste approach to the problem of historical scale in the essay on *la longue durée* had, after all, only appeared in the last issue of *Annales* for 1958, just at the point when Sartre and Lévi-Strauss were about to stage their famous controversy.[52] Braudel looms over Lévi-Strauss's ar-

50. I think we gain a sense of how closely a historiographical theorist like Veyne is working with Lévi-Strauss when we compare the former's remarks on the medial role of "specificity" with the latter's comments on "the special position devolving on the notion of a species considered as a logical operator": "considered in isolation, a species is a collection of individuals; in relation to other species, however, it is a system of definitions" (*The Savage Mind,* pp. 163, 136).

51. This same point is made by Ulrich Weisstein, in his chapter on "Epoch, Period, Generation, and Movement," *Comparative Literature and Literary Theory* (Bloomington: Indiana University Press, 1973), p. 85. Weisstein, however, makes this point as part of a general critique of what he calls "annalization," by which he means to include uses of the year in periodization on any scale; my argument here is that "annalization" in that larger sense is not an expendable but a constitutive component of periodization as we know it.

52. Fernand Braudel, "History and Sciences Sociales: La Longue Durée," *Annales* 13 (July–December 1958): 725–53. Lévi-Strauss's then-recent *Structural Anthropology* (1958) is cited positively as a point of departure for this argument. For an *Annales*-school response to Lévi-Strauss's later elaboration of these views, see Jacques le Goff, *Time, Work and Culture in the Middle*

gument in 1962 even more largely than the latter's citation of the former might suggest. Braudel, of course, pictures the Annales historians as trading upward, in Lévi-Strauss's terms, for greater intelligibility.[53] One might defamiliarize taken-for-granted patterns and procedures by moving on the scale in the other direction, however, trading downward for a gain in information. And this is what more and more began to happen in literary history and cultural studies.

In a useful recent essay on the question of periodization as articulated in the debate between René Wellek and Arthur O. Lovejoy, and renewed in the energetic critical reception of M. H. Abrams' *Natural Supernaturalism* (1971), Mark Parker has given Jerome McGann due credit for formulating a version of these alternatives in the context of English literary history and Romanticism in particular. What McGann suggested in 1972 was, on Parker's account, "a radical reconstruction of periods in either of two ways":

> The first, which makes all literature in the nineteenth and twentieth century Romantic, asks scholars to identify and describe different sorts of Romantic traditions. The second, a prescient description of much future "new historical" scholarship, proposed a difficult task of imposing a "flexible set of interacting limits—formal, substantive, geographical, and historical"—on Romantic literature. The first possibility continues in the search for a regulative or normative set of period concerns (albeit on an impossibly large and diverse body of material), and the second, by looking to the contingencies and particularities of microhistory, tends to defer, by the constant differentiation of "interacting limits," the formation of period concepts on the scale pursued by Wellek, Abrams, and Lovejoy."[54]

This formulation seems to get the matter nearly right, except that Parker, whose account is unsupported by the Sartre/Lévi-Strauss debate, does not seem to recognize that period concepts on the lower scale might be just as crisply differentiated, just as precisely datable, as period concepts on the higher scale.[55]

In Lévi-Strauss's rough mapping of the chronological code, the next level below the secular in exponential power is the annual.[56] One could certainly

---

Ages, trans. Arthur Goldhammer (Chicago: University of Chicago Press, 1980), pp. 235–36. LeGoff suggests that societies cannnot be divided into the chronologically "hot" and "cold" but are rather all more or less "tepid."

53. Paradoxically, however, the "everyday" appears as a concept as one moves up the classificatory scheme of dates away from the daily and even beyond the secular.

54. Mark Parker, "Measure and Countermeasure: the Lovejoy-Wellek Debate and Romantic Periodization," in *Theoretical Issues in Literary History,* ed. David Perkins (Cambridge, Mass.: Harvard University Press, 1991), p. 238.

55. For other meditations on the Lovejoy-Wellek debate and the questions it raised, see Thomas Vogler, "Romanticism and Literary Periods: The Future of the Past," *New German Critique* 38 (1986): 131–60, and Frances Ferguson, "On the Numbers of Romanticisms," *ELH* 58 (1991): 471–98.

56. The role of the decade, which Lévi-Strauss elides, might also be figured into the following account by considering the spread of, for example, courses on "the 1790s" in lieu of eighteenth- or nineteenth-century courses, and of courses in Romanticism, in recent years.

make a structurally consistent move downward to the level of the year, just as one could make that move upward to the level of the millennium. That is, one need not think of the movement upward as conserving the concept of the period and the movement downward as deferring it. On this lower order of exponential power, it would be possible in principle, and with sufficiently detailed documentation, to perform the same sorts of operations as on the higher scales. In other words, it would be possible, by reference to the number of events cardinally dated on *yet lower* orders, to make out "hotter" and "colder" dated periods on which one might choose to work. And, by reference to the sequence of events ordinally dated on those yet lower orders, it would be possible to make out patterns of before and after within the dated period that one chose.

To press the question of chronological scale, as Lévi-Strauss does, is to begin to see that events datable to *any* date on *any* order of magnitude must be both or "at once" narrated in sequence and arrayed as a set. Putting the point somewhat differently, one might say that with Lévi-Strauss's analysis in play we are forced to confront the question of whether it makes sense to refer, as Parker does, to the "formation of period concepts" *on a given scale*—as opposed to the concept of the period as a structure locatable on many different scales. If a period is nothing but a date, and if dates form the kind of structural grid that Lévi-Strauss outlines, then the concept of the date cannot be particularized to any rank on that grid. This in turn, of course, raises a question about whether one can retain the normative function of periods when they are understood in this arbitrary way.

4. From Annalization to Annualization

I have taken the trouble to develop Jameson's speculations in a direction slightly different from his own in order to describe a chronological-conceptual framework that was elaborated and deployed in the wake of the debate between Sartre and Lévi-Strauss. Both the return to history in literary studies and the return to formal self-consciousness in recent historical studies are traceable in some significant part to a reflexive discourse about the dating of cultures in the progressive-regressive method. This problematic of the date, too little attended to in spite of its centrality in recent critical theory and practice, must be at the very least be reckoned with in any conceptual linkage of new historicism and structuralism.[57] It now seems possible to recognize, in any case, that this preoccupa-

---

57. For two recent meditations on the theory of the date and the practice of dating in respect to poetry, see Jacques Derrida, *Schibboleth Pour Paul Célan* (Paris: Editions Galilée, 1986), in which he describes his primary concern as with "la date comme à entaille ou à une incision que le poème porte dans son corps" (p. 36); and Jonathan Goldberg, "Dating Milton," in *Soliciting Inter-*

tion, though it was not routinely identified in relation to the relevant framework of analysis, informed many critical projects in the field of literary and cultural studies in the early 1980s when historicism was gaining force. Such a preoccupation certainly now seems to have informed my own efforts at about that time to frame a course in Romantic literature as a reading of England in 1819 and then to undertake a research project along those same lines.

If I had been more aware of the range of discursive conditions that shaped these projects, I suppose I would have been less surprised in retrospect by the number of studies begun or published, or about to be begun or published, that framed their objects of study on the scale of the annual period. I must have been at least vaguely aware of some of them, for as early as 1976, a year of particular chronological self-consciousness in America, the University of Essex held the first in a series of well-attended conferences on "The Sociology of Literature," all devoted to particular dates. The first was 1848, then 1936, 1642, 1789, and so on; the proceedings of these conferences were subsequently published, and many of the essays have enjoyed considerable influence.[58] As for what may have influenced *them*, it seems fair to point to the reception of French Structuralism in the circles of English materialist criticism in the late 1960s, resulting not least in Raymond Williams' celebrated and apt formulation of the "structure of feeling" in the early 1970s.[59] Williams own contribution to the first Essex conference—"Forms of Fiction in 1848," which begins with a proto–new historicist anecdote about the opening of the first W. H. Smith railway station bookstall in that year—was subsequently reprinted, and it profited from the long overdue enthusiasm for Williams' work that followed on the publication of *Marxism and Literature* in 1978.[60]

After these efforts there followed two book-length studies of Victorian years, Carl Dawson's *Victorian Noon* for 1850 and Richard Stein's more self-

---

pretations: Literary Theory and Seventeenth-Century English Poetry, ed. Elizabeth D. Harvey and Katharine Eisaman Maus (Chicago: University of Chicago Press, 1990), pp. 199–220.

58. Francis Barker et al., eds., *1848: The Sociology of Literature: Proceedings of the Essex Conference on the Sociology of Literature* (Colchester: University of Essex, 1978); *1936: The Sociology of Literature* (Colchester: University of Essex, 1979); *1642: Literature and Power in the 17th Century* (Colchester: University of Essex, 1981); and *1789: Reading, Writing, Revolution* (Colchester: University of Essex, 1982); a number of these essays were collected in Francis Barker et al., eds., *Literature, Politics and Theory: Papers from the Essex Conference, 1976–84* (London: Methuen, 1986).

59. For an account of the genealogy of this concept see Edward Said, "Traveling Theory," in *The World, the Text, and the Critic* (Cambridge, Mass: Harvard University Press, 1983). For Williams' own account, see his *Problems in Materialism and Culture: Selected Essays* (London: Verso, 1980) and *Politics and Letters: Interviews with New Left Review* (London: New Left Books, 1979).

60. "Forms of English Fiction in 1848" was later reprinted in Williams's *Writing in Society* (London: Verso, 1983), pp. 150–65.

consciously ambitious sequel, *Victoria's Year: Literature and Culture, 1837–38.*[61] In German studies, there was Friedrich Kittler's *Discourse Networks,* which divides its pages into two parts, "1800" and "1900."[62] In French studies, Jean Starobinski's *Emblems of Reason, 1789* first appeared in English translation in 1979, and has been followed by an altogether more ambitious project, both collective and institutional in character, Denis Hollier's *New Harvard History of French Literature.* The *New Harvard History* organizes its entries under a noncontinuous sequence of (usually annual) dates—e.g., "1725: The Politics of Epistolary Art," "1727: Portrait of the Philosopher as Tramp," "1734: Intricacies of Literary Production," "1735: The Gender of the Memoir, Novel"—and, for its risks, has won acclaim as "the most current and most advanced exemplar of a nonconvulsive, nonirruptive, linguistically sensitive literary history."[63]

Although the quantity of research in this annualized mode seemed a revelation, I take some small consolation about my failure to theorize the basis of my interests when I look at the difficulty many of these books had in doing the same. Even in Hollier's markedly deliberate and programmatic experiment, one finds surprisingly little self-reflective exploration or rationale for this innovative framework either in the entries themselves or in Hollier's brief introductory essay, preoccupied as it is with the distinctive space or *place* of the project (i.e., outside of France).[64] The Essex volumes, too, refuse to pursue such reflec-

---

61. Carl Dawson, *Victorian Noon: English Literature in 1850* (Baltimore: John Hopkins University Press, 1979); Richard Stein, *Victoria's Year: English Literature and Culture, 1837–1838* (New York: Oxford University Press, 1987). As for literary studies so organized before 1976, there is G. M. Young's notable essay about 1850, "The Victorian Noon-Time," in *Victorian Essays,* ed. W. D. Hancock (London: Oxford University Press, 1962). Dawson's very title, of course, acknowledges his debt to Young as well.

62. In American studies Thomas Lutz's *American Nervousness, 1903: An Anecdotal History* (Ithaca, N.Y.: Cornell University Press, 1991), especially pp. 1–30. See also Rebecca West, *1900* (New York: Viking, 1982). Kittler's *Discourse Networks 1800/1900,* trans. Michael Metteer with Chris Cullens (Stanford, Calif.: Stanford University Press, 1990), is altogether one of the more self-conscious such efforts, partly because it includes an incisive foreword by David Wellbery about just what in Kittler's distinctively post-hermeneutic project lends it to the dated rubrics.

63. Marshall Brown, "Contemplating the Theory of Literary History," introduction to a collection of essays on that "special topic" in *PMLA* 107 (January 1992):13–25.

64. "On Writing Literary History," in *A New History of French Literature,* ed. Denis Hollier (Cambridge, Mass.: Harvard University Press, 1989), pp. xxi–xxv. Among the entries, two notable exceptions to this rule include the first one, "1778: Entering the Date," by John Benton (pp. 1–6), and, inevitably, the entry for 1789, which is subtitled simply "Seventeen Eighty–nine," by Sandy Petrey (pp. 566–720). One of the contributors to the Hollier project, Kristin Ross (author of the entry for "1871"), is also the author of a book-length study, *The Emergence of Social Space: Rimbaud and the Paris Commune* (Minneapolis: University of Minnesota Press, 1988), which deals with a writer, Rimbaud, and an event, the Paris Commune, in the context of France in 1870–71. But, while Ross describes her study as addressing a certain "synchronicity" and is indeed explicit about her methods, it is not even in the first instance an "annualized" study of the sort these other books are.

tions. Indeed, most of the year-studies I mentioned tend not to be method-ologically reflexive, and, insofar as they are so, they by no means reflect on their projects in the same way. Some projects make a connection between what they are doing and structuralism, for example, and some do not. There is also some confusion about the difference between, on the one hand, the very idea of choosing a year as a chronological level of specificity (in, roughly, Lévi-Strauss's sense of that notion) and, on the other, the fact of the choice of some particu-lar year. The choices of the Essex conference are all obviously very "hot years" in the calendars of European historiography, and they also have in common a certain hyperactivity in the public sphere—i.e., they are all, including 1642 (whose events partly occasioned Milton's *Areopagitica*), years of massive pam-phlet wars.[65] But the decision to write the entire history of French literature by way of the year-trope, even though some selectivity is obviously involved in the precise choices, creates a different sort of project, one in which the year-frame as such, rather than the importance of some particular year in question, tends to be foregrounded.

In the face of all this unforthcomingness, questions about the character of such projects nonetheless abound, for, like the "annalization" of history, its "an-nualization" has its problems. How would one describe the new mix of intelli-gibility and information? Is the relation among periods on the secular scale in any sense mappable onto the relation of periods on the annual scale? What hap-pens to the very idea of a period on the lower scale? Does the year frame imply a tendency to make us regard the events of a single year as simultaneous—and thus less of a tendency to narrativize them—than is the case at the secular level of periodization? Are the procedures for typification or exemplification differ-ent on the different scales? Does one "read" differently a given text that is set in a secular literary history and one framed by a single year? Does the difference in framing necessarily alter the object framed, or may one imagine that one is con-sidering the "same" critical object—perhaps a poem—first within one scale and then another?

Whereas, in my introduction, I took pains to establish the importance of 1819 in any chronological terms, it is also true that virtually any year, framed and investigated as such, will suddenly seem crucial in a way that it could not with secular history. In the case of England in 1819, and in British Romanti-cism more broadly, the pursuit of such questions is made yet more complicated by a noticeable explicitness about them in the writings themselves. It is my con-

65. For a recent study of the early modern English public sphere in the months leading to *Areopagitica,* see Sharon Achinstein, *Milton and the Revolutionary Reader* (Princeton, N.J.: Prince-ton University Press, 1994).

tention that much of Romantic "literature" inclines to organize itself around the topics we have associated with the problem of historical specificity—especially after the end of the Napoleonic wars, and most especially in 1819. To demonstrate this tendency will mean drawing on, but also refashioning, some familiar arguments that Romanticism is the age of the spirit of the age—that is, the period when the normative status of the period becomes a central and self-conscious aspect of historical reflection. It will mean recalling that the first years after Waterloo saw the emergence and massive popularity of Scott's historical novels, a literary form whose novelty is widely recognized to consist in its pioneering mode of representing historical specificity in the mode of fiction. It will mean reading certain texts of 1819 as articulating a range of related problems: anachronism, contemporaneity, epochal transcoding, typification, historical casuistry. To read England in 1819, in other words, will prove to be not just a matter of gauging hot chronologies but of coming to terms with texts, events, and symbolic actions, which seek the means of making legible the historical peculiarity of their place and time. Thus, the sonnet *England in 1819* is conceived within just such a project of making history by making it legible. In Shelley's articulation, England in 1819 becomes decipherable as a new kind of case, as a historical moment interpretable in terms of a presiding spirit, alterable under the illumination of that spirit.

In a sense, therefore, my plan to study the year 1819 might be said to resemble the approach to particular nineteenth-century years by Dawson and Stein, insofar as they attempt to justify their research projects by reference to a new historical self-consciousness at work in the writings they study. They can organize the writings they study as a field of contemporaneity because, so the argument goes, writings of the mid-Victorian period (1850) or even the beginning of the Victorian period (1837–38) were organizing themselves in that way, organizing themselves, as Stein puts it, in response to "the problem of what Hazlitt termed 'the spirit of the age.'"[66] In repeating the concept of "the spirit of the age" for the late 1970s and early 1980s—a repetition of M. H. Abrams's earlier repetition of it in *Natural Supernaturalism* (1971)—such studies were perhaps allowing themselves to figure as part of the context for Paul de Man's intricately reflexive opening quip in *Allegories of Reading* (1979), his extended study of Romanticism and deconstruction: "To judge from various recent publications, the spirit of the times is not blowing in the direction of formalist and intrinsic criticism."[67] De

66. Stein, *Victoria's Year,* p. 4. For a detailed discussion of the problem of the spirit of the age in Hazlitt, see below chapter 3.

67. Paul de Man, *Allegories of Reading: Figural Language in Rouseau, Nietzsche, Rilke, and Proust* (New Haven: Yale University Press, 1979), p. 3. Now that de Man's 1967 Gauss Seminar has been

Man evidently judged that the spirit of the times was blowing in the direction of spirit-of-the-times criticism.

5. The "Peculiar Conditions" of British Romanticism

To argue for a reproduced concept of historical specificity one needs to say something about its production. In search of an early articulation in the more familiar annals of literary history, one might begin by pointing to the famous account in Wordsworth's century-closing preface to *Lyrical Ballads* (1800) of the changing contract between poets and their readers.[68] But in 1819, Shelley offered some far more troubled and self-conscious reflections on the topic in his preface to *Prometheus Unbound:* "One word is due in candour to the degree in which the study of contemporary writings may have tinged my composition. . . . It is impossible that any one who inhabits the same age with such writers as those who stand in the foremost ranks of our own, can conscientiously assure himself, that his language and tone of thought may not have been modified by the study of the productions of those extraordinary intellects" (SPP, pp. 133–34). Recognizing the anxiety of this passage, Harold Bloom once cited it to initiate his first study of the romanticization of literary influence, but we must nonetheless note that, insofar as Shelley's concern is only with influence,

---

published, we have some record of that earlier "historical study" of Romanticism he says he gave up to write *Allegories of Reading.* In the last of those just-published Gauss lectures, De Man summarized:

> [T]he changes which the study of romanticism brought about in the conventional methods of literary history are of far-reaching importance. This is not surprising, for in stressing the predominance of a hermeneutically structured temporality in authors of the period, we implied that the poets, conceiving of themselves as the reflective interpreters of experience rather than as the originators or the imitators of unmediated experience, have in fact the concerns of the historian more closely [sic] than those of the visionary or the prophet. One can think of these writers as historians of the self; their main works . . . are such histories. It is perhaps a good sign that no satisfactory histories of romanticism, in the traditional conception of literary history, are available. . . . It reveals the impossibility of the reified concepts of history to deal with a truly historical consciousness. By the time a more valid history of romanticism will come to be written, it may well look very different from what we have come to expect literary history to be." In Paul de Man, *Romanticism and Contemporary Criticism,* ed. E. S. Burt, Kevin Newmark, and Andrzej Warminski (Baltimore: Johns Hopkins University Press, 1993), pp. 96–97.

In a sense, the project that De Man abandoned might be understood in retrospect as the one that I have, perhaps hubristically, taken up here.

68. Explicit chronological self-consciousness (as opposed to awareness of accelerated historical change) is hard to find in the preface, but it was composed in the final weeks of the eighteenth century, roughly contemporaneously with "Michael," which is indeed self-conscious of its chronological position at the turn of the century. For a study of the developing self-consciousness of centuries as such in the 1790s, see Hillel Schwartz, *Century's End* (New York: Doubleday, 1990), pp. 132–56.

however complicated that concern might be, the issue of contemporaneity need not have been brought into play: one can be influenced, after all, by the study of a poet of *any* period.[69] Shelley's concern here is not exactly with contiguity nor with contagion, but rather with a principle that animates the frame of the contemporary body politic, a principle neither expressive nor mechanical in its mode of causality.[70]

Shelley's elaborates this point about contemporaneity in a way that *seems* to qualify it when he makes the following concession: "It is true, that, not the spirit of their genius, but the forms in which it has manifested itself, are due, less to the peculiarities of their own minds, than to the peculiarity of the moral and intellectual condition of the minds among which they have been produced" (SPP, p. 134). This is extraordinarily convoluted syntax, even by Shelley's own standards. It is groping to articulate an elusive and novel distinction between the peculiarity of individuals and the peculiarity of epochs in moral and intellectual history. It is a distinction Lukács would formulate in his effort to sum up the originality of Shelley's contemporary, Scott, whose fiction Lukács credited with being the first to capture the "specifically historical," understood as "the derivation of the individuality of characters from the historical peculiarity of their age."[71]

Shelley also seems close here, however, to anticipating the Marxian dictum that formed the subtext of the Sartre/Lévi-Strauss debate: the dictum that human beings make their own history but under conditions given them from the past. In fact, "the contemporary" in this passage seems divided, just as it is in the opening pages of *The Eighteenth Brumaire,* into a heritage of forms and a capacity for new poesis. Shelley goes on in the preface to *Prometheus Unbound* to try to round out his concession about how form rather than spirit is affected by external considerations: "Thus a number of writers possess the form, whilst they want the spirit of those whom, it is alleged, they imitate; because the former is the endowment of the age in which they live, and the latter must be the uncommunicated lightning of their own mind" (SPP, p. 134). This qualification, however, is itself soon qualified.

69. Harold Bloom, *The Anxiety of Influence* (New York: Oxford University Press, 1973), pp. 103–104.

70. I invoke the terms from the taxonomy of causes appropriated by Jameson from Althusser in *Reading Capital,* pp. 182–93, wherein a third alternative, a Spinozan "structural causality," is promoted at the expense of the other two. In Part Three below I discuss Shelley's work on the "spirit of the age" in relation to his immersion in Spinozan commentary.

71. Lukács, *The Historical Novel,* trans. Hannah and Stanley Mitchell (London: Merlin Press, 1962), p. 19.

Within weeks of composing this preface, Shelley began work on *A Philosophical View of Reform* (in November of 1819) and again found himself meditating on the character of this "uncommunicated lightning" and its relation to the "endowment of the age." Again invoking the greatness of his unnamed contemporaries—among them, presumably, Wordsworth, Coleridge, Southey, Byron, Scott, Hunt, and Keats—Shelley seeks, in the *View,* to distinguish between the power of poetry that abides in these writers and those "portions of their nature [which] have little tendency [to] the spirit of good to which it is the minister" (WPBS, 7:19–20). His effort issues in what seems to have been the first rehearsal of the famous sequence of declarations later incorporated into *A Defense of Poetry:* "It is impossible to read the productions of our most celebrated writers, whatever may be their system relating to thought or expression, without being startled by the electric life which there is in their words. They measure the circumference or sound the depths of human nature with a comprehensive and all-penetrating spirit at which they are themselves perhaps most sincerely astonished, for it [is] less their own spirit than the spirit of their age" (WPBS, 7:20). The "uncommunicated lightning" of the preface to *Prometheus Unbound* strikes again in this passage from the *View* in the form of that "electric life" in the words of the contemporary genius. This principle of animation—it is hard in this connection not to think of electrified revivification in Mary Shelley's *Frankenstein* (1818), subtitled "The Modern Prometheus"—is in its turn associated, precisely, with the spirit of the age. Though there is an apparent discrepancy between this formulation and the emphasis of the preface to *Prometheus Unbound,* it might be reconciled by giving full stress to the word "endowment" in the earlier passage. The "endowment" might be identified as what comes of studying the works of one's great contemporaries, whereas the uncommunicated lightning activates them all together in their historical moment. Or perhaps the two passages are simply at odds, an index of the novelty of the vexed concepts with which Shelley is trying to come to terms.

They are indeed novel concepts. When Stein refers to the problem of "what Hazlitt calls 'the spirit of the age,'" he rightly reminds us that the term was popularized in the remarkable volume of character portraits that Hazlitt published under that title in 1825. As early as 1831, the phrase "spirit of the age" was being denigrated as part of a fashionable cant of faction. The idiom of the spirit of the age is a complex formation in English, but its development from the status of rare locution to the status of cant happens very rapidly, and has much to do with the acknowledged revolutionary energy in the moment of Peterloo. The incoherence of Shelley's various articulations of this new discourse in

1819 might itself be accounted evidence of its relative inchoateness, its close dependence on conditions associated with Peterloo.[72]

Certainly *A Philosophical View of Reform* itself, the text for which Shelley initially composed the famous passage about the spirit of the age and the electric life animating the contemporary corpus of literature, belongs very much in both timing and tone to the spate of literary work produced in the latter months of 1819 as part of the public response to the events in Manchester and their aftermath. Though he was a thousand miles away when it happened, Shelley himself wrote several pieces markedly occasioned by that event: his open letter to *The Examiner,* items in his private correspondence, and poems such as *The Mask of Anarchy.* Even at such distance, Shelley was drawn into the powerful historical contemporaneity of a hyperactive public sphere that made Peterloo thinkable in the first place and that was greatly enhanced by the immediate responses of so many writers in its aftermath.

As I have already begun to suggest, the debate over Peterloo involved writers of many different kinds and positions. It goes without saying that the daily newspapers actively monitored this debate. The weeklies—such as Hunt's *Examiner,* T. J. Wooler's *Black Dwarf,* and Cobbett's *Political Register*—carried articles on Peterloo, the Government response, the fate of the victims, and the prosecutions of the leaders of the demonstration (not only Henry Hunt, but also Samuel Bamford and others) in virtually every issue that appears for the subsequent months. In Scotland, even James Ballantyne, friend to Walter Scott and editor of the normally conservative *Edinburgh Weekly Journal,* raised a question about the "ill-arranged" proceedings of the Manchester Magistrates and the "rash and precipitate" conduct of the Yeomanry.[73] Scott was a part owner of this paper, and his fiction was the bread and butter of the Ballantynes' publishing enterprise, and so, in December, just about the time Shelley would have been hard at work on the early sections of his *Philosophical View of Reform,* it was with special leverage, explicitly noted, that Scott wrote a series of three articles critical of Ballantyne.[74] These were soon recirculated in pamphlet form under

72. A useful but little-cited resource for information about how the early industrial public sphere developed in the decades leading to Peterloo can be found in Leon Soutierre Marshall, *The Development of Public Opinion in Manchester, 1780–1820* (Syracuse, N.Y.: Syracuse University Press, 1946).

73. From Ballantyne's editorial in the *Edinburgh Weekly Journal,* August 24, 1819, p. 289.

74. In a private letter to Ballantyne, inquiring into the production of *Ivanhoe,* Scott not only warned him that his public remarks on the *Journal* "might give you some pain" but threatened to withdraw financial support: "I cannot continue a partner where such mistaken views are inculcated at a crisis of peculiar danger and in relation to any profit which might accrue from the paper conducted on such principles"—*Letters* (London: Constable & Co, 1933), 5:484–85. The

the title, *The Visionary*, in which he not only challenged Ballantyne but also questioned the propriety of the general representations of these events in the popular press.[75] William Hone's *The Political House that Jack Built*, which appeared very quickly after Peterloo and sold with extraordinary rapidity in that same autumn, must have increased the experience of national simultaneity among its many readers, the sense that they were reading the same thing about the same event at the same time (an event that involved a convergence of fifty or sixty thousand Britons on the same grounds in the first place!).

In such a perspective, Shelley's 1819 comments about poet legislators and the spirit of the age can be seen as part of a cycle of intensifying self-consciousness about the historical state of the representation. The Government's response to those who protested its support for the repression at Peterloo was, of course, further repression, to which the radical response was more journalistic representation. This was in part a pattern generalized from the particular example of William Hone himself, a point not lost on alert young writers like Keats. In September, reporting on the recent events in Manchester to his brother and sister-in-law in Kentucky, Keats concluded with a further reference to "the business of Carlisle [sic] the Bookseller," which he said was "of great moment in my mind." As Keats had already reported in February, Carlile was arrested for selling "immense numbers" of Thomas Paine's *The Deist* as well as "many other works held in superstitious horror." But, although there were "above a dozen inditements" [sic] against Carlile, Keats claimed that "they are afraid to prosecute" because his defense "would be published in all the papers all over the Empire" (LJK, 2:194). This strategy—*Offentlicheit* as the best defense—seems to be what Keats had in view when he referred to Carlile in the February letter as "a Bookseller on the *Hone* principle": Hone had been acquitted in December 1817 (as Keats had also reported in his correspondence) by virtue of the embarrassing publicity he generated by printing the proceedings of his trial (LJK, 2:62).[76]

In making its contribution to this cycle of representation, prosecution, and accelerated representation, Peterloo brought very much to the foreground a set of issues that would later be labeled, by Thomas Carlyle and others, the

---

link to *Ivanhoe* is made clear in the chivalric rhetoric of the public letter and in the fact that it is signed "L.T."—as in Lawrence Templeton, the putative narrator of *Ivanhoe*.

75. Peter Garside, ed. *The Visionary* (Cardiff: University College Cardiff Press, 1984).

76. Compare LJK, 1:191–99, for Keats's more extended remarks on the subject. For more detail on the Hone trials, see Frederick W. Hackwood, *William Hone: His Life and Times* (London: T. Fisher Unwin, 1912), pp. 149–73; for more on Hone's mode of defense, see Kevin Gilmartin, *Print Politics: The Press and Radical Opposition in Early Nineteenth-Century England* (Cambridge: Cambridge University Press, 1996), pp. 114–57.

"Condition-of-England" question, one that is later associated with that sense of historical self-consciousness implicit in the spirit-of-the-age (or in Carlyle's own phrase, "sign-of-the-times") idiom discussed by Dawson and Stein.[77] It is in late 1819 that the proto-Carlylean idiom begins to enter the narrative repertoire of Sir Walter Scott. In the weeks after Peterloo, Scott was at work on *Ivanhoe,* a novel that includes a scene-setting overview of, as it were, England in 1194, to launch the panoramic account of the tournament at Ashby-de-la-Zouche. Scott begins this historical overview with the anachronistic formulation, "The condition of the English nation was at this time sufficiently miserable" (Iv, chap. 7)—which might indeed be interpreted as an effort to make the complaints of the lower orders seem less newsworthy than they were being made to appear in the reports of the contemporary public press in 1819. The effort to portray the condition of England in the aftermath of Peterloo structures a wide variety of works in a wide variety of ways in the final weeks of 1819: not only *Ivanhoe,* but also Scott's *Visionary* articles, Shelley's *Ode to the West Wind* and *A Philosophical View of Reform,* the later editions of *The Political House that Jack Built,* and works by other writers and journalists around the country who offered their statements of the case.[78] Again, well attuned to such developments by virtue of the literary packets he was receiving in Florence, Shelley could exclaim in a letter to his friend Leigh Hunt, "What a state England is in!"

77. For Carlyle on "The Condition-of-England Question," see the chapter bearing that title that introduces *Chartism* (1849) and the initial chapter of *Past and Present* (1843), which opens with the following pronouncement: "The condition of England, on which many pamphlets are now in the course of publication, and many thoughts unpublished are going on in every reflective head, is justly regarded as one of the most ominous, and withal one of the strangest, ever seen in this world"—*Past and Present* (London: Chapman and Hall, 1897), p. 1. A subsequent chapter, "The Manchester Insurrection," suggests how strongly the developments represented by Peterloo occasioned Carlyle's meditation on history in this book. For a detailed account, differently slanted from mine, of the changing question of "representation" and "culture" in the condition-of-England debate, see Catherine Gallagher, *The Industrial Reformation of English Fiction* (Chicago: University of Chicago Press, 1985), pp. 264–67. Because I use a broader notion of culture than the Arnoldian one, I see the concept of culture as already crucial to the debate in a writer like Scott, rather than a development that spells its end.

78. Various journals—Whig, Tory, and Radical—chimed in with emergency assessments, often in reviews of other emergency assessments, as in the case of the review article headed "the State of the Nation" in the *Edinburgh Review* for October 1819, which addressed two recent books about the representative crisis itself: Richard Carlyle's *The Democratic Recorder; or Reformer's Guide, a Weekly Publication* (London: Carlile, 1819) and *Radical Reform, the only Remedy for the Disorders of our Country,* by Britannicus (London: Cadel & Davies, 1819), and the review article headed "the State of Public Affairs" in the Tory *Quarterly Review* (January 1820), an omnibus review of published Parliamentary speeches from the November-December debate on the "State of the Country." See also, the first number of the *London Magazine* (January 1820), which offered an account of the "state of public feeling" at the time of the commencement of Parliament on November 23 (1:100).

and then exhort Hunt "to write a paper in the *Examiner* on the actual state of the country."[79] This was the letter in which Shelley produced for Hunt the text of the sonnet "England in 1819," which Shelley knew that Hunt could not print ("I do not expect you to publish it"). All these texts, indeed, were making their bid for representational power on the open field of the press even as Parliament, as if in recognition of how much power there was to contest for, was debating the measures to best restrict it. The measures on which they settled, the notorious Six Acts, were voted into law on the day before New Year's Eve, less than a week after Shelley posted his sonnet to Hunt.

In revisiting the revolutionary literary energy that animates English writing around the time of Peterloo, I have been trying to connect it very specifically with the strong emergence of a discourse on the spirit of the age less to argue that the concept of historical specificity was produced in a particular year than to speculate about what it might mean to think so. I have not yet established that or how the discourse of the spirit of the age in the Romantic period can be articulated on the scale of the year, nor that or how it anticipates the kind of attention to problems of scale in historical epoch or period such as we have seen at work in the return to history in recent discussions of culture. That is, I have not yet tried to demonstrate that Mary Shelley's title, "England in 1819," need not be regarded a kind of anachronistic gesture unavailable for the "glorious Phantom's" contemporary self-characterization in 1819. Such a task will require a more patient sort of exposition. Before turning to that task, however, I would like to conclude the present discussion with some observations about Lévi-Strauss's own genealogical (as distinct from his structural) remarks on the subject.

6. Lévi-Strauss, St. Simon, and the Beginning of History

There is a great deal that I have not explored in Lévi-Strauss's accounts of hot and cold societies, diachrony and synchrony, history and ethnology. I have not pressed as hard as one might on the constitutive role of metaphors—such as the thermometric metaphor—in the arguments that emerge from *The Savage Mind* and related texts. Nor have I considered how one should compare the "simultaneity" of events coded with the same date in a chronological schema to the "simultaneity" of events coded as "past" or "present" in a society without the need or capacity to generate temporal distinctions more refined than "before" and "after." It is not as if Lévi-Strauss's various discussions of these matters achieve tight coherence; he as much as declares his accounts to be so many acts

---

79. To Leigh Hunt, December 23, 1819—LPBS, 2:166–67.

of modern intellectual bricolage. But the temporality of such bricolage raises many questions. In an effort, therefore, at once to outline an approach to some of those questions and to provide at least prima facie plausibility for the notion that what Lévi-Strauss calls the historian's code might, even for him, actually have a genealogy, even one that might broadly be considered "Romantic," I want to turn back briefly to his discussion of history, circa 1960. In particular I want to consider a pair of passages, closely related in date of publication to *The Savage Mind,* where the question is addressed from a different perspective.[80]

Returning to the already-broached topic of hot and cold societies in his conversations with Charbonnier, Lévi-Strauss attempted to redescribe the entire issue in somewhat different terms. He asked Charbonnier to assume, for the sake of argument, that a social field may be said to operate either as a *society* (pertaining to relations its members have with each other) or as a *culture* (pertaining to relations they have with nature), and to assume further that the operations of each are mutually inverse in respect to the question of human order. That is, what we think of as human progress is a process that generates *disorder* (entropy) as a society but generates compensatory *order* as a culture. As if elaborating Benjamin's now-celebrated dictum that every civilized achievement is equally an act of barbarism, Lévi-Strauss proceeds to apply this offhand general theory of culture and society to provide a set of indices to the question of "civilization" itself:

> Primitive peoples produce very little order by means of their culture. Nowadays, we call them the underdeveloped peoples. But they produce very little entropy in their societies. On the whole, these societies are egalitarian, mechanical in type, and governed by the law of unanimity. . . . The civilized peoples, on the other hand, produce a great deal of order in their culture, as is shown by mechanization and by the great achievements of civilization, but they also produce a great deal of entropy in their societies, in the form of social conflicts and political struggles, which as we saw, are the things that primitive people guard against, perhaps more consciously and systematically than we might have supposed.
>
> The great problem of civilization has, therefore, been to maintain differentials. We have seen these ensured by means of slavery, then serfdom, and lastly with the creation of a proletariat. But as the working-class struggle tends to iron out the differences, our society has had to look for fresh ways of establishing differentials—colonialism and the so-called imperialist policies, for instance—that is, it has constantly to try, either within the society itself or by subjecting conquered peoples, to create a differential between a ruling section and a section that is ruled; but such a differential is always provisional, as it is in a steam-engine which tends towards immobility because the temperature of the cold element rises while that of the hot element falls.[81]

80. It might be helpful for this discussion to keep in mind Foucault's account of the shift in thinking about "things" in relation to history that he makes crucial to the transformation in what he calls the "Age of History," in *The Order of Things: An Archaeology of the Human Sciences* (New York: Random House, 1970), pp. 367–73. See below, chapter 2, for a brief comparative discussion of Foucault's account of historicism in this period.

81. Georges Charbonnier, *Entretiens avec Claude Lévi-Strauss* (Paris: Librairie Plon, 1961), p. 41.

This simplified account (which Lévi-Strauss does somewhat complicate in subsequent sessions with Charbonnier) has the virtue of being, I think, the clearest exposition of what is involved in Lévi-Strauss's repeated insistence that the distinction between the societies that anthropologists call "primitive" and those they called "advanced" is not a distinction between societies with and without history but rather a distinction between alternative relations to history. In one a society explains itself in its relation to changes it has undergone, and in the other it does not. It is a distinction metaphorized many times in Lévi-Strauss's work as the distinction between different kinds of machines. I have returned to these issues here at the end of a discussion of structuralism and historicism because of two interesting relations that these formulations have to the period that the historiography of the West's first industrialized civilization calls "Romantic."

This is, of course, the period in which the notion of society as a machine or mechanism enters full blown into the public sphere as part of British culture's self-identification, and it does so perhaps most conspicuously in the rash of writing about the question of "the spirit of the age." In the widely read essay that first made his name, "Signs of the Times" (1829), the young Thomas Carlyle stepped back, as other writers had recently done, to reflect on his epoch: "Were we to characterise this age of ours by any single epithet, we should be tempted to call it, not an Heroical, Devotional, Philosophical, or Moral Age, but, above all others, the Mechanical Age[,] . . . the Age of Machinery in every outward and inward sense of that word."[82] Two years later, writing between the 1830 Revolution in Paris, on which he had reported to the English press, and the first Reform Bill, then under debate, John Stuart Mill returned to the theme in an essay very much in the same new genre, "The Spirit of the Age": "Society demands, and anticipates, not merely a new machine, but a machine constructed in another manner."[83]

Biographers of both Carlyle and Mill have amply demonstrated not only that St. Simonianism is one of the crucial intellectual-historical links between these two essays, but also that the two writers' mutual involvement in the St. Simonian program formed the basis of a long-term intellectual and political relationship between them. St. Simonianism, a doctrine born of mutual relations between England and France over many decades, holds that England's advanced industrial status puts it in a position to reorganize its social structure in a way that the political struggles of the French Revolution could

---

82. Thomas Carlyle, "Signs of the Times, *Edinburgh Review* (June 1829), pp. 441–42.
83. J. S. Mill, "The Spirit of the Age," in *Mill's Essays on Literature and Society,* ed. J. B. Schneewind (New York: Collier, 1965), p. 31.

not.[84] The doctrine only took hold after St. Simon's death, in poverty, in the mid-1820s, when it was promulgated by Auguste Comte and by a number of St. Simon's lesser-known disciples, such as Gustave d'Eichthal and Prosper Enfantin, through the medium of St. Simonian organs with such revealing names as *Le Producteur, L'Organisateur,* and *Le Globe.*[85] The St. Simonians recruited both Carlyle and Mill to their cause. They published an elaborate commentary on "Signs of the Times" in *L'Organisateur* in early 1830 and undertook what Carlyle called an "Apostolic Mission" in 1830 for the conversion of Britain which involved early meetings with both Carlyle and Mill. Mill, for his part, wrote that famous series of essays on "The Spirit of the Age" very much in the spirit of the St. Simonians, whom Carlyle had called "themselves among the *Signs*" he had written about.[86] Mill wrote to d'Eichthal afterward that he had suppressed explicit reference to the St. Simonians in the article only out of fear of adverse political consequences.[87]

There will be more to say about the preoccupation with "the spirit of the age" in the post-Waterloo period. I bring up the relation of Mill's and Carlyle's essays to the St. Simonians in the context of Lévi-Strauss's comments on the dialectic of culture and society in order to focus on the special role Lévi-Strauss assigns to the moment of St. Simonianism in his own historical narrative. Addressing himself to Charbonnier's question of whether this inverse, zero-sum relationship of social entropy and cultural order is "inevitable and irreversible," Lévi-Strauss makes a surprising concession: "It is conceivable that, for modern societies, progress and the achievement of a great degree of social justice might depend on transferring entropy from society to culture. This may seem a very abstract way of putting it, yet I am only repeating Saint-Simon's statement that the problem of modern times is how to effect the transition from the governing of men to the administration of things. 'Government of men' corresponds to society and increasing entropy; 'administration of things' corresponds to culture and the creation of an increasingly varied and complex order."[88] This claim suggests a deeper underlying agreement with Sartre and a more explicit com-

84. Richard Pankhurst, *The St. Simonians, Mill and Carlyle: A Preface to Modern Thought* (London: Sidgwick and Jackson, 1957), p. 24.

85. See Michael St. John Packe, *The Life of John Stuart Mill* (London: Secker and Warburg, 1954), pp. 91–99, and Emery Neff, *Carlyle and Mill* (New York: Columbia University Press, 1926), pp. 254–60.

86. Pankhurst, *The St. Simonians, Mill and Carlyle,* p. 30.

87. Mill wrote to D'Eichthal as follows: "I expect that for a considerable time much obloquy will fall not only upon the St. Simonians, but even on all who venture to hint the possibility of their being other than madmen and rogues. My saying as much for them in the Examiner as I have done est déjà un acte de courage"—*Collected Works,* 12:96.

88. Charbonnier, *Entretiens avec Claude Lévi-Strauss,* p. 42.

mitment to an epochal history than one might have gained from reading the polemics of *The Savage Mind*. Nor can these remarks be dismissed as the casual speculations of an unguarded moment. They were part of Lévi-Strauss's planning for his Inaugural Lecture for the Chair of Social Anthropology at the Collège de France, which he delivered just a few weeks later, on January 5, 1960.

To see more clearly what is at stake, it may help to consider how Lévi-Strauss elaborates the same point about "the industrial revolution of the nineteenth century" in the more formal context of the Inaugural Lecture. He is speculating about how "the anthropologist" might predict the future:

> . . . he would undoubtedly not conceive of it as a continuation or a projection of the present types, but rather on the model of an integration, progressively unifying the appropriate characteristics of the "cold" societies and the "hot" ones. His thought would renew connections with the old Cartesian dream of putting machines, like automatons, at the service of man. It would follow this lead through the social philosophy of the eighteenth century and up to Saint-Simon. The latter, in announcing the passage "from government of men to the administration of things," anticipated in the same breath the anthropological distinction between culture and society. He thus looked forward to an event of which advances in information theory and electronics give us at least a glimpse; the conversion of a type of civilization which inaugurated historical development at the price of the transformation of men into machines into an ideal civilization which would succeed in turning machines into men. Then, culture having entirely taken over the burden of manufacturing progress, society would be freed from the millennial curse which has compelled it to enslave men in order that there be progress. Henceforth, history would make itself by itself. Society, placed outside and above history, would be able to exhibit once again that regular and, as it were, crystalline structure which the best-preserved of primitive societies teach us is not antagonistic to the human condition.[89]

In this address of early 1960, on the very eve of the publication of Sartre's *Critique,* which he would so vigorously attack for its suggestion of a Hegelian *sens d'histoire,* of a meaning and direction in historical process, Lévi-Strauss produces a vision of the future that he articulates in terms of a discourse very much linked with the aftermath of the French Revolution and with the Romantic displacements we now associate with that aftermath. While the future society he envisions is one "outside and above history," it is nonetheless a society that the West would move through history to achieve, a history in which the St. Simonian response to the French Revolution figures prominently. Only through such a narrative construction, one might say, does history find a way to make itself by itself, rather as one might say of Shelley's sonnet, *England in 1819,* that only through such a poetic construction does history find a way to make itself by itself. Shelley's account of the narrative-poem distinction in relation to historicism is a subject I return to in chapter 9 below.

89. Lévi-Strauss, *The Scope of Anthropology,* p. 48–50.

Recalling the final chapter of *The Savage Mind* in the view of these remarks from the Inaugural Lecture, one must, I think, be struck by the concession Lévi-Strauss makes after declaring that the issue of Sartre's *Critique* is reducible to the question: "Under what conditions is the myth of the French Revolution possible?" He is prepared to grant to Sartre, he says, "that the contemporary Frenchman must believe in this myth in order fully to play the part of an historical agent and also that Sartre's analysis admirably extracts the set of formal conditions necessary if this result is to be secured" (p. 254). The work of extracting such conditions is deeply motivated. The Left in France, he says, still clings to what he calls "a golden age of historical consciousness," a period of contemporary history, commencing with the French Revolution, "which bestowed the blessing of a congruence between practical imperatives and schemes of interpretation." But while Lévi-Strauss expresses skepticism about whether the truth of this world-picture is more than "a matter of context," more than "the fortuitous 'focusing of an optical instrument when its object-glass and eyepiece move in relation to each other,'" he does not reflect on the extraordinary coincidence between the account he denigrates and the account he offered before Sartre's text appeared in print.[90]

Especially intriguing is that, in the articulation given the issues from the other side of the Channel in the celebrated essays by Carlyle and Mill, the St. Simonian "period" of industrial consciousness and the Romantic or Revolutionary scheme of historical consciousness appear to go hand in hand. Mill, for example, sees the spirit of the age as involving a certain unprecedented self-consciousness about its own status as a period, as even somehow defined by this self-consciousness. To complicate matters further, Mill goes on to insist that, insofar as the idea the age has of itself has content, it involves a recognition of the age as becoming something other than it is. "The first of the leading peculiarities of the present age is, that it is an age of transition," he says, and thus the idea that characterizes this age, the idea of the spirit of the age itself, is "an idea essentially belonging to an age of change" (p. 34). The double paradox of Mill's formulation of the historicism of his own historical moment then is, first, that it is a period defined by its sense of its own status as a period and, second, that, *as a period,* its identity is essentially transitory. As I am suggesting, the moments of historical contradiction and transformation tend to be conflated in the new Romantic discourse on the spirit of the age.

In Mill's own elaboration of this paradox, the chief point seems to be that the age of the spirit of the age is characterized by a certain skepticism, warranted

90. St. Simon's two kinds of periods do remotely resemble Lévi-Strauss's two kinds of society; cf. Mill, *Essays,* pp. 46–48.

but insufficient in itself, toward traditional figures of authority. The "state we are in," the "condition we are really in," he says, is one in which the "multitude are without a guide; and society is exposed to all the errors and dangers which are to be expected when persons who have never studied any branch of knowledge comprehensively and as a whole attempt to judge for themselves upon particular parts of it." What makes the contemporary state of affairs unstable is that, more than a changed condition, it marks a change in the way conditions change. Mill is interested in "the *mode in which* the old order of things has become unsuited to the state of society and of the human mind" (pp. 34–35). This is what he means when he says that society expects and demands not merely a new machine, but a machine constructed in another manner.

What is the new manner? It is what Mill calls "discussion": "The progress we have made, is precisely that sort of progress which increase of discussion suffices to produce, whether it be attended with increase of wisdom or no." And that sort of progress is to discover erroneous doctrines formerly held on faith, rather than to establish true doctrines on a firmer ground. Discussion does the former much more easily than the latter: "To be rationally assured that a given doctrine is *true,* it is often necessary to examine and weigh an immense variety of facts. One single well-established fact, clearly irreconcilable with a doctrine, is sufficient to prove that it is *false*" (p. 35). Discussion, then, is a second-order mechanism, a mechanism for testing the existing social machinery, a new mode for altering the political modality. To say that the age of the spirit of the age is the age of transition amounts to roughly the same thing as saying that it is the age of discussion.

Both claims, in turn, can be read as closely allied with one made by Thomas Carlyle in his similarly titled essay two years earlier. Alluding to the talk of crisis that he sees permeating public discourse in Britain "for the last fifty years," he claims that "The 'State in Danger' is a condition of things," and that crisis itself is not the defining characteristic of the great age of Revolution. The defining characteristic is machinery. Among the key senses of machinery for Carlyle, however, is what he calls "the great art of adapting means to ends." And among the basic *kinds* of machinery Carlyle has in view, the intellectual machinery of public discussion looms especially large: "every little sect among us, Unitarians, Utilitarians, Anabaptists, Phrenologists, must have its Periodical, its monthly or quarterly Magazine;—hanging out, like its windmill, into the popularist aura, to grind meal for the society." Without such machinery driving home the connection between the machinery of historicist self-consciousness and the machinery of industrialization, says Carlyle, "they were hopeless, helpless; a colony of Hindoo weavers squatting in the heart of Lancashire." Carlyle has an-

ticipated Mill's less straightforward argument with this impressive insight. In
Mill's account, after all, second-order machinery for transforming the social
machine, the machinery he calls "discussion," is just a set of instruments with
their own particular use: testing the validity of established doctrine.[91] The logic
that Carlyle's account supplies is that which connects the notion of making history through publicized literary representation with the notion of making history through industrialized manufacturing technology.

But there is another way to see the connection. Marx's late writings, which
offer extensive commentary on Mill's views of political economy, supply a crucial point of departure for both Lévi-Strauss and Sartre. In a recent commentary on these writings, Moishe Postone has explained the contradiction in the
dual temporality of the labor theory of value. What Marx identified in the duality of commodified labor, first in the *Grundrisse* and then in *Capital,* was a
temporality in which the quantifiable abstract homogeneous time of labor is
used as the basis for assessing value even as machine-enhanced productivity
proved capable of dramatically altering the "socially necessary" average time for
the production of a given task.[92] Carlyle's Hindoo weavers are, in effect, caught
in something like this same contradiction: the value of their labor time is cut in
half by virtue of the machine loom's halving of the socially necessary time for
producing fabric. In this same analysis, Marx develops a picture of the worker
under what St. Simon called the "système industrielle" that resonates with
Lévi-Strauss's own St. Simonian prophecy: "Labour no longer appears so much
to be included within the production process; rather, the human being comes
to relate more as watchman and regulator to the production process itself. . . .
He steps to the side of the production process instead of being its chief actor."[93]
As with Lévi-Strauss's St. Simonian fantasy, Marx's account of this "transformation" involves a new mode of history. And Marx also stresses, as if in response to
Mill's notion of "discussion" as a mode of transformative machinery in the industrial period, that what "holds for machinery holds likewise for the combination of human activities and the development of human intercourse."[94]

91. Writing just after both Carlyle and Mill in yet another similarly entitled essay, "The Intellectual Spirit of the Time," Edward Bulwer-Lytton drew a similar conclusion about the present
state of things but did not date the contemporary period to so early a point in time. Speaking of
his contemporaries, he says that they desire "to see Utility in every branch of intellectual labour,"
and that "it is in this state that the Intellectual Spirit of the age rests, demanding the Useful. . . ."
See *England and the English,* ed. Standish Meacham (Chicago: University of Chicago Press,
1970), pp. 286–87.

92. See Moishe Postone, *Time, Labor, and Social Domination* (Cambridge: Cambridge University Press, 1993), pp. 286–306.

93. Karl Marx, *Grundrisse,* trans. Martin Nicolaus (Harmondsworth: Penguin, 1993), p. 705.

94. Ibid., p. 705.

These speculations linking Lévi-Strauss, by way of St. Simon and Marx, with the English discourse on the spirit of the age aim to make more plausible some of the arguments that will follow. I hope these speculations have also managed to foreground elements of what will become central topics. One has to do with the problematic relation of the theory of uneven development to the concept of homogeneous empty time. Another has to do with "culture" as defined mutually in historiography and anthropology. In his counterfactual description of those Manchester artisans who lacked the machinery to mass produce texts and textiles as so many Hindoo weavers in the heart of Manchester, Carlyle clearly invokes the historiographical-ethnographical analogy that emerges so powerfully in the post-Enlightenment discourse on culture. It is, after all, this same discourse that Lévi-Strauss at once inhabits (as a "contemporary Frenchman" with historical ambitions) and critiques. Examining both the duality of time and the duality of culture—and doing so in relation to the Romantic production of the "historian's code"—will be a central task in the discussion that follows in chapter 2.

In the meantime, I hope to have shown here how Jameson's structuralist genealogy of the so-called return to history can be deepened and "thickened" to enhance the historical intelligibility of the phenomenon. I hope I have also managed to suggest how historicization and politicization over recent years may have gone hand in hand. As Mill and Carlyle both recognized in their St. Simonian moments, to represent a historical state of affairs is to begin to transform it, to make "history" is to begin to "make history." If our academic historicism has not involved quite the same "history-making" effects, that is surely at least in part because its relation to the dominant public sphere is relatively attenuated. Certainly for the U.S. context, the "history-making" function of cultural work in our moment, and in our century more broadly, has been generally taken up by cinematic and televisual forms.[95] D. W. Griffith, the self-styled "man who invented Hollywood," seemed to have recognized as much when he named the film company that would produce *Birth of a Nation* "Epoch Making Productions."[96]

95. For a sampling of recent work addressing such issues, see Robert A. Rosenstone, ed., *Revisioning History: Film and the Construction of a New Past* (Princeton, N.J.: Princeton University Press, 1995).

96. At the same time, however, Griffith's historical cinema is profoundly indebted to the Romantic historicism of Walter Scott, as I have argued at some length in "The Historical Novel Goes to Hollywood: Scott, Griffith, and Film Epic Today," in *The Romantics and Us,* ed. Gene Ruoff (New Brunswick, N.J.: Rutgers University Press, 1991), pp. 237–73; reprinted in *The Birth of a Nation,* ed. Robert Lang (New Brunswick, N.J.: Rutgers University Press, 1994), pp. 225–49.

Chapter Two

AN ART OF "THE STATE" IN ROMANTIC HISTORICISM: THE MEASURES OF UNEVEN DEVELOPMENT

When Lévi-Strauss quipped at the end of his discussion of "History and Dialectic" that, like certain careers, history might lead to anything as long as you get out of it, the remark certainly seemed meant to discourage long-term interest in the field. I have noted some reasons why, in spite of its tone, his account seems to have had the reverse effect of helping to move people *into* the field of history—though often "history" in a revised, revamped, and reflexive mode.[1] Those reasons have to do in the first place with the very extent and quality of attention that Lévi-Strauss invested in the subject. The work of such commentators as Veyne, White, de Certeau, and LaCapra, as well as Leo Braudy, Lionel Gossman, and Suzanne Gearhart, attests in various ways and degrees to the difference that such attention has made. Moreover, by defamiliarizing the aspect of historical specificity which has to do with dating texts and events, Lévi-Strauss's critique of Sartre and the responses it generated not only prompted new methods for the study of literary culture—homological analysis, as Jameson points out, prominent among them—but also indicated what might be involved in shifts of historical scale. By the same token, practicing historical commentary on differing scales further raised critical self-awareness about dates (and dating practices) as such. The notion of anecdotal evidence that emerged from these debates, I have suggested, helped to make possible a range of research explicitly framing itself in terms of a single year.

The claim that Lévi-Strauss was uninterested in history or that he did not take chronology seriously cannot, in any event, stand up to scrutiny. I have al-

---

1. "All signs indicate that the growth of the historical profession after 1970 was spectacular," notes Jacques Revel in his introduction to *Histories: French Constructions of the Past,* ed. Jacques Revel and Lynn Hunt, trans. Arthur Goldhammer and others (New York: New Press, 1995) p. 40—not, of course, that he or I mean to be giving Lévi-Strauss all the credit for this development.

ready reviewed his scattered remarks on the French Revolution and St. Simonianism to indicate one aspect of his investment in history—even if he presents it as a history that might lead beyond itself. And certainly there are contexts in which chronology matters to him in the most apparently straightforward way. The dates he uses in his own narratives—*Tristes Tropiques,* for example—often play quite an important historical role.[2] And in a published interview late in his career, on being asked his opinion of the work of Foucault, he admitted to having the troubling "impression . . . that Foucault takes some liberties with chronology. . . . In a historian of ideas that bothers me."[3] In this chapter, I will note how Foucault's "chronology" for what he called the "Age of History" itself is actually very much in line with most other commentators on the subject, even if his views of it are contrarian. My larger aim, however, is to provide perspective on the genealogy I have been sketching for poststructuralist historicisms by jumping from the debate about history in the heyday of structuralism to the debates on the subject in that earlier age. To prepare for that jump, I wish to return, just briefly, to *The Savage Mind* and to some issues raised in the conflicted reception through which it has been mediated for present readers.

I will be using an important critique of Lévi-Strauss—Johannes Fabian's— in order to show that what the historian's dating system codes is the work of a kind of translation, not only between cultures, but also between the two closely linked approaches to culture, the ethnographical and the historiographical. To establish this claim, I argue that the complex intellectual-historical revolution we call "historicism," which is widely associated with (roughly) the period 1770–1830 in British and European history, can be profitably understood in terms of its production of just this kind of coding—the deployment of a dating system for making intelligible the relationship between the representations of culture in those same, then-emerging discourses, historiography and ethnography. After tracing the transformation in the "state of society" in the eighteenth century and reviewing the conception of "uneven development" in Scottish-

2. Lévi-Strauss introduces his travel account of Brazil by presenting a history of the conquest that began "almost 378 years ago to the day" from the time of his writing and proceeds to date each important event. He also makes repeated comparisons of historically specific moments in European history with aspects he remarks in, for example, Rio de Janeiro: the villas around that city, he says, reminded him "of Nice or Biarritz under Napoleon III." Indeed, it is in this context that he makes his oft-quoted remark: "The tropics are less exotic than out of date." See *Tristes Tropiques,* trans. John and Doreen Weightman (Harmondsworth: Penguin, 1992), pp. 81, 87.

3. The comment is to be found in Didier Eribon, *Conversations with Claude Lévi-Strauss,* trans. Paula Wissing (Chicago: University of Chicago Press, 1991), p. 72. There is an interesting parallel between Lévi-Strauss's complaint in these interviews about Foucault—that he proceeds "as if he knew beforehand what he wanted to prove and then sought to support his thesis"—and Sartre's complaint about idealist marxism in *The Search for a Method* (p. 72).

Enlightenment historical theory, I will argue that the complex terms of the new Romantic-historicist configuration—the signs of the "spirit of the age"—are inscribed in texts such as Anna Barbauld's post-Waterloo meditation on "The Uses of History." I go on to show how such terms are given massively, globally influential articulation in the "necessary anachronisms" of Sir Walter Scott's Waverley novels. These novels provided what contemporaries such as Balzac called Scott's new "model" of a dated historiographical and ethnographical representation of action-in-society, a new form for specifying cultural-historical typologies of character and agency. The "return to history" in our time can be profitably understood as a return, willy-nilly, to this model, though the range of our recognitions and descriptions of its place in current critical practice has indeed been wide.

1. Codifying the Order of History

Anyone familiar with the recent history of the human sciences in France, and in the many quarters of the Anglo-American academy in which French thought has played a major role, knows that Lévi-Strauss's attack on Sartre's conception of the *sens d'histoire* kindled some already-smoldering issues into a controversy that generated an enormous volume of published commentary.[4] The attack was taken by many readers as devastating when it first appeared, and Sartre's failure to produce a timely rejoinder to it did not help his own cause.[5] There were, however, several serious countercritiques leveled against Lévi-Strauss's polemics and then a number of later commentaries on the entire debate.[6] The issues

4. Thus, Lawrence Rosen could write in 1971, "For more than a decade now French philosophical thought has tended to center around the work of two key figures, the existentialist Jean-Paul Sartre and the structuralist Claude Lévi-Strauss." See "Language, History and the Logic of Inquiry in Lévi-Strauss and Sartre," *History and Theory* 10 (1971):269. See also Mark Poster, *Existential Marxism in Postwar France from Sartre to Althusser* (Princeton, N.J.: Princeton University Press, 1975), pp. 306–60. Poster's account includes a list of the works involved in this debate on both sides, including journals that devoted special issues to it (pp. 306–307). For another overview, see Robert D'Amico, "The Contours and Coupures of Structuralist Theory," *Telos* 17 (fall 1973): 70–97. For particular contributions to this debate that include helpful summaries and situations, see G. Lantéra-Laura, "History and Structure in Anthropological Knowledge," *Social Research* 34 (1967): 113–61, and "Histoire et Structure," a special issue of *Annales* 31 (May–June 1971): 1–888. For an important contribution to this debate from the Frankfurt School, see Alfred Schmidt's 1971 monograph, *History and Structure,* trans. Jeffrey Herf (Cambridge, Mass.: MIT Press, 1981), especially the discussion of the progressive-regressive method on pp. 49–52.

5. It was not until much later, and then only obliquely, that Sartre responded to Lévi-Strauss's comments on history and structure in *The Savage Mind,* when he included some remarks on "Anthropology" in an interview of 1965, published in *Situations IX: Melanges* (Paris: Gallimard, 1972), pp. 86–87.

6. Among the earlier interventions, two are noteworthy. In 1963, Henri Lefebvre, on whom Sartre had drawn in formulating his progressive-regressive method, published an important essay,

raised in the Sartre/Lévi-Strauss exchange defined a self-conscious frame of reference in critical debates for at least two decades. Of the later attacks on Lévi-Strauss, Johannes Fabian's *Time and the Other* (1983) merits special attention here because of the way it addresses two questions left hanging from the discussion of the previous chapter, one having to do with the relation of ordinality and simultaneity in the historian's code, the other with the conceptual relationship between the discourses of anthropology and history. Fabian can help us to see the relation between these two relationships and thus move to the next stage of this discussion.

According to Fabian, something odd, perhaps even something intellectually dishonest, occurs in the course of Lévi-Strauss's critique of the Sartrean-historicist conception of time. Fabian points out that Lévi-Strauss begins the chapter on "History and Dialectic" by declaring a need to redress what he perceives (in Sartre and others) as an injustice done to anthropology on the part of historiography. The explicit premise of Lévi-Strauss's challenge was that historians such as Sartre disrespected the symmetrical complementarity that mutually relates these disciplines: "one of them unfurls the range of human societies in time, the other in space[;] . . . the historian strives to reconstruct the picture of vanished societies as they were at the points which for them corresponded to the present, while the ethnographer does his best to reconstruct the historical stages which temporally preceded their existing form."[7] This "symmetry," Lévi-Strauss says, is "rejected" by philosophers who wish to attach some "special prestige . . . to the temporal dimension."[8] Lévi-Strauss here offers his analysis as an adjustment toward the center, and, so introduced, argues Fabian, the ensuing argument is one from which one might expect some redressing of the anthropological or spatially oriented side of the disciplinary balance. Indeed, a similar purpose seems initially to govern the book as a whole: its first chapter begins by trying to claim for the bricolage of mythic thought its rightful place "alongside" the forms of scientific thought wrongfully assumed to have superseded the former. But just as the announced beginning intention to redress this

---

"Réflexions sur le Structuralisme et l'Histoire," which appeared in the same journal where he had laid out the terms of that method a decade before, *Cahiers Internationaux de Sociologie* 35 (Juillet–Décembre 1963): 3–24. Lefebvre's position is complicated, however, in that the 1963 essay is less clearly a defense of Sartre's version of the historical method than a critique of Lévi-Strauss's refusal of it. Second, in 1968, Louis Althusser's radical analysis of historicism that formed a kind of centerpiece for *Reading Capital* actually turned Lévi-Strauss himself into an illustration of just the sort of historicism on which *The Savage Mind* itself had taken aim. See *Reading Capital,* trans. Ben Brewster (London: Verso, 1970), p. 108.

7. Lévi-Strauss, *The Savage Mind* (Chicago: University of Chicago Press, 1966), p. 256.
8. Ibid., p. 256.

imbalance might seem overrun by a drive to establish the priority of the savage mind over the scientific one, so in the final chapter the conclusion might seem less designed to restore a symmetry than to debunk diachrony in favor of synchrony, and historiography in favor of anthropology. This conclusion, for Fabian, betokens little more than bad faith—"structuralist duplicity"—on the part of Lévi-Strauss.[9]

Another reading of the movement of Lévi-Strauss's argument in "History and Dialectic" might be possible, however, for one might view Lévi-Strauss's account as actually recapitulating the synchronic-diachronic binary within the operations of the chronological code. True, insofar as he insists that the historian's date is assimilable to a framework of classification, and a structure of specificity, the emphasis falls on the way in which any given date can be taken either as a member of a class date above it on the structural grid or as a class for member dates below it. If viewed exclusively in these classificatory terms, there would be nothing to prevent any given date from perfectly exemplifying the class above it, or from perfectly containing the class below. What skews this sort of exemplarity, however, is the ordinality of the date, which Lévi-Strauss identifies as its peculiarly historical dimension. Here we might recall his claim early in the analysis that "history's entire originality and distinctive nature lie in apprehending the relation between *before* and *after*."[10] The dated chronological period has an integrity given by the cardinal function of the number, its status as integer, yet it necessarily maintains a further double function as marking moment and sequence. If we say, therefore, that certain events date to some given date, we mean that, in addition to being readable as taking place at the same time—that is, on the same date (August 16, or 1819, or the Romantic period, or the nineteenth century)—they can also be arranged, by means of dates of a different order, in a sequence of moments, each of which can be said to stand as a period that synchronizes still-lower-order dates.

My point is that Fabian seems to overlook the way in which, in Lévi-Strauss's final construction of the historian's code, "order" works along two axes. When produced as a sequence in terms of a higher-order date D, events dated at lower-order dates d_1 and d_2 differ precisely in the *order* of their occurrence. It would follow, then, that the ordinal differences within the specific structure (i.e., distinctive specificity) of the historian's code—those crucial differences of before and after with which Lévi-Strauss begins his discussion—also mark the

9. Johannes Fabian, *Time and the Other: How Anthropology Makes Its Object* (New York: Columbia University Press, 1983), p. 54.
10. Lévi-Strauss, *The Savage Mind*, p. 258 (italics original).

distinctiveness of the historical code among other codes.[11] Similarly, the phrase "specific structure" must be understood to cut both ways: the historian's code as a structure of specificity and the specificity of the historian's code itself in its "peculiar nature."[12] Against Fabian's claim that Lévi-Strauss has skewed the mutual complementarity of the diachronic-synchronic distinction, it seems rather to be the case that the distinction is reconstituted within the apparently diachronic order of the historian's code, though (to be sure) in an avowedly heuristic or nominalist framework.[13]

Whether one accepts or rejects this defense of Lévi-Strauss against Fabian's critique, it is important to register the point that Lévi-Strauss is willing, at the very least, to acknowledge a kind of equivalence between the notion of the historian's period and the notion of the anthropologist's culture. The conceptual framework within which the chronological code operates as a code, in other words, is constituted in terms of the analogy between historiography and anthropology. This analogy—half of which is captured in L. P. Hartley's famous claim that the past is a foreign country, the other half in the notion of a "foreign country" as belonging to the past or future—is historically and conceptually an important component of the practice of historical-cultural specification that Lévi-Strauss and Sartre are debating in the 1950s and 1960s. If the notion of a specifically historical specificity is mutually identified with the notion of a specifically cultural specificity, then some coding is called for to make such an identification patent. Or, to anticipate the way in which I shall consider the problem, the requirement for the sort of "even" or regularized chronological matrix that is developed into the code of dates unfolded by Lévi-Strauss is bound in a necessary but contradictory relationship with the assumptions of "uneven development" in terms of which the historiography-anthropology

11. Not that Lévi-Strauss's stipulation could be quite enough, as Janel Mueller points out to me, to distinguish the historian's code from others that employ before-and-after relations such as the linguistic and musical codes.

12. Seeing that, from the point of view of the anthropologist, the before-and-after of ordinality is crucial to the constitution of historical difference might perhaps provide an answer to Fabian, if it could be shown that the anthropologist, when viewed by the historian, constitutes *similarity* temporally (and difference spatially), which is arguably the perspective that Lévi-Strauss means to be identifying with Sartre's attempt to ground anthropology in the principles of the "progressive-regressive method."

13. Some corroboration of this more symmetrical view of Lévi-Strauss's account of this disciplinary relationship can be found in his remarks on "History and Anthropology," where, as I noted earlier, Lévi-Strauss misquotes Marx's dictum about "men making history" from *The Eighteenth Brumaire* to argue that the approaches of history and anthropology "are inseparable"— *Structural Anthropology,* trans. Claire Jacobson and Brooke Grundfest Schoepf (New York: Basic Books, 1963), p. 23.

analogy is articulated. The evenness implicit in the code, one might say, depends dialectically on the unevenness implicit in the analogy, and vice versa.[14]

What I propose to undertake now is a sketch of the historical emergence of this way of conceiving history—history understood as a periodical coding of relationships among unevenly developing national narratives and temporalities. In doing so, I mean to follow the lead of Michel de Certeau in his response to the structuralist account of history "as *a text* organizing units of meaning and subjecting them to transformations whose rules can be determined":[15] essays written about history from this point of view have not been persuasive, says de Certeau, "to the extent that they have posited the univocality of the genre of the 'historical' over the ages."[16] The aim of my analysis here is to offer, if you will, a conceptual history of the "progressive-regressive method" itself, the method that in various forms, acknowledged and unacknowledged, continues to inform a wide range of academic historicist practice in literary and cultural studies. My claim is that Lévi-Strauss is not mapping out the "historian's code" *tout court,* but rather what might be termed the "historicist's code." This code can be used to date itself, as it were, in the moment I have been calling, with a certain redundancy, "Romantic historicism."[17]

2. Returning to Romantic Historicism

To consult the critical literature on the history of historicism in post-Enlightenment Europe is to confront an oddly sorted range of opinion. The oddity is that, while commentators are quite unanimous in the judgment that European intellectual culture underwent radical historiographical transformation between, say, 1770 and 1830, they are quite divided about what that trans-

14. This dialectic is similar to what Moishe Postone calls the "immanent" and "historical dynamic" of the commodity form in Marx's analysis of capitalism, where evenness corresponds to the dimension of "abstract time" and unevenness to the dimension of "socially necessary time," the later being dependent on the specific state of productive capacity for the social system in question. See *Time, Labor, and Social Domination* (Cambridge: Cambridge University Press, 1993), pp. 287–98.

15. Michel de Certeau, *The Writing of History,* trans. Tom Conley (New York: Columbia University Press, 1988), p. 41.

16. Ibid., p. 41.

17. De Certeau emphasizes that the two reductions of the historiographical operation—the reduction of the past event to its historically specific conditions of productions and of the present explanation to its *own* conditions of production (i.e., why this form of explanation *now*)—do not reduce to each other. See *The Writing of History,* pp. 44–45. See also Susan Stewart's prefatory meditation on "the interplay of philosophy and history" figured as a drawing by Eakins that addresses the problem of "the impossibility of a seeing that could see itself seeing, and consequently of a writing that could write itself writing" in *Crimes of Writing* (New York: Oxford University Press, 1991), pp. ix–xi.

formation actually amounts to: there is more agreement, for example, about the claim that the concept of contemporaneity undergoes major changes in this period than there is about what it means to make such a claim. No doubt, from commentators as diverse as Friedrich Meinecke, R. G. Collingwood, Georg Lukács, Hannah Arendt, Louis Althusser, Reinhart Koselleck, Michel Foucault, Jacques Derrida, J. G. A. Pocock, Hans Blumenberg, Tzvetan Todorov, and Benedict Anderson, one could hardly expect full unanimity. Yet each locates a fundamental change in the recognition and representation of historical time *in* a time that is either called "Romantic" or dated to a period (roughly 1770–1830) that we otherwise associate with the advent of Romanticism in its early (i.e., British) phase. The temporality of that "time-in-which" inevitably makes for a further complication in these accounts, though this complication is not often addressed and seldom even acknowledged in these histories of historiography.

The conundrums, contradictions, or aporias of Romantic historicism appear both within and between the most powerful of these accounts.[18] In *The Order of Things,* Foucault concludes his archaeological account of the human sciences since the Renaissance by looking in turn at the transformations wrought during what he calls the "Age of History" in the discourses of economics, natural science, and linguistics. Although Foucault's dating of the Age of History accords closely with that of other historians, his account is somewhat idiosyncratic. To begin with, he subdivides this age into a transition phase, 1775–95, and a subsequent phase that focuses squarely on the work of Ricardo, Cuvier, and Bopp. Taken whole, the Age of History comprises a great epistemic shift in the order of things, but Foucault's insistence that it pertains precisely to "things" has negative implications for prevailing beliefs about human history. These implications are spelled out in the section called simply "History" in the coda chapter on "The Human Sciences." Here Foucault seeks, on the one hand, to explain the error in the received account of the emergence of historicism in this period. This is the belief "that the nineteenth century, largely for political and social reasons, paid closer attention to human history, that the idea of an order or a continuous level of time was abandoned, as well as that of an uninterrupted progress, and that the bourgeoisie, in attempting to recount its own ascent, encountered, in the calendar of its victory, the historical density of institutions, the specific gravity of habits and beliefs, the violence of struggles, the alternation of success and failure."[19] The extension of this view, according to Foucault, is the conclusion that,

---

18. Some of the antinomies I sketch in Romantic historicism are discussed in terms of the "aporias of the experience of time" and the "circle of narrative and temporality" in Paul Ricoeur's *Time and Narrative,* 3 vols. (Chicago: University of Chicago Press, 1983–85).

19. Michel Foucault, *The Order of Things,* p. 368.

in this period of western European intellectual history, "the study of economies, the history of literatures and grammars, and even the evolution of living beings are merely effects of the diffusion, over increasingly more distant areas of knowledge, of a historicity first revealed in man."[20] One might find some such account in Pocock's argument about how the commerical view of property in the eighteenth century "furnished the human creature with a history."[21]

Foucault's contention is that what happened is exactly the reverse of this: that it was *things* that initially began to receive "a historicity proper to them," freed of the space in which they were thought to share a chronology with humanity, and that then the human being was "dehistoricized" in the sense of being "dispossessed of what constituted the most manifest contents of his history": "[T]he imaginative values then assumed by the past, the whole lyrical halo that surrounded the consciousness of history at that period,—all this is a surface expression of the simple fact that man found himself emptied of history, but that he was already beginning to recover in the depths of his own being, and among all the things that were still capable of reflecting his image (the others have fallen silent and folded back into themselves), a historicity linked essentially to man himself."[22] The historicity of this historical age is thus, for Foucault, "essentially ambiguous," a double reversal of the received view in which one in the end sees the age as the historicization of the human after all, but only after that historicity has been "emptied" by the new histories of things and "refilled" by the new antiquarianism.[23]

The conundrum of the "essential ambiguity" implicit within Foucault's account of a double reversal in the period might, I suppose, be dismissed as a matter of his taking (to reinvoke Lévi-Strauss's indictment) further liberties with chronology. This conundrum has at least a vague analogue, however, in puzzles that appear when one tries to link two distinct but seemingly related accounts of the late-eighteenth century's new historicism. One might, for example, compare two of the most provocative and influential recent commentators on the subject: Reinhart Koselleck, in the series of essays collected as *Futures Past* (1979; English trans. 1985), and Benedict Anderson, in *Imagined Communities* (1983). Neither of these writers takes note of the other's work, and this is unfortunate, in view of the overlap and apparent tension between certain aspects of their arguments. Like most other writers on the subject, they agree in dating the transformation in

20. Ibid., p. 368.
21. J. G. A. Pocock, *Virtue, Commerce and History* (Cambridge: Cambridge University Press, 1985), pp. 122–23.
22. Foucault, *The Order of Things*, p. 368–69.
23. Ibid., p. 369.

question to the late-eighteenth and early nineteenth centuries. What is more, they employ terminologies that seem to resemble each other: where Anderson addresses himself to typification, simultaneity, and temporal homogeneity, Koselleck discusses exemplarity, contemporaneity, and temporal neutrality. Their ways of putting these terms into play, however, suggests some interesting discrepancies.

Working from categories that Walter Benjamin sketched in the "Theses on History," Anderson attempts, in a now well-known argument, to represent the emergence of the concept of homogeneous, empty time as participating in a large-scale shift of paradigms from the medieval dynastic order to the order of the modern nation-state: "The idea of a sociological organism moving calendrically through homogeneous, empty time is a precise analogue of the idea of the nation, which also is conceived as a solid community moving steadily down (or up) history."[24] Anderson goes back to Erich Auerbach's account of temporal representation in the Bible to argue that the notion of simultaneity in question there "views time as something close to what Benjamin calls Messianic time, a simultaneity of past and future in an instantaneous present."[25] In such a view, adds Anderson, "the word 'meanwhile' cannot be of real significance," for it acquires meaning only in the temporal regime that replaces that of the dynastic "simultaneity along time"—i.e., an order centered in Benjamin's "idea of 'homogeneous, empty time,' in which simultaneity is, as it were, transverse, cross-time, marked not by prefiguring and fulfillment, but by temporal coincidence, and measured by the clock and calendar."[26] There is a problem here in Anderson's attempt to narrate as a sequence Benjamin's distinction between opposed historical procedures, but the main tendencies of the scheme become clearer in juxtaposition with Koselleck's account.

When Koselleck speaks of what happens in this (for him) equally crucial period in the history of historical temporality, he puts similar terms into play, but with an apparently different conclusion in view. Koselleck attempts to describe

24. Benedict Anderson, *Imagined Communities,* rev. ed. (London: Verso, 1991), p. 26.

25. Ibid., p. 24.

26. Anderson explains his point by looking at the "meanwhile" structure of bourgeois fiction. A form in which "acts are performed at the same clocked, calendrical time, but by actors who may be largely unaware of one another, shows the novelty of this imagined world conjured up by the author in his readers' minds" (p. 25). The only relation that Anderson wants to claim between the novelty of the novel and the novelty of the nation-state is an analogical one, though he suggests that this modern temporal order in both realms is figured doubly in the phenomenon of the daily newspaper. First, newspaper reading involves the sense that others are reading the same thing at the same time. Secondly, the very arrangement of the parts of the newspaper, what Anderson calls its "essential literary convention," foregrounds calendrical simultaneity: accounts appear side-by-side for no other reason than that the occurrences they chronicle are supposed to have coincided in a given duration.

the "epochal threshold" that he explicitly locates between 1770 and 1830 and that with some hesitation he describes as a temporalization of history.[27] The "new dynamism" of the history in this period demands what Koselleck calls "temporal categories of movement," and hence the "excessive use of the term *Zeit,* beginning around 1800, to gain insight or power or both within the turmoil of social and political movement."[28] One can see the close proximity of this argument to Anderson's in, for example, Koselleck's assertion that, by virtue of this temporalization, "providential anticipation and the exemplarity of ancient histories fade away" or his comment about the "homogenization" of experience that occurs in the new time (p. 253). For Koselleck, however, this new time also involves an important process of differentiation precisely involving "theoretically enriched concepts of time"; this was a history whose "new dynamism demanded temporal categories of movement" (pp. 256–57). Once in play, such concepts contain "structural potential . . . which cannot be reduced to the pure temporal succession of history" (p. 113). Thus, whereas Koselleck posits a new "homogenization of experience" for the decades around 1800 in western Europe, pointing to the development of the new temporal concepts that involve this complex structural potential, Anderson uses similar terms to make a rather different claim. He suggests that homogeneity of experience is a feature closely associated with what he calls "pure temporal succession" but seems to enclose this kind of homogeneous or pure temporality within the respective communal imaginaries of particular nation states. A further problem, internal to Anderson's influential and suggestive account, has to do with the respective roles played by these temporal categories in shaping the story that Anderson tells. In Anderson, though not in Benjamin, the question arises but remains unaddressed: in what temporality is the shift from messianic to homogeneous empty time being recounted?[29]

27. Reinhart Koselleck, *Futures Past: On the Semantics of Historical Time,* trans. Keith Tribe (Cambridge, Mass.: MIT Press, 1985), p. 256. All page references will hereafter appear in the text.

28. To lend empirical support to his claim and his own chronology, Koselleck offers the following philological evidence for the situation in Germany: "For the time between 1770 and 1830, the epochal threshold initially known as *nueeste Zeit,* Grimm's dictionary contains over one hundred neologisms, compounds which qualified *Zeit* in a positive historical fashion," p. 257.

29. In an important study that I discovered too late to integrate properly here, Peter Osborne, *The Politics of Time: Modernity and Avant-Garde* (London: Verso, 1995), reviews the discussion of temporality in Anderson, Koselleck, and Benjamin. See especially his discussion of temporal homogenization, pp. 13–20, and his account of temporal differentiation in Althusser, pp. 23–29. Two earlier accounts of temporal differentiation that should also be cited in any such survey are Norbert Elias, *Time: An Essay,* trans. Edmund Jephcott (Oxford: Basil Blackwell, 1992); and Georges Gurvitch, *The Spectrum of Social Time,* trans. Myrtle Korenbaum (Dordrecht: D. Reidel, 1964), especially pp. 34–38 and 129–41.

To take one last commentator on the problem, Todorov, like Foucault, comes at the issue of historicism through the history of linguistics.[30] He frames his discussion between the usual range of dates: the publication of Beauzée's *Grammaire générale* in 1767 and that of Humboldt's *Linguistic Variability and Intellectual Development* in 1835. What is charted between these dates is an intellectual development in which "to the synchronic variability of languages is joined a diachronic variability" that was actually, however, implicit in it all along, in that, as Todorov makes clear, "synchrony is clearly not opposed to diachrony, but both together are opposed to the panchrony, or even achrony, that is implied by general grammars."[31] Likewise, more broadly for Todorov, what he terms "history (the study of variations in time) is not opposed to ethnology (the study of variations in space)," since, for him, "both arise from the romantic spirit that enthrones difference in the place of identity."[32] Todorov's abstract account seems true enough, as far as it goes, and he signals keen self-awareness about the question of how to relate that account to his own subject: "To observe, during the very process of writing the 'history' of the passage between classics and romantics, that the idea of diversity and history is a romantic and anticlassical idea, is of course to make a statement full of consequences."[33] But while these remarks occur in a chapter called "Openings," they come in the very closing pages of Todorov's *Theories of the Symbol*. Thus, his suggestion that we meditate on the oddity implicit in the "very possibility of describing the romantic ideology today," though it uncannily anticipates the title of Jerome McGann's book of the following year, remains only a suggestion.[34] That "oddity" is precisely the subject before us.[35]

3. The Age of the Spirit of the Age

How, then, to begin addressing some of the long-standing difficulties associated with the notion of historicism in the so-called Romantic period? I suggest we return to the phrase that descends to us as one of the most self-consciously

30. More precisely, Foucault's account considers the genealogy of linguistics out of general grammar—*Order of Things*, pp. 280–302.

31. Todorov, *Theories of the Symbol*, trans. Catherine Porter (Ithaca, N.Y.: Cornell University Press, 1982), p. 286.

32. Ibid., p. 288.

33. Ibid., p. 288.

34. Ibid., p. 289.

35. Three other, and very different, arguments in behalf of the historical novelty of the period 1770–1830 include Hannah Arendt, *On Revolution* (1965; London and New York: Penguin Books, 1990); E. J. Hobsbawm, *Nations and Nationalism since 1780: Programme, Myth, Reality* (New York: Norton, 1990); and Paul Johnson, *The Birth of the Modern: World Society 1815-1830* (New York: Harper Collins, 1991).

novel and distinctive coinages of that period, the term it seems to have coined precisely to identify its own novelty and distinction: "the spirit of the age." The extent of the obsession with this concept by 1830 was testily attested in Blackwood's *Edinburgh Magazine* at the end of that year in an anonymously published letter "On the Spirit of the Age": "That which, in the slang of faction, is called the Spirit of the Age, absorbs, at present, the attention of the world."[36] It was in the following year that John Stuart Mill published his famous series of seven articles on the same subject, partly in response to Robinson, and (conveniently for our purposes) took a stab at dating the new obsession with dates: "The 'spirit of the age' is in some measure a novel expression. I do not believe that it is to be met with in any work exceeding fifty years in antiquity."[37] Mill's periodization of the new notion of the period is thus broadly consistent with the chronology one finds in the commentaries on the history of the emergent historicism.[38] In Hans Blumenberg's terms, it is the crucial moment in "the epochs of the concept of the epoch."[39]

In discussing certain of Shelley's remarks in 1819, I have already addressed one aspect of this new discursive formation: its preoccupation with contemporaneity. One reason why that concept by itself is insufficient for framing an appropriate account is that it might be argued—has been argued, by J. Paul Hunter and others—that the notion of contemporaneity is put into play by British writers at a much earlier moment. For Hunter, indeed, the "commitment to contemporaneity" on the part of the journalistic press of the late seventeenth and early eighteenth centuries amounted to one of the crucial en-

36. [Charles Robinson], "Letter to Christopher North, Esquire, on the Spirit of the Age," *Blackwood's Edinburgh Magazine* 28 (December 1830): 900.

37. Mill, "Spirit of the Age," in *Mill's Essays on Literature and Society,* ed. J. B. Schneewind (New York: Collier, 1965), p. 28.

38. The period Mill identifies would be the five decades that follow 1780, which makes a reasonably good fit with the periodization of the new sense of history discussed above in Foucault, Koselleck, Todorov, et al. But see Friedrich Meinecke's claim that variations on the phrase can be found much earlier; I cite an instance of such an earlier appearance in Boulainvilliers below.

39. Hans Blumenberg, *The Legitimacy of the Modern Age,* trans. Robert M. Wallace (Cambridge: MIT Press, 1983), p. 457. Blumenberg frames his remarks on the "epochs of the concept of the epoch," between two very different uses of the term "epoch" by Goethe on the battle of Valmy, one in 1792 and the other in 1820, explaining that between them "lies his historical experience with the rise and fall of the Napoleonic 'demon,' with *an* epoch that was supposed to have resulted from *the* epoch of the Revolution" (p. 458). The fullest existing account of the British debate about the spirit of the age in the 1820s is probably to be found in A. Dwight Culler, *The Victorian Mirror of History* (New Haven: Yale University Press, 1985), pp. 39–73, though Culler is writing primarily about Victorianism and is therefore less interested in the Scottish Enlightenment provenance of the framework or in its survival in structuralist and poststructuralist discourse.

abling conditions for the rapid development of the early English novel.[40] Hunter's point is not that the concept of contemporaneity was new. He certainly might, if he wished, have pointed to the use of the term "synchronism" by the Renaissance historian John Selden to indicate a much earlier self-consciousness about how, technically, to relate events understood as occurring at or in a given time. The point about the early novel is that journalism is beginning to put in place the conditions for thinking of contemporaneity as a defining idea for ordinary experience. It is likewise possible, however, to differentiate the sense of contemporaneity in a writer like Defoe from what we find in the later discussions of the spirit of the age. What makes Romantic historicism distinctive—and what seems to me to demand the kind of attention I give to it here—is the quality and extent of its interest in what might be called "comparative contemporaneities."[41] As Mill put it, "The idea of comparing one's own age with former ages, or with our notion of those which are yet to come, had occurred to philosophers; but it never before was itself the dominant idea of any age."[42] The dominance of this "idea," I now want to suggest, can be reformulated in terms of a concern with anachronism—or, perhaps I should say, with the emergence of a new conception of anachronism, now understood as a measurable form of dislocation.[43]

Anachronism is not, like the term "the spirit of the age," a coinage of the late eighteenth and early nineteenth centuries. The same John Selden who deployed "synchronism" in the late sixteenth century produced "antichronism" a few years later, and "anachronism" can also be dated to the seventeenth cen-

---

40. Hunter writes: "Long before Samuel Richardson showed readers and writers of fiction how to savor a single human instant a thousand ways, the world of print had begun its long liaison with the up to date, the latest news, and the present moment." *Before Novels: The Cultural Contexts of Eighteenth-Century English Fiction* (New York: Norton, 1990), p. 167.

41. I adopt the notion, but not the term, from Koselleck, who argues that a certain conception of progress meant that what he calls "the contemporaneity of the noncontemporaneous became a fundamental datum of all history." The development of this concept forms a key component in the account I will be offering of the genealogy of the historian's code. Koselleck cites an example of its deployment in Marx that anticipates what I will be saying about its distinctive idiom: "If I deny German conditions of 1843 then, by French chronological standards, I barely stand in 1789, and even less at the focus of the present." See *Futures Past,* p. 249.

42. Mill, "Spirit of the Age," p. 28.

43. To link the discourse of the spirit of the age with the work that refreshed it for our own time is to be reminded how much of what Sartre proposed in *The Question of Method* can be reformulated as a concern with anachronism. His proposed method affirms, he says, "the specificity of the historical event, which it refuses to conceive of as the absurd juxtaposition of a contingent residue and an a priori signification." And "specificity" here means chronological specificity: "the political reality for the men of 1792 is an absolute, an irreducible" (p. 41); "a book written in 1956 does not resemble one in 1930" (p. 49); "The day of the tenth of August, of the ninth of Thermidor, that day in the month of June 1848, etc. cannot be reduced to concepts" (p. 127).

tury.[44] However, a related term, "anatopism," which appears to be a back formation from "anachronism," not only dates to the period of the spirit of the age but also helps to illuminate it. Thomas De Quincey actually sounds as if he thinks he is coining this term in 1850 when he refers to "geographical blunders, or what might be called anatopisms," but it is in fact already recorded in the writings of his mentor Coleridge. In arranging certain books, Coleridge wrote in 1812, "the puzzled librarian must commit anachronism in order to avoid anatopism." The either/or of Coleridge's formulation suggests that the analogy of anachronism and anatopism can assume the character of an inverted mirror structure or chiasmus. Something in its place can be understood as metaphorically out of its time, Coleridge implies; and something in its time, presumably, can be understood as metaphorically out of its place.

This chiastic figure helped to make it possible to conceptualize culture as a shared object of study for the fields of history and ethnography, as the link that has bound those fields in so intimate and uneasy a relationship for more than two centuries. In the literature of this period, one can see a new preoccupation with the dating of the cultural place, the locating of the cultural moment. Some such conception underlies the opening line from L. P. Hartley's *The Go-Between:* "The past is a foreign country; they do things differently there."[45] It is the second part of the quotation that tells you that the concept of culture is at stake: they do [the present tense is important] things differently, they do things in a different manner, they have different manners, different *moeurs,* different norms. In a book that takes its title from Hartley's declaration, David Lowenthal has argued that the perspective that inheres in the metaphor of the past as a foreign country, the one which Lowenthal regards as making possible "the awareness of anachronism," is of relatively recent vintage; he explicitly assigns the date of this awareness to "the late eighteenth century" in Europe.[46] It is roughly

44. Thanks to Claire McEachern for this reference. See Herman L. Ebeling, "The Word *Anachronism,*" *MLN* 52 (February 1937): 120–21. Ebeling suggests that the word may have "acquired its modern currency in consequence of Joseph Justus Scaliger's great work *De Emendatione Temporum* of 1583 (p. 120).

45. L. P. Hartley, *The Go-Between* (London: H. Hamilton, 1953), p. 3.

46. David Lowenthal, *The Past is a Foreign Country* (Cambridge: Cambridge University Press, 1985), p. xvi. A rather different dating is offered by F. J. Levy in *Tudor Historical Thought* (San Marino, Cal.: Huntington Library, 1967). Levy claims that anachronism enters English historiography in the Tudor period as part of the importation of Italian humanism. For Levy, however, this amounts to a claim about a Tudor recognition, less evident in late-medieval historiography, that "the past was different from the present" (p. ix). Lowenthal, in his dating of anachronism to the long Romantic period, refers rather, as I do, to a new *way* of conceiving this difference. This is the conception I describe below as involving a new discourse of "culture" (with its notions of "development," "childhood," "growth," etc.) and as depending on the analogy between historiography and ethnography considered as two approaches to the study of culture.

this same sense in which Georg Lukács argues that Scott's Waverley novels need to be understood in relation to a notion of "necessary anachronism" that is absolutely crucial to their construction.[47]

Extending the claims of Lukács and Lowenthal, then, I want to argue that *both* the specifying of historical cultures in relation to the question of anachronism *and* the conceptualizing of that question in terms of the mutual fit between anachronism and anatopism became major preoccupations for a wide range of writing in British Romanticism. If the literature of this period has not consistently been seen as historicist in this sense, the reasons may partly lie in the prominence certain slogans have achieved in our understanding of its characteristic attitudes. "A poem is the very image of life expressed in its eternal truth," wrote Shelley in *A Defence of Poetry* (comp. 1821), and the same text includes a claim apparently even more resistant to a historicist frame of reference: "A poet," he warns later in his discussion, "would do ill to embody his own conception of right and wrong, which are usually those of his place and time, in his poetical creations, which participate in neither" (SPP, pp. 485, 488). Yet it is this same *Defence* wherein Shelley reproduces the paragraph from *A Philosophical View of Reform* (1819) about how the greatest poets' words are animated by an "electric life" which belongs to the "spirit of their age."[48]

Further, an even more explicit sensitivity to the question of anachronism is on offer in another text of 1819, the Preface to *The Cenci*. "I have endeavoured as nearly as possible," Shelley wrote, in phrasing that precisely anticipates the warning in the *Defence*, "to represent the characters as they probably were, and have sought to avoid the error of making them actuated by *my own conceptions of right and wrong,* false or true, thus under a thin veil converting the names and actions of the sixteenth century into cold impersonations of my own mind" [italics mine] (SPP, p. 240). This anxiety about the problem of anachronism not only structures Shelley's entire conception of *The Cenci,* but also appears, in various forms, in much of his writing for the year he would bring to a close with his famous sonnet.[49] It was during 1819, for example, that Shelley also produced his

47. Lukács, *The Historical Novel,* p. 61.

48. The *OED* is mistaken to cite Shelley's use of the phrase "spirit of the age" in a letter to Hunt of April 1820 as the first in English literature. Since the passage in *A Philosophical View of Reform* was probably composed before April, that is probably not even *Shelley's* first use of it. The passage from the *View,* however, is the first English *analysis* of the phrase that I have found. And, as I have already suggested, there would be many such analyses to come in the course of the next decade.

49. *The Cenci* will be discussed in greater detail below in chapter 9. For more on the awareness of historicity in drama criticism of this period, see Margret de Grazia on Edward Malone's 1790 edition on Shakespeare in *Shakespeare Verbatim* (Cambridge: Cambridge University Press,

striking theorization of literary contemporaneity in the Preface to *Prometheus Unbound*, a passage that, as I noted earlier, Harold Bloom made the starting point for a rather different account of Romanticism's reconception of literary history.

It was in still another of Shelley's more reflective statements of 1819, this one for *Peter Bell the Third,* that he addressed the problem of historicism by vividly dating and placing the new historical orientation with a witty *jeu d'esprit.* The dedication to that poem sketches for Thomas Moore, author of the *Fudge Family* books, the picture of a future in which Regency British culture has become a touristic antiquity. The time will come, the Shelleyan persona declares, "when St. Paul's and Westminster Abbey shall stand, shapeless and nameless ruins in the midst of an unpeopled marsh; when the piers of Waterloo bridge shall become . . . islets of reeds and osiers and cast the jagged shadows of their broken arches on the solitary stream,—[and when] some transatlantic commentator will be weighing in the scales of some new and now unimagined system of criticism the respective merits of the Bells and the Fudges, and of their historians" (SPP, p. 325). The past becomes a country foreign in its system of cultural norms because the future is imagined in a place elsewhere—in this case a place "transatlantic." (One part of what it means to be able to articulate the state of a nation in terms of the chiastic framework of anachronism and anatopism, as we will see in later chapters, is to be able to reconceive the *future* state as well.) In some of the most historiographically suggestive writing from England in 1819, *Peter Bell the Third* among them, the image of an American republican futurity often figures crucially in elaborating the relation between imaginative literature, historical culture, and political representation.

Shelley's graphic picture from the dedication to *Peter Bell the Third*—the vision of England in 1819 as a state of ruin—adumbrates that later adumbration in the sonnet, *England in 1819,* where the conditions of the present moment become so many "graves" in the gaze of those who can read the signs of the times. Yet, while the image might thus be said to clarify a particularly Shelleyan historicist mode, a similar sketch of Regency England in antique decay, made as if from the point of view of a transatlantic observer, had in fact been a central

---

1991), especially chap. 3, "Situating Shakespeare in a Historical Period," pp. 94–131. De Grazia describes the Scottish Enlightenment–influenced antiquarian research by Malone on Shakespeare—the "various particulars emerging from documents coalesced into a period, an integral diachronic division distinct in character and standards from its temporal surroundings"—explaining that, historically, it was only "at this juncture that the word 'period' came to refer not only to a cyclical recurrence but to a singular and definite span of time" (pp. 97, 96). For more on the new markings of historicity in other genres, see Susan Stewart's discussion of "distressed genres" in *Crimes of Writing* (New York: Oxford University Press, 1991), pp. 66–101.

motif in a poem published by Anna Laetitia Barbauld just a few years earlier. The poem offers a protracted dream vision of a time when "England [will] be only known / By the gray ruin and the mouldering stone" and when "ingenuous youth" shall arrive to survey the dust of a former empire "From the blue mountains, or Ontario's lake."[50] The provenance of the conceit merits special attention in this context because Barbauld's poem was titled by a date: *Eighteen Hundred and Eleven*. The reception of this poem in Regency England, moreover, was dominated by a notoriously hostile review that had to do precisely with the conjunction of its title and the gender of the author.

In his study of gender and the literary history of Romanticism, Marlon Ross, noting the unacknowledged relevance of Barbauld to Shelley's political poetry of 1819, implicitly raises a question: should this non-acknowledgment be classified with those that Shelley discusses in the preface to *Prometheus Unbound*?[51] That is, could Anna Barbauld actually have counted for Shelley among those great contemporary writers whose effects on his "tone of thought" were so pervasive as to be acknowledgeable only collectively? Shelley's own understanding of the role of gender in the constitution of the community of electrified writers, its constitution of and by a "few select spirits," is discernible in the differently gendered redemption plots and redemptive outcomes in the action of *Prometheus Unbound*, where Asia's self-reconstitution forms a supplement rather than a complement to Prometheus's. The equivocating treatment of the question of women's suffrage in Shelley's political pamphleteering confirms this sense of invidiousness even in his most utopian picture of gender relations.[52]

Shelley echoed Barbauld in setting the scene for his time, but failed to acknowledge her in so doing. Without better evidence, it is hard to guess how he might have included her in that scene, imagined her in the special circuitry of the spirit of the age. One writer who did paint Barbauld into his picture of the age, however, was Hazlitt. Hazlitt was still a few years from launching the series of magazine essays he published as a book, *The Spirit of the Age,* in 1825. But in the months just prior to and after Shelley's writing of *Prometheus Unbound,* Ha-

---

50. Anna Laetitia Barbauld, *Eighteen Hundred and Eleven* (London: J. Johnson, 1812), p. 10.

51. Marlon Ross, *The Contours of Masculine Desire: Romanticism and the Rise of Women's Poetry* (New York: Oxford University Press, 1989), p. 224. Ross's reading of Barbauld did much to bring her poetry back into critical view.

52. Edward Dowden long ago noted Shelley's 1819 resistance to women's suffrage, in *The Life of Percy Bysshe Shelley,* 2 vols. (London: Kegan Paul, 1886), 2:295–96. For recent critiques of Shelley's gender politics, see Barbara Gelpi, *Shelley's Goddess: Maternity, Language, Subjectivity* (New York: Oxford University Press, 1992), and Nathanial Brown, *Sexuality and Feminism in Shelley* (Cambridge, Mass.: Harvard University Press, 1979).

zlitt produced a survey of the contemporary scene in the last of his *Lectures on the English Poets* (1818). This lecture, "On the Living Poets," in fact begins with a number of observations about women authors of the time. His first remarks set both the patronizing tone and exceptionalist character of what follows: "I am a great admirer of the female writers of the present day; they appear to me like so many modern Muses" (CWWH, 5:146). Hazlitt has high praise, after his fashion, for three female authors—"I could be in love with Mrs. Inchbald, romantic with Mrs. Radcliffe, and sarcastic with Madame D'Arblay" (CWWH, 5:146)—but they are dismissed with a witty allusion. All of them, says Hazlitt, are "novel-writers, and like Audrey, 'thank the Gods for not having made them poetical'" (CWWH, 5:146). As for the trio of women poets whom Hazlitt actually considers (Anna Barbauld, Hannah More, and Joanna Baillie) they supply little more than a short first step in an ascending ladder of masculinization and talent that will rise through Samuel Rogers ("a very lady-like poet"), Thomas Campbell ("of the same school"), Thomas Moore (who has not suffered enough to be a great poet), Lord Byron (who has suffered too much to be one), Walter Scott ("the most popular of all the poets of the present day, and deservedly so"), Wordsworth ("the most original poet now living"), Southey (the talented renegado), and finally Coleridge ("the only person I ever knew who answered to the idea of a man of genius [and] the only person from whom I ever learnt any thing") (CWWH, 5:147–68).

Hazlitt's gendered politics of literary-historical representation are probably now more readily visible than they have ever been. As early as 1981, Gayatri Spivak traced a "programmatic itinerary" of gendered exclusion in the "Great Tradition" of literary studies to the dual Romantic plot of sex and politics in Wordsworth's *The Prelude*.[53] Elaborating Spivak's insight, Mary Jacobus later showed how "High Romantic critical quests might be said to have been waylaid" by what she calls "the Romantic master-plot" of "Natural Supernaturalism," a plot whose by-product has been the "occlusion of woman."[54] More recently, Sonia Hofkosh persuasively argued that the handling of certain episodes in Hazlitt's biography provided "the pattern for the displacement of sexual politics from the discourse of literary history generally": "What Hazlitt did," writes Hofkosh, "and what we have done with Hazlitt, is to make a tradi-

---

53. Gayatri Spivak, "Sex and History in *The Prelude* (1805): Books Nine to Thirteen," *Texas Studies in Literature and Language* (fall 1981), 23:336; reprinted in Spivak, *In Other Worlds: Essays in Cultural Politics* (New York: Routledge, 1988), pp. 46–76.

54. Mary Jacobus, *Romanticism, Writing, and Sexual Difference: Essays on* The Prelude (Oxford: Clarendon Press, 1989), p. 106.

tion of that displacement."[55] Hofkosh helps unmake that tradition by attending to the unacknowledged voice of Sarah Hazlitt in the case of the Hazlitts' divorce to reveal the complexion of that event from a new perspective. Though I will attempt a more rehabilitative reading of Hazlitt on other scores in chapter 3, his articulations of literary contemporaneity from 1818-1820 certainly illustrate Hofkosh's point, even as they introduce my discussion of Barbauld.

They also, as it happens, issue in a backhanded analysis of how gender relates to his new period concept. In a subsequent survey of the contemporary literary scene for the *London Magazine* in April 1820, Hazlitt began with a more sweeping claim of the sort he would put into play in *The Spirit of the Age* itself: "The age we live in is critical, didactic, paradoxical, romantic, but it is not dramatic."[56] As Hazlitt proceeds, he develops the theme of the increasing dominance of the public press over English culture, and the other adjectives momentarily reduce to one:

> In a word, literature and civilization have abstracted man from himself so far, that his existence is no longer *dramatic;* and the press has been the ruin of the stage, unless we are greatly deceived.
> If a bias to abstraction is evidently, then, the reigning spirit of the age; dramatic poetry must be allowed to be most irreconcilable with this spirit; it is essentially individual and concrete, both in form and in power.[57]

The fungibility of identities in an age of public abstraction, and its relation to drama, bears on the role of casuistry in Romantic writing as I will be detailing below. The passage is relevant here because it sets up Hazlitt's suggestive remarks on gender and "spirit of the age" in this 1820 essay. Explaining Joanna Baillie's impressive accomplishments in the drama in an undramatic age, Hazlitt writes: "Miss Baillie has much of the power and spirit of dramatic writing, and not the less because, as a woman, she has been placed out of the vortex of philosophical and political extravagance."[58] Hazlitt means to be paying Baillie a compliment, of course, but its peculiar backhandedness reveals much about his own assumptions of the role of women writers not only in the theater but in the public sphere against which the theater is here defined. Here, indeed, is Hazlitt caught in the act of making a tradition of a gendered exclusion.

55. Sonia Hofkosh, "Sexual Politics & Literary History: William Hazlitt's Keswick Escapade and Sarah Hazlitt's Journal," in *At the Limits of Romanticism,* ed. Mary A. Favret and Nicola J. Watson, p. 132. Anne Mellor, *Romanticism & Gender* (Routledge: New York, 1993), supplies a helpful synopsis to this line of criticism (pp. 13–15).
56. This is the "General Reporter" column on "The Drama" for the second number of *The London Magazine* (April 1820), 1:432.
57. Ibid., p. 433.
58. Ibid., p. 435.

Just as Hofkosh calls on Sarah Hazlitt to speak from the subaltern position of biography, therefore, so I will call on Anna Barbauld to speak from the subaltern position of literary history. In the role that Hazlitt scripts for Anna Barbauld, she stands as the first poet Hazlitt names in his long ascent to the Coleridgean pinnacle of genius, the writer who plays "mother" to Coleridge's "father" in Hazlitt's invidiously gendered account. As I have already begun to suggest, however, there is far more to her story, as her own writings powerfully attest. It is not just that Barbauld's *Eighteen Hundred and Eleven* and her response to its critical fate can tell us much about the conceptual structure of Hazlitt's own spirit-of-the-age discourse, his notion of the state of "literature and civilization" in late Regency Britain. These writings of Barbauld's can also help to advance our understanding of how that discourse is informed by the mirroring concepts of "anachronism" and "anatopism" as they converge in a new way of imagining everyday life.

4. Anna Barbauld and the Measures of History

In 1812, the year that the *OED* records for Coleridge's remark about anachronism and anatopism, the *Quarterly Review* published an anonymous attack on Anna Barbauld's new and curiously titled poetic production. The reception accorded this poem illustrates how the literary representation of the state of the nation became a way of making history in two senses: as the *construction* of a narrative of events in literary form and as the *intervention* in the course of events by the very act of publishing such a construction. Precisely because this kind of activity was regarded as so potent, it was jealously guarded as a male prerogative. Barbauld's date-for-a-title was the very first thing that the reviewer singled out for ridicule:

> The poem, for so out of courtesy we shall call it, is entitled Eighteen Hundred and Eleven, we suppose, because it was written in the year 1811; but this is mere conjecture, founded rather on our inability to assign any other reason for the name, than in any particular relation which the poem has to the events of last year. We do not, we confess, very satisfactorily comprehend the meaning of all the verses which this fatidical spinster has drawn from her poetical distaff; but of what we do understand we very confidently assert that there is not a topic in "Eighteen Hundred and Eleven" which is not quite as applicable to 1810 or 1812.[59]

For the *Quarterly's* reviewer, whom Barbauld took to be Southey but who turns out to be John Wilson Croker, her taking up public satire, with its interest in historical topicalities and practical aims, created a mismatch of gender and genre: "We had hoped, indeed," Croker writes, "that the empire might have been saved

59. *Quarterly Review* 7 (June 1812): 309.

without the intervention of a lady-author."[60] In Croker's account, Barbauld's failure to understand dates—their uses and their specificity—is a symptom of the larger error implicit in her ambition to make history. Meanwhile, the effect of all this on Barbauld was rather like the effect that Croker's review of *Endymion* six years later in the *Quarterly* was mistakenly *thought* to have produced on young John Keats. Barbauld did not wither and die on account of the *Quarterly's* review, as Keats was later thought to have done on reading the contemptuous dismissal of *Endymion,* but, unlike Keats, Barbauld never published again after the attack.[61] She did, however, continue to write in those years, and some of these writings were collected in a posthumous volume called *Advice for Young Ladies.* The most substantial piece in the volume, as it happens, is a protracted four-part essay in epistolary form entitled "The Uses of History."

Though the evidence is inconclusive, the essay can plausibly be read as Barbauld's reply to Croker's charge that women had no place in writing about historical affairs. Her explicit aim, in any case, is to explain to her fictional correspondent, young Lydia, just what kind of knowledge is required to turn the study of history from an affair of mere "adventure," as it must first appear to a young girl in her innocence, into something more serious and substantial. For our purposes here, the utility of "The Uses of History" is that, by spelling out the legacy of historiography in her moment for a young woman, Barbauld makes explicit some of the tacit assumptions that underlay this predominantly male enterprise.

The title of this piece is somewhat misleading, however, in that "The Uses of History" ends up being less about what needs history might serve than about what it needs to serve at all. Lydia is told why on her first approach to the subject, it would not have been good for much: "You could understand nothing of the springs of action, nothing of the connexion of events with the intrigues of cabinets, with religion, with commerce; nothing of the state of the world at different periods of society and improvement: and as little could you grasp the

---

60. Ibid., p. 309. Maria Edgeworth wrote indignantly to Southey, thinking him the reviewer, about the "ungentlemanlike" attack. See William Keach, "A Regency Prophecy and the End of Anna Barbauld's Career," in *Studies in Romanticism* 33 (winter 1994): 569–77. Keach's argument that the poem offended on account of its aspiration to the condition of "prophecy" is not incompatible with the one I am making here. I would rather say that I seek to show the larger understanding of history and history-making in which this notion of prophecy is conceived. For more on the issue of what Shelley called "futurity" in this historical discourse, see below, chaps. 4 and 9.

61. Ina Ferris notes that, prior to this attack, Barbauld had been one of the few exceptions to the rule of dominance in the critical public sphere, and Ferris also discusses attacks in the *Quarterly* on other women writers during the Regency period. See *The Achievement of Literary Authority,* pp. 19–59.

measured distances of time and space which are set between them. This you
could not do, not because the history was not related with clearness, but because you were destitute of other knowledge" (LYL, p. 115). Barbauld's notion
that the "different periods of society and improvement" can be gauged and calibrated in terms of the "measured distances of time and space that are set between them," intimates two important and mutual functions that she will
explicitly name "geography" and "chronology" as the "first studies" necessary
to make the study of history intelligible (p. 139). The two disciplines indeed figure in Barbauld's account as nothing less than what she calls "the two eyes of
History," and she devotes the last two of the four letters to explaining them in
their interrelation (p. 139).

Although, unlike chronology, geography "addresses itself to the eye, and is
easily comprehended," Barbauld also insists, conversely, that every map necessarily indicates the look of a place at a given point in time (p. 148): "[E]ach
country should have the towns and divisions, as far as they are known, calculated
for the period the map was meant to illustrate. Thus geography, civil geography,
would be seen to grow out of history; and the mere view of the map would suggest the political state of the world at any period" (p. 140). Likewise, when she
turns to chronology in the final letter, her discussion repeatedly represents calendrical time as a kind of charted landscape. She says, for example, that with the
proper conception of chronological context, merely a "few dates . . . , perfectly
learned, may suffice, and will serve as landmarks to prevent your going far astray
in the rest" (p. 160). Bringing her impressive learning and intellectual keenness
to the task of teaching what needs to be known about historical time, Barbauld's last letter amounts to an extraordinary meditation on the history and
function of the date, a discussion that is informed by, and that explicitly acknowledges, Joseph Scaliger's and Isaac Newton's studies in ancient chronology, and that recommends consultation with "Dr. Priestley's biographical
chart" (p. 162). It is clear from the start of this letter that one is in the hands of a
writer who saw the full range of the provocation and complication in her act of
giving her political poem a date for a title.[62] Adverting to the difficulty of this
final topic, chronology, she writes, "It is easy to define it by saying it gives an answer to the question, when was it done? but the meaning of the *when* is not quite
so obvious. A date is a very artificial thing, and the world had existed for a long
course of centuries before men were aware of its use and necessity. *When* is a relative term" (p. 148). The artificiality of the date, as Barbauld's culture knows it,

---

62. Cf. Henry Crabb Robinson's similar comment in *Henry Crabb Robinson on Books and their
Writers,* ed. Edith J. Morley, 3 vols. (London: J. M. Dent, 1938) 1:64.

has to do with its way of transcending what she describes as the more natural, which is to say relativizing, answer to the question, "when was it done?"

To establish her point about this naturalness she offers a piece of makeshift anthropology that broadly anticipates, unless I misread it, the distinction made by Émile Benveniste between *temps linguistique* and *temps chronique*[63]—that is, between the time of calendars, which takes its bearings from a fixed event, and the time of tenses, which takes its bearings from the present of the act of utterance: "[T]he most natural application of it [the term *When*] is, how long ago, reckoning backwards from the present moment? Thus if you were to ask an Indian when such an event happened, he would probably say—So many harvests ago, when I could but just reach the boughs of yonder tree;—in the time of my father, grandfather, great-grandfather; still making the time then present to him the date from which he sets out" (pp. 148–49). Even, says Barbauld, in societies possessed of artificially generalized chronologies, we still resort "in more familiar life to this natural kind of chronology—The year before I was married,—when Henry, who is now five years old, was born,—the winter of the hard frost" (p. 149). These, she argues, with pointed reference to the gender barriers to be overcome, "are the epochs which mark the annals of domestic life more readily and with greater clearness, so far as the real idea of time is concerned, than the year of our Lord . . ." (p. 149).

The problem she explicitly raises with these more natural forms of time reckoning is that they are ill-suited to the formation of a written record. When events are recorded, Barbauld explains, the one who relates them may be forgotten, and the *when* question is simply deferred: "When did the historian live? I understand the relative chronology of his narration; I know how the events of it follow one another; but what is their relation to general chronology, to time as it relates to me and to other events?" (pp. 149–50). This relation of relative to general chronology reappears in different forms throughout the final letter in ways that suggest its fundamental importance to what Barbauld wants to tell her protégée about the theory and practice of history in her time. She applies it, for example, to the practice of referring events to the reigns of particular rulers. The situation in which one knows the order of events in a reign but not how to "place them with respect to the history of other times and nations" is explained by way of a geographical analogy: "[It] is as if we had a very accurate map of a small island existing somewhere in the boundless ocean, and could lay down all the bearings and distances of its several towns and villages, but for want of its longitude and latitude were ignorant of the relative position of the island itself.

---

63. Émile Benveniste, *Problèmes de linguistique générale* (Paris: Gallimard, 1974), pp. 67–78.

Chronology supplies this longitude and latitude, and fixes every event to its precise point in the chart of universal time" (p. 150). The solution to the problem is the concept of the calendar based on a "universal date, like a lofty obelisk seen by all the country round, from which and to which every distance should be measured" (p. 152). It is by no means a modern solution, of course, and Barbauld lists a number of different forms of calendrical systems in different cultures before coming to the A.D./B.C. system that governed the writing of history in her own culture for so long as to have become second nature to its users.

Having argued the need for an accurate and generalized chronology, beyond that of the reigns of particular nations, Barbauld returns toward the end of her analysis to remind Lydia of what the chronology is for—that it is the medium of different national histories to each other: "Although I recommend to you a constant attention to chronology, I do not think it desirable to load your memory with a great number of specific dates, both because it would be too great a burthen on the retentive powers, and because it is, after all, not the best way of attaining clear ideas on the subjects of history. In order to do this, it is necessary to have in your mind the relative situation of other countries at the time of any event recorded in one of them" (p. 159). Because of Barbauld's particular conception of social development in relation to general history—one that has to do with what she earlier calls the relation between "different periods of society and improvement," on the one hand, and "the state of the world," on the other—she is committed to the view that general chronology is crucial to the understanding of any given national development one seeks to comprehend. The "state of the world" refers to the transnational simultaneity that makes national-cultural specificity imaginable. It is not just, as she says, that it "may be desirable to keep one kingdom as a meter for the rest" but rather, as she puts it in what I take to be her most forceful and revealing formulation, a matter of mutual illumination: "You do not see truly what the Greeks were, except you know that the British Isles were then barbarous" (pp. 160, 161).

"The Uses of History," as I have been reading it, is Barbauld's attempt to explain to the Crokers of the world all that they failed to comprehend in her performance of 1811. Forty years earlier, in her first volume of poems (1773), Barbauld had included a poem entitled "The Backwardness of the Spring 1771."[64] Although the poem is about a kind of anachronism, it is not a cultural anachronism and has absolutely no significance for public history. In *Eighteen Hundred and Eleven,* however, she surveys what she calls "the state of the world" looking back from a future time on a moment when it is, on the poem's ac-

---

64. Barbauld, *Poems,* pp. 31–32.

count, precariously led by the vast commercial empire of the nation whose recent development had carried it beyond any other in science, technology, literature, military prowess, and reach of influence. The poem includes achievements in the sciences and arts and in the military, by persons singled out for special praise: Shakespeare, Milton, Locke, Newton, Paley, Thomson, Cowper, Oriental Jones, Priestley, Chatham, Clarkson, Roscoe, Barbauld's friend and contemporary Joanna Baillie, Admiral Nelson, and General Moore. What lends Barbauld's survey its disturbing edge, however, is that feature that Shelley seized on in order to lend a historical frame for *Peter Bell the Third*.

Barbauld's survey of Britain in 1811 is conducted from the point of view of future American tourists who come to wander among the ruins of the now-ancient British Empire's great metropolis:

> Yet then the ingenuous youth whom Fancy fires
> With pictured glories of illustrious sires,
> With duteous zeal their pilgrimage shall take
> From the blue mountains, or Ontario's lake,
> With fond adoring steps to press the sod
> By statesmen, sages, poets, heroes, trod;
> On Isis' banks to draw inspiring air,
> From Runnymede to send the patriot's prayer;
> In pensive thought, where Cam's slow waters wind,
> To meet those shades that ruled the realms of mind.[65]

The emerging anxieties in the Regency over Britain's imperial displacement by the expanding U.S. domain in North America will be address more fully below. For now, we can regard this passage as describing a pilgrimage conducted from the present seat of imperial power to its predecessor, much as Augustan Britain was preoccupied with Imperial Rome. Certainly the world is as much present in Barbauld's metropolis as that metropolis is present in the world:

> But who their mingled feelings shall pursue
> When London's faded glories rise to view?
> The mighty city, which by every road,
> In floods of people poured itself abroad;
> Ungirt by walls, irregularly great,
> No jealous drawbridge, and no closing gate;
> Whose merchants (such the state which commerce brings)
> Sent forth their mandates to dependent kings;

65. Barbauld, *Eighteen Hundred and Eleven, A Poem* (London: J. Johnson, 1812), pp. 10–11.

Streets, where the turban'd Moslem, bearded Jew,
And woolly Afric, met the brown Hindu.[66]

The permeability of the Empire's active metropolis, in both directions, makes
it the place of exchange where national currencies of all sorts are converted into
one another, including, as the very title of the poem emphasizes, chronological
currencies.

The survey of Britain in 1811, therefore, retains a sense of the meaning of
the date for other cultures as well. In the terms of the argument of Barbauld's
"The Uses of History," in other words, the poem makes Britain a "meter for the
rest" and, at the same time, so to speak, measures the British achievement in the
context of the state of development or decay among other nations of the
world—as if to say that you cannot see what the British were in 1811 except you
know that Greece was then in slavery to the Turks, the United States on a steep
economic ascendancy, and the unliberated nations of the Americas on the
verge, some of them, of rising up to assert their independence.

5. The Structural Transformation of the Public State

By catching the gendered refraction of the chronological code of British Romanticism first through Hazlitt's survey of the living poets and then through the
episode of Barbauld's meditations on chronology in prose and verse, we have
come to understand something about that code's terms and organization.
Moreover, the poem itself, *Eighteen Hundred and Eleven,* has emerged with a
special relevance to the work of Percy Shelley in 1819, not only to *Peter Bell the
Third* but also to the sonnet, whose pivot on the predicate that opens the penultimate line—"Are graves . . ."—may be seen as a moment when the order of
England in 1819 is itself turned to ruin.[67] In any event, the notorious precedent
of the title, *Eighteen Hundred and Eleven,* attacked in the Tory press as if it bespoke as much about the "slang of faction" as the phrase "the spirit of the age"
would later do in Robinson's account of 1830, stands as evidence that the form
of Mary Shelley's title was not an invention of the early Victorian period. The
title was chosen, in other words, out of a sense of history datable to and placeable in the sonnet's own moment of production.[68]

66. Ibid., pp. 12–13.
67. In taking *Peter Bell the Third*'s picture of England in ruins as projected historical retrospect
rather than as an "apocalyptic vision," I differ somewhat with the account offered in Steven Goldsmith, *Unbuilding Jerusalem: Apocalypse and Romantic Representation* (Ithaca, N.Y.: Cornell University Press, 1993), p. 214; see below chapter 9.
68. Barbauld, *Poems and Prose Writings,* p. 116. This is not to say, obviously, that such titles
could not occur prior to Barbauld. The inscription poem, memorably analyzed by Geoffrey

This is perhaps the time to recall that the sonnet is now generally recognized as the one that, as we have seen, Percy Shelley mentions enclosing in a letter of December 23, 1819, posted from Florence to his friend Leigh Hunt, editor of *The Examiner,* back in London.

> We have just received all your Examiners up to October 27th. I admire and approve most highly of those on religion; there is one very long one that especially pleases me. Added days and years and hours add to my disapprobation of this odious superstition, and to my gratitude to anyone who like you break[s] for ever its ever-gathering bubble.
>
> What a state England is in! But you will never write politics. I don't wonder; but I wish then that you would write a paper in the Examiner on the actual state of the country, and what, under all the circumstances of the conflicting passions and interests of men, we are to expect,—not what we ought to expect or what if so and so were to happen we might expect—but what, as things are, there is reason to believe will come—and send it me for my information. (LPBS, 2:166)

I am going to take it for granted, on the basis of this letter, that the poem Shelley almost certainly enclosed with it can be read as his own effort not only to "write politics" but to do so in verse.

England in 1819 can now appear as a poetic meditation on "the state of England." However, the state of a "state" is not an easy matter to settle. Indeed, the relevant contexts for construing Shelley's exclamation—"What a state England is in!"—will multiply as my discussion proceeds. To establish for now only that Shelley's *England in 1819* is a state plausibly construable on the scale of the year, I want to call attention briefly to how the word "state" functioned in British political journalism as a generic label. It was in effect identified as such by one of the earliest workers in this genre, Guy Miège, in a volume he published in 1707, the year of the English-Scottish Union, entitled *The Present State of Great Britain.* Predictably, the book falls into two parts, "The Present State of England" and "The Present State of Scotland." In the preface to the latter, Miège

---

Hartman, often includes the date of place in its title or subtitle: see "Wordsworth, Inscriptions, and Romantic Nature Poetry," in *From Sensibility to Romanticism,* ed. Frederick W. Hilles and Harold Bloom (New York: Oxford University Press, 1965), pp. 389–414. As Hartman points out, Wordsworth's "Tintern Abbey" is a relatively late instance of the genre. So, too, with the poems that Wordsworth wrote on his excursion to France during the Peace of Amiens, many of which bear the date 1802 in their titles and one of which, *London, 1802,* seems to approach the condition of Shelley's sonnet (even while remaining inscriptive), as it makes the "hour" at hand the virtual subject of its meditation. A stylistically closer precedent for Barbauld, but more remote in time, is Pope's, *One Thousand Seven Hundred and Forty,* not published until long after his lifetime when it was in fact edited with aggressive interpolations by none other than John Wilson Croker. If space permitted a detailed comparison of Pope and Barbauld, I would argue both for a number of similar features *and* for key differences having to do with Barbauld's "future past" historicity and with Pope's focus on "named" persons as the hope for curing Britain's state of corruption in 1740. Pope's "history" is still that of the Horatian imitation: *The Poems of Alexander Pope,* ed. John Butt (New Haven, Conn.: Yale University Press, 1963), pp. 827–31.

notes, apologetically, that "there having been no State of Scotland tolerably well done hitherto, it cannot be supposed that this should be perfect."[69] "State" here, as Miège illustrates, is a genre term.

Miège implies that while there have been no earlier "States of Scotland" there have been earlier "States of England." One of them is his own work of 1691, *The New State of England* (a title which of course implies that there are still earlier examples). In the preface to that volume, the genre term is already in play with evident paranomasia: "Tis the late Revolution that has given birth to this new Piece of Work; a New Face of Things required a New State of England."[70] The piece of work is the new English state, but it is also the new literary production that these words introduce. To "do" a "State," as Miège puts it, at least to do one "tolerably well," is to fulfill generic criteria probably not hard to specify. In fact, the descriptive table of contents on the title page of the first edition of the *New State of England* of 1691 seems to be a reasonably reliable guide to those criteria (see fig. 2). What is most to the point here, however, is how the genre of the "state" changes in the course of the eighteenth century. Miège published many states of Great Britain after 1707 but called each successive publication a new *edition* of the first one he produced. Nor did these editions bear conspicuously generic temporal markings. Their dates appear, in the typical place, after the name and place of the printer or publisher on the title page. Yet, by the end of the century, successive volumes published under the genre-marking title "The State of X" tend to be cast as part of a series of volumes with annual dates featured in their titles.

The transformation in the genre of the state is probably best recounted in the context of that larger set of changes that forms the object of Jürgen Habermas's *Structural Transformation of the Public Sphere.* Although Habermas does not address the problem of the "state" as a literary genre, he does call attention to a publishing event that is crucial to his own narrative: the series of volumes published under the title *The Political State of Great Britain.*[71] Begun in 1711, these volumes offer a public record of Parliamentary debates in the form of year-by-year report. It is a responsibility that, after some interruption in mid-century, was later assumed by William Cobbett and that evolved into the familiar series of Parliamentary reports by Hansard. With this development, the genre of the state now begins to imply the annualized account.

69. Guy Miége, *The Present State of Great Britain* (London: J. Nicholson, 1707), preface to part 2.
70. Guy Miége, *The New State of England* (London: 1691), preface.
71. Jürgen Habermas, *The Structural Transformation of the Public Sphere,* trans. Thomas Burger (Cambridge, Mass.: MIT Press, 1989), p. 61.

Figure 2.   Title page and part of table of contents of Guy Miège, *The New State of England* (London, 1691). The Special Collections Library, University of Michigan.

In eighteenth-century Britain, of course, the history of the periodical forms an important part in any account of the periodization of history. *The Historical Register,* which served functions complementary to *The Political State of Great Britain,* was founded at about the same time, and thus had already been around for a quarter century by the time that Fielding wrote his much-performed antigovernment play of 1737, *The Historical Register for 1736.* The Register stopped publication after 1740, perhaps partly on account of the rivalry of *The Gentleman's Magazine.* Founded in 1731 as a monthly digest of materials from the weeklies, *The Gentleman's Magazine* added an index of the entire year for the assembled issue that made up the 1732 volume. Then, in 1735, it added its annual Supplement, which offered an "Account of the Proceedings and Debates in the Last Session of Parliament Concluded." This was to become a crucial component of the new annualized journalism. Moreover, in the same quarter century (1750–75) when, as Habermas notes, the sale of monthly and weekly journals was doubling in magnitude, the content of the annual Parliamentary reportage extends dramatically in the project begun in 1758 by Edmund Burke and Robert Dodsley. The first publication in this series is called *The Annual Register: Or a View of the History, Politics, and Literature of the Year 1758.* Here the republication of a given annual book appears as a new edition, but each passing new year produces a new volume in the series with a newly dated title.

The distinction is a rich one when we apply it to the ensuing debate on the reform of the British constitution, especially over the question of annual parliaments and regular constitutional review of the sort proposed in the American Constitutional Convention. Burke and Paine debated such questions in terms of the different status of social generations, Paine arguing that generations were real and had to be accorded equality with one another (an argument against prescription) and Burke arguing that the notion of a generational cohort was largely a misleadingly rigid construct placed on the fluid reproductive patterns of natality and fatality. The distinction at stake in this disagreement about the representation of the state as polis seems to me close in character to the distinction I have been making in respect to the state as genre, the distinction between a newly titled annual representation of the nation, on the one hand, and a new annual edition of a national representation bearing the same exact title as the year before, on the other.

The public impact of the *Annual Register* series should not, in any event, be underestimated. It continued well into the nineteenth century and became a valuable and evidently affordable resource of scholars of the time. Thomas Moore, in great financial trouble and at work on a biography of Richard Brinsley Sheridan, whose life spanned the period covered by the *Register,* notes in his journal for August 28, 1818 that his "59 vols. of Annual Registers arrived" (*JTM*, 1:32). That same year, 1818, Hazlitt published an article in *The Examiner,* consisting mainly of Coleridge's *Fears in Solitude,* called "England in 1798." One of the early volumes reviewed in the soon-to-be founded *Westminster Review* was *Men and Things in 1823.*

The "public sphere" that formed the object of Shelley's and Hunt's private correspondence about the "state England is in" in the closing days of 1819 was thus deeply and habitually structured by the annualized representation of society, politics, and culture. When he asked Hunt to match his sonnet with a "paper . . . on the actual state of the country" on the eve of the last week of 1819, Shelley would have been mobilizing the resources of that domain. Moreover, as we have seen, he may also have been recalling Hunt's bold prediction from the first week of the year, that 1819 would be "one of the most important years that have been seen for a long while . . . [for] a spirit is abroad" (January 3, 1819). In addition to giving Hunt credit for his insightful forecast, I want to reemphasize the fact of its annualized framing in the first place. Further, since the sense that the year can be considered an "age" derives in part from its association with that crucial word "spirit," I also want to stress that it is just at this time, perhaps even in this very year , that "spirit of the age" begins to assume the new resonance elaborated by Hazlitt and J. S. Mill in celebrated essays of the coming decade. The phrase is not, as the *OED* would have it, an utterly new combination of words in English. The *OED* indeed errs in listing Shelley's use of the phrase in a letter of 1820 as the first use in English; Shelley himself, we have seen, had used it climactically to close chapter one of *A Philosophical View of Reform,* probably in December 1819. Hume and others actually employed the phrase decades earlier, but not yet with its new stress and inflection. The concept of the spirit of the age in English writing remains an unstable one, and nowhere more so than in writers like Shelley and William Hazlitt who first took it up most explicitly. One persistent source of lability is the problem of historical scale.

Between Hume's use and Shelley's comes an important institutional use of the word *spirit,* not in the phrase "spirit of the age," but still, as it were, in an epoch-making context. Crucially, the scale in the epoch here is that of the single year. I refer to a series very much in keeping with the form of the *Annual Register.* This one was begun, who knows with what prescience, in the year 1798, and entitled *Spirit of the Public Journals for 1798,* . . . for 1799, . . . and so on into the 1820s. In this institution, the notion of a spirit of an age and that of a "state of a nation" converge on the annual scale in the regularized time of the periodical press. When Hunt says, in respect to all the action he looks for in the coming year, that "a spirit is abroad," we may therefore read this as the spirit of the year 1819. It is exactly this sort of idiom, too, that Hunt's friend Keats may have picked up and characteristically ironized, in commenting two months later on his own "1819 temper," and that Canning may have been invoking a year later in referring to late 1819 and early 1820 as two different "epochs" in the nation's history.

It works such as the *Spirit of the Public Journals for 1798* and so on suggest that the annual scale in the recording of British history figures more prominently after the French Revolution, this may owe something to the fame of the new Revolutionary calendar itself. In this respect, Barbauld's *Eighteen Hundred and Eleven* is not just a model for Mary Shelley's title but an example of writing the year as an epoch, of reaping what Barbauld calls "the full harvest of the mental year," in order that, as Barbauld says to her country, "Thy stores of knowledge the new states shall know." As I have already tried to indicate, however, there is also considerable evidence to suggest that the scale of the year was particularly obtrusive in the year of Peterloo, the works and days of which generated so intense a sequence of astonishing revelations, not least because the issue of annual parliaments was arguably as central as that of virtual universal suffrage in radical reformist arguments. The betting on the former plank was certainly less hedged than on the latter, as might be illustrated in the celebrated "Essay on Government" that James Mill planned and executed in the weeks and months following Peterloo (and very much with Peterloo in view), for in that analysis of the system of representation Mill at once supported the change to annual Parliaments and undermined Bentham's support for extension of the franchise to women.[72]

In relating the State to "the state" and its transformations I have more than once invoked the work of Habermas because this relationship seems so much a part of the story he wants to tell about the constitution and transformation of the larger eighteenth-century public sphere in life and letters. That story, in turn, might be said to form part of an answer to the question Jacques Derrida famously put to Lévi-Strauss about the historicity of the concept of structure itself—in this case, the question concerns the historicity of the structure Lévi-Strauss describes as the historian's code. Although Habermas's study appeared in German in 1962, exactly the same year as Lévi-Strauss's *The Savage Mind,* and although both books betray a theoretical concern about the relation between structure and transformation, commentators tend to characterize Habermas's project as historical and Lévi-Strauss's as unhistorical in orientation.

To take one further step in complicating that picture, therefore, we might at least briefly note that, in the course of explaining the value of the procedure of shifting levels on the historical grid, Lévi-Strauss does credit the early eighteenth-century French historian, Boulainvilliers, with the invention of this procedure. Although Lévi-Strauss calls it "Boulainvilliers' transformation," the point is relegated to a long footnote and so is not allowed to ramify as an "event" in Lévi-Strauss's account of historical practice.[73] By the same token, Boulainvilliers plays no role in Habermas's account, which indeed offers very little on the French press before the Revolution. Yet Boulainvilliers is assigned a major

72. James Mill, "Essay on Government," in *Utilitarian Logic and Politics: James Mill's "Essay on Government," Macaulay's Critique and the Ensuing Debate,* ed. Jack Lively and John Rees (Oxford: Clarendon Press, 1978). For Mill's references to the recent "turbulence" in the manufacturing districts, see p. 94.

73. Lévi-Strauss, *The Savage Mind,* pp. 261–62.

role by recent historians in the making of what they describe as a kind of public sphere *avant la lettre* during the controversy over the French succession in 1715–17. It is a nice coincidence, therefore, that Boulainvilliers can also be credited with a *very* early anticipation of later widespread talk of the spirit of the age when, in an epistolary statement "on history and its method," he wrote to one Mademoiselle Cousinot about the importance of getting beyond names and dates "to learn about the genius of each age, [its] predominant opinions, *moeurs,* and ideas."[74] Boulainvilliers is not, of course, advocating that "names and dates" be used to relate the genius of each age, and thus to code comparative contemporaneities. That practice would have to wait for another time and place.

6. Uneven Development

I have been sketching a context, leading to the year of Peterloo, in which to set Shelley's *England in 1819* and Barbauld's *Eighteen Hundred and Eleven*. I have suggested that they can be defined in terms of the even chronology—or what Anderson, following Benjamin, calls the "empty homogeneous time"—of an increasingly periodized (i.e., "periodicalized") public sphere. But there is another side to the articulation of the historicist code of early nineteenth-century British public culture—not the side of even chronology, the chronology of what might broadly be called "secularization," but of uneven development. Barbauld's notion, for example, that the state of the world can be assessed in terms of "different periods of society and improvement" is one that itself belongs to the Scottish-Enlightenment discourse of the evolving states of civil society, a discourse Barbauld would have had access to through her friendships, for example, with Dugald Stewart and Sir Walter Scott. In 1817, Stewart issued a multivolume edition of the works of William Robertson, whose various histories, along with Scott's fiction, probably did as much to change historiography in the West as any two corpuses of work one could name.[75] Robertson's *History of America* alone went through roughly twenty editions in the forty years from 1777 to 1817. More importantly, Barbauld's notion (cited earlier from "The Uses of History") that these "different periods of society and improvement" can be gauged and calibrated in terms of the "measured distances of time and space that are set between them," suggests an understanding of the proverbial relation between geography and chronology (now figured as a relation between

74. *Lettre . . . sur l'histoire et sa methode* (1707), trans. in Harold Ellis, *Boulainvilliers and the French Monarchy* (New York: Cornell University Press, 1988), p. 207.

75. *Works of William Robertson: To Which is Prefixed an Account of His Life and Writings by Alex Stewart* (London: W. Sharpe and Son, 1820).

ethnography and historiography) that is, even on her own account, a relatively new development.

The crucial element in this new Scottish-Enlightenment sense of history, and perhaps implicit as well in the depiction of Romantic historicism in many of the retrospective twentieth-century accounts, is a dialectical sense of periodization in which particular "societies" or "nations," newly theorized as such by just these writers, are recognized as existing in "states" that belong at once to two different, and to some extent competing, orders of temporality. On the one hand, each society is theorized as moving stepwise through a series of stages sequenced in an order that is more-or-less autonomous and stable. Insofar as the stages are also "ages," these sequencings can be said to constitute temporal orders. On the other hand, this same historiographical discourse always implies a second temporality, one in which these different national times can be correlated and calendrically dated in respect to each other.

When this scheme is appropriated by the Germans, especially by Hegel, the larger order is understood to have its own developmental sequence, but this is not necessarily so for the Scottish-Enlightenment writers and their later disciples. In the Scottish-Enlightenment accounts, the emphasis is not on the universal progress of spirit but rather on measurement, comparison, and explanation: rates of historical change are measurable by comparing the progress of different societies with one another and are to some degree explicable by relating the state of a society with the "state of the world" at that same moment. To locate a given state of society within a given state of the world is to establish its age or epoch in a more complete sense and thus to establish a more thorough understanding of it as a culture. When one begins to locate a state of society within a given state of the world, one produces a "historical situation" for the actions of those who inhabit it. However familiar such a concept may be to us in our recent "return to history," its novelty in the discourse of Romantic historicism is what I seek to establish here.

This relational paradigm can be briefly illustrated in John Millar's early study of class and gender, *The Origin of the Distinction of Ranks in Society* (1771). When Millar discusses the "state" of some society, he normally locates that state, explicitly or implicitly, in a sequence of the sort: barbaric, pastoral, agricultural, commercial. Each state, in Millar's account, has its attendant "systems of manners," as is also ostentatiously the case in the apparatus for Hume's *History of England*.[76] Millar is equally concerned, however, with the larger state of things in

---

76. I cite the 1806 edition, which bears a slightly different title: John Millar, *The Origin of the Distinction of Ranks* (Edinburgh: Blackwood, 1806), pp. 2–3.

and to which the society's successive cultural states are related. This latter relationship proves absolutely crucial in Millar's typical form of analysis, though it is not always made explicit there. Consider how implicit it remains, for example, in the following passage from Millar's introduction: "When we survey the present state of the globe, we find that, in many parts of it, the inhabitants are so destitute of culture, as to appear little above the condition of brute animals; and even when we peruse the remote history of polished nations, we have seldom any difficulty in tracing them to a state of the same rudeness and barbarism" (pp. 2–3). In such a framework, one can describe peoples of two different historical moments as belonging to the same state of civilization: in this case the same state of "rudeness and barbarism." Nonetheless, being in the state of barbarism in the present "state of the globe" and being in the state of barbarism in some past "state of the globe" will *not* be quite "the same," in Millar's analysis, because of the different *global circumstances* of such states of a nation—what was also called, in Scottish Enlightenment idiom, the "situation of the world" at the time of a given society's having reached a given social stage.[77]

Indeed, one could not in the same sense even speak of the "state of the globe" in relation to the barbaric state of existing polished nations. The "globe" would signify differently in different times. It likewise matters for Millar whether a certain society reaches the commercial age, for example, in late antiquity, the Renaissance, or the eighteenth century or whether it has not yet reached it at all by the time of his writing.[78] As theories of national development, with the relevant concepts of "backwardness" and "forwardness" begin to become more and more fine grained about the texture and sequence of cultural states, the chronologies become better and better calibrated within the increasingly fined-tuned sense of time and timing of the bourgeois public sphere. This was a public sphere progressively articulated in variously scaled chronolo-

77. This phrase appears prominently in an early pamphlet by William Robertson that explains the timing of Christ's appearance on earth in relation to the geopolitical circumstances of the ancient world: *The Situation of the World at the Time of the Coming of Jesus Christ, To Which is Joined a Short Account of the Present State of the Society in Scotland for Propagating Christian Knowledge* (Edinburgh: Hamilton, Balfour and Neill, 1755).

78. When Millar addresses the question of "the rank and condition of women in different ages," for example, he invokes that sense of age. Thus, his analysis of the pastoral age is that, as the first great improvement in the savage life, the "invention of taming and pasturing cattle" provided for unprecedented leisure, tranquillity and retirement, which in turn fostered a new system of manners with particular consequences for relations between the sexes. But the precise character of that state of manners will depend on when in the course of a larger movement in (for Millar) western history that particular society happens to arrive in it. See *Origin of the Distinction of Ranks*, pp. 14, 57.

gies, a domain of proliferating periodicals measuring out the years and months and weeks in the collective lives of a widening readership.[79]

In social theory such as Millar's we have the basis for what would come to be known in the Marxian tradition as the principle of *Ungleichzeitigkeit*—or "uneven development."[80] It is, roughly, the principle that Leon Trotsky famously used in *The History of the Russian Revolution* (1931) to explain how it is that the most "backward" country in Europe managed successfully to stage the world's first proletarian revolution in 1917. Trotsky derives his version of this principle by considering the impact of capitalism on the older understanding of the repetition of historical cycles. "Unevenness," which he calls the most general law of the historical process, is most visible in the case of backward countries. It means that "under the whip of external necessity," the "backward culture" of less advanced countries "is compelled to make leaps." "Externality," in this context, can be understood to refer roughly to what Millar calls the relation of the state of society to "the state of the globe." In Trotsky's terms, the unevenness of the relation of internal to external states constitutes "the privilege of historical backwardness" by virtue of which the backward nation is permitted, sometimes even compelled, to adopt "whatever is ready in advance of any specified

79. The double sense of "state" here helps to explain how it is, as Raymond Williams points out, that terms like "culture" and "civilization" were being used "interchangeably," and that "each carried the problematic double sense of an achieved state and of an achieved state of development." See *Marxism and Literature* (New York: Oxford, 1977), p. 14. It should be noted here, however, that the history of the genre of the "state" as I have traced it complicates even the larger distinction between "culture" and "society" in Williams, as it does the distinction Hannah Arendt wants to uphold for this same period between the "political" and the "social" in *On Revolution*.

80. See Ronald Meek's groundbreaking essay, "The Scottish Contribution to Marxist Sociology," in his *Economics and Ideology and other Essays* (London: Chapman and Hall, 1967), pp. 34–50. Meek works out the intellectual-historical connections in somewhat different terms from mine, but he does argue for the centrality of the "Scottish Historical School" and John Millar above all, for coming to terms with Marx's understanding of political economy and its critique. See especially pp. 40–47. Meek also tries to answer a question to which Walter Scott's similar answer will figure below: "What was there about Scotland in the latter half of the eighteenth century which made it capable of producing Millar and the other members of the Historical School?" (p. 47). It is the failure to consider Scotland and Scotland's place in Britain after the Union of 1707, that has led to an excessive attention to Germany as, in Ernst Bloch's phrase, "unlike England, and much less France, the classical land of nonsynchronism"—in "Nonsynchronism and the Obligation to its Dialectics," trans. Mark Ritter, *New German Critique* 11 (spring 1977): 22–38. Bloch's reference to "England" rather than "Britain" already goes some way toward making my point and offers a useful note on the difficulty of translating the term. For more on the problem of *Ungleichzeitigkeit* in the Marxian tradition, see Oskar Negt, "The Nonsynchronous Heritage and the Problem of Propaganda," trans. Mark Ritter, *New German Critique* 9 (fall 1976): 46–70. See also Neil Smith, *Uneven Development: Nature, Capital, and the Production of Space* (New York: Blackwell, 1984); and Ernesto Laclau and Chantal Mouffe, *Hegemony and Socialist Strategy: Towards a Radical Democratic Politics* (London: Verso, 1985), pp. 48–54.

date."[81] Scott's narrative of Scottish development in the eighteenth century is very much an account of what Scotland was permitted or compelled to adopt by its more economically advanced neighbor to the south.[82]

That Trotsky's use of dated chronology to calibrate the dialectic of historical states derives, through Marx, from Millar and his contemporaries seems clear enough. That it may have had some influence on Lévi-Strauss's theorizations is a more speculative matter. It is worth noting briefly, at least, that Trotsky's *History* was published, with great *éclat,* at the start of the decade in which Lévi-Strauss began his career as a young Marxist intellectual in Paris and that Trotsky explicitly likened the notion of uneven development to the operations of a steam engine: as neighboring societies move forward rapidly, a society that does not will tend undergo a certain rise in pressure. At a certain point, with some triggering event setting off the mechanism, the pressure is released all at once, and the once backward society is catapulted forward. Lévi-Strauss, of course, would develop a metaphor for conceiving the history of advanced societies that strikingly resembles Trotsky's—the notion of the steam engine with marked temperature differentials for the "hot" societies as distinct from the simple machine of "cold" societies. It seems at least conceivable that this principle of uneven development may have undergirded his conception of historical chronology from the start. Certainly Lévi-Strauss's notion that cultural space and cultural time are mutually transcodable by the historian and ethnographer—"one of them unfurls the range of human societies in time, the other in space"—suggests that he had some such conception in view.[83]

Long before Lévi-Strauss or Trotsky or even Marx himself took it up, however, the Scottish-Enlightenment principle of uneven development became the basis not only of the practice of writers such as Anna Barbauld and Percy Shelley but also of the massively influential new form of historiographical practice that emerges in post-Waterloo British literary culture: Walter Scott's *Waverley* novels. In these works, one can see how the dialectics of uneven development and the dated grid of a homogeneous empty time may be said to go hand in hand. That the logic of uneven development had indeed structured Scott's fic-

81. Leon Trotsky, *The History of the Russian Revolution,* trans. Max Eastman (Ann Arbor: University of Michigan Press, 1957), pp. 4–5. For another discussion of the tradition of uneven development, and in particular Trotsky's place in it, see Michael Löwy, *The Politics of Combined and Uneven Development* (London: Verso, 1981), pp. 70–99.

82. For a more recent account of Scotland and Scottish nationalism in these terms, see Tom Nairn, *The Break-Up of Britain* (London: New Left Books, 1977), pp. 92–195. Some of the subsequent controversy over Nairn's argument is registered in remarks by Eric Hobsbawm and Regis Debray in *New Left Review* (September–October 1977): 1–41.

83. Lévi-Strauss, *The Savage Mind,* p. 256.

tion from his first great experiment had been acknowledged in the final chapter of *Waverley*, "A Postscript, Which Should Have Been a Preface," where Scott famously attempts to situate his project in Scottish intellectual and material history:

> There is no European nation which, within the course of half a century, or little more, has undergone so complete a change as this kingdom of Scotland. The effects of the insurrection of 1745,—the destruction of the patriarchal power of the Highland chiefs,—the abolition of the heritable jurisdictions of the Lowland nobility and barons,—the total eradication of the Jacobite party, which, averse to intermingle with the English, or adopt their customs, long continued to pride themselves upon maintaining ancient Scottish manners and customs— commenced this innovation. The gradual influx of wealth, and extension of commerce, have since united to render the present people of Scotland a class of beings as different from their grandfathers, as the existing English are from those of Queen Elizabeth's time. (Wav, Postscr.)

"Queen Elizabeth's time" is comprehended within the time of England. England's "progress" through the stages or states of society had, until the eighteenth century, been unrivaled in Europe for the speed of its acceleration, but that rate of progress had been utterly outstripped by the acceleration of Scottish development in the century since the Union of 1707. In Scott's reckoning, the time of Scotland, at least in the period we date to the eighteenth century, moves faster than the time of England by a ratio of more than a century to a generation. Elizabeth reigned from 1558 to 1603, and Scott follows the recently standardized sense of a generation as thirty years in making the generation of the grandfathers that of 1745, the date he stresses in the subtitle ("'Tis Sixty Years Since") of the narrative explicitly dated to 1805 in *Waverley*. In each instance— "1745," "the last twenty or twenty-five years of the eighteenth century," "1805"—the calendrical chronology functions as the medium in which different times-in-temporalities can been merged in a yet-higher-order calculus, a historian's code.[84]

Scott offered the most extensive account of his new historiographical form, the closest he came to formulating a theory of the genre, in the Dedicatory

---

84. The argument I am making here about Scott's way of structuring a new form of fiction around the relation between uneven development and the historian's code can be seen as a particularization of arguments that have been made about Scott's relation to the "philosophic history" of the Scottish Enlightenment more generally. See especially Duncan Forbes, "The Rationalism of Sir Walter Scott," *Cambridge Journal* 7 (1953):20–35; David Daiches, "Sir Walter Scott and History" *Etudes Anglais* 24 (1971):458–77; Avrom Fleischman, *The English Historical Novel: Walter Scott to Virginia Woolf* (Baltimore: Johns Hopkins, 1971), pp. 16–36; and Peter D. Garside, "Scott and the 'Philosophical' Historians," in *Journal of the History of Ideas* 36 (1975):497–512. For a suggestive Jamesonian "mapping" of *Waverley* that relies on the notion of uneven development, see Saree Makdisi, "Colonial Space and the Colonization of Time in Scott's *Waverley*," *Studies in Romanticism* 34 (summer 1995): 155–87, and his *Universal Empire* (Cambridge: Cambridge University Press, forthcoming).

Epistle to *Ivanhoe,* which he composed just in time to get the novel into press by the end of 1819. Lukács made this text appropriately central in his own theoretical remarks on Scott's contribution to nineteenth-century realism in *The Historical Novel,* where he was eager to assimilate Scott's project to such Hegelian paradigms as "*necessary anachronism.*"[85] Of course, in view of how the operations of changing times and changing places are mutually defined in the framework of Romantic historicism, it makes sense that Scott should have produced this, his fullest articulation of the temporality of the project, in accounting for the first novel he wrote that was not on a Scottish subject. In other words, shifting geographical ground with *Ivanhoe* prompted Scott to reexplore the historical ground, and to reestablish the historiographical basis, of *Waverley* itself.[86]

The fact that the "Postscript" to *Waverley* appears as the last numbered chapter of the novel, along with other markers, identifies the author of the Postscript to *Waverley* as the "Author of *Waverley*" (to use the phrase that would become famous in the anonymity discussions). By 1819, when *Ivanhoe* was composed, Scott's authorship of *Waverley* and its sequels, though still officially secret, was widely known. The three series of "Tales of My Landlord" (1816–19) had invented a new authorial fiction, that of an editor, Jedediah Cleishbotham, who brings forth narratives of Scottish history, mainly from the 1640s to the 1740s, which had been collected and redacted by Peter Patticson, a deceased schoolteacher from the Scottish lowlands. An altogether different authorial fiction is developed for Scott's novel of medieval England. The Dedicatory Epistle to *Ivanhoe* offers Scott's novel as though from one "Lawrence Templeton," who turns out to be a character from the world of the *Waverley* novels themselves. He is an English antiquary and a friend of the Scotsman Jonathan Oldbuck, title character of *The Antiquary* (1816), the Scottish novel with the most recent setting (the late 1790s) of any he had published at that point.

The fictional dedicatee of the Epistle is an English antiquary and acquaintance of both Templeton and Oldbuck, one Dr. Jonas Dryasdust, whose name of course became synonymous (such was the influence of *Ivanhoe* and its epistle), with the very project of antiquarianism in the nineteenth century.[87] Its dis-

---

85. Lukács, *The Historical Novel,* p. 61 (italics Lukács's).

86. Hazlitt, who writes brilliantly about Scott's relation to uneven development in Britain for the portrait of Scott in *The Spirit of the Age* (p. 62), also noted the implications of Scott's move to England for the setting of *Ivanhoe.*

87. Thomas Carlyle would take up "Dryasdust" as the name for his own antiquarian antihero in *Past and Present* (1843), and eventually it generated such nonce words as "dryasdustic" and "dryasdustism."

cussion employs the convention of the modest author's apology for offering so unworthy a book to so worthy a person. It is introduced by Templeton's reminder of an earlier conversation in which the two men are supposed to have discussed the *Waverley* novels—"that class of productions, in one of which the private and family affairs of your learned northern friend Mr Oldbuck of Monkbarns, were so unjustifiably exposed to the public" (Iv, Ded. Ep. [521–2]). In spite of Dryasdust's criticisms of these novels as having been written "in violation of every rule assigned to the epopeia" and as having succeeded by virtue only of the rich antiquarian stores of which the author had availed himself, Templeton had suggested that such a novel might be written about the English past (Ded. Ep.). The body of the Epistle is taken up with the meeting of objections that Dryasdust is supposed to have raised against such an enterprise.

One of Dryasdust's contemptuous characterizations of the Waverley novels seems to have been especially provocative. Templeton reminds him of his charge that the popular success of these novels stemmed largely from the fact that the "unknown author" had appropriated "real characters" and "real names" from the past—that he had, in short, simply "availed himself, like a second M'Pherson, of the stores of antiquity which lay scattered around him, supplying his own indolence or poverty of invention, by the incidents which had actually taken place in his country at no distant period" (Ded. Ep.). Templeton's response to this criticism indicates just how crucially the logic of uneven development figures in Scott's conception of his project:

> It was not above sixty or seventy years [i.e., since 1739 or 1749], you observed, that the whole north of Scotland was under a state of government nearly as simple and as patriarchal as those of our good allies the Mohawks and Iroquois. Admitting that the author cannot himself be supposed to have witnessed these times, he must have lived, you observed, among persons who had acted and suffered in them; and even within these thirty years [since 1789], such an infinite change has taken place in the manners of Scotland, that men look back upon their fathers' habits of society, as we do on those of the reign of Queen Anne [1701–13]. Having thus materials of every kind lying strewed around him, there was little, you observed, to embarrass the author, but the facility of choice. (Ded. Ep.) [dates are my interpolations]

The calibration of uneven temporalities plays yet a larger role here than in the postscript to *Waverley* in that it is both more fully elaborated and more central to the very conception of the project. Further, there is more than one calibration to attend to here, and more than one set of relations in play. Not only are time-place definitions mutually worked out between Scotland and England, but Scotland itself is divided into two "chronotopic" zones: "the whole north of Scotland" and (by extrapolation) the whole south. Dryasdust suggests an equivalence between the development of manners and habits in the Scotland of 1789 ("within these last thirty years") and that of the England of the first thirteen years of the eighteenth century ("the reign of Queen Anne"). This assignment of an English equivalent (i.e., something over a century) for a Scottish generation (say, thirty years) is broadly consistent with the claim in the *Waverley* Postscript that *two* generations had been equivalent to roughly two centuries of English development. Finally, as for the suggestion that the Highland clan societies of 1745 approached in degree of antiquity to the contemporary societies of the Mohawks and the Iroquois of North America ("our good allies"), it must be said that *that* comparison had been functional for practical decision making in Lowlands institutional contexts since before the time of the Seven Years' War (when the "alliance" in question was solidified). For it was in that period that William Robertson, who would become the great philosophic historian of the Scottish Enlightenment, noted that Scotland's Society for the Propagation of Christianity, in which he was active, was going to add to its ongoing mission of converting Scottish Highlanders to Presbyterianism a parallel mission to the tribal inhabitants of North America, where the threat of Catholicism, as in the Highlands, was likewise perceived as both a religious and a political menace.[88] A savage is a savage, but a Catholic savage is a potential ally to the enemy in France. In Robertson's two great and influential histories, respectively, of Scotland and America, the paradigmatic characterizations of the Highland clansmen in the former and the Native Americans in the latter suggest a similarly parallel relation.[89]

7. Literary Studies and "Historical Epistemology"

I have been demonstrating the literary instantiation of Romantic historicism's complex conceptual framework in the "Postscript That Should Have Been a Preface" to *Waverley* and in the "Dedicatory Epistle" to *Ivanhoe*. In these two texts where Scott reflects on his practice as a historical novelist, I have argued, dates serve to code relationships between societies whose development has newly been theorized as uneven. One objection I can imagine to my procedure is that it places too much weight on so slight an evidentiary base. I should there-

---

88. In his 1755 account of the Society's work, Robertson explained, "Besides their endeavours towards the instructing and improving of the Highlands, the Society have of late been engaged in a new and more extensive undertaking. The late Dr. *Williams,* and some other well-disposed persons in England, confiding in the prudence and fidelity of the Society, have committed to their management certain sums which they ordain to be employed for the instruction of the *Indians* in *America*"—*The Situation of the World . . . To which is Joined a Short Account of The State of the Society in Scotland for Propagating Christian Knowledge* (Edinburgh: 1755), pp. 55–56.

89. This point is made in Robert Crawford, *Devolving English Literature* (Oxford: Clarendon Press, 1992), p. 176. For a comparison of Robertson and Adam Ferguson on this point, see Roy Harvey Pearce, *Savagism and Civilization* (Baltimore: Johns Hopkins University Press, 1965), pp. 82–88.

fore stress the privileged place of these two texts as moments of reflexive theorization at what are commonly regarded as the two primary starting points for
the Waverley series—the first of the Scottish novels and the first of the novels
not about Scotland.[90] What Scott describes in these two texts is a pattern and a
practice that structures the Waverley novels as a whole. Second, I should reemphasize that, in locating the instantiation of this new historical framework in
the Waverley novels, one is identifying it with an oeuvre that is arguably the
most influential single body of literary work produced in English by any writer
since Shakespeare. The Waverley novels, in other words, not only register how
the modern historiographical operation produces its distinctive forms of
meaning, they also, in their massive circulation and impact on the "white
mythologies" of national self-representation in the nineteenth century, play a
significant role in the emergence of modern historiography itself.[91] To forget
Scott's place in "Romanticism" and "historicism" as we have come to know
them is to risk the kind of mistake that those of us in literary studies sometimes
make in attempting to *resist* Romanticism by means of historicism. It is to risk
thinking that the crossing of the disciplinary lines between history and literature in our time is *necessarily* more than a recrossing of boundaries that Scott's
work occupied as if they were themselves discursive locales, just as he himself
made his home in a place called "the Borders."

In relation to the field of literary studies the point has special application.
Certainly, from the point of view of this analysis, the tendency to suppress Romantic historicism in the "return-to-history" movement in recent literary and
cultural criticism is marked by two curious ironies. The first has to do with the
history of literary criticism in our century in relation to work in particular
literary-historical fields. It has been said that, for much of the middle two quarters of our century, a striking number of the dominant literary theorists have
come from the field of Romanticism—the names Richards, Frye, Abrams,
Bloom, Hartman, and de Man should make the claim plausible. The paradigms

90. Judith Wilt deals with these two novels as paradigmatic, for Scott and for the nineteenth
century, for roughly the same reasons, in *Secret Leaves: The Novels of Walter Scott* (Chicago: University of Chicago Press, 1985), pp. 18–48.

91. See Robert Young, *White Mythologies* (London and New York: Routledge, 1990). On the
contribution of the Waverley novels to the work of Andrew Lang, James Frazer, and modern
British anthropology, see Crawford, *Devolving English Literature,* pp. 111–75. On the impact of the
Waverley novels on the writing of history in the nineteenth century, see G. M. Young, "Scott and
the Historians," in the University of Edinburgh's *Sir Walter Scott Lectures 1940–48* (Edinburgh:
Edinburgh University Press, 1950), pp. 78–107; and Hugh Trevor-Roper, "Sir Walter Scott and
History," *The Listener* 86 (August 19, 1971): 225–34; cf. the lectures Trevor-Roper printed under
the title *The Romantic Movement and the Study of History* (London: Athlone, 1969), where he claims
to be the first modern historian to note the dependency of Macaulay on Scott (p. 20).

for general poetics in Anglo-American criticism, likewise, tended to come from Romantic poetry.[92] With the shift (very broadly speaking) from poetics to historicism between the third and fourth quarters of this century, however, Romanticism lost its pride of place as the field of more general theorization in favor of Renaissance and later-American studies. Stephen Greenblatt and Walter Benn Michaels, for example, are critics typically associated with the so-called new historicism.[93] The great paradox is that the move to a form of analysis whose framework is Romantic has occasioned a displacement of Romanticism as the prestige field of methodological advancement. This displacement is abetted by the second ironic development, for Romantic studies have themselves undergone an intense rehistoricization, as Romanticists know full well. If this effort has had relatively less influence beyond its period-specific field of study than other such efforts in other fields, part of the reason may lie in the fact that the Romanticists' variety of new historicism tends to be defined, especially in relation to the "question of history" itself, by way of a disavowal of any genealogical relation to Romanticism and to Romantic studies.

From the point of view produced by recent Romanticists' engagement with new historicism, the relation to history in Romantic literature itself (especially in that literature as it appears as object and source of previous Romanticist criticism) tends to assume one of two forms. Either this literature and its criticism are thought to enact a refusal of history— a denial, displacement, or deferral of the material conditions in which texts were produced— or else they are construable in terms of an identifiably Hegelian historicism. In the negative account, both of these "alternatives" for reading history in the Romantic

92. Annabel Patterson assumes the fact of this tendency in answering the question of "what has happened to the lyric since what was once called the New Criticism was replaced as the ruling methodology in our discipline." She notes that "the still newer criticisms . . . have not . . . been able to disturb the premises of the preceding dynasty with respect to lyric, or even to improve on its work. . . . The modernist view of lyric as an intense, imaginative form of self-expression or self-consciousness, the most private of all genres, is, of course, a belief derived from Romanticism." See "Lyric and Society in Jonson's *Under-wood,*" in *Lyric Poetry: Beyond New Criticism,* ed. Chaviva Hôsek and Patricia Parker (Ithaca, N.Y.: Cornell University Press, 1985), pp. 150–51.

93. Of recent scholars, Greenblatt and Michaels are the "two whose work has become representative" of the new historicism that most interests Brook Thomas in *The New Historicism and Other Old-Fashioned Topics,* p. 6. Attempting to connect the newness of their strain of historicism with the inclusiveness of another, Thomas plots a very different genealogy for the return to history from the one that concerns me here. Thomas does not discuss the Sartre/Lévi-Strauss debate as a framework for these issues, but neither, for example, do the contributors to *Post-Structuralism and the Question of History,* ed. Derek Atridge, Geoff Bennington, and Robert Young (Cambridge: Cambridge University Press, 1987), with the partial exception of William Pietz, in "The Phonograph in Africa," p. 264.

text—the denial ascribed to formalist aestheticism and the *Aufhebung* ascribed to Hegelian organicism—are then posited as the "other" of new-historicist approaches to the Romantic field. Thus, in new-historicist treatments of Romanticism, Romantic texts have typically, where they have been read vigorously, been read against the grain. On this account of the Romantic text, its way of including or occluding history must be resisted, and so must the strains of modern criticism that have been identified with them.

While I share much of the historicist skepticism about the place or displacement of history in Romantic literature and in Romantic studies, I obviously wish to resist some of the characterizations of the literary culture of British Romanticism that have followed from it. Drawing on recent developments in the field of intellectual history, I have begun to resketch, with very different shadings and highlightings, the age of the world picture. The point might be made in respect to Dominick LaCapra's distinction between reading with and against texts in the working out of intellectual historiography, his suggestion that some texts appropriately structure the effort to come to terms with the past of which they form a part. LaCapra suggests that, in the case of some texts and in respect to some questions, the dialectic of these two operations—reading with and against the grain of texts—needs to be more vigorously maintained in the fields of intellectual and cultural history.[94] Part of my motivating suspicion here is that, in respect to the so-called question of history, there has been too little reading with the grain of Romantic texts and thus too little in the way of outlining a "historical epistemology" for Romantic historicism itself. The suspicion, in other words, is that the dismissal of Romantic historicism may prove to be overhasty, if not self-deceived.

That phrase "historical epistemology" comes from recent work in the history of science, where it stands for the attempt to recover and articulate the conditions of intelligibility for the discursive practices of some prior cultural moment.[95] To the extent that one remains committed to the assumption that science means progress, this project of historical epistemology has only an antiquarian justification, but, if historiography itself is what one seeks the history of, the story may be different—perhaps even as different as the one told by

94. La Capra, *Soundings in Critical Theory,* pp. 204–205.

95. See Lorraine Daston, "Historical Epistemology," a response to some queries I put to her in "Proving a History of Evidence," both in *Questions of Evidence,* pp. 275–89. "Historical epistemology," writes Daston, poses a different kind of question from the history of ideas: "not the history of this or that particular use, but the history of the changing forms and standards . . . ; not the history of the establishment of this or that empirical fact . . . , but rather the history of competing forms of facticity . . . " (pp. 282–83).

Siegfried Kracauer in *The Last Things Before the Last*. Kracauer is not the first commentator to dispute consoling opinions of historians who claim to be advancing beyond the work of their predecessors: "The belief in the progress of historiography is largely in the nature of an illusion."[96] Even if one does not go as far as Kracauer's sweeping claim, one may judge that such progress is often wrongly or too quickly supposed—in the "triumphs" of material over intellectual historiography, or vice versa; of social over cultural history, or vice versa; analytic over narrative history, or vice versa; new historicism over literary history, and so on. In a given history of historiography, new historicism certainly can appear to be an historiographical, even a political, advance over any historical paradigm one uncovers in the Romantic era, but that *appearance* may itself depend on covering over—"containing," as we say—the complexity and density of historicist thought in Romantic writing. I take it, then, that only a historicist account that does not begin from the assumption that its history is better than Romantic history will be able to appreciate the intellectual, political, and even moral stakes of Romantic historiographical operations across a range of representative literary forms.[97]

Again, the problem of short-sightedness in historicizing contemporary forms of research and critical practice is not limited to literary criticism but extends across the full range of what we now call cultural studies. Talad Asad has recently cited E. B. Tylor's famous definition of his object of study—"Culture or Civilization, taken in its wide ethnographic sense, is that complex whole which includes knowledge, belief, art, morals, law, custom, and any other capabilities and habits acquired by man as a member of society"—in order to raise a germane question: "it would be interesting to trace how and when this notion of culture . . . was transformed into the notion of a *text*—that is, into something resembling an inscribed discourse."[98] Asad does not "intend to attempt such a history" himself, he says, but raises the question of the textual metaphor for culture in British social anthropology in order to focus attention on the derivative metaphor of "translation" and to "remind ourselves that the phrase 'the transla-

96. Siegfried Kracauer, *History, The Last Things Before the Last*, p. 138.

97. Duncan Forbes observed years ago that the "history of history" in England was a scandalously neglected topic. Part of the great paradox, however, is that what is arguably the most important epoch in this history of history, the Romantic period, is one in which the writing of history is transformed by works not precisely identified with the genre of historiography as such—"*Historismus* in England," *The Cambridge Journal* 4 (April 1951): 388. See my essay on "Romantic Historicism" in Iain McCalman, ed., *The Oxford Companion to British Romanticism* (Oxford: Oxford University Press, forthcoming).

98. Talal Asad, "The Concept of Cultural Translation in British Social Anthropology," in *Writing Culture: The Poetics and Politics of Ethnography*, ed. James Clifford and George E. Marcus (Berkeley: University of California Press, 1986), p. 141.

tion of cultures,' which increasingly since the 1950s has become an almost banal description of the distinctive task of social anthropology, was not always so much in evidence."[99] Asad goes on to stress that he is not talking here about the notion of translating languages between cultures but that of translating languages as cultures, or rather cultures as languages. For Asad's question, as for other questions I have been considering, I am urging a longer conceptual-historical perspective than is routinely assumed. My contention is that Shelley in "England in 1819," Barbauld in *Eighteen Hundred and Eleven,* and Scott throughout the Waverley novels are all writers interested in the textualization of culture in something like Asad's strong sense. Again, Scott's "Dedicatory Epistle" offers a particularly full account of his practice.

8. Translating Cultures

Readers of Lukács's *The Historical Novel* will recall that the problem of how to make an earlier culture intelligible to a later one is the very problem that he identifies as central to the *Ivanhoe* "Epistle," though he does so only to assimilate it to the discussion of "necessary anachronism" in Hegel's *Aesthetics.* In the "Epistle," this problem arises when Templeton fends off Dryasdust's second major objection to his project: that, as an antiquary, Templeton should not stoop to the rhetorical tricks of novelists. Templeton cites the precedents of Horace Walpole and George Ellis to suggest that antiquarian subject matter can be made "interesting" to readers of fiction but worries that such a project runs the risk of creating anachronism along with the "interest." The question then becomes how, without distortion or invention, can the daily life, or "vie privée," of an anterior society, if it belongs to an alien or outdated system of manners, be made "intelligible" to those who can have had no first-hand experience of it? "It is necessary," Templeton insists, "for exciting interest of any kind, that the subject assumed should be, as it were, translated into the manners, as well as the language, of the age we live in" (Iv, Ded. Ep.). And the illustrative analogy, suggestively, is to a handling of that largest of cultural divides available to Scott's imagination, that between "West" and "East" in Galland's *Arabian Nights Tales.*

In developing this analogy—east is to west as past is to present—Scott's persona claims that Galland succeeded because he was able to retain both the splendor of eastern costume and the wildness of eastern fiction, while "mixing with these just so much ordinary feeling and expression as rendered them interesting and intelligible" (Iv, Ded. Ep.). Operating in the analogous divide between national antiquity and national modernity, Templeton produces an analogous so-

---

99. Ibid., p. 141.

lution: "I have so far explained our ancient manners in modern language, and so far detailed the characters and sentiments of my persons, that the modern reader will not find himself . . . trammelled by the repulsive dryness of mere antiquity" (Iv, Ded. Ep.). The "translation" of one culture or system of manners into another, therefore, comes in the form of "explanation" and of giving detail of "characters and sentiments." But it is important to ask at this point just how the difference in manners is supposed to render the action of the Oriental tale or the medieval romance unintelligible to the modern reader of stories in English. Conversely, what kind of "explanation" is required to cast ancient manners in modern language? How is the mixing in of "ordinary feeling and expression" analogous to detailing the "characters and sentiments of my persons"?

Scott introduces the framework for solving these problems when he turns to the negative example of Joseph Strutt's failed historical romance of 1805, *Queen-Hoo Hall*. According to Templeton, the problem with this book, whose posthumous completion and publication were undertaken largely through Scott's good offices, was that it proceeded on the opposite principle from the one followed by Galland. In "distinguishing between what was ancient and modern," Strutt forgot "that extensive neutral ground" that links them, and "in this manner, a man of talent, and of great antiquarian erudition, limited the popularity of his work by excluding from it everything which was not sufficiently obsolete to be altogether forgotten and unintelligible" (Ded. Ep.). This metaphor of the neutral ground between the ancient and modern presides over the rest of Scott's analysis. That it will not be a fully satisfactory solution seems already apparent in Templeton's elaboration of his meaning. He defines this "neutral ground" as "the large proportion . . . of manners and sentiments which are common to us and to our ancestors, which have been handed down unaltered from them to us, or which, arising out of the principles of our common nature, must have existed alike in either state of society" (Ded. Ep.). The metaphor of neutral ground figures here as the insistence on "the principles of our common nature." Common nature makes for common ground, ground shared in a spirit of neutrality. This metaphor is supplemented, however, with the traditionalist metaphor: "what has been handed down unaltered." The tensions between the two metaphors are not sorted out, and Templeton fails, in the end, to provide the warrant for the historical novelist's "license" to translate the manners of one state of society into those of another.

Nor, by the same token, does Scott's persona succeed in providing a fully coherent account of how this license can be held within what he calls "legitimate bounds." It is in explaining just these bounds and the problems they create that Templeton arrives at what he calls "the most difficult part of my task": "However far [the historical novelist] may venture in a more full detail of passions and feelings, than is to be found in the ancient compositions which he imitates, he must introduce nothing inconsistent with the manners of the age; his knights, squires, grooms, and yeomen, may be more fully drawn than the hard, dry delineations of an ancient illuminated manuscript, but the character and costume of the age must remain inviolate; they must be the same figures, drawn by a better pencil, or to speak more modestly, executed in an age when the principles of art were better understood" (Ded. Ep.). The "difficulty" of both Templeton's "task" and his analysis has to do with a distinction that comes in and out of focus between the kind of text that a system of manners amounts to and the kind of text in which it is represented. To rephrase the distinction in Scott's own complex paranomasia, it is between manner as style (mode of textual treatment) and manners as subject (text to be treated). The license of the historical novelist lies primarily at the level of *treatment,* what Templeton calls "a more full detail of passions and feelings than is to be found in the ancient compositions which he imitates" (Ded. Ep.). The restriction the historical novelist respects lies primarily at the level of subject; however drawn, they "must be the same figures." The problem is that the account figures "figure" both at the level of style and subject matter, trope and topos. The historical novelist, one might say, is not only using ancient subjects but also imitating ancient compositions on those subjects. That is, if he is "copying ancient manners," as he sometimes puts it, his sources for these manners represent them *in* a manner—that is, an ancient manner—that leaves them unintelligible. The further step required, therefore, is to copy ancient manners in the modern manner. This is the manner that allows for a fuller treatment of the passions and feelings of the characters involved in the chivalric system of manners. Since the modern manner of representation is to be found most characteristically in the modern mode of romance, which is to say in the novel, the historical novel has to be, in a strict sense, postmodern.

To appreciate this point it is important to see how Templeton locates his work in relation to the prior postmodern form of fiction: Horace Walpole's Gothic novel. Walpole described his aim in *The Castle of Otranto* as an effort to blend ancient and modern romance, explaining that in "the former, all was imagination and improbability; in the latter, nature is always intended to be, and sometimes has been, copied with success."[100] In hoping "to reconcile the two kinds," Walpole couches his program in aesthetic or formalist terms: "Desirous of leaving the powers of fancy at liberty to expatiate through the boundless

---

100. Horace Walpole, "Preface to the Second Edition" (1765), *The Castle of Otranto,* ed. W. S. Lewis (Oxford: Oxford University Press, 1982), p. 7.

realms of invention . . . ; he wished to conduct the mortal agents in his drama according to the rules of probability."[101] Scott's recasting of this language in his critical essay on Walpole is telling: "in *The Castle of Otranto,* it was his object to unite the marvelous turn of incident, and imposing tone of chivalry, exhibited in the ancient romance, with that accurate display of human character, and contrast of feelings and passions, which is, or ought to be, delineated in the modern novel."[102] The signal difference from Walpole is that Scott, following his Scottish-Enlightenment mentors, links romance not with a state of mind but with a state of society: the one made intelligible by virtue of the chivalric code.[103]

Scott merely hints at this link in the Dedicatory Epistle, but he elaborates it quite eloquently in his paired *Encyclopedia Britannica* articles on Chivalry and Romance, especially in that section of the latter where he seeks "to explain the history of Romance."[104] The starting point of the analysis is the observation that the representations of Romance were taken seriously as part of the historical past in the chivalric period itself. And the evidence for this claim is that romances were themselves adduced as evidence. "The fabulous knights of Romance were so completely identified with those of real history," writes Scott, "that graver historians quote the actions of the former in illustration of, and as a corollary to, the real events which they narrate."[105] The puzzle that

---

101. Ibid., p. 7.

102. Scott, "Horace Walpole, Ballantyne's Novelist's Library" (March 1, 1823), included in *Sir Walter Scott on Novelists and Fiction,* ed. Ioan Williams (London: Routledge and Kegan Paul, 1968), p. 85.

103. The way in which literary forms of representation participate in the histories they depict is a topic that looms large in the public discourse of England in 1819. Though my emphasis will remain chiefly on historiography, that is, on literary texts, in *Ivanhoe* itself there is a suggestion that the forms of representation for the "condition of England" in a given state can be nonliterary. This becomes clear in the beginning of the book's central line of narrative, with the narrative of the tournament of Ashby de la Zouche in chapter 7, where the novel seems to begin anew: "The condition of the English nation was at this time sufficiently miserable." After enumerating the principal features of England's "unhappy state of affairs" in 1194, Scott goes on to explain the broad appeal of "the event of the tournament, which was the grand spectacle of the age," and then to recount the event of Ashby de la Zouche itself. In doing so, Scott outlines a complex economy of representation in terms of which the social structure of the tournament's spectatorship—with all of its complex alliances, rivalries, and hierarchies—is acted out in the events on the tournament pitch itself—and the entire event of the tournament figures, both in general and in particular, in the course of social events in that period, very much as Scott says the genre of romance does.

104. Sir Walter Scott, "An Essay on Romance," published in the supplement to the *Encyclopaedia Britannica* (1824), collected in *Essays on Chivalry, Romance, and the Drama* (Edinburgh: R. Cadell, 1834), p. 162.

105. Ibid., p. 170.

Scott poses is how Romance's claim to historicality sorted with its apparently outlandish moral code. The answer, which is intricate, begins by recognizing that the "virtues recommended in Romance," though apparently outlandish, were "only of that overstrained and extravagant cast which consisted with the spirit of chivalry":

> Great bodily strength, and perfection in all martial exercises, was the universal accomplishment inalienable from the character of the hero, and which each romancer had it in his power to confer. It was easily in the composer's power to devise dangers, and to free his hero from them by the exertion of valour equally extravagant. But it was more difficult to frame a story which should illustrate the manners as well as the feats of Chivalry; or to devise the means of evincing that devotion to duty, and that disinterested desire to sacrifice all to faith and . . . which form, perhaps the fairest side of the system under which the noble youths of the middle ages were trained up. The sentiments of Chivalry . . . were founded on the most pure and honourable principles, but unfortunately carried into hyperbole and extravagance; until the religion of its professors approached to fanaticism, their valour to frenzy, their ideas of honour to absurdity, their spirit of enterprise to extravagance, and their respect for the female sex to a sort of idolatry. All those extravagant feelings, which really existed in the society of the middle ages, were magnified and exaggerated by the writers and reciters of Romance; and these, given as resemblances of actual manners, became, in their turn, the glass by which the youth of the age dressed themselves.[106]

I cited earlier Walter Michaels's comment that "the only relation literature as such has to culture as such is that it is part of it." For Scott, and I suspect for many of us, this is an unacceptable reduction. Literature, on this other view, figures in at least two relations to culture—as a reflection of it *and* a part of it, both mimesis and synecdoche, and therein lie the complications. The manner of representation implicit in a given literary form—Romance, for example—is also a part of the manners that the form takes as its object.

In the thoroughgoing mutuality of this dialectic, Scott explains, "the spirit of Chivalry and Romance thus gradually threw light on and enhanced each other" until it was possible to take the one as a reflective index of the other, as "evidence" in the works of those "graver historians." It could thus ultimately be said, with real warrant, that medieval romances "exhibited the same system of manners which existed in the nobles of the age":

> The character of a true son of chivalry was raised to such a pitch of ideal and impossible perfection, that those who emulated such renown were usually contented to stop far short of the mark. The most adventurous and unshaken valour, a mind capable of the highest flights of romantic generosity, a heart which was devoted to the will of some fair idol . . . these were the attributes which all aspired to exhibit who sought to rank high in the annals of chivalry; and such were the virtues which the minstrels celebrated. But, like the temper of a tamed lion, the fierce and dissolute spirit of the age often showed itself through the fair varnish of this artificial system of manners. The valour of the hero was often stained by acts of cruelty, or freaks of rash desperation; his courtesy and munificence became solemn foppery and wild profusion;

106. Ibid., pp. 170–71.

his love to his lady often demanded and received a requital inconsistent with the honour of the object; and those who affected to found their attachment on the purest and most delicate metaphysical principles, carried on their actual intercourse with a license altogether inconsistent with their sublime pretensions. Such were the real manners of the middle ages, and we find them so depicted in these ancient legends.[107]

What Chivalry and Romance share, if I may venture a paraphrase, is the principle of extravagance. A system of manners forms at once part of a society and part of its means of self-representation and thus self-perpetuation. The Chivalric system, according to Scott, offered an extravagant self-representation of medieval society as a culture of perfection. On this view, Romance seems to be nothing more than the set of literary conventions in which this self-representation—the code of Chivalry—is itself encoded. The age's manner of representation is therefore a function of the self-representation of the age through its manners. In this case, the artificialities of Romance are just a function of the difference between what Scott, somewhat confusingly, distinguishes as the artificial system of manners of the period and its real manners. Chivalry-and-Romance, now understood as hyphenated, is an elaborate form of well-meaning social self-deception on a massive scale.[108]

Scott emphasizes that a less extravagant program for achieving the kind of refinement that led the system of chivalry into self-deception and even violence was indeed on the horizon. It arrives, he says, with the advent of the system of modern manners predicated on the systems of commerce and jurisprudence.[109] Such manners are less pure in principle than the chivalric system of manners but also less barbaric than the actual manners of the age. What characterizes modern manners for Scott, indeed, is the closing of the gap between the actual state of things and the manner of their self-representation. The literary form that corresponds to and participates in the modern system of manners is what Scott alternatively called the modern romance and "the novel." Scott's most explicit definition of the novel suggests a deep agreement with Ian Watt's account of "the rise of the novel" in the age of commerce. Taking issue with Dr. Johnson's formulation—"a smooth tale, generally of love"—Scott defined the novel in the "Essay on Romance" as "a fictitious narrative, differing from the

107. Ibid., pp. 171–72.
108. Something very close to this, of course, is suggested by Burke, when he describes the age of chivalry as supplying the "pleasing illusions" that a society requires to veil its power relations from itself. See *Reflections on the Revolution in France & The Rights of Man* (New York: Doubleday, 1973), p. 90.
109. See Pocock on Burke's argument about commerce as an extension of (and as dependent on) the spirit of chivalry, in "The Political Economy of Burke's Reflections," *Virtue, Commerce and History*, pp. 193–212.

Romance, because the events are accommodated to the ordinary train of human events, and the modern state of society."[110]

Glossing the Dedicatory Epistle for *Ivanhoe* with the analyses of the Essays on Chivalry and Romance, then, one might say that the historical novel is not only a form that attempts to fictionalize the past as it really was, but also a form self-aware of its own historicity along two axes: its participation in a contemporary and historically specific system of manners—the manners of commercial society—and in a generic evolution of narrative modes that in turn participated in their *own,* now residual, systems of manners. This account of the historical novel is complicated, I believe, in just the way that the "historian's code" that it articulates is complicated. And while Lukács is eager, like many modern commentators, to assimilate such texts to Hegelian paradigms, I have been emphasizing their place within a specifically British (and, more specifically, Scottish-Enlightenment) intellectual tradition. As further evidence for the propriety of this restoration, I want to cite a forgotten passage by a forgotten commentator on a forgotten work by its forgotten author: that passage is Dugald Stewart's "Memoir" on William Robertson (1802), which deals with Robertson's *History of Scotland* (1777).

Robertson's great *History* would go through nearly two dozen editions by 1819, and Stewart's commentary accompanied most of them after the eleventh. Apropos, precisely, of the differences in representing the Scottish and the English past to the contemporary British reader, the reader informed by the more advanced English state of taste, Stewart explains the problem Robertson confronted in dealing with the remote past of the Scottish people:

> Such is the effect of that provincial situation to which Scotland is now reduced, that the transactions of former ages are apt to convey to ourselves exaggerated conceptions of barbarism, from the uncouth and degraded dialect in which they are recorded. To adapt the history of such a country to the present standard of British taste, it was necessary for the Author, not only to excite an interest for names which, to the majority of his readers, were formerly indifferent or unknown, but, what was still more difficult, to unite in his portraits the truth of nature with the softenings of art, and to reject whatever was unmeaning or offensive in the drapery, without effacing the characteristic garb of the times.[111]

The metaphor Stewart uses for the process is cultural translation:

> The necessity of correcting our common impressions concerning the antient state of Scotland, by translating not only the antiquated phraseology of our forefathers into a more mod-

---

110. "Essay on Romance," p. 129. See Ian Watt's argument about the role of the representation of ordinary life in the new "realism" of the novel form in *The Rise of the Novel: Studies in Defoe, Richardson, and Fielding* (Berkeley: University of California Press, 1957), chap. 1.

111. Dugald Stewart, "Memoir of the Life of William Robertson," prefixed to William Robertson, *The History of Scotland,* 3 vols. (London: Cadell and Davies, 1802) 1:55–56.

ern idiom, but by translating (if I may use the expression) their antiquated fashions into the corresponding fashions of our own times.[112]

Note that here, as in Scott, we have precisely that distinction insisted on by Asad between language in culture and culture as language. And again, here as in Scott, the degree to which we may regard the working assumption as involving what Asad refers to in contemporary social anthropology as the textualization of culture is indicated by that metaphor of translation.[113]

To hold, then, that manners themselves of a past state of society may or must be translated for reception in a later one is to take those manners as a "system," an object of potential intelligibility, a kind of text. It is also, as we have begun to see, to raise questions about cultural representation in this discourse of Romantic historicism that are going to require some further study: questions about the relations between cultural mimesis (representation as a mirror of the whole) and cultural synecdoche (representation as a part of the whole), between cultural specificity and cultural specimen, between culture-produced-as-text and the texts that a culture produces. One question that remains for this phase of the discussion, however, has to do with the *sites* where the cultural differences coded and recoded in these acts of translation are understood to operate. Where is culture bred and where does it do its breeding?

9. "*La vie privée* of our forefathers"

We are considering a question about what Homi Bhabha calls "the location of culture." To address it well we must recognize the real force in the discourses of historicism, old and new, carried by such terms as private life, *vie privée,* domesticity, "privateness-oriented-toward-an-audience," and various other names for ordinary practices so taken for granted that, as Scott suggests, they become visible in the documents of the past only by a hermeneutic exercise of reading between the lines. In recent cultural theory, this category or function is variously labeled: Bourdieu names it "the habitus," and Lefebvre "everyday life." Carlo Ginzburg, addressing himself more specifically to recent developments

112. Ibid., p. 56.
113. The other side of the oddly foreshortened history of current critical practice is the attempt to effect distinction where it arguably does not exist. In her suggestive account of the relation of "our new historicism" to "old historicism," Marjorie Levinson seeks to make this issue of translation decisive: "For the old historicism, the alleged project was to restore to the dead their own, living language, that they might bespeak themselves," whereas, "[b]y contrast, the critical work I've been describing should be called translation" (*Rethinking Historicism,* p. 52). Not only is the metaphor of cultural translation integral to the "old historicism" Scott learned from Dugald Stewart, it coexists for him with the mission of making the dead tell their story (see below, chapter 4).

in cultural historiography associated with his own work and that of Natalie Zemon Davis, identifies it by means of synecdoche as "an interest not only with
the deeds of Trajan, Antoninus Pius, Nero or Caligula . . . but also with scenes
from the private life of Arnaud du Tilh, called Pansette, of Martin Guerre, and
of his wife Bertrande."[114] Ginzburg's is a discussion to which I will return, because it counts as a partial exception to the general repression of the relevance
of forms of Romantic historiography to contemporary practice. He explicitly
associates his and Davis's new brand of history to the nineteenth-century historical novel, although in tracing this genealogy Ginzburg overlooks the
achievements of Scott's fiction, of historicism in Britain more generally, and
certainly of the those underlying theories of Scottish-Enlightenment figures
such as Millar, Robertson, Ferguson, or Dugald Stewart.[115]

Nor does Ginzburg note the congruence between the terms in which he lays
out the project of the new historians and those which the twenty-eight-year-
old Thomas Babington Macaulay employed in the prospectus he published in
Francis Jeffrey's *Edinburgh Review* in 1828 for his own massive project. Macaulay
cited the novels of Scott as showing how to make narrative use of "those fragments of truth which historians have scornfully thrown behind them."[116]
Macaulay, himself, the English-born son of a Highlander, praises Scott for having "constructed out of their gleanings works which, even considered as histories, are scarcely less valuable than theirs," but at the same time he urges
historians to "reclaim those materials which the novelist has appropriated."
Redeploying the ever-strengthening analogy between historiography and
ethnography, Macaulay distinguishes the old from the new student of history
by differentiating two ways of metaphorical travel to the foreign country that is
the past.

The basis of the analogy between the two modes of historiography and the
two modes of travel would have been quite familiar by this time to any reader
conversant with the previous decades of theory in Jeffrey's Edinburgh: it is that
in either mode, the student of history, "like the tourist, is transported into a new

114. Carlo Ginzburg, "Proofs and Possibilities: In the Margins of Natalie Zemon Davis' *The
Return of Martin Guerre,*" *Yearbook of Comparative and General Literature* 37 (November 1988): 125.

115. This omission is all the more curious in that the problem Ginzburg identifies at the start
of his own experimental social history, *The Cheese and the Worms,* trans. John and Anne Tedeschi
(Harmondsworth: Penguin, 1982), is formulated in much the same terms as Scott employs in the
dialogues of the "Dedicatory Epistle" to *Ivanhoe.* The major problem he faced in his research, says
Ginzburg, is the "scarcity of evidence about the behavior and attitudes of the subordinate classes
of the past" (p. xiii).

116. T. B. Macaulay, review of Henry Neele's *The Romance of History, Edinburgh Review* 47
(May 1828): 365.

state of society. He sees new fashions. He hears new modes of expression. His mind is enlarged by contemplating the wide diversities of laws, of morals, and of manners."[117] The equally important *distinction* Macaulay wants to make, however, has to do with exactly how the tourist or history student focuses the powers of attention.

In explaining how it is possible to travel without learning, to move without being moved, Macaulay's own prose seeks at once to teach and to move its readers:

> [M]en may travel far, and return with minds as contracted as if they had never stirred from their own market-town. In the same manner, men may know the fates of many battles and the genealogies of many royal houses, and yet be no wiser. Most people look at past times as princes look at foreign countries. More than one illustrious stranger has landed on our island amidst the shouts of a mob, has dined with the King, has hunted with the master of the stag-hounds, has seen the guards reviewed, and knight of the garter installed; has cantered along Regent Street, has visited St. Paul's, and noted down its dimensions; and has then departed, thinking that he has seen England. He has, in fact, seen a few public buildings, public men, and public ceremonies. But of the vast and complex system of society, of the fine shades of national character, of the practical operation of government and laws, he knows nothing. He who would understand these things rightly must not confine his observations to palaces on solemn days. He must see ordinary men as they appear in their ordinary business and in their ordinary pleasures. He must mingle in the crowds of the exchange and the coffee-house. He must obtain admittance to the convivial table and the domestic hearth. He must bear with vulgar expressions. He must not shrink from exploring even the retreats of misery. He who wishes to understand the condition of mankind in former ages must proceed on the same principle.[118]

The substance of these remarks by Macaulay has, it seems, uncannily been repeated in the new historiography of our time, even by a scholar such as Ginzburg who polemically argues for the model of the nineteenth-century historical novel to contemporary practice. Ginzburg, as I shall explain more fully in chapter 4, cites only Scott's continental emulators, Balzac and Manzoni. It is indeed a curious fact that, even when historiography, per se, is at issue, such historiographically sensitive romantic writers remain uncited, even occluded, as though the form of British Romanticism they stood for itself stood outside the history of historicist writing. In the complex relations of cultural text and cultural texture that structure this discourse, the importance of the sphere Macaulay outlines—the sphere of ordinary business, ordinary pleasures, the convivial table, and the domestic hearth—lies in its functioning as the site where one can see how (to reinvoke Lukács's phrase for identifying the "specifically historical" element in the historical novel) the individuality of character is derived from the historical peculiarity of the age.

117. Ibid., p. 365.
118. Ibid., p. 364.

This point can be illustrated best, I think, by returning briefly to Anna Barbauld's suggestive analogy between the temporalities of primitive and domestic life as both somehow "natural"in respect to the "artificial"systems of public
dates in which they are regularized. Barbauld, we saw, explains that an "Indian,"
in the absence of the sophisticated public dating of contemporary Britain, is
likely to respond to a "when" question with an answer such as "So many harvests ago, when I could but just reach the boughs of yonder tree." However, as a
way of arguing that this form of temporal discourse is indeed more "natural"
than the "universal"system, Barbauld further notes that even in contemporary
British culture, in the circumstances of "familiar life," one is inclined to respond
to a *when* question with what she claims is a similar kind of answer: "The year
before I was married," or "when Henry, who is now five years old, was born."
Both forms of temporal enunciation might fairly be called "more natural," as
Barbauld says, than the "artificial"system of universal dates for correlating states
of society. Even the "natural"states of these two states of society, however, code
time differently from each other. Each form of "natural"time statement might
be understood as "textualizing" the state of society itself, as supplying the texture of the culture that will require "translation" through the artificial code of
dates. The fact that Barbauld is willing to cite as "natural"to the Indian's natural
form of time-reckoning a deictic reference to a "natural" object ("yonder
tree"), whereas the domestic scene in then-contemporary Britain is temporal-
ized by the time of marriage and the age of children, might in turn form a part
of a more subtle cultural unevenness that required translating in terms of a yet
more basic code.

What Scott called "*la vie privée* of our forefathers" comes in his own time to
be understood as the site where historical-cultural difference is inscribed,
where it becomes "character." Hence, the emphasis in Habermas's account of
privacy/publicity in eighteenth-century Britain on "the sphere of the patriar-
chal conjugal family" as the literal "home" of the new forms of "specific subjectivity"in that period.[119] Hence the emerging importance of childhood as a
topic for social theory in the late-eighteenth and early nineteenth centuries,
and indeed, as Carolyn Steedman has suggested, for the new conception of an
interior life that lies hidden in a past.[120] In *Waverley,* Scott traces the historical
"derivation"of the eponymous hero as the passage of an uncharactered character—a kind of cipher—through various forms of inscription: romance, high-

119. Habermas, *Structural Transformation of the Public Sphere,* pp. 43–51.
120. Carolyn Steedman, *Strange Dislocations: Childhood and the Idea of Human Interiority,*
1780–1930 (London: Virago Press, 1995), pp. 1–20. It is worth reemphasizing that Barbauld's
posthumous collection is titled *Advice for Young Ladies.*

land oral song, newspaper report, courtroom argument, and so on. Each is associated with a specific social-historical manner of representation. In 1819, Keats would offer a similar theory of the individuation of the soul in historical circumstance in terms of a similarly inscriptive metaphor—individuated soul as the child who has learned how to read the horn book of the heart in the school room of the world. What the dating system adds to all this—Scott's coding of one culture as equivalent to another, Keats's reference in his most private moments of indolence to his "1819 temper"—is a second-order code, a method of translation from one textually constituted culture/character into another, a way of showing correspondences between "specific subjectivities" formed in different historical states.

Section Two

ROMANTICISM IN THE
REPRESENTATIVE STATE

Chapter Three

REPRESENTING CULTURE,

ROMANTICIZING CONTRADICTION:

THE POLITICS OF LITERARY EXEMPLARITY

I have been arguing for a certain way of conceiving the relationship between poststructuralist and Romantic historicisms, between the current academic discussion of history in English and the public discussion of the question at an earlier moment. I have emphasized how the "return to history" in recent literary studies relies on a particular discursive conjunction: two frameworks for conceiving historiography that worked together to achieve not only intelligibility but also wide currency in what we identify as the Romantic period in Britain. One of these discursive frameworks assumes the system of regularized public periodization on multiple scales that forms the basis, as I have argued, of what Lévi-Strauss came to call the historian's chronological code. The other one assumes a conception of culture based on an analogy between historiographical and ethnographical categories or practices, an assumption that is itself grounded in the practice of correlating the "uneven development" of particular societies to some particular "state of the world." Summarizing the relation between the two frameworks in question, one might say that the regularities of the code make the perception of developmental unevenness possible, while the unevenness of the development makes the perceived regularity of the code necessary.

I do not venture an intellectual history of historicism, at least not in the sense of a narrative account that extends from the eighteenth century to the present. To support the claim about how the discursive conjuncture of current historicism reinstalls the earlier one, however, I have considered recent academic efforts to locate texts within discursive states of affairs, and indeed to "textualize" such states of affairs themselves, and I have related such efforts to the increasingly popular literary genre of the "state" in eighteenth- and early nineteenth-century public writing, especially in Britain. Shelley's *England in 1819,* on my reading, not only locates itself within that genre, but it also performs a self-conscious dramatization of what some writers took to be the genre's revolutionary potential: the spirit of the age as the meaning of a text, a meaning subject to hermeneutic determination according to the sensitivity of its readers. Thus, if the answer I have given to Talal Asad's question about when we began to think of a culture as a text, or as something that could be represented in a text, is roughly "in the Romantic period," it is partly because the Romantic period is when culture in something like the sense Asad understands it was conceived. Its conception and "textualization," from this point of view, should be understood as going hand in hand. Because of the way in which self-consciousness about this kind of activity intensifies in post-Waterloo writings, *England in 1819* proves to be a title eminently iterable as between its own moment and ours, in spite of the fact that the sonnet's own rhetoric seems to insist on the possibility of a radical historical transformation of that which it represents.[1]

Such observations return us now, however, to Jameson's analysis of how the "method of homology" shapes poststructuralist historicism. In Jameson's account, part of the point of the homological method is that it enables the use of "text" to identify a range of seemingly disparate cultural formations and thus to "read" them in juxtaposition as cultural ensembles. We saw that, for Jameson, the issue of cultural-historical "specificity" in structuralist and poststructuralist commentary is bound up precisely with the problem of cultural exemplarity. If we rephrase this problem in terms of a relation between a given culture's specificity and its specimens, then it becomes possible to extend the discussion of correspondences between Romantic and poststructuralist historicisms in light of that relation.[2] We can ask how it is, in each framework, that a text is estab-

---

1. The question thus arises: how is the product of a historical mode or model related to the perpetuation or later reproducibility of that mode/model? This question remains in play throughout the following chapters.

2. The term "specimen," it should be noted, is by no means foreign to debates about literature and the contestation over the national canon in early nineteenth-century Britain. The famous pamphlet war known as "the Pope Controversy" was touched off in 1819, as I noted above, by some remarks in defense of Pope by Thomas Campbell in his *Specimens of the English Poets: With Biographical Notices, and Essay on English Poetry* (London: John Murray, 1819). An earlier collection of literary "specimens," prominently cited by Sir Walter Scott, can be found in the work of George Ellis. Ellis initially published his three-volume *Specimens of the Early English Poets* (London: Edwards, 1790; new edition Bulmer, 1801) and then added a second collection, "intended to supply a chasm" in the earlier collection," *Specimens of Early English Metrical Romances* (London: Longman, 1805), p. iii. Each volume includes a "historical sketch" to contextualize the specimens in question. Also widely influential was Robert Southey's sequel to Ellis's work: *Specimens of the Later English Poets,* 3 vols. (London: Longman, 1807), which Longman's issued with George Burnet, *Specimens of English Prose Writers* (London: Longman, 1807), and Charles Lamb, *Specimens of English Dramatic Poets Who Lived about the Time of Shakespeare* (London: Routledge, 1808). Eventually, the format was also applied to national literary cultures other than English: see *Speci-*

lished as an appropriate specimen of a culture. In pursuing the question, I shall be considering the correspondences between these two moments of historicism (Romantic and poststructuralist) as they form along a contradiction internal, as it were, to the concept of cultural representation itself. This problematic may be glimpsed in the syntactical ambiguity of that phrase, "text of culture," which can be taken either in the genitive or dative senses—i.e., to indicate either a text that belongs to a culture or a culture that can be taken as a text. I shall be referring to this ambiguity as a tension between the "representative" and the "representational" aspects of modern representation, a distinction loosely analogous to the one that Gayatri Spivak has recently made between the activities of *Vertretung* and *Darstellung* in Marx's *Eighteenth Brumaire*—or, as she reformulates it, between the figures of "proxy" and "portrait."[3]

Let me try to concretize these concerns in more recognizable formulations by juxtaposing passages from two of the discussions of historiography I mentioned at the end of the previous chapter. One is from the 1988 essay by Carlo Ginzburg that reflects on recent developments in the new historiography he sees deriving from the historical novel. The other is from the 1828 essay by Thomas Babington Macaulay that projects a new historiography he wishes to see derived from the historical novel. Here first is Ginzburg, writing apropos of the work of Natalie Zemon Davis:

> Davis polemically reminds us that those historians who tend to portray the men of the peasantry (and with even greater reason, peasant women) of this period as individuals almost devoid of freedom of choice, object to Davis's position since it arises from an exceptional case which, therefore, can hardly be considered representative—playing on the ambiguity between the statistically representative (true or presumed) and the historically representative. In reality, the argument should be reversed: it is precisely the exceptional nature of the case of Martin Guerre that throws some light on a normalcy that proves elusive to documentation. Inversely, analogous situations contribute in the integration, through various means, of the *lacunae* in the events Davis has set herself the task of reconstructing: "When I could not find my individual man or woman in Hendaye, in Artigat, in Sajas, or in Burgos, then I did my best through other sources from the period and place to discover the world they would have seen and the reactions they might have had."[4]

---

mens of the German Lyric Poets (London: Boosey and Sons, 1822). As early as 1786, one can find a pair of sermons published together under a title that interestingly anticipates the notion of the specimen of the spirit of the age, but without the historical dimension emphasized: Richard Challoner, ed., *A Specimen of the Spirit of the Dissenting Teachers* (London: Printed for Thomas Meighan, 1736).

3. Gayatri Spivak, "Can the Subaltern Speak?" in *Marxism and the Interpretation of Culture,* ed. Cary Nelson and Lawrence Grossberg (Urbana: University of Illinois Press, 1988), pp. 271–313.

4. Carlo Ginzburg, "Proofs and Possibilities: In the Margins of Natalie Zemon Davis' *The Return of Martin Guerre,*" *Yearbook of Comparative and General Literature* 37 (November 1988): p. 116. All page references will hereafter appear in the text.

Ginzburg invokes Davis's writings both to endorse and to revise them, at once praising her historiographical practice and disputing her characterization of it as "in part [her] invention" (p. 116). Invention is the wrong term, says Ginzburg, because it misses what is crucial about the "margin of uncertainty" in a study that, for the historian (as not for the judge), can have more than a "purely negative significance" (p. 117). For the historian, far from drifting "into a *non liquet*—in modern parlance, a dismissal for insufficient proof"—this uncertainty can actually have the effect of "a deepening of the investigation uniting the specific case to the context"[5] (p. 117). For Ginzburg, a historical culture—the world characteristically seen and reactions characteristically experienced in what Davis calls a "period and place"—is constituted in respect to "a normalcy that proves elusive to documentation" (p. 116). To acknowledge this elusiveness, what Ginzburg elsewhere describes as the double-sided character of the historian's evidence,[6] is to begin to come to terms with the problem of historical culture as he understands it.

Here is the counterpart passage from Macaulay's 1828 programmatic remarks on history in the *Edinburgh Review:*

> The perfect historian is he in whose work the character and spirit of an age is exhibited in miniature. He relates no fact, he attributes no expression to his characters, which is not authenticated by sufficient testimony. But by judicious selection, rejection, and arrangement, he gives to truth those attractions which have been usurped by fiction. In his narrative a due subordination is observed; some transactions are prominent, others retire. But the scale on which he represents them is increased or diminished, not according to the dignity of the persons concerned in them, but according to the degree in which they elucidate the condition of society and the nature of man. . . . The changes in manners will be indicated, not merely by a few general phrases, or a few extracts from statistical documents, but by appropriate images presented in every line.[7]

I do not suggest here that Macaulay and Ginzburg are making the same point, nor that their terminology tallies throughout. Macaulay, for instance, like most western European writers on history in the late eighteenth and early nineteenth centuries, still sees fit to articulate his historicism in relation to something he is willing to call "human nature," a term that, as we shall see, becomes problematic in subsequent debates about historicism. The utility of the comparison lies rather in the way it illustrates a common interest in the problem of what it means to refer, in Ginzburg's phrase, to the "historically representative" as such.

5. See Ginzburg's elaboration of this relationship in "The Historian as Judge," in *Questions of Evidence: Proof, Practice, and Persuasion Across the Disciplines,* ed. James Chandler, Arnold Davidson, and Harry Harootunian (Chicago: University of Chicago Press, 1994), pp. 290–303.

6. Ginzburg, "The Historian as Judge," p. 295.

7. Macaulay, "Review of Henry Neale's *The Romance of History," The Edinburgh Review* 47 (May 1828): 364–65.

The problem can be cast in different ways: as the issue of fictional against nonfictional representation or as the issue of historical representativeness against statistical representativeness. Ginzburg and Macaulay do more than broach, programmatically, the use of fiction in representing historical cultures. They also recognize how such an undertaking might be complicated by a distinction between the representational and the representative and, ultimately, by what follows politically the necessary partiality of historical representation in any form. One can thus hear in both Ginzburg's and Macaulay's comments on history the overtones of what might be called a "politics of representation": Ginzburg's praise for Davis's representation of peasants as possessed of "freedom of choice" and Macaulay's insistence that the scale of historical representations should not depend on the assumed "dignity of the persons concerned in them." Indeed, as Hanna Pitkin has shown, it is difficult to discuss what she calls "the concept of representation" without repeated reference to *political* representation in modern history and theory.[8]

In brief, then, where in the previous chapter I was concerned with the historical invention of the concept of historical culture as such, here I will be concerned with the notions or practices of representation that attend and extend that invention. To suggest a way into this discussion through the idiom of current cultural criticism, I will begin by revisiting the project of one of cultural studies' earliest and most politically oriented theorists, Raymond Williams, who did so much to set, and indeed to historicize, the terms of current practice.

1. Keywords: Culture, Representation, Anecdote

Williams's contribution to the return to history in literary studies is large and complicated. In *Keywords* and elsewhere, he produced a series of analyses of the history and concept of "culture," the term that formed the key to all others in the core lexicon.[9] This work of the mid-1970s remained consistent with Williams's earliest major publications from the 1950s in its tracing of the genealogy of this concept and its most closely related terms to what I have been

8. See Hanna Fenichel Pitkin, *The Concept of Representation* (Berkeley: University of California Press, 1967), especially pp. 244–52. See also, for example, Catherine Gallagher on "The Politics of Representation and the Representation of Politics in the 1840s," in *The Industrial Revolution of English Fiction* (Chicago: University of Chicago Press, 1985), pp. 187–218; and Stuart Hall, on "the shift of the character of representation," in "The Rise of the Representative/Interventionist State: 1880s–1920s," in *State and Society in Contemporary Britain,* ed. Gregar McLennan, David Held, and Stuart Hall (Cambridge: Polity Press, 1984), p. 7.

9. See Raymond Williams, *Keywords: A Vocabulary of Culture and Society* (New York: Oxford University Press, 1976), pp. 76–82. See also his *Marxism and Literature* (New York: Oxford University Press, 1977), pp. 11–20.

calling "the age of the spirit of the age" in Britain. The fundamental historical claim was explicitly formulated in the very opening sentence of *Culture and Society* (1958): "In the last decades of the eighteenth century, and in the first half of the nineteenth century, a number of words, which are now of capital importance, came for the first time into common English use, . . . or acquired new and important meanings."[10] The primary cluster of terms is "industry," "democracy," "class," "art," and "culture," but there is a repeated emphasis on the last of them. "The development of *culture* is perhaps the most striking," writes Williams; indeed, insofar as the terms form mutual connections, the term "which more than any other comprises these relations is *culture*."[11] Opening *Marxism and Literature* almost twenty years later, Williams effectively declared its continuity with the earlier project: "At the very centre of a major area of modern thought and practice, which it is habitually used to describe, is a concept, 'culture,' which in itself, through variation and complication, embodies not only the issues but the contradictions through which it has developed."[12] While the word "history" is not on Williams's list of those keywords he sees undergoing transformation in the late eighteenth and early nineteenth centuries, he emphatically relates the new conception of culture to that same Marxian notion of "men making their own histories" that became such a bone of contention at about the same time in the debate between Sartre and Lévi-Strauss.[13]

Certainly the emphasis on "culture" as a changing and specifiable state of affairs with a decisively differentiating power in shaping the conditions of human experience and productivity is crucial to the dating of Romantic historicism with which I have been working. That is why, in discussing Anna Barbauld, for example, I stressed her attention to the relativity of manners, customs, norms, and ways of life in both *Eighteen Hundred and Eleven* and "The

10. Raymond Williams, *Culture and Society* (New York: Columbia University Press, 1958), p. xi.

11. Ibid., p. xiv.

12. Williams, *Marxism and Literature*, p. 11. These "contradictions" involve the oppositions between "high" and "low" culture, between culture as process and as state, between culture as an internal or external condition of individual human development, and between culture as identified with and as opposed to "civilization," and so on.

13. The notion, says Williams, "of 'man making his own history' was given a new radical content by this emphasis on 'man making himself' through producing his own means of life"— *Marxism and Literature*, p. 19. There is a larger story to tell here about the relation of Williams's cultural Marxism to the Sartrean project, a relation Williams himself attests in his review of the *Critique of Dialectical Reason*. It is hard not to conclude, for example, that Williams's well-known stress on "lived experience" derives in a crucial way from Sartre's equally central concept of "l'expérience vecue," and, when the connection was pointed out to Williams by the *New Left Review* interview team, he acknowledged its justice—see Williams's *Politics and Letters: Interviews with New Left Review* (London: Verso, 1979), p. 168.

Uses of History." It is not by itself Barbauld's metaphor of chronology and geography as the "two eyes of history" that marks her theorization of the "date of place" as belonging to the age of the spirit of the age. That metaphor, indeed, is much older, itself dating to the pioneering era of work on chronology by Joseph Scaliger and others in the Italian Renaissance.[14] What is new about these later formulations—especially with respect to the circulation of public discourse—is the way in which what Williams identifies as "culture" is defined in terms of such metaphors. What is new is the way in which the proverbial link between chronology and geography is refashioned as the gaugeable but contradictory system of equivalencies between the objects of study in the mutually constituting fields of historiography and ethnography.

In recognizing the changing status of culture in the Romantic period—its new state—we must not ignore that other, more familiar sense of the term "state," the political sense, which also undergoes serious transformation in the late eighteenth and early nineteenth centuries. Indeed, what I have described as the mutual constitution of the ethnographic and historiographic fields in terms of state of society was itself often carried out in relation to the celebrated debates over political constitutions of "states" in this same period. "Democracy," after all, is one of those four other "keywords" Williams identifies as being intimately connected with the historical emergence of the concept of culture. To be reminded of these debates, however, and not least the massive and heated debate that came to a head in Britain around the time of Peterloo in 1819, is to recall a keyword— "representation"—that newly assumes importance in and for the historical period to which Williams refers.[15]

This word *representation* does not appear on Williams's short list of crucial terms in *Culture and Society,* nor even on his longest list of several dozen such words in the index to that work. The absence seems even more striking if one

14. Anthony Grafton, *Joseph Scaliger.* Vol. 2: *Historical Chronology* (Oxford: Clarendon Press, 1993), p. 139. For a discussion of the new sense of chronology in early modern England, see Claire McEachern, *The Poetics of English Nationhood* (Cambridge: Cambridge University Press, 1996), p. 179. For subsequent developments in chronological awareness as they bear on English literary history, see Paul K. Alkon, *Defoe and Fictional Time* (Athens: University of Georgia Press, 1979), and Stuart Sherman, *Telling Time. Clocks, Diaries, and English Diurnal Form, 1680–1785* (Chicago: University of Chicago Press, 1996).

15. See, for example, Habermas on new forms of "representative publicity" in the early nineteenth century in *The Structural Transformation of the Public Sphere,* trans. Thomas Burger (Cambridge, Mass.: MIT Press, 1989), pp. 136–140; Jon Klancher on "Radical Representations" in the Romantic period in *The Making of English Reading Audiences, 1790–1832* (Madison: University of Wisconsin Press, 1987), pp. 98–134; Keith Baker, on "Representation Redefined," in *Inventing the French Revolution* (Cambridge: Cambridge University Press, 1990), pp. 224–51; and Dror Wahrman, "Virtual Representation: Parliamentary Reporting and Languages of Class in the 1790s," *Past and Present* 136 (August 1992): 83–113.

recalls that the book begins with a chapter on Burke and Cobbett, whose most telling political writings often amount to sustained reflection on the cultural, economic, and political dimensions of the question, to cite Richard Price, of England's "adequate representation."[16] Over the course of the three decades after the French Revolution, in a number of crucial British writings, it becomes difficult to distinguish the problem of representing a particular state of society from the problem of establishing or maintaining the appropriate monetary or political representation of the *state* itself. In hindsight, and in light of the prominence that term has assumed in cultural-historical studies, we are now as never before alert to the foregrounding of the term "representation" in Burke's *Reflections on the Revolution in France,* or Cobbett's *Paper Against Gold,* or, to take a text of 1819, Shelley's *Philosophical View of Reform.* We must recall, however, that, in books like *Culture and Society,* Williams explicitly tried to focus on words that were for him of "capital importance" not only in the Romantic period but also in his own moment. Since "representation" had not yet come into its own as a critical term in the late 1950s, its omission is perhaps understandable. No one, I assume, would want to deny that the term has been crucial in the post-1970s wave of work carried out under the slogan of the "return to history."[17] The task that Williams left largely unaddressed, therefore, is precisely that of how to understand the problematic of "representation" as it relates to the kind of history and theory of "culture" that his own work so authoritatively established.

There have been efforts in this direction since Williams completed his major work. In addition to Jameson's self-parodic discussion of exemplification in the new historicism, other critiques have appeared, some of them also self-parodic, though often formulated in somewhat different terms—the terms of "detailism" or "localism," for example.[18] My approach here responds in part to

16. I have discussed these aspects of representation in the period elsewhere. See especially "Poetical Liberties: Burke's France and the 'Adequate Representation' of the English," in *The Transformation of Political Culture 1789–1848,* ed. François Furet and Mona Ozouf. Vol. 3 in *The French Revolution and Modern Political Culture* (Oxford: Pergamon Press, 1989), pp. 45–58, and "Ricardo and the Poets: Representing Commonwealth in the Year of Peterloo," *The Wordsworth Circle* 25 (spring 1994): 82–86.

17. It seems indeed inevitable in retrospect that when those scholars whom Jameson singles out as exemplifying the new historicism—Greenblatt, Michaels, and Gallagher—formed a journal in the late 1970s they chose *Representations* for its title.

18. See Naomi Schor, *Reading in Detail: Aesthetics and the Feminine* (New York: Methuen, 1987), passim; Alan Liu, "Local Transcendence: Cultural Criticism, Postmodernism, and the Romanticism of Detail," *Representations* 32 (fall 1990): 83–96; and, more recently, David Simpson, who builds on Liu to link the language of the anecdote with the language of detail in *The Academic Postmodern and the Rule of Literature* (Chicago: University of Chicago Press, 1995), passim. Liu's self-consciously postmodern meditation on the ubiquity of "unit-detail atomism" in con-

a tendency that some observers have found especially vexing in contemporary critical practice. For when it comes to the representational practices of literary-cultural studies carried out under the sign of the "return to history," one of the most frequently recurring questions has to do with its resort to anecdote. The question has perhaps been most wittily posed and pursued in the late Joel Fineman's "History of the Anecdote," a prolegomenon to some future study of Greenblatt's celebrated essay, "Fiction and Friction," where (says Fineman) Greenblatt "anecdotally collates traditional, Galenic, gynecological medical theory with a reading of Shakespeare's *Twelfth Night*" in such a way as to "exemplify" the relation of "New Historicism" to both "literature" and "history" as such.[19] Brushing aside contemporary genealogies of Greenblatt's modus operandi, Fineman traces the history of the anecdote in historiography back to the treatment of the "historically representative" in Thucydides, arguing that the anecdote, as "a specific literary form" is important "because [it] determines the destiny of a specifically historiographic integration of event and context."[20] The representational importance of the anecdote, for Fineman, is that it is, as he says, the "literary form or genre that uniquely refers to the real"; indeed, what he calls the "thesis" of his mock-virtuoso meditation is the claim "that the anecdote is the literary form that uniquely *lets history happen* by virtue of the way it introduces an opening into the teleological, and therefore timeless, narration of beginning, middle and end."[21] In this dialectic, the opening of history that is effected by the anecdote, the "hole" within the totalizing "whole," is plugged up by a teleological narrative that must itself be reopened by anecdote, plugged up again, and so on.

Even as it points to the lack of methodological reflection in the New Historicism, Fineman's analysis sometimes seems, without saying so, to be reading through Greenblatt's work to a methodological text that lies behind it, Kenneth Burke's *A Grammar of Motives*. To see how, we must recall one of Greenblatt's earliest successes in the mode of anecdote-triggered cultural analysis—the final

---

temporary criticism, and its relation to Romanticism, has been especially useful in working out the formulation or reformulation I attempt in what follows. Liu is interested in how "phrases in our matrix such as 'concretely situated,' 'the concrete, the material and the particular,' or 'ordinary, retail, detailed, concrete' build a world that is exactly concrete: a cement aggregate of specific and determinate particularity" (p. 84). It will be clear in what follows how I mean to shift the discussion of the local and concrete into the problematic of the representative anecdote and the dialectics of situationism.

19. Fineman, "The History of the Anecdote," in H. Aram Veeser, *The New Historicism* (London: Routledge, 1989), p. 49.

20. Ibid., p. 56. See below for Reinhart Koselleck's rather differently inflected account of Thucydides's relevance to the question of exemplarity.

21. Ibid., p. 61.

chapter of *Renaissance Self-Fashioning* in which he discusses *Othello* in terms of the "Improvisation of Power." This analysis is developed out of "an incident re-counted in 1525 by Peter Martyr," which concerns the conduct of some early Spanish adventurers in the Caribbean, who, having decimated the native pop-ulation of Hispaniola, visit neighboring islands in what are now the Bahamas to take slaves. Their method in this second, more subtle phase of conquest is to find out the mythic structure of the native cosmology, and, in a virtuoso piece of improvisation, offer themselves as having just arrived from the realms thought sacred by this people for the purpose of taking them there to live in splendor. The precise content of the narrative is less important here than the way it serves as the representative anecdote that provides Greenblatt with terms he claims are apposite for the cultural context of *Othello,* in which he shows Iago learning to improvise power along analogous lines.

In the course of this demonstration, Greenblatt produces a generous foot-note to *A Grammar of Motives,* citing Burke's discussion of *Othello* at some length and reporting as follows: "As so often happens, I discovered that Burke's brilliant sketch had anticipated the shape of much of my argument."[22] As it also happens in this instance, though, *A Grammar of Motives* is a book that makes the problematic of the anecdote—what Burke calls in one of his chapter headings the "representative anecdote"—quite crucial to its massively ambitious and cunningly idiosyncratic investigation. That investigation, for those who have forgotten its ambition or its idiosyncrasy, is self-described as an extended effort to answer the question: "What is involved when we say what people are doing and why they are doing it?" (GM, p. xv). Burke analyzes the forms of thought that are involved in the attribution of motives, in other words, and proceeds to develop, for the purpose, a system that he calls "dramatism." The five central terms of dramatism—act, scene, agent, agency, and purpose—are combined into "ratios," with different ratios being foregrounded and different terms pre-dominating in different philosophical approaches to the problem of motive. "Scene," for example, will be more prominent in materialist philosophies, "agent" in idealist ones.

The protocols of dramatism are described from a number of angles in Burke's protean book, but the relevant description here is the one given in the section on "The Representative Anecdote." "Dramatism," writes Burke, "sug-gests a procedure to be followed in the development of a given calculus, or ter-minology. It involves the search for a 'representative anecdote,' to be used as a

---

22. Greenblatt, *Renaissance Self-Fashioning* (Chicago: University of Chicago Press, 1980), p. 306.

form in conformity with which the vocabulary is constructed. . . . The anecdote is in a sense a *summation,* containing implicitly what the system that is developed from it contains explicitly" (GM, pp. 60–61). The centrality of the notion in Burke's overall project emerges quite powerfully, I think, as Burke proceeds. This "question of the 'representative anecdote,'" he declares at one point, is "itself so dramatistic a conception that we might call it the dramatistic approach to dramatism" (GM, p. 60). The criterion of "representativeness" looms large in Burke's discussion because, as he puts it, "if one does not select a representative anecdote as an introductory form, in conformity with which to select and shape his terms of analysis, one cannot expect to get representative terms" (GM, p. 60). We may well ask: terms representative of what? The answer, which suggests the dialectical character of Burke's argument, is that the terms generated from the representative anecdote must be representative of the subject matter these terms "are designed to calculate."

Burke's dialectic of the anecdote, like Fineman's, turns on a kind of protodeconstructive word play between his description of the representative instance or event and his description of the representational apparatus or framework. Thus, Fineman can insist: "Only through the mutual coordination of a particular event and a generalizing narrative context—a coordination such that the particularity of the *touto,* the 'this,' and the generic, representative urgency of the logic of the *meta* reciprocally will call each other up—is it possible to identify or to attribute an historical significance either to a "this" or to a *meta,* for they co-constitute or co-imply each other."[23] With this dialectic of the representative and the representational, we find ourselves returned to the paranomasia of the phrase, "the text of culture" or, alternatively, to the problem of the "specific" in history as formulated in Paul Veyne's Lévi-Strauss–inspired analysis, where to specify is both to show and to choose. It is a problem Kenneth Burke summarizes with characteristically aphoristic force in *A Grammar of Motives:* "Men seek for vocabularies that will be faithful *reflections* of reality. To this end, they must develop vocabularies that are *selections* of reality" (italics original) (p. 59). The relationship between the mimetic and synecdochic moments of representation is crucial to Burke's critical effort to identify "attitudes toward history" in the cultural texts he considers, and partly through his works it became crucial to much of the work in literary and cultural studies' return to history.[24] But since I have argued that this recent return to history involves,

23. Fineman, "History of Anecdote," p. 53.
24. I echo the title of Burke's great work of the decade before he published *The Philosophy of Literary Form* and *A Grammar of Motives: Attitudes Toward History* (1937; Los Altos, Calif.: Hermes, 1959).

precisely, a return to Romantic historicism of a certain sort, I must now show evidence of a corresponding dynamic in an account of historical representation I have identified as Romantic.[25]

Since the notion of Romanticism I have been considering is so much a part of the early nineteenth-century phenomenon of the historical novel, and perhaps vice versa, there is perhaps no better place to look for the dialectical play of cultural representation, and indeed to show its relation to the operations of the historicist's code, than in Scott's 1819 Dedicatory Epistle to *Ivanhoe*. This, as we have seen, is Scott's playful attempt to theorize the genre of the historical novel on the occasion of his turn, in 1819, from the early sequence of novels about the history of Scotland to a novel about the English past. In other words, having relied on Scott's 1819 Dedicatory Epistle to note how historical specificity is *conceived* within Romantic historicism, it remains for us to see how it is *represented* there. The passage in question is one that explicitly concerns the problem of representing—from within the discursive framework of uneven development—the differences that Scott emphasizes between the respective rates of social development in Scotland and England.

2. The Romantic Type

The Dedicatory Epistle appended to *Ivanhoe* is addressed by the fictive author of the narrative, Lawrence Templeton, to an English antiquarian, the Rev. Dr. Dryasdust, in reference to a prior conversation of theirs in which Dryasdust was

25. I do not, in what follows, try to correlate explicitly the contemporary historicist interest in anecdotes with the spreading practice of writing literary anecdotes in the late eighteenth century, but, as with the notion of the "literary specimen," the literary anecdote rises quickly in popularity and begins to appear all over the culture of early British Romanticism. Indeed, one of the key players in the debate about Pope's place in Campbell's *Specimens* of 1819, Isaac Disraeli, published an early and influential volume, *Curiosities of Literature: Consisting of Anecdotes, Characters, Sketches, and Observation, Literary, Critical, and Historical*, 2 vols. (London: John Murray, 1792). Disraeli later made an important contribution to the debate about Pope in his 1820 review of Joseph Spence's *Anecdotes of Books and Men*—see chapter 7 below. Other such projects include John Almon, *Biographical, Literary, and Political Anecdotes, of Several of the Most Eminent Persons of the Present Age* (London: Longman, 1797); Thomas Leman Rede, *Anecdotes and Biography*, 2d ed. (London: Myers, 1799); and the major series of compilations stretching over much of the period, beginning with John Nichols, *Anecdotes, Biographical and Literary* (London: Nichols, 1778) and stretching through at least nine volumes over the next four decades. In the 1815 volume *Anecdotes*, Nichols offered an account of the genre: "It is not a regular History—it is not a Romantic Tale—nor a Work of Fancy . . . . It is a Mine of literary materials, whence future Biographers and Historians will readily and sparingly collect what may suit their several purposes" (9:1v.). The period of Scott's historical novels is also a time when earlier compilations were newly published. One such miner of materials was Thomas Moore, who recorded spending a late December day in 1818 reading "King's Anecdotes of his own Times, just published by Murray" (JTM, 1:102). See William King, *Poetical and Literary Anecdotes of His Own Times* (London: John Murray, 1818).

critical of the highly popular historical novels about the Scottish past by the Author of *Waverley*. Early in the letter, Templeton reminds Dryasdust that he (Templeton) had speculated on the possibility of attempting such a work and giving it a setting in the *English* past—"to obtain an interest for the traditions and manners of Old England, similar to that which has been obtained in behalf of those of our poorer and less celebrated neighbours" (Iv, Ded. Ep.). In his conversational response to this revelation, Dryasdust had emphasized the disparity of tasks. "You insisted," Templeton reminds him, "upon the advantages which the Scotsman possessed from the very recent existence of that state of society in which his scene was to be laid" (Ded. Ep.). This comment is couched very much in the new idiom of the historian's code, as I have discussed it, in that it understands "recentness" in a temporality other than that of the succession of "states" themselves, invoking instead the terms of calendrical or homogeneous empty time.

One manifestation of the problem posed for the English side of this imagined contest is that, in having to go back so many more generations in pursuing an appropriately anterior state of culture, the English novelist must work from written sources rather than from oral memory. In England, argues Templeton, "civilization has been so long complete, that our ideas of our ancestors are only to be gleaned from musty records and chronicles," and thus to "match an English and a Scottish author in the rival task of embodying and reviving the traditions of their respective countries, would be, you alleged, in the highest degree unequal and unjust" (Ded. Ep.). Dryasdust's metaphor of "embodying and reviving" national traditions under different historical circumstances is elaborated into a complex allegory enriched by an allusive frame of reference. The allegory figures the larger point that the matching of English and Scottish historical novels—i.e., the comparison of historical novelists who attempt to represent equivalent states in different cultures—is "unequal and unjust." Figuring its point as it does, moreover, the allegory also supplies a revealing textual register for some of the contradictions Scott is negotiating in his new historical fiction. For example, although Templeton speaks of "embodying and reviving" as if they were distinct but related activities of the historical novelist, in the allegory the task of historical embodiment threatens to dissolve into the task of revivification, as if there were plenty of bodies but not enough life to breathe into them.

In those opening paragraphs of *The Eighteenth Brumaire,* which have provided such sanction for recent cultural history, Marx made much of the slogan: "Let the dead bury the dead." Scott, in effect, produces the converse injunction—to let the living revive the dead. Thus, in extending his rehearsal of the prior exchange with Dryasdust, Templeton recalls an elaborate and macabre conceit:

> The Scottish magician, you say, was, like Lucan's witch, at liberty to walk over the recent field of battle, and to select for the subject of resuscitation by his sorceries, a body whose limbs had recently quivered with existence, and whose throat had but just uttered the last note of agony. Such a subject even the powerful Erictho was compelled to select. . . . The English author, on the other hand, without supposing him less of a conjurer than the Northern Warlock, can, you observed, only have the liberty of selecting his subject amidst the dust of antiquity, where nothing was to be found but dry, sapless, mouldering, and disjointed bones, such as those which filled the valley of Jehoshaphet. (Iv, Ded. Ep.)

The secondary allusion here is Biblical and seems to be a composite reference to two different passages: one in Ezekiel, on the miraculous revivification of a living body from dusty bones—"Can these dry bones live?"—the other from Joel on the Valley of Jehosaphat. The primary and more recondite allusion is to Lucan's *Pharsalia* (translated as *The Civil War*), a verse history of internecine conflict in the Roman Empire after Pompey the Great. In the aftermath of a particularly vicious battle, Sextus senses that the decisive event of the war may be at hand and seeks prognostic help from the witch Erictho, a powerful and loathsome necromancer whose "tread blights the seeds of the fertile cornfield" and whose "breath poisons the air." Eschewing the more usual and permissible means of augury in favor of bringing a body back to life and forcing it to yield a clear prediction, Erictho can promise Sextus that "no dismal ghost, whose limbs are dried up by the sun, will gibber sounds unintelligible to our ears" but rather that, by her power, "the mouth of a corpse still warm and freshly slain will speak with substantial utterance."[26] The step in Erictho's grotesque ritual that Scott invokes is the first, where she moves among the deliberately unburied dead on the field of the recent battle to choose the corpse best suited to her ends.[27] Writing within short weeks of Scott's composition of the Epistle, at the end of 1819, Shelley had figured the "glorious phantom" of the spirit of the age arising from the "graves" of contemporary conditions understood as passed

---

26. Lucan, *The Civil War* (Pharsalia), trans. J. D. Duff (Cambridge, Mass.: Harvard University Press, 1977), p. 349.

27. It would be well worth pursuing the displacement of Culloden from *Waverley,* where one would have expected it to have been treated. In the context of Templeton's discussion of the recent histories of unevenness between England and Scotland, it is difficult (one can note parenthetically) not to hear in it echoes of the Scottish reaction to the Clansmen who were slaughtered and denied burial by the Duke of Cumberland's orders at Culloden Moor in 1746, the decisive battle in the '45 Rebellion. The English title of Lucan's text is *The Civil War* and the '45 is of course the Civil War that involved the two "countries" whose development Scott is comparing in the Epistle and that, on Scott's own account, defined the conditions of his historiographical practice. For an excellent narrative history of these events see John Prebble, *Culloden* (Harmondsworth: Penguin, 1967).

away. Here Scott imagines the bodies themselves as requiring the life-breath of the historical necromancer.

Three aspects of the Epistle's allegorical complexity deserve special consideration in relation to the new historicism it means to figure.[28] The first involves Templeton's account of the respective "liberties" afforded to the Scottish and English historian. Curiously, the freedom of the one and constraint on the other do not stand in a straightforward relationship of opposition. Templeton's point, though couched in the macabre details of military carnage, might be said to depend on a familiar Rousseauist paradox about civil society: that we must be forced to be free. The Scottish novelist, working on a state of antiquity sufficiently recent in chronicle time, is free to be forced, by the recentness and intactness of the remains he confronts, to choose a "subject," whereas the English novelist, working on an equivalent state more remote in chronicle time, is free to be unconstrained in his selection. It is as if Scott were attempting to unfold the paradoxes implicit in Edmund Burke's famous claim that in their form of constitutional representation the British have made a "choice of inheritance."[29]

We will realize that Scott's sophisticated play with the problem of representing national culture does not stop here—and this becomes the second point— if we ask ourselves the question: How ought one to understand the metaphor of the "field" on which the historical novelist's "subject" lies? When Templeton quotes Dryasdust on the problem faced by the English historical novelist, he speaks of embodying and reviving national traditions. If one thinks of a chosen "body," a selected "subject," as a representation of a tradition, then one might think of the "field" in question as the entire expanse of the national past from which one tradition rather than another is chosen. But if one thinks of the chosen body as a "representative" of a moment or stage of past culture, as the overall logic of the analogy seems to suggest, then the "subject" might be understood as the instance that best speaks for the "field" of the anterior culture in question. But (and this is the third point) more than one kind of "speaking for" or "representation" is in play in the comparison between the Scottish and English historians. It seems that, for the former, the body hails you, as it were, asking

---

28. One aspect of this passage I will not address here, but will return to implicitly in discussing *The Bride of Lammermoor* in chapter 5, is Scott's suppression of the future orientation of Erichtho's necromancy. This suppression crucially excludes Scott from participating in the mode of historicized casuistry that I shall be discussing in Bentham and Shelley toward the conclusion of this chapter.

29. Edmund Burke, *Reflections on the Revolution in France*, p. 16. On Scott and Burke, see, for example, Alexander Welsh, *The Hero of the Waverley Novels* (1963; Princeton, N.J.: Princeton University Press, 1993), pp. 68–77.

to be the *representative* of your subject, whereas, for the latter, the body has to be composed, or recomposed, to make up a *representation* of the past you seek to portray.

Such ambiguities are left undeveloped (and certainly unresolved) in Scott's text, wavering in discursive space between the contradictory aspects of the new concept of historical representation. The very presence of these ambiguities, however, helps us to see the new framework in its incipient form. It must have been some such recognition that prompted Lukács to turn to this same Dedicatory Epistle at the conclusion of his celebrated explication of the historical novel's "classical form," which he gives Scott primary credit for having worked out. In Lukács's account, Scott portrays "the struggles and antagonisms of history by means of characters who, in their psychology and destiny, always represent social trends and historical forces" (p. 34). What Lukács grandly, but not inaccurately, calls the "change which Scott effects in the history of world literature" is thus said to lie "in his novelistic capacity to give living human embodiment to historical-social types" (p. 35). For Lukács, this strategy of embodiment-typification allows Scott to supply what had been lacking in the fiction that preceded him: precisely the element of historical specificity that, as we have seen, Lukács identifies with the derivation of the individuality of characters from the peculiarity of their age. It is this same strategy, I will argue below, that governs Lukács's own representation of Scott as the embodiment of the historical consciousness of his *own* "age," the aftermath of the Napoleonic wars. The ambiguities we have noted, however, raise vexing questions as to which came first, the characters or the age, the bodies or the type. Which is only to say that "historical representation" in our contemporary vocabulary is a difficult notion with a complicated genealogy in which the moment of Romantic historicism must be understood as seminal.

On some accounts, the problem of historical representation is simply the problem of modernity—not that modernity itself can be simple. Heidegger, for example, in his account of the relation between epochal consciousness and representation, argued for identifying the modern age precisely by its development of the age-defining world picture: "The world picture does not change from an earlier medieval one into a modern one, but rather the fact that the world becomes a picture at all is what distinguishes the essence of the modern age."[30] Heidegger speculates that such a picture emerges with the Cartesian analysis of subject-object relations, but eventually his dating falls into line

---

30. In Martin Heidegger, *The Question Concerning Technology and Other Essays,* trans. William Lovitt (New York and London: Garland, 1977), p. 130.

with most other commentators on the history of historicism as he goes on to suggest that the age-defining function of the world picture becomes a major preoccupation only in the decades following the French Revolution. This is the period, says Heidegger, when the "increasing rootedness of the world in anthropology, which has set in since the end of the eighteenth century, finds its expression in the fact that the fundamental stance of man in relation to what is, in its entirety, is defined as a world view."[31] For Heidegger, this stance, with its concomitant forcing back of "what is" into "this relationship to oneself as the normative realm," is precisely the stance of "representation" in the modern sense.[32] In such an account, Romantic historicism would *be* the moment of modernity, and a similar conclusion seems to follow from Lukács's argument in *The Historical Novel*. In both accounts, though, one can sense that tension allegorized in Scott's figure of Erictho between the pictorial and the exemplary in modern representation—that is, between the mimetic and the synecdochic, or (as in Kenneth Burke) between a "reflection" and a "selection" of reality. An analogous distinction, as I noted earlier, appears in Gayatri Spivak's discussion of the difference between "portrait" and "proxy" in relation to the problem of sub-altern representation. Although she does not orient these terms in relation either to Romanticism or modernity, Spivak's particular formulations prove especially helpful in tracing Romantic-historicist genealogies for the idiom of cultural representation in recent criticism. I will presently show how the provocative writings on the spirit of the age by Hazlitt and Shelley, very much a part of England in 1819, invoke, respectively, the metaphorics of portrait and proxy in their reflections on the historical revolution of their time. To prepare for those discussions, however, a further word of clarification is in order about the twin relationships that emerge in the modernity of Romantic historicism between the conceptions of epoch and example and between the practices of periodization and representation.

One of the most suggestive of recent commentaries on historicism-as-modernity, Koselleck's survey of changing interpretations of the time-honored slogan, *historia magistra vitae,* considers the fate of the age-old assumption that "history teaches by example." It was a settled-enough assumption, and

31. Ibid., p. 133.

32. "To represent means to bring what is present at hand, before oneself as something standing over against, to relate it to oneself, to the one representing it, and to force it back into this relationship to oneself as the normative realm"—ibid., p. 131. The significance of Heidegger's and Lukács's emphasis on the *normative* dimension of the new concept of the historical epoch will have to wait until chapter 4 below, where the problem of the historical representative or specimen is reformulated in terms of the history of casuistry and the historical transformation of the case.

one that students of English literature will recall from Sidney's *Apologie for Poetrie* (ca. 1580) where philosophy is said to teach by precept, history by example, and poetry by combining the two modes.[33] A familiar premodern European oeuvre in which philosophy teaches by precept and history by example would be Machiavelli's *The Prince* (ca. 1514), which seems to roam the available historical record to illustrate with concrete instances the precepts of effective historical leadership.[34] The central premise in such a project, as Koselleck puts it, is that "[w]here history indicates the possibility of repeatable events, it must be able to identify structural conditions sufficient for the creation of such an analogous event."[35] Koselleck argues that the possibility of such an identification in history comes increasingly to be challenged with the introduction of *Neuzeit*—the "new time" of modernity—and with those "theoretically enriched concepts of time" that contained "structural potential which cannot be reduced to the pure temporal succession of history."[36] As history comes to be defined by socially constituting movement and movements, moral exemplarity can no longer be understood to operate across period boundaries.[37]

To suggest a broad-brushed illustration of Koselleck's claim about the new paradigm, one might think of Hegel's comments in *The Philosophy of History*: "Rulers, statesmen and nations are often advised to learn the lesson of historical experience. But what experience and history teach is this—that nations and governments have never learned anything from history or acted upon any lessons they might have drawn from it. Each age and each nation finds itself in such peculiar circumstances, in such a unique situation, that it can and must make decisions with reference to itself alone."[38] The point is perhaps overstated

33. "The philosopher, therefore, and the historian are they which would win the goal, the one by precept, the other by example. But both, not having both, do both halt. . . . Now doth the peerless poet perform both," in *Sir Philip Sidney,* ed. Katherine Duncan-Jones (Oxford: Oxford University Press, 1989), p. 221. Even as he articulates the old paradigm, Sidney seems to anticipate the modern concept of representation in his account of how poetry achieves its ambitious goals. He defines the art of poetry as "imitation," which he in turn defines as "a representing," which he in turn defines as "a speaking picture." Speaking picture is very close to the idea of a portrait that can be a proxy in Spivak's attempt to answer the question "Can the Sub-Altern Speak?"

34. Kenneth Burke cites Machiavelli's relevant remarks from the *Discourses on Livy* about those who "read history without applying its lessons, 'as though heaven, the sun, the elements, and men had changed the order of their motions and power, and were different from what they were in ancient times'" (GM, p. 12).

35. Reinhart Koselleck, *Futures Past*, p. 114.

36. Ibid., p. 13. See above, chapter 2, for more on this aspect of Koselleck's argument.

37. Alexander Gelley cites Koselleck to similar effect in introducing a recent collection of essays he has edited on this subject, in *Unruly Examples: On the Rhetoric of Exemplarity* (Stanford, Calif.: Stanford University Press, 1995), pp. 4–6.

38. G. W. F. Hegel, "Introduction: "Reason in History," in *Lectures on the Philosophy of History,* trans. H. B. Nisbet (Cambridge: Cambridge University Press, 1975), p. 21. It is noteworthy for my

by Hegel, but the central issue is that teaching by example depends on iterability, and iterability depends in turn on sufficiently regular conditions of experience and practice.[39] With the new sense of how individual human character could be differentially derived from the peculiarities of different epochs, the iterability of history is dramatically reduced (if not exactly ruled out, as Hegel suggests), and so, therefore, is the possibility of direct instruction through examples from the historical past whether positively, in the form of encouraging emulation, or negatively, in the form of admonishing avoidance. Koselleck particularly stresses, even makes the chief burden of his argument, the key point that the dissolution of iterable exemplarity in *Neuzeit* does not spell the end of history's instructive function. History becomes the means of plotting the vector of structural change itself and thus of indicating the conditions of a possible future that cannot be derived solely from the sum of individual events. Koselleck does *not* stress, or even mention, the possibility that *Neuzeit* does not necessarily spell the end of historical exemplarity as such. Like its teaching function, the exemplifying function in history can indeed be understood as undergoing a transformation.[40]

While Koselleck's conception of exemplarity is classical in its provenance—in addition to Machiavelli, he also cites Thucydides as its own great exemplar—the role it plays in his account corresponds quite closely to Benedict Anderson's notion of the premodern adumbrational typology of the Judaeo-Christian tradition. Indeed, Koselleck assimilates the two traditions to one another when he

revision, below, of Lukács's account of Hegel's relation to Scott, that this passage closely follows Hegel's tendentious misreading of Scott's contribution to historiographical representation in which Hegel suggests that Scott failed to do exactly what, for example, Balzac soon gave Scott so much credit for achieving: capturing the "spirit of the age" in miniature through his narrative art—pp. 18–19.

39. Thus, the argument Koselleck is making tends to contradict Joel Fineman's witty enlistment of Thucydides in his own unruptured (or always already ruptured) "history of the anecdote," at the point where Fineman suggests that Thucydides' concept of the "historical representative" is consistent with the modern notion: "Thus it is, for famous example, that Thucydides can frankly admit that the versions he reports of the speeches delivered at one or another particular deliberative or forensic occasion are not verbatim records of what, in fact, was said, but are nevertheless historically representative, i.e., historical significant examples of what was called for, at the occasion, by the logic of events"—"The History of the Anecdote," p. 53.

40. The argument I have rehearsed from Koselleck was made in slightly different terms in Jameson's early commentary on Sartre's view of how the "scandal" that the "revolutionary event poses for academic historiography lies in the radically new type of event which it offers to historical narration": "In ordinary continuous life, the life of custom and tradition, nothing really changes or happens, there is basically nothing to tell in the narrative sense: there are only 'institutions' on the one hand, and the random stories of individual life on the other, which therefore lose even what existential density they possess and become mere *examples* of the former"—(italics Jameson's) *Marxism and Form,* p. 259.

claims that, in the new time of historicism both "providential anticipation and
the exemplarity of ancient histories fade away." Adapting terms at once from
Koselleck and Anderson, one might then say that as the notion of structural
change becomes definitive of historical temporality itself (what Koselleck elsewhere calls the recognition that events take place not only in but also through
history) then, while one no longer has exemplarity "along time" (to invoke
Anderson's distinction), one would now have exemplarity "across time." Hence
the figure, one might argue, of the culturally representative type and the corresponding "characteristics" and "signs" of the spirit of the age that indeed
emerge and develop rapidly through precisely the period Koselleck is emphasizing: 1770–1830. Periods themselves now have spirits that must be characteristically embodied, corpuses of writing that must be enlivened with a
characterizing spirit, bodies charged (in Shelley's resonant phrase) with "electric life."

3. Exemplary Histories and "Representative Men": Hazlitt's Prismatic Gallery

The very notion of the cultural-historical period, as it has taken shape in modern historiographical practice, seems to be a call for the employment of a representative who can serve as figurehead for the state of things in in given age but
who is precisely not a literal head of state. In pre-Romantic historiography,
when an "age" is identified in respect to a head of state—the Age of Elizabeth,
for example, or of Cromwell—it is normally not the case that the ruler in question is taken to be "representative" of his or her "age" in anything like the modern sense. Hume's *History of England* (1754–62), for example, includes
"Appendices" at the end of the various epochs into which it is divided, and
these appendices give descriptive, mainly synchronic, summaries of the states of
society during the long periods that constitute the major sections of the work:
e.g., "Feudal and Anglo-Norman Government and Manners." The chapters of
Hume's actual narrative of events, on the other hand, are normally entitled simply with the names of England's monarchs. The point is that, whereas the appendices single out no individuals to typify the state of government and
manners, the heads of state associated with sections of the narrative tend not to
be identified with a particular stage of culture. Eighteenth-century biographical writing corroborates the point from the obverse side. Dr. Johnson's *Lives of
the Poets* (1781–83) does not conspicuously offer the subjects of its biographies
as representatives or types of the times in which they lived. Thus, Leopold
Damrosch can argue from the sense that "Johnson's emphasis on the individuality of the imagination is . . . ideally suited to literary biography, rather than to

conventional literary history," to the following conclusion: "In the end, therefore, the subjects of Johnson's *Lives* [though dispersed across centuries] appear
as contemporaries in the fullness of literary achievement."[41] This notion of
"contemporaneity" across period boundaries ties Johnson to the prehistoricist
understanding of historical exemplarity.

The concept of the spirit of the age and the concept of the "representative
man" (in roughly Emerson's sense) thus began to gain currency together, as
functions of one another, and they did so in both England and Germany in the
decades around the turn of the century.[42] This has everything to do with the
changing notion of historical exemplification as I have elaborated it out of remarks by Koselleck and others. When Emerson himself took up this question
in the 1840s, working very much in the English and German traditions he had
learned from the likes of Carlyle, he did not (it must be conceded) consistently
offer his representative men as representative of their respective ages. When he
says, for example, that he admires "great men of all classes, those who stand
for facts, and for thoughts," he does not seem to have historical categories
in mind.[43] His chapters on Plato, Swedenborg, Montaigne, Shakespeare,
Napoleon, and Goethe are presented in that (nonchronological) order, and
their subtitles employ nonhistorical rubrics: the Philosopher, the Mystic, the
Poet, the Man of the World, and the Writer.

In the actual course of his discussions, however, Emerson does relate the two
nineteenth-century figures in the group primarily to the period in which they
lived: "I described Bonaparte as a representative of the popular external life and
aims of the nineteenth century. Its other half, its poet is Goethe."[44] With
Goethe, what is represented is specifically a cultural period, but neither the
sense in which it so appears nor the way in which Goethe is said to represent it
admits of facile application. Goethe, says Emerson, is

> a man quite domesticated in the century, breathing its air, enjoying its fruits, impossible at any
> earlier time, and taking away by his colossal parts the reproach of weakness, which, but for

41. Leopold Damrosch, *The Uses of Johnson's Criticism* (Charlottesville: University Press of
Virginia, 1976), p. 162.

42. See A. Dwight Culler's survey of emergent English cultural history in the early nineteenth century in *The Victorian Mirror of History* (New Haven: Yale University Press, 1985),
pp. 20–73; for more on the eighteenth-century context, see J. G. A. Pocock, *Virtue, Commerce, and
History* (Cambridge: Cambridge University Press, 1985). The two classic intellectual histories of
the larger subject are, of course, Friedrich Meinecke, *Historism: The Rise of a New Historical Out-
look,* trans. J. E. Anderson (New York: Herder and Herder, 1972), and R. G. Collingwood, *The
Idea of History* (Oxford: Oxford University Press, 1945).

43. Ralph Waldo Emerson, *Collected Works,* 5 vols. (Cambridge, Mass.: Harvard University
Press, 1971–94), 4:13.

44. Ibid., p. 156.

him, would lie on the intellectual works of the period. He appears at a time, when a general culture has spread itself, and has smoothed down all sharp individual traits; when, in the absence of heroic characters, a social comfort and cooperation have come in. There is no poet, but scores of poetic writers: no Columbus, but hundreds of post captains with transit-telescope, barometer, and concentrated soup and pemmican: no Demosthenes, no Chatham, but any number of clever parliamentary and forensic debaters;—no prophet or saint, but colleges of divinity; no learned men, but learned societies, a cheap press, readingrooms, and bookclubs, without number. There was never such a miscellany of facts. The world extends itself like American trade. We conceive Greek or Roman life, life in the Middle Ages, to be a simple and comprehensible affair; but modern life to respect a multitude of things which is distracting.

   Goethe was the philosopher of this multiplicity, hundred-handed, Argus-eyed, able and happy to cope with this rolling miscellany of facts and sciences, and, by his own versatility, to dispose of them with ease.[45]

Emerson's handling of Goethe in this, the last of the essays in his volume, thus opens up some of the paradoxes that abide in his notion of the culturally representative individual. Although Emerson's Goethe is the very "type of culture," culture turns out to be so general and spread out as to *require* heuristic epitomizing to become intelligible, legible. He is "the soul of his century," but his was the century of culture's soulless image. It is not that his stature is a summation of the greatness of his period. The age is not one of strength, and Goethe does not lend strength to it; he takes away its weakness. He is the individual capable of standing for an age that has smoothed down all "sharp individual traits."

   Emerson delivered his lectures in England, after much consultation with his mentor Carlyle, and in respect to such paradoxes this discussion certainly bears the marks of writings by both Carlyle and Mill about heroes, hero worship, characteristics, spirits of the age, and signs of the times. Carlyle saw his own age as defined by the penumbra of the French Revolution, but nothing characterizes Carlyle's history of that event so conspicuously (in view of its being written by the man of heroes) as its refusal to represent the Revolution by means of great representative individuals.[46] That Carlyle developed his theory of heroes in an age without them and that Emerson developed his theory of representative great men likewise out of a sense of *their* absence can be taken, perhaps, as another indication of the contradictions that attend the efforts to locate the spirit of the age in a representative body of writing.[47]

   45. Ibid., p. 156. It is Goethe with whom Karl J. Weintraub culminates *The Value of the Individual: Self and Circumstance in Autobiography* (Chicago: University of Chicago Press, 1978): "This whole process whereby an individuality comes to be a unique self, and at the same time a representative of its world, was for Goethe one that consumed a lifetime" (p. 367).
   46. Thomas Carlyle, *The French Revolution: A History.* Vols. 2–4 in *The Collected Works of Thomas Carlyle* (London: Chapman and Hall, 1896).
   47. Carlyle's links to German Idealism are well known, but for an account of his relation to the Scottish Enlightenment, see Robert Crawford, on Carlyle's so-called "Algemeine Mid-

This Romantic-historicist configuration of cultural epochs and exemplary corpuses has continued to structure the presentation of periods in cultural historiography into our own moment. I take it that that is not a point that needs belaboring in view of the hundreds of modern studies that have offered themselves as representations of the age of Chaucer, or of Galileo, or of Pope, Beethoven, or Cézanne. The emergence of such a paradigm in Romanticism has become a matter of explicit recognition on the part of Romanticists themselves in the last quarter century or so, thanks to the influential work of M. H. Abrams in *Natural Supernaturalism* and in the essays that preceded and followed it. Indeed, in showing the continuity between the contemporary field of criticism in which his own work participates and its historical object in the late eighteenth and early nineteenth centuries, Abrams's study might be said to anticipate the argument I am offering here. Among the ways this argument differs from Abrams's, the most crucial lies in its dissent from Abrams's program to assimilate British Romanticism to a Hegelian paradigm. It is in this respect, precisely, that Abrams made himself a target of historically oriented Romantic critics who, in understandably renouncing Abrams's paradigm, fail to acknowledge other possible or necessary relations to Romantic historicist discourse. As I suggested earlier, these two positions—Hegelian Romanticism and its anti-Hegelian counterpart—form the two sides of the main debate about recent historicist work in Romantic studies. Since the problem of how to represent or portray the spirit of the age is crucial in this debate, I want to review it briefly to show specifically why and how the question should be placed on a different footing.

Though published in 1971, *Natural Supernaturalism* has remained an object of critical attention into the 1990s, and its picture still holds some observers captive. The highly successful marketing of British Romanticism to middle-brow America around the bicentennial of the French Revolution, moreover, was largely carried out under Abrams's authority. A major exhibition, covered favorably in the popular press, traveled to three American sites and the volume that emerged from this edition sold extremely well. Abrams's foreword to that volume, *William Wordsworth and the Age of Romanticism,* offers a defense of the titular configuration in terms taken directly from *Natural Supernaturalism:* "His fellow poets would have understood, and approved, putting Wordsworth at the centre of this exhibition celebrating both the spirit and achievements of English Romanticism," says Abrams, for, in spite of reservations they may have had

---

lothianish," in *Devolving English Literature* (New York: Oxford University Press, 1992,) pp. 134–51.

about "some of his opinions and achievements," they "recognized" that he "was the greatest, most inaugurative, and most representative poet of his time."[48]

Playing with that instability I have pointed to in the notion of "representation," Abrams's shift from "greatest" of his time to "most representative . . . of his time" identifies the second dimension to his claim for Wordsworth. What Wordsworth is supposed to be representing *in* his time, as it turns out, is the time itself, the "Age of Romanticism." To prepare for this shift Abrams needs to establish that it makes sense to talk about such things as "ages" in the first place. Conceding that "[t]he 'Age of Romanticism' is a title imposed by later historians on the four decades after 1790," he goes on to argue for the correspondence of this "title" to a contemporary perception, the self-recognition of a certain "spirit" animating contemporary literature on the part of writers such as Shelley. Then, having introduced the concept of the spirit of the age on the authority of Shelley's comments of 1821, as he did in *Natural Supernaturalism* (1971), Abrams cites Hazlitt, as he had done there as well, to support the notion that Wordsworth is the writer "most representative" of that spirit: "'Mr. Wordsworth's genius is a pure emanation of the Spirit of the Age,' and it 'partakes of, and is carried along with, the revolutionary movement of our age.'"[49]

All of this just repeats the thesis of *Natural Supernaturalism* itself, where Abrams had stated outright that the "rationale" for his project "was that Wordsworth (as his English contemporaries acknowledged, with whatever qualifications) was *the* great and exemplary poet of the age" (emphasis mine).[50] Some of Abrams's critics have persuasively advocated the candidacy of other writers to stand as "representatives" of "the Age of Romanticism"—Byron, for example.[51] But if the objections raised against *Natural Supernaturalism* have failed to check its influence, this may be because the critique has been carried out on the wrong level. It is not enough to present new candidates behind the face hole in the painted cardboard figure of "The Representative Romantic."

48. Jonathan Wordsworth, Michael C. Jaye, and Robert Woof, *William Wordsworth and the Age of English Romanticism* (New Brunswick, N.J.: Rutgers University Press and Grasmere, England: Wordsworth Trust, 1987), p. vii.

49. Ibid., p. viii. The authors of the text proper of *William Wordsworth and the Age of English Romanticism* cite the same passage from Hazlitt in their chapter 2, "The Spirit of the Age," and to roughly the same purpose (p. 27).

50. M. H. Abrams, *Natural Supernaturalism* (New York: W. W. Norton, 1971), p. 14. Disputes over the validity of this claim were carried out in reviews of *Natural Supernaturalism* when it appeared, and they have been summarized in Wayne Booth's generous chapter about that book in his *Critical Understanding: The Powers and Limits of Pluralism* (Chicago: University of Chicago Press, 1979), pp. 139–75.

51. See Jerome McGann, "Romanticism and the Embarrassments of Critical Tradition," *Modern Philology* 70 (1973):243–57.

This rendering of the picture of the age picture itself must be called into question. Why the relation of representative writer and represented age is not tied up so neatly will become clearer, I think, if we return to Hazlitt's extraordinary collection of essays in *The Spirit of the Age*. Leaving aside Hazlitt's specific comments about how Wordsworth's poetry is supposed to have been modeled on the political developments of the French Revolution, we need to take up the more general question of Wordsworth's relation to the announced subject of the collection.[52] Does Hazlitt leave unqualified the force of the pronouncement—always cited straightforwardly and out of context—with which he opens his essay on Wordsworth? "Mr. Wordsworth's genius is a pure emanation of the Spirit of the Age" (CWWH, 11:86). In what spirit should this declaration be taken?

It sounds straightforward enough. What might initially give us pause, however, is the recollection that Hazlitt makes similar statements, perhaps not quite so definitively couched, about the claims of other writers to represent the spirit of the age and that these claims are quite adverse to the one Hazlitt advances for Wordsworth. In the essay on Francis Jeffrey, for example, Hazlitt argues that Jeffrey's magazine, *The Edinburgh Review,* is "eminently characteristic of the Spirit of the Age; as it is the express object of the Quarterly Review [earlier discussed by Hazlitt in the essay on Gifford] to oppose that spirit."[53] This seems very nearly as forceful an identification of a true representative of the spirit of the age as the assertion made about Wordsworth. The problem is that, as Hazlitt's portrait of Jeffrey suggests, if one were to single out one antagonist more insistent in his opposition to Wordsworth than any other in the first quarter of the century, it would surely be Jeffrey. Moreover, the spirit of the age is defined in the essay on Jeffrey in terms of intellectual rigor and acumen: the *Edinburgh Review* "asserts the supremacy of intellect" (p. 127). Wordsworth, on the other hand, is said to represent that spirit in spite of "the hebetude of his intellect" (p. 86).

This kind of discrepancy would be easier to ignore if it were the exception in Hazlitt's book, but this is not the case. Consider the opening of Hazlitt's essay on "Mr. Coleridge": "The present is an age of talkers, and not of doers; and the reason is, that the world is growing old. We are so far advanced in the Arts and

52. I have addressed the problems with Hazlitt's more specific claims in *Wordsworth's Second Nature* (Chicago: University of Chicago Press, 1984), pp. 4–6.

53. Every lover of Hazlitt, that great hater, must feel the force of David Bromwich's comment that "We live at a time of immense sophistication in criticism, yet the state of our dealings with Hazlitt might suggest other thoughts than the consoling one that we have advanced beyond him." See *Hazlitt: The Mind of a Critic* (New York and Oxford: Oxford University Press, 1983), p. 13.

Sciences, that we live in retrospect, and doat on past achievements. . . . Mr. Coleridge has 'a mind reflecting ages past'" (pp. 28–29). Mr. Coleridge is the great conversationalist of the age of talkers and the man of retrospection in a time obsessed with past achievements. It is plainly suggested that he is, in these respects, perfectly representative of the age. The opening of the essay on Scott picks out some of the same cultural traits. There Hazlitt calls Scott "undoubtedly the most popular writer of the age" and adds, presumably by way of explanation, "He is just half of what the human intellect is capable of being: . . . he knows all that has been; all that is to be is nothing to him. His is a mind brooding over antiquity" (p. 57). For all this apparent agreement about the retrospectivity of the spirit of the age in the essays on Coleridge and Scott, however, these remarks sort very ill with other comments in the volume—for example where Hazlitt speaks of the age's "rash and headlong spirit" (p. 130), or where, speaking of Gifford's *resistance* to the spirit of the age, Hazlitt says, "He would go back to the standard of opinions, style, the faded ornaments, and insipid formalities that came into fashion about forty years ago. Flashes of thought, flights of fancy, idiomatic expressions, he sets down among the signs of the times—the extraordinary occurrences of the age with live in. They are marks of a restless and revolutionary spirit: they disturb his composure of mind, and threaten (by implication) the safety of the state" (p. 116). Saying that the age is essentially retrospective and also that it is essentially prospective involves a contradiction different from the one involved in identifying one representative of the spirit of the age by his faith in "the supremacy of intellect" and another by his own hebetude of intellect. It is nonetheless a forceful contradiction, and Hazlitt's portrait of the moral and poetical character of Wordsworth does not suggest a subsumption of either of these contradictions.

Nor do we find support for the view of Wordsworth's special centrality in the representation of the spirit of the age in the overall organization of Hazlitt's 1825 collection. The essay on "Mr. Wordsworth" appears as one among many. It is neither placed first, nor last, nor in the middle of the group. The special claim for Wordsworth, or the specification of the spirit of the age along Wordsworthian lines, might easily have been made in a preface or introductory essay, such as Emerson provided in *Representative Men*. Hazlitt was quite capable of producing such a thing; his *Political Essays* of 1819 were prefaced with several pages of remarks that identified common themes and salient interests among those pieces. The collection of pieces in *The Spirit of the Age,* however, appeared without introduction or preface. From the earliest editions, the book begins straightaway with the essay on Bentham; it is a gallery of "contemporary portraits" without a centerpiece or a docent. In view of the pains Hazlitt has taken to avoid simple solutions to this question of representatives and representations, it would seem most unfortunate to take the first sentence from his Wordsworth essay, no matter how definitive it might sound by itself, as that astute critic's last word on the subject (CWWH, 11:127).

The contrast with the 1819 volume of *Political Essays* is relevant in another way in that, while it collects Hazlitt's work from much of the period surveyed in the 1825 volume, it shows no sign of being tempted by the notion of a spirit of the age in the first place. Although the 1819 volume includes several character sketches anticipatory of *The Spirit of the Age,* these earlier essays raise no expectations about how a unified culture might be identified and outlined for, say, 1789–1819. Instead, they tend to make liberal use of specific dates and specific topical references for events across the three decades; Hazlitt speaks freely of parties, camps, and conflicting constituencies; there are discussions of the characters not only of individuals but also of Whigs, Tories, Country People, Courtiers, Reformers, and so on. Openly acknowledging this plurality of factions and features in the post-Revolution decades, the 1819 volume is inclined to dwell on neither the period's singularized "spirit" nor (consequently) its contradictions. When Hazlitt does speak of the "spirit of contradiction" in 1819, he does so in reference to one of several traits he finds in the character of the reformer (CWWH, 7:14).

In *The Spirit of the Age,* on the other hand, in the very act of positing the notion of a unified spirit, Hazlitt has constructed a very scheme of contradictions. Not only are the contradictions discernible; they are emphasized by Hazlitt's arrangement of things. Writers are contrasted with other writers both within essays (Mr. Campbell and Mr. Crabbe), and between essays (Lord Byron and Sir Walter Scott), and, where two paired figures are both accorded representative status, they nonetheless may be said to agree on virtually nothing: "Lord Byron and Sir Walter Scott are of all writers now living the two, who would carry away the majority of suffrages as the greatest geniuses of the age. . . . We shall treat of them in the same connection, partly on account of their distinguished preeminence, and partly because they afford a complete contrast to one another. In their poetry, in their prose, in their politics, and in their tempers, no two men can be more unlike" (p. 69). In addition to contradicting one another, writers also contradict themselves. Robert Southey is first described by Hazlitt as having "a look at once aspiring and dejected." Wordsworth's muse is "distinguished by a proud humility." For most of these figures, it is alleged that their strength lies in their weakness: Coleridge's procrastinating talkativeness, for example, is just the underside of his ability to see all sides of a question. There is no single set of coordinates, however, on which such multiple contradictions can be plotted.[54] Nor, again, is there a single figure either in the sense of a particular contradictory trope (such as Abrams's governing oxymoron "natural supernaturalism") or in the sense of a particular person (Wordsworth as Waverley) in which the entire scheme can be subsumed.[55]

One might plausibly seek such a figure, perhaps, in the initial essay in the collection, on Jeremy Bentham. The self–announced theme of this essay lies in the adage Hazlitt cites to begin it: "A prophet has most honour out of his own country." The contradiction into which Hazlitt elaborates this adage for Bentham's portrait turns on the relation between Bentham's abstraction of humanity and his inability to have influence at the center of the empire from which he operates: "His reputation lies at the circumference; and the lights of his understanding are reflected, with increasing lustre, on the other side of the globe, in the plains of Chile and the mines of Mexico. He has offered constitutions for the New World, and legislated for future times. The people of Westminster, where he lives, hardly dream of such a person; but the Siberian savage has received cold comfort from his lunar aspect" (CWWH, 11:5). The problem with Bentham's project, for Hazlitt, is that, in its abstraction, it admits of no unevenness between cultures. It presumes that, "on pure cosmopolite principles, or on the ground of abstract humanity," it might be possible to "affect an extraordinary regard for the Turks and Tartars" without "neglecting their duties to their friends and next-door neighbors." Skewing the analysis of his "supposed cases" toward the fungible categories of mere "understanding," Bentham becomes the victim of an uneven inversion of his reputation. But such abstrac-

54. It seems to me that Roy Park's rich chapter on *The Spirit of the Age,* and indeed his excellent book as a whole, is diminished rather than enhanced by his drive to reduce Hazlitt's thinking to a polarity of abstraction and particularity. See *Hazlitt and the Spirit of the Age* (Oxford: Oxford University Press, 1971), pp. 206–36. The contradictions summarized above, for example, do not so reduce.

55. John Kinnaird has gone as far as anyone in his insistence on the discrepancies in *The Spirit of the Age—William Hazlitt: Critic of Power* (New York: Columbia University Press, 1978): "What emerges is a composite portrait of the age, whose unity of character is now seen to inhere precisely in its inconsistencies, in the dramatic logic of its discords—a polarity of conflict often very different in its motives from the tensions and contentions of the age as the combatants themselves were defining them" (p. 304). But, perhaps weakened by an underdeveloped sense of contradiction in Hazlitt, Kinnaird's discussion goes on to accept at face value the notion that Wordsworth's genius is given the privileged position in the value "as being thoroughly expressive of its time" (p. 319). See also Herschel Baker's brief but useful comments on the unresolved "antinomy" in Hazlitt's contradictions in *William Hazlitt* (Cambridge, Mass.: Belknap Press of Harvard University Press, 1962), p. 440.

tion, like the abstract formula "spirit of the age" itself, is only one contradictory aspect of the spirit of Bentham's age as Hazlitt represents it.[56]

Reviewing the array of conflicting aspects and figures in Hazlitt's text, then, one might say that, if Hazlitt's own positing of the spirit of the age brings the operative contradictions to notice, then the contradictions in turn have implications for how "the spirit of the age" functions in the discourse of British Romantic, as distinct from Hegelian, historicism. That is, one might say for shorthand, in an idiom often invoked in Jamesonian historicism, that it bespeaks an "overdetermined" causality. We must recall here that Jameson borrows the notion from Althusser who, writing in 1965 in the wake of the controversy between Lévi-Strauss and Sartre, initially deployed the now-familiar term "overdetermination" in order to distinguish between the functions of contradiction in the Hegelian and Marxian conceptions of history and periodicity. If, says Althusser,

> a vast accumulation of "contradictions" comes into play *in the same court,* some of which are radically heterogeneous—of different origins, different sense, different *levels* and *points* of application—but which nevertheless "merge" into a structural unity, we can no longer talk of the sole, unique power of the general "contradiction." Of course, the basic contradiction [between the forces and relations of production] dominating the period (when the revolution is "the task of the day") is active in all these "contradictions: and even in their "fusion." But, strictly speaking, it cannot be claimed that these contradictions and their fusion are merely the pure phenomena of the general contradiction. The "circumstances" and "currents" which achieve it are more than its phenomena pure and simple. . . . This means that if the "differences" that constitute each of the instances in play . . . "*merge*" into a real unity, they are not "*dissipated*" as pure phenomena in the internal unity of a *simple* contradiction.[57]

The period model in which the differences among the instances in play at a given moment are "dissipated as pure phenomena in the internal unity of a simple contradiction" is, for Althusser, Hegel's, and it is the one that I have argued most closely suits the world picture of Romanticism-as-Wordsworth-as-"Natural Supernaturalism"—or for that matter, Romanticism-as-Byron-as-"Faithful Skepticism," or Romanticism-as-Scott-as-"Progressive Conservatism." The simplicity of this kind of contradiction, as Althusser explains, "is made possible only by the simplicity of the internal principle that constitutes the essence of any historical period."[58]

Although Hazlitt's *The Spirit of the Age* brings the reformer's "spirit of con-

---

56. This commitment to abstraction without regard to cultural and historical difference is part of what Halévy refers to as a deficiency in Bentham when he points out that "the idea of a philosophy of history is totally foreign to Bentham's thought." Elie Halévy, *The Growth of Philosophical Radicalism* (London: Faber and Faber, 1952), p. 273.

57. Louis Althusser, "Contradiction and Overdetermination," in *For Marx* (London: Verso, 1977), p 102.

58. Ibid., p. 103.

tradiction" conspicuously into play, he makes every effort to block the identification of a simple contradiction to which his representation of his age could be
said to reduce (in the way that phenomena reduce to an essence). Just this resistance to simplification, it seems to me, is wherein the greatness of the book's
achievement lies. Such resistance is indeed built into Hazlitt's critical style,
which was regarded by some of his first readers as a public menace. In a relatively
well-disposed review, which was nonetheless thoroughly preoccupied with
Hazlitt's "figurative and epigrammatic style," a writer for *The Monthly Review*
wrote of the prose in *The Spirit of the Age:* "Every thing shines as through a prismatic medium. The result is, that we retain nothing distinctly of what he says. It
is a sort of confused memory of sounds, like the clashing of musical instruments."[59] The reviewer's own mixed metaphor bespeaks the contagiousness,
and thus the danger, of Hazlitt's stylistic infection.

But why, if all this is true of the book, does Hazlitt call Wordsworth "a pure
emanation of the spirit of the age"? Any good answer to this question requires
notice of one of Hazlitt's favorite (because anarchic) figures: catachresis. Since
we normally speak of spirits as being "embodied" in persons, the word we
ought to have seen where "emanation" appears is "incarnation." "Emanation"
was used then, and is still now, to suggest a relatively immaterial effluence from
a relatively more material source. Since the spirit of the age is already, for
Hazlitt, immaterial, the notion of an emanation from it, indeed a "pure emanation," is strongly redundant. This might be carelessness or a casual joke, but it
would be more in keeping with what a contemporary reviewer called Hazlitt's
"paradoxical and caustic genius" to see in it a certain mockery of Wordsworth's
pretensions.[60] The essay on Wordsworth attempts to capture what it is that
Wordsworth aspires to, and it would not be difficult to argue, even on the basis
of the poetry Hazlitt would have seen, that Wordsworth's writings aspire to the
condition, exactly, of being read as a "pure emanation" of the spirit of the age.
The "purity," the abstraction, of the claimed representativeness gives the lie
to it.

Hazlitt would not, of course, have seen the completed *Prelude,* though he
would have known something about it and though those parts he would have
seen (such as the "Bliss was it in that dawn to be alive . . ." passage published in
The Friend) would have corroborated such a view of Wordsworth. Furthermore, the Prospectus to *The Recluse* (which Abrams makes his recurring point

59. *The Monthly Review* 10 (May 1825) 107:1. A year earlier, the same periodical's review of
Hazlitt's *Characteristics* noted that "many of these 'Characteristics' are evidently the result of temporary feeling, and are contradicted in different parts of the volume" ([Feb. 1824] 103:221).
60. Ibid., p. 221.

departure and return in *Natural Supernaturalism*) is a text that Hazlitt knew very well. In that ambitious document, Wordsworth represents the "age"—post-Milton, post-Enlightenment—precisely by an act of subsuming it into the patterns of his own mind and character. He makes its hopes his hopes and its disappointments his disappointments. And, by way of sublimation ("pure emanation"?), he also seeks to make *his* recompenses *its* recompenses. In his writings about Wordsworth certainly from the largely sympathetic review of *The Excursion* onward, Hazlitt resisted Wordsworth's "internalization of quest romance"—his way of offering his own experience as an epitome of his historical culture and his narrative of that experience as the resolution of its contradictions. Again, the irreducible multiplicity of representatives and representations of the spirit of the age in Hazlitt's great volume of 1825 aims precisely to refuse, or at least diffuse, such an epitome and such a resolution. Yet Abrams and his followers appeal to Hazlitt's authority for accepting and indeed celebrating the representative status that Wordsworth claimed for himself.[61] No one is allowed such status in Hazlitt's gallery—nor, for that matter, in Walter Savage Landor's counterpart ensemble of the 1820s, the *Imaginary Conversations,* where a similar fantasy is even more pointedly debunked. Landor has his character, General Lascy, say of the arrogance of a typical member of Parliament under Pitt, "He dreamed in his drunkenness that he could compress the spirit of the times."[62]

The larger point that I am trying to establish here, lest it be lost, is that Hazlitt refuses either to capture "the spirit of the age" in a single portrait that could stand as its total representation *or* to select from among the "spirits of the age" one "proxy" (to reinvoke Spivak) whose own "portrait" could be definitely representative. Indeed, in his text as in Landor's, there is evidence to suggest that such a project, so conceived, is to be dismissed as vain. Both texts might be taken to suggest that the contradictions of the new notion of culture under the aegis of the spirit of the age—culture as defined in the chronologically coded domestic manners of uneven social development—are not so easily contained.

61. To their credit, the authors of the text proper of *William Wordsworth and the Age of English Romanticism* attempt to qualify their apparent initial endorsement of Abrams's view when they come to Byron: "It is no longer possible, however, to decide with Hazlitt that Wordsworth was 'a pure emanation of the Spirit of the Age,' and Byron some form of alien. In many ways they seem to be at opposite poles. . . . Yet it is between these two poles that the age must be defined" (p. 45). This sense of what it is no longer possible to decide seems a step in the right direction. But where the authors go wrong, from the perspective of the present argument, is in the simplified view they think Hazlitt holds and in the failure of their own simple "polarity" to measure up to the rich texture of cultural contradiction that I have tried to describe in Hazlitt's book.

62. "General Lascy and the Curate Merino," in Walter Savage Landor, *Imaginary Conversations of Literary Men and Statesmen, The Second Volume* (London: Taylor and Hessey, 1824), p. 85.

4. Shelley's Representative Legislature

To look at the state of this question of representativeness in Shelley, the other authority cited by Abrams in support of his cultural configuration, is to find even less corroboration for the kinds of practices that inform the Hegelianization of British Romanticism. Abrams cites Shelley's more celebrated use of the phrase "spirit of the age" in *A Defence of Poetry,* where it appears in the final paragraph of the existing text and leads to the famous culminating claim that "poets are the unacknowledged legislators of the world." That final paragraph of the *Defence,* as I noted earlier, is a virtual transcription of the conclusion of chapter 1 of a work that Shelley had begun more than a year earlier (in November 1819), *A Philosophical View of Reform.* What the passage indicates in both contexts, however, is that, if Shelley is interested in the question of how and by whom the spirit of the age shall be represented, his way of addressing it is neither simpler nor more direct than Hazlitt's. Wordsworth clearly seems to be one of the writers alluded to in this passage, especially in the remarks about "their system relating to thought and expression," but he is certainly not singled out. From the beginning, Shelley's comments pluralize their referent: "We live among such philosophers & poets as surpass beyond comparison any who have appeared in our nation since its last struggle for liberty."[63]

For Shelley, furthermore, it is not so much that the "spirit" of a privileged writer "corresponds" to the putative spirit of the age but rather that, in manifesting itself through a given writer, the spirit of the age displaces the work of the personal spirit. This historical spirit is not only "unapprehended" by the person it makes its instrument; it can actually stand quite powerfully at odds with his or her personal-authorial opinions and intentions. For example, if we suppose that, in addition to Wordsworth, Shelley is also thinking here of Byron, the contemporary poet whom there is reason to think he held in at least equal esteem with Wordsworth, then he is well aware of being faced with two "representative" writers whose authorial views and intentions were quite deeply at odds. As with Hazlitt, therefore, but for slightly different reasons, Shelley's thinking about how the spirit of the age achieves representation leads him to posit a *plurality* of "representatives" and to incorporate unsimplified contradiction in their representational function.

What lends special distinction and complexity to Shelley's account is his attention to an aspect of the question of representation that is only glimpsed in Emerson and Hazlitt: representation of peoples in such legislative institutions as the English Parliament and the still-young American Congress. Setting up a

63. Ibid., pp. 991–92.

knotty conceit during his introductory remarks in *Representative Men,* Emerson says that "each material thing has its celestial side; has its translation through humanity into the spiritual and necessary sphere, where it plays a part as indestructible as any other." The conceit runs this way: "The gases gather to the solid firmament: the chemic lump arrives at the plant, and grows; arrives at the quadraped, and walks; arrives at the man, and thinks. But also the constituency determines the vote of the representative. He is not only representative but participant."[64] If Emerson's style "calls for philosophy," as Stanley Cavell has suggested,[65] it here seems to call not only for philosophy of science but for political philosophy as well. For, if "the man" in this passage represents the entire diachronic process of phylogeny, the (great) man (also? equally? analogously?) represents the mass of population that ascends toward him in human society. The political metaphor of representation by suffrage—which here incorporates the notion of the political representative as the synecdoche of the represented—itself seems to strive, against some resistance, metaphorically to govern the entire discussion of human representativeness. For his part, Hazlitt, in establishing the representativeness of Byron and Scott, had said that they would "carry away the majority of suffrages as the greatest geniuses of the age." In this age of developing mass readership, Hazlitt's couching of his comments about literary popularity in the terms of political suffrage is, again, by no means an arbitrary metaphor, even if it remains an underdeveloped one.

As I argued earlier, discussions of literary representation or representativeness in this period often intersect with the dominant political topic of the day: the issue of reform in political representation. No one, however, makes the relation between these two aspects of representation so explicit a subject for reflection so early as does Shelley in *A Philosophical View of Reform.* Yet, remarkable as it is, the *View* has not been a widely read essay, partly on account of its presumed eclipse by *A Defence of Poetry,* which, while composed later and also left unfinished, was published eighty years earlier than the *View,* in 1840.[66] It has been too little recognized, certainly among those who cite Shelley's remarks casually, that his discussion of spirits of the age and poet-legislators (i.e., representative men) appears in a discussion of the stages of reform in political representation, or that this is a discussion composed at the moment of severest crisis

---

64. Emerson, *Collected Works,* 4:7.

65. Stanley Cavell, "Emerson's Aversive Thinking," in *Romantic Revolutions,* pp. 244–46.

66. Two exceptions to the rule of neglect can be found in K. N. Cameron, *Shelley: The Golden Years* (Cambridge, Mass.: Harvard University Press, 1974), pp. 127–49, and P. M. S. Dawson, *The Unacknowledged Legislator: Shelley and Politics* (Oxford and New York: Oxford University Press, 1980), passim.

for the reform movement: the months after the Peterloo Massacre. There is no prose text in Shelley's oeuvre, certainly, more apposite to his representation of "England in 1819" in the sonnet he wrote in the final days of the year.

The scope of the *View* is vast, even before Shelley comes to his economic history of England since 1641 in chapter 2 or his prophetic sketch of the theory of passive resistance in chapter 3. His first chapter attempts nothing less than a history of the relation of poetic vitality and political progress since the end of the Roman Republic. This ambitious project was motivated by Shelley's sense of a dilemma in confronting at once a political system he found intolerably oppressive and a reform movement he found intolerably obsessive about changing the mechanisms of parliamentary representation. It was thus, as we have seen, when Shelley wrote in early 1820, that the *View* was "intended as a kind of standard book for the philosophical reformers politically considered, like Jeremy Bentham's something, but different & perhaps more systematic" (LPBS, 2:201). Shelley had been more explicitly critical of Bentham's (and Beccaria's) plans for reform in a letter to Hunt just weeks earlier, on April 5 (LPBS, 2:181). It is perhaps not surprising, therefore, that the doctrine of utility should have special prominence in Shelley's history nor that the outcome of this history is to suggest how circumscribed is the doctrine of utilitarianism both in its horizon of vision and in its theory of representation.

Shelley dates the effective genesis of utility to what he sees as the beginning of the modern period, the enlightened "new epoch" that arrives with the seventeenth century. The heroes of Shelley's seventeenth century are Bacon, Spinoza, Hobbes, Bayle, and Montaigne, writers who "regulated the reasoning powers, criticized the past history, exposed the errors by illustrating their causes and their connection, and anatomized the inmost nature of social man" (p. 8). The stipulation that it is "*social* man" for whom Shelley's philosophic heroes anatomize the "inmost nature" registers a characteristic dissonance in the history he narrates. When he distinguishes a second generation of important metaphysicians in the new epoch—Locke, Berkeley, Hume, and Hartley—he defines their achievement in respect to how they illustrated the consequences of their predecessors' new thought. Their views were "correct, popular, simple, and energetic, but not profound." A third generation of metaphysicians, the French philosophes, were even more popularizing and pragmatic than their English contemporaries, but with a better excuse. Considered as philosophers, the error of this "crowd of writers in France" consisted in their limitedness of view: "they told the truth but not the whole truth" (p. 9). Shelley's excuse for them is that "[t]his might have arisen from the terrible sufferings of their countrymen" which led them "rather to apply a portion of what had already been discovered to their immediate relief, than to pursue one interest, the abstractions of thought, as the great philosophers who preceded them had done, for the sake of a future and a more universal advantage" (p. 9). The writing of the *View* itself is demonstrably caught between these two conflicting impulses, the pragmatic drag on his philosophical aspirations finally achieving strength enough to lead him to abandon the work altogether in favor of embarking on *A Defence of Poetry.*

The doctrine of utility that will come to figure so importantly in 1819 is simply the eighteenth century's application of the principles of the new, still incomplete, metaphysics to the field of politics. Shelley describes the labors and limitations of the political philosophers at some length but summarizes their achievement as "the establishment of the principle of Utility as the substance, and liberty and equality as the forms according to which the concerns of human life ought to be administered" (p. 10). This is the principle, of course, that stands prominent in the Benthamite program for reform that is at once Shelley's topic and point of departure.

How representation and thus "representative men" figure in the argument becomes apparent when Shelley illustrates the powers and limitations of the concept of utility by reference to the revolutions of America and France. The importance of the former, for Shelley, is that it issued in a system of government that he calls "the first practical illustration of the new philosophy" (p. 10). Happy that the American Constitution marks an enormous gain over "the insolent and contaminating tyrannies under which, with some limitation of these terms as regards England, Europe groaned" at the time of the Revolution, Shelley must nonetheless confess that even this new system is also "sufficiently remote . . . from the accuracy of ideal excellence" (pp. 9–10). As compared with the old governments of Europe and Asia, the United States holds forth the example "of a free, happy, and strong people" and of "an immensely populous, and as far as the external arts of life are concerned, a highly civilized, community administered according to republican forms":

> It has no king, that is it has no officer to whom wealth and from whom corruption flows. It has no hereditary oligarchy, that is it acknowledges no order of men privileged to cheat and insult the rest of the members of the state, and who inherit a right of legislating and judging which the principles of human nature compel them to exercise to their peculiar class. It has no established Church, that is it has no system of opinions respecting the abstrusest questions which can be topics of human thought, founded in an age of error and by prosecutions, and sanctioned by enormous bounties given to idle priests and forced thro' the unwilling hands of those who have an interest in the cultivation and improvement of the soil. It has no false representation, whose consequences are captivity, confiscation, infamy and ruin, but a true representation. *The will of the many is represented by the few in the assemblies of legislation and by the officers of the executive entrusted with the administration of the executive power almost as directly as the will of one person can be represented by the will of another.* (p. 11; italics mine)

While it seems as if Shelley's America has it all, the incompleteness of the
American Revolution, and therefore of the utilitarianism that it embodies, and
therefore of its system of representation, becomes clearer when Shelley turns to
his second major case in point: "The just and successful Revolt of America corresponded with a state of public opinion in Europe of which it was the first result. The French Revolution was the second" (p. 13). Shelley regards this
revolution, like the American one, as only a partial success. But in this case, as
not in the American example, the evidence of its flaw is palpable and spectacular in the record of the Reign of Terror.[67] For Shelley, the explanation for the
Reign of Terror, and thus for the failure of the Revolution to achieve what its
proponents had hoped of it, lies less in the history of French politics, in the narrow sense, than in French poetics: "The French were what their literature is [ex-
cluding Montaigne and Rousseau, and some few leaders of the . . .] weak,
superficial, vain, with little imagination, and with passions as well as judgements
cleaving to the external form of things" (pp. 13–14).

The counterpart of this suggestion in Shelley's analysis of the American experiment can be found in the way he qualifies his claim that America is a community administered according to republican forms and is "highly civilized"
only "as far as the external arts of life are concerned." The external arts are the
technological or mechanical arts, what we sometimes call the "useful" arts, and
they are identified here as engaging only with "the external form of things."
The implied internal forms, which they cannot reach, should probably be identified with those "forms of human nature" into which Bacon and his colleagues
inquired. For such purposes, only the internal arts are fit, the arts Shelley summarizes under the name of "literature" or, more typically, "poetry."

To say this much is to begin to respond to the question of how Shelley can
suggest that, in spite of all the indications to the contrary, England stands in a
more advantageous political position in 1819 than do America and France.
Donald Reiman's transcriptions of the *View's* manuscripts include an important and hitherto unpublished note scribbled under the discussion of the
strengths and limitations of the American experiment:

---

67. Of the unhappy response of the "oppressed" against the "tyrants" in the later stage of the
Revolution, Shelley writes: "Their desire to wreak revenge, to this extent, in itself a mistake, a
crime, a calamity, arose from the same source as their other miseries and errors, and affords an additional proof of the necessity of that long-delayed change which it accompanied and disgraced.
If a just and necessary revolution could have been accomplished with as little expense of happiness and order in a country governed by despotic as [in] one governed by free laws, equal liberty
and justice would lose their chief recommendations and tyranny be divested of its most revolting
attributes" (*View,* p. 13).

Its error consists not in the representing the will of the People as it is, but in not providing for the full development of the most salutary condition of that will. For two conditions are necessary to a theoretically perfect government, & one of these alone is adequately fulfilled by the most perfect of practical governments the Republic of the United States. To represent the will of the People as it is. To provide that will should be as wise and just as possible. To a certain extent the mere representation of the public will produces in itself a wholesome condition of it, and in this extent America fulfills imperfectly & indirectly the last & most important condition of perfect government.[68]

Although there are two necessary conditions for good government here—representing the will of the people as it is and providing that it should be as wise and just as possible—to some extent the existence of the first is sufficient for the production of the second, and to that extent there is only one condition. But that extent is evidently limited. The truest representation of the national will is also the best and most beautiful. It is that representation that improves as it reflects. This notion is the basis for the famous claim about poetic legislators that concludes the argument of chapter 1, gives way to the quasi-utilitarian analysis of chapters 2 and 3 of the *View,* and which eventually issues in the full-scale critique of utilitarianism, as personified in Peacock, that one finds in *A Defence of Poetry.*

While its social miseries may be less severe than England's, America lacks the poetic genius to represent its contemporary state—the spirit of its age—to itself. It lacks a public medium in which sympathetic identification and acknowledgment can take place. No one in America in 1819, for example, could have represented the age so effectively as what we find even in a minor sonnet such as Shelley's *England in 1819*—composed contemporaneously with chapter 1 of the *View*—let alone the more celebrated English works of that year. America, Shelley said, has "no false representation . . . but a true representation." In its elected President and Congress, "the will of the many is represented by the few . . . almost as directly as the will of one person can be represented by the will of another." In the writings of great poets, however, the national will represents itself fully, despite even the intentions of the poets themselves to the contrary. Poetic mimesis is the representation not of the will of one person by the will of another but of the national will to itself. This is the kind of representation that improves upon its subject in a powerful way. And, on the Rousseauist principle that it is in the nature of the human will to improve itself, only that kind of will which improves what it represents can be said to represent that will truly.

68. *Shelley and his Circle 1773–1822,* 8 vols., ed. Donald H. Reiman (Cambridge, Mass.: Harvard University Press, 1973), 6:977.

In 1819 Shelley saw this work of a nation's self-representation as a collective enterprise, one that involved a company of poets singing, like the nightingales in *Prometheus Unbound,* both in and of an ever-expanding horizon of inclusion. Many of his works, *Prometheus Unbound* prominent among them, contest the representation, such as he finds it in the writings of his contemporaries, of this work of representation itself. Charles Robinson has suggested that Byron is that "great contemporary" to whom Shelley alludes to in his preface to *Prometheus Unbound.* If "the 'forms' which 'modified' *Prometheus Unbound* were Byron's *Prometheus* and *Manfred,*" Robinson argues, "Shelley borrowed from Byron's Promethean poems only to subvert their metaphysics."[69] I believe this is exactly right, so long as the subverted "metaphysics" can be understood to include Byron's attempt to offer his representation of the Napoleonic or Promethean will as itself representative of an idealized national will. If the representative claims of Byronism are critiqued in *Prometheus Unbound,* the representative claims of Wordsworthianism are critiqued in another great work of Shelley's great year, *Peter Bell the Third,* and likewise those of Rousseauism two years later in *The Triumph of Life.* In representing the work of national representation, indeed, Shelley refused pride of place not only to Byron, Wordsworth, and Rousseau, but also to Coleridge, Southey, Moore, Hunt, Godwin, Keats, and Scott.

In this respect, then, the prose of Shelley's *View* seems to have groped its way toward a position that corresponds to Hazlitt's. In at least one respect, Shelley comes even closer than Hazlitt to a position such as the one from which Althusser offers his critique of Hegelianism. In speaking of Hegelian contradiction as "made possible *only* by the simplicity of the internal principle that constitutes the essence of any historical period," Althusser goes on to explain that "the reduction of *all* the elements that make up the concrete life of a historical epoch (. . . institutions, customs, ethics, art, religion, philosophy, and even historical *events*. . .) to *one* principle of internal unity, is itself only possible on the absolute condition of taking the whole concrete life of a people for the externalization-alienation of an internal spiritual principle, which can never definitely be anything but the most abstract form of that epoch's consciousness of itself."[70] One might not wish to call Shelley's account of "the spirit of the age" materialist, exactly, but it is resistant to just the kind of ideal-

---

69. Charles E. Robinson, *Shelley and Byron: The Snake and Eagle Wreathed in Flight* (Baltimore: Johns Hopkins University Press, 1976), p. 114.
70. Althusser, *For Marx,* p. 103.

ist reduction Althusser synopsizes here.[71] In contemporary commentary on Romanticism, the natural supernaturalism of Wordsworth's Prospectus to *The Recluse* and the faithful skepticism of Byron's *Manfred*—or again, the progressive-conservatism of *Waverley*—are each of them offered as oxymoronic representations of the age's consciousness of itself. From this confident fiction of epochal self-consciousness derives what Shelley called the "didacticism" of such programs; it is what Keats, working out of Hazlitt, called the sense of "palpable design" (LJK, 1:224). Shelley persistently fostered a generous suspicion of this claim of an individual will to represent the general will, even (indeed, especially) for those among his contemporaries whom he regarded as possessed of greatest genius.

How does Shelley's representation of the spirit of the age escape its own critique? Perhaps it simply does not and cannot, but, if one chooses to examine his most famous passage on the subject closely, one might begin to see a way. In that rousing ending of *A Defence of Poetry,* those sentences reprised from the conclusion of chapter 1 in *A Philosophical View of Reform,* we behold a study in unresolved and unresolvable contradictions (SPP, p. 508). Poets are said to measure and plumb a human nature, spatially conceived, and apparently itself unchanging, with a spirit of time and change. In this the spirit of the age seems to be their instrument, what they measure and plumb with. But the metaphor is quickly turned around to suggest that the poets indeed are the instruments wielded by the spirit—trumpets, for example, the insensate means by which a trumpeter inspires a hearer. Two other metaphors seem vaguely to line up this way: the hierophants of the unapprehended inspiration and the words that expressed what they understand not. But the famous last sentence, so often quoted out of context, contradicts the new formation at yet another angle. Following the metaphors of the "trumpet," "hierophant," and "words," one would expect poets to be called "unacknowledging" legislators. Such a formulation would also be consistent with the sense of poets as the influence that moves without being moved. One would have expected, in other words, that it would have been the "spirit" that was unacknowledged as legislator of the world. Indeed, in the famous formulation that Shelley produced, "unacknowledged legislators," it is by no means clear by *whom* poets are to be acknowledged.

Shelley's representation of the spirit of the age disallows reduction to a single formula, oxymoronic or otherwise, about the epoch's consciousness of

71. Shelley not only shares with Althusser a detailed knowledge of Spinoza, he was actually translating Spinoza's *Tractatus* at this time. See below, chapter 10.

itself. In this respect, though Hazlitt could not have seen it, Shelley's passage would have made an appropriate epigraph for Hazlitt's *The Spirit of the Age* four years later. Its style is indeed equally answerable to the synaesthetic description of Hazlitt's by that contemporary reviewer I cited earlier who said that everything in it shines as through a prismatic medium, leaving us nothing but a confused memory of sounds, like the clashing of musical instruments. Indeed, this same reviewer generalized the observation to include more prose writers than Hazlitt: "It would be austere criticism to denounce the figurative and epigrammatic style with which a few of our modern authors are striving to enrich, as they imagine, the prose diction of our nation. . . . It is a little too late to erect a standard of language. The teeming and redundant imaginations of our writers would soon overflow the embankments which a severe taste and a correct judgment might throw up. The authority of academics to fix the speech of a country would be exerted to enslave it."[72] And in a description that resonates uncannily with Shelley's unpublished conclusion to the *Defence* (even as it reminds us of Jameson on new historicism), this same reviewer associates the prose writers of the new spirit of the age with a kind of nominalism: "Words," he says, "or the ideas which they nominally (for the most part *nominally* only) represent, are by far too ungovernable a rabble, as they rush from the minds of gifted and imaginative men, to bow either to the lawgiver or his law."[73] Of Shelley's own famous passage, in any event, one might say that it courts expectations that it will not meet, and it refuses to allow the spirit of the age to reduce to an affair of consciousness or self-comprehension. One of the great ironies in the self-representation of the spirit of the age in Romantic historicism, in other words, is its mistrust of such self-representation.

5. Historicism, Contradiction, and Casuistry

The stylistic solutions to which Shelley and Hazlitt resorted in the face of the new world picture might be more broadly associated with the so-called crisis of reference itself in Romanticism. If the distinctive contradictions of this Romantic historicism could be obliquely registered at the level of style, however, they could not be pursued there. The "spirit of the age" was a figure of speech associated not only with a novel situation but also with a novel understanding of ethical situatedness, and it is in relation to that situation and that concept that its contradictions had to be worked out. Hegel, as we have seen, proclaimed the new historical dispensation when he said that the examples of the past offered no guidance to the agent of the present because a nation in a given age inhabits

72. *Monthly Review,* 52 (May 1825): 1.
73. Ibid., p. 1.

such a "unique situation" that it can only make decisions with reference to itself alone.[74] What is at stake here, though Hegel does not put it that way, is a new understanding of the problem of action-in-circumstance—a new recognition, one might say, of what "the case" was.

In Hegel, the contradictions of the new situation are worked out, as Étienne Balibar suggests, by way of the dialectical progression "from civil society to freedom within the state, through transcending concurrence that expresses the individuality of the 'great men.' "[75] Balibar goes on to describe what he sees as the parallel Marxist account whereby "the movement of the masses is to class antagonism in Engels what the state is to civil society in Hegel."[76] The "very thesis," writes Balibar,

> according to which "it is the masses who make history" therefore takes on a new light, as the equivalent of the role assigned by Hegel to the "great men". . . . Engels' construction suggests that the masses are the *truly* "great men" (of the state) of history; in this sense, it inverts the ideological, statist theme that Hegelian philosophy has taken up. This inversion, however, preserves its Hegelian theoretical structure: both the masses and ideology function, respectively, like the "great men" and the "spirit of the people" in Hegel, namely, as the "spirit of the age" realizing itself.[77]

If Hegel's and Engels's accounts can be understood at this level of abstraction as sharing a paradigmatic form, the contradictions of the new historical situation are differently worked out in the British Romantic context where, at least in some of the most interesting engagements, a crucial mediating role is played by the discourse of casuistry and the form of the case. This mediating role, not widely discussed in the critical literature, will occupy much attention in all the chapters that follow.

The relation of cases and casuistries to the notion of the situation has always, as far as I can tell, been a close one. A "case," most simply understood, is a represented situation, and a casuistry is a discipline for dealing with the application of principles to cases so understood. In important works of late 1818 and 1819, one can see the fascination of Scott and Shelley with this genre and discourse in works like *Prometheus Unbound* and *The Cenci* and in *The Heart of Mid-Lothian*

---

74. Hegel, "Reason in History," p. 21.
75. Étienne Balibar, "The Vacillation of Ideology," in *Marxism and the Interpretation of Culture*, ed. Cary Nelson and Lawrence Grossberg, p. 193.
76. Ibid., p. 193.
77. Ibid., p. 193. To suggest the further relevance of Balibar's analysis to the present discussion, we can note that for the revised version of this essay, "The Vacillation of Ideology," in *Masses, Classes, Ideas* (London: Routledge, 1994), Balibar extensively discusses the intimate relation of the terms "ideology" and "worldview" (pp. 115–19): each term functions as "the middle term of the historical process or *of society's reflecting upon itself*, which permanently engenders its historicity" (p. 114).

and *The Bride of Lammermoor*—all of which involve explicit use of the case form
and identifiable reference to casuistry as a discursive activity. Sometimes these
references appear in familiar passages that are famous for other reasons. Shelley,
for instance, comparing his protagonist with Milton's Satan in the Preface to
Prometheus Unbound, probably just weeks before he began *A Philosophical View
of Reform,* included his notorious epithet about Satan's role in the earlier poem:
"The only imaginary being resembling in any degree Prometheus, is Satan; and
Prometheus is, in my judgement, a more poetical character than Satan because,
in addition to courage and majesty and firm and patient opposition to omnipo-
tent force, he is susceptible of being described as exempt from the taints of ambition, envy, revenge, and a desire for personal aggrandisement, which in the
Hero of *Paradise Lost,* interfere with the interest" (SPP, p. 133).[78] The point of
relevance here has to do with the basis on which Shelley elaborates his distinction between the two heroes he compares. "The character of Satan," Shelley
goes on, "engenders in the mind a pernicious casuistry which leads us to weigh
his faults with his wrongs and to excuse the former because the latter exceed all
measure" (p. 133). The reference to Satan as Milton's hero has attracted much
more attention than this reference to casuistry, a reference that will be repeated
yet more prominently in Shelley's other great dramatic work of the same year.
And in both instances, as well as in the Scott novels and in a number of other influential writings of the post–Waterloo moment, the new "interest" in casuistry
and the case form has everything to do with the discursive preoccupations of
the age of the spirit of the age.

Certainly, the case/casuistry framework encourages a line of inquiry never
quite opened up in Hazlitt's freewheeling critical exercises. It helps to articulate
a series of questions not only about the new forms of periodization specifiable
within the historian's code, or about the new forms of representation thus
brought into play, but also about a series of other relevant issues as well—especially those concerned with institutional circumstance and the explanation of
action, with motivation, agency, and choice. The history of casuistry gives access at once to the historicity of a given normative domain and to the normative dimension of representation in the new age of the world picture. It helps to
chart how historicism redefines the problem of giving reasons—of explaining,
as Kenneth Burke puts it, what is involved when we say what people are doing
and why they are doing it.

78. This remark is sometimes likened to Blake's famous claim that Milton was a true poet and
(therefore) of the Devil's party without knowing it, and yet, if one considers that Milton was
writing an epic pitched against the virtues of classical epic, virtues one might call technically
"heroic," Shelley's appellation for Satan might be understood as literally true.

We should recall here that both the Heideggerian and Lukácsian accounts of the age of the world picture lay stress on the normative dimension of the concept of representation that governs it—Lukács with his stress on the historicity of ethical formations and Heidegger with his formulation of the stance of representation in the modern sense as the forcing of "what is" into a relation to oneself as the "normative realm." To begin to see that normative dimension of modern representation is to take the full force of Kenneth Burke's dialectical pairing of "reflection" and "selection" as it applies to what he called "attitudes toward history" and to understand why it cannot be reduced to the procedural or tropological distinction between, say, synecdoche and mimesis. It is also to see the larger meaning of his claim that from the dramatistic point of view all philosophies and critical systems appear as just so many casuistries.

It would be articulating this recognition only a little differently to say that the internal dialectic of representation as between the mimetic and the synecdochic is best explained by understanding representation as an *activity*, which, precisely because it is an activity, needs to be understood as both motivated and situated. To grasp the historicist problematizing of historical representation, in other words, one must come to terms with the problem of the historical situation, the problem that might be understood to underlie the rest. Burke's term "selection," should certainly recall Lévi-Strauss's emphasis on the historian's partial decisions in his debate over historical specificity between himself and Sartre. It is a connection I have every interest in exploring further in what follows, especially because it helps to identify the value of reformulating the related problems of specificity and representation in terms of the case. After all, the relation of choices to the normative schemes that inform them defines one way of conceiving the "particular nature" of the case form, one way of understanding its peculiar mediation of generality and particularity. And as we have seen, the political aspect of the problem, early and late, is hard to miss in the comparison—implicit in Emerson's *Representative Men* as well as in some Romantic-historicist texts—between a representative *selected* to represent a *historical* state and a representative *elected* to represent a *political* state.[79] Political debate

---

79. It means comprehending the "deliberate" side of representation (to use another of Emerson's favorite words) for the spirit of the age—that is, the relationship of representation to the metaphorics of weighing and the faculty of judgment. Thus we see Jameson summarizing the argument of Sartre's *Search for a Method* with his explanation of how it is that "a nagging uncertainty about *motivation*" (Jameson's italics) haunts Sartre's work: "the past . . . must be formed from the outside, by a decision"—*Marxism and Form*, p. 211. Cf. Kenneth Burke's insistence that "the subject of motivation is a philosophic one, not ultimately to be solved in terms of empirical science"—GM, p. xxiii.

in the context of post-Waterloo British reform tends to be carried out, as I shall be suggesting, as a casuistry of the general will.

I have given preliminary definitions, but it is now time to offer further elaboration of how I will be using the terms "casuistries" and "cases." At the more abstract end of my spectrum of reference, I use "casuistry" as a general term for doctrines and disciplines of decision-making that are designed to handle "cases," by which I mean to invoke the root sense of "befallings," configurations of circumstance identified as such in relation to some normative domain, some principled notion of "rightness." The notion of "rightness," of being *correct,* seems implicit in the concept of grammatical case. Indeed, the grammatical concept seems to capture something of the more abstract description of the case form, as Thomas De Quincey intimates in his essay on "The Casuistry of Duelling": "*Casuistry,* the very word *casuistry* expresses the science which deals with such *cases:* for as a case, in the declension of a noun, means a falling away, or a deflection from the upright nominative (rectus), so a case in ethics implies some falling off, or deflection from the high road or catholic morality."[80] De Quincey refers here to a distinction that goes back to Greek linguistics, especially as developed by the Stoics, between direct and oblique cases. It may not be quite enough, however, to say that the oblique case simply falls away from the upright nominative case, since the uprightness of the nominative might also be said to be established by precisely that falling away into predication. The rightness of the nominative case and the obliquity of the declined case are together constitutive, mutually, of the case form.[81]

At the more concrete end, I use "casuistry" to refer to the tradition of ethical discipline and discourse that was developed after the Third Lateran Council in Rome, revamped by the Jesuits in Spain, satirized by Pascal and the Jansenists in France, revised by Protestant divines in England, and eventually adopted into secular forms such as the novel in various literary traditions through the eighteenth century.[82] Both the most concrete and the most abstract senses of the term "case" come into play in the post-Waterloo British writings that I shall be considering below. In *The Heart of Mid-Lothian,* for example, a novel that in-

---

80. Thomas De Quincey, "The Casuistry of Duelling," in *The Uncollected Writings,* 2 vols. (London: Swan Sonnenschein, 1892), 2:71.

81. See also, Jacques Derrida, "My Chances/*Mes Chances:* A Rendezvous with Some Epicurean Stereophanies," collected, in English translation, in *Taking Chances: Derrida, Psychoanalysis, and Literature* (Baltimore: Johns Hopkins University Press, 1984), pp. 1–32.

82. Albert R. Jonsen and Stephen Toulmin, *The Abuse of Casuistry* (Berkeley: University of California Press, 1988).

cludes explicit references to the Cameronian casuistry of David Deans, Scott has two characters, one called the Master of the Laws of Syntax, the other the Master of the Laws of Scotland, engage in heated dispute over the case of a Latin noun in which the distinction between the erect and fallen forms of naming is explicitly invoked. Since the introduction to *The Heart of Mid-Lothian* also involves a long dialogue between two lawyers comparing novels to cases at law, I should say that the legal case is particularly important to my invocation of the discourse of casuistry here and seems to operate at a level of abstraction somewhere between the high generality of the grammatical case form and the historical particularity of the increasingly secularized tradition of modern Christian casuistry.

The distinction between the legal and moral case is not a sharp one, and it is not hard to find references in the eighteenth and nineteenth century in which moral and jurisprudential casuistry are lumped together. Thus, Adam Smith can negatively link moral and legal cases by arguing that both ethics and jurisprudence should be carried out without resort to a casuistry, and De Quincey (as it happens quite a student of Smith) can, in that same essay on "The Casuistry of Duelling," insist on a metaphorical identification of moral casuists and lawyers:

> The consulting casuist is, in fact, to all intents and purposes, a moral attorney. For, as the plainest man, with the most direct purposes, is yet reasonably afraid to trust himself to his own guidance in any affair connected with questions of law; so also, when taught to believe that an upright intention and good sense are equally important in morals, as they are in law, to keep him from stumbling or from missing his road, he comes to regard a conscience-keeper as being no less indispensable for his daily life and conversation, than his legal agent . . . for his guidance amongst the innumerable niceties which beset the real and inevitable intricacies of rights and duties, as they grow out of human enactments and a complex condition of society.[83]

It is possible that De Quincey is trading here on the knowledge that, as Lucien Goldmann more recently reminded us in *Le Dieu Caché,* the leading theorists of casuistry in Port Royal Jansenism were trained in the law. I cite these comments both on this head and on the subject of the grammatical case to show the flexibility of De Quincey's understanding of casuistry as a modality and of the case as a form. Nor is it impossible to find that kind of flexibility elsewhere.

Toward the end of his discussion of Greenblatt's new historicism, Joel Fineman connects the "history of the anecdote" with the history of the case by claiming that his anecdotal paradigm of the hole and the whole "coincides"

---

83. De Quincey, "The Casuistry of Duelling," p. 66.

with "the logic of event and context established by . . . the medical case history" in Hippocrates.[84] But once again, Kenneth Burke seems to anticipate
both Fineman and Greenblatt in his dramatistic *summa, A Grammar of Motives,*
where he develops the language of the case in such a way as to show its advantage over the language of the anecdote. Perhaps this preference is inevitable in
Burke, given that casuistry's connection with the analysis of *situations* resonates
so strongly with Burke's critical stress on drama and dramatism. In places, it is
true, the terms "anecdote" and "case" seem to be virtually interchangeable in *A
Grammar of Motives.* Burke deploys the terms "representative anecdote" and
"representative case," for instance, with apparent indifference as to their possible distinction, but it is the vocabulary of the case, with its happy correlativity
of cases and casuistries, that eventually offers terms for a wholesale redescrip-
tion of the basic elements of Dramatism as they are initially presented. "One
could," Burke suggests, "think of the Grammatic resources as principles, and of
the various philosophies as casuistries which apply these principles to temporal
situations" (GM, p. xvi).[85]

The notion of the case is useful in what follows here both for its relevance to
the history of Romantic historicism as I have outlined it and for the particular
character of its complexity as (so to speak) a genre term. As it happens, both of
these aspects are evident in a recent collection of essays addressed to "the unexamined status of the case in social science methodology."[86] "What is a case?"
asks Charles Ragin in his introduction to this collection, and his first answer
suggests the relevance of the term for us here. "Comparative social science," he
writes, "has a ready-made, conventionalized answer to this question: Boundaries around places and time periods define cases (e.g., Italy after World War II)"
(p. 5). It might then be said that the present study, though not an exercise in
comparative social science, takes "England in 1819," the time-place represented

---

84. Fineman, "History of the Anecdote," p. 62.
85. Burke has touched on something that seems to run deep in the way we ordinarily talk
about cases. We often speak of getting down to cases, where we mean getting down to individual
cases, and where our emphasis is on the local circumstance, the particularity of the instance. Here
we may be interested in how a general principle applies or does not apply to what Fineman calls
the anecdotal slice of life. But we also speak of something as being "a case of such and such," or
even "just another case of such and such," and here we seem to call attention to the generality according to which anything that is a particular case is a particular case or instance *of* something. The
notion of the case, as we use it, then, is one in which both anecdote and history, particularity and
generality, seem to be mutually implicating.
86. Charles C. Ragin and Howard S. Becker, *What is a Case?* (Cambridge: Cambridge University Press, 1992), p. 4. Page numbers hereafter cited in the text.

in Shelley's sonnet, as a case in this "conventional" sense. But while Ragin concedes to conventional wisdom that "at a minimum, every study is a case study because it is an analysis of social phenomena specific to time and place," he shows a welcome readiness to complicate the received picture (p. 2). In the distinctive prose of his discipline, he goes on to state: "It could just as easily be argued, however, that not countries but rather parallel and contrasting event sequences are cases . . . , or that generic macrosocial processes, or historical outcomes, or macro-level narratives are cases" (p. 5). Or, making a similar point on a different level about what he calls the "slippage" of the term, Ragin offers a hypothetical comparison of an ethnographer and a quantitative researcher who both interview workers in a firm with different goals in view, the one to "uncover its organization," the other to assess variation in the workers' job satisfaction: "Both have data on employees and on the firm, and both produce finds specific in time and place . . . [y]et the ethnographer is said to have but one case and to be conducting a case study, while the quantitative research is seen as having many cases" (p. 4). The case has a way of concerning itself with time-place specificity, in other words, while at the same time offering an internally contradictory mode for its representation, and this double feature makes it especially attractive for my purposes. The fact that the status of the case has been, as Ragin says, relatively unexamined, only enhances that attractiveness.

Not surprisingly the vagaries of this term "case" have earned it more attention in the humanities than in the social sciences as defined by Ragin's disciplinary conception. To look no further than Burke's *A Grammar of Motives,* for the moment, one can note that Ragin's point about the uncertain scale of the case, as well as other related aspects of the problem, was directly anticipated there. Burke wrote in the 1940s: "[W]hereas one philosophic idiom offers the best calculus for one case, another case answers best to a totally different calculus. However, we should not think of 'cases' in too restricted a sense. Although . . . any given philosophy is to be considered a casuistry, even a cultural situation extending over centuries is a 'case,' and would probably require a much different philosophical idiom as its temporizing calculus of motives than would be required in the case of other cultural situations (GM, p. xvii).

In turning now to the Romantic prehistory of the case of culture, and indeed to the history of casuistry in which it must itself be situated, we must heed Burke's admonition not to think of cases in too restricted a sense. At the same time, however, we must understand what the conceptual history of the case can show about the powers and limitations of that discourse and its relatives. One important such related discourse is that of the "situation," a term whose centrality to the Sartre/Lévi-Strauss debate I have already noted in a preliminary way. Part of the point in looking at the case as it figures in Romantic historicism, indeed, is to be in a position to understand how it is that we have come to invoke so routinely the notion that Burke alternately calls "cultural situations" and "temporal situations" or, in an even more familiar idiom, "historical situations."[87]

---

87. I trust this idiom will be immediately recognizable to readers across a range of literary and cultural studies in recent years. It is an idiom that appears, for example, in Bryan Palmer's "contextualized situating of historical agents within structures of determination," John Brenkman's mutual linking of "the interpretation and the text as the two historically—and socially—situated sites of aesthetic experience," and Jonathan Arac's emphatic outlining of "historical situations for postmodern literary studies": Palmer, *Descent into Discourse,* p. xiv; Brenkman, "The Concrete Utopia of Poetry: Blake's 'A Poison Tree,'" in *Lyric Poetry: Beyond New Criticism,* ed. Chaviva Hosek and Patricia Parker (Ithaca, N.Y.: Cornell University Press, 1985); Arac, *Critical Genealogies: Historical Situations for Postmodern Literary Studies* (New York: Columbia University Press, 1987).

Chapter Four

ALTERING THE CASE:
THE INVENTION OF THE
HISTORICAL SITUATION

*W*e have been looking back at Kenneth Burke's brilliantly suggestive work of the 1940s from the other side of that "return to history," which it now seems to have played a role in shaping. In hindsight, one can see not only how Burke's critical meditations anticipate the reliance on the "anecdote" in contemporary criticism but also how the "anecdote" and its "histories" might be discussed in terms of "the case" and its "casuistries." I think it would not be hard, from a simple word search for titles of recent work in literary and cultural studies, to show just how widespread is the tendency of such work to identify its objects of study as "cases."[1] The "case" often seems, indeed, to have replaced "the text" as the generic label for what it is that scholars in the hermeneutic disciplines claim to be investigating. Therefore, as a last step in my argument about the genesis of current historicist critical practice in Romantic historicist writings, I wish to examine how casuistry figures in the period for which I am taking "England in 1819" itself as a case. Such an examination can help both to redescribe the contradictions I have pointed to in Romantic representation and to suggest how Romanticism is itself describable in terms of a massive altering of "the case." In considering "the case of Romantic historicism," then, I will be looking both at how Romanticism figures in the history of casuistry and how casuistry figures in the history of Romanticism.

So understood, the argument follows from an attempt to press the question of what is at stake in that invidious comparison of Prometheus and Satan in

1. For reasons that will emerge below, the turn to the case is also linked to the increased academic interest in metaphorical boundaries, "borders," and "border crossings" in recent years. This connection is explicit in, for example, Mary Poovey's aptly titled *Uneven Developments: The Ideological Work of Gender in Mid-Victorian Britain* (Chicago: University of Chicago Press, 1988), where she explains the organization of her study around issues that she calls "'border cases' because each of them had the potential to expose the artificiality of the binary logic that governed the Victorian symbolic economy," p. 12.

Shelley's 1819 preface to *Prometheus Unbound:* "The character of Satan engenders in the mind a pernicious casuistry which leads us to weigh his faults with his wrongs and to excuse the former because the latter exceed all measure." By way of explication of the significance of casuistry, I have to this point cited only sketchy comments on the subject from scattered sources—a nineteenth-century essayist (De Quincey), a twentieth-century critic (Burke), a contemporary sociologist (Ragin). From one perspective, this may seem odd. The discourse of casuistry has, after all, generated hundreds of volumes of commentary since the early Reformation period. Indeed, generating commentary, as Pascal wittily observed in *The Provincial Letters* (1656), is very much what the discourse of casuistry was all *about*.[2] And yet comprehensive accounts of the case form as such are hard to find. The one *extended* treatment of the case form I know of appears in a remarkable book published in German by André Jolles in 1930 under the title *Einfache Formen,* or *Simple Forms,* which was translated into French in 1946.[3]

Introducing his chapter on the case form, Jolles himself notes the incongruity between the ubiquity of the case form in modern western tradition and the paucity of commentary on its characteristic features:

> Here [in the life and literature of the West], cases are everywhere. The books that could contain them would fill a library. True, the word *casuistry* refers, in its general and ordinary acceptation, to the activity of moral theologians in the Catholic Church chiefly from the end of the sixteenth century. This casuistry has often had very bad press and, since Pascal, all those who had to come to terms with the Church, from the inside or the outside, have made this casuistry their weapon of choice. Casuistry passes for being the measuring instrument par excellence of Catholic morality and, when one speaks of casuistry, one thinks of mental restriction (*reservatio mentalis*) or Jesuitism in the worst sense of the term. . . . I obviously cannot deal with this casuistry in detail: I would like simply to show briefly in what manner the form of the case is realized in it. (p. 197)

Like Jolles, I want to attend to "the form of the case," and I will be relying on his astute account of it in what follows. Unlike Jolles, though, I also wish to keep in view the historical particulars of a specific casuistical tradition. Jesuit-inspired

---

2. See Letter Five, for example, in which Pascal has his Jesuit apologist explain how the number of official Christian commentators—"fathers of the Church"—grew from the ancient quartet to the current myriad, "296 of them," in just 80 years—*The Provincial Letters* (Harmondsworth: Penguin, 1967), p. 86. For more on the role of Pascal and the Port Royal school in the history of probability theory more generally, see Ian Hacking, *The Emergence of Probability* (Cambridge: Cambridge University Press, 1975), pp. 57–72.

3. André Jolles, *Einfache Formen* (1930; Darmstadt: Wissenschaftliche Buchgesellschaft, 1958). Translated into French as *Formes Simples,* trans. Antoine Marie Buguet (Paris: Seuil, 1972). The translation I use below is one I have revised slightly from work done for the present purpose by John Chaimov. All pages references are to the 1958 German edition. My thanks to Lionel Gossman for directing me to Jolles's account of the case.

casuistry from the sixteenth through the early nineteenth centuries has a complicated reception history that can be neither properly recounted nor completely excluded from my account of cases and casuistry in British Romanticism. It cannot be recounted because it is too immense. It cannot be excluded because the figure of the Jesuit reappears in apposite texts. In Scott's *Redgauntlet,* a novel usually read as a commentary on the first raft of "Scotch novels" in the Waverley series, Bonnie Prince Charles returns to Scotland in the guise of a Jesuit confessor. In *The Cenci,* a play written in 1819 intended for the London stage, and set in Catholic Rome of 1599, Shelley makes explicit reference to the casuistical practices of the main characters. Shelley's comment about the "pernicious casuistry" generated by Milton's Satan is as much a specific historical reference as a generalized claim about reader psychology.

Protestant Christian casuistry had been active in Britain at least from the seventeenth century. The notorious casuistical documents of the Jesuits had been an object of critique in Britain at least from the mid-seventeenth century, when Pascal produced his great satire in *The Provincial Letters.*[4] Interest in the subject was clearly recognized as waning by the years just before the close of the Napoleonic Wars, when Dugald Stewart wrote his widely cited account of Pascal for the History of Philosophy he composed as a supplement for the *Encyclopaedia Britannica.* Declaring the *Provincial Letters* the greatest of the great man's works, Stewart allowed that "it is now more praised than read in Great Britain; so completely have those disputes, to which it owed its first celebrity, lost their interest."[5] As the Wars neared an end, however, and the prospect of a Restoration guided by the Holy Alliance came into view, the situation in respect to the Jesuits and their doctrine changed. A papal bull was issued on August 7, 1814 calling for the reinstatement of the Jesuit order that had long since been banned not only by various nations but by the Vatican itself. The fact was not lost on writers for English periodicals, and the *Christian Observer,* for one, was not only monitoring the question of Jesuit revival very closely but also

4. This is a story that has been ably told, for example, in John Barker's account of "Pascal in England during the Age of Reason" as well as in histories of Protestant casuistical traditions in England. See, for example, Benjamin Jowett, "Essay on Casuistry," *Theological Essays* (London: Henry Frowde, 1906), pp. 73–100; H. R. McAdoo, *The Structure of Caroline Moral Theology* (London: Longmans, Green, 1949), especially pp. 64–97; and Edmund Leites, "Conscience, Casuistry, and Moral Decision: Some Historical Perspectives," *Journal of Chinese Philosophy,* special issue on "Conscience and its Analogues: East and West," 2 (December 1974): 41–58.

5. Dugald Stewart, "Dissertation First: Exhibiting a General View of the Progress of Metaphysical, Ethical, and Political Philosophy, Since the Revival of Letters in Europe," in *Encyclopaedia Britannica. Supplement to the Fourth, Fifth, and Sixth Editions* (Edinburgh: A. Constable, 1824), p. 125.

offering a series of articles on the life of Pascal as if in anticipation of a possible rejuvenation of jesuitical doctrine and discipline.

In April 1815, *The Christian Observer* concludes its article on the question of resuming war with Napoleonic France, by resigning itself to the British entry into the new alliance against Napoleon but at the same time issuing a caveat about the consequences of the victory: "Our Government should take care to have it distinctly understood, that in lavishing British blood and treasure for the freedom and independence of Europe, Great Britain must stipulate, that she shalt not be made to contribute, in any degree, to the renewal of a French Slave Trade; to the re-establishment of the papal power; to the revival of the order of the Jesuits; or to the rekindling of the fires of the Inquisition."[6] Such fears, occasioned by the imminent Restoration, explicitly figure in the publication in early 1815 of *A Brief Account of the Jesuits,* which claimed to provide "historical proofs . . . to establish the Danger of the Revival of that Order to the World at large and to the United Kingdom in particular."[7] The *Account* was, of course, favorably reviewed in the *Observer,* in spite of the reviewer's recognition of substantial plagiarisms—one involving a claim about the "pernicious effect" of the Jesuits on civil society—from William Robertson's account of the Jesuits in his celebrated history of the reign of Charles V.[8] Moreover, in the following year, 1816, the first English edition of *The Provincial Letters* to appear in well over a hundred years was published in a volume that also contained the offending papal bull, a brief history of the Jesuits, and a preface citing Stewart's praise for Pascal.[9]

All this evidence makes it difficult to consider Shelley's 1819 comments on Satan and the "pernicious casuistry" associated with his character apart from the specific history of the reception of casuistry in Britain—and of course this point holds a fortiori for Shelley's play of that same year about the casuistry of

6. *The Christian Observer* 14 (April 1815): 271–72.

7. *A Brief Account of the Jesuits* (London: 1815), title page; collected in *The Pamphleteer,* vol 6 (London: Gale and Fenner, 1815).

8. *The Christian Observer* 14 (March 1815): 172. Robertson's own extended account of the Jesuits and their practices appears in *The History of the Reign of the Emperor Charles V* [1767], 7th ed., 5 vols. (London: 1792), 3:188–209. In explaining the overall character of the order, he emphasizes the casuistical character of the leaders in a way that resonates with the critique of this form of casuistry made by his colleague in the Scottish Enlightenment, Adam Smith: "The maxims of an intriguing, ambitious, interested policy," writes Robertson, "might influence those who governed the society, and might even corrupt the heart, and pervert the conduct of some individuals, while the greater number, engaged in literary pursuits, or employed in the functions of religion, was left to the guidance of those common principles which restrain men from vice, and excite them to what is becoming and laudable" (p. 209).

9. Blaise Pascal, *Provincial Letters, Containing an Exposure of the Reasoning and Morals of the Jesuits* (London: Gale and Fenner, 1816).

the Roman aristocracy in 1599 and for Scott's closely contemporary interest in Jesuitism and the Port-Royal monastery in *Redgauntlet*. Jolles is certainly right to identify Jesuit casuistry as central to the larger discourse of casuistry in western Europe, and therefore as crucial to the project of understanding, as he puts it, the case form that is "realized" in that discourse. Jolles's account of the case, perhaps the most complex of the "simple forms" he identifies, ranks with Kenneth Burke's scattered comments as among the very best treatments we have of the matter. And yet the book is almost completely unknown, at least in Anglo-American literary studies; not even Burke himself, for all his interest in related questions of form and casuistry, seems to have been aware of its existence.[10] In order, therefore, to provide the terms for a more subtle rewriting of the idiom of the representative anecdote into that of the case, I begin with a brief exposition of Jolles's analysis.

1. The Form of the Case

Jolles calls his project "morphological," and says it is aimed at supplementing the work in aesthetics and in historical hermeneutics that he sees as having dominated the literary criticism of the eighteenth and nineteenth centuries, respectively. He identifies nine basic forms of thought-in-language and outlines them in individual chapters: the legend, the saga, the myth, the riddle, the proverb, the case, the memoir, the tale, and the joke. Jolles's rangy and provocative chapter on the case takes the nested narratives of the eleventh-century Sanskrit collection, *The Ocean of Story*, as supplying one of its central paradigms but nonetheless identifies casuistry as a dominantly Western phenomenon. Although Jolles sees the Western cultural tradition since the emergence of courtly romance as saturated by casuistry, he is less concerned with the historical fact of European Catholic casuistry than with the cognitive form he sees realized in it, even when he seems interested in rehabilitating the project of casuistry left in the long wake of Pascal's critique. The special relevance of Jolles's account to the question immediately at issue appears in its very opening moves, where he attempts to distinguish the form of the case (*Kasus oder Fall*) from other kinds of forms with which it might be confused (p. 179). The case, says Jolles, is not merely an instantiation of a general scheme or normative system; nor is it just the form in

10. The only English discussion of it I have found is an expository chapter in Robert Scholes, *Structuralism in Literature* (New Haven: Yale University Press, 1974), pp. 42–50. Scholes suggests that an English translation was in the works at that time, but, to my knowledge, no translation of the book into English yet been published. Of Jolles's discussion of the case in particular, Scholes briefly notes, correctly I think, that "this form," as Jolles describes it, "is an important ancestor and ingredient of the short story—as the 'painful cases' of Joyce's *Dubliners* may easily remind us" (p. 46).

which that instantiation occurs. Rather it is the occurrence of an anomaly for such a system or scheme.[11] In the case, we see the posing of a problem for the framework in respect to which the object or event is represented, a dynamic relation rather like one in which the so-called scientific fact itself enters the discourse of early modern natural philosophy.[12]

It is for this reason, as Jolles points out, that the case has been repeatedly associated in many Indo-European languages with the metaphorics of scales and measures. In English we say that cases are "pondered" and "weighed"—that they "pend" or are "suspended," that they hang in the balance:

> The peculiarity of the case form lies precisely in that it poses a question without being able to give an answer, that it imposes on us the obligation to decide without containing the decision in itself—it is the place where a weighing of things is carried out, but not the result of that weighing. The instrument with two plates is the Latin *bilanx*, whence comes the Romance terms for scale, *balance, bilancia*. We Germans have appropriated from this the verb *balancieren*, also having the meaning: to try to find the equilibrium point [one's balance]. There is in the case all the attractions and all the perils of this balancing act, and to use a (German) image, one can say that this form is the place where are realized the swaying and swinging of the mental activity that weighs and ponders [das Schwanken und Schwingen der wägenden und erwägenden Geistesbeschåaftigung verwirklicht]. (p. 191)

I suggested earlier that Shelley's comment about the "pernicious casuistry" attendant on the reader's interest in Milton's Satan seems to echo William Robertson's charge of "perniciousness" in the critique that was being revived around 1815 in response to the threat of the papal restoration of the Society of Jesus. We can now notice how closely this same passage in Shelley's preface to *Promentheus Unbound*—with its insistence on metaphorizing the casuistical process as a weighing and pondering, and its attention to the balance of measures—seems to anticipate Jolles's generalized account of the case form. At a time when interest in casuistry was reviving, Shelley manages, with his characteristic acuity, to articulate its conceptual structure.

While Shelley's elaborations of his notion of casuistry are dispersed among several of his writings, Jolles's account of casuistry and the case, on the other hand, is relatively concise and systematic. It is especially crucial to grasp that, for Jolles, the case names not only the anomaly for a scheme or system, but also the scheme or system itself, as well as those processes by which anomalies

---

11. A self-evidently legal move in a game of fixed rules—pawn to queen 4 as a chess opening—would count as an example of an example. Examples of *cases,* on Jolles's account, appear below.

12. See Lorraine Daston, "Natural Facts and Marvelous Evidence in Early Modern Europe," in *Questions of Evidence: Proof, Practice, and Persuasion Across the Disciplines,* ed. James Chandler, Arnold Davidson, and Harry Harootunian (Chicago: University of Chicago Press, 1994), pp. 245–50.

and norms are adjudicated. The case, to invoke another etymological connection with the scale, is the very form of "deliberation." It is always calling for judgment, and it is by virtue of judgment that it offers formal mediation between the particular and the general, between instance and rule, between circumstance and principle. It mediates between descriptive and normative orders.

By calling attention to the activities of judgment and the metaphorics of the deliberation, Jolles's analysis sheds new light, I think, on those features of the anecdote-case outlined in different terms by Ginzburg's notion of the endless investigation of a "normalcy that proves elusive to documentation," in Fineman's history of "wholes" and "holes," and, quite explicitly, in Kenneth Burke's casuistical dramatism. As Jolles goes on to illustrate in detail, the dynamic *Schwanken und Schwingen* of the scales in the representation of the case suggest a two-way movement in which now the general normative scheme, now the particular event or situation, is being tested. The case has a distinctively dramatic or performative character in that it involves the issuing of judgments or passing of sentences, both *on* scenes of action and *in* scenes of conflict. Thus, comparing it to the other "simple forms" he analyzes, Jolles identifies the case as the form par excellence of "contradiction."[13] The case form answers the needs of our analysis of representation in the spirit of the age, in other words, because it is associated at once with agency, judgment, and normativity, on the one hand, and with the working through of contradictions, on the other.

But perhaps such formulations are too abstract to seem helpful. As a way of concretizing Jolles's account, and bringing his terms closer to home, readers of contemporary fiction might recall Don DeLillo's recent novel *Libra,* a piece of historical fiction about Lee Harvey Oswald and the Kennedy assassination. In DeLillo's tour de force contrivance, the novel is constructed as an alternation between two narratives, odd chapters narrating Oswald's life (each such chapter titled with *place names* from the biography) and even chapters narrating an assassination conspiracy taking shape among disaffected Bay-of-Pigs operatives (each such chapter titled with *dates* from the year 1963). To this twofold narrative modality, DeLillo adds a twofold narrative frame. Half of the frame involves a retired CIA agent, Nicholas Branch, who has been "hired on contract to write the secret history of the assassination of President Kennedy" and been given full access to all state documents he deems relevant to the task. The other part of the frame involves Marguerite Oswald, mother of Lee Harvey, who is testifying be-

---

13. As I will be exploring in chapter 5, apropos of the "scene of explanation" in Scott's historical novels, the case's sayings about scenes—its *captions*—can also be understood (within larger scenes) as sayings in conflict, i.e., as *contradictions*—see below, chapter 5.

fore an unnamed judge and seeks to tell the inner truth about her son's life and fate.[14]

Both Marguerite and Branch describe their objects of representation as cases. With Marguerite this is explicit ("Your honor, I cannot state the truth of this case with a simple yes and no. I have to tell a story. . . . There are stories within stories, judge. . . . I intend to research this case and present my findings. But I cannot pin it down to a simple statement" (pp. 450–51). With Branch it is implicit. He must reconcile "theories that gleam like jade idols, intriguing systems of assumption, four-faced, graceful," to a "strangeness . . . that is almost holy . . . , an aberration in the heartland of the real" (p. 15). At times, to defer the task of resolution Branch "takes refuge in his notes," and, he decides, "it is premature to make a serious effort to turn these notes into coherent history. Maybe it will always be premature" (p. 301). Presenting itself as a quintessential historical case study, *Libra* thus signals again and again its performance of what Jolles describes as the case's perpetual irresolvability, the sustained swinging and swaying of the scales.

The alternation of the two narratives in the novel's interlaced chapter sequences emphasizes the activity of *weighing* over any final settling of the case. The *dated* chapters of the post-Bay-of-Pigs conspiracy against Kennedy in 1963 lead to the point where the conspirators need to invent someone to take the fall, and it is at that same point where the life of Oswald narrated in the *location* chapters begins to reach as far as 1963. That is the point where the apparently speculative, unofficial narrative of the plot against Kennedy by the Bay-of-Pigs operatives begins to take on plausibility as history and where the apparently factual, official biography of Oswald begins to look like a piece of fiction. It is the point of equilibrium in the novel's careful balancing act, one might say, and, in addition to being given titular status in the novel, it is quite pointedly marked in the exchange that takes place when the historical David Ferrie takes the quasi-fictional "Oswald" to meet the historical Clay Shaw:

> "When is your birthday?" Shaw said first thing.
> "October eighteen," Lee said.
> "Libra. A Libran."
> "The Scales," Ferrie said.
> "The Balance," Shaw said.
> It seemed to tell them everything they had to know. (p. 315)

The balancing acts performed in *Libra*'s carefully weighted scales are perhaps not as delicate as one might like, but their very conspicuousness calls attention

---

14. Don DeLillo, *Libra* (New York, Viking, 1988), p. 15. Subsequent citations by page numbers in text.

to how DeLillo claims for what he does a special kind of cognitive power—as if the balance of the case were all one had to know.

Further, lest one missed either the work of balancing or the cognitive function it is assigned in the novel, DeLillo takes pains to foreground the language of the case in his own metacommentary on *Libra*. In a brief "author's note" appended to the novel, rather in the vein of Scott, DeLillo describes his book as "a work of imagination" about "a major unresolved event" which aspires "to fill some of the blank spaces in the known record." Part of the point of the note is to offer a legal disclaimer: "To do this I've altered and embellished reality, extended real people into imagined space and time, invented incidents, dialogues, and characters. Among these invented characters are all officers of intelligence agencies and all organized crime figures, except for those who are part of the book's background." But the last half of the note makes a more substantial claim for something in its methodology:

> In a case in which rumors, facts, suspicions, official subterfuge, conflicting sets of evidence, and a dozen labyrinthine theories all mingle, sometimes indistinguishably, it may seem to some that a work of fiction is one more gloom in a chronicle of unknowing.
>
> But because this book makes no claim to literal truth, because it is only itself, apart and complete, readers may find refuge here—a way of thinking about the assassination without being constrained by half-facts or overwhelmed by possibilities, by the tide of speculation that widens with the years. (n.p.)

It is difficult not to connect and liken these remarks to those of Carlo Ginzburg (reprising young Macaulay), published in the very same year, 1988, about the great potential of the old historical novel genre for contemporary historiography. There Ginzburg described the work of Natalie Davis in terms of the case as, precisely, the form of irresolution, as the means of representing the discrepancy between the historically and statistically representative and of deepening the investigation of uniting the anomalous instance to the context. It is true that Ginzburg redefines the license of "invention" that Davis had invoked and DeLillo here seems to emulate. Then again, we do no violence to Davis's or to Ginzburg's or DeLillo's work if we see them all together making the applicability of Jolles's model patent or at least plausible here.

Just how useful is such a notion of the case form in coming to grips with the problems of representation, contradiction, and normativity in the age of the spirit of the age? How can it offer further illumination of what Lukács calls the "specifically historical" as involving the derivation of the individuality of characters from the historical peculiarity of their age? And how useful in turn might such an analysis be for coming to terms with the case of Scott himself for England in 1819? Is Scott's body of work better understood as an instantiation of or as a case for what I have been calling Romantic historicism? To answer such questions, and thus to mediate the jump I have made from the older history and received form of the case in casuistry to DeLillo's novel, I turn now to a brief analysis of two novels by Scott in which case structure and casuistical history are mutually articulated. The first novel, *Old Mortality* (1816), is widely regarded as the best of Scott's most successful group of novels, the series (within the *Waverley* series) he called "Tales of My Landlord."[15] The second novel I will look at is *Redgauntlet* (1824), which, as I have already noted, has been read as a commentary on the first raft of Waverley novels as an ensemble.

The novels in "Tales of My Landlord" signally concern themselves not only with the history of jurisprudential casuistry in Scotland, like many of Scott's novels, but also more particularly with episodes in Scotland's so-called wars of conscience. They are thus about both legal cases and moral cases, and they tend to put both kinds of cases into a historicized frame of reference. For these reasons, it should become clear how useful these novels are for showing how the case is altered by the historicism that Scott and his contemporaries put into practice. I will show, therefore, how Scott's novels of the decade after the end of the Napoleonic Wars—the novels Lukács sees as the embodiment of the distinctive historicism of that moment—are deeply structured by an interest in casuistical balancing acts of all sorts, including the balancing of trials of persons against trials of laws and the balancing of laws or normative systems against each other. After establishing that point, however, I will suggest the limits to what Scott's distinctive historical casuistry can exemplify about the newly constituted sense of normativity in Romantic historicism. For as Scott reached toward the form and idiom of the case as the means of representing his historical imagination, changes in the general practice of casuistry itself, and in its range of application in (for example) political discourse, were shifting the ground on which he stood.

2. Balancing Acts: Scott and the Wars of Conscience

The action of *Old Mortality* is focused on the career of an enlightened young Presbyterian, Henry Morton, during a notorious period of extremist conflict in Scotland. The narrative opens with the celebrated events of 1679 in which a radical puritan insurgency took on a pro-Stuart regime sympathetic to Catholicism in religion and arbitrary royal power in politics: these events in-

---

15. Scott completed this project in 1819 with the third series, comprising both the novella, *The Legend of Montrose,* and *The Bride of Lammermoor,* which I discuss in chapter 5. It was after completing work on *The Bride* that he turned directly to *Ivanhoe,* managing also to complete that novel as well by the end of his prodigious year's work. *The Bride of Lammermoor* was published together with *A Legend of Montrose* as "Tales of My Landlord," 3d series, on June 10, 1819. *Ivanhoe* appeared on December 18. See John Sutherland, *The Life of Walter Scott* (Oxford: Blackwell, 1995), pp. 226, 235.

clude the assassination of James Sharpe, Archbishop of St. Andrews, the upris-
ing of the Covenanters at the Battle of Drumclog in the west Lowlands, and the
ensuing Battle of Bothwell Bridge. The novel closes in 1689, with the sequence
of political reversals felt in Scotland in the wake of the Glorious Revolution.
Morton's career in volatile political circumstances involves several roles: as a
suitor to a woman from a Royalist family, as an officer in the army of the
Covenanting insurgency, as a religious disputant on both sides, as a prisoner on
both sides, as an exile in America, and, finally, after 1688, as a successful officer
in the service of William of Orange.

Morton's movement back and forth across apparent ideological borders recalls that of Edward Waverley, in the first of Scott's historical novels. And we are
indeed accustomed, after Lukács and others, to likening the protagonist of *Old
Mortality* to that of *Waverley* as figures in the middle, passive mediocrities between active extremities in conflict, not world-historical in themselves but
shaped by world-historical struggle. This account is not wrong, as far as it goes,
but a careful look at *Old Mortality* suggests that Scott is less concerned to show
how Morton's character is specified by the history in whose middle he acts his
part than how his historically specified character might be understood as capable of *acting* in such a middle, choosing and pursuing a line of conduct in a
medium of actual circumstance.[16] In this respect, *Old Mortality* might be seen as
taking a step away from the model of *Waverley* itself. In *Waverley,* the work of
characterological inscription by history is arguably the most fundamental
process recorded in the narrative. It is not only that Edward Waverley has no
character at the start. One might also say that he *is* no character—that he lacks
characterization—and that he acquires characterization by virtue of forces that
operate on him and by genres in which he is allowed to figure: such genres as the
Highland bardic song, the newspaper article, the record of court proceeding,
the epistle, the portrait. Remembering that *Waverley* was initially thought by
some readers to have been written by William Godwin, one might argue that
Waverley's character is shaped in historical circumstance in a fashion suggested
by *Political Justice,* where Godwin argues that actions come from opinions,
opinions from circumstances, and circumstances from historical institutions.[17]

16. Although many commentators follow Lukács's account of the ethical mediocrity or
middleness of Scott's protagonists, there are some exceptions. As Susan Morgan has argued in *Sisters in Time: Imagining Gender in Nineteenth-Century British Fiction* (New York: Oxford University
Press, 1989), the talent for situational decision making importantly characterizes (and genders
feminine) Scott's so-called mediocre protagonists as distinct from the Romantic, fatalist heroes
that inhabit the wings of his moral stage, pp. 71–72.

17. William Godwin, *Enquiry Concerning Political Justice* (Harmodsworth: Penguin, 1976),
pp. 79–163.

In *Old Mortality,* by contrast, where the question of conscience is so explicitly a part of the ideological struggle of the historical period in question, we meet a character quite fully formed at the start of the novel. With Morton, the interest lies in the practical work of conscience, in how he makes difficult judgments in extreme circumstances. Morton's trajectory as it appears in this narrative is indeed largely structured by or as a sequence of casuistical problems or cases of conscience. This sequence is initiated at the very outset of the novel with the difficult case of deciding whether to harbor on his uncle's estate a radical puritan, John Balfour. It is emphasized that Morton knows Balfour to be *both* the assassin who killed Archbishop Sharpe earlier that very day *and* the friend who once saved the life of Morton's father in the civil wars of mid-century. Weighing different forms of obligation against each other, personal gratitude against a more abstract demand for justice, Morton dramatizes a mode of deliberation that will be repeated again and again in the novel.[18]

Morton's balancing acts in this novel are indeed multiple. He must weigh the arguments of Covenanters against those of Anglicans, those of rebels against those of Royalists, the cause of loyalty against the cause of enlightenment. Morton must steer a middle course not merely, however, in the sense that he must split the difference between two political or religious sides. Understood on another level, his difficult via media lies between, on the one hand, acting on principle as if one were beyond circumstance (as Claverhouse, John Balfour, and, most conspicuously, Mause Headrigg do) and, on the other, acting in circumstance as if one were beyond principle—though these extremes do meet. At a time when religious tests were demanded by both sides in a struggle where power often changed hands, the temptation was enormous to play both sides of the street, to say "I believe" to whatever one was asked to swear to. There are characters in the novel who, in effect, do just that: Cuddie Headrigg (Mause's amiable son who befriends Morton in the end), Niel Blane (the pubkeeper-piper who "played whig or jacobite tunes as best pleased his customers" [TML1, conclusion]), and, less innocuously, Basil Olifant, the trimmer who is eventually shot by Cuddie himself for his treachery.

Although this is indeed a novel in which the "lukewarm" shall be vomited from the mouth of the Lord, it is also a novel about the pragmatics of "application," especially about the problems of applying Biblical types to existing situa-

---

18. The casuistical aspect of *Old Mortality* gains added emphasis by virtue of Scott's choice of Archbishop Sharpe's assassination as a triggering occasion for the novel, for Sharpe had himself figured in then-raging controversies over conscience and casuistry in the late seventeenth century with two of his own *Discourses Concerning Conscience* (London: Printed for Fincham Gardiner, 1684).

tions (TML1, chap. 21). Morton appears to change sides as often as Edward Waverley, and like Waverley he ends up commanding a body of troops for an army with whose leaders he lacks full sympathy. But from the start Morton insists on weighing the details of each case of conscience he confronts. Indeed, as he points out in a long discussion with Balfour and the Cameronian minister, Ephraim Macbriar, the one point on which he is agreed with them is that "freedom of conscience" is itself a cause truly worth fighting for. When Morton is offered a command in Balfour's Covenanting army, he deliberates:

> [I]t is not surprising that a natural sense of the injuries of my country, not to mention those I have sustained in my own person, should make me sufficiently willing to draw my sword for liberty and freedom of conscience. But I will own to you, that I must be better satisfied concerning the principles on which you bottom your cause ere I can agree to take a command amongst you. (TML1, chap. 21)

But "principle" here means something much closer to rule-of-application, as Morton makes clear when Balfour expresses surprise that anyone can doubt of principles so explicitly stated as the Covenanters' have been:

> I revere the scriptures as deeply as you or any Christian can do. I look into them with humble hope of extracting a rule of conduct and a law of salvation. But I expect to find this by an examination of their general tenor, and of the spirit which they uniformly breathe, and not by wresting particular passages from their context, or by the application of Scriptural phrases to circumstances and events with which they have often very slender relation. (chap. 21)

In their subsequent dispute, when Morton expresses concern that the campaign will be "carried on by such measures as that with which it commenced" (i.e, the assassination of Archbishop Sharpe) Balfour defends that act with a hypothesis about how the Almighty might permit himself to "raise up instruments to deliver his church of difficulty," and Morton offers the following rebuttal:

> [T]he case you have supposed does not satisfy my judgment. That the Almighty, in his mysterious providence, may bring a bloody man to an end deservedly bloody, does not vindicate those who, without authority of any kind, take upon themselves to be the instruments of execution, and presume to call them the executors of divine vengeance. (chap. 21)

Scott's articulation of a connection between casuistry and history here is neither naive nor simple. It is true that Morton's voice is given what might be called a transhistorical rationality in these exchanges with John Balfour over the issues defined by such terms as "rule of conduct," "general tenor," "particular passages," "context," "application," "circumstances," "temporizing," "falling away," "case," "cause," "conscience," and "judgment." At the same time, this casuistical phraseology itself appears as part of a culturally specific moral discourse.

A similar kind of complexity can be found in *The Heart of Mid-Lothian,* which alone constitutes the second series in the "Tales of My Landlord," where

Jeanie Deans and her father, a man who fought as a Cameronian in the very conflicts narrated in *Old Mortality,* effectively stage a similarly historicized debate, with Jeanie as the voice of transhistorical moral authority. In that novel, too, what might be called a self-consciousness about the case as such—an awareness of its status as a "simple form," to reinvoke that phrase from Jolles—seems to be registered through Scott's way of juxtaposing the legal and moral senses of "the case" in the yoking and framing of the central actions: the legal cases of Wilson the smuggler, Porteous the police captain, and Effie Deans (who stands accused of infanticide) are balanced by the moral case posed to Jeanie, when she is forced to decide, rather like Shakespeare's Isabella in *Measure for Measure,* whether she can engage in wrongdoing to save the life of a sibling accused under a potentially unjust law. The very provenance supplied for the narrative of Jeanie Deans, a tale told to a lawyer who claims to read legal cases as if they were novels, highlights the self-consciousness about the status of the case in *The Heart of Mid-Lothian.* Even the concept of the grammatical case is given some prominence in the diegesis of the narrative itself.

So if, as J. Paul Hunter and others have argued, the early novel can be understood as the elaboration of the secularized case form, then the historical novel—the literary genre associated by Lukács with the new Romantic historicism—can be understood as effecting a self-conscious transformation of the novel by way of a self-conscious transformation of the case.[19] I return below to this self-consciousness about the case in *The Heart of Mid-Lothian* and in *The Bride of Lammermoor,* from the second and third series of "Tales of My Landlord." But one can see how Scott retrospectively reemphasizes the case as a means of self-identification for his new genre in the highly reflexive *Redgauntlet* (1824), a novel in which, as one commentator has recently put it, we encounter "the historical romance as metafiction"—that is, as "the pretext for an elaborate study of [Scott's] own methods as historian and romancer."[20]

3. "A Specimen of All Causes": The Case of *Redgauntlet*

In narrating the historically latest and most fantastic episode in Scott's treatment of the "good old cause" of the Jacobites, *Redgauntlet* posits a final visit of the Young Pretender to Scottish soil in the 1760s, two decades after the failure of the Rebellion, for one last attempt to overthrow the Hanoverians. Centering as it

---

19. See G. A. Starr, *Defoe and Casuistry* (Princeton, N.J.: Princeton University Press, 1971), passim; and J. Paul Hunter, *Before Novels: The Cultural Contexts of Eighteenth-Century English Fiction* (New York: Norton, 1990), pp. 288–94.

20. James Kerr, *Fiction Against History: Scott as Storyteller* (Cambridge: Cambridge University Press, 1989), p. 102.

does on the historical moment when the "good old cause" becomes an object of history, *Redgauntlet* interests itself in the relation between cases and causes of all sorts. This interest becomes clear in the initial comradely epistolary exchanges between the two young would-be lawyers, Alan Fairford and Darsie Latimore, the former of whom has stayed behind in Edinburgh to continue his legal pursuits while the latter wanders the British countryside in search of adventure and romance. The novel is so caught up in self-consciousness about its relation to the case form, and precisely about the formal dimensions of the case, that much of its action actually consists in the work of stating cases. In parallel early sequences, Latimore states a case before an English justice of the peace, and Fairford states a case before a Scottish provost. When the character who sutures the parallel narratives of the separated correspondents (Lilias Redgauntlet) comes to Fairford's legal office in Edinburgh, he hopes to reassure her sufficiently about his inexperience so that she will "remove her scruples to open her case to [him]" (Redg, ltr. 8). Conversing later with Darsie Latimore, she insists to him that her "case is different" than he supposes when he stops himself from flattering her with what he calls the *argumentum ad feminam,* a form of argument, he says, unlike the ad hominem, which can seldom or never be "justified by circumstances" (ltr. 12).

Furthermore, what lends both metaphoric and metonymic organization to the various cases of the novel is the comic cause célèbre which centers the novel's primary relationships: the case of *Peebles against Plainstanes,* that legal-fictional marvel that many readers have recognized as the prototype for Dickens's *Jarndyce v. Jarndyce* in *Bleak House.* The condition of the Peebles case is reported bluntly at the outset: "the carelessness and blunders of Peter's former solicitors had converted [it] into a huge chaotic mass of unintelligible technicality" (Redg, chap. 1). It is a case that turns out to be almost impossible to state. No diegesis is adequate to its complexity, although many are offered in this novel, sometimes offered simultaneously. At the first three-way meeting of Fairford, his lawyer father, and their client Peebles, Fairford's father, having studied the confused heap of documents, proposes "to give the young counsel an outline of the state of the conjoined process, with a view to letting him into the merits of the cause" (ltr. 13). The following diegetic contest is then related:

> "I have made a short abbreviate, Mr. Peebles," said he; "having sat up late last night, and employed much of this morning in wading through these papers, to save Alan some trouble, and I am now about to state the result."
> "I will state it myself," said Peter, breaking in without reverence upon his solicitor.
> "No, by no means," said my father, "I am your agent for the time."
> "Mine eleventh in number," said Peter, "I have a new one every year. . . ."
> "Your agent for the time," resumed my father; "and you, who are acquainted with the forms, know that the client states the cause to the agent—the agent to the counsel." (ltr. 13)

Peter is defeated in the contest over the stating of his case only when he is offered food and his hunger gets the best of his legal pride: "[S]o well," reports young Fairford, "did the diversion engage him, that though, while my father stated the case, he looked at him repeatedly, as if he meant to interrupt his statement, yet he always found more agreeable employment for his mouth, and returned to the cold beef with . . . avidity" (ltr. 13). The statement of the case of Peebles against Planestanes is thus from the start involved in a pair of theatricalized rivalries: the rivalry between Peter and Mr. Fairford to tell it, and then the rivalry of desires within Peter over whether to use his mouth to state his case or to eat his beef. This contestation over the act of diegesis itself is one of the most reflexive features of this, perhaps Scott's most self-referential novel.

The formal dimension of the case will be pressed still harder in this novel, however, for, when Fairford's epistolary narrative finally reaches the point where his father can state the case, the report of that statement is offered as the rival to the story (a piece of *diabolerie* with its own inserted title, "Wandering Willie's Tale") that Darsie Latimer has reported in his previous letter to him. The fungibility of these narratives in *Redgauntlet*'s fictional economy becomes explicit when, at the close of the very paragraph in which he has been describing the diegetic rivalries surrounding the case of Peter Peebles, Fairford writes: "I will endeavour to give you, in exchange for your fiddler's tale, the history of a litigant, or rather the history of his law-suit" (ltr. 13). The structure of exchange that makes possible the substitution of case for tale calls attention at once to the narrative dimension of the case (Fairford will give the *history* of the lawsuit) and the casuistical dimension of the story ("Wandering Willie's Tale" turns on the question of what it means, in an oral culture, for someone to tell a "story he cannot prove" [ltr. 11]). To suggest yet further complication for the structure of *Redgauntlet,* however, Scott allows the figure of substitution (case for case), to be crossed by the figure of interpolation (case within case): after reporting his father's statement of the case, Alan says that his "brain was like to turn at this account of lawsuit within lawsuit, like a nest of chip boxes" (ltr. 13). This structure of interpolated narratives stands in a subtly uncertain relation to the structure of exchange and rivalry, and what happens next in the novel does nothing to clarify the ambiguity.

The relation is uncertain because, at the end of this very letter (ltr. 13 in the exchange of correspondence with which the novel opens), the epistolary form itself abruptly breaks off, and, with only a brief "explanation" having to do with the deficiencies of epistolarity as such, the "Narrative" begins. This third-person narrative runs for only two chapters, which first retell the circumstances that led Mr. Fairford to saddle his son with Peebles's case and then retell the case itself by reference to Alan's brilliant presentation of it on his first day in court against the defendant's lawyer Mr. Tough. Alan's statement of the case is, in turn, interrupted by the letter from Darsie that causes him to depart the courtroom and desert the case, this desertion in *its* turn becoming the basis for Peter's case against Fairford himself for what we might nowadays call "legal malpractice." Hence the larger structural ambiguity of the novel, as registered in its commentaries. Whether this post-epistolary narrative stands as a nest around the earlier representations or on all fours with them is difficult to say, and this indeterminacy as between one of two sides of a case, on the one hand, and its circumscribed integrity, on the other, is itself left a matter of uncertainty in the novel. Like the case of Peebles, the novel itself balances uncertainly and self-consciously on an indeterminate center in a way that is characteristic of the case form. It seems the more explicitly Scott thematizes the case form the more conspicuous the formal features become.

Moreover, when the novel begins to link this sort of jurisprudential "casing" to the traditions of moral casuistry, another area of ambiguity develops in its narrative procedures. Several studies, most notably by Albert Jonson and Stephen Toulmin, have recently attempted to understand the place of casuistry in the history of western European moral philosophy and in such related areas as the history of probability.[21] There have also been a few attempts to link these developments to problems in literary history, especially by those scholars who have argued persuasively that early fiction ought to be read as a body of hypothetical moral cases allowed unprecedented elaboration. Although the work on casuistry and the novel seldom reaches forward even as far as Scott, it is not difficult to show, in discussions of casuistry such as De Quincey's, that the question of casuistry is still being debated by writers well into the nineteenth century.[22] As for Scott himself, it is hard to ignore the many indications of his own deliberate engagement with the casuistical tradition. This is manifest not only in Scott's high-relief juxtaposition of legal and moral casuistry in a novel such as *Redgauntlet,* but also in his explicit identification of its attention to "cases" in relation to the tradition of jesuitical casuistry. That is, while the limited action of *Redgauntlet,* like that of *Old Mortality,* is mediated for the reader by the narrative attention to circumstantial decision making, this line of development receives a particularly pointed inflection when Prince Charles, in whose behalf (or for

21. Albert R. Jonsen and Stephen Toulmin, *The Abuse of Casuistry* (Berkeley: University of California Press, 1988). On the history of probability, see Ian Hacking, *The Emergence of Probability,* and Lorraine Daston, *Classical Probability in the Enlightenment* (Princeton, N.J.: Princeton University Press, 1988).
22. Thomas De Quincey, *Uncollected Writings,* 2:65–112.

whose cause) the largest actions of the novel are being undertaken, finally appears in *Redgauntlet* wearing the guise of a Jesuit priest, Father Buonaventure, and playing the role of confessor, or casuistical *directeur de conscience,* for members of the Jacobite conspiracy. Furthermore, Lilias, whose astute deliberations inform most of the key decisions in the novel, tells Darsie in their late scene of explanation that she escaped her uncle's Catholic and Jacobite moral habits, by virtue of having resided for some years at the convent of the Port-Royal—the site, though not so identified in the text, of Pascal's and Arnaud's famous acts of resistance to the political and theological hegemony of Jesuit casuistry.

The allusive context of casuistry lends a particular frisson to the ironies of the scene between young Fairford and the Pretender in his guise as a French Jesuit. Since Fairford has been granted sanctuary by the hostesses of the establishment, who regard Father Buonaventure as their guest of honor, Fairford's discovery of a Catholic priest in the house leaves him wrestling with a case of conscience, a matter pointed out by the disguised Pretender himself: "You are probably aware," he says, "that you speak to a person proscribed by the severe and unjust laws of the present government" (Redg, chap. 16). Fairford, who is able to cite the precise statute and chapter to which his interlocutor alludes, is immediately caught between loyalties, between the laws of the land and the laws of courtesy, but is clear where his obligation lies: "I consider myself as indebted for my life to the Mistresses of Fairladies; and it would be a vile requital on my part to pry into or make known what I may have seen or heard under this hospitable roof. If I were to meet the Pretender himself *in such a situation,* he should even at the risk of a little stretch to my loyalty, be free from any danger from my indiscretion" [italics mine] (chap. 16). In what follows between them, Alan handles a series of doubtful cases in rapid succession: should he agree to allow the priest to handle the sealed letter he is carrying for Redgauntlet; should he violently resist when the priest decides to break the seal and open it; should he agree to read the contents himself when the priest recommends that his (Alan's) own safety will be better secured by his doing so? In this last instance we are told that his "resolution" was "decided" in the following terms: "If these correspondents, he thought, are conspiring against my person, I have a right to counterplot them; self-preservation, as well as my friend's safety, require that I should not be too scrupulous" (chap. 16). "Scrupulous" is the quasi-technical term that marks this as a part of traditional casuistical discourse. Weighing plot against counterplot, measure against measure, Alan dramatizes that swinging and swaying of the deliberative scales that figure the work of adjudication.

In the action of *Redgauntlet,* however, even this settling of the balance, which occurs long before the conclusion of the novel, proves to be provisional. According to a pattern that Jolles claims is recurrent in casuistical literature, such resolutions seem only to occasion yet more complex cases, more explicitly identified as such. In one such subsequent case in *Redgauntlet's* serial structure, a particularly vexing problem is put to Alan by Prince Charles/Father Buonaventure, and Alan is formally assigned an hour in which to deliberate it. The gist of this later case is as follows: should Alan accept this priest's proposal that he be given his freedom to continue on his mission to deliver the letter to Redgauntlet, along with one from the priest himself, but on condition of foreswearing any appeal to the law (on the grounds that it would risk exposure of those whose hospitality had saved his life)? The Jesuit leaves Alan alone, and two full paragraphs are then given over to his deliberations, in which he is shown considering circumstantial probabilities and weighing the lesser of the imperfect alternatives he faces in his situation. Deliberations of this sort continue to very the end of the novel, as if it could make no sense without them.[23]

I have lavished such detailed attention on *Redgauntlet* here to show how the case form ramifies in the structure of a book widely recognized as the great historical novelist's most astute self-commentary I have shown how, in its deliberate use of the case not just as a theme but also as a formal principle, *Redgauntlet* presses the poetics of the case to the breaking point. Thus, if the historical novel is a symptomatic development of the period 1815–25, the extreme pressure on the form of the case is likewise symptomatic of this new genre as the narrative in which Scott most evidently reflected on his own practice as a pioneering historical novelist.[24] But I have not yet shown how this novel seeks to take the fur-

---

23. The final chapter, for example, when Alan, Darsie, and Lilias face the question of what to do about what they now recognize as Redgauntlet's quixotic scheme to stage another Jacobite rebellion, is especially dense with the idiom of casuistry. Consider the passage in which Lilias, having earlier told her story to Latimer, now relates her story to Fairford:

> Under these circumstances, . . . Fairford heard from Lilias Redgauntlet the history of her family, particularly of her uncle . . . Fairford's acute understanding instantly connected what he had heard with the circumstances he had witnessed at Fairladies. His first thought was, to attempt, at all risks, his instant escape, and procure assistance powerful enough to crush . . . a conspiracy of such a determined character. . . . Lilias exclaimed against this scheme [and] suggested the advice which, of all others, seemed most suited to the occasion, that, yielding, namely, to the circumstances of their situation, they should watch carefully when Darsie should obtain any degree of freedom, and endeavour to open a communication with him, in which case their joint flight might be effected, and without endangering the safety of any one. (Redg, chap. 23)

Their youthful deliberation had nearly fixed on this point, we are told, when, in a moment that internally marks the casuistical seriality of Scott's fiction, the heavy hand of Peter Peebles descends on Alan's shoulders, circumstances change, and the case is altered once again.

24. James Kerr, in *Fiction Against History,* anticipates part of my argument here in his claim about the way in which Scott's novel itself significantly "reproduces" Alain Fairford's work with the case/cause of Peter Peebles: "Alan takes in hand the disparate pieces of Peebles' cause, suit and

ther step of linking the idiom of "the case" with the idiom of "the cause." Concurrent with the private deliberations we have been considering in the novel, Scott portrays discussions on a very different political scale between Redgauntlet and his reluctant confederates. The final scenes of the book indeed produce a complex medley of reverberations between the lost case or cause of Poor Peter Peebles and the lost case or cause of the houses of Stewart and Redgauntlet.[25] The delusions engendered in these unwinnable cases find expression in a recognizable idiom, as we see when the sloganeering appeal of the Jacobites to the "Good Ol' Cause," or even simply to "the good cause," is echoed in Peter's self-aggrandizing elegiac remark to Nanty Ewart: "By my word," says Peter, "it is a gude case, and muckle has it borne, in its day, of various procedure . . ." (chap. 20).[26]

If the goodness of the case of *Peebles v. Planestanes,* as a case, lies in its ability to "bear" diverse courses of action, this is in turn a function of the equilibrium it has managed to sustain over time.[27] As Peter says, reworking the figure of the scales into his own distinctive idiom: "to see a' ane's warldly substance capering in the air in a pair of weigh-bauks, now up, now down, as the breath of judge or counsel inclines it for pursuer or defender,—troth, man, there are times I rue having ever begun the plea wark" (chap. 23). It seems to be precisely because of this sense of suspense and suspension—"capering in the air in a pair of weigh-bauks" being the low Scots equivalent of Jolles's *Schwanken und Schwingen* of the scales—that the novel allows such force to Peter's early boast that his case or cause is "like a specimen of all causes" (ltr. 13). Thus, if the Great Cause of the

---

countersuit, and makes out of them a story calculated to elicit the sympathy of his audience, and thereby to carry his client's claim. Scott uses facts drawn from previous accounts of British history, individuals, events, geographical settings, and arranges them in the form of a compelling story about the past, a story which expresses and endorses a particular ideological bias, a political claim about the meaning of history" (p. 113). This larger case of the novel itself—its story, bias, or claim—is what Alexander Welsh refers to when he argues that *Redgauntlet* is "constructive of a political myth"—in *The Hero of the Waverley Novels* (1963; Princeton, N.J.: Princeton University Press, 1993), p. 230.

25. In the 1832 "Introduction" to *Redgauntlet,* Scott echoes his comments on Peter Peebles in the language of the case as well as the cause when he allows that the "case, too, of Charles Edward must have been a difficult one": *Redgauntlet,* ed. Kathryn Sutherland (Oxford: Oxford University Press, 1985), p. 9. The relation between "case" and "cause" might thus be understood as providing the underlying but unstated "form" of a high Victorian novel such as Gaskell's *Mary Barton* in Catherine Gallagher's reading of it as a novel about "Causality versus Conscience"—*Industrial Revolution of English Fiction* (Chicago: University of Chicago Press, 1985), pp. 62–87.

26. See Judith Wilt, on the connection between Peter's cause and that of the Jacobites, in *Secret Leaves: The Novels of Walter Scott* (Chicago: University of Chicago Press, 1985), p. 151.

27. "As if," says Peter scornfully of Fairford's proposal to "bring an action on the case," his "case hadna as maony actions already as one case can weel carry" (Redg, chap. 20).

book must be read in terms of the cause of Peter Peebles then the cases to be resolved by the conspirators in the Great Cause must be read in terms of the various cases resolved by the allied forces of Lilias, Darsie, and Fairford. Furthermore, following James Kerr's suggestion, we might say this range of analogies between the retrogressive (i.e., Jacobite) and "progressive" conspirators, must itself be understood in terms of another analogical connection: that between the case that Alan Fairford makes of the chaos of documents offered him by Peter Peebles and what Scott offers to us as the case of *Redgauntlet* itself.[28]

The argument I am making about Scott's self-conscious deployment of the case in *Redgauntlet* is not meant to surprise readers familiar with the novel. Many of these points have been made in one or another of the commentaries. I have reopened the case of *Redgauntlet* here because of its special place in the Scott canon as a metafictional commentary—a kind of self-pastiche—on the whole series of "Scotch novels" that reached its apex in 1819.[29] That the form of the case should figure so crucially *here* has more than casual significance for Scott's new historicism in fiction. In view of this understanding of the novel's implications, then, I wish to emphasize two points in particular. The first is that its episodes and its overall action appear as cases in a way that is explicitly connected, in the disguise assumed by the Pretender, with jesuitical casuistry. The second is that its cases lend themselves to theoretical analysis in Jolles's key terms: anomaly, deliberation, and dual normativity. On this second point, I should add that Jolles's discussion is particularly helpful for describing both what I have called the serial relation of cases in a given Waverley novel and the place of that novel in the larger scheme of the Waverley project.

This further relevance of Jolles becomes clearer if, in the light of what Jolles calls the two chief "peculiarities" of the case, we attend to the question of the form of resolution we can expect in cases construed as Scott's are. It was crucial to Jolles's account of the case's "peculiarity," we recall, that the case poses questions without being able to give answers—its mode is always to be calling for deliberation. It is the place where what is realized is the process of judgment but not its result. From this feature of the case, however, follows a "second peculiarity": "that it ceases to be quite itself when, by virtue of a positive decision, the duty to decide is overcome" (p. 181). The resolution of Scott's cases is always

<hr />

28. Kerr, *Fiction Against History*, p. 113.

29. This reflexivity fully justifies Ian Duncan's claim that *Redgauntlet* is one of Scott's two most ambitious and complex novels. See *Modern Romance and Transformations of the Novel: The Gothic, Scott, Dickens* (Cambridge: Cambridge University Press, 1992), p. 110. The other, *The Heart of Mid-Lothian*, is likewise self-conscious about its relation to casuistry and cases, as I argue below, but it does not have *quite* the same quality of self-pastiche that one finds in *Redgauntlet*.

called for but not, insofar as they remain cases, ever actually achieved. To borrow a term from Sartre, only slightly out of context, the case exists in the form of an "appeal."[30] Thus, the so-called simple form of the case tends to situate itself in an implicit or explicit narrative framework that itself continues to pursue its course after one case has been closed, one appeal answered. In Jolles's own words, "hardly has a case been solved, when up surges another, as usually occurs when one lives in a world of norms . . . : the disappearance of one case entails the appearance of another case" (p. 191).[31] The conspicuous nonresolution of many of Scott's novels, *Redgauntlet* among them, is a function of the degree to which casuistry shapes them—i.e., the degree to which the notion of "living in a world of norms" is historically problematized in them. The emphasis on their arrangement in a sequence or collection speaks very much to the same point.

The Heart of Mid-Lothian, which constitutes the second entry in the "Tales of My Landlord" series, is notorious for the distention of its denouement and the openness of the circle we expect to be closed by Jeanie Dean's return to Edinburgh. Although not quite as self-parodic in its main narrative as *Redgauntlet, The Heart of Mid-Lothian* vigorously thematizes the question of the case in its framing materials. Peter Pattieson explains the immediate circumstances of the novel's composition in a conversation between two lawyers and one of their clients, Mr. Dunover, after a mail-coach accident near the Wallace Head Inn:

> [T]he young men . . . gradually engaged [Mr. Dunover] in a conversation, which, much to my satisfaction, again turned upon the *Causes Célèbres* of Scotland. Emboldened by the kindness with which he was treated, Mr Dunover began to contribute his share to the amusement of the evening. Jails, like other places, have their ancient traditions, known only to the inhabitants, and handed down from one set of the melancholy lodgers to the next who occupy their cells. Some of these, which Dunover mentioned, were interesting, and served to illustrate the narratives of remarkable trials, which Hardie had at his finger ends, and which his companion was also well skilled in. This sort of conversation passed away the evening till the early hour when Mr Dunover chose to retire to rest, and I also retreated to take down memorandums of what I had learned, in order to add another narrative to those which it had been my chief amusement to collect, and to write out in detail. (TML2, chap. 2)

What of course makes this passage so much the more apposite to Jolles's point is the parallel drawn between Pattieson's collection of prose fiction narratives and the collection of the *Causes Célèbres* of Scotland, which Halkit says he is contemplating. Can it be a coincidence, in the face of this, that *The Heart of Mid-*

---

30. Jean-Paul Sartre, *What is Literature?* (Cambridge, Mass.: Harvard University Press, 1988), pp. 54–58.

31. Pierre Cariou, in *Les Idéalités Casuistiques* (Paris: Librairie Honoré Champion, 1979), argues that Jacques de Saintebeuve, the seventeenth-century "directeur de conscience" on whom he concentrates, similarly frames the history of the case, as it were, between "le moment de la formulation du Cas, et le moment de sa Resolution" (p. 4).

Lothian, the most case-preoccupied of Scott's novels to date, would be the first of his publications to mark itself as belonging to a "series"? Indeed, although the label "second series" or "third series" would become familiar in nineteenth-century publication practices, it is very much a product of Scott's own historical and historicist moment, very much part of an effort to merge story-telling into the widening sphere of a large periodically oriented reading public.[32]

4. The Representative State and the Transformation of Casuistry

I have used some of the more conspicuous instances to show how Scott's novels are structured by an interest in casuistical balancing acts of all sorts, but this is not to say that this tendency cannot be discerned even in those of his novels where it is less patent. In the denouement of *Ivanhoe,* what is explicitly identified as "the case of Rebecca the Jewess" (Iv, chap. 38) is stated and restated so repeatedly that, just as one can read Natalie Davis's narrative of the return of Martin Guerre in reverse, as her extrapolation from extant court records of that case, so one is induced to imagine the "editor" of *Ivanhoe,* Lawrence Templeton, as working backward from the fictionally extant court records of Rebecca's case.[33] The novel as a whole addresses the balance of Norman-Saxon culture at the time of Richard I, and its final chapters veritably teeter with references to weights and balances: to the "weighty evidence" brought against her (chap. 37), to the "weighty cause[s]" that call for judgment (chap. 38), to the imbalance in weight between the silk glove she throws down to call for trial by combat and armored glove with which Bois-Guilbert matches it.[34] Such language is

32. In this as in much else, Scott takes a lesson from Maria Edgeworth, who, in the preface to the 1809 first edition of *Ennui,* refers to the "Tales of Fashionable Life," to which Scott alludes at the start of *Waverley,* as a "series of moral fictions": *Tales and Novels of Maria Edgeworth,* 10 vols. (London: Henry & Bohn, 1874), 4:211. Although the term was used in eighteenth-century periodical literature, I can find no earlier precedent for the "Series" format in fiction that Scott's massive success with the three series of "Tales of My Landlord," and indeed with the Waverley series as a whole, established as an important publishing mode for nineteenth-century European and American literature. I should add that a more detailed analysis of Scott's relation to cases and casuistry would have to deal with the representation of confession in novels such as *The Heart of Mid-Lothian,* a matter I have scarcely touched on.

33. The narrator of *Ivanhoe,* Lawrence Templeton, explicitly refers late in the novel to "the judicial investigations which followed on this occasion [of Rebecca's trial], and which are given at length in the Wardour Manuscript." The Wardour Manuscript is the fictional source from which Templeton is supposed to be deriving his tale (Iv, chap. 44).

34. Referring to her accuser, Bois-Guilbert, while addressing the court, Rebecca explains her decision not to make a countercharge against him: "[H]e is of your own faith, and his lightest affirmance would weigh down the most solemn protestations of the distressed Jewess" (Iv, chap. 37). When Rebecca casts her silk glove down to call for her exoneration, one of the Knights-Templar observes: "Seest thou, Rebecca, as this thin and light glove of thine is to one of our heavy steel gauntlets, so is thy cause to that of the Temple, for it is our order which thou hast defied" (chap. 38).

worked to the point of self-mocking paranomasia in the discourse of Wamba the Fool—which falls precisely between the trial by testimony and the trial by combat—on the balance of moral trade he sees worked out by the Merry Men of Sherwood Forest.[35]

I see little reason to doubt that Scott was working from David Hume's discussion of the transformation of evidentiary procedures during the Middle Ages in volume one of his *History of England*. But there is a larger set of questions to be dealt with in considering Scott's place in the Romantic historicization of the case. In linking the form of the case in Scott's novels to casuistry as a historical phenomenon in western Europe, I have been referring to casuistry as a *tradition* and taking note of Scott's self-identifying gestures toward it. This procedure, however, has its limits. For the purposes of demonstrating the transformation of the case in Romantic historicism, or Scott's place in that transformation, it is not enough to show that he is a British novelist concerned with the problematics of casuistry and the case, not enough to link him with a tradition. The early novel itself, insofar as it can be identified as a recognized new form of writing in the early eighteenth century, was in part developed out of the literature of secular casuistry—i.e., advice columns and conduct guides for practical decision making in ordinary circumstances.[36] That is why, to see the novelty of Scott—as well as Shelley and other writers of 1819—and thus to recognize the difference made in a distinctively Romantic form of historical representation, one must come to terms with the *history* of casuistry, and in particular with the interrelation of casuistry and its literary representation. How does the Romantic case acquire its historical dimension?

If this were the place to do more than sketch such a history, it would probably begin from the assumption that the conceptual organization of early mod-

---

35. A part of Wamba's exchange with Richard will suffice to indicate how the trope is kept in play:

"Give me an example of your meaning, Wamba—I know nothing of cyphers or rates of usage," answered the Knight.

"Why," said Wamba, "an your valour be so dull, you will please to learn that those honest fellows balance a good deed with one not quite so laudable, as a crown given to a begging friar with an hundred bezants taken from a fat abbot, or a wench kissed in the greenwood with the relief of a poor widow. . . . The merry men of the forest set off the building of a cottage with the burning of a castle—the thatching of a choir against the robbing of a church, the setting free a poor prisoner against the murder of a proud sheriff, or, to come nearer to our point, the deliverance of a Saxon Franklin against the burning alive of a Norman baron." (Iv, chap. 40)

36. See Hunter's discussion of Defoe in relation to John Dunton's advice columns in the *Athenian Mercury*, in *Before Novels*, pp. 292–93. See also illuminating though scattered references to casuistry in Michael McKeon, *The Origins of the English Novel, 1600–1740* (Baltimore: Johns Hopkins Univeristy Press, 1987).

ern casuistry in Christian cultures was one in which a transcendental scheme of norms must be applied to variable human circumstances for the sake of a transcendental purpose, the achievement of the kingdom of heaven and happiness in what was sometime called "the Future State."[37] In its early modern English incarnation, casuistical practice offered itself as the solution to the problem that Camille Slights has summarized this way: "The conscience cannot automatically apply general rules to particular instances but must take into account all the variety of circumstances encountered in the real world."[38] In such a conceptual framework, the process of applying principles involves the identification of situations in generic terms: the "varieties of circumstances" must be classified. Recognizing that to take the grain of another might violate a divine injunction not to steal, one must determine whether the circumstances are such as to amount to the *kind* of case in which such an appropriation is permissible— in the kind of case, for example, where the grain may save a life of another with relatively little cost to its owner. Although one may observe finer or coarser appreciations of an agent's circumstantiality, broader or narrower specifications of the agent's situatedness, I would argue that the moral case continues to be characterized in these "generic" terms through the early modern period of English casuistry. It remains an affair of kind, *tout court.*

So understood, moreover, the case has been shown by several scholars to be a model and an influence for a number of important early modern texts—by Shakespeare, Donne, Milton, and Defoe.[39] The point of crucial importance from the perspective of the present argument, however, is that in all such literature, including the early novel, the case of the agent or protagonist tends to have a *generic* character as opposed to a *historical* character. When you understand the kind of case you confront, when you have classified its species, you know how to deal with it. The case is not as yet organized as a historical state of affairs, or identified in respect to a particular moment in time. The alteration of the case that marks the advent of the concept of culture in Romantic historicism, however, involves just such new modes of organization and identification. It in-

37. I rely here in part on a suggestive discussion of this question by H. D. Kittsteiner, "Kant and Casuistry," in *Conscience and Casuistry in Early Modern Europe,* ed. Edmund Leites (Cambridge: Cambridge University Press, 1988), pp. 185–213. See also the useful historical sketch offered in Leites's own contribution to this volume, "Casuistry and Character," pp. 119–33.

38. Camille Wells Slights, *The Casuistical Tradition in Shakespeare, Donne, Herbert, and Milton* (Princeton, N.J.: Princeton University Press, 1981).

39. In addition to the work of Starr, Slights, Hunter, and McKeon, which I have already cited, one might also mention John Wallace, "'Examples Are Best Precepts': Readers and Meanings in Seventeenth-Century Poetry," *Critical Inquiry* 1 (1974): 273–90, and Amy McCready, "Milton's Casuistry: The Case of *The Doctrine and Discipline of Divorce,*" *Journal of Medieval and Renaissance Studies* 22 (fall 1992): 393–428.

volves the naming of cases with phrases like "England in 1819." It involves the identification of cultural conjuncture in terms of the chronological code.

This is, perhaps, an elusive point, and it does not help that there is so little intellectual historiography on the fate of the case in the eighteenth century, when moral casuistry itself is understood to have "vanished off the face of the theological map."[40] There are some suggestive throwaway lines in Foucault's *Discipline and Punish* about the fate of "casuistic jurisprudence" in this period—i.e., about how "psychological knowledge" of criminal defendants will take over the "modulation of the penalty belonging to casuistry in the broad sense" as a calibration of the variables of "circumstances" and "intention."[41] Likewise, Simon During, in an essay on the "civil imaginary" in the British eighteenth century, writes of a new sociability that "reproduces everyday life in the public domain, reducing the gap between the divine/moral order and the actual behaviour, thereby replacing the old science of casuistry by the modern domination of the life-world by style and civility."[42] Foucault and During both sense that there is an important story to tell about the fate of casuistry, but they do not pursue it. Koselleck's discussion of the fate of the example in historiographical teaching is certainly germane here, with its account of the noniterability of historical situations in the *Neuzeit* of the late eighteenth and early nineteenth centuries. Koselleck does not, however, make the connection to casuistry.

---

40. Leites, "Casuistry and Character," in *Conscience and Casuistry in Early Modern Europe,* p. 119.

41. Michel Foucault, *Discipline and Punish: The Birth of the Prison,* trans. Alan Sheridan (New York: Random House, 1979), pp. 98–101.

42. Simon During, "Literature—Nationalism's Other? The Case for Revision," in *Nation and Narration,* ed. Homi K. Bhabha (London: Routledge, 1990), pp. 142–43. During's sensitivity to the problematic of cases and casuistry enables him also, in his *Foucault and Literature: Toward a Genealogy of Writing* (London: Routledge, 1992), to see the relevance of these terms to the new historicism of Stephen Greenblatt. "His work," writes During,

> remains focused on specific cases. And he forestalls us asking, why *this* instance?—is it typical of, that is, representative of, some larger social force?—by invoking the quasi-aesthetic fascination of, even the weirdness of, his skillfully chosen instances. Perhaps it does not matter that this tactic forestalls rather than answers tendentious questions about the representativeness of a particular example—for those questions merely draw us back into the delirium of mimesis and interpretation. But his appeal to the wonder or fascination of the individual case and his responsiveness to the political use of such fascination, can interrupt another, less easily deferred, set of connections and continuities—those by which old divisive social forces and formations reproduce themselves, religion and colonialism being good examples of such forces. (p. 200)

Although During does not connect his discussions of eighteenth-century and new-historicist casuistries, my discussion here can be seen, in effect, as an attempt to read the transformation of casuistry itself as another "example" of the social forces During sees repeated or reproduced from the past.

In a recent collection of essays on *Conscience and Culture in Early Modern Europe,* the one article that deals at any length with the eighteenth century is H. D. Kittsteiner's. This is a suggestive discussion and I have drawn on it in my account here, but, like the comments by Foucault and During, it seems to presume the disappearance of casuistical discourse, and I begin from the discovery of the strong presence, or at least thematization, of casuistry in post–Waterloo British writing. Nor can the post–Waterloo interest in casuistry be dismissed as an antiquarian fascination with an obsolete practice. It involves, instead, a sense of casuistry's implication for existing life and literature. Hence Scott's references to his own novels about historic cases as cases in themselves and Shelley's insistence on the casuistry of the dramatic audience that bears witness to the spectacle of Beatrice Cenci's self-exculpations. It is not that casuistry goes away but rather that it is refunctioned in response to the material and discursive conditions of Romantic historicism. The problem the persistence of casuistry poses for Kittsteiner's account already becomes apparent, however, at the point where, as part of his narrative of the dissolution of conscience as constituted within the traditional form of casuistry, he discusses Adam Smith. The last pages of Smith's *Theory of Moral Sentiments* (1759), as Kittsteiner notes, address themselves quite explicitly to a critique of casuistry and a reconstitution of judgment in respect to the sentiments.[43] What Kittsteiner does not mention is how explicitly the theory of sympathy with which Smith begins is articulated in respect, precisely, to the idiom of cases.

It is crucial to Smith's analysis that sympathy does not work by identification with the feelings of another person, which Smith rejects as an impossibility, but rather by "conceiving what we ourselves should feel in the like situation."[44] Our sympathetic response to another, as Smith puts it repeatedly, means that "we put ourselves in his case," or, even more frequently, we "bring his case home to ourselves." But it is not, cautions Smith, our "senses" that inform us of the suffering of another: "They never did, and never can, carry us beyond our own person, and it is by the imagination only that we can form any conception of what are his sensations. Neither can that faculty help us to this any other way, than by representing to us what would be our own, if we were in his case" (pp. 47–48). Such a doctrine, formulated in very similar terms, assumes great importance among the theorists of the imagination in the early nineteenth-century. Shelley wrote in *A Defence of Poetry* that "a man, to be greatly good, must imagine intensely and comprehensively; he must put himself in the place

---

43. Smith even offers a historical explanation of the rise of Jesuit casuistry in the early modern period, as will be discussed in chapter 5.

44. Adam Smith, *The Theory of Moral Sentiments* (Indianapolis: Liberty Press, 1969), p. 47.

of another and of many others" (SPP, p. 487). And in *Peter Bell the Third,* Shelley satirized Wordsworth—himself on record in the preface to *Lyrical Ballads* claiming the faculty of the sympathetic imagination as the very demarcation of "the human"—on these very grounds. Of his homely stand-in for Words-worth, Shelley writes:

> He had as much imagination
>   As a pint-pot—he never could
> Fancy another situation
> From which to dart his contemplation
>   Than that wherein he stood. (SPP, ll. 298–302)

We shall see that the kind of reconstitution of the case that we find in the moral philosophy of Smith is itself reiterated in this way through much of what we think of as Romanticism—Hazlitt's essays on imaginative identification, Keats's letter on the chameleon poet, and Byron's stanzas on the dyer's hands in *Don Juan* would be other well-known instances.[45]

The point, however, is that Smith's refiguring of the case takes it out of the domain of Christian casuistry, but not into the domain of history. The situation has not yet been historicized, but Shelley himself, in his own imaginatively sympathetic mode, can illustrate what it means for it to become so. A few months after drafting *Peter Bell the Third,* Shelley wrote to Leigh Hunt from Pisa about the conduct of Ollier, his London bookseller, in terms that spell out a view of the constitution of individuals in social systems:

> And in fact they are all rogues. It is less the character of the individual than the situation in which he is placed which determines him to be honest or dishonest, perhaps we ought to re-gard an honest bookseller, or an honest seller of anything else in the present state of human affairs as a kind of Jesus Christ. The system of society as it exists at present must be overthrown from the foundations with all its superstructure of maxims & of forms before we shall find anything but disappointment in our intercourse with any but a few select spirits.[46]

Shelley's strenuous performance of sympathy with the case of Ollier, his will-ingness to enter into the situation in which a bookseller is placed, is here artic-ulated with a *judgment* on the "present state," on the state of things pictured in his sonnet of a few months before—with a judgment, in other words, on the case of "England in 1819." What might it *mean* to call this state a "case," as I have done? Part of the answer to this question lies in the work of the writer whom Hazlitt listed first in his volume on *The Spirit of the Age,* Jeremy Bentham.

45. For a still-valuable review of the literature on the "sympathetic imagination" of the male Romantic poets, see Patricia Ball, *The Central Self: A Study in Romantic and Victorian Imagination* (London: Athlone Press, 1966), pp. 103–51.

46. Letter to Leigh Hunt, May 1, 1820. LPBS, 2:191.

The prose text in which Shelley attempted to produce a coherent picture of his social theory in 1819 was *A Philosophical View of Reform,* that extraordinary effort launched in the final weeks of the year, precisely the weeks in which the British Parliament was deliberating the Gag Acts passed on December 30. Shelley did not address the question of casuistry explicitly in this dialectical argument, and since he completed only three chapters of a projected longer work it is hard to know if he planned to address it. We have seen, though, that he does take up very seriously the problem of *application* in philosophy, and much of the first chapter takes the form of an admonishment not to move from, as it were, pure to applied philosophy too quickly, no matter how dire the situation in which new theories might be expected to have salutary application.[47] We can recall here that the heading under which he discusses the history of philosophical application in the modern period—i.e., post-sixteenth century—is "utility." Indeed, the history of philosophy and politics since the fall of Rome comes down to "the establishment of the principle of Utility as the substance, and liberty and equality as the forms according to which the concerns of human life ought to be administered" (WPBS, 7.10). That Shelley's age of utility continues into 1819 is manifest by the way in which the *View* itself plays out a quasi-Benthamite argument. It was in Shelley's next letter to Hunt, after writing about Ollier's constitution by the moral system of his time, that, as we have seen, he spoke of the new pamphlet as a standard book for the philosophical reformers, one that would be "like Jeremy Bentham's something, but different & perhaps more systematic" (LPBS, 2:201; May 26, 1820).

The work to which Shelley is almost certainly referring in this letter is Bentham's *Plan of Reform,* which was circulated with an influential introduction first in 1817 and then reprinted, beginning in 1818, in a massively popular edition by T. J. Wooler, the editor of *The Black Dwarf.*[48] It is a crucial and neglected document for understanding the politics of representation in one of its

47. Shelley's critique of contemporary political philosophy is that it was the heir of a "superficial" line of thinkers, who might be forgiven for attempting, in the face of "the terrible sufferings of their countrymen," rather "to apply a portion of what had already been discovered to their immediate relief, than to pursue . . . the abstraction of thought, as the great philosophers who preceded them had done, for the sake of a future and more universal advantage" (WPBS, 7:9). They merely "illustrated with more or less success the principles of human nature as applied to man in political society" (WPBS, 7:9).

48. All references in the text will be by page number to Jeremy Bentham, *Plan of Parliamentary Reform, in the Form of a Catechism, with Reasons for Each Article* (London: T. J. Wooler, 1818). The title of the Wooler's journal seems to have been borrowed from Scott's *The Black Dwarf,* a short novel that appeared with *Old Mortality* in 1816 to round out "Tales of My Landlord," 1st series. No one, to my knowledge, has ever explained the connection.

periods of severest crisis. Bentham's argument proceeds by first giving an account of "the state in which the country lies," then by explaining the causes of
its miseries, then by outlining the solution (what he calls "Democratic Ascendancy"—"representative" as distinct from "self-acting" democracy—with
much of the political power of the monarchy and the aristocracy, as well as the
standing army, left in place) (pp. 9, 15). The state of the country, as Bentham describes it, is one in which the "universal interest" of the vast majority of the
people is subordinated, by the currently constituted system of representation,
to the "two partial and adverse interests" (p. 9): the aristocratic and the monar-
chic. The mechanism, so to speak, of this subordination is a scheme of incentives according to which the monarchy and aristocracy are in a position to
reward the putative representatives of the people with economic benefits in return for acting favorably to monarchical and aristocratic interests. Thus "the
immediate cause of all the mischief of misrule is, that the men acting as representatives of the people have a private and sinister interest, and sufficient power
to gratify that interest, producing a constant sacrifice of the interest of the people" (p. 24; cf. p. 17). The sole solution, therefore, is to reorganize the scheme of
incentives, and the only way to do *that* is to effect a "radical," rather than a moderate, reform of the representative system in Britain: universal suffrage and annual Parliaments were Bentham's call to action (the very slogans under which
demonstrators at Manchester and elsewhere marched in England in 1819).

What I wish to focus attention on, however, is less the conclusions advanced
in Bentham's argument than the mode in which they are argued. One indication of this mode is that Bentham's discussion throughout, originating with his
state of the state, is undertaken in a framework dominated by such notions as
"circumstances," "probability," and "case." For example, in addressing the question of whether the unenlightened multitude might be capable of voting com-
petently, Bentham points to the (for him, successful) example of America and
then tosses the issue, rephrased, back in the faces of his opponents: "in what circumstances belonging to the case are we to look for the *cause* of a state of things,
of the existence of which there cannot be a doubt, but which, in a distant view
of it, presents itself as thus improbable" (p. 18). The answer he provides to *this*
question comes by way of a distinction between self-formed and derivative
judgment and an analysis in terms of cases: there is reason to think that as
people seek authoritative advice in cases from their private life, such as medicine and law, so they would seek advice "in a case such as that in question" (i.e.,
how to choose a ruler) from public life.

This sort of language permeates Bentham's discussion, page by page, and
indeed, he pointedly organizes the "plan of reform" as a sequence of analyses

of probable conduct in systematically arrayed hypothetical circumstances. Bentham divides his overall discussion of the remedy he proposes into two primary divisions that correspond to "the situations to which, to be effectual, the remedy must apply itself." These are: "1. Situation of *Parliamentary Electors*. 2. Situation of *Parliamentary Representatives*" (p. 24). Each of these two discussions is in turn divided into five aspects, and, taken in sum, they constitute the central area of Bentham's attention in this text. In a formulation that anticipates Shelley's discussions of national will, Bentham declares that the "sole use" of the British House of Commons is "the securing on the part of the servants of the Monarch a due dependence on the will of the whole body of the people" (p. 110).[49] His analysis of the situations of the electors and representatives aims principally to show that the incentives of the existing representative system are structured so as to make this outcome impossible. Instead of being answerable to the people who ostensibly elect them, the members of the House of Commons are answerable to the monarchy itself. The primary agency of this perversion of the representative system, in Bentham's analysis, is the office that, on the prerogative of the monarch, dispenses rewards to members of both houses for services rendered. With respect to the situation of the representative, therefore, the system must be restructured in such a way as to effect at once "the due dependence of the representative upon the elector" and the "due independence of the representative towards C_____r General and Co" (p. 27).[50] The "radical" (as opposed to the "moderate") solution combining virtual universal suffrage and annual parliaments provides the only means of reshaping the situation of the Elector to create the proper structure of incentive or "dependence."

It should be clear at this point that Bentham's analysis of the state of the British nation—what he alternately calls "the constitution [in its] present

49. This notion of the "will of the whole body of the people," of course, is not to be linked too closely with Rousseau's concept of the "general will," since the latter is not susceptible of representation. On this point, see Richard Fralin, *Rousseau and Representation: A Study in the Development of His Concept of Political Institutions* (New York: Columbia University Press, 1978), pp. 98–104, and Keith Baker, *Inventing the French Revolution: Essays on French Political Culture in the Eighteenth Century* (New York: Cambridge University Press, 1990), pp. 224–51. For a good account of the appropriation of the Rousseauist "general will" to a politics of representation, by way of Adam Smith's theory of the division of labor, see William Sewell's recent study of the Abbé Sieyes, *A Rhetoric of Bourgeois Revolution: The Abbé Sieyes and "What is the Third Estate?"* (Durham, N.C.: Duke University Press, 1994), pp. 66–108.

50. Bentham explained in a note that "for filling up the *deficit* between the C and *r*, the candour and sagacity of the Reader may employ the letters *onservato*, or any others, if others there be, which in his view may be more apposite" (p. 10). Burke had defended such offices in a way that Bentham attacked directly in his "Defence of the Economy Against the Late Mr. Burke," *The Pamphleteer*, no. 17 (1817):4–47.

state," the "state of things," or "the constitution as it stands" (p. 113)—can be
seen as scheme of political "situations"—a structure of "subject positions" as
one might put it today. In situations sufficiently shaped and grasped, such as
those of the electors and the representatives, the likelihood of an agent's acting
in one way rather than another is taken to be very high, for the "sole clue to political conduct," as Bentham never tires of repeating, is "interest" (pp. 110, 111):

> In this public situation, or in any other, be the *individual* who he may, have you any wish of
> possessing either a clue to his conduct in time past, or a means of foreknowing his conduct in
> time future? Look to the situation he is in, in respect to interest.—Have you any such wish in
> regard to a *body* of men? Look still to interests. (p. 111)

Hence it is true even of him who would seem to be the great villain of
Bentham's political story, the Conservator General himself, that, at least at one
level, he cannot be blamed or faulted for doing what he does, or even being
what he is. There is, Bentham says, "nothing of blame in all this truth" (p. 121).

> [I]t is his *situation* makes him so: it suffices for the purpose: and, to *produce the effect* (and let this
> be well observed), *no overt act—no, nor so much as a thought—is on his part necessary;*—for, were it
> possible for him to have the will, in his *situation,* it would scarcely be in his *power* to avoid be-
> ing C_____r General. (p. 10)

It should be apparent how closely Shelley echoes this passage in his letter to
Hunt about Ollier's blamelessness as an individual in spite of his dishonesty as a
bookseller: "it is less the character of the individual than the situation in which
he is placed which determines him to be honest or dishonest." What Shelley and
Bentham articulate is the new historicist conception of a human environment
as, in the first place, a "system of society" that can be said to have (as Shelley put
it) "foundations" and a "superstructure of maxims and forms" that can be traced
to material historical origins and actually changed, even "overthrown." Marx
has been quoted as having opined that unlike Byron, Shelley, if he had lived,
"would have stood in the vanguard of socialism."[51] Marx could not have
known this passage in Shelley, but he would have recognized Shelley's contribution to early socialist movements. And of course, just months later, in France,
St. Simon would be launching his journal, *L'Organisateur,* with its efforts to rethink the French Revolution in terms of political economy and the new *systéme
industrielle.*

For Bentham, Shelley, and St. Simon, it is the case that virtuous conduct, all
but impossible on the level of individual agency as such, requires the whole
transformation of the normative structure in which human agents are currently
situated as individuals. And they imagine that this transformation must be un-

---

51. Cited in Marx and Engels, *On Literature and Art* (Moscow: Progress Publishers, 1978),
p. 320.

dertaken in respect of an alternative normative structure which will be that of "the Future State" in a reconstituted and secularized sense. But it will be understood as part of a historical future, "posterity," a politically organized version of what Carl Becker famously called "the heavenly city of the eighteenth-century philosophers."[52] Kittsteiner's account of the relation of casuistry to political philosophy over the course of the eighteenth century corroborates this kind of claim. He points out that "casuistry originally operated within a static view of the world and tried to bring the realties of the world into harmony with religious demands that stood in relation to heaven," but the function of moral philosophy, after decades of the "secularizing and psychologizing of the centre of morality," underwent a decisive transformation: "the crucial difference in the bourgeois moral philosophy of the final third of the eighteenth-century consists in its not wanting to leave the world as it is at all."[53] Shelley, who once famously avowed his "passion for transforming the world," claimed for those poet-legislators he described in the *Philosophical View of Reform* the power to apprehend the gigantic shadows that futurity cast on the present, but the other side of this claim is that this futurity will have been in part produced precisely in the historical effort to refashion the state of the representation as it stands. Finishing that letter to Hunt about Ollier, Shelley wrote, "If faith is a virtue in any case it is so in politics rather than religion; as having a power of producing that a belief in which is at once a prophesy & a cause" (LPBS, 2:191). Such a political faith would seem to underlie the pivotal assertion of radical possibility in Shelley's *England in 1819* that all the conditions he mentions "Are graves, from which a glorious phantom / May burst to illumine our tempestuous day." And both the faith in and fear of that radical possibility were, as we have seen, sufficiently widespread in 1819 to have made the possibility seem real enough.

Certainly, Walter Scott's response to the possibility of radical reform in 1819, and to the threat of revolution that gave it greater leverage, speaks volumes about the contradictions in his own historicism. His contribution to the capacity of western writers to depict the "state of society" they inhabited was monumental, but it was a contribution that had to be made backhandedly. Not being able to posit the "future state" in virtue of which the present state of society could be assessed—judged as the case of other cases for that moment—

52. Carl Becker, *The Heavenly City of the Eighteenth-Century Philosophers* (Cambridge, Mass.: Harvard University Press, 1932), especially pp. 119–68. The degree to which Becker's argument anticipates the larger claims of M. H. Abrams's *Natural Supernaturalism* has not been adequately registered in the reception of the latter book.

53. Kittsteiner, "Kant and Casuistry," p. 212.

Scott was left with depicting various past states of society in respect to his unstated sense of the present as the future of the past. As Hazlitt wrote of him in
The Spirit of the Age, trenchantly qualifying his admiration: "He is just half what
the human intellect is capable of being: if you take the universe, and divide it
into two parts, he knows all that it *has been;* all that it *is to be* is nothing to him.
His is a mind brooding over antiquity—scorning 'the present ignorant time.'
He is 'laudator temporis acti'—a '*prophesier* of things past.' The old world is to
him a crowded map; the new one a dull, hateful blank" (CWWH, 11:57–58).
Lukács himself seems to recognize something of the sort in his own admiration
for Scott, when he argues that Scott's move into the past to establish historical
realism was a prelude to a further step in which a realism of the present could be
itself realized in the present. To view Scott in such terms, of course, is to deny
him the status of the perfect exemplar of the historicism we have taken him to
represent. Weighed in this way, that is, Scott's work can itself be understood as a
case in relation to the newly transformed casuistry of Romantic historicism.

5. The Casuistry of the General Will

Because of their willingness to project a secularized normative order in the
future state against which the present state can be measured and assessed,
Bentham, Shelley, and St. Simon, unlike Scott, can take the existing constitution of things as a second-order case—that is, as a scheme of incentive-laden
situations which itself must be considered for judgment. On their side of the issue, however, there is a problem of a different sort from the one faced by Scott.
For them the question has to do with how to understand the status of that
scheme, one's relation to it, one's representation of it. How could one imagine
oneself, that is, in a position to transform the scheme of incentive-laden situations, to alter the case of society's cases? In fact, Bentham himself faces just that
last difficult question toward the very end of the introduction to his *Plan of Parliamentary Reform.* What, he asks, "is the practical use of this display of the state
of interests—of this exposure—melancholy as it is—melancholy and inauspi-
cious, but not the less necessary?" (p. 120).

This is the kind of moment, familiar in texts of this period, even in texts by
writers apparently hostile to "literature," when written arguments about representation are themselves allowed to have representational power, sometimes
even a power to rival the kind of representation they purport to be talking
about. Bentham clearly offers his own text, the *Plan of Parliamentary Reform* itself, as part of an alternative representational system, that of the public press,
that can "display" and "expose" the present state of interests more accurately
than can the system of political representation in its current state. By a logic that

Habermas has made familiar to students of eighteenth-century culture, *this* kind representation—that of what Bentham calls "the *tongue,* the *pen* and the press" (p. 122)—can actually provide the means of altering the political system of representation, precisely by making an accurate representation of the state that it is in. It can, in other words, reveal the larger situation structuring the various local situations that make up the present state of the constitution, and it can indicate how it may be in the interest of the spectator of this "display" or "exposure" to act to change the representative system so exposed.[54]

Thus, in response to his own question about the practical use of his exercise, Bentham has good answers—ostensibly two of them. The first is that the display might inspire certain Whigs, leaders of the movement for moderate (i.e., inadequate) reform, to come forward, lend their help to the cause of radical reform, and receive the glory due to such heroism, in recompense for the price it carries: "*Yes, even in each House, there may, perhaps, be found a few such eccentrically generous minds: and these the people will have for their leaders; and, after death, they will be immortalized.* But, to be thus immortalized, they must have been changed into *People's Men. Whigs* they would be no longer, but *Renegados*" (p. 121). The second answer is that after "these refined spirits are drawn off and lodged in their proper receptacle, the hearts of an adoring people, the power of the mass which they will have left behind, may find itself reduced to its true and proper amount" (p. 121). Obviously, even on Bentham's own accounting, for this outcome to occur it is required that such persons determine it to be in their interest to make the move to the Radical cause. The incentive is adoration and immortalization by the English people. This may seem like a rarefied benefit, but then again Bentham suggests that only superior and generous minds—"refined spirits" (p. 121)—are potential candidates for making the move. This re-

54. The increasing emphasis on the visibility of the political-economic domain in the early decades of this new discourse is a topic insufficiently studied. It is easy to forget that Adam Smith chooses to illustrate the division of labor with the example of his famous pin factory not because that is a particularly good instance of the principle on theoretical grounds, but because it exists on a visual scale that can be comprehended by the peripetetic reader-spectator. The notion of the visualization of scarcity is crucial to the argument of Malthus's *An Essay on the Principle of Population,* ed. Philip Appleman (New York: W. W. Norton, 1976), where Malthus acknowledges that both the "negative" and "positive check to population" must be more or less "obvious to common view" (p. 36) for his own "sketch of the state of society in England" (p. 35) to have efficacy. Hence he concerns himself only with "facts that come within the scope of every man's observation" (p. 31). For a suggestive recent overview of this issue, see Susan Buck-Morss, "Envisioning Capital: Political Economy on Display," *Critical Inquiry* 21 (winter 1995): 434–67. As we shall see below, the spectacular-spectatorial element of this new mode of representation invites Shelley's more-aestheticizing reproduction of Bentham's argument in 1819 with *A Philosophical View of Reform* and then again with *A Defence of Poetry,* and also, perhaps, Hazlitt's painterly representation of the spirit of the age in a "gallery" of literary portraits.

striction of casuistical analysis and moral agency to the oligarchical few recurs as a problem for this kind of argument.

I characterized these answers by Bentham to his own question as "ostensible" because it seems that the final words of his introduction, though not part of the enumerated prolepses, suggest where his "exposure" actually locates its leverage. "ALL THAT RULE—ALL THAT EVEN THINK TO RULE—ARE AGAINST THE PEOPLE. *Causes will have their effects. Sooner or later, unless a change takes place,* THE PEOPLE—*the people, IN THEIR OWN DEFENCE, WILL BE AGAINST ALL THAT RULE*" (p. 123). This suggests a somewhat more complex rhetorical posture informing Bentham's "exposure" of the state of interests. On the one hand, as a printed pamphlet circulating in a widening public sphere, Bentham's text can claim to make a representation of the inadequacy of the state of representation directly to the people it shows the system to be badly serving. The socially determined and historically specific situation they inhabit as a people thus becomes visible to them in a way that, since causes will have their effects, leads them to recognize an interest in changing it—and, since Bentham emphasizes that this is a matter of self-defense, presumably to change it even at the risk of violence. On the other hand, the possibility of this, as it were, alternate form of the people's self-representation through the radical press—i.e., the press that serves the cause of radical reform—as well as the potentially violent response it stands to elicit, itself becomes a part of the perceived historical situation for readers/leaders positioned to change things peacefully.[55]

The point here is not to evaluate Bentham's scare tactics, which would be repeated even in apparently anti-Benthamite texts such as *Hard Times* later in the century—Dickens's narrator warns that things may "take a Wolfish turn" if industrial workers are not shown greater kindness.[56] The point is rather to recognize the way in which the historically determinate political system that structures situations for a given individual to inhabit can also be said to constitute a macrosituation for the will of the people itself. This macrosituation is the represented "state of the interests," including the representation (by, tongue, press, or pen) of that state as susceptible of an alternative form of representation to the political system currently in place.

---

55. For a good exposition of the specifically rhetorical aspects of Bentham's writings about legislation and representation, see Ross Harrison, *Bentham* (London: Routledge, 1983), pp. 196–206.

56. Charles Dickens, *Hard Times* (New York: W. W. Norton, 1990), p. 123. Social casuistry seems to figure as part of the satiric object in Dickens's parodic style throughout the novel: "Is it possible, I wonder, that there was any analogy between the case of the Coketown population and the case of the little Gradgrinds" (p. 24).

What has come into being here is a second-order situation not in the first instance representable by generic label—self-defense, or stealing to save the poor—but rather by what Lévi-Strauss famously called the "historian's code." What has come into being is a situation representable by a place and a date—a "historical situation" very much as Sartre conceived it when he articulated the method Lévi-Strauss set out to dismantle. "England in 1819" indicates a historical situation in this understanding of the term. It becomes possible, in such a framework, not only to suppose the case of a particular elector or representative whose will must make determinations within the system of representation as presently constituted, but also to suppose the case of "the people" whose general or national will must make determinations *about* the system of representation as presently constituted. To spell this point out further, if we can regard casuistry in the older sense as a discourse and discipline established for purposes of guiding confessors in their judgment of the goodness of individual wills, and then later for guiding individual wills in their daily encounters, what we see outlined in the later moment registered in these post-Waterloo writings of Scott, Shelley, and Bentham might be understood as a casuistry of the *general* will.[57]

To make a determination about the system of representation, about the present state of things, is, in both of the relevant senses implied in the Marxian dic-

---

57. What I have been arguing about Bentham's "casuistry of the general will" bears on Mary Poovey's shrewdly reflexive analysis of a debate between two historiographical accounts of Britain in the 1830s in *The Making of a Social Body: British Cultural Formation, 1830–1864* (Chicago: University of Chicago Press, 1995). Showing that the disagreement between historians about whether "the sublime revolution in nineteenth-century government" is a result of Bentham's intervention or of contingent historical change replicates a debate about "charisma" and "bureacracy" in the period itself, Poovey argues that "both of these interpretations . . . fail to recognize that the events typified by the nineteenth-century revolution in government constituted a redefinition *of* agency, which was the necessary counterpart to the redefinition of administration that *was* the Victorian revolution in government" (italics original, p. 113). My claim is that this redefinition of agency was itself already registered, albeit contradictorily, in Bentham's influential late writings on representation, in Shelley's *Philosophical View of Reform*, and, more obliquely, in Hazlitt's writings on the spirit of the age. One might further speculate that the new second-order understanding of will, casuistry, and agency—with its implicit notion of a historical unconscious—corresponds exactly to what Poovey calls the "social body"; hence the Foucauldian medicalization of agency in the form of the new "case history" in nineteenth-century realist writing. See, for example, Lawrence Rothfield, *Vital Signs: Medical Realism and Nineteenth-Century Fiction* (Princeton, N.J.: Princeton University Press, 1992), pp. 33–35. For a historical analysis of the psychiatric case form, see Foucault, "About the Concept of the 'Dangerous Individual' in 19th-Century Legal Psychiatry," *International Journal of Law and Psychiatry* 1 (1978): 1–18. For a formal analysis of the psychoanalytic case, see Steven Marcus, "Freud and Dora: Story, History, Case History," in *In Dora's Case*, ed. Charles Bernheimer and Claire Kahane (New York: Columbia University Press, 1990), pp. 51–91. For a deconstructive account, see Deborah Elise White, "Studies in Hysteria: Case Histories and the Case against History," *MLN* 104 (December 1989): 1034–49.

tum explored by Sartre, to "make history." It is to compose a historical situation in one's representation, and it is to act on that represented state of affairs in such a way as to transform it. In the case of the "England" of Bentham's *Plan,* for example, it is to restructure the local situations constituted by the representative systems in such a way as to enable each member of society—conservator general or bookseller—to serve the general interest by acting in the interest of himself or herself. We come, therefore, to a third sense in which this process is understood to make history: it involves precisely the "concept" of social transformation that is crucial to representing history in terms of periodic shifts in normative frameworks—"history" as we now routinely picture and practice it. Only in thinking about history this way is one led to the concept of the historical situation, and only thus is one confronted with the discourse of a historicized casuistry. Such a concept and such a framework persist in Sartre's Marx, Lévi-Strauss's Sartre, and the Lévi-Strauss of poststructuralist commentators such as Veyne, White, and Jameson.[58]

Reflecting on Bentham's simultaneous contribution to the history of casuistry and to the politics of representation in relation to the question of Romantic historicism, we find in his great project that same conjunction of spirit-of-the-age discourse and the notion of end-means mechanism that we saw in the slightly later surveys of the moment of historicism by Mill, Carlyle, and Bulwer-Lytton. An age that has the capacity to conceive of itself as such will do so in order that it may alter itself. This is at least a partial solution to the riddle of Mill's characterization of his contemporary culture as the first epoch conscious of itself as such, and therefore as a period, quintessentially, of transition. To be able make a case of one's own time is to imagine it otherwise constituted. But it is also in some important way to cease to be able to imagine the cases of one's own time as the cases of another time. Hence we might say that, in the new historical casuistry of Bentham's *Plan,* both casuistry and history cease to play their accustomed roles.

When this analysis is pressed, however, one must eventually come up against the question: how, ultimately, does the general will evaluate the historical situation it confronts, if not in what must be called "general," that is to say, generic terms. After it is understood as defined by a place and a date, in other words, must there not, in the end, occur some reconstitution of the historical situation as a *kind* of state of affairs? It is a difficult question to answer, and its difficulty is related to the vexed debate over the relationship of the claims of history and hu-

---

58. Addressing the question of the novelty of the Age of Revolution, Hannah Arendt makes a similar point from a different perspective, but without seeing the distinction of levels, in *On Revolution* (1965; London and New York: Penguin Books, 1990), pp. 52–53.

man nature in the intellectual tradition that extends from Hume to Marx—both Hume and Marx in particular are writers for whom volumes of commentary have been produced in respect to this very question.[59] At the start of the previous chapter, in comparing remarks on history and the historical novel by Macaulay and Carlo Ginzburg, I mentioned that one important difference between them was that Macaulay, writing in his manifesto for the *Edinburgh Review* in 1828, articulates his new historicism in relation to the concept of human nature. Indeed, one of the founding contradictions of the Waverley novels appears in the very first one, *Waverley* itself, where the framing remarks in the introductory chapter and in the final chapter ("A Postscript That Should Have Been a Preface") seem to be at odds over this very point.

The passage that stands as the locus classicus for the historiographical line of Scott and Macaulay, however, is the brief comment on the uniformity of human nature that Hume composed for the section on "Liberty and Necessity" in the *Enquiry Concerning Human Understanding*. There Hume asks his famous question and gives his own famous answer to it:

> Would you know the sentiments, inclinations and course of life of the Greeks and Romans? Study well the temper and actions of the French and English: you cannot be much mistaken in transferring to the former *most* of the observations which you have made with regard to the latter. Mankind are so much the same, in all times and places, that history informs us of nothing new or strange in this particular. Its chief use is only to discover the constant and universal principles of human nature, by showing men in all varieties of circumstances and situations, and furnishing us with materials from which we may form our observations and become acquainted with the regular springs of human action and behaviour.[60]

59. There have been two book-length studies of this very question in Marx in recent years: George Márkus, *Marxism and Anthropology: The Concept of "Human Essence" in the Philosophy of Marx*, trans. E. de Laczay and G. Márkus (The Netherlands: Van Gorcum Assen, 1978), and Norman Geras, *Marx and Human Nature: Refutation of a Legend* (London: New Left Books, 1983). The problem of history and human nature in Hume is of such long standing that it is hard to know how to date it: Collingwood addresses it in *The Idea of History* (Oxford: Oxford University Press, 1945), and a number of important Hume commentators have made this question central to their studies: e.g., Duncan Forbes, in *Hume's Philosophical Politics* (Cambridge: Cambridge University Press, 1975), and Donald Livingston, in *Hume's Philosophy of Common Life* (Chicago: University of Chicago Press, 1984). The passage I note below as being cited by W. H. Walsh is a crux for all of these discussions. For a guide to the intervening tradition on the British side of the debate, see, for example, *The Scottish Moralists on Human Nature and Society*, ed. Louis Schneider (Chicago: University of Chicago Press, 1967). One of the most thoughtful commentaries on the question, not surprisingly, comes from a Vico scholar, Leon Pompa, in his *Human Nature and Historical Knowledge: Hume, Hegel, and Vico* (Cambridge: Cambridge University Press, 1990), which attempts to adjudicate among several attempts at "finding a framework for understanding history which is not itself ahistorical" (p. 194). See also, Christopher J. Berry, *Hume, Hegel and, Human Nature* (The Hague: Martinus Nigjoff, 1982), especially pp. 172–92.

60. L. A. Selby-Bigge, ed., *Hume's Enquiries,* 3d ed. (Oxford: Oxford University Press, 1975), pp. 83–84.

This was the passage singled out by R. G. Collingwood in his critique of Hume's failure to grasp the idea of history, and it is likewise the passage painstakingly reread by others scholars, such as Duncan Forbes and Donald Livingston, who insist that Collingwood underestimated Hume's historicism. It has also figured in broader discussions of the conceptual problem of human nature and history. It becomes the object, for example, of a meditation on "the constancy of human nature," by the British philosopher of history W. H. Walsh.[61] The philosophical question Walsh poses is apparently a quite simple one: "to what extent do we need to presume the constancy of human nature in making judgments about the human past or present?" (p. 274). The emphasis on "judgment" shows the link with the form of the case, while the complication in the question derives from the analogy we have been examining between historiography and anthropology: the sense that judgments about the present are problematized by the anthropologist's notion of culture just as judgments about the past are complicated by the historian's notion of period. The way Walsh's argument inhabits that analogy is part of what constitutes its relevance to my argument here.

Taking the debate over the passage from Hume's *Enquiry* as his starting point, Walsh announces his agreement with Collingwood that Hume cannot be accounted a historicist in that he "shows no proper awareness of the extent to which man can be described as an historical as opposed to a merely natural being," where a "historical being" is understood as "self-modifying": "It is not just affected by experiences but transforms itself in the light of them" (pp. 277–78). Hume's error about this, Walsh argues, comes from thinking that the causation of actions is not different in kind from the causation of events, and more particularly that the passions, which are for Hume the ultimate springs of action, "operate as causal determinants in the same way that the constituents of the body" do—chemical substances, for example (p. 281). According to Walsh, such views are in error because they fail to register that desires are always mediated by representations or "thoughts" about what is the case: "I want what I do not just because I feel a certain impulse . . . , but because I see the world and my situation in it under a certain description" (p. 281). Once one recognizes the role of "thought" in "desire," one can further recognize that there must indeed be something constant in human nature.

However, that something is not to be understood, with Hume, in terms of the fundamental similarity of human beings in all times and places. What is

61. W. H. Walsh, "The Constancy of Human Nature," in *Contemporary British Philosophy*, ed. J. D. Lewis (London: George Allen & Unwin, 1976), pp. 274–91. All citations to this work appear by page number in the text.

constant, according to Walsh, is not the content of motivation but its structure, not the "principles which govern human action," but the "form of practical thinking itself" (p. 282). Walsh calls this form "the practical syllogism," but in his elaboration it comes to resemble what we have been calling the case: "As a historian or an anthropologist I do not have to believe that men remote from me in time or space share or shared either my view of the world or my ideas about how to behave in it. But I do have to assume that they have or had some coherent conception of the world and their situation in it, together with some notion of what to do in the light of that conception" (p. 282). It is necessary to presume that the person from the past period or other culture must be like oneself in one respect only: "In possessing a more or less intelligible set of rules for dealing with situations of this type or that, [and] in having the ability to put together premises about what is the case and what should be done and draw particular practical conclusions from them." Without the meeting of this condition, says Walsh, "studies such as history and social anthropology would simply not be possible" (p. 282). It is no accident that Walsh singles out the fields of history and anthropology for his discussion of situationism: the conjunction of those fields, I have argued from the start, defines a crucial moment in the history of casuistry. Thus, although Walsh's argument aims to produce an abstract and universalizable formulation of the conditions that must be met if intelligibility is to be achieved across the boundaries of culture, it also seems fair to locate his form of analysis within a Scottish-Enlightenment tradition: at the time he wrote the essay on the constancy of human nature he was a professor of logic and metaphysics at the University of Edinburgh. Whether or not one accepts the argument as it stands, one can certainly read it as corroborating the kind of relationship we have been examining here between the basic premises of Romantic historicism in Britain: the assumption of the analogy between historiographical and anthropological operations, the emphasis on the reflexivity of representation, the reliance on the form of the case.

To conclude this phase of discussion, I would like to return briefly to André Jolles for a possible way of reconceiving the historicization of the case from within his account of the functioning of the form. I pick up his account at the point where he offers an illustration of how the case differs from other forms, especially the example. It comes from what he calls a "vulgar little text" from a Berlin newspaper series entitled *Tragedies and Comedies of Penal Law:*

> A pickpocket stole my wallet in the crowd of a large city. He found in it a hundred marks in small bills and shared them with his friend (female) to whom he recounted his great feat. If they are arrested, the friend is punished as an accomplice. Now suppose that he found in the wallet a single hundred mark bill; if he changed it and gave fifty marks to his friend, she will

not be pursued. Stolen goods are in effect possible only if they concern things directly obtained by a culpable act—and not the change from these bills. (p. 173)

Now if we take only the first part of this text, says Jolles, we do not have a case proper but only an illustration or exemplification of two articles, having to do with theft and trafficking, in the German penal code. Insofar as there is any weighing in this first part of the text, it is only the weighing of the action against a law understood as given and fixed: "In the one dish of the balance," he says, "the law rests with all its weight; as soon as something is laid onto the other dish, it moves up and down and by moving is itself weighed" (p. 175). That is, "the article of law is the weight with which one weighs the acts of this species." The "act" described is just a example or sample (*Exemple oder Beispiel*) of the normative system (p. 177).

With the addition of the second part of this text, however, attention shifts from the "act itself" to the invoked law or norm. All that has changed in the second part of the text is that the thief has stolen a single hundred-mark note instead of fifty one-mark notes, and yet here his friend is not punishable. If the first part simply exemplifies the law, the second part shows its lacunae: "It is no longer the friend whom one evaluates according to a norm; it is the norm itself that one evaluates." Inevitably, one judges that norm according to another normative frame.[62] The text thus turns into a double balancing act in which the balance that weighs an act against the law is balanced with one that weighs one law against another. The form that governs this sort of process is the *Kasus* proper, the simple form that Jolles goes on to explore in richer detail than I can do justice to here. This is his most succinct summary of the matter:

> I would willingly choose for this form [says Jolles] the name that jurisprudence and morals, among others, give to its actualizations: I will call it the Case [Kasus oder Fall]. What lies before us in this ensemble of contradictory parts shows the true meaning of (the) Case: in the mental activity (Geistesbeschaftigung) that imagines the world as an object that can be judged and evaluated according to norms, not only are actions judged against norms, but also the norm is evaluated, at higher and higher levels, against other norms. Each time a simple form results from this mental activity, a process is initiated which is a measuring of measure against measure or, more literally, a measuring from measure to measure [ein Messen von Massstab an Massstab]. (p. 179)

One way to reconceive the historicization of the case, therefore, is to understand that the second set of norms invoked in this dialectical deliberation, this

---

62. I take it that Jolles is lending an analytic framework to the kind of point made more straightforwardly by Camille Wells Slights when, explaining how the "case of conscience arises when a man is doubtful about what to do," she observes that "casuists . . . are sought by men who are torn between conflicting loyalties," in Slights, *The Casuistical Tradition in Shakespeare, Donne, Herbert, and Milton* (Princeton, N.J.: Princeton University Press, 1981), p. 13.

unstable act of weighing, is the set of norms imaginable in a future state no longer conceived as a transcendent or eschatological domain but rather as the projection forward in time of the conditions in which actually existing people are working out their destinies.

The resonance of that phrase, "future state," would not have been lost on the likes of a writer such as Shelley. Among his unpublished papers after he died was a short essay about the doctrine of human immortality that seems to correspond with remarks in some of his earliest surviving letters (from 1811) and that was probably therefore a product of the period before *Queen Mab* (1813). It is published in the collections of Shelley's prose under the title "On a Future State" (WPBS, 6:209). Shelley's conclusion in this essay is that the belief in such a thing is simply a product of the human fear of change: "This desire to be for ever as we are; the reluctance to a violent and unexperienced change, which is common to all the animated and inanimate combinations of the universe, is, indeed, the secret persuasion which has given birth to the opinions of a future state." In his writings of 1819, however, especially in the sonnet, *England in 1819,* Shelley seems sufficiently caught up in the efforts of those poets and philosophers he numbered among his great contemporaries to have reconceived the issue. In that sonnet, we can now say, the steady contemplation of the existing state of things—the statement of the case as it stands—can become the occasion of a recognition, an illumination of the tempestuous day. The content of that recognition is the anticipation of a future day in which the norms brought to bear in judgment on the present state of things will simply have become what the case is.

6. Some Qualifications

It is no easy matter finding the right level of abstraction for the sort of argument I am making here. I hope it is clear that I am interested in concrete historical phenomena at a lower level of abstraction from, for example, Stephen Jay Gould's elegant formulation of the two forms of time ("time's arrow" and "time's cycle") in western thought or from Pitirim Sorokin's account of the alternation of the eternalistic and temporalistic perspectives in this general theory of "social and cultural dynamics."[63] By the same token, I have not, I trust, conveyed the impression that the altering of the case as I have been tracing it

---

63. Stephen Jay Gould, *Time's Arrow, Time's Cycle* (Cambridge, Mass.: Harvard University Press, 1987), pp. 10–16, and Pitirim Sorokin, *Fluctuations of Systems of Truth, Ethics, and Law.* Vol. 2 of *Social and Cultural Dynamics* (New York: Bedminster Press, 1962), pp. 211–41. Sorokin actually produces a table of the fluctuation between these "mentalities" as documented by various representations, which he arranges by both twenty- and hundred-year periods from the sixth century B.C. to the present!

through the long eighteenth century is unattended by confusion and contradiction. Nor would I want to suggest that one could identify any single moment of its occurrence everywhere and all at once in a given literary culture. Some precocious articulations of the new paradigm turn up relatively early and in unexpected places. Bolingbroke's *Letters on the Study and Use of History* (1752), for instance, is a text that has been used by G. H. Nadel and J. G. A. Pocock to illustrate what Nadel calls "exemplary history."[64]

This term, "exemplary history," refers roughly to the notion, which we observed earlier in Koselleck, that prior to historicism history is understood to teach *by* example and to do so *across* period boundaries.[65] And yet, in the course of his *Lectures,* Bolingbroke produces a definition of "epochs" that would seem to imply a framework for the "historicization of the case" in the sense that I have been describing, a framework that identifies the period as a set of macrocircumstances constituted by novel normative structures themselves arising in response not only to "revolutions" but also to far-reaching changes "wrought within the same governments and among the same people."[66] The passage I have in mind from this influential eighteenth-century volume is the following:

> When such changes as these happen in several states about the same time, and consequently affect other states by their vicinity, and by many different relations which they frequently bear to one another; then is one of those periods formed, at which the chain spoken of is so broken as to have little or no real or visible connection with that which we see continue. A new situation, different from the former, begets new interests in the same proportion of difference; not in this or that particular state alone, but in all those that are concerned by vicinity or other relations, as I said just now, in one general system of policy. New interests beget new maxims of government, and new methods of conduct. These, in their turns, beget new manners, new habits, new customs. The longer this new constitution of affairs continues, the more will this difference increase: and although some analogy may remain long between what preceded and what succeeds such a period, yet will this analogy soon become an object of mere curiosity, not of profitable inquiry. Such a period therefore is, in the true sense of the words, an epocha or an era, a point of time at which you stop, or from which you reckon forward. (p. 82)

64. G. H. Nadel, "Philosophy of History before Historicism," in *History and Theory* 3 (1964): 291–315, especially 311–314; and J. G. A. Pocock, *The Ancient Constitution and the Feudal Law: A Study of English Historical Thought in the Seventeenth Century* (Cambridge: Cambridge University Press, 1957), pp. 246–49.

65. In her discussion of seventeenth-century casuistry, Slights points out that some writers of that moment "warn particularly against the uncritical use of biblical examples as precedents for right conduct." The point here has to do less with historical relativism than with the transcendental character of the Scriptures: the caveat is issued "because the actions of even good men are not always imitable and because biblical examples often demonstrate special divine commandments to particular people in particular situations, as in the story of Abraham and Isaac," *The Casuistical Tradition,* p. 21.

66. Lord Bolingbroke, "Letters on the Study and Use of History," in *Historical Writings,* ed. Isaac Kramnick (Chicago: University of Chicago Press, 1972), p. 82. All subsequent citations will be by page number to this edition.

The "new situation" of which Bolingbroke writes here—the new "state of things," to return to our earlier vocabulary—is decidedly a second-order situation, a situation of situations. It involves not just a new combination of circumstances confronting a subjectivity shaped in a given manner and informed by a given set of principles but new "interests," "maxims," and "methods of conduct." A fully achieved epoch of this sort involves nothing less, we are later told, than "a new system of causes and effects" in the moral world (p. 82).

The specific epoch that Bolingbroke means to be introducing with these remarks begins with "the end of the fifteenth century," at least (as he stipulates) "for those who live in the eighteenth century and who inhabit the western parts of Europe" (p. 83). By periodizing on this grand scale—*la longue durée avant la lettre*—Bolingbroke is able to grant room for the operation of the older kind of "exemplary history" *within* the bounds of an altered (modern) condition. Down to the era of the late fifteenth century, writes Bolingbroke, we only "read history"; but from that point down to our own time, we must "study it" (p. 83). The consideration that some movement internal to the long contemporary period might vitiate the exemplificatory capacity of history simply does not figure in this discussion. The "increase in difference" between the present long era and what comes before it seems to be subsumed under its enabling condition: that the "new constitution of affairs" simply "continues."

In certain circles, Bolingbroke's book remained authoritative for decades. Joseph Priestley quotes Bolingbroke's definition of a period in his own influential *Lectures on History,* a work published on the eve of the French Revolution and (as we have seen) cited by Anna Barbauld in her later essay on "The Uses of History."[67] Like Bolingbroke's historical instruction, Priestley's is also ruled by imitation and example—"history may be considered as containing examples of the sciences of *morals* and *politics*" (2:94)—still a distinctly prehistoricist position understood in terms of Koselleck's distinction. Indeed, Priestley's discussion further demonstrates the slipperiness of terms in the more general debate then developing about example and explanation in the field of history.[68] Priestley does emphasize that the alignment of one's situation with some precedent situation requires discrimination: "In proposing to ourselves the imitation of any

---

67. Joseph Priestley, *Lectures on History,* 2 vols. (1788; London: Joseph Johnson, 1793), 2:24. Subsequent citations will appear in the text.

68. It is a debate, after all, that has reappeared in different forms in different times, most recently with the notorious controversy in post–World War II philosophy of history over the question of what Carl Hempel termed "covering laws" in historical explanation. For a review of and contribution to this controversy over "nomothetic explanation" in history, see, for example, Maurice Mandelbaum, *The Anatomy of Historical Knowledge* (Baltimore: Johns Hopkins University Press, 1977).

person or action, we should take care that the circumstances of the two cases be perfectly alike," he says, for otherwise, "a similar conduct will have very different consequences" (2:6). He is even willing to allow for the immense variety of "the circumstances of human conduct" and for "changes . . . imperceptible in the course of time," either of which is capable of leading even persons of the "greatest sagacity" into misjudgment (2:6). Priestley's basic model, however, conforms to the one Koselleck associates with writers like Machiavelli (whom Priestley actually seems to be echoing in places) rather than to the more radically historicist paradigms we have seen in Bentham and Shelley.

For one thing, Priestley does not show the alertness to the problem of scale in historical representation that becomes explicit in Macaulay's 1828 manifesto and crucial to historicism's chronological code. Further, in spite of his early, staunch, and personally costly commitment to the cause of reform, Priestley's scientific orientation leads him to expect a future that will be fundamentally explicable in the term of the past. Thus, under the heading of attending to cause and effect in history, he urges that one "endeavour to trace all the circumstances in the situation of things which contributed either to produce, or facilitate; to hasten, or to retard it, and clearly see the manner of their operation; by which we shall be better able to form a judgment of the state of political affairs in a future time, and take our measures with greater wisdom, and a more reasonable prospect of success" (2:7). It is true that Priestley's *Lectures* are informed by a careful study of Scottish-Enlightenment theory: he explicitly cites the work of Hume, Robertson, and Millar. He does not, however, invoke the notion of cultural textuality that informs Dugald Stewart's and Scott's later descriptions of translating manners between historical ages. Nor yet does he enter the discursive framework dominated by the post-Waterloo obsession with the "spirit of the age." Though that particular concept was beginning to take shape in British discourse at that moment, it did not figure in the discussion of politics and culture before the French Revolution as it would do after the close of the Napoleonic Wars.[69]

69. It is instructive to compare the rhetoric of political debate in the 1790s and in the post-Waterloo period. In the former, the frame of reference tends to be some notion of "reason," "nature," "righteousness," or "rights" and to involve philosophical and theological categories. In the 1790s, reform is "necessary" because it is "right." In the post-1815 debates, the frame of reference tends to involve some notion of political movement, social change, demographic shift, industrial transformation, and periodic shift. In the post-Waterloo debates, as Shelley made explicit, reform is "necessary" not only because it is "right" but also because it is historically determined—its moment has arrived. See Shelley's account of this distinction at the start of the chapter "On the Sentiment of the Necessity of Change," in *A Philosophical View of Reform,* p. 21. Bentham advertises the same second sense of the term, a sense backed up by the threat of revolution, when he refers on his title page to the "necessity for radical [as distinct from moderate] reform."

One way to consider the altered sense and scale of the epochal paradigm between the one shared by Bolingbroke and Priestley, on the one hand, and the ones I have identified in texts from around the time of Peterloo, on the other, is to reexamine the speech, famous in its time, by George Canning: the address to his constituents in Liverpool, at the celebration of his fourth election, March 18, 1820. Here the victorious Canning first surveys retrospectively what he calls "the situation of the country in November 1819," when the outrage over Peterloo was at its highest and Parliament commenced deliberations on measures to address it (measures that would take shape as the Gag Acts passed in the final days of the year), and then pauses to reflect on "the situation of the Country now."[70] In a few scant months, he claims, a historical threshold has been passed that seems in every sense comparable to the one which Bolingbroke saw dividing history between what came before and what has come after the late fifteenth century: "I would appeal to the recollection of every man who now hears me . . . whether any Country, in any two epochs, however distant, of its history, ever presented such a contrast with itself as this Country in November 1819, and this Country in February 1820" (p. 7). It is as if the radical implications of a text like Shelley's sonnet of December, though Canning could obviously not have seen it, had been coopted in an antiradical polemic against the reform movement.

I have already noted some of the events that separate these two "epochs" in the rapidly developing social and political history of post-Waterloo Britain: the debate on and passage of the Six Acts, the death of George III, the Cato Street Conspiracy, the beginnings of the Affair of Queen Caroline. By the same token, though, I have also given evidence that the microhistorical sense of scale implicit in Canning's gauging of these epochs was already in place beforehand. Bolingbroke and Priestley can begin to adumbrate the new historical paradigm. But it is in the difference between their diminishment of its import and the central place given it in the representations of Canning and Shelley that we can gain a sense of the change that Lukács and Hans Blumenberg see taking place, in this epoch, in the concept of the epoch itself. The concept of the epoch—homogeneous in its "spirit" but heterogeneous in its manifestations—recognizes changes in what Koselleck calls the "structural conditions of history", conditions the likes of which were summarized by Wordsworth in 1798

70. *Speech of the Right Hon. George Canning, to his Constituents at Liverpool, On Saturday, March 18th, 1820* (London: John Murray, 1820), pp. 7–8. We might note here that Canning pays an indirect compliment to the power and influence of Bentham's *Plan of Reform* when he declares that he has "never yet heard any intelligible theory of Reform, except that of the *Radical* Reformers" (p. 33).

when he spoke of that "multitude of causes, unknown to former times, . . . now acting with combined force" in British society.[71]

There are two potentially more troubling forms of contradiction implicit in the discussion of Romantic historicism to this point. One has to do with the contradictions that structure the relation of temporal and generic categories (i.e., the date and the case) in this analysis, the other with those that structure the relation of normative and arbitrary categories in the historicist conception of the period. Both demand some additional attention here. As for the first point, about time and genre, it is perhaps simply a matter of making explicit an unstated connection between the arguments in chapters 2 and 4. In chapter 2, I followed the transformation of the genre of the literary "state" to show how the date assumed a titular function in eighteenth-century writings on politics and society. The logical extension of this argument is that the date itself comes to invoke generic expectations. This is, of course, precisely what we find in Marx's *Eighteenth Brumaire of Louis Bonaparte*, where the date is used to name a state of affairs repeatable in different times and places. And there is an interesting anticipation of Marx's trope twenty years earlier in the letters of J. S. Mill. Explaining to his St. Simonian correspondents in Paris that he had to be wary of overstepping himself in writing "The Spirit of the Age," Mill suggested that it is was untimely "to seek a hearing for any 'vues organiques' in England now [1831], as it would have been for your master St Simon in the height of the revolution." Then, to explain, Mill adds: "our 10 août, our 20 juin, and perhaps our 18 Brumaire, are yet to come."[72] Thus, in the age of the spirit of the age can the *date* of a particular event come to signify a *kind* of event.[73]

In chapter 4, conversely, I tried to show how, by way of the historicization of the concept of the case, what had once been understood primarily in generic terms—"a case of self-defense" or "a case of stealing in order not to starve"—had come to be understood in temporal terms. That is, the new *historical* situation could be understood as the case, say, of England in 1798 or 1811 or 1819 or 1823, or any mo-

71. William Wordsworth, *Prose Works*, 3 vols. Edited by W. J. B. Owen and Jane Worthington Smyser (Oxford: Clarendon Press, 1974). Wordsworth's own list of "the most effective of these causes" includes "the great national events which are daily taking place, and the increasing accumulation of men in cities, where the uniformity of their occupations produces a craving for extraordinary incident, which the rapid communication of intelligence hourly gratifies" (1:28).

72. John Stuart Mill, "Letter to Gustave d'Eichthal, 30 November 1831," in *Collected Works*, 33 vols., ed. Francis Mineka and Dwight Lindley (Toronto: University of Toronto Press, 1963–91), 12:89.

73. It should be noted that this is also the period when we begin to see the now-common practice of naming political movements and parties after dates: those who embraced the terms of the violent defense of the new republic established in France in 1792, for example, soon became known as "Septembrists."

ment identified by a date of place, in which microsituations are all but determined by the macrosituation or historical "condition" of society in question, which condition in turn becomes the object of a "national" or "general will." To say this much is perhaps only to acknowledge that my object of study here is something like what John Bender and David Wellbery have recently called "the chronotype," though I mean to be framing a discussion of this hybridized object in terms that themselves are, self-consciously, at once generic and historical.[74] In associating this problematic conjunction with some time/thing called "Romanticism," I am elaborating a point made by Derrida in "The Law of Genre," where he set out to consider what he punningly called "the most general concept of genre, from the minimal trait or predicate delineating it permanently through the modulations of its types and the regimens of its history."[75] It suits my argument nicely, of course, that Derrida's meditation on this problem leads, as it were inevitably, to what he alternately calls "Romanticism" and "the Romantic era" (the classificatory term alternating with the temporalizing one).[76] "Such a 'moment,'" writes Derrida, "is no longer a simple moment *in* the history and theory of literary genres [for] Romanticism simultaneously obeys the naturalizing and historicizing logic," and we cannot say we have been "delivered from the Romantic heritage . . . as long as we persist in drawing attention to historical concerns and the truth of historical production in order to militate against abuses or confusions of naturalization."[77] The very debate, as he suggests, "remains itself a part or effect of Romanticism," a formulation in which the second-order joke involves the performance of the terms of the debate by the appositive disjunction: "part or effect."[78]

The second and perhaps less remarked contradiction I wish to highlight, like the first, strongly inheres in present-day historicist practice. It has to do with the way in which, after Romanticism, we identify period concepts as normative in respect to the subjects we locate within them. René Wellek is emphatic on this point in his widely cited work on periodization: "A period is not a type or a class, but a time section, defined by a system of norms embedded in the histori-

74. John Bender and David E. Wellbery, *Chronotypes: The Construction of Time* (Stanford, Calif.: Stanford University Press, 1991), p. 4.

75. Jacques Derrida, "The Law of Genre," *Critical Inquiry* 7 (autumn 1980): 60. For Derrida on the date, see *Schibboleth Pour Paul Célan* (Paris: Editions Galilée, 1986), pp. 11–40.

76. Derrida, "Law of Genre," pp. 61–62.

77. Ibid., pp. 61–62.

78. Ibid., p. 62. A similar argument is made about the relation of a genre, and a "moment" in Paul de Man's "Lyric and Modernity," in *Blindness and Insight* (New York: Oxford University Press, 1971), pp. 166–86; cf. final pages of "Literary History and Literary Modernity" in the same volume, pp. 162–65. See also Michael McKeon's "dialectical literary history" of genre in *Origins of the English Novel*, pp. 25–64; and Herbert Lindenberger, *The History of Literature: On Value, Genre, Institutions* (New York: Columbia University Press, 1990), pp. 109–28.

cal process, irremovable from its temporal place."[79] In his parallel discussion of the concept of Romanticism, an account later attacked by A. O. Lovejoy and reargued back and forth by innumerable scholars since, Wellek famously defends the validity of the period term "Romantic" and even the claim for "the unity of European Romanticism," but without managing to identify the Romantic period as an age normatively defined at least in part by the emergence of the normative concept of the period itself.[80] As I have suggested, though, the work of Benjamin, Kracauer, Althusser, Habermas, Kubler, and Anderson has helped us to understand the historical contingency of the very notion of the "time-section," as it appears in such work as Wellek's. The "time section" is thus doubly arbitrary: arbitrary in respect to its being available to a culture *and,* even for cultures that have it, in respect to its mode of organization.

Both forms of arbitrariness are foregrounded, and indeed exacerbated, by the way in which the increasingly influential periodic press, especially in Britain, effectively encoded the public sphere into the measures of homogeneous empty time. The contradiction between the arbitrary and the normative, in other words, runs as deep in the developing discourse on "the Spirit of the Age" as does the presupposition of period-specific normativity itself. The contingent fact that a number of texts happened to be printed in British "public journals" for the year 1798, 1808, or 1818, would not seem to constitute serious grounds for positing a "spirit" that one could say, with Leigh Hunt, was "abroad" in those years. How could such a fact provide the warrant, or the terms, in virtue of which such texts could be framed together in a single interpretative scheme?[81] The aporia implicit in such a measure is only aggravated by the way in which, as the time section becomes more critically normative, it also becomes more arbitrary as to scale.[82] And yet such a measure is precisely the one taken in, if not quite constitutive of, the self-conscious historical practice of the age of the world picture.[83]

79. René Wellek, "Periods and Movements in Literary History," *English Institute Annual, 1940* (New York: AMS Press, 1965), p. 90. This formulation appears as the answer to a question Wellek poses at the start: "The solution lies in the attempt to relate the historical process to a scheme of values or norms" (p. 88).

80. René Wellek, "The Concept of 'Romanticism' in Literary History," *Comparative Literature* 1 (winter 1949): 1–23 and 147–72.

81. Imagine demanding a hermeneutic *warrant* for "cross-reading" items in a periodical—the "old game of reading across rather than down columns of print to produce unexpected juxtapositions," which Kevin Gilmartin has discussed for this period, *Print Politics,* p. 95.

82. Although it is not always identified in the terms I have used, this aporia tends to figure in arguments about the so-called impossibility of literary history. See for example Peter Burger, "On Literary History," and Siegfried J. Schmidt, "On Writing Histories of Literature, Some Remarks from a Constructivist Point of View," both in a special issue of *Poetics,* ed. Siedgfried J. Schmidt, 14 (1985):202, 279–80.

83. In the writings of 1819, a spirit can be understood to preside over a time defined as sev-

Or should we say the world picture in England in 1819, or perhaps in Britain more generally, through the extraordinary post-Waterloo period whose literary culture was dominated by Scott's historical fiction? I have up to this point been deploying categories developed on either side of the Channel to characterize the historicism of this period. The gallery of authorities I cited at the start of chapter three—Meinecke, Collingwood, Gadamer, Foucault, Lukács, and so on—was deliberately eclectic with respect to national and critical tradition. At this point, however, I would like to attempt a discrimination—or, more precisely, both to resist one discrimination and make another—between the new theories and practices of social-political-historical representation in British and in those of continental romanticisms. Since the influential work of Fredric Jameson has been a point of reference throughout this discussion, it may be helpful to return to it one last time as a way of taking bearings for my final step in the argument of part 1.

7. The Continental System

Let me therefore return to the critical injunction that was my point of departure in the first chapter, the words ("Always historicize!") that open Jameson's great critical study of 1981, *The Political Unconscious*—this time, however, in order to raise a question about the sentence that follows it: "This slogan—the one absolute and we may even say 'transhistorical' imperative of all dialectical thought—will unsurprisingly turn out to be the moral of *The Political Unconscious* as well."[84] The question I want to raise about this sentence concerns the word "unsurprisingly": why "unsurprisingly"? These are the very first words of Jameson's preface. Why should we be unsurprised that the "thought" of the book that follows will be dialectical?

The reason, presumably, lies in the declared commitment to the dialectic in Jameson's already twenty-year publication record to that point, the centerpiece of which, surely, being the magesterial study that opened the decade of the 1970s (as did *The Political Unconscious* the 1980s and *Postmodernism* the 1990s): *Marxism and Form: Twentieth-Century Dialectical Theories of Literature* (1971). For readers already familiar with Jameson's first decade of publication, beginning with *Sartre: The Origins of a Style* (1961), it was perhaps already unsurprising that *Marxism and Form* should have taken the shape of a sequence of critical exposi-

---

eral decades, or as a year, a day, or even, in *Prometheus Unbound,* an hour. To "The Spirit of the Hour" is given the long stunningly beautiful speech reporting on the changed world at the end of act 3 (scene 4, ll. 98–204).

84. Jameson, *The Political Unconscious: Narrative as a Socially Symbolic Act* (Ithaca, N.Y.: Cornell University Press), p. 9.

tions of Adorno then, in chapters of increasing length and density, of Benjamin, Marcuse, Bloch, and Lukács, and should have culminated in a one-hundred-page chapter, "Sartre and History," in which Jameson patiently lays out the argument of the two works (*Search for a Method* and *Critique of Dialectical Reason*) that Sartre published in the year that Jameson's own earlier study of Sartre's style would have gone to press—the same works, as we have seen, that formed the object of Lévi-Strauss's polemic in *The Savage Mind*. It is "Sartre's enormous book," says Jameson at the start, that "yields the techniques for a genuine Marxist *hermeneutics*," by virtue of the way in which it poses the central questions of mediation: "How do we pass . . . from one level of social life to another, from the psychological to the social, indeed, from the social to the economic? What is the relation of ideology, not to mention the work of art itself, to the more fundamental social and historical reality of groups in conflict, and how must the latter be understood if we are to be able to see cultural objects as social acts, at once disguised and transparent?"[85] These were to become some of the central questions of criticism in the quarter century since Jameson posed them.

To suggest the further relevance of *Marxism and Form* as articulating a framework for the issues of the "return to history" movement, we can note that Jameson's enormous chapter on Sartre's enormous book begins with an effort to show the connection between the *Critique* and those earlier writings by Sartre to which Jameson's first book had been attentive, especially the fiction and drama. The basis of this connection lies in the way in which the *Critique* illustrates the importance that the "problem of *biography*" has played throughout the Sartrean oeuvre. In particular, it centers in the relation of biography and the past, and in the recognition that the past is that "about which one must 'make up one's mind,'" that the past "must be formed from the outside, by a *decision*" (p. 210). It has to do with "the basic indeterminacy of the past," a "dizzying possibility of the rearrangement of models" which "takes the form of a nagging uncertainty about *motivation*." In such formulations, Jameson's account shows its affinity with the kind of casuistical dramatism that Kenneth Burke helps us to recognize in both Romantic historicism and in its recent revivals under other names.[86] In support of this suggestion, I wish to offer a brief argument that I hope can lead to a larger point.

85. Jameson, *Marxism and Form: Twentieth-Century Dialectical Theories of Literature* (Princeton, N.J.: Princeton University Press, 1971), p. xv. Hereafter cited by page number in the text.
86. Kenneth Burke, too, we must recall, like Jameson's Sartre, produced a "critique of the idea of motivation as self-contradictory." See *Marxism and Form*, p. 211. Burke's critique goes this way:

We may discern a dramatistic pun, involving a merger of active and passive in the expression, "the motivation of an act." Strictly speaking, the act of an agent would be the move-

The brief argument has to do with the role of Lukács in Jameson's book. For the enormous chapter on Sartre is set up by a long chapter on Lukács, which itself builds toward a reading of Lukács's relatively late critical study, *The Historical Novel*. The important role assigned to this book in Jameson's account should not seem odd if we recall how Jameson's interest in Sartre centers, strongly and justifiably, on Sartre's own way of working out some working notion of "the historical situation"—a term that forms, with its cognates ("concrete social situation," "actual situation itself," "Concrete situation itself," "the specificity of its own historical and cultural context," etc.), a kind of refrain in Jameson's discussion of Sartre, and in *Marxism and Form* as a whole.[87] It is indeed in terms of this difficult concept that the two key problems Jameson finds in Sartre—the problem of mediation and the problem of biography—might be said to come together.

This conjunction emerges as Jameson's particular point of emphasis in his use of Lukács to prepare for the analysis of Sartre, and it organizes the other central topics. Thus, when Jameson takes up the key question of "typicality" in Lukács's theory of the historical novel he stresses that, for Lukács, "realist characters are distinguished from those in other types of literature by their *typicality*: they stand, in other words, for something larger and more meaningful than themselves, than their own isolated individual destinies. They are concrete individualities and yet at the same time maintain a relationship with some more general or collective human substance" (p. 191). Insisting that the notion of typicality was already present in the "the first full-scale specimen of Marxist literary criticism" (Marx's epistolary exchange about Lasalle's *Franz von Sickingen*), Jameson argues for its utility in a summary paragraph that makes up in suggestiveness what it might lack in precision or grace:

> For if its relevance to other forms of literature may be questioned, there can be at last no doubt that the historical work, aiming explicitly at a picture of a whole period of history, bears thus in itself a standard by which it may then be judged, so that the question as to whether the characters and situation of a historical work are adequate to reflect the basic historical situation it-

---

ment not of one *moved* but of a *mover* (a mover of the self or of something else by the self). For an act is by definition active, whereas to be moved (or motivated) is by definition passive. Thus, if we quizzically scrutinize the expression, "the motivating of an act," we note that it implicitly contains the paradox of substance. Grammatically, if a construction is active, it is not passive; and if it is passive, it is not active. But to consider an *act* in terms of its *grounds* is to consider it in terms of what it is not, namely passive. (GM, p. 40)

87. A sampling of such occurrences in *Marxism and Form* can be found on pp. xviii, 192, 203, 223, 280, 298, and 333.

self has validity in terms of the form itself. The problem is one of the accidental and of the necessary in the work of art: Does the free shaping power of the historical playwright or novelist extend to certain kinds of liberties with the subject matter which he has (through his initial free choice) assigned himself? (p. 192)

What Jameson provides here, though curiously not with his wonted clarity, is a gloss on his account of Sartre's project-on-projects in *The Critique of Dialectic Reason,* and indeed a retrospective gloss on the entire Sartre/Lévi-Strauss debate. And it is a gloss that links precisely the issues of historical situationism and historiographical constructivism into a single problematic, which Jameson associates, precisely, with Lukács's account of the historical novel and with the emergence of what might be properly be called a "Marxist criticism."[88]

If we were to construe the unclarity of this important passage in Jameson as the effect of a repression, or perhaps a willful suppression, then the object being pushed back or down would be the fiction of Scott and thus by extension British Romantic historicism as I have described it. Lukács identifies Scott's fiction, after all, as the starting point and centerpiece for the entire argument of *The Historical Novel.* Nor does Jameson seem inclined to allow this identification when he praises Lukács for his conservative critique of modernism from the point of view of a history that posits an epochal break with the literature of the past. Lukács, as we have seen, locates this break with a historiographical epoch that he sees commencing with the Waverley novels: "What is lacking in the so-called historical novel before Sir Walter Scott is precisely the specifically historical, that is, the derivation of the individuality of characters from the historical peculiarity of their age."[89] Jameson suggests that the critique of modernism is indeed based on a "fundamental fact," which is "the observation of a qualitative leap in recent times, of an absolute difference between that literature which is ours . . . and the classical literature which preceded it" (p. 199). The surprising thing is that, without explicitly taking issue with Lukács's own account, Jameson locates the break in question not in the post-Waterloo Britain

---

88. Furthermore, in linking Lukács's account of Scott's achievement with one of Sartre's complaints about the role of "types" in "sociological Marxism," Jameson invokes the category, precisely, of the "historical situation" to make his point: "Sartre has pointed out that such categories are themselves idealistic, in that they presuppose immutable forms, eternal Platonic ideas, of the various social classes: what they leave out is precisely history itself, and the notion of the unique historical situation, to which Lukács himself has always been faithful in his criticism" (*Marxism and Form,* p. 193). Jameson does not address the question, crucial to the present discussion, of how to understand the "notion of the unique historical situation" as a "form" or "idea" that is not "immutable" or "Platonic."

89. Lukács, *The Historical Novel,* p. 19.

dominated by Scott's fiction, as Lukács does, but rather "around the time of Baudelaire and Flaubert" (p. 199).[90]

Of course, Jameson is aware that such an act of dating will be to some extent arbitrary, but in his very act of acknowledgment and adjustment one can see precisely the degree to which the history he produces here is itself a motivated one. "No doubt," he adds, "depending upon the width of our historical lens, this absolute break could be located earlier, perhaps around the beginning of the nineteenth century, with the French Revolution and German Romanticism" (p. 199). The motivated aspect of such speculations appears in Jameson's restriction of the discussion to the continental side of late-eighteenth- and early-nineteenth-century European culture. He elides the new dialectical discourse of antiquity and modernity that, as Lukács himself suggests, was taking shape in Britain around a number of new material elements (unequally stressed in his account), including British industrialism, the two revolutions, the reform movements, and, not least, such ethnographic relationships as were shaping and taking shape in Scotland and England, Britain and America, Highlands and Lowlands, and, to be sure, England and the Continent.

I have suggested that there may be motivation to discern in Jameson's complete elision of British Romanticism as the moment for defining the "absolute break" that begins modern culture in favor of locating that break in the literature of "the French Revolution and German Romanticism." The evidence for such motivation is not really so far to seek. In fact, it is spelled out two hundred pages earlier, in Jameson's preface, when he calls attention to the most insidious of the several obstacles he imagines his book will have to face:

> Less obvious, perhaps, is the degree to which anyone presenting German and French dialectical literature is forced—either implicitly or explicitly—to take yet a third national tradition into account, I mean our own: that mixture of political liberalism, empiricism, and logical positivism which we know as Anglo-American philosophy and which is hostile at all points to the type of thinking outlined here. One cannot write for a reader formed in this tradition—one cannot even come to terms with one's own historical formation—without taking this influential conceptual opponent into account; and it is this, if you like, which makes up the tendentious part of my book, which gives it its political and philosophical cutting edge, so to speak. For the bankruptcy of the liberal tradition is as plain on the philosophical level as it is on the political: which does not mean that it has lost its prestige or ideological potency. On the contrary: the anti-speculative bias of that tradition, its emphasis on the individual fact or item at the expense of the network of relationships in which that item may be embedded, continue to encourage submission to what is by preventing its followers from making

90. In fairness to Jameson's account, it should be recognized that in another context Lukács is capable of giving 1848 a more pivotal role. See "Narrate or Describe?" in *Writer & Critic and Other Essays,* ed. and trans. Arthur D. Kahn (New York: Grosset & Dunlap, 1970), pp. 110–48.

connections, and in particular from drawing the otherwise unavoidable conclusions on the political level. It is therefore time for those of us in the Anglo-American tradition to learn to think dialectically, to acquire the rudiments of a dialectical culture and the essential critical weapons it provides. (pp. x–xi)

I want to be clear in saying that I endorse the aspiration of this manifesto. And, certainly, there was far more reason for it to have been issued when it was than may appear in hindsight at a time when, thanks in part to Jameson's own efforts, assumptions in critical practice have changed. I do think, however, that the passage badly oversimplifies its presumed adversary. To glimpse why, E. P. Thompson's polemics notwithstanding, one need only think of the unfolding work of Raymond Williams in Britain, moving between Continental and British models of analysis, but always returning to British culture and society after 1780 as a point of reference.[91] Surely if there is a postwar critic whose work paradigmatically embodies both the effort to "come to terms with one's own historical formation" and the refusal to "submit to what is," it is Williams. The larger problem here, therefore, is that Jameson's representation weakens the cultural-historical argument that he wishes to mount in behalf of a refashioned cultural historicism. If I am right in judging that Jameson's struggle against the "conceptual opponent" of an Anglo-American "national tradition" (posited as homogeneous down to the ground) lies behind, say, the somewhat tendentious rewriting of Lukács's account of Scott, or the willingness to consign a dialectician like Shelley, whom Marx so admired, to any such characterization as the one provided for the British quietist-positivist, or the failure to heed the admonition of Althusser, who constantly emphasized the importance of Scottish-Enlightenment thinking behind Marx's work, then it may be necessary to reconsider some aspects of the manifesto in behalf of which these representations are made.[92]

The self-consciousness in British Romanticism about the relation between language, narrativity, and the various modes of representation—in economics, politics, literature, and aesthetics—is everywhere present in the period, from its most to its least "progressive" writers. Moreover, Jameson seems at times to be forgetting that Marxian injunction to which he elsewhere subscribes, that history can progress on its bad side, that one can learn from historical conservatives, even, as Jameson says in *Marxism and Form,* suddenly conjuring the name

---

91. I refer here, of course, to E. P. Thompson, *The Poverty of Theory* (London: Merlin, 1978).

92. Dialectic and historicist criticism had its share of enemies in the third quarter of this century, though some were also hostile to British Romanticism and not all of them were oriented primarily in the Anglo-American tradition. For a good sorting out of such issues, see David Simpson, *Romanticism, Nationalism, and the Revolt Against Theory* (Chicago: University of Chicago Press, 1993).

from midair, from "Burke himself" (p. 199). The very case of Burke, indeed, reveals the flaw in Jameson's stereotype even as he ("Burke himself") apparently epitomizes it. Burke's best writing is antispeculative, but primarily in a sense tied to metaphors of financial speculation, for he was also regarded by many readers as an impossibly obscure metaphysician. It is anything but positivist, and by no means committed to items and facts at the expense of the networks in which they are embedded—that, after all, was precisely part of his critique of the "oeconomists" and "calculators" of his day.[93] And he is certainly a dialectician when it comes to the relation among materials and their uses, signs and their signifiers. Indeed, that Burke, Cobbett, and Shelley agree on so much about the history and theory of representation in this period says something about the multiple levels of complexity involved in their categories of analysis.[94] The point, again, is that the caricature version of Anglo-American thought, while rightly challenging some tenets of its critical legacy, further occludes what that criticism itself occludes: a form of historical dialectic not reducible to Hegelianism.

8. Bretagne en 1799, *History in 1988*: *The Historical Novel* Redivivus

Although Jameson's *Marxism and Form* deals with a number of philosophical texts, he says it is intended not as philosophy but as "literary criticism, or at least a preparation for literary criticism" (p. xi). It was indeed such a preparation, and not just for Jameson's own extraordinary sequence of subsequent writings. By a complex series of connections and associations, I have tried to show how one might view the Anglo-American criticism generated by the engagement of Jameson and others with the Sartre/Lévi-Strauss controversy as being carried out under the sign of "the historical situation." I have also been arguing that this criticism has operated less as a form of resistance to a monolithic "Romantic ideology" than as a reinstallation of a dimension of Romanticism that has received too little notice during the years of the New Criticism. I have emphasized from the start, however, that the renewed interest in history for recent literary criticism has been matched by a renewed interest in form for recent historiography. Turning once more to the history side of this mutual articulation of fields, we

---

93. Burke, *Reflections on the Revolution in France,* p. 88.

94. I address some of these strange conjunctures in "Ricardo and the Poets: Representing Commonwealth in the Year of Peterloo," *The Wordsworth Circle* 25 (spring 1994): 82–86, and in "Poetical Liberties: Burke's France and the 'Adequate Representation' of the English," in *The Transformation of Political Culture 1789–1848,* ed. François Furet and Mona Ozouf. Vol. 3 in *The French Revolution and Modern Political Culture* (Oxford: Pergamon Press, 1989), pp. 54–57.

can fill out a pattern, already briefly glimpsed, similar to the one I have described in the case of Jameson but perhaps ultimately starker in its outline.

In his 1988 essay on recent methodologies in historiography, we recall, Carlo Ginzburg attempted to explain some of the powers and limitations of the new programmatic efforts to represent the underrepresented in history, a project in which his own work and that of Natalie Zemon Davis, the specific subject of the analysis, has been at the forefront. We saw that Ginzburg is especially keen on framing his account in such a way as to save the new forms of historical practice from the charge of relativism. We also saw that, in sorting out how the historian should decide on the representation of underrepresented cases, Ginzburg takes minor issue with Davis's own provocative use of the term "invention" to describe what she does, and argues instead for a model of extrapolation that he locates in the history of modern fiction.

Now, the crucial moment in this history for Ginzburg, as for Lukács (who does not figure in Ginzburg's account), is in the development of the historical novel. The great innovators in this crucial genre, according to Ginzburg, are Balzac, who "vindicated the private life of the individual, contrasting it to the public life of nations," and Manzoni, who tried to portray what one of his characters called "the private effects of the public events that are more properly called historical" (p. 121). Both novelists, Ginzburg argues, adumbrate the practice of historians such as Davis and himself. They provide what he calls an unmistakable "prefiguration of the most notable characteristics of historical research of the last decade: from the polemic against the limitations of an exclusively political and military history to the claim for a history of the mentality of individuals and of social groups, and even (in the case of Manzoni) a theorization of microhistory and the systematic use of new documentary sources" (p. 121). This seems to me an astute acknowledgment, and of a sort not often made in contemporary literary criticism. And, of course, it is also a wonderfully ironic tactic: Ginzburg avows the heritage of *fiction* behind his and Davis's historiographical practice precisely to save that practice from the charge of "invention" and "relativism."

He can have it both ways because he sees the practice of historical novelists, with Defoe and Fielding in the deep background behind them, not as dispensing with the concept of the factual but of immensely complicating its role in historiographical representation: "A century needed to pass [Ginzburg does not say why] before historians began to take up the challenge issued by the great novelists of the nineteenth century—from Balzac to Manzoni, from Stendhal to Tolstoy—confronting previously disregarded fields of research with the aid of more subtle and complex explanatory modes than the traditional ones"

(p. 121). Like Jameson in *Marxism and Form,* Ginzburg here seems to be establishing both a continuity where one was not imagined and a break where one may or may not have been imagined. The *continuity* is between contemporary academic practice (one arguably in both cases informed by the debate about history between Lévi-Strauss and Sartre)[95] and a literary tradition in Romanticism. The *break* is between that Romanticism and what lies beyond or behind it.

Needless to say, neither the continuity nor the break (notwithstanding Jameson's momentary suggestion) should be regarded as "absolute." As Jameson suggests in his own account, one needs to allow for adjustments of the date relative to the width of the lens through which one regards the past. What seems extraordinary, however, is the fact that, like Jameson, Ginzburg disregards the role of Scott, the Scottish Enlightenment, and British historicism in his effort to be compendious about the early tradition he is describing. Indeed, Ginzburg's genealogy leaps directly from Defoe and Fielding to Balzac and Stendhal, without so much as gesturing to British writing in between on the subject of history, except for a reference to Gibbon's reliance on "conjecture" in *The Decline and Fall of the Roman Empire.*[96] Ginzburg's occlusion of Scott and, by synecdoche, the Scottish Enlightenment and British Romanticism does not, like Jameson's, seem particularly motivated. Nor is he, like Jameson, working directly from an account (Lukács's) that itself cites Scott as the key figure in the historical-historiographical paradigm shift in question. Nonetheless, in framing his account to occlude Romantic historicism in Britain, Ginzburg does manage to overlook some conspicuous evidence that he might be missing something.

To begin with, Balzac is recognized as having taken part in the competition among his fellow young writers of the 1820s to become "the French Walter Scott." He actually attempted an imitation of *Ivanhoe* before turning to a novel whose very subtitle gestures to the historical code Scott explained in *Ivanhoe*'s dedicatory epistle: *La Dernier Chouan ou Bretagne en 1800* (1829). This novel—later retitled *Les Chouans ou la Bretagne il y a trente ans* (echoing the subtitle of *Waverley*), then *Les Chouans ou Bretagne en 1799,* and finally just *Les Chouans*—

95. In this same essay, Ginzburg cites the work of Hayden White, for instance, in describing the recent discussion of "the narrative dimension of historiography"—"Proofs and Possibilities," p. 118, and, elsewhere recounting his path of approach to historiographical problems, Ginzburg speaks of the "pull" of his encounter with Lévi-Strauss's *Structural Anthropology,* trans. Claire Jacobson and Brooke Grundfest Schoepf (New York: Basic Books, 1963)—preface to the Italian edition of *Clues, Myths, and the Historical Method,* p. xi.

96. This is especially odd, since "conjectural history" is one of the names given to the historiographical practices of Gibbon's contemporaries and, indeed, mentors, in Scotland. In a flattering letter to William Robertson, Gibbon wrote that he had ever sought only "to find my name associated with the names of Robertson and Hume"; see Dugald Stewart, *Biographical Memoirs* (Edinburgh: Thomas Constable, 1858), p. 228.

would become the earliest entry to be included in *La Comédie Humaine*. This grand series of novels accumulated as his own answer to the Waverley novels, and in the avant-propos to the 1842 edition of *La Comédie Humaine* he offered a stirring tribute to his Scottish mentor.

As for *Le Dernier Chouan*, its reliance on Scott is quite impossible to ignore. Early responses to the novel certainly did not shrink from pointing out the novel's emulation of Scott's practice, mediated by Cooper's prior emulation in the Leatherstocking Tales. After speculating on what Sir Walter might have done with such scenes of carnage and piety as are presented in the spectacle of the counterrevolution in the Vendée, one early critic could only despair. "Malheuresement . . . pour lui-même," sighs the critic, "l'auteur du *Dernier Chouan* n'est point un Walter Scott."[97] What is perhaps yet more striking even than this strongly worded dismissal is the *Avertissement* that Balzac wrote but did not publish for the serialized version of the novel, then titled *Le Gars*, in 1828. A dizzying hall of mirrors, the *Avertissement* ostentatiously imitates the tactics of Scott's playful prefaces, especially the Dedicatory Epistle to *Ivanhoe*, to create a cast of characters that include both a drole editorializing narrator (very like Jedediah Cleishbotham from Scott's "Tales of My Landlord") and an autobiographical stand-in, here called Morillon, who was, the editor-narrator suggests, changed forever by his reading of one of Scott's novels. Confronted with the question of his literary debt by the editor himself, Morillon is reported to have produced the following apology:

> Je ne crois pas, nous répondit-il, qu'une nation soit assez injuste pour repousser comme imitateur l'homme courageux qui prend pour sujet de ses compositions, l'histoire et la Nature de son pays parce qu'il essayera de les peindre dans une forme nouvellement consacrée. Je ne sache pas qu'en Allemagne les critiques aient arrêté M. de Goëthe en lui opposant qu'il ne serait que le singe de Shakespeare. . . . Le poète qui compose le second quatrain ou la seconde églogue a-t-il été accablé sous cette effrayante raison qu'il marchait dans un chemin trace par un autre. Existe-t-il un *école* pour ceux qui veulent pendre des paysages, des costumes et des hommes réels et parce que Téniers a montré le peuple hollandais fumant du taback et buvant de la bière, est-il interdit à un peintre de représenter le retour des vendanges du people napolitain?[98]

And if the self-ironizing use of Scott's own ironic tactics in this *Avertissement* were not enough to identify exactly who corresponds to Shakespeare and Téniers in this conceit, Morillon eventually spells everything out plainly:

> Quant à moi, messieurs, je ne pretends attacquer en aucune manière sir Walter Scott. C'est pour moi un homme de génie, il connaît le coeur humain, et s'il manque à sa lyre les cordes sur lesquelles on peut chanter l'amour qu'il nous présent tout venu et qu'il ne montre jamais naissant et grandissant, l'histoire devient domestique sous ses pinceaux; après l'avoir lu, on

97. From *Trilby, Album des Salons* (July 22, 1829), reprinted in the Livre de Poche edition of *Les Chouans*, ed. René Guise (Paris: Librairie Générale Francaise, 1983), p. 426.
98. Reprinted in *Les Chouans*, ed. René Guise, pp. 448–49.

comprend mieux in siècle, il en evoque l'esprit et dans une seule scène en exprime le génie et la physionomie.[99]

Summarizing the point briefly in the preface he *did* publish for the first edition of *Le Dernier Chouan* in 1829, Balzac writes that following the new "systême" has meant "mettre dans ce livre l'esprit d'un époque et d'un fait."[100]

The talk of "manner," and "form," and "system" is crucially germane to Ginzburg's argument, for it is precisely what he calls the "model" of the historical novel that he says underlies contemporary historical practice. What stronger testimony could one want, both in the reception of Balzac's trial run for his great series and in his own unpublished anticipation of that reception, that the model in question comes from another author and another time and place? Furthermore, if we think of Edinburgh in 1828, the year before Balzac in France published *Le Dernier Chouan ou Bretagne en 1800,* we can recall that Macaulay had already not only explained the uses of Scott's new model of historical narrative for the practicing historian but actually made arguments that anticipate the suggestions of Ginzburg himself. And again, Scott's earliest proselytes, both in fiction and history, understood that what he offered them was not just a new wrinkle in the novel but a new model for historical narrative, not just a variation within a genre but a new representational conceptual framework in which "l'histoire devient domestique."[101]

That such a conceptual framework still operates in fiction itself is sufficiently evident, I hope, in the case of Don DeLillo's *Libra.* Among that novel's balancing acts, as I described them at the outset, is one that might be used for a summary formulation of what I have been trying to suggest about the altering of the case in Romantic historicism. I mentioned that DeLillo used the strategy of alternating chapters to construct two different narratives in his account of Oswald and the Kennedy assassination: in one set of chapters, a narrative of the life of Oswald, as it is known from the existing records; in the other, a narrative of a conspiracy to kill Kennedy in which disgruntled veterans of the Bay of Pigs develop the need for a fall guy of roughly "Oswald's" description. The argument that I have offered here depends on a similar crossing of narrative lines. On the one hand, there is the story of casuistry and its transformation by the events of what we have loosely been calling the Romantic period. On the other

99. Ibid., p. 449.
100. Ibid., p. 455.
101. Balzac's formulation of how "history becomes domestic" in the novels of Scott points to his crucial place in the history of domestic fiction, which raises some troubling questions about the hiatus around the career of Scott—the "gap" between the work of Austen and the Brontës—in Nancy Armstrong's *Desire and Domestic Fiction: A Political History of the Novel* (New York: Oxford University Press, 1987), p. 161.

hand, there is the story of the Romantic writers such as Scott and Shelley and Bentham who turn to the case form in order to articulate their distinctive sense of their historical moment. The equilibrium point between these narratives is the one, I claim, that holds us still in place.

Assuming, then, that the case of Romantic historicism remains our own case—the case of those of us who take seriously the interrelation of literature, politics, and culture—we must be clear about what this does and does not mean. It means that we inhabit a frame of reference that has a history of relatively modern vintage, a history that I have partially outlined. It does not mean that we all inhabit it in the same way, nor that various Romantic writers in Britain did when they elaborated its structures and practices. As I have already begun to suggest, if Romantic historicism counts as a case in respect to the prehistoricist world that preceded it, one can nonetheless differentiate a variety of historicist casuistries (ways of taking historical cases), within Romantic historicism, and even within the literary culture of England in 1819. I turn presently to an examination of the rich particulars of that literary culture without, I hope, losing sight of the coherence with which I have tried to invest it. We will consider in some detail a series of cases of and for the case of England in 1819. These cases involve some materials that are quite familiar and others that are less so, but each case will prove to have anticipated some aspect of the casuistry of historical criticism today.

PART TWO

Reading England in 1819

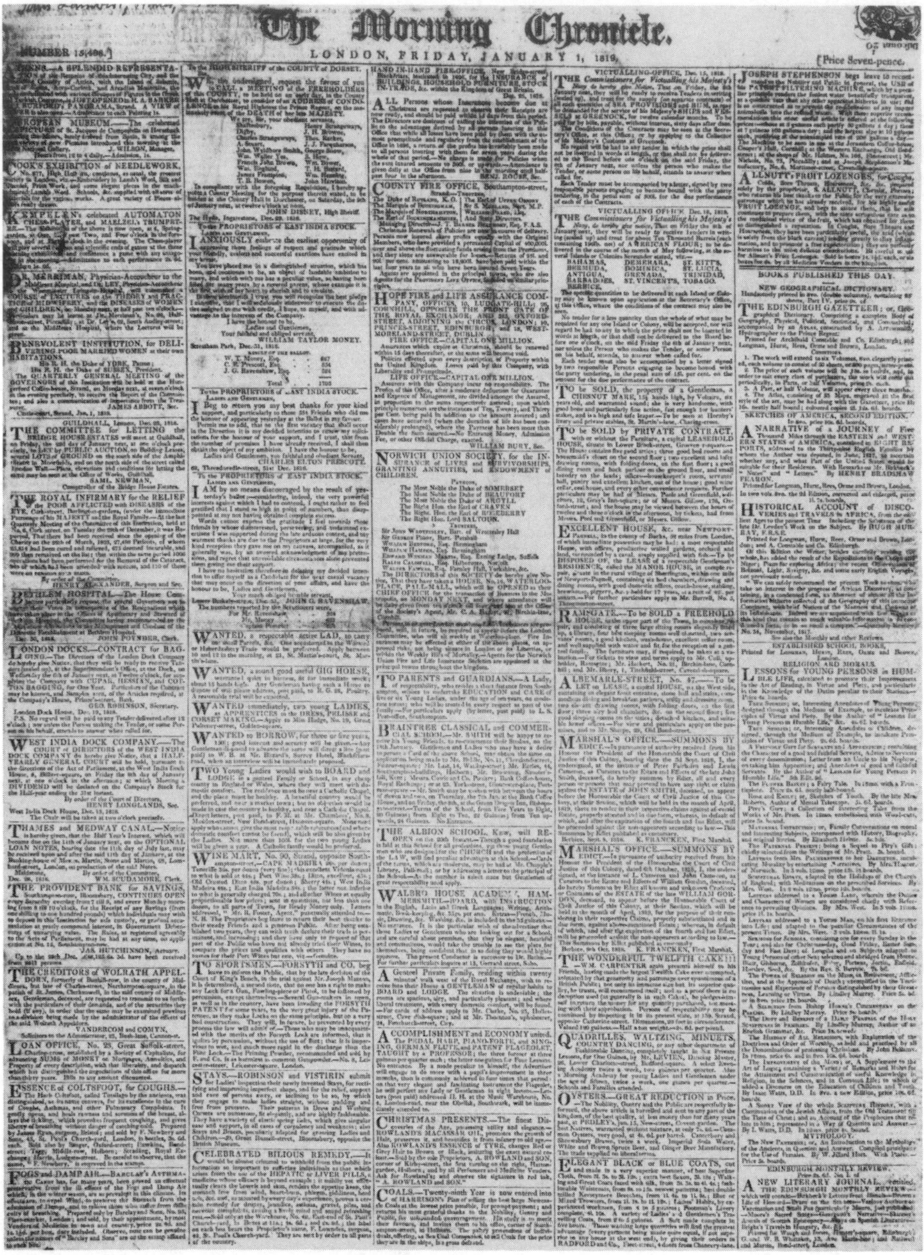

Figure 3. Front page of *Morning Chronicle* for January 1, 1819. Courtesy of the British Library

Interchapter

THE SCENE OF READING IN 1819:
LITERATURE, POLITICS, AND MOORE

How, in the light of the foregoing considerations, does one best set out to represent "England in 1819"? How does one depict in words that historical scene of literary activity so preoccupied with its own history-making possibilities, with the illumination that *may* burst forth to change the course of things? As a way into the particular texts and topicalities of the chapters to follow, I propose a conjectural thought experiment similar, perhaps, to the sort that Carlo Ginzburg has described, and prescribed, for meeting the challenge of a difficult or obscure past record. I propose that we imagine a beginning for the literary life of England in 1819 in the experience of the Irish writer Thomas Moore, who was known as the English Anacreon (oddly), in his role as a writer of lyrics, and as "Tom Brown," in his role as a writer of satire. I propose that we initially imagine Moore in a scene of reading on New Year's Day 1819, a setting with such loose parameters as can be extrapolated from the evidence we have at our disposal. It is reasonable to conjecture that Moore was preoccupied that day with both a particular London newspaper and a particular novel, and this cultural coincidence rewards speculation in allowing us to juxtapose the even time that structures the periodical with the uneven development that structures the spirit of the age. Moore's extraordinary status and fame in the literary culture of his time means that my choice of him cannot exactly be called arbitrary. Then again, since he has all but vanished from the literary history of our time—there may well be no British writer of the period who has fallen more dramatically in reputation—I begin with a brief sketch of his life and letters.

After Scott and Byron, Moore was arguably the most visible English writer of his day, a part of what one of his admirers called "the Triangulum Major" of England in 1819 (JTM, 1:147).[1] He did have a talent for verse, as Hazlitt

---

1. It was a "visibility" that Moore did nothing to diminish. In September 1819, he cites, with a certain pride, a remark he noted "after looking over Peter's Letters to his Kinsfolk": "he says of

pointed out, and some of Moore's lyrics—"Believe me, if all those endearing young charms," for example—survive even now in the popular repertoire for Irish tenors.[2] He wrote in many literary genres. Like Robert Burns, whose monument he helped build and whose son he helped to fête and finance in 1819, Moore had enchanted the English metropolis with songs and ballads from, as it were, the Celtic fringe; already seven volumes of his *Irish Melodies* had appeared by 1819 (in multiple editions), with others yet to come. Moore's Orientalist romance, *Lalla Rookh* (1817), which went through a score of editions in his own lifetime, enjoyed a degree of success in the literary marketplace surpassed only perhaps by the very best-selling volumes of poetry of Scott and Byron and earned Moore an advance in the extraordinary sum of 3,000 pounds. Moore's political poetry, especially the humorous verse epistles published as *Intercepted Letters; or, The Twopenny Post-Bag* (1813) and *The Fudge Family in Paris* (1818), placed him near the head of the company of contemporary satirists. He was an accomplished biographer, playwright, and novelist. His several volumes of *National Airs* (1818-27) showed that he could work in a variety of ethnically marked lyric styles. His judgment was sufficiently respected that he was offered the editorship of the age's most powerful periodical, the *Edinburgh Review* (which he turned down), in 1823. He had already refused an offer from John Murray, his and Byron's publisher, to start up a rival to the *Edinburgh Review* some years before.

We find perhaps the most telling evidence of Moore's high reputation among his contemporaries in his journal entry for March 2, 1819, when he reported a recent exchange of letters in which Murray is said to have made the following suggestion: "I wish you would write a Tom Brown on the literature, manners, & characters of the day & we would sell a billion" (JTM, 1:153). Murray knew the literary scene in England as well as anyone then alive, and he was a shrewd entrepreneur. We may think of the hyperbole of this fantasy ("we would sell a billion") as a commercialized measure of the intensity observed by Shelley when, months later, he testified to a feeling among the contemporary Britons that theirs was "*a memorable age,*" or by Leigh Hunt in the first *Examiner* of the New Year when he predicted that 1819 would be "one of the most important years that have been seen for a long while" (WPBS, 7:19).[3] More ab-

---

Jeffrey's dress at some assembly—'in short he was more of a *Dandy* than any great author I ever saw—always excepting Tom Moore'" (p. 209).

  2. Evidence that this lyric was already one of the favorites of Moore's earliest readers is suggested by the fact that was one of those singled out for mockery in the *New Whig Guide* compiled by Tory writers such as Croker and Palmerston in 1819.

  3. *The Examiner* (January 3, 1819).

stractly, we may think of Murray's hyperbole as indexing the sense of historical eventfulness that Lévi-Strauss would later seek to capture with his notion of the so-called hot chronology. Granting all this, we must also recognize that the optimism of Murray's forecast derived not only from the quantity and quality of impressive writing in this period but also from his professional assessment of Moore's talent and position. Whether or not the "Tom Brown" on England in 1819 that Murray proposed to Moore would have met his high commercial expectations, it would surely, in light of Moore's acuity and vantage point, have proved a valuable survey of contemporary literary culture.

Moore did not compose it, alas, forming instead a resolve "never to have any thing more to do with Satire."[4] One reason for the decision was that he was already engaged in a major undertaking for a different publisher, the project for which he purchased the fifty-nine existing volumes of Burke's *Annual Register* in the latter part of 1818. These volumes were to serve as reference works for a historical biography (to be published by Longmans) of another of the "great men" from the previous age in British history, Richard Brinsley Sheridan— Burke's national compatriot, literary contemporary, and Parliamentary colleague.[5] It was this biography, praised in the *Edinburgh Review* as "the best historical notice yet published of the events of our time,"[6] that primarily occupied Moore's literary energy in 1819, though his attention was anything but undivided at this time. The year before, Moore had learned that he was to be charged with responsibility for repaying 6,000 pounds embezzled by the deputy he had long before named to serve in his place as Registrar of a naval prize court in Bermuda, a post to which he had been appointed in 1803. Though apparently not dishonest, Moore had been inattentive and irresponsible in his handling of this middle-level imperial sinecure. It was perhaps his own experience with imperial scandal that led him to pay so much attention in the Sheridan biography to the impeachment trial of Warren Hastings in which Sheridan, like Burke, played so important a role. At the start of 1819, Moore was already well along with the work on his *Life of Sheridan,* but Moore's life, especially in 1819, offers an impressively rich subject for biography in its own right. Indeed, if Moore rivaled Byron and Scott in literary reputation so did he

4. A few days after forming this resolve, still in March, Moore reports that he "Determined, as I walked home, to write A Farewell to Satire by Thomas Brown, &c, &c" (JTM, 1:153, 154). This may be taken as a weakening rather than a maintenance of the resolve, perhaps, in that Moore did eventually return to the satirical Tom Brown mode with *The Fudges in England* (1835).

5. To consult the *Life of Sheridan* is to see why Moore needed the *Annual Registers,* for the narrative of Sheridan's biography is glossed by the year numbers in the margins.

6. Howard Mumford Jones, *The Harp that Once: A Chronicle of the Life of Thomas Moore* (New York: Henry Holt and Company, 1937), p. 251.

as well in the glamorous and controversial episodes of his public career, some of which returned to haunt Moore in 1819.

Before going to Bermuda to take his post. Moore had gained early notoriety when, after being welcomed as a celebrated visitor to North America in 1803, he published some distinctly unflattering verses about his American hosts in Washington. These verses stung American readers so deeply that Moore's barbs were still being flung back at British visitors to America in the renewed travel of the years after Waterloo. Byron, for one, explicitly drew a connection between Moore's satire on Americans and the financial problems arising from what Moore called "my Bermuda business" in 1819.[7] As the months passed in this year of personal and national crisis, it became clearer to Moore that he would not find adequate means to repay a debt he acknowledged his own. He suffered from uncharacteristic anomie and, as he put it in April, often wished he "had a *good cause to die in*" (JTM, 1:164 [Moore's italics]). Eventually he found himself confronted with a fugitive course of action. He initially considered taking flight to Scotland to seek sanctuary in Edinburgh's Holyrood Palace, an episode straight out of the fiction of Scott. Eventually he decided instead, at the invitation and encouragement of Lord Russell, on exiling himself to the Continent.[8] He sailed from Dover to Calais and arrived in Paris in early September to some fanfare.[9] As if completing some agenda of the paradigmatic Romantic career in this period, Moore embarked, de rigueur, on the walking tour of Geneva and the Alps. It included all the already-standard Romantic moments: an ascent of the Jura ("caught sight of the stupendous Mont-Blanc—It is impossible to describe what I felt" [JTM, 1:216]), a crossing of the Simplon Pass, and a tour of Lake Como. From the Alps, he descended to Venice, that most fashionable of destinations, where he was received with great warmth by Byron. Such was their intimacy that, on their parting, with Moore bound for Florence and Rome before returning to Paris, Byron entrusted him with his memoirs. It was these memoirs, to the great consternation of Moore and many readers since, that would be cast into John Murray's London fireplace after Byron's death in

7. In a letter to John Murray from Bologna in 1819, Byron wrote of Moore: "It seems his Claimants are *American* merchants. *There* goes *Nemesis.* Moore abused America. It is always thus in the long run.—Time the Avenger" (BLJ, 6:207). "Bermuda business" is from entry for January 29, 1819 in JTM, 1:138.

8. Russell would become Moore's editor as Moore became Byron's: see *Memoirs, Journal, and Correspondence of Thomas Moore,* ed. Lord John Russell, 7 vols. (London: Longman's, 1853).

9. Moore reports that his arrival was "announced in Gagliani," and then two days later that "a poem on my arrival in Paris" was published there (JTM, 1:214–15). Moore's celebrity was sufficient to cause his movements to be followed in the London press when he was in England. On June 8, 1819, he noted sarcastically in his journal: "The Morning Post kind eneough to tell me what I was last night" (1:185).

1824, though one positive consequence of this disaster was Moore's undertaking the *Life of Byron,* whose publication in 1830, it has been said, "took on the proportions of a national event."[10]

Much history had already linked the affairs of Byron and Moore by 1819. In 1810–11, before they had ever met, a quarrel of honor had erupted, occasioned by some remarks of Byron's in *English Bards and Scotch Reviewers* about a still-earlier dueling episode between Moore and Francis Jeffrey about a review of the former by the latter.[11] The quarrel was patched up to avert a duel, and a dinner was arranged soon after by Samuel Rogers. From the time of this first meeting, Byron and his posthumous biographer became fast friends. By the beginning of 1819, Byron had already thought well enough of Moore to have urged John Murray to call him in to decide on the case of *Don Juan*—the question, specifically, of whether its inaugural two cantos were fit for publication. In late January 1819, Moore read the poem, and praised it, but discouraged Murray from going ahead with the plan to print it, and indeed Murray did back off temporarily.[12] Moore also read at least one of the private letters to Murray of 1819 in which Byron described his active erotic life in Venice. The reply that William Lisle Bowles wrote to Thomas Campbell to ignite the Pope Controversy in 1819, a seven-years war of words in which Byron figured centrally, was initially supposed to be framed as an address to Moore, who accounted himself a sympathizer with Bowles's anti-Pope camp.[13] Later in the year, Shelley would

10. Jones, *The Harp that Once,* p. 276.

11. Byron's verses were as follows:

> Can none remember that eventful day,
> That ever glorious almost fatal fray,
> When LITTLE's leadless pistol met his eye,
> And Bow-street Myrmidons stood laughing by? (ll. 463–66)

Byron appended the following note to the passage: "In 1806, Mssrs. Jeffrey and Moore met at Chalk Farm. The duel was prevented by the interference of the Magistracy; and, on examination, the balls of the pistols, like the courage of the combatants, was found to have evaporated. This incident gave occasion to much waggery in the daily prints." Byron later emended the note in Moore's favor. CPWB, 1:407.

12. On a typically (for Moore) busy Saturday afternoon in literary London, January 30, 1819, Moore records, among myriad other encounters, a conversation with Byron's friend Hobhouse: "Asked him had I any chance of a glimpse at Don Juan [still in MS] & then found that Byron had desired it might be referred to my decision" (JTM, 1:139). Moore's private impressions about *Don Juan,* which he recorded in his journal, are among the most often-quoted remarks about the poem's early reception history: JTM, 1:136–37; 139–40. See below, chap. 6.

13. This particular entry on Bowles in Moore's journal also serves to indicate the "literary" emphasis in political writing and the political dimension of literary topics, and the confusion between the two at this time: March 28, 1819: "Bowles called, according to appointment, having given me the proofs of a pamphlet he is about to publish (on the Increse of Crimes, Poor Laws

in fact dedicate his quasi-Popean, quasi-Byronic satire, *Peter Bell the Third,* in a gesture mocking Wordsworth's and Southey's solemnity, to "Thomas Brown, Esq., The Younger, H.F." (Historian of the Fudges). Moore's allegiances to these mutual enemies, Bowles and Byron, show that, as Hazlitt pointed out, Moore had a capacity to unite opposites.[14] He also had an extraordinary capacity to win friends and influence people. Finishing the year 1819 as a debtor-in-exile in Paris, he soon met (among others) Washington Irving, flush with the early success of *The Sketch-Book of Geoffrey Crayon, Esq.,* a book preoccupied precisely with the history of U.S.–Great Britain relations in which Moore had played so conspicuous an early role (JTM, 1:371–72).[15] Irving, too, became a fast friend and literary confidant, as would both Walter Scott and Mary Shelley in the coming years. Irving consulted Moore on his *Tales of a Traveler.* Moore dedicated the *Life of Byron* to Scott. Mary Shelley sent to Moore a personally inscribed copy of the 1839 edition of her husband's poetry that contained the hitherto-unpublished sonnet "England in 1819."

Moore would remain in Paris from the end of 1819 until near the end of 1821, though he did disguise himself in a false mustache to return briefly on business to the British Isles in 1820. If Moore's ballyhooed arrival in Paris in 1819 and his need for disguise in leaving it alike suggest his high visibility, then a more oblique but no less telling index of his high profile can be found in the letters of an envious John Keats, who recorded his desire for the glamorous contemporary reception that Moore repeatedly enjoyed. Writing to his brother George in the "Western Country" of America on January 2, 1819, for example, the twenty-three-year-old Keats, sensitive himself to social ridicule, mocked Moore's dinner speech at the Dublin banquet where Moore had been lionized and his father honored with him, the event Byron would call Moore's "Apoth-

---

&c.) to look over—I had marked with a pencil the things I had particularly objected to—but the truth is, the whole is weak and confused—his head, however, is now full of his answer to Campbell, which his present intention is to publish in the shape of a letter to me—Mentioned to him that Foscolo told me he had a design of publishing a Parallel between Italian & English poetry in Four Letters addressed to Crabbe, Campbell, Rogers, & myself" (1:155). A month later Moore records seeing his reaction to Bowles's pamphlet: "Received Bowles's answer to Campbell—tells me in a note he left with it that Lord Lansdowne considers his position indisputable & so I think it is—" (1:164).

14. Evidence of the extent of Moore's ability to make connections abounds in the journal he began in 1818. Even when he was still in England, it was not uncommon for him to dine out four or five nights in a week and to have breakfast or lunch with several literary and political celebrities as well: poets of such recognized merit as Samuel Rogers and George Crabbe were among his regular dining companions, as were the publishers Longman and Murray.

15. See Jones, *The Harp that Once,* p. 245, for Moore's consultation with Irving on the latter's *Tales of a Traveler.*

eosis" in Ireland (BLJ, 6:67): "Perhaps you may have heard of the dinner given to Thos Moore in Dublin, because I have the account here by me in the Philadelphia democratic paper—the most pleasant thing that occurred was the speech Mr Tom made on his Farthers health being drank" (LJK, 2:20). Keats tracked Moore for many reasons, some having to do, I suspect, with the still-unexplored parallels between the respective critical attacks they suffered. On this occasion, the newspaper in front of Keats would have been *The Democratic Press,* published in Philadelphia, for October 24, 1818 (which reprinted the article on Moore's June 7 dinner from the *Dublin Evening Post).* Keats reasoned, no doubt, that, if *The Democratic Press* managed to reach him back in London, surely it might have found its way to George and Georgiana in the Ohio River Basin.

We may perhaps conclude from the fact that Moore had such an invitation to Philadelphia that, by the end of 1818, the barbs of the 1803 tour had begun to be forgotten in America in favor of the nationalist and orientalist felicities of the *Irish Melodies* and *Lalla Rookh.* And we may conclude from the way in which the newspaper form linked into a single chronology such different cultures as England and America in 1819—and America was indeed perceived to occupy a different state of society from that of England—that the sense of conjunction between the periodical coding of empty homogeneous time and the discourse of uneven development would have become especially acute in such encounters. Moore was made for such encounters. Indeed, one reason he could play his various parts so well was that given his ethnicity and his mobility, he could so plausibly represent the relation of England in 1819 to other parts of the expanded United Kingdom and to the present and former British Empire.

For the thought experiment in historical stage setting, then—to frame a scene of reading for 1819—I propose that we conjure up the image of Moore on the day before Keats wrote to his brother (that is, on New Year's Day of 1819) and that we picture him with his own newspaper in front of him. Moore was then living in Wiltshire, where he had moved in 1817, with his wife Bessy and their children, to be near Bowood, the estate of his noble friend Lord Lansdowne, a powerful Whig in the House of Lords who would take a prominent role during the special sessions on Peterloo at the end of the year.[16] As for Moore's active daily life, social and literary, at this time, we know a great deal about it because of the detailed journal Moore began to keep in August 1818— one of the best sources we have for the daily life of British intellectual elites for

---

16. Landsdowne's speeches can be found in Hansard's Parliamentary Record for the session convened specially to deal with the crisis over Peterloo in November 1819.

this period. It is because of the journal that we know, for example, that at the start of 1819 Moore was at work on his *Life of Sheridan,* and that Longmans promised him a badly needed thousand pounds for the right to publish it. We also know at least one newspaper that he read at this period because of a journal entry for January 9. At the start of 1819, William Hazlitt's *Lectures on the English Comic Writers* were being offered concurrently at the Crown and Anchor Tavern with an equally important lecture series by Samuel Taylor Coleridge. The January 9 entry records, "Hazlitt's Lecture on Sheridan (quoted in the Chronicle of this morning) and containing a warm eulogium on me led us to talk of humour . . ." (JTM, p. 131). To imagine the scene of reading that I have proposed is, in effect, to place in conjunction two surviving chronicles of daily life for England in 1819, Moore's journal and the London *Morning Chronicle.*

What then do we find on offer in the *Chronicle* for January 1, 1819? Because of the holidays, that day's paper was relatively thin on news, and some of its regular year-round features were absent. Of course, not all of the news that was reported in daily newspapers of this period had happened only the day before it was printed: news arrived from foreign correspondents whose reports reached London on variously extended travel schedules (a matter of days from Paris, or weeks from North America). The main news story printed on January 1 concerned French affairs in the last days of 1818. Its lead sentence—"A French ministry is, it seems, at last formed"—conveys a sense of relief at the defeat of the Duke of Richilieu and the Ultra Royalists of the Restoration and at "the triumph of the party of the constitution in France." "The friends of liberty, in general, must rejoice that the attempts to trample on the rights of a great nation are, for the present defeated; while those who view the affair only with reference to our own national interests, must rejoice at a defeat which averts the disturbances that could not have failed to take place—disturbances which might soon have extended beyond France."[17] In the *Chronicle's* article on France, the optimism is qualified by the specific recognition that the French army remains royalist. Hence the question for the New Year: "will Royalists, *with swords in their hands,* look on quietly while Royalty is once more proscribed?" If such comments raise the question of revolution or counterrevolution in 1819, the question is clearly posed for France, not for England. Indeed, the *Chronicle* that Moore would have read reports directly on the "state of England" only in its social column, "The Mirror of Fashion," which appeared daily under the verse epitaph: "To shew / The very age and body of the time, / Its form and pressure."

17. It was just two days later, on January 3, that Hunt's report on the "state of the world" and his forecast for 1819 appeared in The *Examiner.*

To distinguish the "body of the time" from the "spirit of the age" is beyond my purpose here, but certainly the relation of fashion to periodization becomes a subject of particular interest toward the end of the Napoleonic Wars when the rage for Scott's historical novels sweeps across various reading publics at home and abroad. Nor is the connection merely fortuitous. In that same introductory chapter of *Waverley,* where Scott explains his choice of name/title, "Waverley," he goes on to allude precisely to "that part of a newspaper entitled the Mirror of Fashion." He explains the setting and the subtitle of the first of the Waverley novels, as an attempt to establish a middle ground between the fashion for the up-to-date as coded in such genre-marking phrases as "A Tale of the Times" and the fashion for the old, in such subtitles as "A Tale of Other Days." Moreover, it is just at this historical juncture that Cruikshank launches an annual series of satirical cartoons—*Monstrosities of 1814, . . . 1815, . . . 1816,* and so on—bringing to bear the annually changing normativity of high fashion on various forms of sartorial extravagance (see fig. 4).

In regard to the *Chronicle,* of course, it is fair to say that not just that segment on the "Mirror of Fashion" but really the entire issue of each newspaper carried out the task of showing the time's age and body, form and pressure. The front page of the paper for January 1, 1819, for example, offered its typically dense array of advertisements, including some for books whose claims to fashionability and novelty urged their appropriateness as gifts for the New Year. Many are marked by a kind of popularizing cosmopolitanism: Leigh's *New Views of London,* for example, for the visitor to the metropolis, and Feinaigle's *New Art of Memory,* which featured a system for projecting the map of the world in a three-dimensional mnemonic scheme. Byron refers to Feinaigle's system in canto 1 of *Don Juan,* just as Coleridge had recently done in the *Biographia Literaria.* Evidence, more particularly, of the fashionable appetite for antiquity appears in the extraordinary amount of space given to a letter to the editor about the Portland Vase, the kind of object that a would-be cosmopolitan Keats would make the occasion of his ekphrastic historism in May.[18]

What was new in the theater, as the dramatic notice related, was in a sense antiquity itself, in the form of a play just opened at the Drury Lane: *Flodden Field,* "a new dramatic Romance, in three acts," and "taken from Walter Scott's popular poem of *Marmion.*" Scott himself, of course, had some time since begun to drift away from poetry and toward fiction. The second series of his "Tales of My Landlord"—the first of Scott's publications to bear the name of "series"—had

18. See Theresa Kelley's nuanced reading of *Ode on a Grecian Urn* in her "Keats, Ekphrasis, and History," in *Keats and History,* ed. Nicholas Roe (Cambridge: Cambridge University Press, 1995), pp. 212–37.

Figure 4. "Monstrosities of 1819," part of an annual series by George Cruikshank. Reproduced by permission of the Huntington Library, San Marino, California.

been published recently enough to be mentioned on the front page of the *Chronicle,* but in a mediated context. That is, one of the books advertised that day was "The Monthly Review for December 1818" and—such was the "hypertext" structure of the periodical press—this volume in turn offered a brief guide to its contents: " . . . containing copious accounts of Milman's Samor— New Tales of my Landlord—Fearon's Sketches of America—Gourgoud on the Campaign of 1815—Irish Melodies, No. 6 and 7, &c. &c." Later that month, Moore would see the magazine itself and respond cynically in his journal to the review of his new volumes six and seven: "A Review of the Melodies in the Monthly, vulgarly written, but good-natured enough—& will be serviceable among the country clods, who read this & such other precious guides in Taste" (1:135). The *Irish Melodies* were themselves deeply involved in the movement that brought Scott early fame with *The Minstrelsy of the Scottish Border,* and he and Scott had profited together from approving notices in the various "precious guides in Taste."

This paradox of what might be called "novel antiquities"—the basis for the success in 1819 of the rash of historical dramas and of the "Scotch novels" from which they derived—was already a crucial component of the earlier lyric volumes by Burns, Hemans, and Moore himself and indeed forms a very large element of literary popular culture in the period.[19] In the period from the publication of John Brand's massive and massively circulated *Observations on Popular Antiquities* (1813) to William Hone's equally successful *Every-day Book; or Everlasting Calendar of Popular Amusements, Sports, Pastimes, Ceremonies, Manners, Customs and Events* (1825–27), the (antique) culture industry boomed in its literary production. It was, moreover, a kind of participation sport. Hone would solicit letters from readers about their local customs so that, in future editions, "the *Every-Day Book* would become what it is designed to be made,—*a storehouse of past and present manners and customs*" (Hone's italics).[20] Precisely the novelty of such a storehouse of the past, generated by the power of print capitalism and an organized postal service, had everything to do with its distinctive frisson.[21] Nor did Hone view these things as static. Indeed, his boast was that "the Every-Day Book has presented a more striking view of the changes in manners and customs than any book which has gone before it."[22] Moore himself solicited readers for additional Irish melodies. Walter Scott's *The Antiquary* (1816), characters from which were reprised for the Dedicatory Epistle to *Ivanhoe*, was both a spin-off from and spur to these developments. And so, of course, was Irving's American literary-cultural miscellany, *The Sketch-Book of Geoffrey Crayon*.

Indeed, the United States as a whole was another large and complex site of

19. Later in the year William Hone would capitalize on the taste being whetted by the Brand-Ellis collection of *Popular Antiquities* with his *Sixty Curious and Authentic Narratives and Anecdotes Respecting Extraordinary Characters* (1819)—for a helpful survey of these developments in the wake of Brand-Ellis see Dorson, *The British Folklorists: A History* (Chicago: University of Chicago Press, 1968) pp. 17–43. Dorson's good account suffers from being a mere preface to a discussion of Victorian folklore, so that he is primarily interested in books such as Brand's and Hone's as examples of what would have been on a shelf in a typical Victorian library rather than for their impact on or relations to the immediate post-Waterloo period.

20. Hone, 1838, vol 2, col. 73. "Thus," writes Richard Dorson of Hone's campaign, "did Hone through his columns and on his wrappers train his readers in scholarly habits" (Dorson, p 37). And Hone would provide encouraging signs that this training was effective, as when he cited a letter from a reader who explained that the "character and manners of a people may be often correctly ascertained by an attentive examination of their familiar customs and manners" (Dorson, p. 37). In chap. 7 below I shall be discussing Keats, a Hone watcher, in respect to "The Eve of St. Agnes" as a popular antiquity.

21. This industry is indeed one of the literary by-products of the regularization of the postal industry, as discussed in Mary Favret, *Romantic Correspondence: Women, Politics, and the Fiction of Letters* (Cambridge: Cambridge University Press, 1993), pp. 203–13.

22. Hone, vol. 2, col. 1577 (St. Clement).

anachronism in which "novel antiquity" was perceived to be the operative paradox in 1819—a nation at once primitive in manners and advanced in methods, a state newly constituted in an anciently republican form. And perhaps the most heatedly discussed of books on America at the turn of 1819 was the one listed in the *Monthly*'s advertisement as "Fearon's Sketches of America," which was independently advertised elsewhere in the *Chronicle* for January 1 (as having just appeared in its second edition). It is a book that comes up several times in Moore's journal for this period, appearing initially in the entry for December 19, when Fearon's study is recommended to him by Lord Lansdowne as "the most acute work upon the subject he had seen" (JTM, p. 102). It is not just Moore's personal experience in America that aroused his interest, however, nor just Moore who was interested, nor again just Fearon who was generating the interest. The American question—the question of how popular manners would be shaped in the first generation of citizens raised under the Constitution—poses itself as part of a complex cultural discourse of issues and influences in which the phenomenon of the Waverley novels and their rapidly spreading popularity are major factors to be considered.[23]

Fearon and America come up again December 30, when, as was his habit, Moore dined at Bowood in illustrious company. On the present occasion at Lansdowne's he was seated next to James McIntosh, the celebrated political contemporary of Burke and Sheridan. Moore saw McIntosh often in 1819, and, while he freely availed himself of McIntosh's company to do informal research on his Sheridan biography, this time the subject of America became the main topic: "[T]alked of Fearon, Birkbeck—the singularity of two such men being produced out of the middling class of society at the same time—proof of the intelligence now spread through that rank of Englishman—It must make those in the higher regions look about them & be on the alert—every man now feels that kind of warning from the man immediately beneath him & the stimulus is propagated—what it will come to God knows" (p. 105). What happens in this instance—the topic of America occasioning an analysis of the state of British society—is very much a part of a consistent pattern of conversation *and* letters in 1819. The "Birkbeck" referred to in this conversation, Morris Birkbeck, is the main reason why Keats's brother was in America when Keats wrote to him on January 2. George Keats had read about Birkbeck's settlement the previous year in Birkbeck's *Letters from Illinois* and had decided to join Birk-

---

23. In emphasizing Scott's power to synthesize and circulate narrative materials into an influential paradigm I don't mean to be excluding the enormous contribution of the whole series of novelists and collectors of literary antiquities arrayed and discussed in Katie Trumpener, *Bardic Nationalism* (Princeton, N.J.: Princeton University Press, forthcoming), passim.

beck in the "Western Country" in October 1818. George, too, might be taken as an example of "the intelligence now spread through that rank of Englishman," a subject that, indeed, much exercised John Keats in his correspondence with George.

The actual title of Fearon's book is not *Sketches of America*—Moore may have been thinking here of Irving's *Sketch-Book of Geoffrey Crayon,* just published that month—but rather *Narrative of a Journey of Five Thousand Miles Through the Eastern and Western States of America.*[24] In the coming months, William Cobbett would engage in polemic with both Fearon and Birkbeck in the memoirs of his American exile, which were published under a similar title, *Journal of a Year's Residence in the United States of America* (1819). Another book advertised in the *Chronicle* in these weeks, dissimilar in title but likewise part of the discourse on America, is John Bristed's *America and Her Resources.* Moore soon got his hands on this book as well, again evidently looking for references to himself. In the journal entry for March 12, 1819, we find: "Read Bristed's 'Resources of the United States'—This is the person who has accused me of 'swinging into the opposite extreme' about America—His book is full of information" (JTM, p. 149). This is a judgment that Moore sustained through the conclusion of his reading five days later: "Finished Bristed—a very *wordy* book, but sometimes eloquent & full of information about America" (p. 150). Fearon, Birkbeck, Cobbett, and Bristed all helped to make the newly constituted United States the celebrated *case* that it became for the likes of Bentham in his *Plan of Reform* and Shelley in *A Philosophical View of Reform.*[25]

Renewed travel, and especially the prospect of major waves of emigration

24. The full title helps to associate Fearon's book generically with other books recently advertised in the *Chronicle,* especially those clustered in an advertisement of "Important Works" from Henry Colburn on December 16: *Narrative of a Residence in Algiers, Narrative of a Residence in Ireland* ("by Anne Plumptre, author of Narrative of Three Years Residence in France"), and *Narrative of my Captivity in Japan, Narrative of Ten Years Residence at the Court of Tripoli* ("domestic manners of the Moors, Arabs, and Turks").

25. Both the genre of the exotic travel narrative and the increasing attention to a new America inscribed within it have been a neglected part of the story of late-Regency literary culture. The settlement of the post–Congress of Vienna French ministry punctuated the sense that this was distinctively a postrevolutionary, post-Napoleonic world—a "new world order"—where accounts of the Napoleonic wars, even their final moments as in Gourgoud's narrative of the Hundred Days, increasingly appear as history rather than journalism. It is true that one of the other books advertised in the New Year's Day edition of the *Chronicle* is *An Appeal to the Honour of the English Nation in the Behalf of Napoleon Bonaparte,* which, with its advertised motto (*Audi alteram partem*) may well be taken as a sign of the viability of Bonaparte's name and fame. However, in a few months' time Richard Whately's pamphlet, *Historic Doubts Relative to Napoleon Bonaparte* (1819), would offer arguments that call into question whether such a person as the historical Napoleon ever actually existed.

from Britain to America, lent the "narratives" of American travels and residencies a kind of urgency not present in those that tell of Japan, or Tripoli, or Russia. Indeed, the most serious threat to a Pax Britannia in 1819 no longer came from France, or even from America as a military force, but rather from the internal challenges of the four-year post-Waterloo period that set the high-watermark for popular radicalism in Britain. And since the American narratives are most of them keyed to the question of middle-class British flight from, as they put it, the oppressions of a corrupt political system, these narratives were especially pointed. They certainly seemed to penetrate the British publishing market with an extraordinary ease, and cross-cultural encounters dominated conversation, accordingly, as both returning foreign travelers and their many published reports circulated through the social circles of southern England: Leigh's new tourist maps of London and Feinaigle's mnemonic maps of the world being mapped, as it were, on to each other.

Describing Moore with his morning paper at the start of 1819 has enabled me to set out much of the culturally specific *topics* and *materials* to be addressed in what follows, but a I would like to venture something further about the *forms* and *modes* of cultural specificity that appear in Moore's literary life at this time. The *Chronicle*'s notice about *Flodden Field,* an adaptation of one of Scott's verse romances, should remind us of the extent to which the adaptations of Scott's *novels* dominated the British stage in 1819. Historical drama adapted from Scott's narratives, or composed after his manner, would indeed be the fashion that year. Theatrical versions of *Rob Roy* had played to considerable audiences in 1818, 1819, and in years to follow: Moore saw either the Isaac Pacock adaptation or the George Saone adaptation on March 20, 1819 (JTM, 1:153).[26] In the first week of 1819, at the invitation of Sarah Egerton, Thomas Dibdin composed an adaptation of *The Heart of Mid-Lothian* that would run for 170 nights at the unlicensed Surrey Theatre in London. Another London adaptation of *Heart,* by Daniel Terry, would play Covent Garden before the year was out. It was because the taste for historical dramas was so seriously whetted that in the spring of 1819, on the Isle of Wight, Keats would be enlisted by his opportunistic patron, Charles Brown, to write *Otho the Great,* a potboiling piece for

26. For a general survey of Scott's dramatic adaptations, see Henry Adelbert White, *Sir Walter Scott's Novels on the Stage* (New Haven: Yale University Press, 1927); and the more recent, more quantitative work in this area by Barbara Bell, "Sir Walter Scott and the National Drama," in *Scott in Carnival: Papers from the 4th International Scott Conference, Ediburgh, 1991,* ed. J. H. Alexander and David Hewitt (Aberdeen: Association for Scottish Literary Studies, 1993), pp. 459–77.

the theater about a tenth-century Holy Roman emperor. While in just these months Shelley would stake his bid for a popular audience on a domestic tragedy whose setting was Rome in 1599.

Moore would not have seen the opening of *Flodden Field* on Thursday, December 31, since, in spite of his debts, he and his wife had given a New Year's Eve party that evening. But Walter Scott figured prominently in Moore's routine on the morning of the first, as he did in the everyday life of so many literate Britons at his time. Here is how the first entry of the year in his journal begins: "January 1st.—Weary and resting after last nights gaities—visitors in the morning—read to Bessy the Scotch Novel in the evening. . . ." The Scotch novel in question, as is clear from earlier entries, is indeed *The Heart of Mid-Lothian,* the sole entry in the second series of Scott's "Tales of My Landlord."[27] Moore's scene of reading at the start of 1819, we might therefore say, involves the conjunction of the "Scotch novel" and the London paper we can presume to be in front of Moore on January 1. It is marked by a coincidence, therefore, of what Benedict Anderson describes as the two great literary forms of coincidence itself in this period.[28]

As we have seen, the emphasis in Anderson's historical epistemology of nationalism is on the empty homogeneity of the public sphere of letters—what he calls print capitalism. But, insofar as the nationalism in question is a "cultural nationalism," and is thus implicated in the historicization of culture in Romanticism, the empty homogeneity of print culture amounts to only half the story. The other side of that story has to do with the sense of unevenness in the everyday life of culture that requires just such chronological coding in the first place. In the "Tales of My Landlord," of which *The Heart of Mid-Lothian* forms the second series and 1819's *The Bride of Lammermoor* the third, the medium where cultural difference is registered tends to be the conversation. In the following chapter, I examine the place and function of "conversation" in these two novels as having a special role in Scott's metaphorization of the case form. The narrative proper of *The Heart of Mid-Lothian* is framed by a introductory scene in which the tale itself emerges from a conversation among travelers. The narrative proper of *The Bride of Lammermoor*—its central diegesis or statement of the case— is framed by an introductory scene in which the compiler of the "Tales of My Landlord," Peter Pattieson, is confronted by a painter who criticizes his practice exactly on the ground that his novels rely too much on dialogue.

27. December 19, 1818: "Read to Bessy in the evening the Scot novel, The Heart of Mid-Lothian, which have just received from the Book Society." December 20: "the Scotch novel in the evening. December 23: "read The Heart of Mid-Lothian to Bessy in the evening" (JTM, 1:103).
28. See Benedict Anderson, *Imagined Communities,* rev. ed. (London: Verso, 1991), pp. 50–65.

If it is fair to suggest that in such novels as *The Heart of Mid-Lothian* Scott is developing a technique for using conversation as an index to historical culture, we might by extension consider the conversations recorded by Moore in a similar light. As Peter Burke has noted, the history of conversation is notoriously difficult to document, but Moore's journal around the turn of the year 1819 is an especially rich record of the oral commerce of the many centrally located writers and politicians with whom he associated.[29] Moore is peculiarly self-conscious about the structure of conversation, about what it means to write it down, about how a conversation signifies. The genre of recorded conversation was not new with this period—books with titles like *Table Talk* had been around for decades—but its cultural role was understood to be changing in its representation of literature, characters, and manners.

Hazlitt, in his 1817 *Round Table* (a collection of essays on, precisely, "literature, men, and manners"), had tried to explain this historical shift. "A hundred years back, when the mode of living was different from what it is now, and taverns and coffee-houses made the persons of the wits familiar to every body," wrote Hazlitt, there was a need on the part of those wishing to publicize their conversation to disguise themselves. They were already public. Now times are different: "we have not the same occasion for disguise; and, therefore, as we prefer at all times a plain, straightforward behavior, and, in fact, choose to be as original as we can be in our productions, we have avoided the trouble of adding assumed characters to our real ones; and shall talk, just as we think, walk, and take dinner, in our own proper persons."[30] It is true that Moore himself was "familiar" enough in his time to warrant his donning a disguise for his return to England in 1820, but the larger point here is that, when recorded conversation is associated with privacy, domestic propriety, and sincerity, it arguably has a newly representative role in figuring culture, a role that promotes Scott's interest in the unknowable conversations of the past and the *vie privée* of the forefathers.[31] In Moore's journal, I want to suggest, the conversations often turn on the very aspects of contemporary life and discourse in which the new role of conversation itself is being redefined.

Here, in effect, we return to the question of the anecdote, its historical form

---

29. On conversation's connection with the "spirit of the age," see Peter Burke, *The Art of Conversation* (Ithaca, N.Y.: Cornell University Press, 1993), pp. 89–122. Mark Twain understood all of this perfectly well, as Patricia Connelley reminds me, in his satire of this particular symptom of the "Sir Walter Scott disease": see Samuel L. Clemens, *"1601" or Conversation as It Was at the Fireside in the Time of the Tudors* (New York: Golden Hind, 1933), pp. 11–20.

30. Hazlitt, *Table Talk*, 2 vols. (Edinburgh: Constable, 1817), 1:1–2.

31. Walter Savage Landor's ambitious multivolume series of *Imaginary Conversations* might be cited as one example of a new, culturally exemplary role given to conversation in this period.

and function. In chapters 3 and 4, I discussed how the new emphasis on literary "specimens" and "anecdotes" in the Romantic period might be understood as part of the effort to find forms of representation for a new sense of culture.[32] Moore's journal has entries that thematize the anecdote in an especially interesting way, including a passage recording a conversation with Lord Lansdowne, purely anecdotal in itself, about the Jacobite William King's *Political and Literary Anecdotes of his Own Times* (1818) and another passage recording deliberations over "insertion of the anecdote about the Sermon" in the *Life of Sheridan* (JTM, 1:102, 164). The anecdote is very much a part of the conversational model of representing culture described by Hazlitt in his 1817 *Round Table*. Since anecdotes are related in terms of an appositional conversational logic, the way in which they might be understood to represent a culture is through the reconstruction of that principle of apposition in relation to the larger movement of a conversation. The anecdote must be "topical" to be intelligible.[33]

It is not too much to say that Moore was obsessed with the making and recording of conversation, and the holiday period of the winter of 1818–1819 was no exception. The conversational anecdotes recorded in Moore's journal can be seen as representing "culture," so understood, in the interstices of the account of that dinner party at Bowood on December 30, 1818. The journal registers how the conversation moved by a seemingly inevitable segue from Fearon and Birkbeck to more spectacularly self-conscious episodes of cultural dislocation and transcoding. Consider the following reported conversation around Lord Lansdowne's dinner table, for example:

> Sir J. McIntosh told of "*Barry Close*" the well-known East Indian officer—that, not having learned anything previous to his going to India, he got every thing he knew through the medium of Persian literature—studied logic in a translation (from Arabic into Persian) of Aristotle—and was a most learned & troublesome *practitioner* as well as theorist in dialectics—Some one brought him a volume of Lord Bacon (of whom he had never heard) and said here is a man who has attacked your friend Aristotle tooth & nail—"Who can the impudent

32. The notorious Pope controversy in which Moore was so intimately involved in 1819 was decidedly couched within the new rhetoric of the literary-cultural specimen: the response that Bowles wrote to trigger the episode, the one intended to be addressed to more himself, was occasioned, after all, by Thomas Campbell's *Specimens of the English Poets: With Biographical Notices, and an Essay on English Poetry* (London: John Murray, 1819). On January 3, Moore was delivered a table of contents for a similar kind of collection, "begging of me to omit or insert as I think proper." "Received from the Longmans the List of Poems they mean to put in the Selection from the English Poets which they are about to publish—begging of me to omit or insert as I think proper—" (JTM, 1:128; cf. 1:136).

33. For analysis of how conversation signifies culturally, see the published lectures of Harvey Sachs, especially *Lectures on Conversation,* 2 vols., ed. Gail Jefferson (Oxford: Blackwell, 1992); see especially 2:3–83. I thank John Frow for the lead. For a Romantic-era analysis, see Isaac Disraeli, *Dissertation on Anecdotes* (London: Kearsley and Murray, 1793), especially pp. v–vii.

fellow be?" said Close—"Lord Bacon"—"Who the devil is he! what trash people do publish in these times"—After reading him however, he confessed that Lord Bacon had said some devilish sensible things. (1:106)

The implicit joke, at this stage of the conversation, seems to depend on seeing that, as middle-class *hommes d'affaires* such as Fearon and Birkbeck were setting their deep stamp on things, Lord Bacon, the very paradigm of British thought, could have been misrecognized as a recent interloper in an Orientalized Aristotelian discourse. But, eventually, the anecdotes circulated around the table at Bowood, and the implicit levels of meaning and value that govern their exchange, gradually begin to disclose a kind of logic. Indeed, the involvement of this conversation in the new discourse of culture becomes clearer and clearer, especially in relation to the crucial question of cultural translation and misrecognition. Thus, after Lord Lansdowne mentioned an amusingly mistranslated line from Oliver Goldsmith's Anglo-Irish poem, "The Deserted Village," Moore records that he himself chimed in with a story of his own:

> I told an anecdote mentioned to me by Lord Moira of a foreign teacher of either music or drawing at Lady Perth's in Scotland—as he was walking round the trottoir with Lord M. the latter said "Voila le Chateau de Macbeth—" "Maccabée, milor" said the artist—"Je crois que c'est Macbeth," modestly answered Lord M. "Pardon, Milord—nous le prononçons Maccabée sur le Continent—Judas Maccabéus, Empereur Romain!" (JTM, 1:107)

It is not clear that Moore supplies enough information for another reader of his journal actually to see the funny part of this story, but the joke evidently turns on several related forms of confusion—of English and French pronunciation, Scottish and Roman antiquities, Hebrew and pagan heroes—all suggesting the variety of cultural translations in play. Whatever the purport of the Maccabée-Macbeth joke, Moore's journal indicated that it prompted yet another, which involves a cross-cultural error of historical identity: "Talked of the egotism of foreign writers—the Abbé de Pradt begins one of his books 'Un seul homme a sauvé l'Europe—c'est moi.' The best of it is he read this in a company where the Duke of Wellington was; and, on the Abbé making a pause at the word 'l'Europe,' all eyes were turned to the Duke—but then came out to their no small astonishment 'C'est moi'" (p. 107). This, Lukács might say, suggests a movement from cultural error at the level of everyday life to cultural error at the level of the world historical individual, but we begin to see emerging here an implicit ethical critique that is consistent with Moore's Whiggish political orientation. Moore's life is all about forms of exchange, and egotism of the sort shown here by the Abbé is exactly anathema to the mobile commerce of Whig society. Moore's own dexterous social chamelionism, by contrast, stood him in good stead with such company in such conversations.

It was not just foreign writers, however, who could be afflicted with this sort of debilitating egotism. Just as Keats, following Hazlitt, contrasted the work of the "camelion poet" to that of the Wordsworthian or egotistical sublime, so we can see something of Moore's resistance to the egotistical sublime when he first met Wordsworth during his exile in Paris. Moore's report of the encounter is unmistakably stinging on the question of egotism: "[October] 27. Wordsworth came at half past eight, and stopped to breakfast—Talked a good deal [so very smugly]—Spoke of Byron's plagiarisms from him—the whole third Canto of Childe Harold's founded on his style & sentiments—the feeling of natural objects, which is there expressed not caught by B. from Nature herself but from him, Wordsworth, and spoiled in the transmission—Tintern Abbey the source of it all" (p. 355). In view of Byron's recent remarks about the English provincialism of those contemporaries such as Wordsworth, Coleridge, and William Lisle Bowles, who sought, in the name of "Nature" to diminish Pope's place in the English canon, it seems easy to read English jingoism between the lines here as well.[34] The record of the later conversation with Wordsworth goes on directly to mention the new literary form in which, as we have seen, the new post–Scottish Enlightenment discourse of culture in Britain was given its most elaborate articulation: "Spoke of the Scotch Novels—are sure they are Scott's—the only doubt he {has} ever had on the question did not arise from thinking them too good to be Scott's, but on the contrary, from the infinite number of clumsy things in them, common-place contrivances, worthy only of the Minerva press, and in such bad vulgar English as no gentleman of education ought to have written" (pp. 355–56). It is hard to tell from this entry just who introduced the subject of Scott into the conversation. The juxtaposition of Scott and Byron, as the two most dominant writers of the moment, is fairly conventional, but the figure of Scott as the antithesis of Wordsworthian egotism also has its own associative logic here. When Hazlitt expanded his claims about Wordsworthian egotism in his essay on "Mr. Wordsworth" in *The Spirit of the Age,* the writer whose portrait he opposes to Wordsworth's in this respect is Scott, for whom Hazlitt's claim is that, in poetry and prose alike, he lost himself in the pastness of his imaginative objects.

The enormous popularity of the Scotch novels on the page and the stage alike in this moment must be construed at least partly in terms of the sorts of cross-culturalist topics that organize not only conversation at the Bowood dinner party but also the materials of newspapers, the weeklies, the monthlies, and

---

34. Moore commented on Bowles's egotism after an encounter in 1819: "How lucky it is that self-love has always something comfortable to retire upon!" (JTM, 1:143).

the book trade. Moore was surely invoking a sense of the massive influence of Waverley translations abroad when, on the day before he met with Wordsworth in Paris, he identified what he took to be the first "historical novel" written by a French author.[35] What we begin to see in Moore's literary encounters with Scott on New Year's Day—the *Chronicle's* review of *Flodden Field* and his reading to Bessy Moore from "Tales of My Landlord"—is the way "influence" operates closer to home, in the everyday scene of reading in 1819.

In the next chapter I elaborate what might be called the "cultural dramatism" of *The Heart of Mid-Lothian* and *The Bride of Lammermoor.* There I explain the complex structures and movements of these works in some detail. For now I mean only to have stressed how the two texts we are picturing in Moore's hands on the morning of New Year's Day 1819—*The Heart of Mid-Lothian* and the *Morning Chronicle*—might each be understood as participating in the discursive conjuncture of the theory of uneven development and the code of even empty time. Whether such themes would have emerged in the book that John Murray encouraged Moore to write in 1819—a "Tom Brown on the literature, manners, & characters of the day"—is beyond my ability to speculate.[36]

Calling attention to the place of "conjecture" (not to say "invention") in the work of such historians as Natalie Zemon Davis, Ginzburg has suggested that

35. It is in this context of some interest that the historical novels of the author of *Waverley* were routinely referred to as the Scotch novels, as if to suggest the interchangeability of the ethnographical and historiographical categories.

36. That trait targeted by Hazlitt, Moore's lack of a sense of continuous identity, makes it as difficult to predict what one might find with Moore as it is easy to predict that it will touch important matters. To be sure, what Moore does *not* do can be as interesting as what he does. One would certainly have thought, for example, that Moore would have taken some stand in print, or at least offered some views in his Journal, on the Peterloo Massacre and its aftermath. The political members of his circle were crucial to the parliamentary debate that took place at the end of the year, and many of his writer friends took their stands pro or con on this great question. We find evidence for the plausibility of this expectation in a publication from later in the year, probably after Moore had left for the continent. When Moore was attacked in the *New Whig Guide* of 1819 by Croker and others, a new "Tom Brown" appeared in the form of a verse satire called *The Field of Peterloo,* a title significantly echoing Southey's chauvinistic laureate performance, *The Field of Peterloo* (1815). *The Field of Peterloo* (London: J. Fairburn, 1819). The title page of this publication reads: "*The Field of Peterloo:* a poem : written in commemoration of the Manchester massacre: with an admonitory epistle to the P—e R—t : the whole being an anti-sympathetic response to 'The new Whig guide:' proving him to be no pilot in a storm. by Thomas Brown, Esq., Author of the 'Replies to the Letters of the Fudge Family in Paris'; . . ." The satire is not Moore's own work, however, but rather an appropriation of his nom de plume to address a topic he might plausibly have addressed. Moore himself seems to have been strangely silent on this issue. The journal contains no mention of Henry Hunt, or Peterloo, or even Manchester for 1819—nor, as far as I can tell, for any year afterward.

our new cultural histories do and should reprise the narrative and representational tactics of the historical novel. If one were to explore further the role of Moore for a new cultural history of "England in 1819," how might one best describe his representative status? In chapter 4, I pushed Ginzburg's genealogy of his own practice in the tradition of historical fiction back further than he does himself, arguing that Scott provided the model for the fiction by Balzac and Manzoni to which Ginzburg, in behalf of others, avows a debt. To take another step in applying Scott's conjectural model to the literary scene of England in 1819, we might now ask what it would mean to think of Moore as a kind of Waverley character in relation to the historical peculiarity of his own culture. How might Moore serve to figure the literary culture of England in 1819? Is Moore himself to be taken as a "case" of his historical culture in the sense that I have described? That is, do his writings characteristically stand in a relation at once illustrative of and problematic for the "spirit of the age"? Do they reveal a sense of the stakes in the invention of the historical situation, the transformation of history's exemplary function, the alteration of casuistry itself?

In chapter 3, analyzing the distinctive historicism of Hazlitt's *The Spirit of the Age,* its peculiar way of structuring contemporaneity and contradiction, I argued that Hazlitt's writing was notorious for manifesting its difficulty—its sense of the complex new historical situation—chiefly at the level of style. Hazlitt did not, I maintained, resort to the concept of the case that served some other writers of his age who addressed its spirit such as Shelley, Bentham, and Scott. Hazlitt's Moore might well have been a good candidate for conceptualization in such terms. For one thing, in the year before the publication of *The Spirit of the Age,* we know that Moore had been involved in one of the most controversial "cases" in the history of the modern literature—a complex deliberation after the death of Byron in 1824 that resulted in the destruction of the memoirs of the already-legendary poet. It was an occasion that Moore's own best biographer has described as one in which "five high-strung gentlemen got themselves entangled in a problem of casuistry which an earlier resort to the documents of the case might have simplified."[37]

Even within the terms of Hazlitt's own account, though, one might have expected to see Moore—Moore the writer, Moore his work—taken and presented as a case, as an exemplary anomaly for the new cultural regime of the spirit of the age. Certainly, Hazlitt defines Moore's life and character by way of a series of contradictions: an Irish commoner (son of a Dublin grocer) who be-

37. Jones, *The Harp that Once,* p. 243. And for sometime afterwards, writes Jones, "Moore's friends in London insisted upon going over and over again the casuistical problem of the Byron memoirs" (p. 245).

comes the darling of Whig aristocrats; a figure of talent rather than genius who insists on genius in his literary associates; a writer of prettified lines ("he can write verses, not a poem" [CWWH, 11:173]) who would at the same time mount a substantial threat to tyranny with his satirical writings;[38] a British subject who makes use of his Irishness among the English and his Englishness among the Irish. Moore's contradictions, his myriad hypocrisies, stand in sharper relief for being juxtaposed with the portrait of Hazlitt's close friend Leigh Hunt, with whom Moore shares an entry in Hazlitt's collection. Indeed, the sin for which Hazlitt does not forgive Moore is his alleged "personal injury" to Hunt, the author with whom Hazlitt himself most obviously identifies in *The Spirit of the Age*. Before he turns to his flattering picture of the injured Hunt, Hazlitt offers some concluding remarks on Moore that are among the most scathing in the book:

> Because he is genteel and sarcastic, may not others be paradoxical and argumentative? Or must no one bark at a Minister or General, unless they have been first dandled, like a little French pug-dog, in the lap of a lady of quality? Does Mr. Moore insist on the double claim of birth and genius as a title to respectability in all advocates of the popular side—but himself? Or is he anxious to keep the pretensions of his patrician and plebeian friends quite separate, so as to be himself the only point of union, a sort of *double meaning* between the two? (CWWH, 11:176)

Not just a run-of-the-mill exposé of literary hypocrisy, Hazlitt's analysis represents in the figure of Moore a principle of connection, even of contradictory union, across the deepest division of contemporary society. Rather than invoking the form of the case, however, Hazlitt's account of Moore figures him, at least in the first instance, as a local verbal effect—a paronomasia, a play on words.[39] This returns us to the distinction between the case and the pun— between the contradictions working at the level of form and of style, which I tried to develop in discussing Hazlitt's volume more broadly in chapter 3. That distinction will itself be challenged in what follows. It can be maintained heuristically for now as the difference, roughly, between a formal and a local ambiguity—or better, perhaps, between judgment of action and judgment of meaning.

But what, precisely, is the pun, the *double entendre,* to which Hazlitt alludes?

---

38. By 1819, Moore had arguably become the "most efficient satirist of the Whigs" (Jones, *The Harp that Once*, p. 196). Certainly, the virulence of Tory counter-attacks lends support for this view. See, for example, Palmerston's *New Whig Guide* and *The Fudger Fudged,* both of 1819.

39. Moore is thus personified as an instance not only of the sort of stylistic panache that characterized Moore's own writing in Hazlitt's account—"a play of fancy, a glitter of words, a shallowness of thought"—but also of the kind of thing that characterized Hazlitt's writing in the accounts of others (p. 173). The parallel is not one that could have been acknowledged, however, in that Hazlitt emphasizes the "polish" of Moore's style, whereas Hazlitt prided himself on the rough-and-tumble character of his writing.

A clue to the answer, I suspect, lies in a series of Tory satirical responses to Moore, which increased in crudity and vulgarity as his own lampoons gained in sting. These Tory counterattacks, comparable to contemporary Tory debunkings of Keats, attempt to expose Moore's literary elegances as a kind of foppery of the lower orders or "fringe" ethnicities—and they did so by making their jokes turn on broad puns. Examples abound in the various versions of the *Irish Melodies Illustrated,* where, in each illustrated line, each ridiculed caption, the key pun perforates the surface of Moore's style to reveal the degraded material conditions from which it was supposed to have issued. Thus, a drawing of two peasants next to a dilapidated thatched cottage, pig on the threshold (emphasizing the connection with Burke's "swinish multitude"), illustrates Moore's line: "Here we dwell in hole-iest Bowers" (see fig. 5). The very book that relies so much on the pun to mock Moore, however, bears a title page in which a rumpled Irishman in a "paddy" hat being led by a pig down the opposite fork in the road from the one he indicates. Its heading is itself a most telling play on words: *More-Irish Melodies Illustrated*[40] (see fig. 6).

Thus, evidently, Moore became More. If Hazlitt is punning on Moore's own name in this same way, we may speculate that, in the rather different terms of Hazlitt's differently motivated critique, the "double meaning" points to the trait of a man always seeking "more" from all sides in his social commerce. His many mediations, like those of the commercial party with which he is affiliated, involves the expectation of a surplus, a kind of "interest." "Interest" is a term that derives from *interesse:* being between.[41] Hazlitt certainly describes Moore's in-betweenness in *The Spirit of the Age* as if "interest" were what Moore was all about—the surface interest of his verses, the personal interest of his career, the political interest of some of the highest circles of Regency society. For Hazlitt, then, Moore is also Less. Thus, in his comments on Moore in "On the Living Poets" (1818), Hazlitt declared that the "fault of Mr. Moore is an exuberance of involuntary power." Moore's overindulgence in all sentiments "prevents him from giving their full force to the masses of things, from connecting them into a whole." His writing "lacks the same principle to make us thoroughly like poetry, that makes us like ourselves so well, the feeling of continued identity" (CWWH, 5:151). Moore's excess makes him less than he ought to be, less than a person.

Thomas Moore will thus appear in what follows less (or less obviously) as a case than as a kind of historical pun or go-between, a figure of interaction or interest whose *excess* can provide a means of *access* for each of the cases to follow.

40. Claude Scott, *Comic Illustrations to T. Moore's Irish Melodies* (n.d, n.p.).
41. See "interest" in the *OED.* For the modern development of the term, see Hirschman, *The Passions and the Interests,* passim.

Figure 5.   "Here we dwell in hole-iest Bowers," from *More-Irish Melodies Illustrated*

Indeed, thinking of these cases very loosely as a Waverley-esque series of cultural-historical studies, a Leatherstocking Tales of literary criticism, one may also regard Tom Moore as a character in virtue of whom they gain a sense of connection, a Hawk-eye of the forest of symbols. In this sense, Moore's punning name suits him for the role of eponymous hero, the figure of literary interest and excess. Scott himself, after all, supplemented his historical case histories with a similar kind of word play on the names of the historically representative title characters of his first two novels: *Waverley* and *Guy Mannering*.[42]

In insisting that I do not take Moore himself as a case, moreover, I do not mean to imply that he was immune to the contemporary fascination with the rapidly transforming discourse of casuistry in the England of 1819. Evidence of his interest in the historicization of the case can be found in his major literary project for that year, *The Life of Sheridan*. That same March 2 journal entry

42.   The pun on the surname of Edward Waverley is actually alluded to within the diegesis of the novel, when reference is made in a news article about the "wavering honour of Waverley-honour." See Judith Wilt, *Secret Leaves: The Novels of Walter Scott* (Chicago: University of Chicago Press, 1985), pp. 20-21, for an insightful comment on how such names work in Scott's fiction.

Figure 6.   Title page from *More-Irish Melodies Illustrated*

where Moore quotes Murray's suggestion for a new project actually begins with a reference to a book that had recently brought the Hastings affair back into memory, James Mill's *History of British India* (1818): "Read Mill's India, and made notes for my remarks on Hastings's Trial" (p. 153). The journal for 1819 records a host of other such investigations into the case of Warren Hastings. Hastings, Governor of Bengal and later Governor-General of India, was pursued for years by Edmund Burke and others, including Sheridan, before being impeached for high crimes and misdemeanors in 1788. The celebrated Parliamentary hearings ran for seven years before Hastings's acquittal in 1795. Toward the end of his detailed treatment of the Hastings affair, Moore addresses the question of why he has dilated so on that episode:

> I have dwelt so long upon the circumstances and nature of this Trial, not only on account of the conspicuous place which it occupies in the fore-ground of Mr. Sheridan's life, but because of that general interest which an observer of our Institutions must take in it, from the clearness with which it brought into view some of their best and worst features. While, on one side, we perceive the weight of the popular scale, in the lead taken, upon an occasion of such solemnity and importance, by two persons brought forward from the middle ranks of society into the very van of political distinction and influence, on the other hand, in the sympathy and favour extended by the Court to the practical assertor of despotic principles, we trace the

prevalence of that feeling, which since the commencement of the late King's reign, has made the Throne the rallying point of all that are unfriendly to the cause of freedom. Again, in considering the conduct of the Crown Lawyers during the Trial—the narrow and irrational rules of evidence which they sought to establish—the unconstitutional control assumed by the Judges, over the decisions of the tribunal before which the cause was tried, and the refusal to communicate the reasons upon which those decisions were founded—above all, too, the legal opinions expressed . . . , in which almost the whole body of lawyers took the wrong, the pedantic, and the unstatesman-like side of the question; while in all these indications of the spirit of that profession, and of its propensity to tie down the giant, Truth, with its small threads of technicality and precedent, we perceive the danger to be apprehended from the interference of such a spirit in politics, on the other side, arrayed against those petty tactics of the Forum, we see the broad banner of Constitutional Law, upheld alike by a Fox and a Pitt, a Sheridan and a Dundas, and find truth and good sense taking refuge from the equivocations of lawyers. . . .[43]

Moore deals with this cause célèbre as itself a second-order case, the case of the case of Hastings, as it were, and thus puts the trial itself on trial. The judicious weighing of the two sides of this proceeding, punctuated as it is by the use of the very figure of the scales as part of the assessment of this act of judicial deliberation, nicely illustrates the account of the case form that I elaborated earlier from the work of André Jolles. It is, in a sense, the historical institution of the British system of justice itself that is being pondered in this account: the weight of the "popular scale" (in the role granted to such men as Burke and Sheridan in the trial) as against the weight of the royal and aristocratic prerogative (in the sympathy granted to despotism) on the other side; or, in Moore's second formulation, the weight of procedure and the local technicalities of the legal apparatus balanced by the truth and good sense of "Constitutional Law" understood in its broadest terms. In chapter 5, I will argue that Scott figures the tension between civil law and equity law to similar effect in *The Bride of Lammermoor.*

The burden of Moore's discussion of "The Impeachment of Warren Hastings" is to display it as "one of those pageants in the drama of public life, which show how fleeting are the labours and triumphs of politicians" (pp. 378–79). That is, Moore tries to resolve the discrepancy between "the importance which the great actors in that scene attached to it" and the sense that "all that splendid array of Law and of talent has dwindled away, in the view of most persons at present, into an unworthy and harassing persecution of a meritorious and successful statesman" (p. 379). Moore's weighing of the judicial process in the case of Hastings, therefore, is carried out in the light of what he insists is a *historical shift in the situation of judgment.* It is not just that the times have changed but that there are new views about what it means to live in a certain time and place. Fur-

43. Thomas Moore, *Memoirs of the Life of The Right Honorable Richard Brinsley Sheridan* (London: Longman, 1825), pp. 384–85.

ther, part of the explanation of that new "current of opinion," in Moore's account, has to do with a new sense of the complexity of the circumstances in which Hastings acted: "There are also, without doubt, considerable allowances to be made, for the difficult situations in which Mr. Hastings was placed, and those impulses to wrong which acted upon him from all sides—allowances which will have more or less weight with the judgment" (p. 380).

Moore's phrasing, "impulses to wrong which acted upon him," strives for a casuistry of the historical situation, a location of motive in the historical scene. To this end, Moore spells out the circumstances of Hastings's alleged crimes in some detail: "The incessant and urgent demands of the Directors upon him for money, may palliate, perhaps, the violence of those methods which he took to procure it for them; and the obstruction to his policy which would have arisen from a strict observance of Treatise, may be admitted, by the same gentle casuistry, as an apology for his frequent infractions of them."[44] In addition to identifying the motives of Hastings's unique scene of action in India, Moore also adduces the new forms of publicity in the administration of India's affairs as an extenuating circumstance in considering the case of Hastings: "such a system of exposure—submitted, as it was in this case, to still further scrutiny, under the bold, denuding hands of a Burke and a Sheridan—was a test to which the councils of few rulers could with impunity be brought."[45] Moore's thus becomes another in a series of higher- and higher-order representations—a *review* of a *scrutiny* of an *exposure* of a situation.

In light of Moore's own scandal in the episode of the funds embezzled by his office in Bermuda, it speaks well of him that, while he brings the extenuating circumstances of the Hastings case to bear on the question of the shift of public opinion and on that of the higher-order justice of the trial, his position in the end is that Burke and Sheridan were in the right and that the British people should not let "excuses for rapine and oppression pass muster" so easily.[46] Nor does he resort to "gentle casuistry" to excuse the flaws of Sheridan himself, although he is known to have contemplated doing so (JTM, 1:178–79).[47]

44. Ibid., pp. 380–81.
45. Ibid., p. 381.
46. Ibid., p. 380.
47. May 30, 1819: records "A good deal of conversation with Mackintosh, chiefly about Sheridan, & the politics of his time." Then May 31: "Mackintosh, who seemed yesterday to think that I must hold a veil up before Sheridan's criminalities, told me this morning he had been thinking of the subject the greater part of the night, & had come to the decision that I ought to do no such thing." As for the status of the term "literary" at this time, it is interesting to note that in 1819 Moore could still use "literature" to include published political addresses: "Burke's Speeches alone, of all modern oratory, deserve to take a rank in the literature of the country—they altogether display a talent almost super-human." JTM, 1:159.

Moore's discussion of Hastings in the book on which he was at work in 1819 thus invokes the discourse of casuistry and the case, and does so in relation to a framework of dual normativity and to an assumed historical shift in the framework of evaluation. Nor is this the only place, as I show presently, where Moore's writings involve this frame of reference.

I invoke the figure of Moore to introduce readers to certain cases, rather than as a case in himself, but, as is clear from his treatment of Hastings, the case tends to intrude itself as a form and a topic in the everyday literary practice of Moore's moment. Certainly it is there in the novel and newspaper we are imagining in Moore's hands on January 1, 1819: *The Morning Chronicle* and *The Heart of Mid-Lothian.* Although there was no regular column of legal cases for the New Year's Day edition of the *Chronicle,* there was a report entitled "Extraordinary Case of a Criminal Recently Pardoned," which told of how an Irish servant sentenced to death for robbing his master had been pardoned after efforts by Sidmouth and Hobhouse to show his innocence. To the reader of *The Heart of Mid-Lothian,* such a story may well have resonated in various ways, not the least of which is the notion of an extraordinary pardon for a convicted criminal in a position of social subordination. A more curious connection, however, can be drawn between Moore's thinking about Scott's cases and one of the important senses of case in that novel. For when it came to speculation about the authorship of the Waverley novels—and we have seen that it is still a question that Moore and Wordsworth were discussing in 1820—Moore had some weeks earlier offered reflections that frame the issue in terms close to those of the novel Moore began reading to his wife in December.

The crux of *The Heart of Mid-Lothian,* as I argue in chapter 5, is the relation between a legal case (actually a series of legal cases) and a case of conscience, the latter turning on the question of whether a woman might, under certain circumstances, lie under oath to save the life of a sister accused of murder. Meeting with Samuel Rogers at Bowood on October 22, nearly a month before his own copy of *The Heart of Mid-Lothian* had arrived, Moore had discussed the case of the authorship of *Waverley* in strikingly similar terms:

> Talked of the Scotch Novels—When Wilkie, the painter, was taking the portraits of Scott's family, the eldest daughter said to him "We don't know what to think of those Novels—We have access to all Papa's papers—he has no particular study—writes every thing in the midst of us all & yet we have never seen a single scrap of the MS. of any of these Novels—but still we have *one* reason for thinking them his & that is that they are the only works published in Scotland, of which copies are not presented to Papa"—The reason *against* is stronger than the reason *for*—Scott gave his honour to the Prince Regent they were not his. . . . Another argument between us on the justifiableness of a man asserting so solemnly that a book was *not his,* when it really was—I maintained that no man had a right to put himself into a situation which re-

quired lies to support himself in it—R. [Rogers] quoted Paley about the expedience of occasionally lying, and mentioned extreme cases about murder &c. which had nothing at all whatever to do with the point in question & certainly did not convince me that Scott could be at all justified in such a solemn falsehood [if he really is denying, on his honour, that he wrote them, if he really did] . . . .(1:71)

This casuistical analysis of the question of Scott's hypothetical solemn lie about his authorship of such novels as *The Heart of Mid-Lothian* resonates in several ways with the novel itself. Not only is the moral case posed to Jeannie Deans a case about the justifiability of lying under oath, but the issue of authorship and its relation to conscience—i.e., to the heart—is very much in play in Scott's introductory chapter, which supplies a framing action for the production of the central narrative about the Deans family and the Porteous riots of 1736. *The Heart of Mid-Lothian* offers a sustained investigative experiment on the literary-historical problems attending the relations of the historical frame to the historical picture, the preface to the diegesis, the title to context, the case-at-hand to the heart of the matter. Moreover, in its 1819 sequel, *The Bride of Lammermoor* ("Tales of My Landlord," third series) the negotiation of such issues of contextualism, in effect, begin to constitute the substance of the historical action itself. This exposition will be the burden of the next chapter, but before turning to it I should briefly sketch the organization of part 2.

Moore's friend Samuel Rogers wrote of him that his "Life [was] a good poem, bad matter of fact" (Jones, p. 244), and I mean to invoke both its poetic and its factual dimensions in my use of Moore in what follows. While Moore's life and letters touch on the subjects of all the chapters that follow, he figures centrally in none of them. Instead, he sets the scene for these cases, or rather he lends a sense, not illusory, that these cases might share a scene: the scene I call "England in 1819." To be sure, the means by which I construe or construct the coherence of these cases are varied, but, to recall my account of the case in part 1 and to provide one additional gloss for my use of the case idiom in part 2, I reinvoke Thomas De Quincey.

Toward the end of the essay on "The Casuistry of Duelling," De Quincey summarized his own working understanding of the key terms as follows: "Casuistry . . . is the moral philosophy of *cases*—that is, of anomalous combinations of circumstances—that, for any reason whatsoever, do not fall, or do not seem to fall, under the general rules of morality."[48] When De Quincey speaks of the "general rules of morality" here, we may understand him to be referring to the normative precepts of "moral philosophy" in the broad sense, the sense in

---

48. Thomas De Quincey, "Casuistry of Duelling" in *The Uncollected Writings,* 2 vols. (London: Swan Sonnenschein, 1892), 2:91.

which "natural philosophy" and "moral philosophy" divide between them the things that are dreamt of in philosophical meditation. It is a distinction that corresponds to the differentiation between "natural sciences" and "human sciences" that still persists in our own time, in the sense that, broadly considered, moral philosophy is the science of the human.[49] This view of De Quincey's formulation is corroborated by what he goes on to say about how the specific case he is considering "arises out of a great dilemma, with difficulties on both sides," on which point he declares that "in all *practical* applications of philosophy, among materials so imperfect as men, just as in all attempts to realize the rigour of mathematical laws amongst earthly mechanics, inevitably there will arise such dilemmas and cases of approbrium to the reflecting intellect."[50]

The claim for analogy between the mode of explanation in natural and moral philosophy has received a great deal of attention in major commentaries on eighteenth-century thought—R. G. Collingwood's *The Idea of History* perhaps chief among them. And for many of these intellectual historians, including Collingwood, the pursuit of that analogy by Enlightenment figures such as Hume led logically to the development of historicism understood as an attempt to give the category of "period" normative status in explanation.[51] Historicism is indeed, for Collingwood, the only possible "science" of human nature. But the period of British history that develops normative status for the period as such necessarily breaks with the scheme of things in which historical periods are *not* understood as normative. It is, as we recall from the discussion of Koselleck, the extent to which periods were not seen as normative in pre-Romantic historiography that one was enabled to generalize across their boundaries. The moment of historicism—call it "Romanticism" or "England in 1819"—thus poses itself as a "case" for the normative (i.e., traditional) understanding of the period concept. It poses itself as a case by virtue of its seeming departure from the principles of generalization that were understood to govern that series of epochs—principles summed up, as we have seen, in the notion that history teaches by example. To call the "Romantic period" or "1819" itself a case is thus to understand it as both an instance of and a challenge to earlier ways of conceiving a historical epoch.

The "historicism" of a moment identified as "England in 1819," however,

49. Whether "moral philosophy" understood as the science of the human could actually boast a normative dimension in the strong sense was of course a point of controversy in Kant's critique of the British tradition. For a contemporary neo-Kantian account of these matters, see Christine Korsgaard, *The Sources of Normativity* (Cambridge: Cambridge University Press, 1996).

50. Ibid., p. 99.

51. Collingwood, *Idea of History*, pp. 327–28.

can itself become in its turn normative for a range of cases that both instantiate and challenge it as a normative system. Each of the cases I take up in the chapters that follow are at once exemplary and anomalous for Romantic historicism as defined by a new understanding of the "historical situation" in its bearing on human action and society. The four chapters (5–8) of section 3 "Cases, Causes, Casuistries" all center on particular texts that were composed and/or published in that year and that foreground thematic and formal issues having to do with the historicization of the case itself. Some of these connections are more direct than others. In Scott's back-to-back novels from "Tales of My Landlord," *The Heart of Mid-Lothian* and *The Bride of Lammermoor,* to which I turn in chapter 5, the interest in the historicization of the case and the cause is explicit. In chapter 6, I argue that *Don Juan,* which first saw the light of day in 1819, is preoccupied with the problem of historical explanation and typicality in a way that has yet to receive proper emphasis. I also suggest that Byron is particularly interested in the relation of moral explanation to natural explanation in *Don Juan,* and, by virtue of its much-overlooked emulation of Scott's historical novels, keen to explore the role of what might be called "cultural history" as a problem in the representation of the various cases he considers there.

I would not want to deny—in fact, I will explicitly argue—that the way in which *Don Juan* rivals Scott's fiction has to do with their shared aspiration to the condition of epic, and their shared effort to revise epic form for the modern period. Issues of explanation and typicality, one might say, naturally arise in such cases. I am concerned, however, not to limit the implications of my larger argument in this way. Thus, in chapter 7, I turn to certain aspects of Keats's nonepic writings in 1819 to show a set of preoccupations related to those I outline in the Scott and Byron chapters. Until just recently, scholarship on Keats has paid much more attention to a narrative of *poetic* development, his own, than it has to the way in which his new style of poetry depends on new conceptions of literary-cultural development and on the new forms of explanation and representation that attend them. Here I reread two of the great odes of Keats to consider how what he self-consciously termed his "1819 temper" manifested itself in his lyric art both *in* particular historical circumstances and *with* a particular understanding of historical circumstantiality, the historicity of the soul, and the immanence of the future state.

My account of the case of Keats involves both his brother's emigration to southern Illinois in mid-1818 and the literary representations of early U.S. culture—"American manners"—that began to circulate through the British public sphere with dramatically increasing intensity in the years just following the Napoleonic Wars. It was to these representations that Washington Irving addressed himself in the chapter entitled "English Writers on America" in *The Sketch-Book of Geoffrey Crayon,* published just before the turn of the year 1820. Such accounts, which supply the subject matter of chapter 8, are much concerned with the cultural "state" of America vis à vis England (ca. 1819). They explore both the "case" (as it was called) of U.S. culture and the comparative question of the respective cases of both nations taken as historically specific cultural and institutional systems.

Finally, in section 2, I revisit what Frederick Pottle famously called "The Case of Shelley" in order to extend and recapitulate the discussion of the four previous case studies. Three important works of 1819—*The Cenci, Peter Bell the Third,* and the *Ode to the West Wind*—provide three different angles of access on the difficult question of Shelley's way of representing the "state of the representation" in his time, a question in which the case of U.S. culture figures prominently. What contributes to the difficulty of the question is Shelley's theoretical insistence that a poet must be oblivious to the spirit of the age that animates his or her work, even as he (Shelley) evidently writes in distinct awareness of its power. This last section reviews some of the primary questions about historical writing, repetition, specificity, and genre that will have been addressed along the way. Moreover, it tracks a set of allusions to the way in which the general literary culture of 1819 was understood as a domain in which to "catch the conscience" of the nation, much as Hamlet used a staged drama to catch the conscience of the king. The allusion is explicit in Shelley's *Peter Bell the Third,* whose preface is supposed to be written by "Miching Mallecho"—the name that Hamlet uses in that famous speech ("the play's the thing") to Ophelia. I read this textual interplay as a commentary on the overt treatment of casuistry as a topic in and for his 1819 play, *The Cenci.* Since *The Cenci* is set in Rome in 1599, and keenly alert to the problem of anachronism in representing the moral culture of the past, it also provides an occasion to revisit and clarify my argument in chapter 4 about the invention of the "historical situation" in British Romanticism.[52] Chapter 10, a short chapter consisting primarily of a reading of the *Ode to the West Wind,* serves as a coda, if not conclusion to the whole. It tries to establish the poem as a history deploying "structural causality" in the lyric mode.

52. *Peter Bell the Third* is also helpful for showing Shelley's astute recognition of the problem of how to identify a case in or of a literary culture—whether it is by text, or by author, or by character. Through his dark comic ballad, *Peter Bell* refers (in all three generations) to, at once, a poem by Wordsworth, the protagonist of that poem, and Wordsworth himself (as prototypical Lake Poet). In the chapters below, I will be claiming similar license for the literary culture of England in 1819, referring sometimes to the case of *Don Juan,* sometimes to the case of Jeanie Deans, sometimes to the case of Keats.

The cases of part 2 are sequenced in such a way as to suggest how addressing one set of issues can issue in another, thus at least gesturally mimicking the structure of the case series that, with Jolles's help, I described in chapter 4. Each chapter of part 2 addresses a text (or cluster of texts) that can count as a case—count, that is, by the logic I have traced in Kenneth Burke, as posing an exemplary anomaly for a normative frame of reference. However, each chapter also finds implicit in its case a certain casuistry that facilitates the mediation between case and norm, (historical) situation and (historical) scheme. This again follows from the logic of Burke's analysis. Beyond these connections, moreover, each chapter seeks to construct the case it addresses in such a way as to show at work in that case an adumbration of the form of critical commentary later brought to bear on it. Thus, Scott's way of representing the historical scene of agency and deliberation in the Waverley novels anticipates the most influential attempts (following Lukács) to place Scott in his own historical scene. Byron's obsession with causality and explanation in the historical period of *Don Juan* anticipates the explanatory procedures of his most aggressive recent commentators. Keats's reflexive meditation on the place of his own writing in the history of psyche anticipates the recent deployment of the "progressive-regressive method" to show the origins of his style. The early English writers on America (Cobbett, Birkbeck, Brougham, Fearon) used the western settlements of the United States as a laboratory for developing a model of historically constituted subjectivity now commonly taken for granted in the critical practice of U.S. cultural studies. And finally Shelley, so alert to those shadows cast by futurity on the present, jokingly prophesies a transatlantic commentator with a system of criticism that can properly weigh his own work of this moment against that of his friend Thomas Moore, to whom, addressing him by his pen name "Thomas Brown," he dedicates the poem.[53]

53. I am not ruling out that other works written or published in 1819 might be similarly deployed as cases/casuistries: many of these I have cited in passing comment already to this point. These are simply the cases that I have found easiest to work with in respect to the multiple criteria I have outlined here: (1) explicit thematization of the case and the cause in conjunction with a marked historicism; (2) implicit casuistry for relating the case to the normative scheme; and (3) a claim that the historical casuistry implicit in the case plausibly anticipates critical historicism in our own time.

Section One

CASES, CAUSES,
AND CASUISTRIES

Chapter Five

REOPENING THE CASE OF SCOTT

The commentary on Moore's famous burning of Byron's memoirs in John Murray's fireplace represents it as a case, as we have seen, the arguments on various sides as so many exercises in casuistry. It was an event that haunted Moore long after it took place, and his subsequent references to it suggest that he conceived the episode in similar terms. Here is the full entry from Moore's journal for January 25, 1826:

> Hardman's gig called for me at two to take me to his house to dinner—Dressed at Scott's where I was to sleep—Company at Hardman's, Lord & Lady Ashtown, Scott, Miss Armstrong, & a Mr. Pipon—Rather agreeable some amusing stories of Lord Bellamont—his duel with Lord Townsend—taking off his hat to him when he wounded him—Lord A. mentioned some French remarks upon Pope, in which on the line "he oped his snuff-box first and then the case"—the commentator says "Comment peut-on ouvrir une tabatière sans ouvrir l'étui qui la contient."—Walked home with Scott and slept at his house—Received an answer, by the bye, this morning from Hobhouse, in which, after saying that he will "of course do what he promised," he proceeds to discuss the question of the destruction of the Memoirs on other grounds.—This evasion, if I had not motives enough to justify to myself in what I have done, would have made me uncomfortable. (JTM, 3:914)

Hobhouse's "promise" was to leave some written record of a comment made to him by Byron on their last meeting, apropos of the memoirs he had consigned to Moore, that "he [Byron] regretted having put such a document out of his own power & was only restrained by delicacy toward me [Moore] from recalling the gift" (3:912). Moore requested this bit of documentation, which he felt helped his own cause, after Hobhouse reported a new public attack on Moore's decision by an American writer.[1] It is clear that justification was still in order. The case was not closed. It was still a case.

Looking at this passage in the context of the whole entry, we note that

---

1. The attack has been identified as that of J. W. Simmons in *An Inquiry into the Moral Character of Lord Byron* (New York: E. Bliss and E. White, 1824): see JTM, 3:992.

Moore segues to the case of Byron's destroyed memoirs from the anecdote about the Frenchman's ignorant commentary on the ingenious line from Pope's *The Rape of the Lock* and that he then segues to the anecdote about the Frenchman from the topic of a duel. Is there a "cultural logic" in these transitions? De Quincey, in "The Casuistry of Duelling," argued not only that dueling might be justified casuistically but also, and more suggestively, that the institution of dueling offered a kind of alternative court for handling *cases,* a "supplementary code of law, reaching those cases which the weakness of municipal law was . . . unavailable to meet."[2] To the extent that some such conception of dueling was available to Moore, and certainly the norms and practices of the duel were well known to him of all people, the passage from the journal might be seen as structured thus: two anecdotes focused on problems of justification in "cases" ambiguous in respect to the legal code are linked by the humorous story about the Frenchman missing Pope's joke about case, the joke that the assembled British wits at the dinner party obviously congratulate themselves on recognizing.

The "Scott" who hosted the dinner party Moore attended is not Sir Walter, though the latter was much in Moore's thoughts in those days—Moore had only two days earlier heard about Scott's "ruin," by which he was deeply saddened, and a week later he would receive a gift from Sir Walter of the complete Waverley novels to that point. Sir Walter's looming financial catastrophe would have made him a more than usually plausible subject for conversation that evening: we have seen how both the form of the case and the semantic play in the very term were patent in Scott's fiction. Indeed, just as Moore's analysis of the justifiability of Scott's lying about his authorship of the Waverley novels seemed to echo the portrayals of case thinking that figure so prominently in novels such as *The Heart of Mid-Lothian,* so here a Popean pun on the case is replicated in a pun installed at the very heart of that same novel. In what might be the central scene of *The Heart of Mid-Lothian,* when Jeanie "pleaded her sister's cause," the "case of her kinswoman" (TML2, chap. 38), before Queen Caroline with the Duke of Argyle at her side, the Queen rewards her in kind, as it were, by presenting her with "a housewife's case" (which Jeanie herself calls a "hussy case") (chap. 39).[3] And this pun resonates with another, for when the case is opened Jeanie discovers that on "the inside of the case were the usual as-

2. Thomas De Quincey, "The Casuistry of Duelling" in *The Uncollected Writings,* 2 vols. (London: Swan Sonnenschein, 1892), 2:95.

3. Making the cause/case substitution that illustrates the connection between cases and explanations, Jeanie will later describe the Duke himself as a "true-hearted nobleman who pleads the cause of the poor" (chap. 38).

sortment of silk and needles, with scissars, tweazers, &c; and in the pocket was a bank-bill for fifty pounds." Unsure that the money in the secret recess of the case is meant for her, Jeanie raises a question with the Duke. Argyle replies, "there is no mistake in the case" (chap. 38).

If these cultural linkages suggest a discourse of the case at work just beneath the surface of this banter, the allusive linkage between Scott's and Pope's puns on *case* suggest a particular point in its invocation. In the quoted verse from *The Rape of the Lock,* Pope plays with a double reference of the word—*case* both as the container of the snuff box and the "matter" of the offense about to be investigated (the unsolicited cutting of Belinda's hair). In missing the joke, what the Frenchman misses is precisely the play on the notion of "content": *Comment peut-on ouvrir une tabatière sans ouvrir l'étui qui la contient?* A similar attention to what it means for a case to contain or be contained seems to play around the edges of Scott's passage. Even when the hussy case remains closed, the value of what it holds remains open to negotiation—*depends* on negotiation for its value. If we consider that the "heart" of the title signals that this is a book about modes of circulation,[4] and that the case at the heart of the book contains notes that have value only by virtue of their power to circulate, we might speculate that *The Heart of Mid-Lothian* plays with the figure of container and thing-contained in a way that the Frenchman's naive reading of Pope's pun seems obliquely to capture—a confusion between the case as substance and the case "qui la contient."

I hope it is clear that my point about the play with "cases" in Scott is not going to be that no one ever punned on the word before what I have called the invention of the historical situation. The point is going to be that, at the peak of his powers and his popularity as a historical novelist—that is, in the later entries for his series on the wars of conscience—Scott makes central to his work (if anything is) a searching elaboration of the case form. This elaboration, I argue, is in a sense the primary work of this fiction, at once the form and content of its self-presentation, and it ramifies in a number of directions. Consider what Scott does with the very title of *The Heart of Mid-Lothian.* In its most explicit application, "The Heart of Mid-Lothian" refers to the prison known as the "Edinburgh Tolbooth." We learn this much in chapter 1's frame narrative, in which the redactor of the "Tales of My Landlord," Peter Pattieson, witnesses the overturning of the local mail coach and then enters into conversation with two of its passengers, the lawyers Halkit and Hardie, in reference to a third, Mr.

4. For a suggestive reading of the novel in relation to this metaphor of circulation, see Andrea Henderson, *Romantic Identities: Varieties of Subjectivity 1774–1830* (Cambridge: Cambridge University Press, 1996), pp. 130–62.

Dunover, an unfortunate former client of Hardie's. Referring to the lawyer's
mishandling of "the case of that honest man [Dunover]," Halkit adds that
Dunover "looks as if he were just about to honour with his residence the
HEART OF MID-LOTHIAN" (chap. 1). Later in this same exchange, Hardie
returns to this subject: "And as to the old and condemned Tolbooth, what a pity
the same honour cannot be done to it as has been done to many of its inmates.
Why should not the Tolbooth have its 'Last Speech, Confession, and Dying
Words?' The old stones would be just as conscious of the honour, as many a
poor devil who has dangled like a tassel at the west end of it, while the hawkers
were shouting a confession the culprit had never heard of" (chap. 1). When such
a suggestion has been planted, it is hard not to read the narrative that Peter
Pattieson redacts to form this novel as the "confession" of the personified Tolbooth, for the story that begins in chapter 2 is said to be compiled from notes
taken by Pattieson on the subsequent conversation among the two lawyers and
the client: "Jails," explains Pattieson, "like other places, have their ancient traditions, known only to the inhabitants, and handed down from one set of the
melancholy lodgers to the next who occupy their cells" (chap. 1).

But Hardie has already undercut any sense that the "confession" from the
"HEART" can be grounded in the sincerity it seems to presume, or in any other
aspect of authorship, with his suggestion that the autobiographical subject of
the "Last Speech, Confession, and Dying Words" in his culture is not at all likely
to have been conscious of, let alone compositionally responsible for, the production that appears over his or her name. The problem of authorship is complicated everywhere in Scott, but in this novel it is especially vexed by the sheer
number of candidates with a claim to authorial credit. On the evidence of the
introductory frames, one could make an argument for any or all of the following as the author of the narrative that begins with chapter 2: the Tolbooth of
Edinburgh itself; Peter Pattieson, who redacts the materials for the story; Mr.
Dunover (the debtor who inhabited the Tolbooth long enough to learn its secrets); the lawyers Halkit and Hardie (who supplied crucial details for the narrative); Jedediah Cleishbotham (editor of "Tales of My Landlord"); the Author
of Waverley; or Sir Walter Scott. A confession ought to be a pure disclosure of
the state of one's heart, but the genre of confessions to which this story belongs—one of which, the hanged Meg Murdruckson's own "Last Speech,
Confession, and Dying Words" appears *within* the story, and in a crucially evidentiary role—is enmeshed in the materiality of its signifying circumstances.[5]

5. Copies of this broadside figure in the scene involving the execution of Murdrockson
(TML2, chap. 41) and then reappear prominently in the novel's closing pages, where their status
as evidence is contemplated at some length and given some weight.

We are not likely to find the heart of the case, therefore, in the centralized integrity of an authorizing subject. Here, as in other contemporary novels, confessions are contrivances: think of the fabulous array of nested confessions in Mary Shelley's *Frankenstein,* a novel Scott favorably reviewed in 1818, the year he wrote *The Heart,* or the bizarre *Confessions of a Justified Sinner* contrived by his friend James Hogg six years later. Each of these Romantic novels, like the broadside genre to which Hardie alludes, involves reported *confession,* and in each there are notorious complications of reliability generated by the nested frames. When confessions become part of the general commerce of culture, the virtue of the open heart risks the displacement of personal authority and integrity, and thus the case is left unresolved after all.

At several points in part 1, I made use of Scott's case histories and their many prefaces in discussing the representative practices of Romantic historicism. I have not addressed the relation of the introduction of the case to its diegesis, the preface to the story, the framing narrative to the one "that it contains." To enlist Scott in an effort to address these matters, and thus to advance the analysis of the case into its next phase, it will eventually be necessary to explicate the insistent "dramatism" of his fiction. A case, I will argue, may be understood as a scene of conflict to be resolved in another scene conceived as a court. This reinvocation of Kenneth Burke should recall another relationship, broached but yet not properly accounted for in my discussion to this point. I mean the relationship between dramatism and casuistry, so utterly crucial to *The Grammar of Motives.* Scott's fiction of 1819 provides a kind of literary laboratory for thinking through these questions. And the appositeness of such questions for us now, today, lies in the practices of "scene setting" more generally that, in contemporary criticism, link the emphatic interest in "contextualizing" literary works with the emphatic interest in the "performative" dimension of texts. Scott foregrounds, though in a more ordinary idiom, just those questions about historiographical performativity that have recently claimed attention under a variety of slogans and rubrics: the dramatization of an "attitude toward history," the presentist dimension of the "historiographical operation," the historian's "transferential dialogue" with the past, the "framing" of the historical sign, and the dialectic of "pedagogy and performance" in nationalist historical narrative.[6]

6. These rubrics and slogans will be familiar enough to most readers. They derive, respectively, from the following writers and critics: Kenneth Burke, *Attitudes Toward History* (Boston: Beacon Press, 1961); Michel de Certeau, *The Writing of History,* trans. Tom Conley (New York: Columbia University Press, 1988), chap. 2, pp. 56–114; Dominick LaCapra has worked out his transferential notion of context in a series of studies, especially *Rethinking Intellectual History: Texts, Contexts, Language* (Ithaca, N.Y.: Cornell University Press, 1983), pp. 23–71, and *Soundings*

Not all such topics have their origins in Scott, needless to say, but the originality of the Waverley novels consists largely in his inventive handling of them. Recent work in this vein, anyhow, forms one important context on which I
consider my own critical performance with Scott to have bearing.

In looking at two of Scott's linked case novels from the second and third series
of "Tales of My Landlord," then, I will be attending both to their handling of
cases and to their own prefatory narratives and framing structures. But I will also
be considering how each novel establishes the broader relevance of such issues
by associating casuistry with what De Quincey calls "a supplementary code of
law"—an alternative to the official court system, a rival normative framework in
which the hegemony of the central system comes in for challenge and possible
modification. Not only can a case be weighed in different kinds of courts, but
the constellation of case and court, from the perspective of Scott's new historical novels, will vary from era to era and culture to culture. This historicity of
modern casuistry De Quincey also registers, but obliquely. Although he defines
cases, as we have seen, as "anomalous combinations of circumstances" that do
not clearly fall "under the general rules of morality," he also admits the historicist
understanding of moral rules as culturally relative. He recognizes that the duel,
for example, once had a different status in the system of courts and cases in part
because of the different composition of armies "from a large variety of
different nations, whose peculiar usages, points of traditional honour, and even
the oddness of their several languages to the ear, formed a perpetual occasion of
insult and quarrel" (p. 91). Thus, when De Quincey sums up this point with the
claim that "Fluellen's affair with Pistol . . . was no rare but a representative case,"
he is using "representative case" in an importantly dual frame of reference
(p. 99).

The notion of the representative case, we might say, acquires the divided
character of an oxymoron, one corresponding roughly to "typical anomaly":
that is, a moral anomaly that typifies its historically-specific code of manners.
De Quincey makes the same point about the primary subject of his essay, his
own "case," which involves an injury that he allegedly suffered "through his female connexions" from one of the "mercenary libellers, whose stiletto is in the
market" of early nineteenth-century print culture (p. 86). In insisting that his
own is not an "extreme case," the implicit frame of reference in which the "ex-

in *Critical Theory* (Ithaca, N.Y.: Cornell University Press, 1989), pp. 182–209; Jonathan Culler,
Framing the Sign: Criticism and Its Institutions (Norman: University of Oklahoma Press, 1988),
pp. 57–68; and Homi K. Bhabha, "DissemiNation: Time, Narrative, and the Margins of the
Modern Nation," in *Nation and Narration,* ed. Homi Bhabha (London: Routledge, 1990)
pp. 297–99.

tremity" or "ordinariness" of the case is gauged would seem to be the culture of contemporary commercial Britain (p. 91). The implicit "court" before which De Quincey argues what he calls "the case of dueling" (p. 71) itself is ultimately called into being in and by the literary-historical performance of this very essay.[7] De Quincey, that famous child of his Romantic age, fully internalized its form of appeal to the court of contemporary literary culture—just the form of appeal that so markedly characterizes the dominant work of Scott.[8]

I begin by examining *The Heart of Mid-Lothian*—a novel in which the primary or overarching case at issue is difficult to identify—for what I see as Scott's return to and revision of Adam Smith's sentimental case against casuistry in *The Theory of Moral Sentiments*. Then, after indicating my sense of what the case is and how its "resolution" remains provisional, I argue that its problem, finally understood as a problem about the scene of its own articulation, is in effect displaced or deferred to the next major case narrative in the series of "Tales of My Landlord," *The Bride of Lammermoor*. The very plot of that latter novel, I argue, is framed and constituted in virtue of an almost obsessive attention to acts of making and taking cases and to anatomies of the casuistical act—as if such activity were all there was to the plot itself. The novel's preoccupying attention to the dialectics of word and scene, caption and conversation, implies a mode of representation of human action wherein, on the one hand, every case could be explained by its name, as if to name a case were to assign it a cause, but, on the other, every naming of a case itself necessarily stood in need of further explanation. It is, I will argue, a working through of the "historiographical operation" *avant la lettre*. In the end, I return to *The Heart of Mid-Lothian* with an explanatory word of my own about the relation of Romantic historicism to the notorious problematization of reference in the literature of the period.

1. The Theory of Sentiment and the Case of *The Heart*

On January 4, 1819, Moore reached the final page of the new novel he had been reading aloud to his wife since before the turn of the year: "Finished the 'Heart of Mid-Lothian' to Bessy in the evening—A most extravagant and incredible story, but full of striking situations, & picturesque sketches—the winding up disagreeable & unsatisfactory" (JTM, 1:128). Since this is the extent of the en-

---

7. He published it in *Tait's Magazine* in 1841, where it was included in a series, "Sketches of Life and Manners: From the Autobiography of an English Opium Eater."

8. Sartre seems to play on the notion of the audience as a kind of contemporary court for writers when he insists that all literature should be thought of as a kind of appeal made from the writer to his or her first readership. See *What is Literature?* (Cambridge, Mass.: Harvard University Press, 1988), chap. 2.

try for January 4, it is plausible to surmise that Moore spent a good part of the day reading through the last of the novel's four volumes to the end. Why was he, like so many commentators since, so disappointed when he got there? There is indeed a considerable literature, dating back to Scott's early reception, on the problem of closure in this novel. Readers of many critical persuasions have addressed the strange distension and open-endedness of the plot, the issue of the novel's resolution, and thus of its formal integrity.[9] One reason for the trouble, I suggest, lies in the structuring of what Moore calls the novel's "striking situations" from the first book of the novel forward.

For this is a novel that juxtaposes two very different kinds of situation deriving from two very different episodes in the historical record. One historical episode is routinely called the "case of Porteous." In 1736, Jack Porteous, Captain of the Edinburgh City Guard, was convicted of firing on a stone-throwing crowd after the unpopular execution of a smuggler. His trial became one of the recognized causes célèbres of Scottish jurisprudence, and, when he was pardoned (again contrary to intense popular sentiment), a second Edinburgh crowd rioted and lynched him. The other historical episode involves the striking situation of Helen Walker (the prototype for Jeanie Deans), a young Cameronian peasant who, after the fashion of Shakespeare's Isabella in *Measure for Measure,* found herself faced with having to violate a sacred commandment in order to save a sibling from a controversial but strictly legal charge of murder under a rewritten infanticide statute. Helen Walker would not lie to save her sister from being convicted in an Edinburgh court, but she did determine, and manage, to make her way on foot from Scotland to London to secure her a pardon from the Queen. The problem of formal integrity for the novel, in effect, is the problem of how these two central episodes are finally to be articulated in or as one narrative, one diegesis, one case. The question that might initially be put to this novel, then, is roughly: what is the case of *The Heart of Mid-Lothian*? Or, even more simply, what is the case of the heart, or the heart of the case?[10]

Reading back into *The Heart* from *Redgauntlet,* we might suppose that, inso-

---

9. Among representative recent commentators on the oddity of the distended "Highland Arcadia" epilogue, see, for example, Jane Millgate, *Walter Scott: The Making of a Novelist* (Toronto: University of Toronto Press, 1984), pp. 162–67; Susan Morgan, *Sisters in Time: Imagining Gender in Nineteenth-Century British Fiction* (New York: Oxford University Press, 1989), pp. 135–37; and Ian Duncan, *Modern Romance and the Transformation of the Novel: The Gothic, Scott, Dickens* (Cambridge: Cambridge University Press, 1992), pp. 165–76.

10. Many genres of case statement are identified in the course of the novel, for example, the various references to the genre of "confession," discussed above, and in the narrator's reference to the "Information for Porteous (the paper, namely, in which his case is stated)" (TML2, chap. 4).

far as *Peebles v. Planestanes* can be read, *pace* Peter Peebles himself, as "a specimen of all causes," or cases, then the case of *The Heart* must have at least two sides, like Peter's, each of which is itself a cause or a case. It is easy to see the two sides argued in the novel's portrayal of the case of Porteous, and, just as vividly, the two sides argued in the case of Effie Deans. The records for the celebrated trials of Scotland were indeed available to Scott, and the legal cases on which this novel was based would be published before the end of 1818 in a spin-off volume brought out by Constable, *Criminal Trials, Illustrative of the Tale Entitled "The Heart of Mid-Lothian."* [11] However, if, as I have suggested, the two central cases in the novel are those of Porteous and Jeanie Deans, the Helen Walker figure, it would seem that they are *not cases of the same kind.* Porteous's is a legal case, but Jeanie Deans is charged with no crime and involved in no suit. Clearly, she is the subject of a *moral* case, a case of conscience, and plays this role perhaps more conspicuously than any character in English literature after Isabella herself. [12] And just as the "case of Porteous" can stand for the other legal cases of the novel—those of Andrew Wilson or Effie Deans—so Jeanie's case of conscience is echoed in the casuistical deliberations in which we see other characters involved. Thus, late in the novel when the Deans family is about to settle on the land given them by the Duke of Argyle, some reference is made to "the case of David Deans" (Jeanie's father), as if it were the most casual possible reference to his situation (chap. 43).

But in fact the ensuing pages show David Deans still caught up in a long series of casuistical issues. One such case concerns his friend and now son-in-law:

11. *Criminal Trials, Illustrative of the Tale Entitled "The Heart of Mid-Lothian"* (Edinburgh: Constable and Company, 1818). The trial of Andrew Wilson, the smuggler, is included here, though not, as such, the trial of Helen Walker's sister. The Porteous trial was reproduced in a modern series of "Causes Célèbres of Scotland" rather like those said to be planned by Hardie in Scott's fictional frame for *The Heart of Mid-Lothian:* William Roughland, ed., *The Trial of Captain Porteous* (Glasgow and Edinburgh: William Hodge, 1909). This volume actually advertises a series by Hodge & Co. entitled "Notable Scottish Trials." The book is dedicated to "The Honourable Lord Ardwall, A Former President of the Edinburgh Sir Walter Scott Club."

12. By the time he wrote *The Heart of Mid-Lothian,* Scott had so much heeded the suggestion that he might be the Shakespeare of his age that he began cultivating more marked connections between his novels and Shakespeare's plays: *Hamlet* and *The Bride of Lammermoor, Henry IV* and *The Legend of Montrose, The Merchant of Venice* and *Ivanhoe.* Further evidence of the rewriting of *Measure for Measure* as *The Heart of Mid-Lothian* lies in reprise of the civil magic of Shakespeare's "fantastical Duke of the dark corners" in the description of the Duke of Argyle as the "benevolent enchanter" whose "rod" effects such wondrous changes in Jeanie's world in the later chapters (chap. 43). Scott makes the comparison of himself and Shakespeare explicit in the brief envoy with which he closes *The Legend of Montrose,* and the "Tales" series as a whole: "Mr. Cleishbotham bore the same resemblance to Ariel, as he at whose voice he rose doth to the sage Prospero; and yet, so fond are we of the fictions of our own fancy, that I part with him, and all his imaginary localities, with idle reluctance" (TML3, *Legend,* chap. 15).

"Ought Reuben Butler in conscience to accept of this preferment in the Kirk of Scotland, subject as David at present thought that establishment was to the Erastian encroachments of the civil power" (chap. 43). Deliberation on this point leads David "to lay down his own rules for guiding the conscience of his friend" (chap. 43) and to engage in a series of other vaguely comic encounters, including "his lengthened argument for and against the holy state of matrimony" (chap. 43). Indeed, by the final chapters of the novel, when David and Reuben are still involved in discussing "many cases of nicety, such as in owning certain defections, and failing to testify against certain backslidings of the time," it is Jeanie Deans herself who becomes "a mediating spirit, who endeavoured, by the alkaline smoothness of her own disposition, to neutralize the acidity of theological controversy" (chap. 47). This is the literalization of the figure of the "hussie case," or the figurative extension of the object itself.

Suppose, then, we take legal and moral casuistry as the two sides of the discipline of *The Heart of Mid-Lothian* and the legal case of Porteous and the moral case of Jeanie as the two sides of the case itself. What sort of case is defined as a relation between a legal and a moral case? We find an answer to this question, I think, in the work of one of Scott's most powerful Scottish-Enlightenment mentors, Adam Smith. It should be recalled that the concluding chapter to Smith's *Theory of Moral Sentiments* provided a thumbnail history of casuistry. In that same section, by way of a laborious analysis of the case of whether one must honor a promise extorted by a highwayman, Smith attempts to "shew wherein consists the difference between casuistry and jurisprudence" and then qualifies his point:

> But though this difference be real and essential, though those two sciences propose quite different ends, the sameness of the subject has made such a similarity between them, that the greater part of authors, whose professed design was to treat of jurisprudence, have determined the different questions they examine, sometimes according to the principles of that science, and sometimes according to those of casuistry, without distinguishing, and perhaps without being themselves aware of when they did the one and when the other.[13]

The "different ends" proposed by the sciences of jurisprudence and casuistry had already been distinguished by Smith in respect to their scope of reference— the one being concerned with right, the other (roughly) with goodness:

> Those who write upon the principles of jurisprudence, consider only what the person to whom the obligation is due ought to think himself entitled to exact by force; what every impartial spectator would approve of him for exacting, or what a judge or arbiter, to whom he had submitted his case, and who had undertaken to do him justice, ought to oblige the other person to suffer or to perform. The casuists, on the other hand, do not so much examine what it is that might properly be exacted by force, as what it is that the person who owes the obligation ought to think himself bound to perform, from the most sacred and scrupulous regard

13. Smith, *Theory of Moral Sentiments* (Indianapolis: Liberty Press, 1969), p. 525. All page references will hereafter appear in the text.

to the general rules of justice and from the most conscientious dread either of wronging his neighbour or of violating the integrity of his own character. It is the end of jurisprudence to prescribe rules for the decisions of judges and arbiters. It is the end of casuistry to prescribe rules for the conduct of a good man. (pp. 520–21)

Given the seeming clarity of this distinction, one might wonder that any confusion between the two ways of writing about the rules of morality could arise, but Smith himself locates the level on which these "sciences" can be likened to each other at the very start of this section: "Of the Manner in Which Different Authors have Treated of the Practical Rules of Morality." His own "treatment" proves acutely relevant to Scott's fable.

Smith's opening gambit is to distinguish justice from the other virtues by suggesting that justice is the only one for which "precise and accurate" rules of morality can be established—"those of all the other virtues are loose, vague, and indeterminate." And just as there are different degrees of accuracy for the different virtues' rules of morality, Smith goes on to say, so there are differences in literary treatment of these rules. "Those authors who have endeavoured to collect and digest them into systems," he says, "have [accordingly] done it in two different manners" (p. 517). One set of authors has treated all of morality with the looseness appropriate to the virtues other than justice, while another set of authors has treated all of morality with the sort of accuracy of which only justice is susceptible. Since he is speaking of *authors* and their modes of composition ("collection" and "digestion"), Smith describes these two modes of moral inquiry in literary terms. The first group (those of the loose method) "have written like critics, the second like grammarians" (p. 516). It is, thus, insofar as scientists of jurisprudence and scientists of casuistry are both "grammarians" of the moral life that they are liable, in spite of differences of approach that Smith carefully spells out, to being confused with each other, even in their own writings. This large group of moral grammarians includes "all the casuists of the middle and latter ages of the Christian church, as well as all those who, in this and in the preceding century, have treated of what is called natural jurisprudence" (p. 520). Not content with general characterizations of "that tenor of conduct which they would recommend to us," this set of moralists tries "to lay down exact and precise rules for the direction of every circumstance of our behaviour." They deal, in other words, in the handling of cases. That is what makes them "grammarians." Further, since "justice is the only virtue with regard to which such exact rules can properly be given, it is this virtue that has chiefly fallen under the consideration of those two different sets of writers." They deal, to use a distinction that is itself grammatical, in the handling of cases where the issue, paradigmatically at least, is the relation of obliquity to "rightness."

Understanding this much about Smith's analysis, we are in a position to rec-ognize how it informs Scott's way of structuring *The Heart of Mid-Lothian* in the juxtaposition of the two kinds of cases, moral and legal, and also how the novel follows Smith's characterization of jurisprudence and casuistry as, at one level, alike. In an early comic scene, for example, Scott introduces us to two pedants, Bartoline Saddletree and Reuben Butler. Saddletree is a saddle maker hobby-horsical about the Scottish legal system, who leaves his wife to tend his business while he attends court and gossips about the proceedings. Butler, who matures into a character worthy of Jeanie Deans by the end of the novel, begins his career in this story as a supercilious tutor in Latin. Playing out their little farce in the dire circumstances of the Porteous affair, they are ironically identified, re-spectively, as the masters of "the laws of Scotland" and "those of syntax" (TML2, chap. 4). Saddletree, master of the laws of Scotland, is characteristically holding forth with his neighbors, "laying down, with great precision, the law upon Porteous's case" for some acquaintances outside his shop in the Lucken-booths quarter of Edinburgh (chap. 4). (He will later do the same for "the case of Effie (or Euphemia) Deans" pronouncing it "one of those cases of murder presumptive" [chap. 5].) He is in the midst of making the absurd argument—accurately summarized by his neighbor, Plumdamas, as claiming that "John Porteous's case wad hae been better if he had begun firing before any stanes were flung at a'" (chap. 4)—when he is interrupted by Reuben Butler, who will lay down the law on a different aspect of case in Saddletree's discourse, charging that Saddletree mistook the dative *cuivis ex populo* for the nominative *quivis ex populo*. He mistook an oblique case, in other words, for a right or true one.

We recall that De Quincey, in "Casuistry and Duelling," summarizes his ar-gument for the necessary supplement of a moral system with a casuistry—casu-ists are "moral attorneys," he says—by insisting that doubtful cases occur every day to thinking persons because the conditions of ordinary life are necessarily imperfect. His metaphor was also from linguistics: "*Casuistry,* the very word *ca-suistry* expresses the science which deals with such *cases:* for as a case, in the de-clension of a noun, means a falling away, or a deflection from the upright nominative (rectus), so a case in ethics implies some falling off, or deflection from the high road of catholic morality."[14] What makes it inconvenient to dis-miss this connection in *The Heart of Mid-Lothian* is that Reuben Butler, in the second half of his conversation with Saddletree, makes the same distinction in pedantically attempting to enlighten Saddletree a second time, with still further explanation, on the usage of *quivus* and *cuivus:*

---

14. De Quincey, "Casuistry of Duelling"-see above, chapter 4.

"Give me your patience, Mr. Saddletree, and I'll explain the discrepancy in three words," said Butler, as pedantic in his own department, though with infinitely more judgment and learning, as Bartoline was in his self-assumed profession of the law—"Give my your patience for a moment—You'll grant that the nominative case is that by which a person or thing is nominated or designed, and which may be called the primary case, all others being formed from it by alterations of the termination in the learned languages, and by prepositions in our modern Babylonian jargons. . . . And the dative case . . . is that in which any thing is given or assigned as properly belonging to a person, or thing—You cannot deny that, I am sure."

"I am sure I'll no grant it though," said Saddletree.

"Then, what the *deevil* d'ye take the nominative and the dative cases to be?" said Butler, hastily, and surprised at once out of his decency of expression and accuracy of pronunciation. (chap. 5)

Scott's comic allegory elaborates Smith's point about the scientists of justice as case-conscious "grammarians" by producing a grammarian whose concern is with the law of the case, and particularly with the "erect" or "right" case as opposed to the oblique. To see what larger issue might be at stake here it is necessary to understand Smith's particular criticism of casuistry in both its moral and jurisprudential form, and this in turn requires some attention to Smith's logic of distinction (as distinct from his logic of similarity).

Smith's first point is that, since justice is only one of the virtues, it does not exhaust the possibilities or demands of the moral life. For Smith, as we have seen, justice involves a system of *rights,* in the first place, and *obligations* only as a consideration of "what the person to whom the obligation is due ought to think himself entitled to exact by force, or what a judge . . . ought to oblige the other person to perform." Legal obligations occur only as required by the system of rights that is encoded in positive law—positive law itself being understood as an incarnation of the "natural rights" of natural jurisprudence.[15] What follows from this, for Smith, is that jurisprudence should concern itself only with rules for the decisions of judges, not with rules for the conduct of a good person. The conduct of a good person, the person who deserves not only to be unpunished by the law but also praised by other persons, is the result of a judgment otherwise guided. The problem with the "works of the casuists," says Smith, is that they tried "to direct, by precise rules, what it belongs to feelings and sentiment only to judge of" (p. 533). The effort to produce a rational and minute calibration of precept to situation must necessarily fail, and because it does fail the casuist also fails to achieve influence in the only ethical domain that counts. This domain is where feelings and sentiments have their proper place. Smith calls it "the heart": "That frivolous accuracy which they attempt to introduce into subjects which do not admit of it, almost necessarily betrayed

15. See p. 535: "Every system of positive law may be regarded as a more or less imperfect attempt towards a system of natural jurisprudence."

them into those dangerous errors, and at the same time rendered their works dry and disagreeable, abounding in abstruse and metaphysical distinctions, but incapable of *exciting in the heart* any of those emotions which it is the principal use of books of morality to excite" (my italics) (pp. 534–35).

The ability to speak of and to the heart, it turns out, is the special province and power of that other set of writers on moral issues, the ones whom Smith calls the "critics" (as opposed to the grammarians). This group, says Smith, "have not affected to lay down many precise rules that are to hold good unexceptionably in all particular cases. They have only endeavoured to ascertain, as far as language is capable of ascertaining, first, wherein consists *the sentiment of the heart,* upon which each particular virtue is founded . . . ; and, secondly, what is the general way of acting . . . to which each of those sentiments would direct us" (p. 518). It is clear from Smith's tone here, and indeed from the general tenor of his argument in *The Theory of Moral Sentiments,* that he not only valorizes the work of these "authors" but also that this book itself would in some sense place him among their number. In the final pages of the last section of this very long discourse, Smith spells out his conclusion about the various approaches to writing about morality. Only two of the three parts of moral philosophy, he says, ethics and jurisprudence, are useful. Jurisprudence is useful in determining the relation of positive to natural law, while ethics is useful in the study and gradual strengthening of the character who judges in particular circumstances. "Casuistry," however, which confuses the tasks of both in its obsession with formalizing applications of law to circumstance, "ought to be rejected altogether."

In proposing that we read *The Heart of Mid-Lothian* as assimilating to itself the conceptual structure of Smith's massively influential treatise, then, I mean initially to suggest that, in the novel, too, a "grammarian's" discourse of casuistry (a conjunction of a mistaken ethics and a mistaken jurisprudence) stands opposed to a "critic's" discourse of sentimentality. The heart of the case of *The Heart of Mid-Lothian* would therefore be understood as an opposition between the case *and* the heart. But just as Smith uses the case of "the man who promises a highwayman under duress" to explain the failure of casuistry to do the work of honorable sentiment, so Scott too must be understood to be exploring the relation between the case and the heart in the form of a higher-level case.

The triggering episode of the Porteous affair involves Captain Porteous's handling of an unruly crowd during the execution of Andrew Wilson, a convicted smuggler. Here is how Scott sets up the prior case of Wilson, the one that aroused such popular support in the first place:

> The county of Fife, bounded by two friths on the south and north, and by the sea on the east, and having a number of small seaports, was long famed for maintaining successfully a contra-

band trade; and as there were many seafaring men residing there, who had been pirates and buccaneers in their youth, there were not wanting a sufficient number of daring men to carry it on. Among these, a fellow, called Andrew Wilson, originally a baker in the village of Path-head, was particularly obnoxious to the revenue officers. He was possessed of great personal strength, courage, and cunning,—was perfectly acquainted with the coast, and capable of conducting the most desperate enterprises. On several occasions, he succeeded in baffling the pursuit and researches of the king's officers; but he became so much the object of their suspicious and watchful attention, that at length he was totally ruined by repeated seizures. The man became desperate. He considered himself as robbed and plundered; and took it into his head, that he had a right to make reprisals as he could find opportunity. Where the heart is prepared for evil, opportunity is seldom wanting. This Wilson learned, that the Collector of the Customs at Kirkaldy had come to Pittenweem, in the course of his official round of duty, with a considerable sum of public money in his custody. As the amount was greatly within the value of the goods which had been seized from him, Wilson felt no scruple of conscience, in resolving to reimburse himself for his losses, at the expense of the Collector and the revenue. He associated with himself one Robertson, and two other idle young men, whom, having been concerned in the same illicit trade, he persuaded to view the transaction in the same justifiable light in which he himself considered it. (TML2, chap. 2)

Wilson's process of deliberation demonstrates what Smith describes as the conflation of jurisprudence with moral casuistry. Confronting a situation in which he must settle on an appropriate course of action, Wilson operates by the jurisprudential notion of, as Smith explains it, the rightness of exacting by force that which one is rightly due, but Wilson fails to see that the judgment of what one is rightly due is for judiciary officials to determine. He allows the corrupt form of jurisprudential thinking to become one with a casuistical impulse to invent a rule of application of principle to his own circumstances. The principle of justice becomes the pretext of justification. These are conditions in which "character" lacks strength, the conscience lacks appropriate scruple, and "the heart" is prepared for an opportunity, never long in coming, to do evil.

How does the "heart" shore itself up against the dual danger of a perverted jurisprudence and a pernicious casuistry? Smith's answer to this seems to lie in what might be called a "theory of communicative exchange" (taking Habermas only slightly out of context) and said to be informed by a loose ideal of sincerity. The heart strengthens itself by sharing itself and encouraging others to do likewise:

> We all desire . . . to feel how each other is affected, to penetrate into each other's bosoms, and to observe the sentiments and affections which really subsist there. The man who indulges us in this natural passion, who invites us into his heart, who, as it were, sets open the gates of his breast to us, seems to exercise a species of hospitality more delightful than any other. No man, who is in ordinary good temper, can fail of pleasing, if he has the courage to utter his real sentiments as he feels them, and because he feels them. It is this unreserved sincerity which renders even the prattle of a child agreeable. How weak and imperfect soever the views of the open-hearted, we take pleasure to enter into them. . . . (pp. 531–32)[16]

16. Smith actually discusses the case of infanticide at some length on p. 342.

The natural pleasures of openhearted communication make it possible for a human subject to learn a better way with cases than the one proposed by the grammarians. It is the mode of "sympathy," touted from the start of Smith's book, as the capacity to enter into "the case of another." Indeed, case is used throughout *The Theory of Moral Sentiments* as if it were synonymous with "bosom" and as if both were synonymous with "heart." One's "heart," in this sense, is just sensibility to the specific situation one inhabits. Insofar as another can share that sensibility, two hearts can beat as one, as we are in effect asked to imagine in the cases of Jeanie Deans and Reuben Butler in the distended Arcadian epilogue. On this account, the case of *The Heart of Mid-Lothian* is kept open by the openheartedness that it posits as its highest value.[17]

However, insofar as sensibility involves the capacity to be moved by one's immediate situation, such a capacity is itself inexorably conditioned on one's *historical* situation. The general state of the "manners" of an age, both in Smith's account and in Scott's fiction, deeply conditions the possibilities for ethical formation. The same holds true for legal-political formation. The whole issue of "accuracy and precision" with which Smith begins that final section—that justice admits of it in a way that the other virtues do not—turns out to have an important historical dimension. The science of jurisprudence presumes that, in well-governed states, rules are prescribed for regulating the decisions of judges, and that "these rules are, in general, intended to coincide with those of natural justice." In a striking litotes, Smith then concedes that it "does not, indeed, always happen that they do so in every instance." The "warping" of positive law from natural justice can derive from either government interest or individual interest. Then there is the larger historical consideration:

> In some countries, the rudeness and barbarism of the people hinder the natural sentiments of justice from arriving at that accuracy and precision which, in more civilized nations, they naturally attain to. Their laws are, like their manners, gross, and rude, and undistinguishing. In other countries, the unfortunate constitution of their courts of judicature hinders any regular system of jurisprudence from ever establishing itself among them, though the improved manners of the people may be such as would admit of the most accurate. In no country, do the decisions of positive law coincide exactly, in every case, with the rules which the natural sense of justice would dictate. Systems of positive law, therefore, though they deserve the greatest authority, as the records of the sentiments of mankind in different ages and nations, yet can never be regarded as accurate systems of the rules of natural justice. (p. 536)

The historicity of sentiments, a condition here underlined in the claim that systems of positive law are nothing more (though also nothing less) than "records of the sentiments of mankind in different ages and nations," emerges against the

---

17. Jeanie's case for sister Effie, her plea for her cause, carries the day precisely because of the open-hearted "eloquence" that so moves the Queen (TML2, chap. 37).

presumed background of the timeless rules of natural justice. In the positing of that relationship between historically determinate systems of sentiment and the pure principles of jurisprudence as such, Smith knows he has pursued his "ethical" inquiry, the "critical" (as opposed to the "grammatical") moral inquiry, as far as it will go. It only remains for him to promise to address such topics in another book—that is, (in the words of his final paragraph) to "give an account of the general principles of law and government and of the different revolutions they have undergone in the different ages and periods of society" (p. 537).

From this perspective, then, one which is at least implicit in Smith's *Theory of Moral Sentiments,* we might say that "history" suspends the case of *The Heart of Mid-Lothian,* keeps it unresolved. For we may ask: if open heartedness is natural and an aid to virtue, how is it that hearts ever close? How is it that sensibility fails to be shared in such a way as to strengthen the hearts of a community to the tasks of virtue? Just as Scott's answer to such questions seems to have to do with the institutional conditions of life in early eighteenth-century Scotland, so Smith points to specific institutional formations of, and medieval legacies left to, early modern Europe more generally. In this connection, indeed, Smith offers a brief history of the origin of works of casuistry, which traces them to the historical function of the Catholic Church in relation to "the custom of auricular confession, introduced by the Roman Catholic superstition, in times of barbarism and ignorance" (p. 525). Auricular confession imposed an ecclesiastical form of regimentation on the free and easy commerce that human hearts should naturally enjoy with each other. In the distress of conscience, as in other distress, people "are naturally eager to disburden themselves," and whatever shame they feel is "fully compensated by that alleviation of their uneasiness which the sympathy of their confidant seldom fails to occasion" (p. 526). Formalized auricular confession enabled the Catholic priesthood to arrogate power to itself by exploiting this natural sentiment and thus increasing the range of their monopoly in cultural capital:

> A numerous and artful clergy had, in those times of superstition, insinuated themselves into the confidence of almost every private family. They possessed all the little learning which the times could afford, and their manners, though in many respects rude and disorderly, were polished and regular compared with those of the age they lived in. . . . Being considered as the great judges of right and wrong, they were naturally consulted about all scruples that occurred . . . It was not difficult for the clergy, therefore, to get it established as a general rule that they should be entrusted with what it had already become fashionable to entrust them. (pp. 526–27)

To "qualify themselves" for this more official role, they began to collect and codify "what are called cases of conscience," and "hence the origin of books of casuistry." In Smith's account, the codification of confessional cases goes hand

in hand with the ecclesiastical usurpation of the natural impulses of human beings to confide freely in each other.

Scott's novel, as I read it, registers the limitations of Smith's account in its acknowledgment of Smith's fantasy of disembodiment. Others have written on
the way in which *sexuality* poses an obstacle to Smith's conception of social
sympathy.[18] What I have in view here is a similar problem in relation to *institutionality*. Smith seems to imagine a mode of confidentiality beyond institution-
alized media or genres, as if "confession" could literally occur, as we say in a
familiar figure of speech, heart to heart. Scott extends the historicization of the
case implicit in Smith to a point Smith does not reach. In framing of the larger
"confession" of the HEART by way of a reference to the contemporary genre
of the execution day broadside, with its motivations and expediencies ("the
hawkers . . . shouting a confession the culprit never heard of"), Scott refuses
himself Smith's fantasy of transcendence. It is not by naive openheartedness, as
such, but rather by insisting at every turn on the institutionality of the media,
genres, and practices of his commitment to the court of "sentiments and feelings," that Scott keeps the case of the heart open—disclosed—in the end.

2. Caption and Conversation: Scott's Explanatory Words

I have offered, by way of a familiar formalist logic, that the problem of integrity
in *The Heart of Mid-Lothian* can be understood in terms of the problem of its
closure or nonclosure. The gap in the unclosed circle of Jeanie's journey opens,
in the final chapters, into the distended pastoral epilogue with Jeanie and
Reuben Butler in the "Highland Arcadia" of book 4. Apropos of Jolles's notion
that the case form is always defined by its irresolution, by its tendency to generate a series, I suggested earlier that the notorious problem of closure in this
novel is a function of its self-conscious commitment to the case form, a function of the degree to which casuistry is conspicuous there, and that the emphasis on the placement of this story in a sequence or collection speaks likewise to
this point. We recall here Peter Pattieson's account of the immediate circumstances of his composition of the narrative that his first chapter frames and introduces: "This sort of conversation passed away the evening till the early hour
when Mr Dunover chose to retire to rest, and I also retreated to take down
memorandums of what I had learned, in order to add another narrative to those
which it had been my chief amusement to collect, and to write out in detail.
The two young men ordered a broiled bone, Madeira negus, and a pack of

18. See, for example, Martha C. Nussbaum, *Love's Knowledge: Essays on Philosophy and Literature* (New York: Oxford University Press, 1990), pp. 338–46.

cards, and commenced a game at picquet" (TML2, chap. 1). The pleasures of the card table may make it unlikely that Halkit will ever get to that collection of "the Cause Célèbres of Scotland" that he claims to have planned, and they will soon, the narrative informs us, be caught up again in their quotidian legal work: "Both have been since engaged in the great political cause of Bubbleburgh and Bitem, a summary case, and entitled to particular dispatch; but which, it is thought nevertheless, may outlast the duration of the parliament to which the contest refers" (chap. 1). But the author of these words—call him Pattieson/Cleishbotham/Scott—both works at the lawyer's game and plays at their work. Through earnest and game, this author, however we name him, carries on with "Tales of My Landlord," second series—not to mention with Waverley novels as a larger enterprise. Like the lawyers, he will keep the case in play beyond the duration of the institutions "to which the context refers."

In the conclusion to *The Heart of Mid-Lothian,* the short paragraph addressed simply to "READER" appears (below a break marked by three asterisks) after the final words of the narrative proper: ". . . this simple pair lived beloved, and died lamented":

> READER—This tale will not be told in vain, if it shall be found to illustrate the great truth, that guilt, though it may attain temporal splendour, can never confer real happiness; that the evil consequences of our crimes long survive their commission, and, like the ghosts of the murdered, for ever haunt the steps of the malefactor; and that the paths of virtue, though seldom those of worldly greatness, are always those of pleasantness and peace. (chap. 52)

One might be tempted to conclude that this conclusion amounted to something, that it is meant to supply the moral sentence that brings the disjointed narrative syntax of this rambling story into coherence. There is a question, however, about how we situate this summary. Who speaks it? The fact that it is bears its own salutation—"READER"—seems to place it outside the frame defined by the previous narrative act. Is this Peter Pattieson or Jedediah Cleishbotham? To complicate matters, there is yet a further paragraph that follows this conclusion, one that marks it as a conclusion, and that bears its own mark of separation:

> L'Envoy. by JEDEDIAH CLEISHBOTHAM.
>
> ---
>
> Thus, concludeth the Tale of "THE HEART OF MID-LOTHIAN," which hath filled more pages than I opined. The Heart of Mid-Lothian is now no more, or rather it is transferred to the extreme side of the city, even as the Sieur Jean Baptiste Poquelin hath it, in his pleasant comedy called Le Médecin Malgré lui, where the simulated doctor wittily replieth to a charge, that he had placed the heart on the right side, instead of the left, "*Cela étoit autrefois ainsi, mais nous avons changé tout cela.*" Of which witty speech, if any reader shall demand the purport, I have only to respond, that I teach the French as well as the Classical tongues, at the easy rate of five shillings per quarter, as my advertisements are periodically making known to the public. (chap. L'Envoy)

If there is no way of ruling Cleishbotham out as a candidate author of the moral that precedes the "envoy," then to take the sententious summary of the novel's account as a resolution of its complex case is to risk crediting a country pedant hawking his meager learning with powers of judgment not obviously within his capacities. In other words, to accept the "resolution" of the case of *The Heart of Mid-Lothian* as provided is to raise again, on a different level, the question of the relationship of situation to judgment, scene to explanation. Pursuing this reading in the light of Jolles's analysis, we would expect to see that as one case in the series is "resolved," another crops up in its wake. So we will, though within a newly articulated sense of "scene."

Although the first series of "Tales of My Landlord" (1817), the one featuring *Old Mortality,* was followed by *Rob Roy* (1817), the second series, constituted solely by *The Heart of Mid-Lothian* (1818) was followed directly by *The Bride of Lammermoor* (1819). As it happens, this novel is one in which the relation of primary narrative to primary frame is peculiarly vexing.[19] What I am provisionally calling the "primary frame" of *The Bride of Lammermoor,* only one of many frames in the book, is the one that relates the narrative to the fictional horizon of the "Tales of My Landlord," the domain of the tales' narrator, Peter Pattieson.[20] Pattieson's narrative of origin for the story told in *The Bride,* perhaps the most enigmatic of his many frame narratives, has to do with his friend Dick Tinto, a hard-luck painter, and with Pattieson's recollections of some "conversations" in which the story of the ill-starred lovers was first broached by Tinto. The main subject broached in these conversations, in a reflexive move characteristic of Scott's prefatory strategies, is Pattieson's progress, to date, as a writer of narrative, especially in *Old Mortality* and *The Heart of Mid-Lothian.* As in the instance of the witty Dedicatory Epistle to *Ivanhoe* (written just months later), the text that Lukács used for his theorization of the Waverley novels, the introductory material for *The Bride of Lammermoor* can be immensely illuminating of Scott's narrative self-understanding.

19. In addition to terminating perhaps the most sophisticated of the subseries within the larger project loosely termed the Waverley novels, the publication of *The Bride of Lammermoor* in "Tales of My Landlord," 3d series, also marks the end of a phase of Scott's career as the last entry in the first published collection of the Scott's novels, *Ballantyne's Waverley Library* (1819), and as the last in the unbroken series of "Scotch novels" before Scott turned to English subject matter in *Ivanhoe.*

20. The deceased Pattieson was a retired schoolteacher of Gandercleugh, in the Scottish Borders, who made a hobby of redacting various documents and traditionary stories into written narratives. These he left behind to one Jedediah Cleishbotham, who, as I have noted, is editing them seriatim for publication. In chapter 1, we find a humorously self-referential account by Pattieson of how he came by the particular tale he is about to relate: in this instance the tale of how a secret vow of engagement between two lovers was broken through the interposition of a second engagement on the part of the young woman's mother and how the broken engagement led to catastrophe for all parties concerned.

The central conversation in the introductory chapter of this novel is triggered when Tinto's initial praise for Pattieson's works gives way to what he offers as a searching criticism: " 'Your characters,' he said, 'my dear Pattieson, make too much use of the *gob box;* they patter too much . . . there is nothing in whole pages but mere chat and dialogue' " (TML3, chap. 1).[21] In an important aside, Pattieson informs us that Tinto had learned such "elegant phraseology" as *gob box* "while painting the scenes of an itinerant company of players" thus implicitly defining a "scene" as a context for dramatic exchange—as distinct from, say, a picturesque landscape (TML3, chap. 1). This connection proves relevant both in the elaboration of the critique and in its applications, for it indicates that a "scene" is a spectacle of human conflict. A "scene" necessarily involves the staging of some incident for which dialogue would be an imaginable (although, to Tinto, an inferior) mode of representation. It may thus be likened to the sense in which Kenneth Burke uses the term when, in the course of elaborating his dramatistic framework for the investigation of motive, he allows that "variants of the scene-agent ratio abound in typical nineteenth-century thought" because of its peculiar interest in motive.[22]

What Tinto prefers to the dramatic or dialogical mode of representing a scene is not at first clear. When he responds to Peter's reply that, in accordance with an ancient injunction ("Speak, that I may know thee" [chap. 1]), he needs dialogue for purposes of characterizing his dramatis personae, Tinto's positive claim is expressed as a preference for the image over the word. Whatever may be the place of dialogue in ordinary human affairs, argues Tinto, things are different in the sphere of art, or more precisely in what he calls the "fine arts": "I will not allow that a professor of the fine arts has occasion to embody the idea of his scene in language, in order to impress upon the reader its reality and its effect" (chap. 1). Tinto's ensuing comments make it clear that when he speaks against the artist's embodying the idea of his scene in language, the reference is not to language in general, but to *dramatic language,* to what he will call "talk" as distinct

21. Fiona Robertson's recent edition of *The Bride of Lammermoor* (Oxford: Oxford University Press, 1991), based on the Magnum edition of 1830, has an extraordinarily thorough set of notes and a useful introduction.

22. GM, p. 9. For various suggestions about how to use Burke's dramatism in performance-oriented critical analysis, see Timothy C. Murray, "Kenneth Burke's Logology: A Mock Logomachy," *Glyph* 2 (1977): 144–61, and, more recently, Art Borreca, "Political Dramaturgy: A Dramaturg's (Re)View," *The Drama Review* 37 (1993):56–79. For more on Burke, see Frank Lentricchia, *Criticism and Social Change* (Chicago: University of Chicago Press, 1983). For more on performance, see Mária Minich Brewer, "Performing Theory," *Theatre Journal* 37 (1985):13–30. See also Erving Goffman, *Frame Analysis: An Essay on the Organization of Experience* (Boston: Northeastern University Press, 1986), passim.

from "words."[23] Pattieson thus correctly takes Tinto to be arguing that, in prose fiction, the descriptive mode of representation should prevail over the dramatic.[24] The point is further revised and refined in response to Pattieson's next reply—that Tinto's critique fails to recognize the responsibilities to the ear as well as to the eye—when Tinto elaborates an analogy between the function of description in "fictitious writing" and the function of drawing and tinting in painting.[25] The crucial—and, as I shall argue, deeply ironized—application of Tinto's principle will be made only at the point when Pattieson acquiesces in Tinto's critique and in return is offered a subject that Tinto himself has "studied with a view to his own art" (chap. 1).

Tinto's mode of introducing the new narrative subject matter is to show Pattieson a sketch he has made of one of its climactic scenes, Pattieson's failure to respond to which sends Tinto into comic contortions:

> He held it at arms' length from me,—he held it closer,—he placed it upon the top of a chest of drawers, closed the lower shutters of the casement, to adjust a downward and favourable light,—fell back to the due distance, dragging me after him,—shaded his face with his hand, as if to exclude all but the favourite object,—and ended by spoiling a child's copy book, which he rolled up so as to serve for the darkened tube of an amateur. I fancy my expressions of enthusiasm had not been in proportion to his own, for he presently exclaimed with vehemence, "Mr Pattieson, I used to think you had a eye in your head." (chap. 1)

Having expressed chagrin at Pattieson's failure "to discover the subject and meaning" (chap. 1) of his sketch at a single glance, Tinto explicitly links this failure to Pattieson's mode of writing. The critique that had previously been grounded in Tinto's preference for the pictorial over the verbal, the narrative-

---

23. The distinction between "talk" and "words" is explicit in Tinto's ensuing remarks, which are discussed below. Tinto's "word," as I shall be suggesting, is a *logos* in the Platonic sense that includes the notion of providing an explanation or giving a reason.

24. "Description" does not oppose narration here, as it would do later, for example, in "Narrate or Describe," Lukács's famous essay on European realism before and after 1848. Rather, narrative and description are presented as going hand-in-hand, and both are being opposed to the dramatic or dialogical mode. Whereas, in "Narrate or Describe," Lukács had emphasized that narration is the mode of action, and description that of observation, here in Tinto's account both narration and description are associated with action, while the dramatic mode is invidiously associated with mere talk: Georg Lukács, "Narrate or Describe?" in *Writer & Critic and Other Essays,* ed. and trans. Arthur D. Kahn (New York: Grosset & Dunlap, 1970), pp. 110–48.

25. "The same rules, he contended, applied to both, and an exuberance of dialogue, in the former case, was a verbose and laborious mode of composition, which went to confound the proper art of fictitious narrative with that of the drama, a widely different species of composition, of which dialogue was the very essence. . . . But as nothing," said Dick, "can be more dull than a long narrative written upon the plan of a drama, so where you have approached most near to that species of composition, by indulging in prolonged scenes of mere conversation, the course of your story has become chill and constrained, and you have lost the power of arresting the attention and exciting the imagination . . . " (TML3, chap. 1).

descriptive over the dramatic, doing over saying, is now given a new formulation:

> You have accustomed yourself so much to these creeping twilight details of yours, that you are become incapable of receiving that instant and vivid flash of conviction, which darts on the mind from seeing the happy and expressive combinations of a single scene, and which gathers from the position, attitude, and countenance of the moment, not only the history of the past lives of the personages represented, and the nature of the business on which they are immediately engaged, but lifts even the veil of futurity, and affords a shrewd guess at their future fortunes. (chap. 1)

This last phrasing of the invidious distinction, perhaps the most invidious of all, plainly seeks to align Pattieson's mode with partiality and Tinto's with totality.

Ina Ferris has suggestively read this passage as implying Scott's criticism of Tinto: "[M]oments for Scott have neither constitutive nor inherently revelatory power," she writes, but rather "exist as traces, as highly complex traces of the working of diverse and unobservable forces that it is the business of the historical novelist to attempt to uncover."[26] I agree that a critical perspective is opened up on Tinto's position, but, while Ferris finds implicit in this passage Scott's distrust of "the whole idea of the moment," I want to read it, in the first instance, as Tinto's consideration of "the moment" in relation to some idea of the whole. For the power of synopsis to which Tinto lays claim is not limited to the "moment" in time but extends as well to the larger course of affairs—history of the past, immediate business, future fortunes—in which such a moment might be said to take place. The "uncovering" of the moment, in Tinto as in Ferris, occurs not as a "self-revelation" but as a *dis*covery by the historian whose sees its place in an overall scheme. The articulate form of such a discovery is the account of the traces of the moment, the "happy and expressive combinations of a single scene," in relation to the forces that produce them and follow from them.

To produce such an account of a moment or scene is to explain it, to give its logos. This concept of explanatory logos, the "word" of the scene as distinct from its "talk," is not only central to its introduction, but will also figure most crucially in the ensuing novel. Thus, for example, when on her wedding night Lucy attempts to murder the husband she is forced to marry in the place of Ravenswood (to whom she has been secretly betrothed), she enters a state of delirium from which she never recovers: "Convulsion followed convulsion, till they closed in death, without her being able to utter a word explanatory of the fatal scene" (chap. 32). Her inability to produce the logos for the scene of her catastrophe is signaled as the most noteworthy feature of her premature demise

---

26. Ina Ferris, *The Achievement of Literary Authority* (Ithaca, N.Y.: Cornell University Press, 1991), p. 221.

and, indeed, of the state to which she has been reduced by her mother's coercive methods. In short, the Tinto introduction prepares for the complexities of the novel's diegetic case by complicating a relation it makes crucial to the case dynamic—that of the "explanatory word" to the "scene."

At the start, Tinto criticizes Pattieson's narrative art by way of an invidious distinction between the pictorial and verbal, but he proves to be more invested in an equally invidious distinction between two different aspects of verbal representation: the dramatic use of words (Pattieson's way) as distinct from the narrative-descriptive use. Tinto's metaphorization of this distinction as that difference between the partiality of the "twilight detail" and the totality of the "lightning flash," however, permits us to refigure the distinction as between alternative ways of *placing* words in relation to a scene. That is, the words may be understood as spoken by characters in a scene, in which case they would count only as "talk" and would remain partial (in the sense that they would belong to one of the parties of the scene). Or they may be understood as placed outside the scene to synopsize it, in which case they would count as action rather than mere talk and achieve a total (as distinct from a partial) representation of the scene. In this latter event, the words might be said to capture—or more precisely, to *caption*—the scene. Hence the notion of the scene as the basis for the distinction between conversation and caption, for the latter is simply the distinction between words understood as placed inside or placed outside a frame of human conflict.

This kind of analysis in terms of language, scene, and explanation can also show how Tinto's own exemplary claim to totalization in chapter 1 is ironically qualified. After Tinto's riposte to Pattieson's modest suggestion that the sketch Tinto has shown him may involve "some reference to a love affair" between the young man and woman, Tinto mocks his reticence—"Do you really presume to form such a bold conjecture?" (chap. 1)—and then goes on to offer his own elaborate speculation about the meaning of the scene depicted. It is true that Tinto's ekphrasis proves quite consistent with the narrative about Edgar, master of Ravenswood, his love affair with Lucy Ashton, their secret troth-plight, and her mother's insistence that she break off this engagement in favor of one she has arranged between Lucy and Frank Hayston of Bucklaw. It is also true that this story in turn is broadly consistent with one that, in a yet later introduction for *The Bride,* Scott tells as part of his effort to identify the historical source for the novel, with historical prototypes of the various characters identified by name and family.[27] Yet, if Tinto is allowed to anticipate the conception of the

27. This is the introduction added to *The Bride of Lammermoor* for the Magnum edition of the novel in 1830.

story of the broken betrothal, it will be a matter of at least equal significance that that story itself—the one Donizetti relied on, with alterations, for virtually the whole of his celebrated operatic adaptation, *Lucia di Lammermoor* (1835)—is relegated to roughly the last third of Scott's novel.[28] The rest of the book really just establishes the framing for this narrative of the defeated love affair itself, just as that framing is in turn framed by the Tinto-Pattieson discussion of scene, captions, and conversational comments.

We can now recognize the force of the irony that works through that entire discussion. Every point that Tinto registers in his critique of what might be called Pattieson's "dramatism" is itself represented in the dramatic mode. What we are reading, after all, is precisely a conversation between the two characters, a fact that is pointedly signaled by one of Tinto's own critical comments: "I will be judged by most of your readers, Peter, should these tales ever become public, whether you have not given us a page of talk for every single idea which two words might have communicated, while the posture, manner, and incident, accurately drawn, and brought out by appropriate colouring, would have preserved all that was worthy of preservation, and saved these everlasting said he's and said she's, with which it has been your pleasure to encumber your pages" (chap. 1). This exchange itself is marked by exactly such indicators of speaker and speech throughout—"said he's and said she's"—as the passages I have already cited will attest. This very comment is introduced in Pattieson's narrative by the same sort of linguistic indicator: "said Tinto."

It is but an easy step from here to conclude that Tinto's pronouncements against conversational representation in favor of representation by caption are themselves placeable in a scene. And this conclusion must extend as well, and tellingly, to the summary comment Tinto produces for the sketch he shows to Pattieson: the comment that purports to synopsize that scene in a flash. Tinto's captioning of that scene, after all, is part of a conversation in another—that is, in the scene he is playing with Pattieson. The sense of that conversation as constituting a scene gains additional force when, in later illustrated editions of Scott's novels, the scene of the Tinto-Pattieson exchange over the sketch would be the first illustration a reader would come across in the novel—in effect a sketch of the encounter of Tinto and Pattieson over the meaning of the encounter shown on Tinto's sketch (fig. 7).

One can therefore imagine Tinto's synopsis of the Lammermoor sketch as

28. Ferris shows that since the earliest reviews, Scott's novels have been criticized for being "too slowly opened, and too hastily summed up." See *Achievement of Literary Authority*, p. 200. But the deferral of the titular narrative in *The Bride of Lammermoor* is protracted, even by Scott's own standards.

DICK TINTO AND THE AUTHOR.

Figure 7.   Dick Tinto shows Peter Pattieson the sketch that inspires the central narrative for *The Bride of Lammermoor.*

inscribed in a kind of caricaturist's word-balloon pointing to the mouth of Tinto, with a caption at the bottom explaining the scene in relation to the totality of the novel. Scott and his readers would have been quite familiar with such a layout of words and images from the growing circulation of political caricatures by George Cruikshank and others, which typically involved both forms of inscription at this time. Cruikshank was capable of producing strikingly reflexive instances of this form, sometimes in multiple receding frames of caption and conversation (fig. 8). In such an anatomy of the scene one can begin to visualize, as it were, the larger dialectical relation governing conversation and caption in Scott's text. It is as if he recognized in such a picture that the implicit subject of a conversation in a scene is always another scene, and the effort

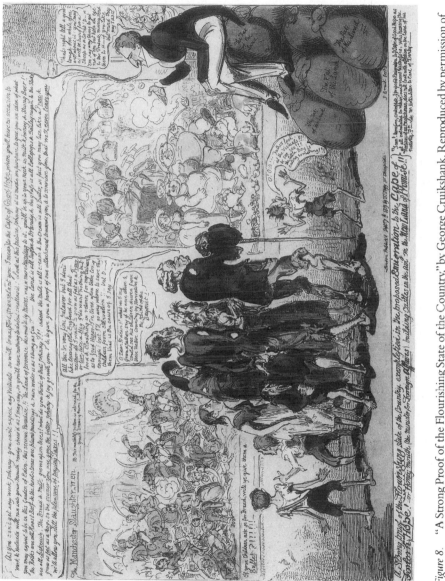

Figure 8. "A Strong Proof of the Flourishing State of the Country," by George Cruikshank. Reproduced by permission of the Huntington Library, San Marino, California.

to capture a scene can always be construed as occurring in the setting of another scene, which is not to say that the *mode* of scene setting must be uniform throughout. This dialectic, I believe, strongly governs the narrative of *The Bride of Lammermoor* as a whole, and indeed Scott's fiction more generally.

3. Making a Scene in *The Bride of Lammermoor*

If we therefore turn, for example, to the scene that corresponds in the novel to the sketch by Tinto, where Edgar Ravenswood confronts his fiancée, Lucy Ashton, and her mother, we note that it is played as a dramatic struggle over the meaning of an earlier scene, the scene of the lovers' secret betrothal. Ravenswood and Lady Ashton, here and elsewhere, wage a contest for the power to caption that scene, and each offers the strongest candidate captions he or she can contrive—Ravenswood describing it as a solemn engagement sworn between consenting adults, Lady Ashton as an agreement, according to holy writ, requiring the consent of the woman's parents. But as I have already suggested, the entire sequence of scenes in that final phase of the narrative, the rapid passage from betrothal to catastrophe, takes place in relatively few chapters. The first two thirds of the book narrates, in effect, a contest of scene setting for this denouement.

It is difficult to convey abstractly the degree of Scott's engagement with this contest through the greater part of his novel, though just a brief concrete sampling of this distinctive narrative strategy is possible here. The contest begins with the actual Lammermoor narrative itself, when, in the very first chapter of the story proper, we are presented with what is called, in a phrase that unmistakably echoes the Tinto vignette, a "scene . . . worthy of an artist's pencil" (TML3, chap. 2).[29] The scene in question is that of the funeral of the protagonist's father, the former Lord Ravenswood, whose death had been hurried along by the successful legal maneuvers of William Ashton to win from him his chief estate, Ravenswood Castle, and much of his wealth. The funeral takes place at the desolate castle to which son and father had repaired after the loss, and the main event of the "scene" in question arises out of a conflict between the young Master of Ravenswood, who contrary to Scottish law has arranged for his father's body to be received by an Episcopal priest, and the agent authorized by William Ashton to enforce the law proscribing the practice:

29. Most of the *Waverley* novels involve an opening act or movement of about a half-dozen chapters, usually followed by a conspicuously marked "new beginning": e.g., chap. 6 in *Waverley,* chap. 8 in *The Heart of Mid-Lothian,* chap. 6 in *Ivanhoe,* and so on. The technique, especially in view of its routinization, lends the sense of yet another formal layer in the arrangement of nested frames.

The presbyterian church-judicatory of the bounds, considering the ceremony as a bravading insult upon their authority, had applied to the Lord Keeper [Ashton], as the nearest privy-counsellor, for a warrant to prevent its being carried into effect; so that, when the clergyman had opened his prayer-book, an officer of the law, supported by some armed men, commanded him to be silent. An insult, which fired the whole assembly with indignation, was particularly and instantly resented by the only son of the deceased [Ravenswood]. . . . He clapped his hand on his sword, and, bidding the official person to desist at his peril from further interruption, commanded the clergyman to proceed. The man attempted to enforce his commission, but as an hundred swords at once glittered in the air, he contented himself with protesting against the violence which had been offered to him in the execution of his duty, and stood aloof, a sullen and moody spectator of the ceremonial, muttering as one who should say, "You'll rue the day that clogs me with this answer." (chap. 2)

How this scene is captioned—that is, how it is captured for representation and by which party—becomes very much the question at issue in the opening movement of the novel. Indeed, this first scene proves to be the subject of the very next scene, in which we shift to Ravenswood Castle and to William Ashton, the usurping lawyer who now presides there.

Just how the first scene figures—gets figured—in the second begins to make patent the narrative scheme I mean to be illustrating. The second scene opens with Ashton, at his desk, in conversation with the emissary who had been thwarted in his effort to enforce the ban on episcopal rituals at Wolf's Crag the day before. On hearing what is called "an exaggerated account" (chap. 3) of the affair, Ashton takes careful notes and then meditates on the sort of representation he will make of this scene in a report to the Scottish Privy-council. We are given access to Ashton's initial deliberations in the form of his mutterings to himself about how he must press his advantage against young Ravenswood lest some turning of the political tide enable Ravenswood to recoup the losses sustained by his father in earlier legal battles with Ashton: "These memoranda, properly stated to the Privy-council, cannot but be construed into an aggravated riot, in which the dignity both of the civil and ecclesiastical authorities stand committed. A heavy fine might be imposed—an order for committing him to Edinburgh or Blackness Castle seems not improper—even a charge of treason might be laid on many of these words and expressions . . . " (chap. 3). "Aggravated riot" and "treason" are—in the terms I have been developing—captions, abbreviated explanations, of that scene in which Ravenswood's own words to the officer had been part of the conversation.

The importance placed on the work of captioning this first scene may be measured by Scott's dilation of the moment of Ashton's decision to include the events of almost three chapters. Ashton's momentary hesitation over which label to apply is enough to permit his immediate circumstances to change. Into the library comes his daughter Lucy, who persuades him to take a walk with her before finishing his business. With the representation of the funeral episode still pending, Ashton and Lucy stroll the estate, talk with Blind Alice the prophet, hear her dire forecast, find themselves threatened by the charge of a runaway bull, and are saved by a musket shot by Ravenswood himself, who had come to his father's estate to try to settle matters with Ashton. It is Ashton's interpretation of the meaning and consequences of Ravenswood's rescue—together with his sense of Ravenswood's potential interest in his daughter and the uncertainty of the political situation—that induces him to write a far more lenient report of the funeral episode than he had planned: "Bred to casuistry, and well accustomed to practise the ambi-dexter ingenuity of the bar, it cost him little trouble to soften the features of the tumult which he had been at first so anxious to exaggerate" (chap. 5).

The first movement of *The Bride of Lammermoor* thus manages to conclude with chapter 5's account of the delivery of Ashton's report to the Privy-council and a representation of the debate on that report among its members. In the final sentence of this chapter and movement—"And so we close the scene on the Privy-council of that period" (chap. 5)—the use of the theatrical idiom is no more casual than when the funeral episode is described as a "scene . . . worthy of an artist's pencil." Both call up the dialectic that governs the Tinto exchange, in that the question of how Ashton will represent the earlier scene is crucially dependent on his sense of the scene *in which he is making his representation*. The Privy-council is the focus of the scene Ashton imagines himself operating in, but we come to see that there is a yet wider horizon in which to understand the changing scene of the Privy-council itself. This horizon provisionally circumscribes the narrative's yet wider range of reference, including the struggles between the Court of St. James in London and the exiled Court of St. Germain and between Whigs and Jacobites more generally. Indeed, these struggles themselves are defined in relation to the play of major social and economic forces as registered in the neighboring village of Wolf's Hope, especially in the emergent though tentative solidarity of the "feuars," who prove capable of some resistance to feudal claims on their wealth.

This first movement of the novel, then, is one in which verbal stage setting, while preparing the ground of later episodes in the book, is both conditioned by certain material circumstances and at the same time constitutive of the action to this point. The history is being made, but not under conditions of the maker's own choosing.[30] The limits of this kind of making are revealed

30. As we move on to the later scenes, we find that the terms of the Tinto exchange, at least as I have construed it, continue to define the terms of the narrative, for they too are scenes in which the action amounts to the framing of other scenes, and in which the theatrical metaphors

nowhere more clearly than in the comic theatricality of the Caleb Balderstone subplot, which so delighted Scott's early readers and audiences. The novel is relentless in exposing the effects of large scale economic and social changes—much for the better among the feuars in the village of Wolf's Hope, and much for the worse in the waning aristocratic household of Wolf's Crag.[31] Caleb, the faithful servant, vainly presumes on his master's increasingly archaic feudal authority in an effort to secure provisions for the empty castle larder, and goes to absurd lengths to hide or excuse the absence of provision. Caleb's art, too, is played by Scott very conspicuously as an affair of the sort of framing and stage setting introduced in the Tinto discussion. Indeed, Caleb's greatest triumph of artful captioning—which occurs when a thunderstorm lands Ravenswood, Ashton, and Lucy at Wolf's Crag, unannounced, and he is caught completely unprepared—is set off, in an unmistakable echo of the exchange in chapter 1, by "a flash of lightning" (chap. 10). In Caleb's case, the lightning bolt does not so much illuminate the scene of desolation of the castle as it becomes the occasion for him to exercise his narrative or "captioning" talents—while the lightning bolt "stunned all who were within hearing of it," it "had only served to awaken the bold and inventive genius of the flower of Majors-Domo" (chap. 11). In an outrageously transparent deployment of the rhetorical *occupatio*, Caleb interrupts Ravenswood and his guests to describe in detail the elaborate multicourse dinner that he had on hand but that had just been destroyed by the hand of nature. When Ravenswood, in mortification at the thinness of Caleb's cover story, attempts to silence him, Caleb resourcefully threatens him with

---

that we now associate with the problematic of the frame become especially prominent. For example, in the first scene of the novel's second movement or act, we find two conspirators against the Whig government awaiting Ravenswood in a tavern. Against the background of their citations from Dryden's dramatic poetry, they refer to themselves as stage-players "acting . . . in the Fatal Conspiracy" (TML3, chap. 6); it is a script in which Ravenswood, when he arrives, will refuse to play the role assigned him. It is as if he had overheard their conversing about "the risk belonging to these two terrible words, art and part" (TML3, chap. 6).

31. As in many narratives plotted as tragedy, it is for a long time unclear that *The Bride of Lammermoor* will not in fact sustain at least a modified comic outcome. As James Kerr puts it: "The fascinating twist of *The Bride* is that Scott provides the possibility of resolving the novel's central social conflict through the affair of Ravenswood and Lucy Ashton, but then describes the historical and psychological processes by which the projected marriage is thwarted." See *Fiction Against History: Scott as Storyteller* (Cambridge: Cambridge University Press, 1989), p. 12. For a fuller account of the thwarting and its implication for the larger issues of the novel, see Ian Duncan, *Modern Romance and the Transformation of the Novel: The Gothic, Scott, Dickens* (Cambridge: Cambridge University Press, 1992), pp. 135–46. For another good account of *The Bride* in relation to the Gothic novel—a form in which the problem of interpolation assumes a different character—see Fiona Robertson, *Legitimate Histories: Scott, Gothic, and the Authorities of Fiction* (Oxford: Clarendon Press, 1994), pp. 214–25.

what the narrator calls "scenes yet more ridiculous": "[I]f ye let me gang on quietly, I'se be moderate in my banquet; but if ye contradict me, de'il but I dress ye a dinner fit for a duke!" (chap. 11).

Caleb's futile attempt not so much to capture scenes as to explain them away provides a low-comic parallel to the stage setting undertaken by Ashton in this crucial midnovel sequence. Over the course of three successive scenes, Ashton attempts to explain or explain away the scenes of his legal confrontations with the Ravenswood family, including the most recent affair of the report to the Privy-council, and here again the very narrative is carried along by the work of casuistry. This is the point where Ashton begins, for entirely political reasons, to take seriously the prospect of a marriage between his daughter and Ravenswood, and Ashton believes that such a match might make an effective hedge against the possibility that the political tide of the times might turn against him and in favor of Ravenswood thus reversing the decisions that put him in possession of the Ravenswood fortune and estate. To assuage Ravenswood's enmity, Ashton therefore cast his prior court battles against the Ravenswood family in the most favorable light possible. Arriving at Wolf's Crag on a pretext, Ashton thus "seemed in the situation of a performer who has ventured to take upon himself a part which he finds himself unable to perform" (chap. 10).

The part that Ashton seeks to play in these central scenes is to offer a diegesis of the case between him and Ravenswood, a "statement of the matters which had been in debate betwixt their families" but framed in such a way as to serve his most immediate ends: to "stun and confuse Ravenswood's ideas" (chap. 16). In a displacement of the quarrel over the marital contract that is the novel's presumed subject, Scott here makes the (literally) central issue of the novel another contract, one between the two fathers. And it is the struggle over this contract that Ashton seeks to capture when he "commenced the history of a bond for twenty thousand marks, advanced by his father to the father of Allan Lord Ravenswood" (chap. 16). By contrast, the part that young Ravenswood plays in this scene of a struggle over the meaning of prior scenes is to suggest that it is inappropriately set: "'It is not in this place,' he said, 'that I can hear Sir William Ashton's explanation of the matters in question between us. It is not here, where my father died of a broken heart, that I can with decency or temper investigate the cause of his distress. I might remember that I was a son, and forget the duties of a host. A time, however, there must come, when these things shall be discussed in a place and in a presence where both of us will have equal freedom to speak and to hear'" (chap. 16). Ashton's reply to this is a statement that we may take as true in principle but misapplied to the present situation: "Any time, . . . any place, was alike to those who sought nothing but justice" (chap. 16). Ashton seeks far more than justice, or far less. He will be described pages later as someone who had spent a life "in securing advantages to himself by artfully working upon the passions of others" (chap. 16). It is also made clear that he has chosen this time and place with some care.

Although Ashton's talent for casuistry is evident from the start, this is the part of the novel when the play of word and scene begins to be figured more explicitly as a relationship of cases and courts. And if we think of a case as a scene of conflict to be resolved in another scene conceived as a court, a double question crucially arises, as it indeed it does for Edgar Ravenswood: not only what counts as an appropriate verbal specification of a scene? but also what counts as an appropriate court-scene for the resolution of a case? Ravenswood's countering summary of the case between himself and Ashton offers a long perspective on the dispute and summarizes one side of the larger ideological issue that the novel places at stake:

> [T]he lands of Ravenswood which you now occupy were granted to my remote ancestor for services done with his sword against the English invaders. How they have glided from us by a train of proceedings that seem to be neither sale, nor mortgage, nor adjudication for debt, but a non-descript and entangled mixture of all these rights—how annual-rent has been accumulated upon principal, and no nook or coign of legal advantage left unoccupied, until our interest in our hereditary property seems to have melted away like an icicle in thaw—all this you understand better than me. (chap. 16)

But when Ashton, the "consummate courtier," rejoins that his superior legal understanding ought be a reason for him to "explain the points of difference between them," Ravenswood counters that "it is in the Estates of the nation, in the supreme Court of Parliament, that we must parley together" (chap. 16). Of course, the very question of where such matters ought to be debated *is* being debated here, in the struggle to caption the case of *Ashton v. Ravenswood* in one way rather than another, to explain it in terms of one history rather than another (e.g., a history of the emergence of commercial merit or a history of the threatened extinction of aristocratic virtue). The question is how, where, and by whom the determination will be made as to what, in the words of the Magnum edition's version of this passage, is the "court of last resort."[32]

4. Scott and Sign Value

I cite these "twilight details" from *The Bride of Lammermoor* to show how deeply constitutive of the action of this novel is the dialectic of the scene and frame,

---

32. Sir Walter Scott, *The Waverley Novels,* 48 vols. (Edinburgh: Robert Cadell, 1829–33) 14:108.

drama and narrative, caption and conversation. Scott's engagement with the historiographical operation, as de Certeau calls it, is worked out in just these terms, much as the argument about the two irreducible reductions of that operation is worked out in de Certeau. I do wish to pose a further question about this dialectic in *The Bride of Lammermoor,* however, which has to do with what might be called the scene of the novel itself, the question of how, as it were, to characterize Scott's own scene in producing it. It is a question absolutely insisted on, it seems to me, by the way in which the progress of the narrative is structured, though at the same time it is strongly resisted by the novel's defensive tactics. It is insisted on by virtue of the novel's apparent disallowance of a form of representation beyond rhetoric and of caption outside conversation. It is resisted both by the novel's general posture of representational neutrality and by certain specific, though sometimes implicit claims it makes for its special discursive status.

By the posture of representational neutrality, I mean both a certain idiom—what Roland Barthes famously called the "preterite-dominated style" of the nineteenth-century novel—and a certain set of presuppositions.[33] The preterite narrative style means to be invisible, so it is not easy to identify its features. One might, however, look to the way in which episodes are introduced at the level of the paragraph. Consider the opening of the funeral narrative, for example: "It was a November morning, and the cliffs which overlooked the ocean were hung with thick and heavy mist, when the portals of the ancient and half-ruinous tower, in which Lord Ravenswood had spent the last and troubled years of his life, opened, that his mortal remains might pass forward to an abode yet more dreary and lonely" (TML3, chap. 2). The style here does not avoid affective characterization ("dreary and lonely"), but neither is it willing to go very far with it. It invokes a vaguely pathetic fallacy of the implicit metaphor "shroud of mist" but does not make the fallacy explicit. It speaks of death, and will shortly go on to narrate a (superficially) religious quarrel over the funeral, but it does not make a theological statement or take a theological stand. No mention is made of the place where the *spirit* of old Ravenswood might be headed when his "mortal remains" pass forward to their abode in the ground.

A passage such as this one thus prepares us to accept at face value the initial description I quoted earlier of the events at the funeral—the so-called scene worthy of an artist's pencil. It encourages us to read them naively, in spite of the

33. "The teleology common to the Novel and to narrated History," writes Barthes, "is the alienation of the facts: the preterite is the very act by which society affirms its possession of its past and its possibility"—*Writing Degree Zero and Elements of Semiology,* trans. Annette Lavers and Colin Smith (Boston: Beacon Press, 1967), pp. 32–33.

fact that precisely the representation of that scene becomes such a bone of contention in subsequent action. It discourages us from asking why that account should be accorded a place beyond all scenes of representational struggle. It would not, I think, be hard to construct a rhetorical analysis of the passage to suggest its idiomatic and ideological biases: an obvious place to start would be with the echo between those "hundred swords [that] at once glittered in the air" to resent the "insult" to the Ravenswood family and the "ten thousand swords" in Burke's *Reflections* that ought to have "leaped from their scabbards to avenge even a look that threatened [Marie Antoinette] with an insult" in 1789.[34] Nor will it do to lay off the rhetorical problem on to the narrative persona of Peter Pattieson, if only because there seems to be no discernible stylistic or narratological feature that distinguishes the actual telling of the story in the "Tales of My Landlord" from the earlier Waverley novels. Pattieson's defenses seem, for all the world, to be Scott's defenses and vice versa.

Perhaps the most important of these defenses comes from the part of the introductory chapter (just before Pattieson's conversation with Tinto) that has posed the greatest problem for commentators on the novel, what George Levine has called "the extraordinarily irrelevant narrative of Dick's career." Levine's reading of chapter 1 is that Scott is "merely playing" and that he thus misses opportunities to problematize the narrative and historiographical issues in which his project is involved: "Comfortable among narrative conventions, unalarmed by confusions between fiction and fact, Scott feels no need to push these games to their logical or illogical conclusions."[35] But the case is more complicated than this account allows.

Pattieson narrates Tinto's career as that of a visual craftsman caught between identities as a painter of pub signs, on the one hand, and an ambitious pursuer of the fine arts, on the other. The history of the pub sign matters some to this account, and with it the notion of the caption, though this part of the account relates word and image rather than word and scene. In contemporary Britain, the pub sign typically appears as a what might be called a redundant conjunction of word and image: an establishment can be identified both by the image of the nag's head and by the caption "The Nag's Head" that would customarily now be painted in below it. Pattieson suggests that in his Scotland, however, image and word are alternative forms of representation, and do not coinhabit the space of the sign. The relation, moreover, is sequenced: first the image signifies,

---

34. Edmund Burke, *Reflections on the Revolution in France & The Rights of Man* (New York: Doubleday, 1973), p. 89.

35. George Levine, *The Realistic Imagination: English Fiction from Frankenstein to Lady Chatterley* (Chicago: University of Chicago Press, 1981), p. 90.

and then the word. Pattieson explicitly relates the life of Tinto to the history of the supplanting of the image by the word. He tells us that, in Tinto's birthplace of Langdirdum, the pub sign was still a simple and illiterate affair that bore only an image associated with the name by which it was called.

> The age had not yet adopted, amongst other unworthy retrenchments, that illiberal measure of economy, which, supplying by written characters the lack of symbolical representation, closes one open and easily accessible avenue of instruction and emolument against the students of the fine arts. It was not yet permitted to write upon the plaistered door-way of an ale-house, or the suspended sign of an inn, "The Old Magpie," or "The Saracen's Head," substituting that cold description for the lively effigies of the plumed chatterer, or the turban'd frown of the terrific soldan. That early and more simple age considered alike the necessities of all ranks, and depicted the symbols of good cheer so as to be obvious to all capacities; well judging, that a man, who could not read a syllable, might nevertheless love a pot of good ale as well as his better educated neighbours, or even the parson himself. Acting upon this liberal principle, publicans yet hung forth the painted emblems of their calling, and sign-painters, if they seldom feasted, did not at least absolutely starve. (chap. 1)

The economy in which the image stood in for the word is also one that enforced no strong distinction between the fine and the useful arts and thus made it possible for a painter of middling ability, such as Dick Tinto, to find a means of life between feasting and starving.

The sad story that Pattieson goes on to relate about Tinto is the story of an artist whose life spans the transition between this economy and another, less "liberal" one, a transition effected in part by Tinto's own ambition to move from the province to the modern metropolis. In the modernized context, having foregone a living as a painter of pub signs and then exhausted the possibilities for portraits of wealthy villagers, Tinto strives to make it as a practitioner of the fine arts in the age of Wilkie. But the fine arts admit of no place for the mediocre talent, and Tinto, lacking what it takes to become a great success, fails utterly. The "great truth" of which Tinto's life supplies the "proof," according to Pattieson, is "that in the fine arts mediocrity is not permitted, and that he who cannot ascend to the very top of the ladder will do well not to put his foot upon it at all" (chap. 1). The distinction involving image and word in the representative sign of the public house—the "liberal," universal language of the image as opposed to the stingier demand for literacy—thus becomes a function of the distinction between two modes of economy and two conceptions of the arts, both latter distinctions depending at bottom on a contrast between graduated degrees and absolute thresholds of difference.[36]

36. A more exhaustive consideration of these relations would have to take into account the rather different economic distinction, Adam Smith's, between productive and the unproductive labor—the distinction Kathryn Sutherland shows Scott to be invoking in the "Epistle" to *The Fortunes of Nigel:* "Fictional Economies: Adam Smith, Walter Scott, and the Nineteenth-Century

Pattieson's "great truth" bears on the novel in supplying a possible means of arresting the dialectic of scene and representation. In the action of the novel itself, the world to which the ancièn régime of violence and force gives way is one in which conflict is carried on by the commerce of representation. Conquest gives way to casuistry, capture to caption. In Pattieson's account, the move into that world is one in which the word takes the place of the image, but both then undergo a split into the two kinds of arts. Such a split suggests, however, that there is in the commercial order such a thing as representation outside of use, which is to say outside of motive—a representation for which the analysis of motivation in the scene-agent ratio would be irrelevant. Romance writing of the sort that Pattieson (and Walter Scott) might be said to pursue is clearly on the fine arts side of the divide, a point that Scott made explicit in his *Essay on Romance,* when he argued for the same grand truth about the fate of mediocrity in the fine arts:

> In the useful arts, a great equality subsists among the members, and it is wealth alone which distinguishes a tradesman or a mechanic from the brethren of his guild; in other points the respectability is equal. The worst weaver in the craft is still a weaver, and the best, to all but those who buy his web, is little more—as men they are entirely on a level. In what are called the fine arts, it is different, for excellence leads to the highest points of consideration; mediocrity, and marked inferiority, are the object of neglect and utter contempt.[37]

These remarks form that part of Scott's effort to "explain the history of romance" in which he attempts to explicate how romance writers, in spite of the once close alliance of romance and history, fell from their more privileged place in early societies where every tribe was a family and every nation a union of tribes. Scott not only thus places romance on the fine arts side of the distinction, he seems to make the development of that distinction the basis for his separation of history and romance in the first place, as if romance amounted to a historical narrative without (first-order) utility.

On the one hand, then, the "great truth" illustrated by the life of Tinto puts Pattieson—like Scott—in a position to exempt his own narrative from the dialectic of scene and representation. His posture as narrator can be neutral because nothing is at stake for him. His narrative has no use. Furthermore, the risk he assumes in striking this posture is the escalation of the standards against which it will be judged: if it is not excellent it will be execrable, although of course, since Pattieson's and Scott's prior efforts have been widely acclaimed,

---

Novel," *ELH* 54:1 (spring 1987): 97–127. The complication is that in that text the "Author of Waverley" argues that his is a form of productive labor, whereas (so I argue below) he tended to classify romance writing with the fine arts rather than the useful.

37. Sir Walter Scott, *Miscellaneous Prose Works,* 6 vols. (Edinburgh: Robert Cadell, 1834), 6:167.

there is no reason for much worry on that score. On the other hand, however, unlike the distinction between the good and the bad posited within the world of the fine arts as a threshold distinction, the means of distinguishing the useful from the fine arts are by no means thresholdlike in character. They are, indeed, not even perspicuous. Moreover, insofar as we regard the fine arts/useful arts distinction and the history/romance distinction as correlatives of one another, we will be inclined to call the former into question in situations where the latter is called into question. But of course to call the history/romance distinction into question was the distinctive province of the new literary form that Scott invented with the first of the Waverley novels in 1814.[38]

5. Making a Scene for *The Bride of Lammermoor*

At work in these novels, then, is not Levine's "mere playing" but a strange double game, and its tensions surface in an particularly telling way in *The Bride of Lammermoor*. Commercial society of the sort that Scott and his readers inhabited in 1819 constituted itself in struggles of representation, signs produced at once in scenes as conversation and about scenes as captions, with the history of the past, present, and future all at stake.[39] Scott's novels can be read as just this sort of comment on the scenes he depicts from the great episodes of Scottish and British history, episodes whose meaning and implication were hotly contested in his own time: the rebellion of 1745 in *Waverley,* the rebellion of 1715 in *Rob Roy,* the Porteous Riots of 1736 in *The Heart of Mid-Lothian,* and, of course, the 1707 Union of Scotland and England in *The Bride of Lammermoor.* All this would seem to commit Scott to acknowledging that his is a deeply invested and high-stakes symbolic act in the Waverley novels. And, yet, the other side of this game is that he seeks to offer himself only as a romancer, a practitioner of the fine arts whose risk is defined chiefly in terms of the threshold that separates success from failure in the world of the fine arts market.

One might wish to say in Scott's behalf that he had no reason to believe his work could be taken seriously as historical scene setting, but that would be a very difficult argument to make. To see the problem with it one would not have

---

38. There is, of course, a large and interesting body of criticism on the history/romance distinction as it operates in Scott's *Waverley* novels, one reaching back to contemporary responses. Two recent approaches to the question can be found in Ferris, *The Achievement of Literary Authority,* pp. 195–236, and in Kerr, *Fiction Against History,* pp. 1–17 and passim.

39. One must recall Tinto's claim here that the "vivid flash of conviction, which darts on the mind from seeing the happy and expressive combinations of a single scene" captures not only the moment but also "the history of the past lives of the personages represented," "the nature of the business on which they are immediately engaged," and even "affords a shrewd guess at their future fortunes" (TML3, chap. 1).

to look further than the early reception of the first series of the "Tales of My Landlord." The main entry in that series was *Old Mortality,* a novel whose action leaves off roughly where that of *The Bride of Lammermoor* picks up and whose topics overlap with the latter in several particulars. *Old Mortality* indeed centers on episodes still being discussed with passion by characters in *The Bride:* the events of the often-violent insurgency of the Covenanters between the assassination of Archbishop Sharpe in 1679 and the aftermath of the 1688 Revolution settlement. That might seem to modern readers a less explosive subject than, for example, the Forty-Five Rebellion, but the evidence suggests otherwise. This is perhaps explainable, as Ina Ferris has suggested, by virtue of the Lowland Covenanters' special status in Scotland, where they were "venerated as defenders of its civil and religious liberties": Ferris notes, tellingly, that the site of the battle of Drumclog, a 1679 military victory by the Covenanters memorably depicted in the novel, had as recently as June 1815 become a rallying point for artisans and textile workers in the early days of the "Radical War." However one explains the sense of relevance, though, there can be no question that the novel occasioned a heated debate about the accuracy, fairness, and relevance of its historical account, including two-hundred-odd pages of critique in the *Edinburgh Christian Instructor* by the fierce polemicist, Thomas M'Crie.[40]

No one familiar with this controversy can believe Scott innocent of the ways in which his novels might have been taken as history rather than just romance or naive about their possible uses or motives. Indeed, Scott entered this controversy in his own defense, and when he did so, his tack was not to explain away his narrative as mere romance but to insist on its broad historical accuracy and impartiality. It is because it so relentlessly seems to call claims of impartiality into question that the featured novel in the third series of the "Tales" requires the hedging deployment of the distinction between the useful and fine arts or the one between history and romance. The fantasy of transcendence offered by the threshold of excellence in the fine arts is no more acceptable than the fantasy of indifference offered by Ashton's suggestion that all times and places were the same for purposes of his negotiation with Ravenswood.

The question, then, about the "scene" of the enunciation that is *The Bride of Lammermoor* seems fair enough, and of course such questions have been posed and answered by every critic who has ventured a political reading of this novel

---

40. Ferris, *Achievement of Literary Authority,* p. 142. As part of her effort to show how seriously the novel in Scott's hand could be taken, Ferris lays out this whole controversy, and M'Crie's role in it, in very helpful terms (pp. 141–60). See also George Goodin's discussion of this controversy in "Walter Scott and the Tradition of the Political Novel," in *The English Novel in the Nineteenth Century,* ed. George Goodin (Urbana: University of Illinois Press, 1974), pp. 14–24.

and others in the Waverley series. Different ways of captioning the scenes of various novels may themselves be explicable in turn by a characterization of the critical scene in which those constructions are offered. I do not mean to survey those captions or speculate about the scenes of the critics who have made them—though, understandably, many tend to focus on the scene called "Scotland," even when the Union with England is seen to be the key issue.[41] By way of conclusion, I offer my own brief sketch of the scene of *The Bride* and Scott's role in it. My sketch deals with the affairs of Scotland less than with those of Britain and, perhaps predictably, directs attention less to the eighteenth-century debates on national identity than to the post-Waterloo debates on Parliamentary reform. I do take seriously arguments such as Peter Garside's that this novel straddles, displaces, and remains preoccupied with the Act of Union in 1707. The question is how far such an account of the book locks it into the nationalist politics of the long-standing conflicts between Scotland and England. Might one not instead reasonably take the events of 1707 as having constituted the status quo for the British Parliament in 1819, when Scott composed and published *The Bride of Lammermoor?*

The British Parliament had, after all, undergone relatively few major changes since 1707. The constitution of that Parliament was indeed under siege when Scott wrote and published *The Bride* in 1819, but this was less for ethnic or national conflict between England and Scotland than for social and economic conflict throughout Britain more generally, or at least in the newly industrialized areas of Britain. The crisis over the state of Parliamentary representation came severely to a head in the demonstration and massacre at St. Peter's Field in Manchester, an episode that took place just two months after the publication of *The Bride of Lammermoor* and which had been brewing all through the months of Scott's work on it.[42] Before the year was out, Scott would write anxious, angry, and even threatening public letters to his friend James Ballantyne, editor of *The Edinburgh Weekly Journal*. These letters, quickly collected in pamphlet form, supported the decision of the Manchester magis-

41. For various accounts of the novel that might be construed as describing its "scene," see the following: Robert C. Gordon, "*The Bride of Lammermoor:* A Novel of Tory Pessimism," *Nineteenth-Century Fiction* 12 (1957):110–24; Andrew D. Hook, "The Bride of Lammermoor: A Re-examination." *Nineteenth-Century Fiction* 22 (1967):111–26; David Brown, *Walter Scott and the Historical Imagination* (London: Routledge & Kegan Paul, 1975), pp. 129–50; Graham McMaster, *Scott and Society* (Cambridge: Cambridge University Press, 1981), pp. 165–78; Peter Garside, "Union and *The Bride of Lammermoor,*" *Studies in Scottish Literature* 14 (1984):85–89, a meticulous account of both the textual problems and historical references to the Union; Kerr, *Fiction Against History,* pp. 85–101; and Ian Duncan, *Modern Romance,* pp. 135–46;

42. For a careful sorting out of the myth of Scott's composition of this novel, see Millgate, *Walter Scott,* pp. 169–71.

trates who ordered the dispersal of the August demonstration and urged the British government to hold the line against the activities of the Reformers.[43] Let us imagine, then, that Scott's novel seeks a role in this more extended theater of national representation.

Two of the principles I take to be crucial to the ideological work of the reform movement are, first, the equality of freeholders in determining the election of Parliament (even though not all reformers held out for "one man one vote") and, second, the related principle of the equality of persons before the law. Such issues are very much in play from early on in *The Bride of Lammermoor.* Peter Pattieson's characterization of the novel's historical setting emphasizes, right from the start, that it was a period in which social hierarchy had been deranged. After James VI left Edinburgh to assume the crown of England in 1603, rival parties had formed among the aristocrats to contend for control in the power vacuum. This historical situation is then subjected to a straightforward Hobbesian argument for the greater stability of hierarchy over equality and for monarchy in particular:

> There was no supereminent power, claiming and possessing a general interest with the community at large, to whom the oppressed might appeal from subordinate tyranny, either for justice or for mercy. Let a monarch be as indolent, as selfish, as much disposed to arbitrary power as he will, still, in a free country, his own interests are so clearly connected with those of the public at large, and the evil consequences to his own authority are so obvious and imminent when a different course is pursued, that common policy, as well as common feeling, point to the equal distribution of justice, and to the establishment of the throne in righteousness. (TML3, chap. 2)[44]

There is nothing in the tone or diction of this passage, or in its relation to the rest of this novel or the other Waverley novels, that diminishes the sense of Scott's full endorsement of this principle. Further, as Daniel Cottom observes of this passage, it is the "personal character" rather than the institutional function of the monarch that Scott means to emphasize: "Scott's good monarch is simply a feudal lord on a larger scale."[45] But the principle itself seems to harbor an internal inconsistency in that what the monarchical hierarchy exists to preserve is the equal distribution of justice. One is reminded of the paradox that is so basic to the argument of Burke's *Reflections:* the notion of a "noble equality . . . handed down through all of the gradations of social life."[46]

43. See Sir Walter Scott, *The Visionary,* ed. and introd. Peter Garside (Cardiff: University College Cardiff Press, 1984).

44. Cf. Thomas Hobbes, *Leviathan* (1651; rprt. Harmondsworth: Penguin Books, 1968), pp. 239–51.

45. Daniel Cottom, *The Civilized Imagination: A Study of Ann Radcliffe, Jane Austen, and Sir Walter Scott* (Cambridge: Cambridge University Press, 1985), p. 186.

46. Burke, *Reflections,* p. 90.

Pattieson's more particular comments on law only heighten the paradox. When the narrator tells us that "[t]he character of the times" (chap. 2) in which the story is set aggravated contemporary suspicions that Ashton had won his court victories against the older Ravenswood by playing politics, it is explained that Scottish political culture was in chaos on account of rivalry of aristocratic factions and that the judiciary system in particular was "infected": "Scarce a case of importance could occur, in which there was not some ground for bias or partiality on the part of the judges, who were so little able to withstand the temptation, that the adage, 'Show me the man, and I will show you the law,' became as prevalent as it was scandalous" (chap. 2). It certainly sounds as though the implicit legal norm being violated in this historical aberration is the principle of equality before the law, and yet so much in this novel conspires to produce a very different picture of social relations. It offers a clear hierarchy of what, in the older system of orders, was called "dignity" among the general cast of characters in this book. This is not exactly the kind of dignity that Caleb Balderstone is constantly trying to salvage with his efforts on behalf of the honor of the household, but rather a criterion, as it is explained by theorists of the ancièn régime, that allows one to rank entities in a social hierarchy according to the clarity of the internal hierarchy in any given entity. On this theory, the first estate of France—the clergy—was the highest in dignity, and thus ranked above the second and third estates, because the principle of hierarchy within that estate was more pronounced than in theirs. Likewise for the precedence that the second estate takes over the third. Within any given estate, the ranking of persons, in theory, had to do with the internal hierarchization of their faculties.[47]

Some such theory as this governs the characterological ranking of the male characters who might be said to represent their respective classes in the novel: Ravenswood, Ashton, and, in the village of Wolf's Hope, Gibbie Girder, the cooper whose prosperous household Caleb targets in his raid on the village in search of provisions to support the unexpected visit of the Ashtons to Wolf's Crag. The point can be illustrated by Scott's representation of the marital state of each of the men. Gibbie Girder cannot hold sway in his household, in spite of threatening his wife with the use of force; Ashton cannot hold sway in his household, in spite of his attempts to outmaneuver his wife by cunning. Ravenswood would hold sway over Lucy, as is clear from all evidence in their courtship, but the wedding is blocked. The novel's gender politics and class politics thus go hand-in-hand.

47. See Charles Loyseau, *A Treatise on Orders,* trans. Sheldon Mossberg and William H. Sewell, Jr., in *The Old Regime and the French Revolution,* ed. Keith Michael Baker (Chicago: University of Chicago Press, 1987), pp. 13–31.

We gain some evidence of the novel's specific resistance to the notion of the equality of "men" before the law, in spite of its apparent criticism of the partiality of the courts in the century after the Union of the Crowns, when we see what an "impartial" settlement of the case between Ravenswood and Ashton might look like. This picture begins to clarify with Ravenswood's final words on the matter to Ashton, which are given authority not only by Ravenswood's straightforward eloquence but also by virtue of what the reader is told, beyond even Ravenswood's own suspicions, of Ashton's thoroughly undignified manipulation of the situation at hand. In refusing Ashton's wish to argue out their differences at Wolf's Crag, and in rejecting Ashton's principle that "any place was alike" to such men as themselves, Ravenswood insists that there is only one place in which they can speak on the question and that is the Supreme Court of the Scottish Estates. His reason for insisting on that venue as "the court of last resort" in their case is precisely because in that place all men are *not* understood as equal before the law.

> The belted lords and knights of Scotland, her ancient peers and baronage, must decide, if it is their will that a house, not the least noble of their members, shall be stripped of their possessions, the reward of the patriotism of generations, as the pawn of a wretched mechanic becomes forfeit to the usurer the instant the hour of redemption has passed away. If they yield to the grasping severity of the creditor, and to the gnawing usury that eats into our lands as moths into raiment, it will be of more evil consequence to them and their posterity than to Norman [i.e., Edgar] Ravenswood—I shall still have my sword and my cloak, and can follow the profession of arms wherever a trumpet shall sound. (chap. 15)

Again, it is not just that this is supposed to be such rousing stuff but that the exchange between Ashton and Ravenswood epitomizes their relationship—conniving manipulation against honest courage, fraud against strength, corruption against virtue. Everything about the scene conspires against the notion that they deserve, as least in the first instance, equal treatment under the civil law.

As it happens, Scott's revisions to this speech by Ravenswood have become the occasion of much debate in the commentaries over the question of whether the historical setting of *The Bride* is pre-Union or post-Union.[48] For the Magnum edition of 1830, Scott substituted the phrase "in the British House of Peers" for "in the estates of the nation, in the Supreme Court of Parliament" and the phrase "belted lords of Britain" for "belted lords of Scot-

48. Millgate addresses the question in *Walter Scott: The Making of a Novelist*, pp. 171–76. Garside takes issue with some of Millgate's findings in "Union and *The Bride of Lammermoor*," pp. 72–93. For the politics of the Act of Union see P. W. J. Riley, "The Structure of Scottish Politics and the Union of 1707," in *The Union of 1707: Its Impact on Scotland* (Glasgow: Blackie and Son, 1974), pp. 1–29.

land."[49] These changes have had their share of critical attention, but perhaps we should be no less attentive to the fact that Scott could make them in a passage that he left otherwise basically untouched. This fact might suggest that, whatever the problems of inconsistency to be sorted out in the historical cross-references, the force of this crucial passage in which honest Ravenswood comes closest to stating his own case against the manipulative Ashton is aimed less at the issue of nationalist conflict between England and Scotland than at the issue of class disharmony in Britain as a whole. Scott after all chose to focus on a feature of the post-Union Parliamentary settlement that preserved the equity function of the Supreme Court of the Estates.

A final way of considering Scott's framing of the contemporary political scene, of course, would be to view it in terms of this very preoccupation with the scene as a framing topos. In *A Grammar of Motives,* Kenneth Burke attempts to correlate the featuring of one of his five key dramatistic terms with various philosophical orientations, and for "the featuring of *scene,* the corresponding terminology is *materialism*" (GM, p. 9). Compared to some of the other correlations—the feature of *act* with *realism,* for example—the suggestion seems straightforward enough. Moreover, as applied to *The Bride of Lammermoor,* it corroborates Ian Duncan's well-argued conclusion about the novel that it poses "a gruesome conservative and materialist critique of the idealism of individual subjectivity of Richardson and Radcliffe."[50] But to take seriously the dialectic of caption and conversation in relation to the scene is to recognize that the novel's materialism, though crucial, may be only half the story. It is to recognize that the novel is concerned not only with the category of the scene but also with what Burke calls the "scene-agent ratio," the perspective that he sees governing "nineteenth-century thought" more broadly. The scene-agent ratio in *The Bride* plays itself out *both* as gruesome materialist critique of subjectivity *and* as acknowledgment of the material power of representation in the construction of the contexts of action: something like Marx's notion about making one's history but not just as one pleases.

Although the novel does not embrace the notion of the level field of intellectual contest, it by no means abandons the picture of a world where agents engage in a struggle for representation—not, at least, insofar as its male characters are concerned. For the characters gendered female, the story is far more complicated. The power of their word tends to be either more or less than that of male legal subjects, beyond the range of inequality that allows men their differently weighted representations in either the Supreme Court of the Scottish Es-

49. Sir Walter Scott, *The Waverley Novels,* 14:108.
50. Duncan, *Modern Romance,* p. 141.

tates *or* the British House of Peers. The verbal power of the woman is more, in the case of what Duncan has described as the demonic matriarchy constituted by Blind Alice the prophet (who foretells the doom of the lovers), Ailsie the witch (who destroys Lucy with her stories), and Lady Ashton, whose word surpasses that of all others.[51] But the price is paid for this power on the same side of the gender ledger, when Lucy is bereft of her powers of agency—or what amounts to the same thing, logos—and dies without being able to utter the "word explanatory" of the scene that sealed her fate.

6. Laws of Scotland, Laws of Syntax

More could be said about the scenes of explanation in *The Bride of Lammermoor*.[52] Instead of pursuing such topics here, I will return instead now, very briefly, to the initial scene of explanation in the framing narrative for *The Heart of Mid-Lothian* where we are introduced to the novel's title phrase for the first time. The two lawyers, Halkit and Hardie, are trading gibes in an explanatory framework derived from King Lear's famous comment about causality:

> "That's not my fault, Jack," replied the other. . . . "You are to give me all your business, you know; and if you have none, the learned gentlemen here knows nothing can come of nothing."
> "You seem to have brought something to nothing, though, in the case of that honest man. He looks as if he were just about to honour with his residence the HEART OF MID-LOTHIAN."
> "You are mistaken—he is just delivered from it—Our friend here looks for an explanation." (TML2, chap. 1)

The explanation comes in the form of a riddle, and the answer to the riddle is the title of the book:

> "Then the Tolbooth of Edinburgh is called the Heart of Mid-lothian?" said I.
> "So termed and reputed, I assure you."
> "I think," said I, with the bashful diffidence with which a man lets slip a pun in the presence of his superiors, "the metropolitan county may, in that case, be said to have a sad heart."
> "Right as my glove, Mr. Pattieson," added Mr. Hardie, "and a close heart, and a hard heart—Keep it up, Jack."
> "And a wicked heart, and a poor heart," answered Halkit, doing his best.
> "And yet it may be called in some sort a strong heart, and a high heart," rejoined the advocate. "You see I can put you both out of heart."
> "I have played all my hearts," said the younger companion.
> "Then we'll have another lead," answered his companion. (chap. 1)

51. Ibid., p. 143.
52. The obvious place to turn next would be the extraordinary scene of the charging of the bull at Lucy and her father in chapter 5, where multiple modes of explanation—from history, from sociology, from psychology, from biology, finally from physics ("the progressive force of [the bull's] motion rather than any operation of limbs, carried him up to within three years of the astonished Lord Keeper"—(TML3, chap. 5)—are put into play in rapid succession.

And with this we come to the suggestion that the *Heart of Mid-Lothian* must have its "Last Words, Confession, and Dying Will." The title phrase of this puzzling novel is here, by way of explanation, made the subject of a verbal riddle, and then of a series of puns, as if the thing it named were inextricable from the circumstances of the signifying medium in which it is named. It is as if naming were only possible in the context of obliquity and indirection, like the refractions of Edmund Burke's "dense medium" of "common life."[53] The circumstantiality of linguistic usage—the fact that two words like *case* and *cause* can mean the same thing in some contexts but different things elsewhere, or that case can refer sometimes to what you *take* and sometimes what you *make* in argument—amounts to the "fallenness" of our words from that upright nominative posited in the very declension. This fallenness or situatedness, in turn, is what the case as a form is supposed to reckon with. "Case" situates nouns in predication as "cases" situate agents in events.

But is Peter's paronomasia here really captured in the silly efforts of his social superiors to emulate it? Peter says: "The metropolitan county may, in that case, be said to have a sad heart." Perhaps the charged phrase in Pattieson's sentence is not "sad heart," which the ingenious lawyers seize on, but "in that case." "In that case" might well be heard as an echo of, and deictic reference to the sad "case of that honest man," Dunover, who stands before them. It might be an architectural pun; a case is the outer part of a house or building, or in the suggestive phrase of nineteenth-century architectural terminology, the "carcass of a house." As we have seen, however, this is a novel in which confusion over grammatical case forms assumes the status of a topic for broad humor. There is thus another dimension with which to reckon in this paronomasia with "case" here, a suggestion that reflexively refers the linguistic playfulness to the discourse of linguistics itself. In English, it is recognized that the object of the preposition in phrases of the form "the x of y" can be assigned either of two Latin cases: the dative or the possessive. Thus, in the phrase "the Heart of Mid-Lothian," the metropolitan county might technically be said to possess a sad heart. The confessional crux for the county named in the title would then turn on the question of whether it will own or acknowledge the (criminal) heart it has.[54]

53. Burke, *Reflections,* p. 74.

54. Hazlitt's section "Of Case" in his *New and Improved Grammar of the English Tongue* (London: M. J. Godwin, 1810) discusses some of the ambiguities of grammatical case in the English language, including the problem of how in English "we use the words in precisely the same way" (i.e., without difference in termination) "whether . . . they are governed by a preposition or not." Hazlitt goes on to invoke the term "situation" to explain why we have grammatical case in the first place: "Perhaps what is here called the nominative case might more properly be called the *noun* simply; and wherever in the technical construction of sentences it is necessary to distinguish

If we assume that Scott's games are to some degree in earnest here, we can read all this word play with semantics and syntax alike as extending the revision of Smith's account of moral life beyond the domain of the institutionality and into the domain of language itself. When Bartoline Saddletree insists to Reuben Butler, in the midst of their debate about grammatical and legal cases, that "Institutes and Substitutes are synonymous words" (chap. 5), he provides a comic version of Smith's commercial utopia of disembodiment: "institute" and "substitute" cannot be substituted for each other in English as it is itself instituted. While Smith repeatedly emphasizes that he is concerned with literary representation—"the manner in which different *authors* have treated of the practical rules of morality" (italics mine)—the circumstantialities and contingencies of language itself are not allowed much play in his analysis. The fantasy of a confidentiality beyond all forms of institutional mediation is matched by a fantasy of meaning beyond all forms of linguistic codification. Scott does not let us forget such mediating forms. And in this connection, between the case as a form for the application of rule to circumstance and paronomasia as a trope registering the circumstantial play in language itself, we see why Hazlitt and Shelley were led to represent the spirit of the age in a style so marked in its inconsistencies.

---

the situation of the noun with respect to other words, instead of saying the *nominative case* and the *objective case* . . . we might uniformly say, the *subject of the verb* and the *object of the verb.*" CWWH, 2:30–31.

Chapter Six

BYRON'S CAUSES:

THE MORAL MECHANICS

OF *DON JUAN*

On January 31, 1819, Thomas Moore registered two pieces of news about Walter Scott. First, that he was "to be made a Baronet" and, second, that he had indeed been paid "in one year £14,000" by Constable the bookseller. In that same journal entry, Moore also recorded his reaction to a new manuscript by Lord Byron, the other great literary lion of the period. At Byron's suggestion, Moore had been called in, along with Byron's friends John Hookham Frere and John Cam Hobhouse, to advise John Murray on the publishability of *Don Juan*. Moore recorded his early reaction to the poem in Journal entries such as the following:

> [January 31, 1819]—Went to breakfast with Hobhouse, in order to read Lord Byron's Poem—a strange production,—full of talent & singularity, as every thing he writes must be—some highly beautiful passages & some highly humourous ones—but, as a whole not publishable—Don Juan's mother is Lady Byron—and not only her learning, but various other points about her ridiculed—he talks of her favourite dress being *dimity* (which is the case)—dimity rhyming very comically to sublimity—& the conclusion of one stanza is "I hate a dumpy woman"—meaning Lady B. again—This would disgust the Public beyond endurance—There is also a systematic profligacy running through it which would not be borne—Hobhouse has undertaken the delicate task of letting him know our joint opinions—The two following lines are well rhymed.
>
> But, oh ye Lords of Ladies intellectual,
> Come, tell us truly, have they not hen-peck'd you all? (JTM, 1:141–42)

In singling out the rhymes he did, Moore may have recognized that, while a distinctive mark of Byron's new comic style, they also reveal a debt to Moore's own satiric practice as a poet. Indeed, of the many "sources" that have been identified as contributing to Byron's style in this poem—Pope, Pulci, Sterne—it is surprising how little attention has been paid to the immensely popular satirical verse of Byron's close friend and confidant.

In the *Twopenny Post-Bag* (1813) for example, Moore included a verse dream vision in which the written works of the Viscount Castlereagh take on a life of their own and mutiny against their author. The following is a sample of Moore's way with rhyme:

> When lo! the Papers, one and all,
> As if at some magician's call,
> Began to flutter of themselves,
> From desk and table, floor and shelves,
> And, cutting each some different capers,
> Advanc'd, oh jacobine papers!
> As though they said, "our sole design is
> "To suffocate his Royal Highness!"
> The Leader of this vile sedition
> Was a huge Catholic Petition. . . .
> But, oh the basest of defections!
> His Letter about "predilections"—
> His own dear Letter, void of grace,
> Now flew up in its parent's face!
> Shock'd with this breach of filial duty,
> He could just murmur "et Tu, *Brute*"?[1]

The lines seem to intimate that Moore's own poem has as much a life/mind of its own as do Castlereagh's writings, the all-but-built-in jocularity of the poly-syllabic rhymes conveying a sense of autonomy in the poem analogous to the independence of the Jacobin papers, a subversive rhyme echoing a subversive rationality.[2]

In the terms we have been developing, we might say that Moore resolves the case of *Don Juan's* publishability by determining that the poem poses no case against the reigning normative framework it superficially seems to flout. Its particularizing references to Lady Byron, Moore judges, offend in their very particularity, even when they do not offend in their indecorous language. The particularity itself is indecorous and fails to observe, without successfully challenging, a social and literary norm. Where the poem does aim for a normative framework of its own, some form of reasoned generality, it manages only "systematized profligacy."

1. Thomas Moore, *Intercepted Letters; Or, The Twopenny Post-Bag*, 16th ed. (London: J. Carpenter, 1818), pp. 44–45.
2. For another representation of the personified autonomy of the text in this period, see my discussion below of *Peter Bell the Third*, a quasi-Byronic satire, with similar rhymes, and dedicated to Thomas Moore—chap. 9. On the role of rhyme in Byronic satire, see W. H. Auden, *The Dyer's Hand* (New York: Random House, 1962), pp. 395–98.

This was not Moore's first vetting of the poem. He was already conversant with the text the previous day, as is clear from his brief consultation with Frere, where the subject of "systematized profligacy" had already been broached:

> Frere came in . . . —was proceeding to talk to him about our joint umpireship on Byron's poem, when he stopped me by a look, & we retired into the next room to speak over the subject—he said he did not wish the opinion he had pronounced to be known to any one except B. himself, lest B. should suppose he was taking merit to himself among the *righteous* for having been the means of preventing the publication of the Poem—spoke of the disgust it would excite, if published,—the attacks in it upon Lady B.—and said it is strange, too, he should think there was any connection between patriotism & profligacy—if we had a very puritan court indeed, one can understand *then* profligacy being adopted as a badge of opposition to it, but the reverse being the case, there is not even that excuse for connecting dissoluteness with patriotism, which, on the contrary, ought always to be attended by the sternest virtues. (JTM, 1:140)

This analysis by Frere, as edited and, evidently, endorsed by Moore, sheds light on Moore's comments on the following day. While the indecorum of the poem's conduct will excite only disgust in the court of public judgment, the one possible basis for this indecorum—that is, the basis in the "system" that seems to assume a reliable correlation of profligacy and patriotism—fails in the end to support it. And it fails because it does not resist but rather flatters the moral principles of the nation's *ruling* "court"—the court of the chief dandy and leading profligate of the realm, the Prince Regent. As a case against national mores, a case construed in principled political terms, *Don Juan* amounts to very little indeed on this analysis. For Moore and Frere, the case of *Don Juan* lacked a cause and thus could not ultimately be taken seriously as a case.

It was in these same weeks of 1819, when the fate of *Don Juan* was hanging in the balance, that Moore acknowledged his low spirits and expressed his recurring sense of how they might be offset: "[April] 24—A wet, gloomy day— my spirits of the same hue—Often do I wish I had a *good cause to die in*" (JTM, 1:164). The "good ol' cause" of Jacobitism that was so prominently reinvoked in Scott's *Waverley* novels of these years would seem to have supplied one kind of fulfillment of Moore's wish. But none of the most likely candidates in this kind—neither Irish independence, say, nor Catholic Emancipation (the cause which had taken the young Shelley to Dublin for pamphleteering a few years earlier)—apparently carried much weight with Moore.[3] Byron himself, on the

---

3. Both of these causes are mentioned in numerous places in Moore's journal, but, in spite of his real support for them, Moore kept a certain distance and was seldom moved to anything like passion about them. Thus, even when he later socialized and corresponded with Daniel O'Connell, praising him in a public speech at Dublin, Moore still "did not believe in pressure groups, such as represented by O'Connell" and "regarded himself as a regularly enlisted member of the English liberal group which respected the right of private political judgment"—Howard Mumford Jones, *The Harp that Once: A Chronicle of the Life of Thomas Moore* (New York: Henry Holt and Company, 1937), p. 296. For Moore's Dublin speech of 1838, see JTM, 5:2001.

other hand, with almost unexampled celebrity, did indeed soon find a "good cause to die in." Byron's noble cause was that of "Greek independence." Though construed, to be sure, in a European "Liberal" perspective, this cause appears in late lyrics like "On This Day I Complete My Thirty-Sixth Year" as a kind of passion whose fatal implications had become prophetically evident to him. It is clear that *Don Juan* is the grand opus whose serial publication and production so preoccupied Byron from the time of Moore's comment about dying in a good cause to Byron's actual death in 1824. Were Frere and Moore right in their sense, as I have described it, that *Don Juan* was a case of a poem without a cause?

It is a question that may be difficult to answer, but I think it cannot even be properly considered without recognizing the poem's extraordinary attention to what might be called the very idea of the "cause" and to such related topics as the theory of explanation, the practice of casuistry, the Romantic invention of the historical situation, and the linguistic embodiment of the case. If the grammatical appositeness of the terms "case" and "cause," long established in English usage, becomes in Scott's writings the pretext for a playful exploration of the relation of casuistry to explanation, a similar appositeness is discernible in Byron's usage. It appears, for example, in canto 16, where the phrases "tell / The cause" and "state the case" appear to be virtually interchangeable formulations (16:32–33). And Byron, too, offers a meditation on the affinities of casuistry and causality in relation to a historicized sense of modernity. Having a cause, being cause, counting as a case—these, I hope to show, are all part of the complex moral-historical mechanics of the world with which Byron professed to be reckoning. It is a world that he could neither tolerate in its new historical unintelligibility nor fully resolve into a sustainable grammar of motives.

1. The "Common Case" of Robert Southey

This complex set of connections can be glimpsed in Byron's treatment of Robert Southey, still understood by Byron as the leader of "the Lake School" of poetry, as he was for Francis Jeffrey when Jeffrey coined that term in 1802.[4] The centrality of Southey to *Don Juan* is immediately evident in the ironic dedication of the poem to him (suppressed when the first canto was published in 1819) and in the characterization that takes shape in the very first stanzas, which famously begin :

> Bob Southey! You're a poet—poet laureate,
>   And representative of all the race;

---

4. On Southey's perceived representativeness of the Lake School, see Marilyn Butler, "Plotting the Revolution," in *Romantic Revolutions,* p. 141.

> Although 'tis true you turned out a Tory at
>   Last, yours has lately been a common case—
> And now my epic renegade, what are ye at
>   With all the Lakers, in and out of place? (DS:1)

The "common case" of Southey—would-be representative of England and, by
imperial extension, of the human race—is identified in terms of the *period* of
contemporary history ("lately"), the *genre* of epic, and the *norm* of political
good faith ("renegade"/"place"). The common case of Southey has to do, in
other words, with the grand ambitions of post–French Revolution English
writers and the notorious question of their fidelity to a cause.

The first draft of the Dedication is dated just above this first stanza "Venice
July 3d 1818," but the Southey-like figure of the poet without a cause, the common case of the age, makes a dramatic reentry into the poem in late 1819, when
Byron decides to resume composition after the publication of cantos 1 and 2 that
summer. Byron wrote the first one hundred stanzas of canto 3 in September and
October of 1819. Many of these stanzas (sixteen of them) are devoted to the
interpolated poetic performance that young Don Juan witnesses on the Greek
Island where he has shipwrecked and fallen in love with Haidée, daughter of the
pirate Lambro. A roughly equal number of stanzas (st. 78–95) are devoted to the
introduction of the poet and to commentary on his art. Two of the stanzas that
portray the literary character of the island bard will suffice to make the point:

> He was a man who had seen many changes,
>   And always changed as true as any needle;
> His polar star being one which rather ranges,
>   And not the fixed—He knew the way to wheedle:
> So vile he 'scaped the doom which oft avenges;
>   And being fluent (save indeed when fee'd ill),
> He lied with such a fervour of intention
> There was no doubt he earn'd his laureate pension. . . .
>
> Their poet, a sad trimmer, but no less
>   In company a very pleasant fellow,
> Had been the favourite of full many a mess
>   Of men and made them speeches when half mellow,
> And though his meaning they could rarely guess,
>   Yet still they deigned to hiccup or to bellow
> The glorious meed of popular applause,
> Of which the first ne'er knows the second cause. (3:80–82)

To recognize the "common case" of Southey in these lines, we do not really need to know that the first line of the second quoted stanza appeared in an early manuscript as "Their poet—a sad Southey." Nor do we need to know that, in response to an 1817 attack in Parliament on Southey's renegadism by William Smith, the Member for Norwich, Southey had written a defense of his political conduct, also published by Murray, and that this *Letter to William Smith* explained Southey's apparent change of politics as a result of keeping his own "needle" fixed on the "pole star" while the "the world went round."[5] We do not need to know these things because the reference to the Greek poet's "laureate pension" would already be enough itself to connect him with the Southey of the first stanza—indeed the first line—of the poem.

What is of particular interest in these stanzas, though, is their connection of "the common case" of Southey with, on the one hand, the notion of a political "cause" (a *renegado* is a person who deserts such a cause) and, on the other, the ability to understand causality—that is, to explain things. I frankly cannot con-

---

5. The "case" of Southey began to take shape in 1817 when, after a blistering attack on the new reform movement in the *Quarterly Review*, Southey was embarrassed by the publication of a long lost play from his radical youth in the early 1790s, *Wat Tyler.* Smith marched into Parliament with a copy of the *Quarterly Review* issue in one pocket of his coat and a copy of *Wat Tyler* in the other, and, holding up now the one publication and now the other, delivered a scathing attack which concluded with the claim that of all forms of political expression in the world, "what most filled him with disgust, was the settled determined malignity of a renegado." The event was highly publicized and called for a public answer. The relevant passage from Southey's publication is as follows:

> The one object to which I have ever been desirous of contributing according to my power, is the removal of those obstacles by which the improvement of mankind is impeded; and to this the whole of my writings, whether in prose or verse, bears witness. This has been the pole star of my course; the needle has shifted according to the movements of the state vessel wherein I am embarked, but the direction to which it points has always been the same. I did not fall into the error of those who having been the friends of France when they imagined that the cause of liberty was implicated in her success, transferred their attachment from the Republic to the military Tyranny in which it ended, and regarded with complacency the progress of oppression because France was the Oppressor. "They had turned their faces toward the East in the morning to worship the rising sun, and the evening were looking Eastward still, obstinately affirming that still the sun was there." I, on the contrary altered my position as the world went round. For so doing, Mr. William Smith is said to have insulted me with the appellation of Renegade. *Letter to William Smith,* 2d ed. (London: John Murray, 1817), pp. 27–28.

For a fuller account of this episode in the context of post-Waterloo charges of "tergiversation" against the Lake Poets see my "'Wordsworth' After Waterloo." in Johnston and Ruoff, eds., *The Age of William Wordsworth,* pp. 84–111. Byron alludes to the attack on Southey by "the upright and able Member for Norwich" in "Some Observations Upon an Article in *Blackwood's Edinburgh Magazine—No—August 1819,*" in Lord Byron, *The Complete Miscellaneous Prose,* ed. Andrew Nicholson (Oxford: Clarendon Press, 1991), p. 101. The *Blackwood's* article was an attack on the first two cantos of *Don Juan.*

fidently parse the final line: "Of which the first ne're knows the second cause." If pressed, I would take "first cause" to be a reference to the "mess of men" made speechless by the performance, and the "second cause" to refer to the immediate reason in the poet's performance deemed applause worthy: they cannot guess the poet's meaning. Such a reading is consistent with, though not much supported by, the earlier version of the lines: "Of which the Causers /Never know the Cause" (CPWB, 5:187). That the line itself is obscure, early and late, suggests the kind of performative dimension to Byron's own practice to which I return below. But the question that the passage darkly poses seems to be something like the following: what kind of cause does it make sense to pursue in one's writing when one labors under the burden of such explanatory ignorance?[6]

It deepens the sense of connection among the terms and concepts in question—"case," "cause," "causality"—that Southey's own impressively articulate self-defense in the *Letter to William Smith,* depends on his argument for a particular kind of relationship between them. "I did not," wrote Southey, "fall into the error of those who having been the friends of France when they imagined that the *cause of liberty* was implicated in her success, transferred their attachment from the Republic to the military Tyranny in which it ended, and regarded with complacency the progress of oppression *because* France was the Oppressor" (my emphasis).[7] However we explain such suppressed but powerful verbal echoes, Southey's linkage of cause and causality in this notorious apologia becomes crucial to the understanding of his own case. Indeed, this explicit proposition—that one can only participate in a moral "cause" insofar as one fully understands the causal relations of the moral world that pertains to it—is presumably a part of what must be understood in Byron's reminder that Southey's had lately become "a common case." *The Letter to William Smith* was, unquestionably, the definitive statement of Southey's case.

Like Scott—to some extent even *following* Scott—Byron elaborated these topics with an eye to their bearing on the history and historicism of his moment. He may well have seen his taking on of questions made central by Scott as a way of rejoining Scott at the very peak of the contemporary literary pyramid that he so ridiculed.[8] Understood in the framework I have been develop-

6. In *A Philosophical View of Reform,* moreover, Shelley argued strenuously that what he saw as the seventeenth-century scientific revolutions in the understanding of causality served the cause of liberty more profoundly than any other modern development—see below, chapter 9.

7. Southey, *Letter to William Smith,* p. 27.

8. Part of the idea may also have been to dismiss the vain pretensions of epic renegados, such as Wordsworth. In June 1818, Byron wrote to Moore to protest Leigh Hunt's "skimble-skamble about [Wordsworth] being at the head of his own *profession,* in the *eyes* of *those* who followed it? I

ing here, *Don Juan* emerges as Byron's ambitious effort to rival Scott's campaign to modernize the writing of epic in the post-Revolution period, and of course Byron was the only contemporary writer with the literary reputation—the "sign value"—to take Scott on. Unlike Scott, however, for better or for worse, Byron's ambitious effort to modernize the epic after Waterloo has not yet had its Georg Lukács. In our own century, Byron's literary reputation suffered much as Scott's has done (if nothing like so much as Moore's or Felicia Hemans's), while the reputations of Wordsworth, Blake, Austen, and Keats have all soared by comparison. Scott has been fortunate to have had a Lukács to make fully palpable for *our* contemporaries the basis of the strong reactions of his work by its first readers. And, as we have seen, Lukács *performed* the distinctive operation of Scott's fiction in describing it, making the form of explanation and typicality in Scott's historical novel so crucial to the operations of *The Historical Novel,* the book in which the genesis of that form is explained and typified.

Among recent commentators on Byron, the two who have come closest to stating his case with the kind of power and performative self-consciousness that Lukács brought to Scott are probably Jerome McGann and Jerome Christensen. Both commentators call attention to the poem's vocabulary of causality, representation, and circumstance. Both are discussing what I would call "Byronic casuistry," though neither phrases the point quite in those terms. Both books, *Don Juan in Context* and *Lord Byron's Strength,* even less obviously but more importantly, amount to apologies for Byron in a distinctly Byronic mode. They redeploy Byronic casuistry in making Byron's case—hence McGann's preoccupation with what he calls Byron's "style" or "method" and Christensen's preoccupation with the Byronic mode of "commanding belief."[9] Of course, readers familiar with Christensen's study know that he frames both his method and his matter as a critique of McGann's. He contends, for example,

---

thought that Poetry was an *art* or an *attribute,* and not a *profession;* but be it one, is that ****** at the head of *your* profession in *your* eyes: I'll be curst if he is of *mine,* or ever shall be. He is the one of us (but of us he is not) whose coronation I would oppose. Let them take Scott, Campbell, Crabbe, or you, or me, or any of the living and throne him;—but not this new Jacob Behmen" (BLJ, 8:47).

9. See McGann's account of Byron's mode of poetic experimentation—of moral experimentation in poetry—in *Don Juan in Context* (Chicago: University of Chicago Press, 1976), pp. 116–31. See Christensen's interest in Byron's "strength" as the capacity to repeatedly pose questions about the "basis" on which he commanded a belief in his right to command, and to answer them "differently every time. The strong poet answers not so much with a rightness that fits the occasion . . . but with a rightness that decides the occasion"—*Lord Byron's Strength* (Baltimore: Johns Hopkins University Press, 1993), pp. xvii–xviii. In introducing the terms of his argument, furthermore, Christensen takes pains to distinguish his notion of "strength" from "force": e.g., pp. xvi, xxiii–xxiv, 5–6, 33.

that McGann "objectifies" Byron's styles, texts, authorship, and period in a way that fails to honor Romanticism's resistance to the commodity as the modern, commercialized form of ancient sacrifice.[10] But Christensen's oppositional distinction between McGann's (or Marjorie Levinson's) so-called objectification and his own so-called resistance—"Tis against *that* that I am writing," Christensen wittily paraphrases Wordsworth at one point—proves to be one of those unstable "lines" that, quite pointedly in Christensen's sketch, seem to "lose themselves," like those "little lines . . . run wild" in "Tintern Abbey."[11] Christensen is particularly interested, throughout his study, in moments where relationships of "opposition" get figured or refigured as relationships of "apposition." But what Christensen, echoing Byron, calls "circumstantial gravity" in Byron does not stand so much in a relation of opposition as in one of apposition—or perhaps greater particularization—with what McGann, himself already echoing Byron, calls "the force of circumstance."[12] Taking great pains to insist that everything depends on his rewriting of McGann's phrase, "*Don Juan* in Context," to become "*Don Juan* as Context," Christensen misses the extent to which *Don Juan* takes place both in *and* as "context" in both books.[13]

Building, then, on the work of McGann, Christensen, and others, I would like to address the question of whether there is a cause in Byron's case by considering the question of whether there might be such a thing as a Byronic casuistry. The notion of the "force of circumstance" or of "circumstantial gravity" will be important for this question of a Byronic casuistry because of Byron's emphatic resort to metaphors drawn from mechanics. Pausing to reflect, in "The Casuistry of Duelling," on how his "case arises out of a great dilemma," De Quincey generalizes about particularity in the following terms: "in all *practical* applications of philosophy, amongst materials so imperfect as men, just as in

10. On McGann's alleged reifications and objectifications, see *Lord Byron's Strength,* p. 214–15. On the larger claim about the commodity and the "logic of sacrifice," see pp. xxi–xxii.

11. Ibid., p. 351.

12. For McGann's scene-setting discussion of "Byron and the Force of Circumstance," see *Don Juan in Context,* pp. 1–10. For Christensen's counterpart discussion see "The Circumstantial Gravity of *Don Juan,*" in *Lord Byron's Strength,* pp. 214–57.

13. Suggesting that his discussion of the poem might bear the spectral title "*Don Juan* as Context," Christensen then wittily parodies the *Crede Byron* which is his homiletic text: "Believe me, on the distinction between *in* and *as* rests the different betweeen and ironical book and a revolutionary text" (p. 215). The joke here is that one cannot tell which is which, I take it, and the form in which *in* and *as* stand in apposition to each other is the case itself. It might even be called the form in which the relation between opposition and apposition itself breaks down. Note that the same point could be made with Christensen's subtitle: "Romantic Writing and Commercial Society," which translates sometimes as "*in* Commercial Society" (where the stress is on the history of texts), and sometimes as "*as* commercial Society" (where the stress is on the textualization of history).

all attempts to realize the rigour of mathematical laws amongst earthly mechanics, inevitably there will arise such dilemmas and cases of opprobrium."[14] We will see that Byron deploys the metaphor of a mechanics to similar effect. Indeed, the question of a Byronic casuistry takes us into what might be called the "moral mechanics" of *Don Juan* and of the place of fallen languages in explaining both the fall of apples and that of "men."

2. "Explaining Explanation": Wordsworthian Whys and Wherefores

Epics have always explained. That much is clear from the narrative convention that has most consistently distinguished the genre: the beginning in medias res. Since *Don Juan* declares itself as an epic, the question of its relation to explanation is raised early when Byron announces his departure from the conventional narrative structure:

> Most epic poets plunge in 'medias res,'
> (Horace makes this the heroic turnpike road)
> And then your hero tells, when'er you please,
> What went before—by way of episode . . . . (1:6)

That, says Byron, "is the usual method, but not mine—/ My way is to begin with the beginning" (1:7). Commenting on this passage in his seminal chapter on "Form" in *Don Juan in Context,* McGann concludes that Byron's declaration should be taken as a disclaimer of the poem's interest in explanation:

> [E]pic poets continually begin *in medias res* because such a narrative procedure establishes the need for an explicatory context. The convention of *in medias res* puts the reader in suspense, not about what will happen, but about how and why the present state of affairs came to be. *In medias res* enforces the desire to understand events in terms of an orderliness that springs from causes and natural consequences. To begin *in medias res* is to ensure that the events of the epic will be set only in the context of what is relevant to them. It is a probability device.
> *Don Juan* is different. It explicitly does not begin *in medias res* and its arrangement scarcely covets probability.[15]

Don Juan is different—McGann is certainly right about that—and perhaps if we look only at this issue of ordonnance, we can see the poem as uncovetous of "probability." But other indicators suggest that the relation of the poem to explanatory ambition is at the very least one of deep ambivalence, for it sometimes seems to verge on downright obsession. If we look instead to diction, for example, we can actually go some way toward quantifying the poem's preoccu-

14. Thomas De Quincey, "The Casuistry of Duelling" in *The Uncollected Writings,* 2 vols. (London: Swan Sonnenschein, 1892), 2:98.
15. McGann, *Don Juan in Context,* p. 100.

pation with the topic. The conjunction "because" occurs one hundred four-
teen times in *Don Juan*, more than four times the number of its appearances in
all of Wordsworth's poetical works. The word "cause" occurs fifty-six times in
the poem, a figure that puts it near the top of the poem's most frequently appearing nouns and verbs—higher, for example than such staples of Byronic
diction as *passion, war, word, words, age, sun, light*, and *water. Cause* also happens to
appear exactly the same number of times as *women*, a coincidence one might dis-
count as meaningless if it were not that gender categories do so much explanatory work in the poem. There are about a dozen instances of some form of the
word "explain" itself, some of which directly thematize explanation as an issue.

Byron wrote to his publisher, John Murray, in 1819 that he had no other intention in the poem than "to giggle and make giggle," and herein lies another
way to recognize *Don Juan*'s strong interest in explanation (BLJ, 6:208). The
poem's great faculty of pleasure, its celebrated wit, exercises itself most flam-
boyantly in the making of explanatory jokes. These jokes are not all of the same
kind, and they are not all equally funny or pleasurable. There is a range of them,
for example, that are not particularly funny or pleasurable because they parody
what is itself already a tonally bizarre strain of explanatory comment in
Wordsworth's "The Thorn," the poem invoked as the mock narrative framework for *Don Juan* in Byron's prose preface. Wordsworth's anthropological
ironies appear paradigmatically in response to the whys and wherefores of the
poem's internal balladic dialogue:

> "Now wherefore thus, by day and night,
> In rain, in tempest, and in snow,
> Thus to the dreary mountain-top
> Does this poor woman go?
> And why sits she beside the thorn
> When the blue day-light's in the sky,
> Or when the whirlwind's on the hill,
> Or frost air is keen and still,
> And wherefore does she cry?—
> Oh wherefore? wherefore? tell me why
> Does she repeat that doleful cry?"
>
> I cannot tell; I wish I could;
> For the true reason no one knows. (ll. 78–90)[16]

16. This and subsequent citations from the 1798 text of the poem as republished in
Wordsworth, *Lyrical Ballads and Other Poems, 1797–1800*, ed. James Butler and Karen Jones
(Ithaca, N.Y.: Cornell University Press, 1992).

The old sea captain who narrates the poem, and who is the object of Byron's first lampoon in *Don Juan*, offers several such disavowals of his explanatory capacity: "I'll give you the best help I can . . . " (p. 111), "No more I know; I wish I did . . . " (p. 155). Yet, while these comments may be cast in the form of disclaimers of his explanatory authority, their effect is to call attention to the narrator's explanatory obsessions. Indeed, he often succumbs to the temptation to offer surmises in spite of protests about his incapacities. It is anyway clear from Wordsworth's famous note to "The Thorn," a text that comes in for particular ridicule in Byron's prose preface, that Wordsworth attempted to frame the poem as an investigation of how causal categories function in what anthropologists such as Lévy-Bruhl came to call the "primitive mentality."[17]

Byron appropriates Wordsworth's disclamatory idiom pervasively in *Don Juan*. When Don Alfonso invades Julia's bedroom during her liaison with Juan, the narrator says he is at a loss to account for it: "I can't tell how or why or what suspicion / Could enter Don Alfonso's head" (1:139). Introducing Juan's premonition of disaster before Lambro's return in canto 4, which the narrator will go on to describe as "feelings causeless, or at least abstruse," he says,

> I know not why, but in that hour to-night
>   Even as they gazed, a sudden tremor came,
> And swept, as 'twere, across their heart's delight. . . . (4·21)

Of Dudù's blush in canto 6, the narrator says, "I can't tell why she blushed, nor can expound / The mystery of this rupture of their rest" (6:85). Of the disappearance of Juan's infantry corps during the siege of Ismail, he says:

---

17. Lucian Lévy-Bruhl, *Primitive Mentality,* trans. Lilian A. Clare (London: Allen & Unwin, 1923); the question of causation is perhaps the central one in Lévy-Bruhl's famous study. Wordsworth's long note to "The Thorn" explains his sea-captain narrator as his own kind of "common case":

> The character which I have here introduced speaking is sufficiently common. The Reader will perhaps have a general notion of it, if he has ever known a man, a Captain of a small trading vessel for example, who being past the middle age of life, had retired upon an annuity or small independent income to some village or country town of which he was not a native or in which he had not been accustomed to live. Such men having little to do become credulous and talkative from indolence, and from the same cause, and other predisposing causes by which it is probable that such men have been affected, they are prone to superstition. On which account it appeared to me proper to select a character like this to exhibit some of the general laws by which superstition acts upon the mind. (Butler and Green, eds., *Lyrical Ballads,* pp. 350–51)

Although Byron wrote (without publishing) a preface for *Don Juan* parodying the specificity of Wordsworth's characterization (CPWB, 5:683–84), the project of *Don Juan* often comes very close to that of "The Thorn," as I argue below. The animus seems driven in part by the narcissism of fine differences. For a good discussion of how proto-anthropological discourses shape

the gods know how! I can't
Account for [every thing] which may look bad
In history. (8:31)

There are moments, as we shall see in looking at the stanzas on Catherine the
Great (in canto 9), when Byron will indeed project a capacity, and an apparatus,
that will enable him precisely to explain "everything which may look bad / In
history." It will not necessarily prove to be a historical way of explaining, however, and the confidence does not last for long. Thus, of Juan's sickness during
his "service" for Catherine in canto 10, the posture (at least) of intellectual
modesty is reassumed:

Perhaps—but sans perhaps, we need not seek
    For causes young or old. . . .
I don't know how it was, but he grew sick. (10:38–39)

With "I don't know how it was," we return to the idiom of Wordsworth's
naive sea captain, though now in the context of a suggestion about venereal
disease.

The Wordsworthian *occupatio* remains available to Byron, or his narrator (the
distinction is notoriously difficult to maintain), even through the late English
cantos, as one can see in the review of various speculations on the cause of the
unearthly music that occasionally sounds through the arches of Norman
Abbey: "The cause I know not, nor can solve, but such / The fact: I've heard it—
once perhaps too much" (13:64). The ironies that operate in these jokes are
both labile and heterogeneous. While some (like the Norman Abbey joke)
seem to indicate skepticism about assigning causes to clear up mysterious
events, others (like the joke about Juan's sickness) appear to point to causes that
could be inobvious only (it is implied) to the most repressed or obtuse among
Byron's readership. Likewise the relation of these jokes to their Wordsworthian
target is difficult to ascertain. It is hard to tell whether Wordsworth's "I cannot
tell" is being mocked as an escape from the responsibilities of explanation or, on
the other hand, as a too-simple irony that conceals a concomitantly naive optimism about the poet's ability to explain such matters as the psychology of superstition in the first place. It is hard to tell, indeed, what telling might *mean* in
many of these instances.

One can also find in *Don Juan* a second form of causal humor, certainly related to the first but more effective as humor and probably more salient in the

---

Wordsworth's major poetry, see Alan Bewell, *Wordsworth and the Enlightenment* (New Haven: Yale
University Press, 1988).

poem. These are the jokes of a narrator who is in fact quite cavalier about the problem of identifying causes behind what he observes. The tone is set for these moments early on when, in a pastiche of Montesquieu's climatological analysis, the narrator asserts in canto 1 that the sexual mores of southern European countries are "all the fault of that indecent sun, / Who cannot leave alone our helpless clay, / But will keep baking, broiling, burning on" (1:63). Or again in canto 5:

> The Turks do well to shut—at least sometimes—
>   The women up—because in sad reality,
> Their chastity in these unhappy climes
>   Is not a thing of that astringent quality,
> Which in the north prevents precocious crimes,
>   And makes our snow less pure than our morality. (5:157)

These are explanations *of* sexuality, but a more common version of this more confident Byronic joke involves an explanation *from* sexuality. For example, in an early episode explicitly satirical of Wordsworthian sublimity, where the narrator has occasion to report Juan's distracted ruminations between encounters with Donna Julia, Juan is said to be wandering and wondering in "self-communion with his own high soul":

> 'Twas strange that one so young should thus concern
>   His brain about the action of the sky;
> If *you* think 'twas philosophy that this did,
>   I can't help thinking puberty assisted. (1:93)

If one recognizes in these explanatory jokes the stuff out of which the poem is made, one also recognizes that they are characteristically "antiphilosophical," which is to say "materialist" in orientation. The explanations of "philosophy"—which Byron tends to identify with Coleridge, Plato, and Berkeley— lead one to mistake ideas for things. Byron's explanations set out to expose this delusion. They deal in things themselves—material "facts," as Byron likes to stress. Berkeley may be allowed to introduce canto 11 with his dictum that "there was no matter," but it is met immediately by Byron's witty rejoinder: "'twas no matter what he said" (11:1). When he strikes this posture, Byron seems to presume a certain easy access to his "facts," and he gestures openhandedly toward providing such access for his readers as well. In this role, Byron shows unqualified confidence in his talent for lucid explanation: "I wish to be perspicuous," he says in canto 5 with no apparent doubts about his ability to do so—no doubts, that is, in spite of the lability of the ironies that attend his use throughout the poem of the "I-know-not-why" idiom from "The Thorn."

It takes little investigation to learn that this will-to-explain is an old habit with Byron and that, if we can believe him, it dates back at least to when he himself was of the age (about sixteen) that Juan had attained by the Donna Julia episode in canto 1. In his Aberdeen youth, Byron summered in the Highlands and saw much of what Moore calls their "wild beauties." It was, according to Moore, "about this period, when [Byron] was not quite eight years old, that a feeling partaking more of the nature of love than it is easy to believe possible in so young a child took, according to his own account, entire possession of his thoughts, and showed how early, in this passion as in most others, the sensibility of his nature was awakened."[18] A little Scottish girl named Mary Duff was the object of this attachment. And though Moore's evidence on this point is a passage from a journal Byron kept in 1813, seventeen years after the fact, Moore does not invoke the notion of an "anachronism in the history of his own feelings"[19] to explain it away:

> I have been thinking lately a good deal of Mary Duff. How very odd that I should have been so utterly, devotedly fond of that girl, at an age when I could neither feel passion, nor know the meaning of the word. And the effect!—My mother used always to rally me about this childish amour; and, at last, many years after, when I was sixteen, she told me one day, "Oh, Byron, I have had a letter from Edinburgh, from Miss Abercromby, and your old sweetheart Mary Duff is married to a Mr Co." And what was my answer? I really cannot explain or account for my feelings at that moment; but they nearly threw me into convulsions. . . . Now, what could this be? . . . How the deuce did all this occur so early? where could it originate? I certainly had no sexual ideas for years afterwards: and yet my misery, my love for that girl were so violent, that I sometimes doubt if I have ever really been attached since. . . . Next to the beginning, the conclusion has often occupied my reflections, in the way of investigation. That the facts are thus, others know as well as I, and my memory yet tells me so, in more than a whisper. But, the more I reflect, the more I am bewildered to assign any cause for this precocity of affection.[20]

Trying to explain himself to himself, Byron documents or displaces his amorous obsession by an obsession with its cause. What *kind* of cause would have satisfied Byron in this, a serious effort at self-analysis of his own primordial case?[21] Is this satire self-directed? Does it mark a "change of heart"?

Byron's tone here seems straightforward enough, and yet he is apparently engaging in the same sort of explanatory quest that comes in for satire in the early cantos of *Don Juan*. Uncannily, what would seem to be the moment of supreme

18. Thomas Moore, *The Life of Lord Byron; With His Letters and Journals,* 2 vols. (Philadelphia: Carey and Hart, 1846), 1:14.

19. Ibid., 1:14.

20. Ibid., 1:15–16.

21. An alternative direction in which to take this discussion would be through Peter Manning's suggestion that "the 'one beloved playmate' invoked by 'Childe Harold's Good Night' is the type of the perfectly benevolent mother" in *Byron and His Fictions* (Detroit: Wayne State University Press, 1978), p. 26.

self-delusion in canto 1 is the moment of Juan's "self-communion with his own high soul," explicitly marked as a Wordsworthian-Coleridgean idealization, where Juan's reflections sound for all the world like a rewriting of Byron's Journal entry on Mary Duff:

> He thought about himself, and the whole earth,
>   Of man the wonderful, and of the stars,
> And how the deuce they ever could have birth;
>   And then he thought of earthquakes, and of wars,
> How many miles the moon might have in girth,
>   Of air-balloons, and of the many bars
> To perfect knowledge of the boundless skies;
> And then he thought of Donna Julia's eyes. (1:92)

The very next scene, dated "the sixth of June—I like to be particular in dates" (1:103), is the one in which Juan and Julia "fall" through their inattention to the laws of sexual attraction. How the deuce are we to understand the connection between the two "how the deuce's" juxtaposed here?

What is in order is some closer attention to Byron's moral mechanics, to the formalities of explanation in his poetic laboratory, and to the grammar of the terms he deploys there. The labilities of the Byronic vocabulary make it difficult to conduct a "materialist" analysis of his project, or for that matter a "historical-materialist" analysis, and this is at least partly because he himself seems to anticipate and complicate the very operations of such accounts.

3. "Man Fell with Apples"

Some of the problems about Byron's "materialism" in relation to his understanding of human motivation can be illustrated in what is probably his most explicitly formulated meditation on the problem of causality in *Don Juan*, the passage that deploys the metaphor of a moral mechanics I cited earlier in De Quincey's essay on "The Casuistry of Duelling." I refer to the witty exordium to canto 10, which contemplates the relation between explanation in natural philosophy and in (what the eighteenth century called) "moral philosophy":

> When Newton saw an apple fall, he found
>   In that slight startle from his contemplation—
> 'Tis *said* (for I'll not answer above ground
>   For any sage's creed or calculation)—
> A mode of proving that the earth turned round
>   In a most natural whirl called "Gravitation,"

And this is the sole mortal who could grapple,
Since Adam, with a fall, or with an apple.

Man fell with apples, and with apples rose,
  If this be true; for we must deem the mode
In which Sir Isaac Newton could disclose
  Through the then unpaved stars the turnpike road,
A thing to counterbalance human woes;
  For ever since immortal man hath glowed
With all kinds of mechanics, and full soon
Steam-engines will conduct him to the Moon. (10:1–2)

This passage has the look of perspicuity, but its juxtaposition of natural mechanics and moral mechanics could scarcely be more problematically framed, as just a modest analysis of the central conceit can show.

Certain post-Newtonian philosophers, such as Hume, attempted to work out the possibilities of extending the Newtonian method beyond natural science. To accept the Humean premises to which Byron often seems so committed, premises that William Godwin accepted wholesale in *Political Justice* and that for years had Shelley's full endorsement, is to see natural and moral mechanics as analogues of one another, two sciences united by a single method. On this view, the sense of necessity that underwrites an account of the operations of nature—the operations of the stars, for example—is exactly the same *in form* as the sense of necessity that underwrites what can be told about the operations of human nature. Such a picture, however, is Pelasgian in character, and if we take account of Byron's use of Genesis as the framework for the moral side of the question, we find that the analogy no longer seems to hold. For, whether one locates the consequences of a fall in the blindness of the subject's understanding or in the corruption of the subject's will—i.e., in the theory of knowledge or the theory of action—the physical-science/moral science analogy breaks down. It is a problem of comparing apples with, well, apples that you just cannot compare them with. Thus, *Don Juan* both creates and erases the structure of analogy between physical science and moral science, and herein lies the discrepancy in Byron's own "mode of proving" or "showing." This is the source of friction in the mechanics with which *he* "glows."[22]

22. Manning's discussion of this passage rightly notes how "the allusions to Prometheus and Adam suggest that *Don Juan* is not only epic action and Romantic introspection but also a version of history." The version of history that Byron has in view, for Manning, is "the history of consciousness seen as a movement from a past hypostatized as univalent, conscious only of the pre-

What further raises the stakes for Byron's poetic gamble in passages like this one is the way in which he uses the issue of explanation in attacking his poetic adversaries. Central to this critique is Byron's allegation of the failure of the Lake Poets to achieve perspicuity in their writings. As early as in the second of the poem's Dedicatory Stanzas, we find the witty dismissal of some of Coleridge's recent work on the grounds of its opacity. The reference is probably to the *Lay Sermons* (1816–17):

> And Coleridge, too, has lately taken wing,
> > But, like a hawk encumber'd with his hood,
> Explaining metaphysics to the nation—
> I wish he would explain his Explanation. (DS:2)

It is not clear that Byron could have known so, but in the first of his *Philosophical Lectures* for 1819 (lecture 3, on January 4) Coleridge was "explaining explanation" in Democritus by way of accounting for the invention of gravity in ancient materialism.

Attempting to reverse Zeno's subjectivist account of metaphysics, Coleridge pointed out, Democritus "took the direct opposite system," placing the "whole" in the "outward object and in the parts."[23] Democritus called the parts "atoms," but he needed some "something" to explain "why these atoms came together at all, how they came to connect and form essence" (p. 131). He was obliged, therefore, according to Coleridge, "to imagine, that is to invent, a *power,* the very thing which he had been anxious to avoid, which he called gravity, a something which was no longer either an atom or any thing capable of being conceived of by the mind, but [nonetheless] a notion altogether borrowed from what he found within himself, namely, the sense of power" (p. 131). And out of this, Coleridge explained, "came the whole notable system of material or mechanic philosophy taken as the base and groundwork of human knowledge" (p. 131). Coleridge's judgment about this philosophy is that "as instrumental" it cannot be too highly valued but that, as a critique of Zeno, it is a groundless, "a perfect fiction, as complete a dream as ever formed any imagined image" (p. 131). The point I wish to stress, however, is that, for all his attitudi-

---

sent, hence innocent, to the ambiguities and temporal self-consciousness of the modern era." Manning's *Don Juan,* in other words, is the history of historical consciousness itself, in roughly the sense identified by R. G. Collingwood, to whom Manning specifically refers. See *Byron and his Fictions,* pp. 214–216. I will try below to resituate this interesting claim about the poem, and likewise Manning's observation about Juan's "passivity," when I take up the problem of *Don Juan* as a historical novel.

23. Coleridge, *Philosophical Lectures* (New York: Philosophical Library, 1949), p. 130.

nizing against Coleridge in *Don Juan,* Byron's representation of the philosophy of mechanism is also a kind of pure fantasy, or "perfect fiction," operating in a most impure and imperfect human environment.

Two stanzas after the satirical remarks about Coleridge's opaque self-encumbrances, his poetical partner comes in for criticism along similar lines:

> And Wordsworth, in a rather long 'Excursion',
>   (I think the quarto holds five hundred pages)
> Has given a sample from the vasty version
> Of his new system to perplex the sages . . .
> And he who understands it would be able
> To add a story to the Tower of Babel. (DS:4)

Byron's practice is at odds with his preaching. The pun on "story" would seem to compromise the perspicuity of this very comment about Wordsworth's lack of it and thus to compress into a single line one major pattern of irony in the poem. Both of these early keynote passages, in any event, couch the issue we are investigating in terms of intelligibility (to borrow a distinction from modern philosophy of explanation) rather than those of causality.[24] Coleridge *explicates* metaphysics, one might paraphrase Byron, but needs to explicate his explication; Wordsworth's system (this critique derives from Francis Jeffrey) is faulted for writing incomprehensible defenses of his poetry in the preface to *Lyrical Ballads* and other essays. We have already seen that there is a problem, in view the labile ironies in *Don Juan,* about the poem's own general intelligibility. We can now note that there is a further problem concerning the relation of intelligibility and causation in those parts of the poem most involved with the topic or practice of explanation.

The question of intelligibility figures prominently in that description of Juan's wanderings in the woods just before he falls for, and with, Donna Julia, a passage in which, as we have seen, causal humor is particularly intense. When Juan wanders through "leafy nooks" (1:190), in self communion with his own high soul, he attempts to imagine his sexual interest in Julia as a merely specula-

---

24. This distinction has been in play at least since Peter Winch's Wittgensteinian critique of the nomological view of explanation held by Carl Hempel and the Berlin school; see *The Idea of a Social Science and its Relation to Philosophy* (London: Routledge & Kegan Paul, 1958), especially pp. 18–21. For a more recent formulation, also sympathetic to Wittgenstein, see Anthony Giddens, *Central Problems in Social Theory* (Berkeley: University of California Press, 1979). Speaking of Hempel's neo-Humian position, Giddens writes: "Explanation, most broadly conceived, can be more appropriately treated as the clearing up of puzzles or queries; seen from this point of view, explanation is the making intelligible of observations of events that cannot be readily interpreted within the context of an existing theory or frame of meaning" (p. 258).

tive curiosity. In his very act of inquiring into the causes of general ("man") and external ("the stars") objects of his observation, Juan becomes mystified about his own motives, and thus grows unintelligible to himself. The apparently casual disposition of the items in the catalogue would seem to betoken a certain insouciance of disposition *toward* those objects. That *affect*, on the other hand, can be read as an *effect* of Juan's self-deception. We can, that is, read the last object in the catalogue, Julia's eyes, as the one that counts, and the one that provides means of explaining the wandering of his attention in the first place.

The question of intelligibility becomes explicit, indeed, when Byron likens Juan's confusion in these "leafy nooks" to the sort of confusion to which Wordsworth fell prey during those wanderings in nature that he made the subject of his most celebrated poetry:

> There poets find materials for their books,
>   And every now and then we read them through,
> So that their plan and prosody are eligible,
> Unless, like Wordsworth, they prove unintelligible. (1:90)

As I read it, the line "so that their plan and prosody are eligible" is itself unintelligible here, which is to say that Byron is once again performing the confusion he says he deplores. As for the analogy of the confusions imputed to Juan and Wordsworth, it becomes so strong that it threatens to become a confusion of Juan and Wordsworth themselves, or at least this is a plausible inference from the narrator's having to enter the ensuing semantic clarification: "He, Juan (and not Wordsworth), . . . pursued / His self-communion with his own high soul" (1:91). Further, the locution that the narrator has taken from the "The Thorn"—"I know not why"—is now modified to apply to the class of persons (such as Juan, and Wordsworth himself) who tend to mistake the effects of philosophy for those of puberty:

> In thoughts like these true wisdom may discern
> Longings sublime and aspirations high,
> Which some are born with, but the most part learn
> To plague themselves withal, *they know not why*. (1:93; emphasis added)

The Lake poets as a group appear in the poem as writers whose failure to achieve perspicuity in explanation is a function of a failure to acknowledge material causality, especially sexual causality, in everyday life.

To see how much reinforcement *Don Juan* lends to this linkage between one's acknowledgment of certain kinds of causes, one's having a cause, and the intelligibility of one's writing, we need only consider how it forms the basis, in turn, for a linkage between the Lake Poets and the poem's preeminent bogeyman, the Viscount Castlereagh, England's Foreign Minister and chief negotiator at the Congress of Vienna (and thus a principal architect of the European Restoration after Waterloo). Byron's Castlereagh, the two-faced embodiment of tyranny and sycophancy in the poem, is the figure par excellence at once of verbal unintelligibility and suppressed sexuality. He appears in the Dedicatory Stanzas, after the lampoon on Southey, Coleridge, and Wordsworth, and as their master—and thus is in the position of one whose character can explain theirs. The set-piece lampoon of Castlereagh with which Byron closes his Dedicatory Stanzas is as trenchant as anything that one might find in the satire of, say, Swift and Pope, whom Byron so admired. It far exceeds in its trenchancy the then-celebrated satire on Castlereagh's literary production that we find in Moore's *Twopenny Post-Bag*.

The subject of this lampoon is initially called the "intellectual eunuch Castlereagh" and is subsequently referred to only with pronouns of neutral gender, yet Byron's description of Castlereagh does not finally represent him as without sexual passion:

> Cold-blooded, smooth-faced, placid miscreant!
>   Dabbling its sleek young hands in Erin's gore,
> And thus for wider carnage taught to pant,
>   Transferr'd to gorge upon a sister-shore;
> The vulgarest tool that tyranny could want,
>   With just enough of talent, and no more,
> To lengthen fetters by another fix'd,
> And offer poison long already mix'd.
>
> An orator of such set trash of phrase
>   Ineffably, legitimately vile,
> That even its grossest flatterers dare not praise,
>   Nor foes—all nations—condescend to smile:
> Not even a *sprightly* blunder's spark can blaze
>   From that Ixion grindstone's ceaseless toil,
> That turns and turns, to give the world a notion
> Of endless torments, and perpetual motion.
>
> A bungler even in its disgusting trade,
>   And botching, patching, leaving still behind
> Something of which its masters are afraid,
>   States to be curb'd, and thoughts to be confined,
> Conspiracy or Congress to be made—
>   Cobbling at manacles for all mankind—

A tinkering slavemaker, who mends old chains,
With God and man's abhorrence for its gains.

If we may judge of matter by the mind,
    Emasculated to the marrow, *It*
Hath but two objects—how to serve, and bind,
    Deeming the chain it wears even men may fit. (DS:12–15)

Though Byron will go on to say that Castlereagh is "fearless, because *no* feeling dwells in ice," this is a description of one whose sexuality is not inert, but sado-masochistic. It is not that Castlereagh is without desire. Rather, the desire that he has is only to serve and bind. He pants to wreak wider carnage with his sleek hands. The alleged perversion, furthermore, appears as a displacement that comes of a disavowal. It develops as part of a process of self-emasculation understood as sexual self-denial, the denial of the *place* of sexuality in one's life. Castlereagh's language is what it is because he has tried to debar passion from entering it. In this respect, ironically, Byron's implied argument resembles one that Wordsworth had made, though not published, in *The Prelude,* where he describes the theory-justified violence of the Reign of Terror as conduct in which passions exert their power without ever hearing the sound of their own names.[25] Byron's Castlereagh cannot manage his language because he does not own it, and he does not own his language because he does not own up to his passion. His phrases are manacles, to recall Blake's terms, not in that they are "mind forg'd" but in that they are unforged by their own user. The chains in which he would sadistically bind others are the same chains in which he himself has been bound, figured here as the "set trash of phrase" that issues in the mechanical operations of his oratory.

When Moore composed his allegory of the mutiny of Castlereagh's writings against their author, he invested the papers with a sense of revulsion at their own content that in turn induced their revolt against Castlereagh. If we read back to the squib in *The Twopenny Post-Bag* through Byron's account, however, Moore's critique acquires a different dimension. In having no cause of his own, we

---

25. Apropos of the "abstract philosophy" of the later phases of the French Revolution, Wordsworth writes:

        Tempting region that
    For zeal to enter and refresh herself,
    Where passions had the privilege to work,
    And never hear the sound of their own names.

The Prelude, ed. by Jonathan Wordsworth, M. H. Abrams, and Stephen Gill (New York: W. W. Norton, 1979), book 10: ll. 810–14 of 1805 text.

might say, Castlereagh can invest his writings with none. His cause is not theirs. This is why the papers must instead be understood as pursuing causes of their own. In Byron's account the notion of the autonomous cause, the cause that becomes the principle of autonomy, is associated with "passion." Byron's passion would, on this account, ensure that he retains command of his written words, a command that, in turn, ensures their intelligibility and virtue. These traits, in their turn, would be understood to operate in the service of general liberation. Unlike Castlereagh, Byron might then be understood as writing with a clear and forceful passion for the liberal cause. But the case is not so simple.

The difficulty can be highlighted by the way in which Byron's sense of the matter is mediated, predictably, through Wordsworth's. "All I have written," Byron wrote in response to an 1819 attack on *Don Juan* "has been mere Passion, passion it is true of different kinds, but always passion."[26] But it was Wordsworth who declared, in that same note to "The Thorn" where he described the old sea-captain, that "Poetry is passion; it is the history or science of feelings." Moreover, in his widely read apologia of 1815, the "Essay, Supplementary," Wordsworth elaborated the concept dialectically, explaining that while "passion" is "derived from a word which signifies *suffering,*" suffering has an "immediate and inseparable" connection with *action;* "To be moved . . . by a passion, is to be excited, often to external, and always to internal, effort; whether for the continuance and strengthening of the passion, or for its suppression, according as the course which it takes may be painful or pleasurable."[27] This paradoxical paradigm, which Byron and Wordsworth share, is the one defined by what Kenneth Burke calls the "dramatistic pun" in the phrase "the motivation of an act." Looking closely at the matter, Burke says, we find that "an act is by definition active, whereas to be moved (or motivated) is by definition passive" (GM, p. 40). There is a difference between Wordsworth's and Kenneth Burke's formulation here, in that for Wordsworth the suffering occasions or "excites" action, where as in Burke it grammatically constitutes it. In Byron, it seems that acknowledging the unintelligibility of passion—perhaps definable as its unsortable mix of what one does and suffers—is the ground of the intelligibility of one's expression. But here too there are complications.[28]

---

26. *Complete Miscellaneous Prose,* p. 110. Byron actually quotes David Deans from *The Heart of Mid-Lothian* in denoucing the apostasies of his moment (p. 119).

27. *Prose Works,* 3 vols. Edited by W. J. B. Owen and Jane Worthington Smyser (Oxford: Clarendon Press, 1974), 3:81–82.

28. For a good fresh discussion of the discourse of passion in poetry from Dennis and Pope through Wordsworth and Byron, see John Morillo, "Uneasy Feelings," Ph.D. dissertation, University of Chicago, 1994.

4. Byron's Waverley Novel

The issue of intelligibility in Castlereagh's prose reappears more explicitly in lines that introduce Juan's encounter with Catherine the Great, in canto 9, after the account of Juan's involvement in the siege of Ismail. Juan is about to achieve cabinet-level status in the Russian state by virtue of Catherine's sexual preference for him, her decision to elevate Juan over "him who, in the language of his station, / Then held that 'high official situation'" (9:48). Byron takes it upon himself to "explain" the phrase "high official station":

> Oh, gentle ladies! should you seek to know
> 　　The import of this diplomatic phrase,
> Bid Ireland's Londonderry's Marquess show
> 　　His parts of speech; and in the strange displays
> Of that odd string of words, all in a row,
> 　　Which none divine, and every one obeys,
> Perhaps you may pick out some queer *no*-meaning,
> Of that weak wordy harvest the sole gleaning.
>
> I think I can explain myself without
> 　　That sad inexplicable beast of prey—
> That Sphinx, whose words would ever be a doubt,
> 　　Did not his deeds unriddle them each day—
> That monstrous Hieroglyphic—that long Spout
> 　　Of blood and water, leaden Castlereagh! (9:49–50)

Here, the figure of the chain made by one's oppressor and inflicted on one's victim reappears as the meaningless "string of words" in Castlereagh's prose. Byron thus reformulates the charge against Castlereagh's bureaucratic cant explicitly in terms of its unintelligibility—his "queer no meaning"—and the punning phrase "bid [him] show his parts" (of speech) articulates a suspicion about the soundness of Castlereagh's grammar as a suspicion about the soundness of both his sexual and intellectual parts as well.[29]

Byron's own capacity for self-explanation is defined not only by his act of self-definition against Castlereagh but also, paradoxically, by his claim that he does not need Castlereagh to make himself "perspicuous." The implicit contradiction here is only aggravated by the general sense that Byron's resort to

---

29. I am indebted here to an unpublished talk by my former colleague, Sherwood Williams, about the relation between verbal and sexual "ambiguity" in Melville's fiction, and also, more generally, to Eve Kosofsky Sedgwick, *The Epistemology of the Closet* (Berkeley: University of California Press, 1990).

Castlereagh (or Southey, or Coleridge, or Wordsworth) for purposes of invidi-ous self-definition recurs so routinely in this poem as to become a kind of nar-rative tic. How else to explain this tic if not by positing an anxiety about the uncertain state of Byron's and his poem's own forms of (self-)intelligibility? The labile ironies in the poem's recurrent explanatory jokes, like the mutual in-compatibilities of its deep explanatory paradigms, already offer ample grounds for such anxieties.

While the passage in canto 9 portrays Castlereagh in his writings as a Sphinx to be unriddled and thus suggests a defining antithesis to Byron's self-repre-sentation in *Don Juan,* some lines near the end of canto 8 take stock of the poem in a way that, even before the fact, calls such a self-characterization into question:

> Reader! I have kept my word,—at least so far
>   As the first Canto promised. You have now
> Had sketches of love, tempest, travel, war—
>   All very accurate, you must allow,
> And *Epic,* if plain truth should prove no bar;
>   For I have drawn much less with a long bow
> Than my forerunners. Carelessly I sing,
> But Phoebus lends me now and then a string,
>   With which I still can harp, and carp, and fiddle,
> What further hath befallen or may befall
> The Hero of this grand poetic riddle,
> I by and bye may tell you, if at all. . . . (8:138–39)[30]

The riddle of *Don Juan,* then, is perhaps how it can be both a riddle and not a riddle—or, if we concede that it is a riddle, how its riddling differs from that of its adversary, who evidently stands for all that the poem professes to abhor.

Byron stresses that his is a "grand poetic"—that is to say, an "*Epic*"—riddle. We might wish to suppose here that the riddle of *Don Juan* differs from the riddle of Castlereagh's writings by virtue of the way it registers exactly that complex relation—just as we might say that Byron's contradictory deployment of explanatory idiom differs from Wordsworth's by virtue of registering *that* relation, the one between him and Wordsworth. The epic dimension of *Don Juan* would then more generally be understood in terms of its capacity for ac-commodating a variety of such relations. This will not quite work, however,

---

30. This passage offers an example of *syntactic* unintelligiblity to go with the other forms that we have noted. The clause, "What further hath befallen or may befall . . . ," constitutes the direct object, incompatibly, of both "fiddle" and "tell."

since, from the very first stanza of the dedication, *Don Juan* represents the genre of its poetic enemies as, precisely, epic—the pretentious, renegado, moderniz-ing, anti-Popean verse productions on a grand scale such as Southey's *Thalaba the Destroyer* (1801) and Wordsworth's *The Excursion* (1814). There was, how-ever, another version of modernized epic available to Byron, a version, as it happens, for which he showed nothing less than a passion. This is the version of "modern epopée" available to Byron in Scott's Waverley novels. Though the topic of Byron's connection with Scott has enjoyed some recent attention, and although the notion of *Don Juan* as "novelistic" has long been a commonplace in the commentaries, the precise relation of Byron's epic to the new form of the historical novel has remained curiously unexplored.[31]

This is curious for several reasons. The first is that Byron's letters for the pe-riod of the composition of *Don Juan* make it clear that he is a man obsessed with reading Scott's fiction. References to Scott are nearly as numerous as those to Shakespeare, and show a far greater degree of absorption. Less than two weeks after Byron sent off to John Murray the packet containing cantos 3 and 4 of *Don Juan,* he wrote Murray as follows (on March 1, 1820):

> Pray send me W. Scott's new novels—what are their names and characters? I read some of his former ones at least once a day for an hour or so.—The last are too hurried—he forgets Ravenswood's name—and calls him *Edgar*—and then *Norman*—and Girder—the Cooper—is—styled now *Gilbert* and now *John*—and he don't make enough of Montrose—but Dalgetty is excellent—and so is Lucy Ashton—and the bitch her mother. . . . Don't forget to answer forthwith—for I wish to hear of the arrival of the packets—viz. the two Cantos of Donny Johnny. . . . (BLJ, 7:48–49)

Writing again to Murray less than two months later on April 23, he resumes:

> My love to Scott—I shall think higher of knighthood ever after for his being dubbed—by the way—he is the first poet titled for his talent—in Britain—it has happened abroad before now—but on the continent titles are universal & worthless.—Why don't you send me Ivanhoe & the Monastery—I have never written to Sir Walter—for I know he has a thousand things & I a thousand nothings to do—but I hope to see him at Abbotsford before very long, and I will sweat his Claret for him— . . . I love Scott and Moore—and all the better brethren—but I hate & abhor that puddle of water-worms—whom you have taken into your troop in the *history* line I see. (BLJ, 7:83)

31. There are two brief biographical essays in *Byron and Scotland,* ed. Angus Calder (Totowa, N.J.: Barnes and Noble, 1989): P. H. Scott, "Byron and Scott," pp. 51–64, and J. Drummond Bone, "Byron, Scott, and Scottish Nostalgia," pp. 119–31; and a footnote in McGann's "The Book of Byron and the Book of a World," p. 269, n. 21. Andrew Rutherford takes up the ques-tion of Byron's relation to Scott's fiction toward the latter half of his "Byron, Scott, and Scotland," in *Lord Byron and His Contemporaries,* ed. Charles Robinson (Newark: University of Delaware Press, 1982), pp. 43–65. Perhaps the most provocative discussion of the subject, especially in re-spect to their mutually constructed relation to the literary market, is Sonia Hofkosh's "The Writer's Ravishment: Women and the Romantic Author—the Example of Byron," in *The Ro-mantic Woman,* ed. Anne K. Mellor (Bloomington: Indiana University Press), pp. 99–104.

That Byron invidiously compares Scott, and even Moore, with Murray's "troop in the *history* line," betrays a recognition on Byron's part that the "history" that is being made in this age of historicism is not in the genre of historiography as such. Byron's own work, by extension, deserves such comparison. This particular sequence closes, unsurprisingly, with Byron's acknowledging receipt of, and offering simple emphatic praise for, Scott's longed-for last novel of 1819: "I have received *Ivanhoe;—good*" (June 7—p. 113). But his letters of this period often show the process by which Byron's appetite is whetted for other novels— *The Monastery* and *The Abbott,* for example—and then gratified when the desired books have been delivered and perused.

In those instances, furthermore, where Byron expresses even the slightest disappointment with Scott's novels, as in his criticisms of *The Bride of Lammermoor,* it is often the case that his opinions improve with continued and compulsive rereading. Here is Byron's subsequent response to *The Bride:* "[January 5, 1821] Read the conclusion, for the fiftieth time (I have read all W. Scott's novels at least fifty times) of the third series of 'Tales of my Landlord',—grand work— . . . wonderful man! I long to get drunk with him" (BLJ, 8:13). Although it is safe to assume exaggeration in these numbers—Byron has a stanza-long joke, after all, about the number "fifty" (BLJ, 1:108)—it is worth recalling that this passage is not from a letter but from the journal Byron kept during his time in Ravenna, where hyperbole seems less in order. And while the fact that the character of Ravenswood in *The Bride of Lammermoor* was modeled on Byron's characters (and even his character) clearly might have influenced his judgment, just as clearly the entire series of "Landlord" tales struck a responsive chord with Byron. In the two critical essays he wrote during the period 1820–21, for example, Byron cited both of the early series, alluding to David Deans's deathbed lamentation on his time at the close of his public response to *Blackwood's* and borrowing an epigraph from *Old Mortality* for his *Letter to* **** ***** [John Murray] on the Pope Controversy.[32]

Not only does Byron laud Scott in private writings and related prose essays, but he also praises him openly in the stanzas of *Don Juan* itself. In the poem's dedicatory stanzas, Scott is the first of the contemporary writers offered by Byron in lieu of the renegado trio "Wordsworth, Coleridge, Southey" (DS:7). He is cited as Byron's "buon camerado" when it comes to the question of representing aberrant morals (12:16). He also figures prominently in the famous passage where Byron, while discussing the *Edinburgh Review,* comes to terms

32. Byron, *Complete Miscellaneous Prose,* pp. 119, 120.

with his own Scottishness (10:17–19). Beyond the fact of the praise incorporated into the poem, though, there is the further issue of what Scott is praised for. Late in the poem, when he calls Scott "the superlative of my comparative," the particular talent that Byron identifies is Scott's way with comparative description: "Scott, who can paint your Christian knight or Saracen, / Serf, lord, man with such skill" (15:59). One could argue (as Byron seems to recognize) that Scott's innovations in historical epic are built on a power to describe the typical characters and elements of various cultures, past and present, and to see the connection between such a literary mode and those popular travel books that Moore would have seen advertised in his *Morning Chronicle* for New Year's Day 1819.

This sort of comparativist cultural representation is a literary technique Byron seeks to redeploy to his own epic purposes, and nowhere more evidently, Byron being Byron, than in the canto where he denies that he will do so:

> I won't describe; description is my forte,
>> But, every fool describes in these bright days
> His wond'rous journey to some foreign court,
>> And spawns his quarto, and demands your praise—
> Death to his publisher, to him 'tis sport;
>> While Nature, tortured twenty thousand ways,
> Resigns herself with exemplary patience
> To guidebooks, rhymes, tours, sketches, illustrations. (5:52)[33]

Canto 5, written in the fall of 1820, marks the beginning of the third major block of the poem's composition-publication, and arguably the block where its comparative scheme of national-cultural critique begins to emerge. On February 16, 1821, soon after completing it, Byron confronted a jittery John Murray and addressed the possibility of the poem's being suspended while Murray assessed public reaction. At this point, he stressed that the five completed cantos formed "hardly the beginning," and outlined a scheme in which Juan would be taken on "the tour of Europe—with a proper mixture of siege—battle—and adventure—and to make him finish as *Anarcharsis Cloots*—in the French revolution" (BLJ, 8:78). Byron writes that he is uncertain of the number of cantos he would live to write but adds that he also "meant to have made him [Juan] a Cavalier Servente in Italy and a cause for divorce in England—and a Sentimental 'Werther-faced man' in Germany—so as to show the different ridicules of

---

33. Cf. "I won't describe—that is, if I can help / Description" (10:28).

the society in each of those countries" (BLJ, 8:78). It is in cantos 3 and 4, and then more dramatically in canto 5, where "description" is formally abjured, that Byron begins with steadily increasing deliberateness to move his protagonist into determinate cultural contexts that require the extraordinary descriptive virtuosity, the Scott-like "skill," to paint your Greek pastoral, Turkish harem, your English military, your Russian court, your English manor—those diverse scenes where Juan acts and is acted on.[34]

In establishing the relation of Byron to Scott, it is important to understand that they were not only the two recognized "kings" of the literary realm but that they had also, in a sense, been taking turns appropriating each other's reader-ships. Scott built an unprecedented public taste for romantic poetry in the first decade of the century, when he emerged as far and away the most widely read and acclaimed verse writer in Britain. Byron capitalized on this newly established audience with the first cantos of *Childe Harold* and with the early Oriental verse tales. Meanwhile, Scott turned his talents to the innovative series of Waverley novels, which reached their zenith just in the years (1818–19) when Byron composed and published the early cantos of his most "novelistic" verse production to date. Byron's use in *Don Juan* of so many elements of the Waverley format results in a poem in which it is hard not to see the general stamp of Scott's new form of "modern epopée."

In Juan we confront a distinctively and notoriously "passive" or "mediocre" hero, very much in line, in spite of his famous name, with such cipher-ish pro-tagonists as young Waverley and Ivanhoe.[35] Byron traces the historically condi-tioned and conditioning education of Juan in some detail, paying close attention to the culture of private or everyday life. He deftly steers Juan through situations that are identified in relation to stages of society—from the most "primitive" to the most "advanced." Further, as we have seen, if there is one Ro-mantic-era project that is as fully absorbed in the problematics of explanation as *Don Juan* is, it is surely Scott's attempt in the Waverley novels to bring Edin-burgh "philosophical history" to bear on the practice of fiction. Scott's is the lit-erary form in which the problem of what it means to "be of one's age" was given the fullest and certainly its most influential realization, and this certainly included the new mode of explanation in which, as Lukács wrote of Scott, we

34. In August 1819, when Byron told Murray he had "no plan" for *Don Juan,* he also had no plan to continue it: "If it don't take I will leave it off where it is with all due respect to the Public" (BLJ, 6:207). In the seventeen months that follow, apparently the period of his most intense en-gagement with Scott, he reaches a point where he can already describe the plan of the poem in the past tense.

35. See Alexander Welsh, *The Hero of the Waverley Novels* (1963; Princeton, N.J.: Princeton University Press, 1993), pp. 21–39.

understand the "specifically historical" as the derivation of the individuality of characters from the historical peculiarity of their epoch.[36] This in turn, as I have argued throughout, involved a new notion of typification—the moral exemplification of historical or age-specific "peculiarity"—and thus both a new sense of the historical situation and a concomitant transformation of casuistry.

I want to suggest, then, that *some* of the difficulties of the epic riddle that is *Don Juan,* some of its causal conundrums in particular, can be helpfully addressed in relation to the Waverley model. One such difficulty is the kind of contradiction that seems to be implicit in the relation of Byron's own literary practices in *Don Juan* and those of the figures he denounces, such as Castlereagh and Southey. To the extent that Byron is understood to be working within a "spirit-of-the-age" model of literary culture of the sort implicit in the Waverley novels, or in Shelley's contemporary observation that all writers must willy-nilly participate in the spirit of the age in spite of their avowed doctrines and systems, to that same extent must Byron see himself, like Shelley and Scott, as in some sense a party to contemporary developments he professes to abhor. On such an account, Byron would be inscribing himself into the representation of an epoch in which, much as he might wish to lampoon his fellow representative men, we can make out a dim recognition that he is of their number.

It may be well to recall in this connection what Byron said on the subject of contemporaneity at about this time, when he took part in the controversy that erupted in 1819 over the canonical status of Pope. Here again, the issue is broached by way of a problem about intelligibility, although here Byron is more explicit in seeing it as a problem in his own writings. The rhetorical crescendo of his *Letter to* ★★★★ ★★★★★★ [John Murray], published in 1821, occurs as an elaboration of his charge that the present enemies of Pope "have raised a mosque by the side of a Grecian temple of the purest architecture; and, more barbarous than the barbarians from whose practice I have borrowed the figure, they are not contented with their own grotesque edifice, unless they destroy the prior, and purely beautiful fabric which preceded, and which shames them and theirs for ever and ever."[37] Byron then answers the charge of hypocrisy on this score by conceding its truth: "I shall be told that amongst these—I *have* been—(or it may be still *am*) conspicuous;—true   and I am ashamed of it. I *have* been amongst the builders of this Babel, attended by a confusion of tongues. . . ."[38]

---

36. Lukács, *The Historical Novel,* trans. Hannah and Stanley Mitchell (London: Merlin Press, 1962), p. 19.

37. *Works of Lord Byron,* ed. R. E. Prothero and E. H. Coleridge, 13 vols. (London: 1898–1904), 5:559.

38. Ibid., 5:559.

The appositeness of this passage to *Don Juan* is punctuated by Byron's castiga-
tion of those disciples of Wordsworth who, understanding his poetry, "would
be able / To add a story to the Tower of Babel" (DS:4). What Byron goes on
to say in his own defense—i.e., that at least he has not been among the detrac-
tors of the pure classical temple erected by Pope—is no more directly relevant
here than his acknowledgment that when it comes to the production of romantic unintelligibility he cannot escape being of his age any more than Pope
could have escaped being of his.[39] Byron, Scott, Moore, Shelley, Southey,
Wordsworth, Coleridge, and even Castlereagh (insofar as his speeches would
have been taken as "literature" and thus susceptible to poetic analysis)—each
becomes a case *in relation to* the normative scheme of the epoch, the "common
case" of degenerate Babel.

   Don Juan is thus haunted by a historicism with which it can neither dispense
nor quite come to terms. To see how this poem poses a kind of case for the new
Romantic historicism, it is useful to ask exactly how, reading *Don Juan,* we best
construct the poem's "historical situation." In Christensen's study, as its subtitle
suggests, the "historical situation" of *Don Juan* is "commercial society." In
McGann's, especially in the coda essay he published after *Don Juan in Context,*
the answer is somewhat more chronologically specific. The poem's historical
situation, for McGann, is defined by "the period 1789–1824," and it offers the
"history" or " *wholeness* of [this] period," at the same time that it dramatizes its
participation in its repetition compulsions.[40] What I wish to emphasize here is

---

   39. Byron's chief ally in the defense of Pope was Isaac Disraeli, whose contributions to the
campaign Byron knew and praised. Reviewing Joseph Spence's *Anecdotes of Books and Men,*
Disraeli explained his position as follows:

   In the contrast of human tempers and habits, in the changes of circumstances in society, and
   the consequent mutations of tastes, the objects of poetry may be different in different periods; preeminent genius obtains its purpose by its adaptation to this eternal variety; and on
   this principle, if we would justly appreciate the creative faculty, we cannot see why Pope
   should not class, at least in file, with Dante, or Milton. It is probable that Pope could not have
   produced an "Inferno," or a "Paradise Lost," for his invention was elsewhere: but it is equally
   probable that Dante and Milton, with their cast of mind, could not have so exquisitely
   touched the refined gaiety of "the Rape of the Lock."

"Cast of mind" here clearly designates a historically-determinate sensibility, a culturally relative
normative framework of aesthetic judgment: *Quarterly Review* 66 (July 1820): 410. Disraeli had
in fact elaborated such a framework in *The Literary Character,* 2 vols. (London: John Murray,
1818). For a more detailed account of Byron's position on this subject see my "The Pope Controversy: Romantic Poetics and the English Canon," *Critical Inquiry* 10 (spring 1984): 481–509.
   40. McGann, "The Book of Byron and the Book of a World," in *The Beauty of Inflections: Literary Investigations in Historical Method and Theory* (Oxford: Clarendon Press, 1985), pp. 287, 291,
288.

the way in which the poem offers an implicit critique of the very idea of the "commercial" phase of society or of a "period" like 1789–1824, even as it so crucially deploys such conceptions. It is useful here to reconsider one of the standard exhibits in talking about Byron's grand scheme for his poem.

Responding to a review of the poem about a year after spelling out his vision of the poem for Murray, Byron rearticulated his plan of *Don Juan* for his friend Medwin: "[W]hat the Writer says of DJ is harsh—but it is inevitable—He must follow—or at least not directly oppose the opinion of a prevailing & yet not very firmly seated party—a review may and will direct or 'turn away' the Currents of opinion—but it must not directly oppose them—D Juan will be known by and bye for what it is intended a *satire* on *abuses* of the present *states* of Society—and not an eulogy of vice" (BLJ, 10:68). Byron's echo of the Scottish-Enlightenment idiom—"states of society"—clearly establishes Byron's assimilation of the cultural-historical model and identifies his resistances to it. First, Byron seems willing to see society itself in global terms, rather than positing a relation between a "state of society" and a "state of the world" of the sort we traced back to John Millar in Scottish-Enlightenment theory. Second, in his curious phrase "present *states* of society," Byron emphasizes the simultaneity of such states with each other in his scheme of things. In the *Letter to ★★★★ ★★★★★★*, this simultaneity of states is figured in the fact that Byron has the romantic poets of his own age building their grotesque mosque "by the side of" the temple erected by Pope. In *Don Juan*, this simultaneity is figured in the fact that Byron has Juan traverse the states of society in just a brief interval of a relatively short lifetime. That Juan is young at the Siege of Ismail (late 1790) but will die in the Reign of Terror (1793–94) conveys a strong sense of the copresence of the "states" through which he passes in the contemporary world order. Indeed, after his flight from polite Spanish society in canto 1, Juan is taken through a series of social arrangements corresponding at least *roughly* to the kind of sequence familiar from the schemes of the philosophic historians: a bucolic natural state on the island with Haidée, an eastern despotic state in canto 5, a medieval siege in cantos 6–8, an absolutist court in Catherine's Russia, a commercial oligarchy in the English cantos.[41] Finally, Byron's satirical emphasis on the "abuses" of these states of society, like his insistence on the "degeneracy" of the age of Southey and Castlereagh in Britain, suggests a stronger emphasis on decline and decay in the course of history than we have seen in the

---

41. None of these "states" is pure, the way that Pope's temple is supposed to be. Thus, notoriously, the idyllic largesse of Haidée's apparently innocent island proves to be supported by a particularly ambitious and violent network of piracy.

Scottish Enlightenment accounts of the "progress" and (albeit uneven) development of societies.

What Byron's comments to Medwin help to highlight, then, are the ways in which *Don Juan* manages to reopen the question of what counts as "a society" in the discourse on the "State of Society" and, what amounts to the same thing, to expose the aporia in the relationship established by writers like Millar between the "state of society" and the "state of the world." The problem, in a sense, has to do with the question of what you hold constant as part of an explanatory framework and what you allow as variation to be explained. The problem also marks the contradiction between the first and last chapters of *Waverley*—turning on the question of whether Scott undertook this experiment with historical narrative to preserve evanescent manners or to identify the unchanging features of human nature. Significantly, when Scott seems to be arguing the latter point, as he does in the opening chapter of *Waverley,* he identifies the explanatory substratum as the domain of "the passions." Taking his metaphor from the language of heraldry, the narrator distinguishes between the changing colors by which the passions are differently expressed in different times from their underlying "bearings":

> The wrath of our ancestors, for example, was coloured *gules;* it broke forth in acts of open and sanguinary violence against the objects of its fury. Our malignant feelings, which must seek gratification through more indirect channels, and undermine the obstacles which they cannot openly bear down, may be rather said to be tinctured *sable.* But the deep-ruling impulse is the same in both cases; and the proud peer who can now only ruin his neighbour according to law, by protracted suits, is the genuine descendant of the baron who wrapped the castle of his competitor in flames, and knocked him on the head as he endeavoured to escape from the conflagration. It is from the great book of Nature, the same through a thousand editions, whether of black-letter, or wire-wove and hot-pressed, that I have venturously essayed to read a chapter to the public. (Wav., chap. 6)

To focus on the subtext in this palimpsest, the book of human nature, the same through all editions, is presumably to operate in a code that is always already evened out. It is not a respecter of the unevennesses of cultural development. Byron, however, has his own way of flattening the emergent sense of historical specificity into the grammar of the passions. To see how, and to conclude with *Don Juan,* I would like to turn briefly now to the representation of Juan's encounter with Catherine the Great, who, like Castlereagh, is a world-historical individual in *Don Juan,* and who is perhaps the only character in the poem to surpass Castlereagh in demonic power. This episode, perhaps more obviously derivative of one of Scott's inventions than any other in the poem, also points to Byron's crucial departure from Scott's narrative practice in the Waverley novels, especially in regard to explanation.

5. Catherine and Castlereagh: Worst Cases, Worst Causes

To consider the kind of episode from the Waverley novels on which Byron partially modeled his encounter between Juan and Catherine the Great, one need only think of Edward Waverley's meeting with Bonnie Prince Charles, Henry Morton's with Claverhouse (in *Old Mortality*), or Jeanie Deans's with the Duke of Argyle (in *The Heart of Mid-Lothian*). All show how this sort of incident is handled in Scott. The reason that this sort of episode—the encounter between the mediocre protagonist and the "world-historical individual"—recurs so often in Scott's fiction is that, as Lukács has explained, it is so crucial to the fundamental representational dynamics of Scott's new form. In such episodes, Scott tends to draw the historical figure in such a way as to typify a specifically historical formation or sociological group of the cultural epoch in question; the encounter serves to place the mediocre hero in connection with such forces. Certain residual tendencies of this narrative strategy survive in Byron's handling of the Juan-Catherine episode. Seeing the poem as moving through a series of "stages of society," from the barbarism of the shipwreck episode to the commercial manners of the English cantos, we might say that Catherine and her modernized court typify something about the social structure of Europe's developing nation states in the eighteenth century. Something of this historical particularity is suggested in the way in which Byron dresses Juan for the part he will play in this meeting. We are asked to "suppose" Juan as "Love turned a Lieutenant of Artillery":

> His Bandage slipped down into a cravat;
>   His Wings subdued to epaulettes; his Quiver
> Shrunk to a scabbard, with his Arrows at
>   His side as a small sword, but sharp as ever;
> His bow converted into a cocked hat;
>   But still so like, that Psyche were more clever
> Than some wives (who make blunders no less stupid)
> If She had not mistaken him for Cupid.

But, just as the particularity of Juan's role as late-eighteenth-century military officer is overshadowed by the mythic type he is said to embody, so Catherine will be made to play Psyche to his Cupid here, as well as Helen to his Paris.

Nor does Byron quite observe the kind of relations Scott tended to portray between mediocre protagonist and world-historical individual as those relations were set forth and analyzed by Scott. Indeed, when it comes to issues of explanation and causality, which are intensely foregrounded here, explanation from period specificity tends to give way to an overriding explanatory axis, just as the third-person narrative decorum of the passage gives way to an apostrophe that is extraordinary even by the wide-ranging standards of this poem:

> Oh, thou 'teterrima *Causa*' of all 'belli'—
>   Thou gate of Life and Death—thou nondescript!
> Whence is our exit and our entrance,—well I
>   May pause in pondering how all Souls are dipt
> In thy perennial fountain—how man *fell,* I
>   Know not, since Knowledge saw her branches stript
> Of her first fruit, but how he falls and rises
> *Since, thou* hast settled beyond all surmises.
>
> Some call thee 'the worst Cause of war,' but I
>   Maintain thou art the *best:* for after all
> From thee we come, to thee we go, and why
>   To get at thee not batter down a wall,
> Or waste a world? Since no one can deny
>   Thou dost replenish worlds both great and small:
> With, or without thee, all things at a stand
> Are, or would be, thou Sea of Life's dry Land!
>
> Catherine, who was the grand Epitome
>   Of that great Cause of war, or peace, or what
> You please (it causes all the things which be,
>   So you may take your choice of this or that)—
> Catherine, I say, was very glad to see
>   The handsome herald, on whose plumage sat
> Victory; and, pausing as she saw him kneel
> With his dispatch, forgot to break the seal.
>
> Then recollecting the whole Empress, nor
>   Forgetting quite the woman (which composed
> At least three parts of this great whole) she tore
>   The letter open with an air which posed
> The Court, that watched each look her visage wore,
>   Until royal smile at length disclosed
> Fair weather for the day. Though rather spacious,
> Her face was noble, her eyes fine, mouth gracious. (9:55–58)

The addressee of the apostrophe in stanzas 55 and 56, the *causa* in question, as the Latin allusion makes clear, is the Horatian *cunnus,* and Byron's figurings of it at this key juncture in the poem mark some of the most complex poetry he ever composed. Stylistically, these lines comprise one of those rare passages in his work where his Augustan sensibility fully merges with both a Cavalier poetic subject matter and Metaphysical poetic talent for complicating the witty conceit. The conceit itself, the female genitalia as *cause* or case, is a familiar one in seventeenth-century bawdy comedy of the sort that Byron knew and often cited.[42]

Some of the complications of the metonymy in question here are elaborated by an ostentatious logic that seems to call attention to Byron's "wish to be perspicuous." Although the *cunnus* is the worst cause of war, he argues, it is also the best, since of all causes of war this at least can also replenish the populations that war destroys. In stanza 57, which returns from apostrophic to narrative mode, Byron extends the analysis of the *cunnus* as the cause of war by an implicitly syllogistic line of thought that runs thus: if the *cunnus* is the cause of all things, and if war is a thing, then it is necessarily the cause of war as well. And yet the complications generated here are not so easily held in check. In the passage leading up to these lines, Byron has prepared the undoing of Catherine's historical specificity by the strong suggestion that the Siege of Ismail is a replay of the Homeric account of the Siege of Troy, a siege he represents as carried out on very much, as it were, the same grounds. At first, one might take Byron's dehistoricizing move here as a simplification of Scott's practice in such episodes. Where Scott makes such scenes occasions for the applications of his explanatory frameworks for relating characters to one another, Byron turns one of his characters, Catherine, into the "Epitome" of what he insists on calling the cause of all things, the great (w)hole itself. This is Catherine as Woman, Woman as Eve, Eve as the absent cause (in the meditation on Newton and the apples) of all of Man's fallings and risings. This very reduction, however, is articulated in terms of tropes that seem to defy it and to recomplicate the question with a vengeance. In Kenneth Burke's terms, the passage might be said to conflate the dramatistic functions of scene and agent (GM, 7–20). For the *cunnus* in this passage is figured both as a part of the scene—the gate of our exits and our entrances—and as a part played in the scene, in the person of Catherine, who is said to be epitomized by it. The *cunnus* as *causa,* in other words, shares a struc-

---

42. Eric Partridge cites Shakespearean puns on *case* as "pudend" in both *The Merry Wives of Windsor* and *All's Well that Ends Well*—in *Shakespeare's Bawdy* (London: Routledge, 1947), pp. 84–85. In *Merry Wives,* the puns also involve grammatical jokes of the sort Scott makes in the

tural principle with the *causa* as case: the sense of being ambiguous as to the question of frame and subject, container and thing contained.[43]

One of the obvious problems with Byron's taking the *cunnus* as what Burke would call the "representative case" of his philosophic casuistry, however, is that it inadequately engenders generality in respect to the question of gender itself. The problem shows in Byron's deployment of the first-person-plural pronoun, which seems to wobble along an axis very close to that which can been seen in Byron's self-conscious paranomasia with "man" as marking both gendered and ungendered humanity.[44] In calling the *cunnus* the scene of "our exits and our entrances," he even seems to be giving himself away on this point, since (in view

---

chaster context of *The Heart of Mid-Lothian*. Mistress Quickly, who performs the famous eulogy over the "cold" genitals of Falstaff in act 2 of Henry IV, is at the center of things in this scene of education between the boy William and his Master, Sir Hugh Evans:

> WILLIAM Articles are borrow'd of the pronoun, and be thus declin'd, "Singulariter, nominativo, hic, haec, hoc."
> EVANS "Nominativo, hig, hag, hog." Pray you, mark: genitivo, jujus. Well, what is your accusative case?
> WILLIAM "Accusativo, hinc."
> EVANS I pray you, have your remembrance, child. "Accusativo, hung, hang, hog."
> QUICKLY "Hang-hog" is Latin for bacon, I warrant you.
> EVANS Leave your prabbles, 'oman. What is the focative case, William?
> WILLIAM O—"vocativo, O."
> EVANS Remember, William, focative is "caret."
> QUICKLY And that's a good root.
> EVANS 'Oman, forbear.
> MRS PAGE Peace!
> EVANS What is your genitive case plural, William?
> WILLIAM Genitive case?
> EVANS Ay.
> WILLIAM "Genitivo—horum, harum, horum."
> QUICKLY Vengeance of Jenny's case! Fie on her! Never name her, child, if she be a whore.

The Complete Works of Shakespeare, 3d ed. (Glenview, Ill: Scott, Foresman, 1980), p. 347.

Elsewhere, in the *Dictionary of Slang,* 8th ed. (New York: Macmillan, 1984), Partridge points to the same pun in *The Chances,* by John Fletcher, a playwright of whom Byron was known to be fond. Interestingly, in that play, whose hero is a philanderer named "Don John," the language of the case is linked to the "cause of honour" in a central dueling scene and to the issue of probability, as indicated in the title. *The Chances* (London: R. Bentley, 1692).

43. And there is the further issue of whether *tetterima causa* is not better translated as "worst case," making Catherine's scene the worst case scenario of war.

44. There are a number of passages in *Don Juan* that acknowledge the problem of the gender specificity of humanist idiom. Even in the stretch between this encounter with Catherine and the "Man fell with apples" passage at the start of the next canto, we find one that marks this semantic wobble, a stanza in which the Shakespearean epicene idiom—"what a strange thing is man"—is immediately undercut: "and what a stranger / thing is woman!" (9:64). For a good discussion of related gender questions in the poem, see Susan Wolfson, "Their She-Condition: Cross-Dressing and the Politics of Gender in *Don Juan,*" *ELH* 54 (fall 1987): 585–613.

of Catherine's notorious heterosexuality) the first "our" indicates a nongen-
dered first-person plural and the second a gendered one. The representative
case of the *cunnus* likewise has limited application in the domain of sexuality
and sexual preference, a limitation that seems particularly acute in view of recent studies of Byron's own homosexuality. The notion that the *cunnus* might
not mean the world to a man of passion, might not be (to paraphrase Wittgenstein) "all that is the case," ought to have been available to a writer of Byron's experiences—a writer so well-versed in what Andrew Elfenbein, applying D. A.
Miller's term to the case of Byron, calls the "open secret" of Regency sodomy.[45]
Thus, on the one hand, the case of Catherine is elaborated as a prophylactic measure to sustain the myth of hetrosexual normativity embodied in the figure of
Juan/Byron. On the other (though it may be the same hand), it becomes a kind
of Byronic escape hatch from history, a passage into unproblematized passion as
such, the element of pure unintelligibility that is supposed to lend meaning to
all around it. For Byron, Catherine lacks sense because she embodies it.

It is here, I think, that the great bogey figure of Castlereagh returns to haunt
that of Catherine. In *Byron and Greek Love,* Louis Crompton actually deals at
some length with the case of Castlereagh, but his concern is chiefly with the
"historical" Castlereagh, and with the possibility that his suicide in 1822 was
occasioned by attempts to blackmail him for (actual or contrived) homosexual
liaisons. Oddly, Crompton does not address the "textual" Castlereagh, the character whose sexuality is made an issue in *Don Juan* three years before either the
suicide of Castlereagh or the arrest of Bishop Clogher on charges of homosexuality. Does Byron's Castlereagh become the epitome of all that lies beyond the
causal field of the all-causing *cunnus* of which Catherine is the epitome? In calling Castlereagh an intellectual eunuch, can he be suggesting that the explanatory confusions of this monstrous sphinx are what they are because "it" has
attempted to place itself beyond the power of what the poem represents as the
primum mobile? And if so, then where does this sort of placement leave "Byron"
itself in the poem's epic framework of erotics and explanations?[46]

Perhaps the most vexing questions of all for the poem, in the end, have to do
precisely with the way in which "Byron" figures as a site of motivation for what
we read in *Don Juan.* At the beginning and the end of the long set-piece description of Donna Julia there are editorial interjections: "Her eye (I'm very
fond of handsome eyes) / Was large and dark" and "Her stature tall—I hate a
dumpy woman" (1:60–61). Causal relations are very much in play here but it is

---

45. Elfenbein, *Byron and the Victorians* (Cambridge: Cambridge University Press, 1995),
pp. 209–10.
46. Louis Crompton, *Byron and Greek Love* (Berkeley: University of California Press, 1985).

hard to judge how they run: are the editorial comments occasioned by the picture of such charms, or are they meant to explain why the character is drawn
that way in the first place?[46] To put it another way, do such comments explain
Byron's masquerade of masculinity or does it tend rather to explain them? We
are still early in the Byron revival, and criticism has only begun to broach such
questions for the perspicuous perplexity of this text. When they are pursued
further it may prove that the poem does covet probability after all, but that it is
confused by this very desire and quite at a loss to explain it. Meanwhile, the
question of whether the case of *Don Juan* may be said to have a cause remains
suspended in its contradictions. Perhaps the poem is too quick to take refuge in
the very charm of contradiction:

> If people contradict themselves, can I
>   Help contradicting them and everybody,
> Even my voracious self? But that's a lie;
>   I never did so, never will. How should I?
> He who doubts all things nothing can deny,
>   Truth's fountains may be clear, her streams are muddy
> And cut through such canals of contradiction
> That she must often navigate o'er fiction. (15:88)

Here Byron's casuisty reaches its limit, not by attaining resolution but by giving
way to Pyrrhonian skepticism. Forsaking the possibility of rational deliberation, the poem can no longer, in such a view, continue to suspend our judgments or prolong our work of explanation.

Chapter Seven

AN "1819 TEMPER":
KEATS AND THE HISTORY
OF PSYCHE

*D*uring Thomas Moore's stay in Venice in the fall of 1819, Byron assigned him to a friend named Scott and encouraged him to "sall[y] out to . . . to see the sights" (JTM, 1:224). Moore obliged. On the first day, he went to the Ducal palace, in which he saw that mysterious blank space among the "portraits of the Doges in the Library" where the portrait of Marino Faliero should have hung. Byron intended "to write a tragedy" about Faliero, Moore noted, and soon would do so—his answer, quite pointedly, to the dramatic casuistry of Shelley's *The Cenci*.[1] For the second day's outing, on October 9, Moore visited the Grimani Palace, and then recorded that one of the things that struck him there was "a Cupid of Guido's" (fig. 9). It was here, too, he recalled, that he found "the story of Cupid & Psyche in one of the rooms, and we were much amused with two Englishmen who could not be made to understand what Favola di Psyche meant—what brings such men to such places?" (JTM, 1:226).[2] I cite this anec-dote, and particularly the "amusement" of Moore and his friend at the two Englishmen, to raise the question of "what Favola di Psyche meant" beyond the trivial issue of a title in a foreign language. I wish to explore what the fable of Psyche might have meant not just to two English tourists in Venice but to a larger literary culture—indeed to consider how the story of the soul, in the hands of a writer such as Keats, could come to figure the history of culture itself.

The "story" that Moore would have seen depicted in one of the rooms of the Grimani Palace has its classical source in Apuleius's *Golden Ass*. In an era when

---

1. In the preface to *The Cenci,* as it happens, Shelley claimed that the play was inspired by the portrait of Beatrice in Rome he attributed to this same artist—SPP, p. 242—though the attribu-tion to Guido has recently been called into question by D. Stephen Pepper, *Guido Reni* (Oxford: Phaidon, 1984), p. 304.

2. In *The Journal of Thomas Moore,* the place is identified as "Giovanni Palace," but this appears to be a mistranscription. I thank Charles Cohen for help on Venetian art history.

Figure 9.   Detail from *Sacred and Profane Love,* Guido Reni, Museo Civico, Pisa. Probably similar to the Guido "Cupid" seen by Moore in 1819. Alinari/Art Resource, New York.

"the soul" and "psychology" were contested concepts, both philosophically and politically, the Psyche myth enjoyed fresh attention and took on new significance. In 1795, for example, Blake's hero, Thomas Taylor, the neoplatonic classicist whom Isaac Disraeli called "the modern Pletho" and Coleridge "the English Pagan," issued a translation of Apuleius's story with a commentary on the announced "meaning of the fable" as an allegory of the soul's "fall" from "the intelligible world."[3] In the terms I have been developing, Taylor construes

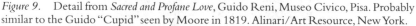

3. Taylor, *The Fable of Cupid and Psyche* (London: Leigh and Sotherby, 1795), pp. 4–5. Disraeli's epithet appears in his essay on "Modern Platonism," where he moves from a discussion of Gemisthus Pletho, the late-medieval scholar credited with massive influence on Florentine Platonism, to his own moment: "a *modern Pletho* has risen in Mr. Thomas Taylor, who, consonant to the platonic philosophy, in the present day religiously professes *polytheism!*" See Isaac Disraeli, *Curiosities of Literature,* 4 vols. (New York: Thomas Crowell, 1881), 1:295. Coleridge's epithet appears in his Letter to Thelwall, November 19, 1796, cited in James Dykes Campbell, *Samuel Taylor Coleridge* (London: Macmillan, 1894), p. 58.

the myth of Psyche as a kind of primordial "case," a situation explicitly defined by a "fall" from ideal principle and calling for judgment. I will later argue that this account, understood as an attempt to recuperate the soul from its near annihilation by an "enlightened" philosophy of mechanism, made it possible to achieve new purchase on the case of Psyche and on the casuistry of "psychology"—the study of the soul's "explanatory words." Eventually, for Keats, immersed in neopagan lore but self-conscious of his modern moment, the question of history would become particularly salient. But perhaps a reminder about the tale itself is in order.

Once upon a time, a king and queen had three daughters, the last of whom, Psyche, was so beautiful that she began to be worshipped by the people of her country. The goddess Venus noticed this new practice with envy, enraged that the homage owed to her own immortal beauty was being slighted in favor of a mere girl. In order to punish and humiliate Psyche, Venus asked her son Cupid, also known as Eros, to make Psyche enamored of an unworthy lover. On seeing Psyche's beauty, however, the unruly boy fell in love with her himself. Through the offices of the Apollonian oracle, he had Psyche delivered to a forest bower, where, after a sumptuous feast and a shower of precious gifts, he married and made love to her by the dark of night, leaving at daybreak to ensure against his being seen. This visitation was repeated often, and so they lived and loved, darkling, until Psyche allowed her jealous older sisters to arouse her doubt about her lover's good faith.

Against his explicit warnings, Psyche agreed to act on her sisters' plan to reveal her lover's identity. One night, as Cupid lay sleeping next to her, she examined him by the light of a lamp she had hidden for this purpose. Newly infatuated by the beauty of his form, Psyche accidentally spilled a drop of lamp oil on his shoulder, whereupon he awoke and discovered the betrayal. He fled back to his mother to be healed, leaving Psyche in a state of desperate longing. She implored Venus for clemency and was eventually charged with a series of three arduous tasks to be performed as acts of appeasement. Completing these tasks, with the help of various supernatural agents, Psyche was assigned a fourth, to descend to Hades and return to Venus with a box containing the beauty of Proserpine. Having nearly passed this test as well, Psyche ignored advice not to look in the box, again letting her curiosity overwhelm her, and thus apparently lost all hope of being reunited with Cupid. But Cupid, now healed, and moved by Psyche's efforts to reclaim him, sued successfully to Jupiter for redress. In spite of Venus's antipathy, Jupiter declared Psyche's promotion to the state of immortality to be a fit spouse for the god of Love. At length, a daughter, Pleasure, was born to them.

Although the "meaning" of this story has long been a matter of debate, most recently in Rachel Blau de Plessis's gender-based critique of Erich Neumann's influential Jungian commentary, I wish to restrict attention here, at least at first, to the meaning of the Psyche fable for Moore's contemporaries. What it meant to Byron, for example, is a matter we have already considered, in looking at his ironized portrayal of young Juan's appearance before Catherine the Great in canto 9 of *Don Juan*. Byron first describes Juan as the historical materialization of the idealized character of Love—Cupid's bandage slipping to form the cravat and his wings drooping to become the epaulettes of a late-eighteenth-century officer's uniform. After materializing Cupid in the character of Juan, Byron eternalizes Psyche as the very principle of the body itself in the character of Catherine, a body that becomes at once scene and agent of all "causes" in the poem. Byron, we might say, uses the myth of Cupid and Psyche to move into "history"—history staged as a Scott-like encounter between mediocre heroes and world-historical individuals—only to move out of it again into a metaphysics, or at least a metaphorics, in which reproductive erotics appear as the soul's final cause.

We know that Moore, the day after he saw Guido's Cupid in 1819, reported that Byron read to him "what he has done of the Third Canto of Don Juan" (JTM, 1:225). And although two years would pass before Byron painted his own version of the Cupid and Psyche scene in the Juan-Catherine encounter, it seems likely enough that he would have known the paintings in the Grimani Palace—and by no means improbable that he would have had a hand in shaping the itinerary that led Moore to that spot. But the contemporary appeal of the *Favola di Psyche* in 1819 was such that we do not need to look to Byron to establish Moore's interest in it. Indeed, at the time when Moore saw the paintings in Venice and sneered at the ignorant English tourists, he could boast that the author of the most influential treatment of the story in recent years—the Irish poet Mary Tighe—had been a compatriot and personal friend of his. Tighe's not inconsiderable posthumous fame in the Regency rested chiefly on her *Psyche; or The Legend of Love,* a long Spenserian verse narrative that enjoyed both critical and popular success in the years leading to 1819. Although Tighe died of consumption in Dublin in 1810, five British editions of her volume, as well as an American edition, appeared between 1811 and 1816. Moore's own connection with Mrs. Tighe and her famous poem, however, began long before. They were dinner companions both in London, during Tighe's stay there in 1805, and in Dublin, when Moore would revisit his place of birth.[4] When

4. Moore noticed Tighe's absence when she was not available company, which is not to say he was fully respectful of her or her talent. On a visit in 1806, he wrote: "You cannot imagine how

Tighe first published *Psyche* in 1805 in an edition of one hundred copies for her own circle of friends, Moore read it and expressed his pleasure in it with a short lyric addressed to Tighe *as* Psyche.[5] When Tighe died in 1810, he eulogized her as the protagonist, again, in her own Spenserian allegory, with a lyric that became part of the *Irish Melodies.*[6]

In the spring of 1819, a few months before Moore's visit with Byron, another English poet, John Keats, had already produced what probably still stands as the most important treatment of the *Favola di Psyche* in the history of lyric poetry: the *Ode to Psyche*. Moore and Byron could not have known about Keats's unpublished manuscript of the Ode—nor Keats, of course, about Byron's use of the myth in canto 9 of *Don Juan*. Tighe's *Psyche,* on the other hand, is a composition Keats knew intimately. The number of echoes of Tighe in Keats's poetry is indeed large enough to have generated a book-length tally and commentary of "parallel passages."[7] It says something about the reputation of Tighe, something not *necessarily* good, that she was strongly admired by the young Keats. And it says something about Tighe's perceived connection with Moore—not only personal but also stylistic and aesthetic—that, when Keats singled Tighe out for great praise in a lyric of 1815, *To Some Ladies,* he did so in a poem imitative of Moore's style:

> If a cherub, on pinions of silver descending,
>> Had brought me a gem from the fret-work of heaven.
> And, smiles with his star-cheering voice sweetly blending,
>> The blessings of Tighe had melodiously given;

---

desperately vulgar and dreary this place is: I have not even Mrs. Tighe to comfort me, but I expect she will be in town in a week or two. I regret very much to find that she is becoming so '*furieusement littéraire:*' one used hardly to get a peep at her blue stockings, but now I am afraid she shows them up to the knee." Thomas Moore, *Memoirs of the Life of The Right Honorable Richard Brinsley Sheridan* (London: Longman, 1825), 1:185.

5. "To Mrs. Henry Tighe, On Reading Her 'Psyche,'" in Moore, *Poetical Works,* 2 vols. (New York: Thomas Crowell, 1895), 1:95.

6. "I Saw Thy Form in Youthful Prime," *Poetical Works,* p. 185. The last stanza of this poem exemplifies Moore's way of figuring Tighe as Psyche:

> If souls could always dwell above,
>> Thou ne'er hadst left that sphere;
> Or could we keep the souls we love,
>> We ne'er had lost thee here, Mary!
> Though many a gifted mind we meet,
>> Though fairest forms we see,
> To live with them is far less sweet,
>> Than to remember thee, Mary!

7. Earle Vonard Weller, ed., *Keats and Mary Tighe* (New York: Century for the MLA, 1928).

> It had not created a warmer emotion
>> Than the present, fair nymphs, I was blest with from you,
> Than the shell, from the bright golden sands of the ocean
>> Which the emerald waves at your feet gladly threw. (ll. 17–24)[8]

Readers of the immensely popular *Irish Melodies*—"Believe me if all those endearing young charms / Which I gaze on so fondly today . . . "—would undoubtedly have recognized in the precious diction and the anapestic cadences of Keats's little exercise just so much warmed-over Moore.

Indeed, when he turned his hand to a sequel to this lyric, Keats wrote not only in Moore's style to express gratitude for a shell mentioned in *To Some Ladies* but also, appreciatively, *about* Moore. In "On Receiving a Curious Shell and a Copy of Verses from the Same Ladies," the "copy of verses" in question is indeed a hand-copied manuscript of Moore's *The Wreath and the Chain,* and it prompted Keats to redundant gushings of delight:

> So, when I am in a voluptuous vein,
>> I pillow my head on the sweets of the rose,
> And list to the tale of the wreath, and the chain,
>> Till its echoes depart; then I sink to repose.[9]

My intent here is not to poke fun at the young Keats, as he would later do at Moore. It is rather to show a connection between Moore and the author of *Psyche; or the Legend of Love* in the emulative eyes of a talented nineteen-year-old aspiring to become, as it were, the kind of poet who could produce an *Ode to Psyche.* And the reason it is worth showing that connection is to be in a position to see three things: first, how Keats articulated the development of his own "psyche" in relation to a condition he saw emblematized by Moore and Tighe; second, how his notion of "psychic" development became historicized; and, third, how his poetry of the annus mirabilis dramatized the story of Psyche—figure of human breath or spirit—in relation to what we have been calling the "spirit of the age."

This elaboration of the status of the soul and the myth of its immortality in early 1819—in the *Ode* and in the famous letter on "the vale of soul-making"—helps explain a major change both in Keats's circumstances and in his concept of circumstance as such. As we watch Keats working through or

8. "To Some Ladies," in PJK, p. 10.

9. For a poem even more obviously imitative of Moore's lyric mode, see also "O come, dearest Emma! the rose is full blown," a poem possibly written to Keats's future sister-in-law Georgiana (LJK, pp. 11–12).

beyond the developmental stage for which Tighe's *Psyche* is a primary case, we discover that his claim to be reaching another stage involves a new historicist understanding of both the stage and the case as such.[10] Keats, I contend, self-consciously addresses the problem of situational intelligibility, the "meaning" the human psyche finds or makes in the circumstances of its experience. In the hands of *this* Englishman, who had not yet traveled to Italy himself, the *Favola di Psyche* takes on a new meaning altogether—even, he suggests, for other poets of his age, like Wordsworth. Keats sees in Wordsworth and others a collective revision of the Psyche myth that is never quite explicit in their own work. Psyche becomes, for Keats in 1819, at once a representation and a representative of the spirit of the age. Wordsworth's own famous poetry on the soul's immortality and on the Mind as the "haunt and region" of his song themselves, as Keats intimates, belong to an age-specific, post-Enlightenment exploration of the relation of "psychology" to "idéologie," of gender to reproduction, and of historical and political movements to religious doctrines about the fate of the soul. The meaning of the fable of Psyche for England in 1819 has to do not only with a new cultural understanding of the historicity of the soul but also with the immanence—not to say imminence—of the "future state."

1. Smokeability

Keats's social position, as Christopher Ricks has shown, made him painfully susceptible to embarrassment of all sorts. A particularly recurring occasion of embarrassment for Keats was the thought of his own prior work and of the conditions in which it was produced.[11] It was a response in which we can imagine Keats identifying, in effect, with the posture of superiority struck by the notoriously hostile reviewers of his early published work.[12] Through a succession of embarrassed disavowals of his own prior writings, Keats effectively created a sense of staged progress in his literary career. The resulting scheme in turn has

10. Keats was in effect taking seriously the Byronic joke at the start of *Don Juan,* canto 12: "Of all the barbarous Middle Ages, that / Which is the most barbarous is the middle age / Of man" (CPWB, 12:1).

11. Christopher Ricks, *Keats and Embarrassment* (Oxford: Clarendon Press, 1974), especially pp. 115–42.

12. See Marjorie Levinson's account of the Byronic response, *Keats's Life of Allegory: The Origins of a Style* (Oxford: Basil Blackwell, 1988), pp. 9–25; Paul Hamilton, "Keats and Critique," in *Rethinking Historicism,* ed. Levinson (Oxford: Basil Blackwell, 1989), pp. 108–42; and the early reviews helpfully synthesized in *Keats: The Critical Heritage,* ed. G. M. Matthews (London: RKP, 1971). See also, Donald H. Reiman, *The Romantics Reviewed: Contemporary Reviews of British Romantic Writers* (New York: Garland, 1972), and the helpful chapter on the reception of "the Cockney School," in John O. Hayden, *The Romantic Reviewers: 1802–1824* (Chicago: University of Chicago Press, 1968), pp. 176–215.

enjoyed much influence since. As Keats's letters appeared and his biography was written and rewritten in the century of so after his death, his notion of his own development became a model of the poet's *Bildung,* a model I wish both to put in play and in question.[13]

Moore, for example, is one of the poets to whom Keats attached himself early on, as we have seen, but Keats would eventually disavow Moore and his distinctive style in no uncertain terms. "The undersigned," he wrote with mock legal formality to George and Georgiana in Kentucky, "doth not admire . . . Thomas Moore" (LJK, 2:69). This remark, from March 3, 1819, forms a part of the evidence that Keats wished to see his new phase of work of that year defined against the work of Moore. It was indeed in a journal-letter entry dated to January 2, 1819, that Keats commented snidely to the George Keatses on Moore's toast to his father at the widely reported Dublin dinner in the poet's honor. Two days earlier, in the entry for December 31, 1818, however, there is an even more explicit declaration about his entry into a new personal epoch with the turning of the year. In this passage, one of Keats's markedly "philosophical" reflections, Tighe herself forms the backdrop of his claim to have entered a new stage of development:

> The more we know the more inadequacy we discover in the world to satisfy us—this is an old observation; but I have made up my Mind never to take anything for granted—but even to examine the truth of the commonest proverbs—This however is true—Mrs Tighe and Beattie once delighted me—now I see through them and can find nothing in them—or weakness—and yet how many they still delight! Perhaps a superior being may look upon Shakespeare in the same light—is it possible? No—This same inadequacy is discovered (forgive me little George you know I don't mean to put you in the mess) in Women with few exceptions—the Dress Maker, the blue Stocking and the most charming sentimentalist differ but in Slight degree, and are equally smokeable—But I'll go no further—I may be speaking sacrilegiously—and on my word I have thought so little that I have not one opinion upon any thing except in matters of taste—I never can feel certain of any truth but from a clear perception of its Beauty—and I find myself very young minded even in that perceptive power—which I hope will encrease—A year ago I could not understand in the slightest degree Raphael's cartoons—now I begin to read them a little—and how did I lea[r]n to do so? By seeing something done in quite an opposite spirit—I mean a picture of Guido's in which all the Saints, in stead of that heroic simplicity and unaffected grandeur which they inherit from Raphael, had each of them both in countenance and gesture all the canting, solemn melo dramatic mawkishness of Mackenzie's father Nicholas. (LJK, 2:18–19)

13. There are many examples of this kind of work on Keats. For a straightforward instance, see Hugh I. Fausset, *Keats: A Study in Development* (1922; New York: Archon, 1966). For a provocative critique of developmental narratives in Romantic-influenced criticism more generally, see Siskin, *The Historicity of Romantic Discourse,* though Siskin's paradigm is Wordsworthian "growth"—or what he calls "the manner in which a self written by the literary innovations of a Wordsworth became normal for Darwin, Freud, and every 'developing' individual" ([New York: Oxford University Press, 1988], p. 14).

In the Guido reference, Keats is, as it were, taking the part of his friend Haydon, whose paintings he called one of the three wonders of his age.[14] Keats's new aesthetic regime more broadly, his sense of an epochal change in the development of his "taste," no doubt stems in part from his recent sputtering efforts on *Hyperion,* the epic poem in which he explicitly tried for a new mode of writing.[15] This was a mode that he had predicted would distinguish the unwritten *Hyperion* from the already-written *Endymion* by avoiding what he called the "deep and sentimental cast" of the latter: "and one great contrast between them will be—that the Hero of the written tale being mortal is led on, like Buonaparte, by circumstances; whereas the Apollo in Hyperion being a fore-seeing God will shape his actions like one" (LJK, 1:207). *Hyperion* was a poem in which Keats attempted to imagine himself beyond the veiling mists of circumstance, and the "nature" of the poem would lead him to "treat it in a more naked and grecian Manner."[16]

But the claim to advance himself by way of *Hyperion* also proved suspect, for *Hyperion* would not be sustained or sustaining. Although Keats refers to his work on *Hyperion* in this same letter of December 31, 1818, as "scarce begun," he would make little further headway with it: by March 8 he would admit to Haydon that he was "not exactly on the road to an epic poem," (LJK, 2:42) and by April, he had sent the manuscript fragment to his friend Woodhouse refusing to complete the poem he had planned. Significantly, however, as every reader of his biography knows, it was in those same early spring days of 1819 that Keats would begin to hit his stride with the much-celebrated run of poetic compositions that produced, in the space of a few months, the six Great Odes, as well as *Lamia,* and the fragment of another blank-verse epic, *The Fall of Hyperion*—that is, most of the work on which his poetic reputation has come to rest. If we ask what occupied Keats between his December 31 announcement to George and Georgiana about surpassing Mary Tighe and his

14. Hyder Rollins notes that when this passage was first published in Milnes's edition of Keats's letters, in 1848, the young pre-Raphaelites hailed it and made it the basis for enshrining both Keats *and* Haydon in the pre-Raphaelite cause, with Guido as one of the villains (LJK, 2:19).

15. I sketch a part of the "historical situation" that helps to explain this shift in Keats's project in the following chapter.

16. Ibid. For good accounts of the "cosmo-politics" of the portrayal of history in *Hyperion,* see Marilyn Butler, *Romantics, Rebels, and Reactionaries* (New York: Oxford University Press, 1981), pp. 151–54, and Alan Bewell, "The Political Implications of Keats's Classicist Aesthetics," *Studies in Romanticism* 25 (summer 1986): 220–29; Ronald Paulson, *Representations of Revolution (1789–1820)* (New Haven, Conn.: Yale University Press, 1983), pp. 283–85; and Thomas A. Reed, "Keats and the Gregarious Advance of Intellect in *Hyperion,*" *ELH* 55 (1988): 195–232.

great spate of work that ran from April to September, we can find some interesting answers.[17]

We know that Keats's one substantial composition of the first month of 1819
was *The Eve of St. Agnes*, a narrative poem in forty-two Spenserian stanzas. What
makes this choice of poetic form appear curious is that two of the most noteworthy recent avatars of the Spenserian stanza in Keats's era were Mary Tighe
and James Beattie, the very poets he declared smokeable on New Year's Eve.[18]
Since we know that Keats wrote the poem just around the time of *St. Agnes Eve*
itself (January 21), we are therefore confronted with an interesting sequence of
events. On December 31, Keats renounces the latest avatars of a form of
Spenserianism he once admired, proclaiming that his own new stage of development can be indexed by this renunciation, and then three weeks later composes a long Spenserian poem of his own. I think we best address this puzzle by
investigating how Keats uses Tighe's stanza form and her related formal devices
as a way, precisely, of surpassing her achievement. But this, necessarily, means
coming to terms with Keats's own criteria of "smokeability" as a means of
working through the analysis. What makes a situation "smokeable," in Keats's
understanding of things?

As a piece of argot the verb "to smoke" is not new with Keats's time, but it interestingly appears and disappears in his letters roughly with the coming and
going of his annus mirabilis.[19] It has a transitive and an intransitive form, as De
Quincey pointedly illustrated some years later: "The orator grew urgent; wits
began to SMOKE the case, as active verbs—the advocate to smoke, as neuter
verbs."[20] As a "neuter," or intransitive verb, smoking means to be embarrassed
by or simply "to blush"—which establishes the special relevance of this term for
the social Keats that Ricks has sketched for us.[21] What De Quincey's grammatical illustration further establishes for us is that, when "smoke" is used transi-
tively, as it tends to be in Keats, it not only requires a substantive in the objective

---

17. Scholars interested in pursuing the day-by-day developments of Keats's annus mirabilis
now enjoy the kind of tool that Mark Reed long ago made available to Wordsworth scholars: see
F. B. Pinion, *A Keats Chronology* (London: Macmillan, 1992).

18. Byron's *Childe Harold's Pilgrimage* was actually the best-selling recent instance of the
Spenserian mode. For a valuable survey of the uses of Spenser's poetic form in this period, with
good attention to Keats, see Greg Kucich, *Keats, Shelley, and Romantic Spenserianism* (University
Park: Pennsylvania State University Press, 1991).

19. Although Keats uses forms of the term "smoke" often during 1819, it appears in his letters for the first time as late as mid-December 1818 and for the last time in mid-January of 1820.

20. Thomas De Quincey, *Works*, 14 vols. (Edinburgh: D. and C. Black, 1862), 11:86.

21. For the definition of "to smoke" as "to blush" see Francis Grose, *A Classical Dictionary of
the Vulgar Tongue*, ed. Eric Partridge (London: The Scholartis Press, 1931), p. 271. For Ricks on
blushing in Keats, see *Keats and Embarrassment*, pp. 19–49.

case, but also calls for an object that is paradigmatically describable as a "case."

With this much established, one can discern in the variety of Keats's deployment of the term a rough range of meanings that is consistent with the history of its slang usage. This range runs from "understand" to "make fun of." A good example of the latter end of this spectrum is Keats's comment in a letter of 24 January 1819 about being persuaded to "wear [his] Shirtcollar up to [his] eyes" and his fear that he is being ridiculed about it behind his back (LJK, 2:36). A good example of the former end would be passages in which "smoking" seems to imply "grasp" without any suggestion of mockery. Two weeks before the New Year's Eve comment about his coming to see Tighe's poetry as "smokeable," he had written in this more neutral sense to George and Georgiana on December 16, 1818: "I have been so little used to writing lately that I am affraid you will not smoke my meaning so I will give an example." (LJK, 2:5) Or again on September 20, 1819: "As far as I could smoke things on the Sunday before last, thus matters stood in Henrietta street . . . " (LJK, 2:206).

Most typically, though, "to smoke" involves a blending of these two senses: an act of *comprehension* that implies an act *condescension,* toward "weakness" or "inadequacy." This blended sense is what Keats calls on when he writes on New Year's Eve that Tighe now appears to him as vulnerable and transparent, and it is again close to the connotation that Keats is still invoking, nine months and several famous poems later, when he speaks of his unwillingness to publish what he now regards as one of the lesser productions of the year:

> I will give you a few reasons why I shall persist in not publishing The Pot of Basil—It is too smokeable—I can get it smoak'd at the Carpenters shaving chimney much more cheaply—There is too much inexperience of live, and simplicity of knowledge in it—which might do very well after one's death—but not while one is alive. There are very few would look to the reality. I intend to use more finesse with the Public. It is possible to write fine things which cannot be laugh'd at in any way. Isabella is what I should call were I a reviewer "A weak-sided Poem." (LJK, 2:174)[22]

Keats thought of *Isabella, or The Pot of Basil,* as "smokeable" in spite of the pains he took to craft its obscurity. Most critics, as Jack Stillinger has noted, have met the poem with only "puzzlement," and the same point holds a fortiori for *The Eve of St. Agnes.*[23] We must not fail to recognize the extent to which Keats's sen-

---

22. Even *The Eve of St. Agnes* itself, another poem of earlier in the year, comes in for criticism here. "There is no objection of this kind," Keats continues, "to Lamia—A good deal to St. Agnes Eve—only not so glaring" (LJK, 2:174).

23. Stillinger, *The Hoodwinking of Madeline and Other Essays on Keats* (Urbana: University of Illinois Press, 1971), p. 37. For an account of Keats's programmatic effort to encrypt his Spenserian narrative, see Andrew Bennett, *Keats, Narrative, and Audience* (Cambridge: Cambridge University Press, 1994), pp. 82–95.

sitivity to being "smoked" by the reviewing establishment contributed to the hermeneutic density for which he is now revered. "Smokeability" here implies a conception of intelligibility or understanding that is itself understood, in its circumstance, as a vulnerability to being grasped—*captured*—by a higher-order intelligence. It implies a hierarchy of minds, souls, or sensibilities arranged according to the capacity to "see through" another, as Keats says of his new perception of the author of *Psyche; or the Legend of Love.* The "smoke" metaphor itself seems to have to do with clearing the smoke from a situation, attaining relative clarity, fineness, *finesse.* Contrariwise, however, it also suggests a metaphorically inconsistent sense involving the injection of smoke into a situation: smoking out one's quarry.

That there is something very *unfine*—indeed, vaguely predatory—about this metaphor is confirmed by the way in which, writing to the George Keatses on March 19, 1819, Keats analogizes being a writer to having the position in a great natural food chain: both, to use one of Keats's associated terms, are in a kind of "mist":[24] "The noble animal man for his amusement smokes his pipe— the Hawk balances about the Clouds—that is the only difference of their leisures" (LJK, 2:79). This is the "only difference" because both cases—the deliberative "man" and the balancing bird—are otherwise alike on account of the purposive fixation that organizes their attention. It is this purposiveness, he says,

> that makes the Amusement of Life—to a speculative Mind I go among the Feilds and catch a glimpse of a stoat or fieldmouse peeping out of the withered grass—the creature hath a purpose and its eyes are bright with it—I go amongst the buildings of a city and I see a Man hurrying along—to what? The Creature has a purpose and his eyes are bright with it. . . . Even here though I myself am pursueing the same instinctive course as the veriest human animal you can think of—I am however young writing at random—straining at particles of light in the midst of a great darkness—without knowing the bearing of any one assertion of any one opinion. Yet may I not in this be free from sin? May there not be superior beings amused with any graceful, though instinctive attitude my mind m[a]y fall into, as I am entertained with the alertness of a Stoat or the anxiety of a Deer? (LJK, 2:80)[25]

24. "I have no meridian to date Interests from, or measure circumstances—To night I am all in a mist": Keats to John Hamilton Reynolds, September 21, 1819 (LJK, 2:167).

25. In the third of his weekly series of *Philosophical Lectures* (New York: Philosophical Library, 1949), the first given on January 4, 1819, Coleridge discussed the emergence of the philosophic impulse among the pre-Socratics in Greece as well as a continued account of "the probable states of Religion, Arts & Sciences of Egypt, Persia and India at that period." Using the history of Greek thought and culture as evidence against the "natural 'proofs' of religion" brought forward by anti-Christian Deists of the eighteenth century, Coleridge challenged the idea that one could aspire to give, on the basis of "the human reason, of itself," what he called "demonstrable proofs, which no man could reject, of the being and attributes of God and a future state." Here is Coleridge's historical refutation of that notion on the basis of the conclusion that would be reached in a culture (pre-Socratic Athens) where the human reason was still, according to Coleridge, unaided by Revelation:

I shall be returning below to the connection of these predatory metaphors with Keats's meditation on imagination and "power" in early 1819, occasioned as they were—as indeed this passage was—by his fascinated engagement with Hazlitt's just-published *Letter to William Gifford* about Shakespeare's sympathy with "the arbitrary side" of the power issue in *Coriolanus*. For now it is enough to see how "smoking" is linked with a form of "superiority" that enables the pleasurable capture of a lower-order creature in the mystery—mist, midst (Keats himself sustains this paranomasia)—of its circumstances. "Circumstances," says Keats in this same passage, "are like Clouds continually gathering and bursting" (2:79).

Just what it was that Keats found "smokeable" in Mary Tighe's rendition of the fable of Psyche he does not say. We may reasonably conjecture, however, that part of Keats's objection has to do with Tighe's handling of allegory—her missing the necessary "mystery" of allegory—and that this in turn is for Keats, at least at one level, a gendered competence. As Keats's New Year's Eve remark on the smokeability of "Women" makes clear, he regards the capacity to smoke a piece of writing, to surpass its stage, as the capacity to establish it as feminine and oneself as masculine. It is in this context that Keats's famous remarks two months later (February 19, 1819), also to the George Keatses, about Shakespeare as exemplifying "a life of Allegory," need to be read as similarly gendered: "[T]hey are very shallow people who take every thing literal[.] A Man's life of any worth is a continual allegory— and very few eyes can see the Mystery of his life—a life like the scriptures, figurative—which such people can no more make out than they can the hebrew Bible. Lord Byron cuts a figure—but he is not figurative—Shakespeare led a life of Allegory; his works are the comments on it" (LJK: 2:67). In Keats's most typical usage the phrase "See the Mystery of"

It might have been a matter of surprise that the philosophers of old did not arrive at this [conclusion] that they were extremely puzzled that when Simonides was asked the question, he required day after day to solve it; and that the arguments which they bring forward independent of revelation the philosophers of old would have treated either with abundant contempt or as mere proofs of what they admitted, namely that for every motion in nature there was a motive power, that when a man said he prove [*a fate or power with control*] over the person but not the intention, they would say, "All the [*same thing*] Just as bees in a beehive all pursue one object." And from thence would produce a system of [*either panhylism or hylozoism*] which alone could have been derived from such argument. While the arguments of a higher kind go into pantheism which again instantly brought round the effect of [*polytheism*]. (pp. 126–27)
Coleridge's subsequent account of world history as the triumph of Judaic monotheism and ultimately Christianity over the "cruelty and brutality" of polytheistic cultures reads as if it were the very target of Keats's historical argument, as I shall be outlining it, in the *Ode to Psyche*, written shortly after an encounter with Coleridge on April 11, just days after the lecture series had concluded.

would be a fair enough paraphrase of "smoke"—and by punning extension, "see (in or through) the mist (midst) of." The key point, though, is twofold: the un-smokeable life is the allegorical life, and the most allegorical life is the most manly.

When Keats gives George examples of what it means to construe the world with a "shallow literalness," he at once confirms the gendering of the noun "man" and, less directly, complicates the relation of the smoker to the smoked. We need to learn, he says, "that the man who rediculies romance is the most ro-mantic of Men—that he who abuses women and slights them—loves them the most" (LJK, 2:67). In the predatory chain, the hawk and stoat and fieldmouse are linked, successively comprehensible in a chain of successively higher orders, *because* they are finally involved in the same "amusement": call it stalking. The hawk understands the stoat because the stoat, too, is a hunter, and his hunting instincts lend sense to his movements in the eye of his natural superior. One can smoke a poet—Tighe, Baillie, John Keats—because one identifies, though in a superior way, with that poet's instincts. Keats has revised his earlier theory of the "cameleon poet's" negative capability. In 1818, this was the capacity for selfless-ness that enabled Shakespeare to take "as much delight in conceiving an Iago as an Imogen" (LJK, 1:387). Now, though, in 1819, it has been recontextualized within a kind of self-conscious realism about power and predation. In 1819, negative capability is roughly what makes this kind of smoking possible.

2. Mary Tighe and the Tenses of History

Having gained some understanding of the complexity and density implicit in Keats's figure for relative transcendence—the capacity to smoke—we can re-turn to his remarks about the developmental stage he thinks he has reached on the eve of 1819 and to the question of how *The Eve of St. Agnes* is intelligible as an articulation of that stage. Since "man" is situated in a chain of predatory dis-cernment, he cannot help both smoking and being smoked. Thus, on the principle that, as we say, it takes one to know one, smoking also implies identi-fication with the intelligible object. It follows, then, that a Keatsian "man" can smoke a woman (say)—blue stocking or sentimentalist (Mary Tighe was both)—only to the degree that he is able to identify with *her* instincts.[26] This is why gender relations in Keats's late work, not least in *The Eve of St. Agnes* itself, are at once so conventional in gesture and so unstable in practice. If we accept this crucial point about identification, we can say that Tighe and Beattie are sin-gled out by Keats on New Year's Eve because, as Spenserians, they are—like the

---

26. For an account of the expansion of the term "bluestocking" after 1800, see Sylvia Harc-stark Myers, *The Bluestocking Circle: Women, Friendship, and the Life of the Mind in Eighteenth-Century England* (Oxford: Clarendon Press, 1990), pp. 290–303.

poet who deems them "smokeable"—so obviously in pursuit of allegorical game, so obviously in the game of allegory.

This is especially clear with Mary Tighe. It is not just that the fable of Cupid and Psyche appears in the allegory of *The Faerie Queene* but, more to the point, that Tighe made the topic of allegory so explicit and self-conscious in *Psyche*.[27] In her prose preface, for example, Tighe resorts to a traditional personification of allegory as a mysterious and seductive "veiled form" whose allure she acknowledges irresistible.[28] But while justifying her practice on the grounds that the "choicest fables of the poets" are typically "wrapt in perplexed allegories," she makes a major concession to readers who can resist allegory's charms: "If I have not been able to resist the seductions of the mysterious fair," she says, "I have remembered that my verse cannot be worth much consideration, and have therefore endeavoured to let my meaning be perfectly obvious."[29]

Accepting Marlon Ross's conclusion that Tighe is self-conscious of her identity as a female poet and that her general public diffidence is a function of that recognition, we can extrapolate from her prefatory disclaimer that Tighe and Keats stand in basic agreement on both the "smokeability" of her allegory and on the (gendered) explanation for it. Certainly, Tighe tends to spell out— or make "literal," as Keats might say—the figures of her narrative in relatively straightforward and often sententious terms. Thus, toward the end of the final canto, when Psyche is struggling to reach the place where she hopes to be reunited with Cupid, Tighe delivers explicatory stanzas that are relatively characteristic of the poem's overall mode of editorializing on the case of the soul:

> But one dear object every wish confines,
> Her spouse is promised in that bower of rest;
> And shall the sun, that now so cheerful shines,
> Indeed behold her to his bosom prest,
> And in his heavenly smiles of fondness blest?
> Oh! 'tis too much! exhausted life she fears

27. Spenser's stanzas on Cupid and Psyche are in *Faerie Queene,* book 3, st. 50–53. For an extended commentary on their importance to Spenser see A. C. Hamilton, *The Structure of Allegory in The Faeire Queene* (Oxford: Clarendon Press, 1961), pp. 138–48.

28. "I much regret," writes Tighe, "that I can have no hope of affording any pleasure to some, whose opinion I highly respect, whom I have heard profess themselves ever disgusted by the veiled form of allegory, and yet

> Are not the choicest fables of the poets,
> Who were the fountains and first springs of wisdom,
> Wrapt in perplexed allegories?"

Mary Tighe, *Psyche; or, The Legend of Love,* ed. D. H. Reiman (New York: Garland, 1978), p. v.

29. Tighe, *Psyche,* p. v.

Will struggling leave her agitated breast,
Ere to her longing eyes his form appears,
Or the soft hand of Love shall wipe away her tears.

Oh! how impatience gains upon the soul
When the long promised hour of joy draws near!
How slow the tardy moments seem to roll!
What spectres rise of inconsistent fear!
To the fond doubting heart its hopes appear
Too brightly fair, too sweet to realize;
All seem but day-dreams of delight too dear!
Strange hopes and fears in painful contest rise,
While the scarce trusted bliss seems but to cheat the eyes.[30]

In making the allegorical "meaning" of the fable of Psyche "obvious" (to recall those terms from her preface), Tighe *sentimentalizes* it, in the somewhat technical eighteenth-century sense of "sentiment."[31] That is, she reduces the allegory to a set of communicable representations of Psyche's narrative situation—what might be called the case of the soul as such. And she does so, it would seem, precisely to make it possible at various points in the story to "sympathize" with Psyche as the generalized soul. In spelling out the allegory in generally applicable, generally intelligible terms, Tighe makes Psyche the very sign under which the act of sympathy itself takes place. The governing discipline of Tighe's poem, then, is that of "Psychology," the explanatory science that takes the soul for its object.

It makes sense to think of Keats as having been invested in Psychology, so understood, early on in his brief career as a poet. But in his annus mirabilis of 1819, he also imagined that he had reached a new stage in his appreciation of Psyche's "mysteries," of the allegorical mode in which they are represented, and of the work of the soul's circumstantial individuation—three formulations which prove to be so many ways of saying the same thing. To return to Tighe's preface, we might say that Keats is *neither* the reader who can resist the allure of allegory's mysteries *nor* the one who seeks to have them fully explicated.[32] Moreover, in spite of his class position, or possibly because of it, Keats persuaded himself (as Tighe said she could not in her own case) that his verse was worth sufficient "consideration" to enable him to forego sententious explication. He counted on attentive readers. Indeed, in spite of the partial worry Keats later felt in be-

30. Ibid., pp. 199–200.
31. See the discussion of Adam Smith on sentiment and sympathy above in chapter 5.
32. We have no guarantee that Keats saw the 1805 preface to *Pscyhe,* but in its terms he would have classified himself in a category Tighe implies but does not identify.

half of the forty-two Spenserian stanzas he produced for St. Agnes Eve, the tradition of commentary on his *Eve of St. Agnes* suggests both that his poetry
would gain ample "consideration" *and* that it would not be easily smokeable.[33]

Keats's "winter's tale" about Madeline and Porphyro—the story of a woman
who undergoes the virginity rites of St. Agnes in order that a husband might
materialize from her dreams—is not dissimilar in narrative content from that of
the fable of Psyche. Both poems, after all, deal with a succubus myth.[34] Compared to Tighe's poem, however, *The Eve of St. Agnes* appears distinctively un-
moralized, unsentimental, and indeed un-"psychological" in its execution.
Even its basic story or diegesis is notoriously ambiguous and labile.[35] Keats's
well-documented echoes of Tighe in *St. Agnes,* moreover, suggest that this was
a deliberate effect.[36] A key echo appears in the final lines where Keats employs

33. The problems of unintelligibility and tonal dissonance in *The Eve of St. Agnes* come up
routinely in commentary on the poem. See, for example, Stillinger, *The Hoodwinking of Madeline,*
pp. 72–74.

34. The tradition of illustrating what the French call "l'histoire de Psyche," the scenes chosen for exemplifying the tale, often results in pictures that make the connection between the
fable and Keats's *Eve of St. Agnes* particularly evident. See Christiane Noireau, *La Lampe de Psyché*
(Paris: Flammarion, 1991), especially illustrations 57 and 58 on p.236.

35. In the opening half-dozen stanzas, for example, the modulation from a kind of associative logic—what Marjorie Levinson calls an "image logic" (*Keats's Life of Allegory,* p. 135)—into a
narrative representative of the events is a major source of confusion in a reader's tracking. Likewise the conflation of Madeline and the narrator as dreaming subjects—Madeline conjuring
Porphyro even as the narrator conjures her act of conjuring.

36. We can compare, for example, the notorious passage in *The Eve of St. Agnes* where
Porphyro, the succubus incarnate, steals into Madeline's chamber to gaze on her sleeping body
with the equivalent lines in Tighe's *Psyche:*

> Sto'n to this paradise, and so entranced,
> Porphyro gazed upon her empty dress,
> And listen'd to her breathing, if it chanced
> To wake into a slumberous tenderness;
> Which when he heard that minute did he bless,
> And breath'd himself: then from the closet crept,
> Noiseless as fear in a wide widlerness,
> And over the hush'd carpet, silent, stept,
> And 'tween the curtains peep'd, where lo!—how fast she slept. (*St. Agnes,* st. 28)

> Wrapt in a cloud unseen by mortal eye,
> He sought the chamber of the royal maid;
> There, lull'd by careless soft security,
> Of the impending mischief nought afraid,
> Upon her purple couch was Psyche laid,
> Her radiant eyes a downy slumber seal'd;
> In light transparent veil alone array'd,
> Her bosom's opening charms were half reveal'd,
> And scarce the lucid folds her polish'd limb conceal'd. (Tighe's *Psyche,* st. 20)

a device very like the one with which Tighe closes her own Spenserian adventure poem. Psyche and Cupid have—in Tighe's altered account—at last successfully passed their test, and then the narrator breaks in, with a distinct change in direction and tone:

> Dreams of Delight farewell! your charms no more
> Shall gild the hours of solitary gloom!
> The page remains—but can the page restore
> The vanished bowers which Fancy taught to bloom?
> Ah, no! her smiles no longer can illume
> The path my Psyche treads no more for me;
> Consigned to dark oblivion's silent tomb
> The visionary scenes no more I see,
> Fast from the fading lines the vivid colours flee! (p. 209)[37]

In Tighe's poem, this is the last in a sequence of passages having to do with her own, as it were, psychological relation to the story of Psyche. Although the story yields stable moral sentences about the human soul, Tighe's relation to its visions is itself fleeting—confined to the phenomenology of reading and writing. When the act of reading has finished, and the page is merely *seen,* the vivacity of the narrative "lines" fades accordingly.[38]

In the concluding lines of *The Eve of St. Agnes,* Keats likewise zooms away from a close involvement with the sequence of events that make up the escape of Porphyro and Madeline from the hostile castle. But here the shift is from a past perspective whose vivacity is marked by the use of the historical present tense (i.e., the present tense of the past) to a perspective in the historical present itself. In the newly altered perspective with which Keats's poem closes, all that had been solid in the foregoing narrative melts into air, or turns into dust:

> They glide, like phantoms, into the wide hall;
> Like phantoms, to the iron porch, they glide;
> Where lay the Porter, in uneasy sprawl,
> With a huge empty flaggon by his side:
> The wakeful bloodhound rose, and shook his hide,

---

37. For drawing attention to the Tighe-Keats connection, I am indebted to Marlon Ross's groundbreaking discussion in *The Contours of Masculine Desire* (New York: Oxford University Press, 1989), pp. 155–72. In respect to this particular passage (p. 164), though, my reading diverges from his, in that I focus specifically on the conclusion to *St. Agnes,* and see the issue as historicity rather than ephemerality.

38. Tighe's ending gambit is one on which Keats would play several variations in the coming months, as in the "fading" of the "plaintive anthem" at the end of the *Ode to a Nightingale.*

But his sagacious eye an inmate owns:
By one, and one, the bolts full easy slide:—
The chains lie silent on the footworn stones—
The key turns, and the door upon its hinges groans.

And they are gone: ay, ages long ago
These lovers fled away into the storm.
That night the Baron dreamt of many a woe,
And all his warrior-guests, with shade and form
Of witch and demon, and large coffin-worm
Were long be-nightmar'd. Angela the old
Died palsy-twitch'd, with meagre face deform;
The Beadsman, after thousand aves told,
For aye unsought for slept among his ashes cold. (st. 41-42)

Like Tighe's ending, this is an objectifying gesture, a withdrawal of sympathetic perspective on the medievalized Spenserian action of the narrative. But Keats emphasizes the difference between the cultural state in which he is reproducing the Spenserian anachronisms and that of a specific Christian-chivalric past of troubadours, chapels, knights, Beadsman, "aves," and courtly manners. What is peculiar in Keats's rewriting of Tighe's ending is that he produces the sense of a *historical* shift of perspective.[39]

From one point of view, therefore, we can say that Keats makes this final stanza a mark of his developmental "superiority" to the cultural state or stage epitomized by the diegetic content of the "old romance" presented in *The Eve of St. Agnes*. Medieval romance, like Tighe's allegory, is a form that he has "smoked" from his advanced historical position. Stillinger has taught us to understand the humor and irony of *The Eve of St. Agnes,* and one might say that much of Keats's "amusement" is purchased at the expense of those characters who most epitomize medieval Christian culture, characters like the pathetic celibate Beadsman who told his "thousand aves" in vain.[40] Keats is on record,

---

39. For Keats's reading in medieval history, see Daniel Watkins, *Keats's Poetry and the Politics of the Imagination* (Rutherford, N.J.: Fairleigh Dickinson University Press, 1989), pp. 65–75. Watkins' aim is to "historicize the place names in the narrative and to focus on the tension between an old feudal aristocracy and an inchoate commercial culture" (p. 75), though he articulates his conclusions at a level of abstraction rather more distant from Keats's texts themselves than I have attempted here.

40. On the ironization of the Christian imagery in the poem, see Jack Stillinger, *The Hoodwinking of Madeline,* pp. 74–76. One gains some sense of Keats's air of "amusement" in this poem, and in the related "Eve of St. Mark," when his remark to the George Keatses: "you see what fine mother Radcliff names I have" (LJK, 2:62).

though, in his New Year's Eve letter, as arguing that the man who abuses romance is the most romantic. Thus, the poet who smokes sentimental allegory or Christian ritual can only do so—and must only do so—because of the sense that he is in or after the same game.

"The Eve of St. Agnes" thus articulates as a *historical* relation—"ages long ago"—the kind of identity-in-superiority that Keats works out, first, in terms of his own aesthetic development in the passage about Tighe and Guido on New Year's Eve and then in terms of the food chain in the "stoat and field-mouse" passage. I wish to argue here, against a very long tradition of Keats scholarship that has emphasized the hermetic self-containment and aesthetic perfection of his 1819 poetry, that part of what distinguishes the writing of Keats in his "living year" is a particular kind of awareness of an epochal cultural history. Indeed, the sort of moment we see in the final stanza of *The Eve of St. Agnes*—a moment of extreme historical self-consciousness complicated by its own sense of implication in its object—plays a crucial role in Keats's two most famous poems, both composed in the next few months.

We are, by now, so used to thinking of the Grecian urn as a symbol of visual art, or art in general, or of the relation of art in general to truth and beauty in general, that we often fail to register that the moment even formalists recognize as the turning point of the poem is the one in which Keats is led to see the urn as an archaeological deposit of a former civilization, one whose little towns will silent be for ever more, except insofar as Keats can make out the ways of life they left embossed, indexed (as it were), on this object. We are so used to thinking of the *Nightingale Ode* as a poem about poetic flights and bowers of bliss that we can fail to register that the commonly recognized turning point in that poem occurs when the consciousness of the historical Ruth invades the poem with sobering force. I point to these examples to show how the consciousness of history shapes Keats's writing of 1819 even, or perhaps especially, when he dramatizes himself as resisting its power. I now turn, however, to the relatively neglected poem that arguably spawned them both, the composition that most evidently bridges the personal "epochs" between Keats's turn-of-the-year announcement about the surpassing of Tighe's *Psyche* and his entry into high productivity in late spring. The *Ode to Psyche* versifies the celebrated "vale of soul-making" passage that Keats worked out for George and Georgiana just days after recording his meeting with Coleridge in the journal-entry of April 21. "With this evening," as Walter Jackson Bate declares in his biography of Keats, "begins the extraordinary productivity of Keats's final five months of writing."[41]

---

41. Walter Jackson Bate, *John Keats* (New York: Oxford University Press, 1963), p. 473.

3. Rehabilitating *Psyche*

Characteristically, Keats himself gives us reason to regard the *Ode to Psyche* as a new beginning in his poetic development. Enclosing a copy to George and Georgiana on April 30, Keats prefaces it by saying the it is "the last I have written" and "the first and the only one with which I have taken even moderate pains—I have for the most part dash'd of [f] my lines in a hurry—This I have done leisurely—I think it reads the more richly for it and will I hope encourage me to write other thing[s] in even a more peacable and healthy spirit" (LJK, 2:105–106). It seems fair to say that one reason for the special "pains" Keats took with this poem—"pains" becomes a loaded term in the context of a fable involving arduous tasks and trials—was that its subject matter, the fable of Psyche, had just come to *mean* so much to him. It allegorized what he took to be issues of moment. That Keats composed the *Ode to Psyche* to be a kind of manifesto poem is evident from the way in which it signals connection with other poems that had themselves been offered or regarded as poetic manifestos: Wordsworth's prospectus to *The Recluse* and several of his related lyrics, Shelley's response to the Wordsworthian program in *Alastor* and *Mont Blanc,* and less immediately, Milton's *Ode on the Morning of Christ's Nativity.* The fable of Psyche afforded Keats the opportunity to write his own psychic development large and to do so in terms most apposite to what he would call, later in 1819, the "present struggle" of his own historical situation (LJK, 2:193).

Though Keats, like Tighe, drew on Apuleius, and says as much, even the most cursory glance at the *Ode to Psyche* reveals that, unlike Tighe, and indeed unlike most earlier writers on Psyche, Keats does not actually retell the fable itself—not even (like Tighe) in modified form. It is not that Keats tells the story and then withdraws from it in the final moment, as he does in his succubus narrative in *The Eve of St. Agnes.* It is not even that Keats merely *starts* to tells the story before interrupting himself, as happens with a later nineteenth-century Psyche lyric cited in Andrew Lang's edition of the fable.[42] In the *Ode to Psyche,* the

---

42. The first stanza of J. W. Mackail's *Cupid and Psyche* runs as follows:

> Once in a city of old
> > Lived a king and a queen:
> These had three fair daughters,
> > But the fairest of all was the third,—
> How, in the ages of gold,
> > Where summer meadows were green,
> By welling of pastoral waters
> Did the story begin to be heard?

The poem appeared long after Keats's death, but it dramatizes a poetic tactic—the folktale interrupted by the folkloristic meditation—that he did not choose. See Andrew Lang, ed., *The Marriage of Cupid and Psyche,* trans. William Adlington (London: David Nutt, 1887), p. vi.

story as such never even begins. In lieu of retelling the fable, Keats offers an act of historiography in the unlikely form of a verse apostrophe, a form signaled at the outset: "O Goddess! hear these tuneless numbers, wrung / By sweet enforcement and remembrance dear, / And pardon that thy secrets should be sung / Even into thine own soft-conched ear" (ll. 1–4). How the poem moves from the present tense of this apostrophe into a tense of the historical present (as opposed to a historical present tense) is crucial to understanding how the poem achieves its "history effect" within the severe constraints of the lyric form.

The question of history in this poem has been obscured, even vexed, because of a striking feature of its structure: the chiastic arrangement of its stanzas. The first and last of the four stanzas address Psyche while offering different set-piece descriptions of her and her situation; the middle two stanzas address Psyche while offering set-piece accounts of the rites, instruments, and institutions of her proper worship. Invoking the manifesto aspects of the *Ode to Psyche* to launch an argument about the unfolding of the Odes as a sequence, Helen Vendler interprets this project in terms that neutralize the historical dimension of the poem's argument. On the theory that each of the Odes has a particular master trope, Vendler ventures, reasonably, that the master trope of the *Ode to Psyche* is repetition. The problem is that, for Vendler, "repetition" reduces all movement to an effort at mere reduplication, as if the suggestive chiasmus of the *abba* stanza structure were not merely suggestive but all there is to it. This thesis is itself repeated in several claims throughout Vendler's chapter on the Ode.[43] Vendler does not ignore the fact that the repetitive structure goes unful-

---

43. Helen Vendler, *The Odes of John Keats* (Cambridge, Mass.: Harvard University Press, 1983). For example:

The implicit boast of Psyche is that the "working brain" can produce a flawless virtual object, indistinguishable from the "real" object in the mythological or historical world. (p. 47)

The shape of the *Ode to Psyche* is, in its essence, . . . a reduplication-shape; we might compare it to the shape made by a Rorschach blot. Everything that appears on the left must reappear, in mirror image, on the right; or, in terms of the aesthetic of the ode, whatever has existed in "life" must be, and can be, restored in art.

The notion of art which underlies Keats's continual use of the trope of reduplication in the ode is a strictly mimetic one. The internal world of the artist's brain can attain by the agency of Fancy—so the trope implies—a point for point correspondence with the external worlds of history, mythology, and the senses. The task of the poet is defined in excessively simple terms: he is, in this instance, first to sketch the full presence of Psyche and her cult as they existed in the pagan past—that is, to show the locus of loss—and then to create by his art a new ritual and a new environment for the restored divinity. (p. 47)

The ode declares, by its words and by its shape, that the creation of art requires the complete replacement of all memory and sense-experience by an entire duplication of the ex-filled in the Ode: she is too careful a reader not to notice the discrepancies and too honest a critic not to report them. Yet she misidentifies the more profound question that these discrepancies, and ultimately the repetitive structure itself, are meant to raise.

On the reading I propose, the iterations function historiographically, though perhaps, as in Marx's notion of repetition, with generic variation in the repeated events. The catalogue is introduced in stanza two:

> O latest born and loveliest vision far
>   Of all Olympus' faded hierarchy!
> Fairer than Phoebe's sapphire-region'd star,
>   Or Vesper, amorous glow-worm of the sky;
> Fairer than these, though temple thou hast none,
>   Nor altar heap'd with flowers;
> Nor virgin-choir to make delicious moan
>   Upon the midnight hours;
> No voice, no lute, no pipe, no incense sweet
>   From chain-swung censer teeming;
> No shrine, no grove, no oracle, no heat
>   Of pale-mouth'd prophet dreaming. (ll. 24–35)

Without actually rehearsing anything that might count as a version of Apuleius's narrative, Keats has effected a key displacement of it in this catalogue of failed obeisance and subsequent compensation. For in Apuleius's account, the worship of Psyche as a mortal leaves Venus neglected, and it is because *Venus's* rituals are going unobserved and her fanes unattended that she calls in her son Cupid against Psyche in the first place.

The impression of the centrality of stanzas 2 and 3 in the poem is deepened by the conspicuous length of the catalogue that is repeated in detail in the poet's entreaty to the goddess Psyche that he be allowed to compensate her:

> . . . let me be thy choir, and make a moan
>   Upon the midnight hours;

---

ternal world within the artist's brain. . . . *Psyche* asserts that by the [duplicative and] constructive activity of the mind we can assert a victory, complete and permanent, over loss. (p. 49)

The Rorschach blot might even be said to have that shape named by the term Psyche insofar as she is visible to the human eye: the butterfly. The gendering of activities in the first of Wordsworth's poems *To a Butterfly*—hunting for the speaker and preserving for "Emmeline"—suggests that Tighe's *Psyche* is the subtext for that "nature lyric" as well.

> Thy voice, thy lute, thy pipe, thy incense sweet
>> From swinged censer teeming;
> Thy shrine, thy grove, thy oracle, thy heat
>> Of pale-mouth'd prophet dreaming. (ll. 43–49)

The substitution of the "no" by the "thy" (or by the "my"-*as*-"thy") is obviously foregrounded by the wholesale repetition of the other terms, but it is simply impossible to understand how the iteration functions in the poem without addressing the passage (i.e, the opening lines of stanza 3) that is itself given such emphasis by virtue of its bridging of the two catalogues.

The transition between the two appearances of the catalogue is effected by the following difficult and finely worked verses:

> O brightest! though too late for antique vows,
>> Too, too late for the fond believing lyre,
> When holy were the haunted forest boughs,
>> Holy the air, the water, and the fire;
> Yet even in these days so far retir'd
>> From happy pieties, thy lucent fans,
>> Fluttering among the faint Olympians,
> I see, and sing by my own eyes inspired.
> So let me be thy choir. . . . (ll. 36–44)

The difficulties here lie in part in the syntactical ambiguities created by Keats's use—throughout the poem but here particularly—of participle forms in different grammatical positions (e.g., "believing," "haunted," "retir'd," "fluttering"). The tense or time of these participles is not in every case clear. As with the crucial syntactical confusion of the speaker and the nightingale in Keats's next great Ode ("'Tis not through envy of thy happy lot, / But being too happy in thine happiness, / That *thou* . . . "), the indicators of reference here are hard to make out. "Fluttering," for example, itself flutters among a variety of possible times and cases in the syntax of these lines, as if replaying at large that most clichéd of Spoonerisms (but most apposite for Psyche): "butterfly" / "flutter by."[44] But even as they make ambiguous the issues of time and circumstance in the poem, these lines already begin to recreate a narrative in which to reestablish intelligibility for the iterated elements in the two catalogues. This narrative is not itself being offered as a version of Apuleius's fable but instead as a devel-

---

44. The intransitivity of "sing" tends to break the directness with which one can take Psyche's fluttering as the grammatic object of the apparently transitive "see," thus grammatically raising a doubt about the claim in the present to see Psyche "fluttering" in the past.

opmental history of Western culture that can actually be laid out in a subtextual time line plotting the poem's crucial points of reference in the past, a line on which Apuleius's moment itself can be located. Thus, where in the final distancing moment of *The Eve of St. Agnes* the speaker withdraws to a perspective on the historical present tense of the action in which it all now appears as having happened "ages long ago," the *Ode to Psyche* gives historicist force to the old cliché by actually tracing out these ages over time.

It is not just that the *Ode* is an epochal history in which Apuleius's moment itself has a place. It is also that the stages of this history, indeed, are projected backward and forward from the post-Augustan moment of Psyche's mythologization in Apuleius, as if the mythical apotheosis of Psyche, instead of the mythical incarnation of Christ, were being offered as the pivot of western religious history. Keats acknowledges his reliance on Apuleius in the late-April journal-letter entry to George and Georgiana: "You must recollect that Psyche was not embodied as a goddess before the time of Apulius the Platonist who lived afteir the Agustan age, and consequently the Goddess was never worshipped or sacrificed to with any of the ancient fervour—and perhaps never thought of in the old religion—I am more orthodox [than] to let a hethan Goddess be so neglected" (LJK, 2:106). The poem's first major historical shift is premised on the distinction between early and late antiquity, whereby the "old religion" of early antiquity is explicitly associated with "antique vows" and the "fond believing lyre." Later antiquity is marked by a skepticism that we may hold responsible for the faintness of the older Olympian gods and the fading of their hierarchy. This gradual disappearance or demotion coincides with the "appearance" of the beautiful Psyche and her promotion to divine status. Apuleius's fable, in other words, which dates to about the mid-second century A.D., is not only a *late story* of Psyche as a goddess but also, explicitly, an account of her *late apotheosis.* Psyche begins as a human being in a plot of the gods but is promoted to divinity and granted immortality at the end.

Further, if we stop to ask what, apart from her beauty, characterizes Psyche in Apuleius's fable, we find that it is not her faith or her piety toward the existing divinities. Psyche represents the apotheosis not of fideism but of skepticism, or at least of an empiricism that insists on the proof of the senses. The eighteenth-century connection of Psyche with empirical sense is clear from Voltaire's *Philosophical Dictionary,* which informs its readers that "the Greeks had invented the faculty *Psyche* for the sensations."[45] It is precisely Psyche's empiri-

---

45. Voltaire, *Philosophical Dictionary,* trans. and ed. Peter Gay (New York: Harcourt, Brace & World, 1962), p. 470.

cal curiosity about her invisible lover, her wish to see for herself, that sets her on the course to immortality. And this will-to-seeing remains unreformed in the course of her arduous travails, as evidenced in her inability to refrain from opening the box containing Proserpine's beauty in the final stage of the last quest. The Keatsian speaker alludes to this skeptical, show-me brand of empiricism in the *Ode to Psyche* and makes it part of the assimilation of Psyche to his own psyche. Just as she can be described as "too late for the fond believing lyre," so, when the speaker identifies the modernity of his own frame of reference, his fitness to make amends for centuries of neglect, he declares: "I see, and sing, by my own eyes inspired" (l. 43).

The late-antique period on the poem's underlying time line, then, is one implicitly characterized by a skeptical empiricism. The next period that follows it on that time line, though less explicit, is just as clearly built into the poem's historical frame of reference. We can bring its contours to light by asking why, given her deification, Psyche has neither temple nor any of the usual accouterments of divinity. Keats noted for the George Keatses that Psyche was not embodied as a goddess until after "the Agustan age, *and consequently* was never worshipped or sacrificed to with any of the ancient fervour" (my emphasis). The skepticism that attended the fading of the Olympians from popular consciousness presumably had something to do with this, but so too, surely, did the Christianization of Rome, which dates roughly to the era of Apuleius. Christianity took over the doctrine of the immortality of the soul, but removed it from the history in which, from Plato himself to the writer Keats refers to as "Apuleius the Platonist," it was developing. In orthodox Christianity, one might argue, the deification of the soul is not purchased at the expense of the Sky God's "fading"—at the expense of the many gods, but not of the One God.

This is where the echoes of Milton's *Nativity Ode,* astutely tallied in Vendler's account, can be most helpful, for they strongly suggest that Keats is producing a late riposte to the Christian challenge to the authority of pagan mythologies. Milton, in terms that reappear all over Keats's poem, produced an ode on the birth of Christ in which that moment spells the end of polytheism and the fulfillment of the plan of the God of Scripture. One stanza from the *Ode* suffices to illustrate:

> The Oracles are dumb,
> No voice or hideous hum
>   Runs through the arched roof in words deceiving.
> *Apollo* from his shrine

Can no more divine,
　　With hollow shriek the steep of *Delphus* leaving.
No nightly trance, or breathed spell,
Inspires the pale-ey'd Priest from the prophetic cell. (173–80)[46]

At the same time, however, as a poet of the English seventeenth century, Milton himself belongs to the historical moment when the Christian challenge to paganism and classicism was beginning to meet stronger and stronger resistance—Milton was staving off a perceived threat. And Keats, aware of Milton's historical position, implies an intellectual history, familiar enough to us, that was just in his time becoming conventional: after more than a millennium and a half of the Christian epoch, a period notorious for the perversities of chivalry and romance of the sort "smoked" in *The Eve of St. Agnes,* the neoclassicism of the Renaissance and the New Science of the seventeenth and eighteenth centuries are understood to undermine the ecclesiastical hegemony, to systematize the powers of observation, awaken the senses, and liberate the peoples of Europe from the dark ages. This was very much the story that Keats's friend Shelley would be narrating independently later that year in *A Philosophical View of Reform.*

Implicit in Keats's developmental history, then, is an epoch of "enlightenment," in which superstition is explained and the political uses of superstition are exposed. The way was now open to recover the "prior orthodoxy" (as Keats wryly calls it) of heathenism, to return to the developing course of pagan mythological consciousness—to pick up, so to speak, where Apuleius left off, with the decline of the sky gods and the myth of the elevation of the human soul to divine immortality through the agency of love. But what it means to pick up where Apuleius left off is not so simple a matter, since the skepticism implicitly celebrated in his account led first, as it were, to the blind faith of Christianity and then to the sensational skepticism of an Enlightenment that, in certain moments, lost sight of the soul altogether. Thus, Voltaire, in the same *Dictionnaire Philosophe* where he had defined "Psyche" in terms of mere sensation, included an entry on the soul (*âme*), in which he analytically dismantled all the "fine systems about souls that your philosophy has fabricated" without offering another in their place.[47] The "neglect" of Psyche that Keats playfully describes himself as too "orthodox" a heathen to countenance is thus a double neglect: the neglect of the pagan-Platonic "Psyche" in favor of the Christian

---

46. *On the Morning of Christ's Nativity,* in John Milton, *Complete Poems and Major Prose,* ed. Merritt Y. Hughes (Indianapolis: Bobbs-Merrill, 1957), p. 48.

47. Voltaire, *Philosophical Dictionary,* p. 66.

"soul" and the neglect of the Psyche/soul in any form by the mechanist strain in Enlightenment moral philosophy.

Vendler's question about Keats's *Ode* therefore needs to be reformulated. The question does not reduce to whether the poet can completely reduplicate an external world said to be constituted by the triad she calls "history, mythology, and the senses." The question is rather: Must the future be exactly like the past? That is, need history repeat itself, or what is the relation between our understanding of the soul's "immortality" and our expectations about the "future state"? Or, more elaborately, can we trace the historical logic of Psyche, the transformations in the concept and character of the soul, from the mythology of the ancients to the enlightened sensory empiricism of the moderns without suffering either the soul's superstitious and retrograde debasement by the Christian church or its complete elimination by a hyperanalytic enlightened mechanism? Putting the problem this way allows one to register the full force of those allusions to Milton's *Nativity Ode* as establishing the place of Renaissance Christianity in a scheme of development. It also allows one to see that "picking up where Apuleius left off" involves neither striving to recapture Apuleius's moment nor interpreting the discrepancies between the *ab* of stanzas one and two and the *ba* of stanzas three and four as failures to achieve this. Rather, it involves continuing a process that Apuleius had advanced and that a millennium and a half of Christianity had interrupted. That the process was already underway with Apuleius is clear from the way in which he is given credit for aiding in the promotion of the human Psyche to divinity as the Olympians fade.

That it is being further advanced, in the same direction, is clear from the way in which Keats handles the final stanza:

> Yes, I will be thy priest, and build a fane
>   In some untrodden region of my mind,
> Where branched thoughts, new grown with pleasant pain,
>   Instead of pines shall murmur in the wind:
> Far, far around shall those dark-cluster'd trees
>   Fledge the wild-ridged mountains steep by steep;
> And there by zephyrs, streams, and birds, and bees,
>   The moss-lain Dryads shall be lull'd to sleep;
> And in the midst of this wide quietness
> A rosy sanctuary will I dress
> With the wreath'd trellis of a working brain,
>   With buds, and bells, and stars without a name,

With all the gardener Fancy e'er could feign,
     Who breeding flowers, will never breed the same:
And there shall be for thee all soft delight
     That shadowy thought can win,
A bright torch, and a casement ope at night,
     To let the warm Love in! (ll. 50–67)

The thought is "shadowy" here, and the allegory is not easy to smoke.[48] One might say that Keats guards himself against smokeability in a future moment by attempting to anticipate that moment. The "fair attitude" depicted here, both of Keats toward Psyche and Psyche toward "Love," is a posture of expectation, and the stanza is dominated by the future tense. The implicit topic is, precisely, the future state of the soul. But what is the *scene* of this utterance? The scene depicted *in* the utterance is clear enough. It is the "mind" of the speaker become an internalized landscape, a domain in which "shadowy thought" and the "working brain" can recreate an alternative world, like the alternative world of Cupid's nightly visits to Psyche, in Apuleius's fable.

If this were all there were to the final stanza, then Vendler's reduplication model would be adequate to capturing it. But the poem is massively invested in the effort to show that this act of mimesis takes place *in* a scene, one now given a historical dimension. How might we understand the scene of the utterance that describes such a scene? I suggested at the start that the present tense of the poet's initial address is historically indeterminate. The present tense implicit in the end of the poem, on the other hand, is a historically determinate one. We are led by this line of analysis to inquire into the contours of the present scene, the present "time" (as distinct from what Keats calls "the time of Apuleius") regarded as a scene or situation. There are many ways to come at such a question, and much of what follows here and in the next chapter can be take as successive attempts to describe Keats's scene in 1819.

4. The Politics of "Soul-Making"

As a problem for the *Ode to Psyche* itself, the question of the present scene might redirect attention to the opening stanza to see if what is initially understood there as an ahistorical present must not be reread in the light of the poem's conclusion. Looking again at that opening stanza, we can now observe that after the salutation to Psyche we are given a brief description of the poet's recent vision.

---

48. Martin Aske has offered suggestive comments on this stanza in *Keats and Hellenism* (Cambridge: Cambridge University Press, 1985), pp. 107–109.

After asking the goddess Psyche to "hear these tuneless numbers, wrung / By sweet enforcement and remembrance dear," the speaker shifts into a past-tense report:

> Surely I dreamt to-day, or did I see
>   The winged Psyche with awaken'd eyes?
> I wander'd in a forest thoughtlessly,
> And, on the sudden, fainting with surprise,
> Saw two fair creatures, couched side by side
> In deepest grass, beneath the whisp'ring roof
> Of leaves and trembled blossoms, where there ran
>   A brooklet, scarce-espied. (ll. 5–12)

Now, one way of seeing this first stanza as taking place in historical time would be to identify the historicity of this little lyric narrative: "I wandered. . . ." Is it possible to place this mode of utterance in a discursive history? The answer, I believe, is decidedly yes, in that Keats's lines so neatly mimic what was already a well-known lyric of his own time (as it has remained for ours). It is Wordsworth's stanzas on the daffodils from the 1807 *Poems,* which had been recently reprinted (in 1815) as part of his major round of publication in 1814–15: "I wandered lonely as a cloud / . . . When all at once I saw . . . ."[49] The echo of Wordsworth's lyric would count for less here, if it were not also a signal of Keats's appropriation of Wordsworth's characteristic structural device for these memory lyrics. A first stanza of "thoughtless" vision, followed by meditation, followed by a revisiting of the scene of the first stanza "in thought"—to use the phrase from the *Immortality Ode* ("We in thought will join your throng").

But what kind of sense does it make to think of the historically present "scene" of the *Ode to Psyche* as one somehow presided over by Wordsworth's poetry? We know from independent evidence that the contemporary poet whom Keats personally regarded as most influential in setting the scene for his (Keats's) own writing was almost certainly Wordsworth. He is also the poet whom Keats read as most promising in his impulses to urge this twofold modern challenge, i.e., to mount resistance at once to enlightenment and to Christianity. We know that Keats regarded *The Excursion* as one of the three great wonders of his age, but we also know precisely which part of it most attracted his interest: the Wanderer's account in book 4 of the appeal of ancient mythology to a deracinated modernity. The appeal was dramatized in more precise form in the famous sonnet "The World is too Much With Us":

49. Wordsworth, *Poems in Two Volumes, and Other Poems, 1800–1807* (Ithaca, N.Y.: Cornell University Press, 1983), p. 331.

> Great God! I'd rather be
> A Pagan suckled in a creed outworn;
> So might I, standing on this pleasant lea,
> Have glimpses that would make me less forlorn;
> Have sight of Proteus rising from the sea;
> Or hear old Triton blow his wreathed horn.

Wordsworth's writings about pagan mythology betray deep ambivalences in that one can find as much evidence of his renunciation of it as of his endorsement of it.[50] When, at Benjamin Haydon's insistence, Keats recited his *Hymn to Pan* to Wordsworth at their only meeting in 1817, a poem using some of the older poet's own material, Wordsworth responded with chilling curtness: "A Very pretty piece of Paganism."[51] Nonetheless, Keats clearly saw in Wordsworth's most programmatic work the signs of tendencies he took to be more "advanced" and less superstitiously Christian than such a comment would indicate.[52]

Some of the evidence that Keats saw these tendencies lies in the way he deploys Wordsworthian terms, idioms, and structures in the *Ode to Psyche,* especially the echoes of the lines that Wordsworth appended to *The Excursion.* These lines, we recall, were meant to serve as a "prospectus to the design and scope" of the massive modernizing poetic project of which *The Excursion* and the yet-unpublished *Prelude* formed a part. The "remembrance dear" of line two of the *Ode,* for example, echoes the famous opening of this text:

> On Man, on Nature, and on Human Life
> Musing in Solitude, I oft perceive
> Fair trains of imagery before me rise,
> Accompanied by feelings of delight

---

50. See Alex Zwerdling, "Wordsworth and Greek Myth," *University of Toronto Quarterly* 33 (July 1964): 341–54.

51. Hyder E. Rollins, ed., *The Keats Circle,* 3 vols. (Cambridge, Mass.: Harvard University Press, 1948), 2:143–44.

52. One of the key texts of the Waterloo moment in respect to this question, I believe, is Godwin's *The Pantheon; or Ancient History of the Gods of the Gods of Greece and Rome for the Use of Schools and Young Persons of Both Sexes* (London: M. J. Godwin, 1814). Not only does it include a chapter "Of Allegory—Historical Origin of the Gods of the Greeks," but another, far more apposite to Keats, "Of the Gods Representative of the Faculties and Conceptions of the Mind." The work of Taylor, not only the 1795 translation of and commentary on Psyche, but also the 1793 *On the Gods and the World,* seems to have played some role in Godwin's etiologies, as it may have done in Blake's famous comments on the subject of the human invention of the deities in *The Marriage of Heaven and Hell* (1793): see G. M. Harper, *The Neo-Platonism of William Blake* (Chapel Hill: University of North Carolina Press, 1961).

Pure, or with no unpleasing sadness mixed;
And I am conscious of affecting thoughts
And dear remembrances, whose presence soothes
Or elevates the Mind, intent to weigh
The good and evil of our mortal state.[53]

We follow the echo to a textual site in which the *Ode to Psyche* seems to have been conceived. Here is Wordsworth defining his project as the attempt to make his poetry out of his own unconscious associations ("affecting thoughts" and "dear remembrances") and to make his subject the "individual mind" in its relation to the soul and to the world of outward circumstances. He goes on to explain:

—To these emotions, whenceso'er they come,
Whether from the breath of outward circumstance,
Or from the Soul—an impulse to herself,
I would give utterance in numerous Verse.

    . . .

Of the individual Mind that keeps her own
Inviolate retirement . . .
I sing: "fit audience let me find though few!" (ll. 10–23)[54]

Toward the end of the *Ode to Psyche* Keats will speak of building a fane for Psyche "in some untrodden region of my mind," a distinct echo of Wordsworth's later claim in the prospectus to look boldly into what he calls "the Mind of Man, / My haunt and the main region of my song." The added word, "untrodden," is itself a Wordsworthian importation, this time from "She dwelt among the untrodden ways."[55]

53. Ernest de Selincout and Helen Darbishire, eds., *The Poetical Works of William Wordsworth,* 5 vols. (Oxford: Clarendon, 1949), 5:3. And see, of course, M. H. Abrams book-length commentary on the Prospectus in *Natural Supernaturalism* (New York: W. W. Norton, 1971), passim.
54. Wordsworth, *Works,* 5:3.
55. A further complication in the reverberations of this literary echo chamber involves the fact that the phrase "dear remembrance" that Keats echoes from Wordsworth's *Excursion,* as I believe, was itself already echoing, in inverted form, the very opening stanza of canto 1 of Tighe's *Psyche* (a description in medias res of Psyche's state after losing Cupid), where it also appears in the neighborhood of "untrodden":

Much wearied with her long and dreary way,
And now with toil and sorrow well nigh spent,
Of sad regret and wasting grief the prey,
Fair Psyche through untrodden forests went,
To lone shades uttering off a vain lament.
And oft in hopeless silence sighing deep,

My point is not that Keats wishes to "smoke" Wordsworth with his *Ode to Psyche*. It is rather that Keats echoes Wordsworth in such a way as to mark the latter's most important work as already a kind of *Ode to Psyche,* a poetry with implications similar to those that Keats is arguing for. Both texts present themselves as modern acknowledgments of the notion that true divinity resides not with the sky gods, in the heaven of heavens, but, as Wordsworth puts it, in a world "to which the heaven of heavens is but a veil" (l. 30). More specifically, Wordsworth's emphasis on the soul—here and, just as famously, in the *Immortality Ode*—needs to be seen, as Keats intuitively understood, against the backdrop of enlightenment attempts to dissolve the soul into the mechanics of the body.

I have argued elsewhere that Wordsworth defined his great post-1797 literary project against the intellectual background of *Idéologie*.[56] This was the program of the Directory, that hyper-Enlightenment phase of the French Revolution between the end of the Reign of Terror and the Napoleonic coup (1794-98). It was at that time that the Institut National was founded in Paris under the leadership of Destutt de Tracy for purposes of regrounding the work of the enlightened Girondist party on a purer scientific basis. The word itself, "idéologie," De Tracy's coinage, was supposed to name the core discipline of this new educational scheme in such a way as to keep it free from all ambiguity or superstition. One of the terms explicitly rejected by De Tracy's committee was "psychology," and it was ruled out precisely because it carried associations with the concept of the "soul."[57] A similar set of developments can be traced in late-eighteenth-century England, where debates about mind and body engaged by the likes of Richard Price and Joseph Priestley were repeatedly articulated in relation to the question of the soul's immortality and inevitably given a political cast. Addressing these debates on the reconception of the soul in this

---

> As she her fatal error did repent,
> While dear remembrance bade her ever weep,
> And her pale cheek in ceaseless showers of sorrow steep. (1:1)

For a sensitive account of the orchestrating of these and other echoes in Keats's allusive text, see Donald C. Goellnicht, "'In Some Untrodden Region of My Mind': Double Discourse in Keats's 'Ode to Psyche,'" *Mosaic* 21 (spring 1988): 91–103. For a comprehensive tally of Keats echoes and recorded readings of Wordsworth, see Beth Lau, *Keats's Reading of the Romantic Poets* (Ann Arbor: University of Michigan Press, 1991), pp. 11–69.

56. See my *Wordsworth's Second Nature* (Chicago: University of Chicago Press, 1984), pp. 216–34.

57. See Emmet Kennedy, *A Philosophe in the Age of Revolution* (Philadelphia: American Philosophical Society, 1978), pp. 44–47, and Jan Goldstein, *Console and Classify: The French Psychiatric Profession in the Nineteenth Century* (Cambridge: Cambridge University Press, 1987), p. 246.

period, Simon Schaffer concludes that the "combination of a philosophical materialism and conjectural history implied a revised account of a future state."[58] And this "revised account" is the one I claim Keats takes as his point of departure in working out the meaning of the Psyche fable in 1819.

All this becomes reasonably evident in Keats's long meditation on a new theory of the soul in the journal-letter entry to George and Georgiana written a few days before the *Ode to Psyche* itself, on April 21:

> The common cognomen of this world among the misguided and superstitious is "a vale of tears" from which we are to be redeemed by a certain arbitrary interposition of God and taken to Heaven—What a little circumscribe[d] straightened notion! Call the world if you Please "The vale of Soul-Making" Then you will find out the use of the world . . . I say "*Soul making*" Soul as distinguished from an Intelligence—There may be intelligences or sparks of the divinity in millions—but they are not Souls till they acquire identities, till each one be personally itself. I[n]telligences are atoms of perception—they know and they see and they are pure, in short they are God—how then are Souls to be made? How then are these sparks which are God to have identity given them—so as ever to possess a bliss peculiar to each ones individual existence? How, but by the medium of a world like this? This point I sincerely wish to consider because I think it a grander system of salvation than the chrystain religion—or rather it is a system of Spirit-creation. (LJK, 2:101–102)[59]

The posture of "enlightenment" is conspicuous here. Keats explicitly opposes his comments to the views of the "misguided and superstitious" at the start, and, in reviewing his speculations a few sentences on, he claims to have sketched a "a system of Salvation which does not affront our reason and humanity" (LJK, 2:103). At the same time, this exercise is just as obviously an effort to recuperate the concept of the soul from those who would deny it outright. The sense of a historical present, defined by the tension between enlightenment analysis and Christian superstition, seems very much assumed in Keats's rhetoric here.

In his effort to understand the meaning of the Psyche fable in relation to the historicity of the concept of the soul, Keats was almost certainly abetted by Thomas Taylor's commentary for the English translation of Apuleius's tale in 1795. It is not just that Keats identifies the tale's author for the George's Keatses as "Apuleius the Platonist" and that Taylor's interpretation of the fable is so relentlessly Platonizing. Nor is it just that the pagan Keats would certainly have been attracted to a classicist familiarly referred to by Coleridge as "the English

---

58. Simon Schaffer, "States of Mind: Enlightenment and Natural Philosophy," in *The Languages of Psyche,* ed. G. S. Rousseau (Berkeley: University of California Press, 1990), p. 285. This is not to imply that the question did not continue to be contested in the years after the French Revolution.

59. This notion of the medium, developed by Burke and Wordsworth in the traditionalist mode and very differently by Shelley in the modern mesmeric mode, remains itself mediational for many of the various concepts of culture that emerge in the discourse of Romantic historicism.

Pagan." Nor that Keats wrote the "soul-making" letter just days after his meeting with Coleridge, who was himself fresh from the last of his 1819 *Philosophical Lectures,* in which, explaining the history of polytheism in Greece, Coleridge is known to have consulted Taylor's works.[60] Rather, the argument for this connection rests primarily on striking parallels in the topic and formulation.

Thus, where Keats's Platonizing account locates the origins of human souls in "intelligences or sparks of divinity," Apuleius anticipates this move with an genealogy couched in very similar terms. In Taylor's interpretation, the fable "was designed to represent the lapse of the human soul from the intelligible world to the earth." It is designed to represent, in other words, the "fall" or, as I prefer, the "case" of the soul and to do so in such a way as to present this event as a moment of unintelligibility. Where cases are, causes cannot be far away. Thus, in terms profoundly resonant of those Keats will later use to explain the "earth" as a "vale of soul-making," Taylor frames the entire commentary in respect to the status of a cause which is not a pure or "first" cause:

> In the first place, the gods, as I have elsewhere shown, are super-essential natures, from their found union with the first cause, who is super-essential without any addition. But though the gods, through their summits or unities, transcend essence, yet their unities are participated either by intellect alone, or by intellect and soul, or by intellect, soul, and body; from which participations the various orders of the gods are deduced. When, therefore, intellect, soul, and body are in conjunction suspended from this super-essential unity, which is the center flower or blossom of a divine nature, then the god from whom they are suspended is called a mundane god. In the next place, the common parents of the human soul are the intellect and soul of the world; but its proximate parents are the intellect and soul of the particular star about which it was originally distributed, and from which it first descends.[61]

Keats's own "soul-making" account distinguishes, likewise, three elements or "grand materials" in the process. What in Apuleius had been intellect, soul, and body, become in Keats the triad of intelligence, heart, and world. On his account, the system of salvation, he says, "is effected by three grand materials act-

---

60. Neither Taylor, nor the "soul" as such, appears in Keats's humorously long list of topics discussed by himself and Coleridge in a walk that probably did not last an hour. But Coleridge did refer elsewhere to Taylor as one of the "metaphysical dreamers" of the age, and both "metaphysics" and "dreams" do appear on this list, along with some topics having to do with ghosts and pagan divinities. Writing to John Thelwall in 1796, Coleridge had mentioned his interest in Taylor as a foil for his distaste for history:

> I have read & digested most of the Historical Writers—; but I do not *like* History. Metaphysics & Poetry, and "Facts of mind:"—(i.e. [*sic*] accounts of all strange phantasms that ever possessed your philosophy-dreamers, from Theuth the Egyptian to Taylor, the English Pagan) are my darling Studies.

By 1819, however, Taylor's work on Greek polytheism would figure in Coleridge's *historical* account of Western culture from the Greeks to the present. Samuel Taylor Coleridge, *Selected Letters,* ed. H. J. Jackson (Oxford: Clarendon Press, 1987), p. 30.

61. Taylor, *The Fable of Cupid and Psyche,* pp. 4–5.

ing the one upon the other for a series of years—These three Materials are the *Intelligence*—the *human heart* (as distinguished from intelligence or Mind) and the *World* or *Elemental space* suited for the proper action of *Mind* and *Heart* on each other for the purpose of forming the *Soul* or *Intelligence destined to posses the sense of Identity*" (LJK, 2:102). Sometime in the next few days, Keats put himself to work on the *Ode to Psyche,* the first poem with which he had ever taken real pains.

My own sense is that Keats not only worked closely from Taylor's text but also that he made the connection between it and Wordsworth's Platonizing account of the progress of the soul in that other great contemporary poem on the "future state" of Psyche: the *Immortality Ode.* When Wordsworth shifted attention from "ideology" to "psychology," from the brain to the soul, in poems such as the *Immortality Ode,* the occasion of the new poetic articulation is, famously, the lost sense of the "visionary gleam." And, as he explained in a later commentary on the poem, his default framework for writing his way through the difficult issues of the poem was the Platonic myth of the soul's preexistence. Wordsworth referred to his use of Plato in the *Ode* as a kind of convenience, an Archimedean point on which to stand—just as, in invoking the Platonizing cosmology for use in his prospectus, he calls his own poem a domain in terms of which the Heaven of Heavens is but a veil.[62] In both poems by Wordsworth, as in Keats's account, the soul, Psyche, enjoys a kind of provisional, self-consciously post-Enlightenment rehabilitation. The relevant difference is that Wordsworth represses the historical dimension of his argument, resting content with making quantitative comparisons to Milton, claiming (for example) that he needs a "greater muse." Keats, by contrast, stresses the chronological dimension, suggesting a temporal development in which both he and Milton (and Wordsworth, for that matter) have their part. The emphasis on what is (necessarily) "greater" in Wordsworth shifts to what is (historically) "later" in Keats.[63]

---

62. The relevant part of Wordsworth's well-known note to the Immortality Ode, also invoked (comically) by Shelley in *Peter Bell the Third* (see chapter 9 below), runs as follows:
   [A] pre-existent state has entered into the popular creeds of many nations, and among all persons acquainted with classic literature is known as an ingredient in Platonic philosophy. Archimedes said that he could move the world if he had a point whereon to rest his machine. Who has not felt the same aspirations as regards the world of his own mind? Having to wield some of its elements when I was impelled to write this poem on the "Immortality of the Soul," I took hold of the notion of pre-existence as having sufficient foundation in humanity for authorizing me to make for my purpose the best use of it I could as a Poet.
   Poems, in Two Volumes, ed. Jared Curtis, p. 428.
   63. Lyrics sometimes perform their "attitude toward history" in the structure of their tense shifts. If, as I argue elsewhere, the tense loop of the characteristic Wordsworthian lyric creates a kind of traditionalist structure, in which past and present aspire to a condition of preliterate in-

Reinvoking that conjunction of "linguistic" and "calendar time" that I discussed above in relation to Anna Barbauld, we might say that the historical "present" of the speaker's final utterance in the *Ode to Psyche,* its place on his time line, is 1819. This is the moment when the poet offers his individual mind as the site of a divinity, the principle of human life, newly reacknowledged and only now, in the history of Psyche, able to be celebrated as it ought to be, and married, as it ought to be, with the principle of love that enables it to reproduce itself. On this reading, I would argue, the conclusion of the poem is not so "private" as it is often thought. For the putative internality of poem's final vision appears at the end of a public history. The Psyche who will lodge in Keats's mind—become *Keats's* psyche—has a history, is indeed partly constituted by a history, which tells of how she has been conceived over time. She can be what Keats now claims she is by virtue of his way of following Wordsworth's lead in seeing her that way. The ways of soul-making in 1819, in other words, will assume a more highly developed form by virtue of the recognition that *that* is all we know on earth and all we need to know. Anything else is just what Keats calls superstition.

5. The Week when Keats Wrote *To Autumn*

I began this discussion of Keats by describing how his acute vulnerability to embarrassment led him to see his poetic career as a succession of stages, defined in terms of successive modes of writing. I then invoked his notion of "smoking" as a term of relative transcendence in order to complicate the developmental model implicit in his remarks on his own poetic development. By looking at the peculiar place of Mary Tighe and the myth of Psyche in Keats self-representation of his new personal epoch (that of 1819), I further tried to suggest that Keats's newly acquired sense of historical culture supplied a new frame of reference for the work of his annus mirabilis. This new frame of reference is one in which the poet comes to terms with the past in order to understand his historically present moment—his contemporary scene—as historically conditioned. And it is an effort to understand *that,* in order to be guided in future projects—that is, in order to become, like Apollo, a "fore-seeing God." What I have outlined, in short, is Keats's anticipation of something rather like the "progressive-regressive method" as it was worked out by Sartre from Lefebvre and then *applied* to Keats in Levinson's provocatively "social" or "historical" critical commentary. Keats was there first, after his fashion, self-conscious of the new framework for explaining

---

distinguishability, then Keats's replay of this form in the *Ode to Psyche* can be read as an exposure of the historicism implicit in the attempt of traditionalism to efface it. See *Wordsworth's Second Nature,* pp. 212–14.

his own case. Part of what he foresaw in this process—exemplified in his expressed conviction that he would someday have sufficient critical attention to require some "mystification"—was us. I have not yet said much about how Keats managed to achieve this acute historical self-consciousness in the way he did, or when he did, but I shall return to that topic in the next chapter. In the closing pages of this chapter, I wish first to shore up my argument about Keats's cultural historicism by considering the end of the legendary five-month period of composition that, as Bate observed, began in mid-April 1819. Then, I will add a brief word about the immense scope of Keats's ambition in representing the history of Psyche.

In a journal entry for September 18, 1819, Keats recorded for George and Georgiana his most explicit statement on the historical moment he had come to see himself occupying. That was a Saturday. The next morning, Keats took his daily walk through Winchester, presumably just as he described it for George and Georgiana: crossing the square past the cathedral, past Westminster College (and also the house where Jane Austen had died three years earlier, though Keats took no note of the fact), through the Abbey of St. Croix, and on to the sallows of the River Itchin. Given that the cathedral had a Romanesque foundation and a Gothic superstructure, and that the college and abbey were monuments to medieval Christianity and its teachings, and that the River Itchin was the well-known topos for what Coleridge (and later W. K. Wimsatt) hailed as the birth of a distinctively Romantic mode of nature poetry at the hands of Bowles, it is not too much to claim that the walk is already itself a historical allegory.[64] When he returned from his walk, he composed *To Autumn*. Like *Psyche,* this poem has suffered from a critical horizon drawn too narrowly, though key essays by Geoffrey Hartman and Jerome McGann have helped to open it up. The New-Critical tendency, which survives in Vendler's nuanced commentary, is to regard it as Keats's—even England's—most perfect poem and in turn to see this perfection as a function of its ability to satisfy the canons of poetic autonomy and self-referentiality. Hartman challenged this judgment (and those canons) by insisting on the poem's relation to English literary history as a larger context of meaning.[65] McGann challenged Hartman by insisting on

64. Keats describes the walk for George, humorously takes him along, in his journal letter of Saturday, September 21, three days after he provides the history of English politics discussed below: LJK, 2:189–90. For Coleridge's account of his generation's epoch-changing reception of Bowles's sonnets to the River Itchin, see *Biographia Literaria,* ed. W. J. Bate (Princeton, N.J.: Bollingen Press, 1983). For Wimsatt's often-anthologized essay on "The Structure of Romantic Nature Imagery," see *The Verbal Icon* (Lexington: University of Kentucky Press, 1954), pp. 103–16.

65. Geoffrey Hartman, "Poem and Ideology: A Study of Keats's 'To Autumn'," in *The Fate of Reading* (Chicago: University of Chicago Press), pp. 124–46.

its relation not only to literary history but also to the immediate context of English social conditions.[66]

The problem with McGann's salutary revision of Hartman is that he sees Keats's relationship to these conditions primarily in terms of escapism, whereby Keats recognizes his historical situation only to turn away from it in an act of aesthetic pseudotranscendence. What is not adequately registered is the near certainty that less than a week earlier Keats was in London moving through the crowd that gave Henry Hunt a triumphal welcome on his return from Manchester to stand trial for chairing the session at Peterloo.[67] We can place Keats along that route at the time when the crowds would have begun assembling, as he would have been returning from his sister's in Walthamstow down the North Road though Islington and on into the City in the late morning of September 13.[68] What is more, Keats described the scene to George and Georgiana just five days later (September 18) as if he had witnessed it:

> You will hear by the papers of the proceedings at Manchester and Hunt's triumphal entry into London—I[t] would take me a whole day and a quire of paper to give you any thing like detail—I will merely mention that it is calculated that 30.000 people were in the streets waiting for him—The whole distance from the Angel Islington to the Crown and anchor was lined with Multitudes. As I pass'd Colnaghi's window I saw a profil Portrait of Sands the destroyer of Kotzebue. His very look must interest every one in his favour. (LJK, 2:194–95)

The words "As I passed" seem to indicate that this whole account is the description of someone moving among the "Multitudes" he is describing. As

---

66. McGann, "Keats and the Historical Method," pp. 49–62. For a different account of the *Psyche-Autumn* connection, see Stuart Curran, *Poetic Form and British Romanticism* (Oxford: Oxford University Press, 1986), pp. 84–85.

67. A volume that has appeared in the late stages of preparing the present book for the press has helped to rectify this situation. Nicholas Roe, ed., *Keats and History* (Cambridge: Cambridge University Press, 1995). Several of the essays address the question of Keats and Peterloo, a most welcome development, especially Roe's and Vincent Newey's, each of which makes something interesting of the participle "conspiring" in stanza one of *To Autumn* (see pp. 186–87 and pp. 199–201). Writing about the question of history for the *Ode to Psyche* in this same volume, Daniel Watkins revisits Christopher Caudwell's 1930's attempt to explain the interest of the poem in what Watkins calls "*identity* and *circumstance*" all "within the strict terms of commodity exchange" (pp. 96, 91); my aim here has been to show how Keats's work can be seen as just one contemporary case of the massive reconceptualization of "identity and circumstance" in this post-Waterloo moment. Thus, while our readings tally on certain points, there is a difference: while I agree with Watkins' conclusion "that the poem's importance is not diminished but enhanced by recognition of its historical situation" (p. 104), I have tried to show its part in, or version of, the very discourse that establishes the possibility of such a "recognition."

68. Both Bate's and Aileen Ward's biographies won major awards when they appeared in 1963. One of the most useful indexes to the way in which Aileen Ward's biography of Keats offers perspectives unavailable in Bate's lies in her handling of these events, which Bate largely overlooks. See her *John Keats: The Making of a Poet* (New York: Viking, 1963), pp. 316–18.

we shall see, at least one other reference to this occasion tends to confirm that hypothesis.

The *Times* estimated the crowd for this entry at 300,000, which was probably an exaggeration, but if it was even one-fourth of that size it would have surpassed Peterloo itself as Britain's largest-ever ordered public demonstration. Keats would have faced this energized throng, moreover, after weeks of deep solitude in Winchester and an entire summer of quasi-solitude in the company of Charles Brown on the unpopulated Isle of Wight. The event could scarcely have failed to make an impact, to convey a sense of involvement in the movement of history. It was this crowd, once the great "triumph" had come to its destination in front of St. Paul's, that Hunt described as "unexampled" in its spirit.[69] There is no evidence that Keats heard the comment, but the claim is roughly the one that he is addressing in writing the George Keatses on September 18:

> All civil[iz]ed countries become gradually more enlighten'd and there should be a continual change for the better. Look at this Country at present and remember it when it was even though[t] impious to doubt the justice of a trial by Combat—From that time there has been a gradual change—Three great changes have been in progess—First for the better, next for the worse, and a third time for the better once more. The first was the gradual annihilation of the tyranny of the nobles. when kings found it their interest to conciliate the common people, elevate them and be just to them. Just when baronial Power ceased and before standing armies were so dangerous, Taxes were few. kings were lifted by the people over the heads of their nobles, and those people held a rod over kings. The change for the worse in Europe was again this. The obligation of kings to the Multitude began to be forgotten—Custom had made noblemen the humble servants [of kings—Then kings turned to the Nobles as the adorners] of the[i]r power, the slaves of it, and from the people as creatures continually endeavouring to check them. Then in every kingdom therre was a long struggle of kings to destroy all popular privleges. The english were the only people in europe who made a grand kick at this. They were slaves to Henry 8th but were freemen under william 3rd at the time the French were abject slaves under Lewis 14th[.] The example of England, and the liberal writers of france and england sowed the seed of opposition to this Tyranny—and it was swelling in the ground till it burst out in the french revolution—That has had an unlucky termination. It put a stop to the rapid progress of free sentiments in England; and gave our Court hopes of turning back on the despotism of the 16 century. They have made a handle of this event in every way to undermine our freedom. They spread a horrid superstition against all inovation and improvement—The present struggle in England of the people is to destroy this superstition. (LJK, 2:193)

This passage, which is only just recently receiving the attention it deserves in Keats studies, is unremarkable as a piece of political analysis, of course, but it is interesting as Keats's application to the history of England of the developmental scheme he had used to organize the more abstract history implicit in the *Ode*

---

69. For Henry Hunt's remarks to the London assembly on this occasion, see Introduction above.

to Psyche. That history, too, had proceeded in such stages: a change for the better (the birth of Psyche in late antiquity), change for the worse (the Christian appropriation of the doctrine of the immortal soul), and change for the better again (the overthrow of Christianity by enlightened romanticism). Still more apposite for the *Ode to Psyche,* however, is the explicit identification of the moment of the text's production as a historically determinate, politically charged condition—what Keats refers to as "the present struggle." And the object of this struggle, Keats declares outright, is a form of superstition, just as with his lyric history of Psyche.

The ensuing discussion of Carlile the bookseller and Paine also makes it clear both that the superstition in question is Christianity and that the answer lies in some form of refashioned post-Enlightenment form of religion. Keats's account of the English people's "present struggle" thus pushes forward into the following elaboration:

> What has rous'd them to do it is their distresses—Per[h]aps on this account the present distresses of this nation are a fortunate thing—tho so horrid in the[i]r experience. You will see I mean that the french Revolution [p]ut a tempor[a]ry stop to this third change, the change for the better—Now it is in progress again and I thin[k] in an effectual one . . . I know very little of these things. I am convinced however that apparently small causes make great alterations. There are little signs whereby we may know how matters are going on—This makes the business about Carlisle the Bookseller of great moment in my mind. He has been selling deistical pamphlets, republished Tom Payne and many other works held in superstitious horror. He even has been selling for some time immense numbers of a work call[ed] "The Deist" which comes out in weekly numbers—For this Conduct he I think has had above a dozen inditements issued against him; for which he has found Bail to the amount of many thousand Pounds—After all they are affraid to prosecute: they are affraid of his defence: it would be published in all the papers all over the Empire: they shudder at this: the Trials would light a flame they could not extinguish. Do you not think this of great import? (LJK, 2:193–94)

Keats said of his first great ode of the spring, the *Ode to Psyche,* that it was the first with which he took any real pains, and "pains" in his account of "soul-making," clearly formed part of his account of how to revise the "superstitious" story of salvation that was still dominant in his English culture. Here, in the post-Peterloo letter, pains, "distresses," are a fortunate thing in their capacity to rouse the people to engage in their present struggle.

The "deism" of Paine and Carlyle is one kind of answer to the superstitious Christianity against which the English people must struggle to resume the course of political progress.[70] And Keats's Sunday-morning poem of the next day, rather like the more explicit Sunday-morning poem of his American dis-

---

70. For more on the intellectual context of these questions see Albert J. Kuhn, "English Deism and the Development of Romantic Mythological Syncretisim," *PMLA* 71 (1956): 1094–1116.

ciple Wallace Stevens, is another kind of answer: we can think of them both as neopagan hymns. That Christianity appeared to offer an answer to the problem of death, after all, went far toward explaining its powerful appeal. At least for the select number of souls who submitted to its doctrine and discipline, and counted themselves elect, it offered a hope, the intimation of immortality. The decisive invasions of history-as-death in the middle *Odes*—both *Nightingale* and *Grecian Urn,* for example—dramatize Keats' sensitivity to the question despite his young age. If *To Autumn* is his greatest piece of writing, as has so often been said, it is because in it he arguably set himself the most ambitious challenge of his brief career and managed to meet it. For the poem is decidedly a thanatopsis, a view of death, and as such it addresses the issues which the various forms of "deism" in Keats's age have had most difficulty handling.[71]

Apropos of his claims about the "revised account of a future state" in Romantic-period materialism, Schaffer turns to Bentham's celebrated willing of his body to science as exemplifying the point that, "the materialists needed to define their own art of making a good end."[72] I argued above in chapter 4 for Bentham's importance in shaping the new concept of the "historical situation" that is so crucial to the revision of "the future state." What I am claiming about *To Autumn* is that, in a cultural domain that represented an alternative within, or to, the scientific domain, Keats was working through his own historical case to make a good end.[73] Indeed, we may assess his project, so understood, in terms analogous to those I have developed for Bentham's understanding of the historical situation as the case of all cases in a given state of society. When Shelley wrote his beautiful elegy for Keats in 1821, he decidedly represented his friend's survival not in the form of a carcass—like Bentham's—that could be encased for annual faculty meetings at the University of London but rather in the form of the circumstantial materiality of his own verse practice in poems like *To Au-*

---

71. Although he focuses primarily on the two *Hyperions,* Robert Ryan offers helpful background comments on Keats, paganism, and Deism, quite compatible with those I have outlined here, in "The Politics of Greek Religion," in *Critical Essays on John Keats,* ed. Hermione de Almeida (Boston: G. K. Hall, 1990), pp. 261–79.

72. Schaffer, "States of Mind," in *Languages of Psyche,* p. 285.

73. On the topic of Keats and science, there has been a fair amount of work prompted by Stuart Sperry's suggestive account of the role played by pharmocology in Keats's poetry. See *Keats the Poet* (Princeton, N.J.: Princeton University Press, 1973), especially pp. 30–71. See, for example, Donald C. Goellnicht, *The Poet–Physician, Keats and Medical Science* (Pittsburgh: University of Pittsburgh Press, 1984); and Hermione D'Alemeida, *Keats and Medicine* (New York: Oxford University Press, 1991), for whom "Keats's portrait of life in autumn stands at the point of consensus on the subject among the physiologists and philosophers of his time" (p. 319).

tumn. Indeed, the long reception of the poem suggests that it at least partly has done the work that Keats intended it to do in providing an alternative to a politically retarding superstition.[74] In Keats's humanist neopaganism, for example, if the immanent Soul as the principle of life, and immanent Love as the principle of reproducing life, are the only divinities at work in the world, then nothing is allowed to gainsay the fact that life expires even as it is reproduced. Where, then, are the consolations of Keats's paganism? Aye, where are they, the poem asks, but suggests that we think not of them but attend instead to the appeal of the dying sounds themselves when mellowed by the finest tones and turned by the finest tropes that Keats can muster.

I will not offer a full "reading" of the poem in these terms. Such a reading, I think, is unlikely to differ greatly from the existing tradition of commentary, with just two exceptions. First, the poem would be understood to be somewhat differently motivated, or motivated on another level, from what has typically been assumed. Second, the issue of "motivation" as figured in the poem itself would merit some attention, especially around that notion, so crucial to the grammar of "smoking," of *transitivity* itself in the first stanza, as would the catachretic misuse of intransitive verbs in transitive syntactic circumstances throughout. Witness the line where those "barred-clouds" ungrammatically "*bloom* the soft-dying day" (l. 25). Likewise, I would not venture that it is the greatest lyric in English, but I do think it is certainly the most powerful of those consolation poems that refuse to resort to Christian comfort and that it therefore has had special appeal for those readers who share Keats's skepticism about that question. In the film version of *The Prime of Miss Jean Brodie,* when Maggie Smith stands at the window gazing on the turning foliage and breaks into a rapturous incantation of "Season of mists and mellow fruitfulness . . . ," she at once emblematizes the place of this lyric in the Anglo-American poetry curriculum and extends its reach to popular audiences who may have forgotten they ever heard it before.

In this respect, *To Autumn* forms the last step in Keats's attempt at once to tell and shape the history of Psyche. Like the *Ode to Psyche,* then, it is thus a terribly ambitious poem. For although Keats's implication is that every individual mind must, in its internal region, cultivate the principle of its own divinity and accept its completion as a spirit, he offers himself as the one who knows how to show

---

74. On these themes in "Adonais," see two excellent recent essays in particular, one by James Heffernan, "*Adonais:* Shelley's Consumption of Keats," *Studies in Romanticism* 23 (fall 1984): 295–315; and Susan Wolfson, "Keats Enters History: Autopsy, 'Adonais,' and the fame of Keats," in *Keats and History,* ed. Roe, pp. 17–45.

the way, even better than did Wordsworth, whom Keats after all saw as in certain respects a greater power for good in the world than Milton himself.[75]

6. Emperor and Clown: Keats's Literary Imperialism

The post-Waterloo context provided the circumstances in which this sort of ambition could arise. It is a kind of historical chaos in which, as in modern chaos theory, (to requote Keats) "apparently small causes make great alterations." The massive influence of the press and the grand scale of the assemblies for public speeches gave verbally talented young men and women the impression that they could do anything. The urgency of the reform issues, sharply raised during the French Revolution and then suspended for twenty years, supplied the necessary pressure. Three days after writing *To Autumn,* Keats announced that he was going to see Hazlitt about a decision he had just taken to go into journalism. He wished, he said, to contribute to "the liberal side of the question." And that picture of Hunt's being met by tens and tens of thousands of his countrymen left its impression on Keats, as we can surmise from a letter he wrote a couple of weeks later to his friend Benjamin Haydon about an English public of whom he often expressed distrust. But here, with only a trace of irony, he concedes, "I have no cause to complain because I am certain any thing really fine will in these days be felt. I have no doubt that if I had written Othello I should have been cheered by as good a Mob as Hunt" (LJK, 2:219). Placing himself in the position, by turns, of Shakespeare and "Orator" Hunt, Keats betrays an ambition for reshaping the state of the nation.

And yet Keats sometimes betrayed even greater ambition, fantasies of international power and influence through his writing, as if in recognition of Anna Barbauld's point that one cannot effectively come to terms with the state of England at a given moment without doing so for other nations at the same time. To be sure, Keats's fantasies tended to be articulated with a certain irony or tonal instability, a certain air of "amusement." When the poet identifies the bird's song in *Ode to a Nightingale* as the same that "was heard / In ancient days by emperor and clown" (ll. 63–64), he effects a telling conjunction between the imperial and the risible that marks much of his writing in 1819. True, too, Keats did not set foot out of England until his tour of Scotland with Charles Brown

---

75. As early as May 1818, Keats wrote about Wordsworth and Milton as follows: "[Milton] did not think into the human heart, as Wordsworth has done—Yet Milton as a Philosop[h]er, had sure as great power as Wordsworth—What is then to be inferr'd? O many things—It proves there is a really grand march of intellect—It proves that a mighty providence subdues the mightiest Minds to the service of the time being, whether it be in human Knowledge or Religion" (LJK, 1:282).

in mid-1818, and he did not leave the British Isles until well after he had written the last of his major poetry. One did not have to travel to experience the empire, however, for it shaped one's everyday life of sensations in the imperial capital. Long before Rossetti's *Burden of Nineveh* epiphany at the British Museum, Keats reported seeing "a Sphinx there of a giant size, & most voluptuous Egyptian expression" on March 31, 1819 (LJK, 2:68).[76] Colnaghi's import store windows likewise seemed to hold a special attraction for him. And the "man-tiger organ" that finds its way into *The Cap and Bells (The Jealousies)* in late 1819 is an item that he probably saw on display at the East India Company.[77]

The empire also impinged materially on Keats's "life of thoughts," making itself felt in his most intimate personal connections. In the annus mirabilis, after the departure of George and Georgiana and the death of Tom Keats in 1818, Keats's most constant companion was probably Charles Brown, who took him in for a nominal rent after Tom died.[78] Brown's effect on Keats's horizon of interest begins with his urging the walking tour of Scotland just before Keats began work on *Hyperion,* but it later began to work in far more subtle ways. The shelter Brown offered Keats at Wentworth Place and Brown's largesse, such as it was, on which Keats was dependent in 1819, both derived from the legacy of Brown's brother, who made his money in the East India Company. Brown himself had been working for the Company, after a long stint abroad in Russia, when the sudden death of his brother brought him the funds to pursue his commercial literary and theatrical interests instead. Certainly by 1819, probably earlier, Brown had determined to make these latter ambitions Keats's own. The two large projects on which Keats collaborated with him in that year—*Otho the Great* and *The Cap and Bells*—were not only conceived as commercial enterprises; they were also both conspicuously about emperors and empires, even more so than the post-Napoleonic epic, *Hyperion* (in preparing for which, nonetheless, Keats had read Gibbon's *Decline and Fall*) (LJK, 1:237).

These same two late works of 1819, despite the fact that one is a history play and the other a comic fairy tale, can also lay claim to being the most tonally

76. Keats's plan for a new career in the periodicals, in late 1819, called for him to be in walking distance to the Museum for daily visits (LJK, 2.174, 220).

77. See Stillinger's note in PJK, p. 483.

78. George and Georgiana had departed for Kentucky just before Tom died. George's aim was to try his fortunes in the wilderness, and the failure of his first investment enterprises caused Keats untold woes in 1819. Some of Keats's greatest letters, indeed greatest writing, as I shall argue in the next chapter, derived from his ingenious contrivances to span the cultural distance that the earlier British empire had created between the capital and the frontier. Reading them one is constantly reminded, for example, of arguments in Burke's 1770s speeches about the American colonies to the effect that one cannot rule a land that one has no experience of.

bizarre works in a corpus notorious for tonal difficulties. Anyone who has read even as far as the first act of *Otho,* for example, will have been struck by the extraordinary moment in which, during an anxious father-son confrontation that appears to be headed for premature tragic confusion, the emperor suddenly reveals, with corny slapstick humor, that he was only jesting about taking umbrage with his son. Far from demanding death or exile, as any audience would have expected, he now says he intends to see him married to the woman whom he (Otho) had formerly found objectionable (act 2, scene 1). If such moments in the play seem perplexing to us, it may be some consolation that they were downright frustrating to Brown. Of a later tonal oddity in the play, he wrote to their mutual friend Dilke in the midst of composition: "Keats is very industrious, but I swear . . . he is obstinately monstrous. What think you of Otho's threatening cold pig to the new-married couple? He says the Emperor must have a spice of drollery."[79] "Spice" is itself an imperial joke on the part of Brown, a term chosen with the showy cleverness characteristic of the Keats circle. But why is it that with Otho, as with Elfinan in *The Cap and Bells,* and even (though more subtly) with *Hyperion,* Keats's Emperors must have a spice of drollery?

It is a matter of understanding how Keats imagined himself in the world and the world in his imagination. Consider how Keats framed the major career decision he faced in May 1819 when Brown decided to rent the house at Wentworth Place. "I have the choice as it were of two Poisons," he writes to Sarah Jeffery, "the one is voyaging to and from India for a few years; the other is leading a fevrous life alone with Poetry" (LJK, 2:112–13). This might seem a choice between adventuring into the world and some poetic alternative, and thus between ambition and idleness. But in the proximate example of Brown, these career paths had not differed much in degree of ambition. Further, Keats explains that he inclines toward the latter because he would "rather conquer his indolence and strain [his] nerves at some grand Poem—than be in a dunderheaded indiaman" (LJK, 2:113). Indeed, his next letter to Jeffery suggests that this grand poem will make its way in a world much larger than what the Indiaman will give him access to: "An Indiaman is a little world. One of the great reasons that the english have produced the finest writers in the world; is, that the English world has ill-treated them during their lives and foster'd them after their deaths. They have in general been trampled aside into the bye paths of life and seen the festerings of Society. . . . For all this I will not go on board an Indiaman" (LJK, 2:115–16). To illustrate the social inferiority of England's great writers, Keats

---

79. Charles Dilke, *The Papers of a Critic,* 2 vols. (London: J. Murray, 1875), 1:9.

cites the cases of Shakespeare and Ben Jonson. In a kind of master-slave dialectic, their sufferings as a class humanize their writings, and eventually promote their fame. This fame will not come until posthumous lionization—but in losing "the English world," they gain the larger world (LJK, 2:115). Thus, when Keats imagined himself "among the English poets" after his death, he was also imagining himself among the first poets of the world (LJK, 1:394).

Keats often spoke of writing for "the world," of course, and we do wrong to underestimate the scope of the ambition thus implied in such remarks. Back in December, writing to George after Tom's death, he wrote jealously of literary kings but, as the context makes clear, meant literary emperors:

> We have seen three literary kings in our Time—Scott—Byron—and then the scotch nove[ls.] All now appears to be dead—or I may mistake—literary Bodies may still keep up the Bustle which I do not hear—Haydon show'd me a letter he had received from Tripoli—Ritchey was well and in good Spirits, among Camels, Turbands, Palm Trees and sands—You may remember I promised to send him an Endymion which I did not—however he has one—you have one—One is in the Wilds of america—the other is on a Camel's back in the plains of Egypt. (LJK, 2:16)

Byron had not yet called himself the "grand Napoleon of the realms of rhyme," but the identification was clear enough from the post-Waterloo reflections on Europe in canto 3 of *Childe Harold's Pilgrimage*. Keats's unhidden jealousy of Byron clearly has to do with more than just money and rank. It has to do with cultural influence in "the world."[80] Keats's suggestion to George that Scott and Byron were dead as literary bodies, might seem less like imperial regicide if it were not that Keats goes on to dream, with the fantasy of *Endymion's* progress across northern Africa and midwestern America, that he may already be taking their place. In February Keats had written to George about how David Lewis had "[s]aid a thing I am not at all contented with—Says he 'O, he is quite the little Poet' now this is abominable—you might as well say Buonaparte is quite the little Soldier." In his famous next sentence—"You see what it is to be under six foot and not a lord"—both of the negative characteristics happen to single out himself—and rule out Byron—as the leading candidate for the Napoleonic position in literature (LJK, 2:61). It is hard not to see the little poet playfully imagining himself here as emperor of the literary world.

Keats's fantasies of imperial conquest in literature go back at least as far as the

---

80. In *The Cap and Bells*, Keats would make Byron a composite part—along with the Prince Regent and Keats himself—in the characterization of the emperor Elfinan. On the satirical topicality of this, Keats's last major poem, see Martin Halpern, "Keats and the 'Spirit that Laughest'," *Keats-Shelley Journal* 15 (1966): 69–86; Howard O. Brogan, "'The Cap and Bells, or . . . The Jealousies'?," in *Bulletin of the New York Public Library* 77 (1974): 298–313; and Claude Lee Finney, *The Evolution of Keats's Poetry* (Cambridge: Harvard University Press, 1936), pp. 732–37.

chestnut conceit in the sonnet on Chapman's Homer when Keats imagines himself a literary Cortez (for Balboa), considering the prospects of a newly discovered ocean. And in 1819, the famous April 21 discussion of the vale of soul making is prompted by Keats's reading of Robertson's *History of America* and Voltaire's *Siécle de Louis XIV,* literary experiences Keats described as "like walking arm and arm between Pizarro and the great little Monarch" (LJK, 2:100).[81] These are fantasies of reading one's way through the world, however, and the stress in the references to Byron and Scott and Napoleon seems to be on writing one's way through it. We know that Bonaparte was the model of the displaced emperor in what Hunt called the "transcendental cosmopolitics" of *Hyperion,* but there is a more explicit frame of reference for the question of literary–cultural imperialism in Keats. Perhaps the most powerful articulation of the emergent postwar jingoism under which Keats matured occurs in the rhetorical climax of that 1814 publication that Keats called one of the three wonders of his age, Wordsworth's *Excursion,* where the Wanderer recasts the global vision of a commercial *Pax Britannia* from the conclusion of Pope's *Windsor Forest.* In the Wanderer's fantasy of the "glorious destiny" for Britain's "imperial realm," the emphasis is not (as in Pope) on the physical riches—balm, amber, coral, rubies, pearls and gold—that British ships will import back to the Thames, but rather on the cultural riches that Britain will export to an uncivilized world too much ruled by France as Pope's world had been, he thought, too much ruled by Spain. "Vast the circumference of hope," the Wanderer tells his nation, "and ye / Are at its centre":

> Change wide, and deep, and silently performed,
> This Land shall witness; and as days roll on,
> Earth's universal frame shall feel the effect;
> Even till the smallest habitable rock,
> Beaten by lonely billows, hear the songs
> Of humanised society; and bloom
> With civil arts, that shall breathe forth their fragrance,
> A grateful tribute to all-ruling Heaven.
> From culture, unexclusively bestowed
> On Albion's noble Race in freedom born,
> Expect these mighty issues: . . . (Book 9, ll. 384–94)[82]

Keats's jingoistic endorsement of English poetry over the French school in *Sleep and Poetry* showed the impact of this passage on him as early as 1817. The

81. See chapter 8 below.
82. De Selincout and Darbishire, eds., *The Poetical Works of Wordsworth,* vol. 5, pp. 298–99.

Wordsworthian project of exporting the songs of humanised British society to the wider world was never far from Keats's wildest dreams, even if his understanding of how those songs became "humanized" differed from Wordsworth's.

In contending, therefore, that the conjunction of "emperor and clown" as stand-ins for the poet of the *Ode to a Nightingale* may be less adventitious than we have thought, I mean that it may belie deep ideological ambivalence. For the emperor and the clown represent two mutually related aspects of the imperial subject—calculation and folly, grandeur and pathos. The chameleon poet, to be sure, identified with an Otho as much as with an Imogen or a Iago, but he also recognized, with Hazlitt's help, something Otho-like, hawklike, in the English poet's act of such imaginative appropriations. Hazlitt's criticism was the second of Keats's three "wonders" of the modern world—Haydon's paintings were the third—but Hazlitt's importance for Keats has not always been well understood, and the vexed question of Shakespeare brings this out.

Keatsians have tended to look to Hazlitt primarily for influence on Keats's aesthetic views, but in March 1819 Hazlitt published a pamphlet that can lay claim to being a crucial text for the topics of imagination, power, and empire in the Romantic period. Hazlitt's *Letter to William Gifford*, a bristling counterattack on the editor of the *Quarterly Review*, not only argues that romantic "imagination" serves the interests of tyrannical power; it also identifies that power as specifically imperialist in character. This identification is made implicitly, in the framing of the discussion between references to Shakespeare's *Coriolanus* at the start of the discussion, and Domitian and Nero at its close—between two references to the decline of the Roman Empire. It is also made explicitly in Hazlitt's response to specific challenges. For example, Hazlitt quotes Gifford's question—"Do we read with more pleasure of the ravages of a beast of prey than of the Shepherds' pipe upon the Mountains?"—and then answers it thus:

> No, but we do read with pleasure of the ravages of a beast of prey, and we do so on the principle I have stated, namely, from the sense of power abstracted from the sense of good; and it is the same principle that makes us read with admiration and reconciles us in fact to the triumphant progress of the conquerors and mighty hunters of mankind, who come to stop the shepherd's pipe upon the mountains and sweep away his listening flock. (CWWH, 9:37)

In making Gifford's beast of prey a metaphor for an imperialist conqueror, Hazlitt also transforms the image of the piper and flock into a figure for the pacifist poet-leader and his constituent audience, the listening flock. Hazlitt then goes on to ask some questions of his own:

> Do you mean to deny that there is anything imposing to the imagination in power, in grandeur, in outward shew, in the accumulation of individual wealth and luxury, at the expense of equal justice and the common weal? Do you deny that there is anything in the 'pride, pomp and circumstance of glorious war, that makes ambition virtue,' in the eyes of admiring

multitudes? . . . Is it a paradox of my making that 'one murder makes a villain millions a Hero!' Or is it not true that here, as in other cases, the enormity of the evil overpowers and makes a convert of the imagination by its very magnitude? (CWWH, 9:37–38)

Hazlitt had begun his article by accusing Gifford of being a "government critic" and the secret link between government and the police, but the emphasis on scale here shows clearly that empire still more than domestic tyranny is the true subject of his discussion, and that his critique is therefore aimed specifically at what Shelley, in a different context, called "the imperial imagination." Keats contrived to obtain a copy of Hazlitt's three-shilling pamphlet and to absorb its content within days of its appearance in March 1819. Then, remarkably, he copied from Hazlitt's discussion, in successive journal-letter entries, *passages totaling nearly two thousand words*—including the entire discussion of the imperial imagination, beginning with Coriolanus and ending with Nero (LJK, 2: 74–76).

As I have already begun to suggest, Keats's interest in Hazlitt's topics should not come as a complete surprise to the attentive reader of the letters, especially of those to George and Georgiana. Keats's associative processes in a December letter to George, for example, are uncannily proleptic of Hazlitt's discussion:

What are you doing this morning? Have you a clear hard frost as we have? How do you come on with the gun? Have you shot a Buffalo? Have you met with any Pheasants? My Thoughts are very frequently in a foreign Country—I live more out of England than in it—The Mountains of Tartary are a favorite lounge, if I happen to miss the Allegany ridge, or have no whim for Savoy. There must be great pleasure in pursuing game—pointing your gun—no, it wont do—now no—rabbit it—now bang—smoke and feathers—where is it? Shall you be able to get a good pointer or so? (LJK, 2:9)

Embedded in this predatory reverie, travel fantasies assume a more sinister look, despite the comic tone, and help to explain why Keats was so taken a few weeks later with Hazlitt's more explicit linkage of hunting targets and thoughts that turn to foreign places.

In his March journal entries on *A Letter to Gifford,* Keats made no mention of how Hazlitt invoked his theory of disinterestedness in reproaching Gifford, though this was discussed in Hunt's *Examiner* review that week.[83] In resuming the journal-letter six days later, however, Keats ventured the notion that "very few men have ever arrived at a complete disinterestedness of Mind" and he then elaborated it in the now famous passage about what it would be like to push the feeling of benevolent disinterestedness to extremity:

For in wild nature the Hawk would loose his Breakfast of Robins and the Robin his of Worms The Lion must starve as well as the swallow—The greater part of Men make their way with the same instinctiveness, the same unwandering eye from their purposes, the same animal ea-

83. *Examiner,* 14 March 1819, pp. 171–72.

gerness as the Hawk—The Hawk wants a Mate, so does the Man—look at them both they set about it and procure on[e] in the same manner—They want both a nest and they both set about one in the same manner—they get their food in the same manner. . . . (LJK, 2:79)

It is just here that Keats delivers his claim for symmetry between the case of the Hawk balancing in the clouds of the sky and the case of the Man deliberating in the smoke of his pipe.

Keats manages to make Hazlitt's predatory analogy his own, by owning up to the "cause" that Hazlitt intended it to expose. In the long passage earlier copied out from the *Letter to Gifford,* Hazlitt summed up the difference between his own reading of *Coriolanus* and Gifford's by suggesting that whereas he (Hazlitt) has admitted that there are such things as tyrants and slaves abroad in the world, Gifford would hush the matter up. Further, argues Hazlitt, "I have explained the cause, the subtle sophistry in the human mind, that tolerates and pampers the evil, in order to guard against its approaches." (CWWH, 9:38) Gifford, on the other hand, would "conceal the cause in order to prevent the cure" (CWWH, 9:38). Like Hazlitt's account of Shakespeare's alignment with power, Keats's use of the predatory metaphor likewise aims at a deep and difficult acknowledgment. What calls for acknowledgment in Keats's account is a proto-Nietzschean impulse even darker than what Hazlitt smokes in Gifford's sophistry. It is the tendency of the imagination to go further—to *identify* itself with hunters and conquerors. "Men"—this seems to be a gendered argument for Keats—are susceptible to the power of the Nimrods of the world, Keats comes to believe, because of something in them that seeks to be Nimrod. This deep impulse is dramatized in Keats's discussion of the implications of the hawk-man analogy for a disinterested conception of writing. Yet, paradoxically, in that very recognition he found the hope of his redemption from predatory sin. This was the possibility that his imperial ambitions and predatory instincts might amuse the superior beings of a generation generated in part by his own poetry, readers led on by the march of intellect, the history of Psyche, the progress less of knowledge than acknowledgment, which, and in which, Keats strove to advance. Who is to say that his hope was vain?

Of course, the age's imperial fantasies had another side and another look in the writings of its great authors. For the obverse of the hope that one can do everything is the fear that one can do nothing at all. Measured against the heights to which these writers' ambitions could reach, even extraordinary accomplishment could seem negligible. How else do we explain the number of manuscripts of brilliant poetry, meant for publication, that were left unpublished or that were published belatedly or reluctantly in or around 1819? Hence the irony that, having reached the midpoint of what many critics have judged to be the greatest year any poet ever had, Keats felt compelled to confess his sense of idleness. Explaining to Sarah Jeffrey in June why he has not yet attacked his "grand poem" and has nothing recently in print to send to her, he writes: "You will judge of my 1819 temper when I tell you that the thing I have most enjoyed this year has been writing an ode to Indolence" (LJK, 2:116). The very idea of his describing his mood as an *1819* temper suggests how fully he locates the history of his own psyche in more public terms. More specifically, though, the concern about his "Indolence," after a half-year that had already seen the production of such remarkable poems, indicates the scale on which Keats conceived of the question of just what "great alterations" the cause of poetry could effect.

Chapter Eight

CONCERNING THE INFLUENCE OF AMERICA ON THE MIND: WESTERN SETTLEMENTS, "ENGLISH WRITERS," AND THE CASE OF U.S. CULTURE

𝒰nder the heading, "New Books Published this Day," in the *Morning Chronicle* that Thomas Moore would have seen on January 1, 1819, the first advertised item was the fourth part of the "New Geographical Dictionary" for the *Edinburgh Gazetteer*, brought out jointly by Walter Scott's publisher in Edinburgh and Moore's own publisher in London. It promised to comprise a "complete body of Geography, Physical, Political, Statistical, and Commercial" to satisfy the rapidly increasing British demand for this kind of information in the years after Waterloo. The second advertised item dealt with the part of the world where this kind of demand was most intense among English readers (fig. 10). The first edition of Fearon's American *Narrative* had appeared a few months before and had enjoyed sufficient success to warrant the "new and enlarged" edition. In Moore's journal for the end of 1818, we find some testimony to the book's capacity to reach and impress its British readership. Moore records that on December 19 his friend and patron Lord Lansdowne recommended "Fearon's Book upon America . . . as the most acute work upon the subject he had seen" (JTM, 1:102).

This was not the first mention of Fearon's *Narrative* in the journal, for Samuel Rogers had told Moore in late November that "Fearon in his account of America describes the conversation there as very much occupied" with "two personages": Lord Byron and Moore himself. There was a difference, however, in how the conversation of the Americans was occupied with these two poets. With Byron, Americans were occupied much as everyone else was—by his talent and glamour. With Moore, the recognition of talent and glamour was often overshadowed by resentment and indignation. Unlike Byron, Moore had actually visited America and had indeed been very warmly received there as the "English Anacreon" long before *Lalla Rookh* and the *Irish Melodies* established his extraordinary celebrity in Britain and on the Continent. Moore traveled ex-

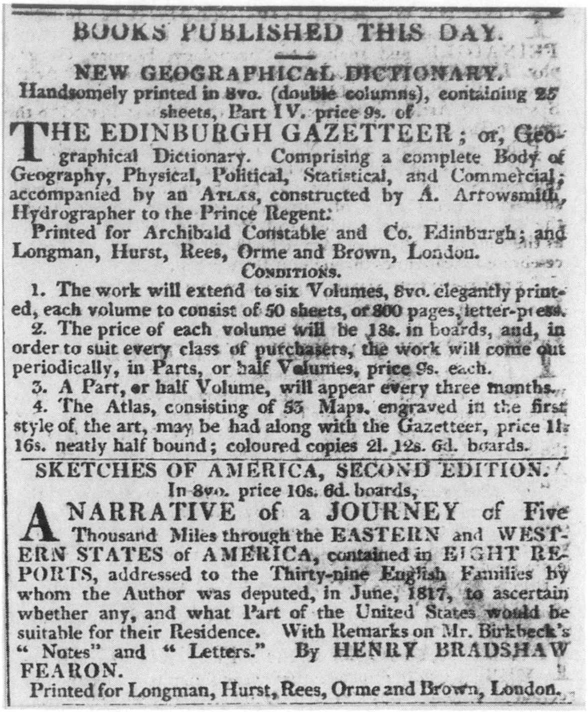

BOOKS PUBLISHED THIS DAY.

NEW GEOGRAPHICAL DICTIONARY.
Handsomely printed in 8vo. (double columns), containing 25 sheets, Part IV. price 9s. of

THE EDINBURGH GAZETTEER; or, Geographical Dictionary. Comprising a complete Body of Geography, Physical, Political, Statistical, and Commercial; accompanied by an ATLAS, constructed by A. Arrowsmith, Hydrographer to the Prince Regent.
Printed for Archibald Constable and Co. Edinburgh; and Longman, Hurst, Rees, Orme and Brown, London.

CONDITIONS.

1. The work will extend to six Volumes, 8vo. elegantly printed, each volume to consist of 50 sheets, or 800 pages, letter-press.
2. The price of each volume will be 18s. in boards, and, in order to suit every class of purchasers, the work will come out periodically, in Parts, or half Volumes, price 9s. each.
3. A Part, or half Volume, will appear every three months.
4. The Atlas, consisting of 53 Maps, engraved in the first style of the art, may be had along with the Gazetteer, price 1l. 16s. neatly half bound; coloured copies 2l. 12s. 6d. boards.

SKETCHES OF AMERICA, SECOND EDITION.
In 8vo. price 10s. 6d. boards,

A NARRATIVE of a JOURNEY of Five Thousand Miles through the EASTERN and WESTERN STATES of AMERICA, contained in EIGHT REPORTS, addressed to the Thirty-nine English Families by whom the Author was deputed, in June, 1817, to ascertain whether any, and what Part of the United States would be suitable for their Residence. With Remarks on Mr. Birkbeck's "Notes" and "Letters." By HENRY BRADSHAW FEARON.
Printed for Longman, Hurst, Rees, Orme and Brown, London.

Figure 10. Advertisement from the *Morning Chronicle* for January 1, 1819 ("Books Published This Day," the British Library)

tensively on the East Coast in 1803, and then, when he returned to England after his brief stint in Bermuda, published *Odes and Epistles* (1806), a volume that included a section of "Poems Relating to America." This section was set off by its own dedication and by a preface that explained the poems' occasion in Moore's American tour and, more pointedly, in the great disappointment that he felt on visiting the nation he had admired from afar. The poems themselves elaborate these sentiments. As Moore would have quickly discovered on opening his volume of Fearon in late December 1819, the sting these poems carried for Americans was still remembered when Fearon retraced some of Moore's footsteps in Washington, D.C., fifteen eventful years after Moore's visit.

These years had witnessed not only the major battles of the Napoleonic Wars—Austerlitz, Trafalgar, Leipzig, Waterloo—but also the momentous round of hostilities on North American soil in 1812–14, including the burning of the new public buildings in Washington, D.C., by British Rear Admiral Sir George Cockburn in 1814. In fact, Moore's name is first introduced in Fearon's narrative just at the point when Fearon reflects on the reputation of Cockburn among the residents of Washington. Noting that "the children . . . have a dread of the name of 'Admiral Cockburn,' similar to that I used to entertain of Buonaparte and the Devil," Fearon goes on to relate his encounter with a Senator from Pennsylvania, General Lacock, who "amused me one evening by a humourous detail of what foreign travellers have said against America, especially the celebrated poet Thomas Moore, who had visited America in 1803."[1] Fearon then proceeds to cite a long passage from one of Moore's American poems with which "the general was particularly familiar." The long passage was from an "epistle, dated from Washington" which ran, in part, as follows:

> Oh, great Potowmac! Oh, you banks of shade,
> You mighty scenes! in nature's morning made;
> Say, were your towering hills, your boundless floods,
> Your rich savannahs, and majestic woods;
> Oh! was a world so bright but born to grace
> Its own half-organised, half-minded race
> Of weak barbarians, swarming o'er its breast
> Like vermin gender'd in the lion's crest?
> Were none but brutes to call that soil their home,
> Where none but demi-gods should dare to roam?
> O'er lake and marsh, through fevers and through fogs,
> 'Midst bears and Yankies, _____ and frogs,
> That foot shall follow me; thy heart and eyes
> With me shall wander, and with me despise.[2]

By contrast with their half-organized cultural object, these verses display themselves as fully organized and strong in confidence about the state of civilization they represent—i.e., the one in Britain that produced them. This organization and strength are supposed to be manifest, for example, in the assured handling of the couplet, with its ingenious syntactic variation: "Were none but brutes . . . / Where none but demi-gods. . . ." In Fearon's more loosely managed text in which this verse is embedded, the association that leads Fearon from Admiral Cockburn to Thomas Moore, though unmarked, seems clear enough: the

1. Henry Bradshaw Fearon, *Narrative of a Journey of Five Thousand Miles through the Eastern and Western States of America* (London: Longman, 1818), p. 326. All page references will hereafter appear in the text.
2. The longer passage is cited by Fearon, ibid., pp. 326–27. The poem is *To Thomas Hume, Esq. M.D., From the City of Washington,* in Thomas Moore, *Poetical Works* (New York: Appleton, 1846), p. 179.

one man burned down the completed capital city, the other had burned up its reputation before it was even finished. Moore's sharp Juvenalian satire struck Americans where they were most sensitive, for the problem Moore found with the capital was the national character—the level of morals and manners—that *it* represented in its lack of discipline and cultivation.

If Moore's tone seems harsh, his particular exemplification makes his general target appear sufficiently monstrous to warrant strong feelings. At an earlier moment in the long verse passage recalled by Fearon and Lacock in 1818, Moore suggests that the representatives convened in the public buildings of the new capital are capable of representing only a general state of depravity and hypocrisy: "The weary statesman for repose hath fled / From halls of council to his negro's shed, / Where, blest, he woos some black Aspasia's grace, / And dreams of freedom *in his slave's embrace.*" A note in Fearon's text explains that these lines are "[s]upposed to refer to a charge made by the federalists against a celebrated politician of Virginia" (p. 326), a gloss that both points a finger at Thomas Jefferson and acknowledges the impropriety of naming him. Taking Jefferson as the representative American representative, and seeing his moral constitution in this light, we might judge Moore's critique both earnest and deserved.[3] Fearon certainly did.

Moore himself backed off from his own harsh words when he saw them quoted in Fearon. Reporting on his reading of Fearon in late December, Moore said he was "amused" that Fearon should take seriously his own "boyish opinions about America" (JTM, 1:103). In thus making light of his comments, furthermore, Moore aligns himself with Fearon's Washington interlocutor, Senator Lacock, who, Fearon reports, simply "laughed at Moore's conceit" (p. 327). Lacock not only dismissed Moore's critique as the kind of thing that such disappointed European "friends of liberty" typically say when they come to America, he also suggested that Moore's published attack did him little credit, since Moore "*had received while here much personal attention*" (p. 327). This latter comment, Fearon writes, was typical of Americans, characteristic of their conception of being judged and of judging others. The "standard" by which they "estimate different parts of their own continent, as well as of Europe" is not "what they saw" but, rather, "how they were personally treated" (p. 328).

This characteristically American framework of evaluation, however, involves an assumption to which Fearon takes serious exception: "That a distinguished individual receiving attentions in a foreign land is a proof of the

3. This note is Fearon's. Moore's own note runs as follows: "The 'black Aspasia' of the present ********* of the United States, inter Avernales haud ignotissima nymphas, has given rise to much pleasantry among the anti-democrat wits in America" (p. 178).

existence of the common habits of civilized society is unquestionable," Fearon admits, "but that that should be the criterion by which he is to judge of the whole mass of a country, requires no refutation" (pp. 327–28). It is as if Fearon had detected a now-familiar American attenuation of the concept of manners from a system of culture (in the Scottish-Enlightenment sense) to the sententious observations of an etiquette book—as if he had recognized that, for an American, "manners" were something you either had or you did not. To "have manners," to show etiquette, is to have all the civilization one needed. To be shown manners is, in the American system, to compel mannerly respect. In the American view of Moore, *he* is the one without manners, as he proved in speaking ill of those who had extended him their hospitality. But Fearon, the Quaker, thinks otherwise: "[O]n the contrary, the man who tells the honest truth of a nation is . . . its best friend. Seeing it with the eye of a stranger, he discerns defects which, perhaps, custom has rendered invisible to the eye of the native" and saying so "affords an opportunity of amendment which would not otherwise be gained" (p. 328).

Fearon's comments focus on a question that had achieved extraordinary currency in England by 1819: how to judge American manners. This topic, we recall, had come up in Moore's meeting with Mrs. Cobbett just a couple of weeks before Moore left for the Continent and a couple of months before William Cobbett returned from exile on Long Island. It is, indeed, the only issue that Moore reports from that conversation of August 26: "[W]hen we talked of the rude manner of the Americans, Mrs. Cobbet said it was the Republican part of them [the Americans] that deserved this character, for the Royalist or Federal party were very different in their manners" (JTM, 1:208). The way in which party affiliation affects the question of manners, as in the instance of the "antidemocratic" revelation about Jefferson, remains an important one for Fearon. But where Moore simply lampooned the kind of manners that would condone the conduct of a statesmen who left the public halls to find sexual pleasure in the arms of a woman he held as a slave, the more complicated framework developed by Fearon from his conversation over this episode with Senator Lacock suggests a new level of sophistication and the possibility of a dual normative system for weighing the matter. It was not just a question of judging American manners but of how to go about making such a judgment, of what norms and forms to use. For English writers of the post-Waterloo period, American manners had become a *case,* in short, a circumstantial challenge to a normative frame of reference.

Somewhat later in 1819, a Philadelphia writer named Robert Walsh would publish a formal review of the charges brought by British writers against

American manners: *An Appeal from the Judgments of Great Britain, Respecting the United States of America.*[4] Walsh's *Appeal,* both in its title and its tactics, brings into sharp relief the casuistical character of the British confrontation with American culture in 1819. Certainly, the degree to which Walsh was arguing a case would have been clear to his readers. Taking notice of the *Appeal* in early 1820, for example, the *British Critic* could not be more explicit about this point, nor about the extent of Walsh's credibility for adjudicating it. Walsh's book, says the reviewer, "professes to be an appeal from the *judgments* of Great Britain, but to whom the appeal is made, or who are to act as the umpires in this case of calumny, North America *versus* England, we are not yet informed" (p. 395).[5] For its part, needless to say, the *British Critic* has its doubts.

Since (the *British Critic* argues) Walsh "takes the law into his own hand," neither will the *British Critic* himself scruple to affect impartiality: "As . . . we ourselves are parties concerned; for among 'British writers,' against whom a true bill has been found in Philadelphia, the British Critics are specially named,—we should feel inclined to insist upon being satisfied as to the competency of the court and the impartiality of the witnesses, before we allowed the prosecutor, Mr. Walsh, to proceed one step further in following out his action for damages" (p. 395). And while the *British Critic* is impressed with Walsh's casuistical skills in making his arguments—"in the exercise of this Old Bailey wit and Billingsgate rhetoric, we give the palm to America" (p. 395)—the *Review* itself makes this concession only tactically. Granting Walsh local victory on the strength of his rhetoric, the reviewer goes on to argue, with no negligible skill of his own, that the larger case Walsh is prosecuting will not carry. "It looks ill for Mr. Walsh's cause," the reviewer notes with restraint, that even those in Britain who disagree most violently about all other issues, "differ very little" when it comes time to "speak of American manners and institutions" (p. 395). The British consensus against America accrues such force, the argument goes, because it occurs in the context of such heated political debates.

To its credit, the *British Critic* admits that its captioning of the general British political scene at this time with a label such as "Consensus Against America" is not undertaken from a position *hors de combat.* But while the *British Critic*'s claim must be slightly qualified, it is on balance true enough that, notwithstanding Paul Johnson's recent suggestion that the period 1815–30 is the period that es-

4. Robert Walsh, Jr., *Appeal from the Judgments of Great Britain Respecting the United States of America* (Philadelphia: Mitchell, Ames, and White, 1819). Walsh's Dedication is dated September 1819 (p. iv). Page numbers hereafter cited in text.

5. Review of Walsh's *Appeal from the Judgments of Great Britain* in *The British Critic* (April 1820), p. 395. Page numbers hereafter cited in text. The problem of "scene" that the *British Critic* raises here is discussed above (Chapter 5) in relation to Scott.

tablishes the "special relationship" between Britain and the United States, the level of animosity runs at extremely high levels on both sides for much of this period.[6] A survey of those whom Washington Irving called "English Writers on America" suggests that levels of anti-American sentiment ran higher than what Tom Moore expressed in 1803, and higher even than some reached during the open hostilities of 1812–14. The charges escalate in 1819 for the simple reason that the perceived stakes were higher, and the pronounced hyperbole in the representation of America among English writers in 1819 betrays anxieties of a different order from those that we find in earlier writings.

The appearance abroad of a new and specific understanding of U.S. culture goes some way to account for the new British historical discourse in the years after Waterloo, even as it is in other respects a product of this same developing discourse. Not that the issue of America was altogether a new topic in English writing—obviously far from it. Rather, a particular conjuncture of developments—its Constitution, the Napoleonic Wars, the emigration push after 1815, the reform movement, the increased correspondence between Britain and America in print—brought a new America newly into focus in Britain. Much work has been done on the question of how the literature of the British Romantic period registered in American culture.[7] Yet, though the case of America helped shape a concept of culture in which Britons could reimagine their own culture in its historicity, there is surprisingly little on the question of how American culture registered in the literature of the British Romantic period. To be sure, the projects are less symmetrical than this chiastic formulation suggests. The so-called literary backwardness of the early American republic, itself a prominent topic of debate at the time, has obvious implications for the kinds of materials available for study. What one consults in studying the literary representation of America in Britain will not precisely correspond to what one consults in studying, say, Emerson's debts to the Wordsworth circle or the emulation of Scott's Waverley Novels (what Mark Twain called "the Sir Walter disease") in American historical fiction of the nineteenth century. My contention, nonetheless, is that the importance of investigating the British reception of America is as compelling as when the question is put the other way around, and that the question so posed has relevance for both American and British studies. In the years just following the Napoleonic Wars, English writers

6. Paul Johnson, *The Birth of the Modern: World Society 1815–1830* (New York: Harper Collins, 1991), pp. 43–44.

7. The former and more familiar topic has been called "the Burden of Britain": see Robert Weisbuch, *Atlantic Double-Cross: American Literature and British Influence in the Age of Emerson* (Chicago: University of Chicago Press, 1986), pp. 3–35.

produced an elaborate ethnography of the early U.S. republic, and, like all ethnographies, these surveys of "American manners" need to be read as cutting both ways—that is, as carrying implication for *both* cultural identities at a crucial moment in their modern development and, further, an implication for the development of ethnographic practice. The case of post-Constitution America—U.S. culture—is crucial to understanding the "historical situation" of British Romanticism both in form and in fact.

In this chapter, then, the last in a sequence of four linked case studies for England in 1819, I discuss some of these now largely neglected writings on America. My broad aim is to offer a critical and historical framework that tries to make some of these writings more vivid and to establish their claim upon the interests of contemporary cultural studies. I wish, more particularly, to provide an explanatory framework for some of the earlier cases I have examined, and especially that of Keats, to whom I turn later. To that end, I want to consider the case of U.S. culture itself, the sense in which the newly constituted system problematized conceptions of national character and everyday life. Since this case is defined mostly sharply in the post-Waterloo period, peaking in 1819, it helps to clarify four key distinctions that are crucial in the present argument. One is the distinction between the politics of English literary culture in the post–French Revolution period—1789 through, let us say, the Peace of Amiens—and the politics of literary culture in the post-Waterloo period.[8] A second distinction is that between representations of the state of England in 1819 and those of America in the same moment. A third is the distinction between first- and second-generation U.S. citizens, especially when understood as the difference between the original colonies who ratified the Constitution in 1790–91 and the so-called Western Country recently opened up by virtue of the Louisiana Purchase of 1803. Finally, to return to a topic I have addressed in both Scott and Shelley, there is the relationship between a literature of "utility" and a literature of "imagination," especially when understood as a difference articulated by the "case" of America versus Britain in 1819. Though a further distinction between "history" and "literature" becomes very difficult to maintain in an argument of this kind, it could be added in shorthand that the key historical figure in this discussion will be Morris Birkbeck and that the key literary figure will be John Keats. Keats's connection with Birkbeck was decidedly mediated and indirect, but it was serious and also consequential for what Keats was able to accomplish in his annus mirabilis. To round off part three of my ar-

8. The latter, as I have already suggested at various points, involves strongly epochal or historical distinctions rather than oppositional distinctions of the "reason"/"tradition," or "natural society"/"civil society," or "nature"/"second nature," varieties.

gument and to anticipate part four, I will conclude with a word about Shelley's judgment in the case of America in 1819 and about the considered "opinion" he offered in support of it.

1. Washington Irving and the "English Writers in America"

If one seeks to rectify the bias in transatlantic studies that leads critics to emphasize the reception of English Romanticism in America, it might well seem that a focus on the generation of the 1790s would best serve one's interest. For, in the Britain of that decade, it could be argued, the emergence of the U.S. republic was a major enough event for British writers and intellectuals. In pursuit of such a study, one could examine (for example) the early work of the great English journalist, William Cobbett. Writing from Philadelphia under the name of "Peter Porcupine," Cobbett produced voluminous and unsympathetic accounts of American life that enjoyed considerable influence with English readers. Or one might conduct a detailed inquiry into the representations of America that shaped the "Pantisocracy" scheme conceived by Coleridge, Southey, and others in 1794–95 in which and English utopian community was to be established on the banks of Pennsylvania's Susquehanna River. It was surely no coincidence that this plan preoccupied these key authors at just the moment when what would be called the "Lake School" of poetry was about to produce the work that would transform English literary history. One could also point to several passages in the poetry and fiction of the 1790s that indicate some notice of America on the part of writers like Blake, Wordsworth, and Robert Bage.[9]

The limitations of such strategies, however, lie in the fact that England's concern with America in the 1790s is so far overshadowed by its concern with France that the former often appears merely as a function or displacement of the latter. Cobbett's overriding preoccupation in the Peter Porcupine series was with the possibility that America would take the part of France in the conflict that escalated by stages into the Napoleonic Wars. The Pantisocratic scheme was generated in the wake of France's so-called Reign of Terror, which, as countless commentators have told, inaugurated the beginning of the end for radical hopes on the part of the future Lake poets. The English reputation of Thomas Paine in the 1790s was primarily that of an ideologue of the French Revolution, the opponent of Burke on the same question: that both Burke and Paine had a strong hand in the American War of Independence may not have

9. Blake verses on the Ohio River, Wordsworth American references in *Lyrical Ballads,* and the American moments in Robert Bage's *Hermsprong* are additional places to which one would turn in studying the British literary response to America in the 1790s.

been entirely forgotten in the Great Debate on the French Revolution, but neither was it much discussed then.[10] Even as late as 1803, when Moore visited America during the Peace of Amiens, the terms of his Juvenalian critique of the American character still conformed with the earlier British tendency to regard its failures as a function of its gallicization—of its having, as Moore put it, imbibed "the drug of French philosophy."[11]

For these reasons, we do better to look for England's constitution of America in the decade immediately following the conclusion of the wars with France (roughly 1815–25), and thus beyond the literary generation of Wordsworth and Coleridge to that of Keats and Shelley. Not until the end of the wars did the English begin in earnest to develop a sense of a specific U.S. national identity, development profoundly related to a simultaneous crisis over the question of English identity. The available criticism and historiography for this period suggests that the force of this delayed impact does need arguing, in spite of the extraordinary volume of literary work in which it was registered. The sheer bulk of these writings can be quite startling to confront, and they are certainly difficult to synopsize. Readers of Washington Irving's still popular *Sketch Book of Geoffrey Crayon* (1819–20), however, may perhaps be more prepared than others if they recall the essay whose title I have already alluded to, "English Writers on America."

This essay, which for reasons that might themselves be interesting to explore, follows "Rip Van Winkle" in Irving's miscellany, announces its occasion very explicitly in its opening paragraph:[12] "It is with feelings of deep regret that I observe the literary animosity daily growing up between England and America. Great curiosity has been awakened of late with respect to the United States, and the London press has teemed with volumes of travels through the republic; but they seem intended to diffuse error rather than knowledge; and so successful have they been, that, notwithstanding the constant intercourse between the nations, there is no people concerning whom the great mass of the British public have less pure information, or entertain more numerous prejudices."[13] When Irving goes on to locate his concern about "literary animosity" in the context of

10. For a recent study of Britain's self-definition of national character against the example of France, see Seamus Deane, *The French Revolution and Enlightenment in England* (Cambridge, Mass.: Harvard University Press, 1988), passim.

11. *To Thomas Hume, Esq. M.D., From the City of Washington,* in Moore, *Works* (New York: 1846), p. 179.

12. On the relation of "Rip Wan Winkle" to such topics as are treated in "The English Writers on America," see Jeffrey Rubin-Dorsky, *Adrift in the Old World* (Chicago: University of Chicago Press, 1988), pp. 73–76, 100–15.

13. Washington Irving, *The Sketch Book of Geoffrey Crayon, Gent,* ed. Haskell Springer (Boston: Twayne, 1978), p. 43. All page references hereafter cited in text.

what he calls "the all pervading influence of literature in the present day, and how much the opinions and passions of mankind are under its control" (p. 46), it is clear that his terms "literature" and "literary" do not refer only to what we now call creative or imaginative writing but to "letters" more generally. The distinctively "creative" connotation for the "literary" is to some extent being worked out in these very controversies. In this context, clearly, Irving means primarily to be pointing a finger at English reportage and to be suggesting that, whatever England's more general claims to literary genius (and he takes them to be real), soundness of health in the body politic depends on the virtue of the public press: "If England is willing to permit the mean jealousies of trade or the rancorous animosities of politics to deprave the integrity of her press, and poison the fountain of public opinion, let us beware of her example" (p. 48). Irving's move here, anticipating the rebuttal of the *British Critic* against Robert Walsh, is to suggest that, whatever "consensus" there may be against America in the British press, it is an artifact of economic and political motivations and is by no means evidence of the accuracy of the portrayal. The attacks of the "English Writers" only reflect ill on themselves.[14]

At stake in the contamination of *American* public opinion, for Irving, is the corruption of the very national character that has been misrepresented, and Irving seeks to guard his compatriots against their being provoked into a literary warfare that could only debase them and weaken the distinctive "integrity" of their "literature." "We attach," he insists, "too much consequence to these attacks":

> The tissue of misrepresentations attempted to be woven round us are like cobwebs, woven round the limbs of an infant giant. Our country continually outgrows them. . . . All the writers of England united . . . could not conceal our rapidly growing importance and matchless prosperity. They could not conceal that these are owing, not merely to physical and local, but also to moral causes. To the political liberty, the general diffusion of knowledge, the prevalence of sound moral and religious principles, which give force and sustained energy to the character of a people, and which, in fact have been the acknowledged and wonderful supporters of their own national power and glory. (p. 45)

Here, Irving's counterfactual "all the writers of England united . . . could not conceal" would seem to give the lie to the so-called consensus claimed by the *British Critic*. The overall rhetoric of the passage amounts to an impressive piece of mimicry. In explaining American prosperity in terms of character rather than resources, and in explaining character in terms of political institutions, Irving is dramatizing for his English readers a procedure that, as he comes close to conceding, he has learned from the English themselves. Hazlitt, after all,

14. Walsh's opening chapter explicitly addresses this question: "Of the Political and Mercantile Jealousy of Great Britain," *Appeal from the Judgments of Great Britain,* pp. 1–34.

judged Irving a writer sufficiently relevant to the English context to have included a portrait of him in *The Spirit of the Age*.[15] As for Irving's American readers, he asks them to trust that their own representative institutions will effectively manifest, in spite of British misrepresentations to the contrary, the extraordinary moral growth he claims to see in the space of a single post-Constitutional generation (i.e., from 1789 to 1819).[16]

Irving's text thus obliquely broaches the great question of the post–Waterloo discourse on America: what effect do the institutions of the new constitutional republic have on the citizenry? This issue received perhaps its most explicit attention in Charles Ingersoll's *Discourse Concerning the Influence of America on the Mind*. This was an American pamphlet, published in London in 1824, which carried a preface by Richard Flower (who turns up later in this story) explaining why English readers should attend to yet another discussion of this subject in the face of "the numerous works which for the past six years have been laid before the public by writers of different descriptions."[17] In Ingersoll, and in much of the British writing, one is confronted with a distinctively Godwinian way of framing the question.[18] Indeed, couched in more general terms, the issue of how character is constituted in the experience of political institutions had been a hotly contested one in Britain from as early as the 1790s. It was then, as Hazlitt vividly testified in *The Spirit of the Age*, that Godwin's account of the institutional formation of character in his *Enquiry Concerning Political Justice* became the obsession of English intellectual circles. Godwin had argued that, since people's actions depended chiefly on their opinions, their opinions on their circumstances, and their circumstances on their social institutions, to change the way people acted one had to change their institutions.[19]

15. The problem with Irving, as far as Hazlitt was concerned, was not that he was too American but rather that he was not American enough. See Elia and Geoffrey Crayon, in *The Spirit of the Age,* CWWH, 11:184.

16. On the contemporary atmosphere of hostility and the fate of Irving's own volume at the hands of the British press, see Rubin Dorsky, *Adrift in the Old World,* pp. 38–41. See also David Simpson's discussion of James Kirke Paulding in this connection in *The Politics of American English* (New York: Oxford University Press, 1986), pp. 122–30.

17. Charles J. Ingersoll, *Discourse Concerning the Influence of America on the Mind* (London, 1824), pp. vi–vii.

18. "Things as they are," the famous slogan taken as subtitle to *Caleb Williams,* is echoed in the final words Faux's preface, for example, and indeed also at the end of his long title. William Faux, *Memorable Days in America, Being a Journal of Tour to the United States Principally Undertaken to Ascertain, by Positive Evidence, the Condition and Probable Prospects of British Emigrants; including Accounts of Mr. Birkbeck's Settlement in the Illinois: And Intended to shew Men and Things as they are in America* (London: Simpkin and Marshall, 1823), p. 9.

19. It is an argument that risks a begging of the main question, like that of Bentham's, discussed above in chap. 4.

It seems reasonable to assume that reports of the American Constitution may have played a role in Godwin's way of thinking through these issues.[20] However, a central tenet in Godwin's influential doctrine is that social institutions do not achieve their effects instantaneously. Observers of a Godwinian persuasion would therefore have to await the pudding that would show the proof. No foreign nation could be better positioned to test the American pudding than Britain, but then there were those intervening distractions: the French Revolution, Jacobinism, Napoleon. Further, the process of "Americanization" that the United States underwent during this time—well-documented by historians of the early republic—gained strength from the degree of isolationism effected by the Anglo-French conflict.[21] The outcome of all this was not lost on Henry Fearon, for example, who argued that after the Napoleonic Wars it was no longer possible to hold the view that Americans lacked national character—which is not to say that his picture of this character was a particularly flattering one. So, having lacked for so long either the opportunity or the motive to consider empirically (as it were) the way the United States functioned as a cultural system, the British also began to see a more distinct cultural system there to be considered: some would even call it a *rival* system. America-watching soon became something of a British national hobby.

Of course, the English system itself had begun, since the anticipation of the end of the wars, to come in for more and more severe internal scrutiny and challenge from activist reformers. If the wars effected a suspension of English speculation on the U.S. experiment, they also occasioned a suppression of the more immediate political agenda that called for the refashioning of England's own political structure. In the 1790s, the Pitt administration had responded to an earlier stage of the reform movement with a series of repressive statutes, but it had also forestalled consideration of the radical agenda by appeal to the notion of solidarity in the face of the foreign enemy that was France.[22] After the wars, the English reform movement sufficiently renewed itself to create, in the

20. In spite of his anti-contractarian position on constitutions, Godwin was a great admirer of Thomas Paine. We know that he met with the American writer Joel Barlow on ten separate occasions, consulting several of Barlow's republican writings during the months of his most intense work on *Political Justice* in 1792. See Peter Marshall, *William Godwin* (New Haven, Conn.: Yale University Press, 1984), pp. 84–85.

21. For a good account of how the process of Americanization worked itself out in the literary domain, see Michael Warner, *The Letters of the Republic: Publication and the Public Sphere in Eighteenth-Century America* (Cambridge, Mass.: Harvard University Press, 1990), pp. 118–50.

22. Henry Brougham and other post-Waterloo reformers made specific references to this government strategy. See my "Wordsworth after Waterloo," in *The Age of William Wordsworth*, ed. Kenneth Johnston and Gene Ruoff (New Brunswick, N.J.: Rutgers University Press, 1987), pp.104–105.

years between 1815 and 1819, that "heroic age" of popular radicalism that I have discussed above. Among the closest watchers of America in England in 1819 were two groups in particular, the supporters of reform and their opponents, which taken together formed a very large portion of the literate public.

Although it is a major limitation of Irving's "English Writers on America" that it makes no mention of the English reform movement, this is perhaps part of a more general limitation: his refusal either to name the names of the "English Writers" in question or to pursue the details of his analysis. Since his explicit concern is to reduce the literary animosity between England and America, he will not risk its escalation with an account of the specific interests that fueled it; he conspicuously declines the rhetorical low road that he claims English writers on America have been traveling. However, in the one brief passage where he discusses the ulterior purposes of the hostile commentators, he demonstrates awareness of what it was that many contemporaries claimed was motivating those attacks. England, he says, "may deem it in her interest to diffuse error and engender antipathy, for the purpose of checking emigration; we have no purpose of the kind to serve" (p. 48). The issue of emigration to America makes it possible to see how the theory of national character and the practice of political reform come together in the English writers on America. To pursue it is to recognize immediately how misleading is Irving's (and the British Critic's) suggestion that English writers on America were uniformly hostile at the time. One might even argue that a good deal of the anti-American animosity that existed in the post-Waterloo years was as heated as it was precisely because of other English writers on America who were depicting it in excessively attractive terms.

2. The English Columbus

If Irving *were* to have named names in this controversy, he would certainly have included Fearon's, as well as those of other authors already in print—William Cobbett, Thomas Hulme, John Bristed, Henry Brougham, Joseph Johnson, and Francis Jeffrey—or yet other authors, themselves still traveling in 1819 but soon to publish their accounts: William Faux, John Woods, and Adam Hodgson, for example, all of whom came to America in 1819 but issued their accounts afterwards.[23] Irving might well have begun his list, however, with the name that ap-

---

23. This is not to mention scattered essays and reviews: Walsh includes a hundred-page survey chapter, "Of the Hostilities of the British Reviews," in his *Appeal,* pp. 211–305. Nor would the new tide of activities end in 1819. The early 1820s would see a number of other such surveys, including Frances Trollope's *Domestic Manners of the Americans,* 2 vols. (London and New York: Whittaker Treacher, 1832). Hodgson, who arrived at the end of 1819, did not publish his account

pears in the advertisement to Fearon's American *Narrative* and stands linked with Fearon's in the conversation of Moore's English circle on December 30, 1819: "[T]alked of Fearon, Birkbeck—the singularity of two such men being produced out of the middling class of society at the same time—proof of the intelligence now spread through that rank of Englishman—It must make the higher regions look about them & be on the alert" (JTM, 1:105).

By no means anti-American, Morris Birkbeck was indeed a frightening presence for many British observers by the end of 1818, and would only grow more frightening to them in the coming year. He was a Surrey farmer—a Quaker, like Fearon—who emigrated to America in 1817 to join his friend George Flower (whose father wrote the preface to Ingersoll's *Discourse Concerning the Influence of America on the Mind*), in founding a new settlement just beyond the frontier state of Indiana in the Illinois territory. After making his way from the East Coast to this frontier, Birkbeck quickly entered 26,400 acres just west of the Wabash River (in what is now Edwards County, Illinois)—not far from Harmony, Indiana, where George Rapp (Byron's "Rapp the Harmonist") had settled a small community (CPWB, 5:599). It was here, after the departure of the Rappites and at the suggestion of Flower, that Robert Owen would found his utopian community in 1825. In the fall of 1817, Birkbeck published a Philadelphia edition of *Notes on a Journey in America from the Coast of Virginia to the Territory of Illinois,* in which he surveyed the American scene, explained his reasons for settling in Illinois, and, in a brief preface, articulated the aims of his project. The first English edition appeared in 1818. This was closely followed by his *Letters from Illinois* (also 1818), in which he described the natural and cultural features of the region and narrated the early days of the settlement. Though Birkbeck lived long enough to play a role in early Illinois state politics, including its resistance to slavery, he drowned in the Wabash River in 1825—recrossing on horseback after a visit to the newly arrived Robert Owen at New Harmony. The Birkbeck settlement neither grew large nor survived long. Birkbeck quarreled with Flower early on, and so the initial idea of a single settlement was realized as two communities: Birkbeck's was called Wanborough, Flower's Albion. While the great house of Flower's settlement still survives, Birkbeck's colony has vanished without a trace.[24] Indeed, it is hard to come to terms with Birkbeck's importance in his own time when in ours he is so little

---

for five years, but when he did he addressed the reputation of Birkbeck's settlement in some detail and dwelt for many pages on the issues of American manners and the American character. See *Letters from North America* 2:64–88 (on Birkbeck) and 25–42 (on American character and manners).

24. Neither site has been commemorated in the manner of Owen's New Harmony.

known. Yet it was said of him by William Faux, a British contemporary who surveyed the situation in 1819, that "no man, since Columbus, has done so much towards peopling America."[25]

One index of Birkbeck's impact is that his *Notes on the Journey across America* and *Letters from Illinois* went through, respectively, eleven and seven editions in England and America within just a couple of years. There were scores of responses in reviews, pamphlets, and in other books, often with extensive quotation. It was on Birkbeck's account that, as one historian of the American Midwest puts it, without exaggeration: "For perhaps a dozen years a tract of land in southeastern Illinois, containing no more than 100 square miles . . , was known to more people in the United States, Great Britain, and western Europe than almost any other place in North America."[26] In calculating the "prodigious" effects of Birkbeck's writings, Faux estimated that, "if all could have settled in Illinois, whom he had tempted to cross the Atlantic and the mountains, it had now been the most populous state in the Union."[27] These quantifications convey little of the *affect* of Birkbeck's contemporary reception, however, nor of the way it managed to establish U.S. culture as a new kind of case.

Fearon's *Narrative* is helpful for establishing the contemporary sense of the stakes—moral, political, economic, psychological, emotional—in the controversy that centered on Birkbeck. When Fearon spoke with General Lacock about Thomas Moore and American manners, he had just come from a visit to Birkbeck in the Western Country. Fearon journeyed to America in behalf of thirty-nine English families just a little after Birkbeck arrived but a few months before the publication of Birkbeck's *Notes* on his American journey:

> I was deputed by a circle of friends, whose persons and whose interests are most dear to me, to visit the United States of America, in order to furnish them with materials to regulate their decision on the subject of emigration. Into the motives and the views which led to this proposed measure on their part, it is not requisite that I should enter much in detail; they are, I fear, known and *felt* too generally to render description necessary.
>
> Emigration had, at the time of my appointment, assumed a totally new character: it was no longer merely the poor, the idle, the profligate, or the wildly speculative, who were proposing to quit their native country; but men also of capital, of industry, of sober habits and regular pursuits, men of reflection who apprehended approaching evils; men of upright and conscientious minds, to whose happiness civil and religious liberty were essential; and men of do-

---

25. W. Faux, *Memorable Days,* p. 298. It is Faux who tells the world the inside story of the break-up of the community having to do with Birkbeck's and young Flower's love for the same woman, and who reports, playing Mr. Lockwood to Birkbeck's Heathcliff, on the forbidding aspect of Birkbeck as he first approached the gate of his Illinois prairie in 1819.

26. Paul M. Angle, "Historical Introduction," to John Woods, *Two Years' Residence on the English Prairie of Illinois* (London: 1823; reprt. ed. Chicago: R. R. Donnelley, 1968), p. xiii.

27. Faux, *Memorable Days,* p. 298.

mestic feelings, who wished to provide for the future support and prosperity of their offspring.

Under such circumstances as these it was, that my friends turned their thoughts, in the way of enquiry merely, upon the subject of emigration to America. Having done so, they naturally set themselves seriously to investigate the state of the country and the character of the people. . . . It was, at length, resolved that some one should visit the country to make the necessary enquiries—the lot fell to myself. ("Introductory Remarks," n.p.)

Fearon learns about the Illinois settlement early in his travels, corresponds with Birkbeck (one of the "Letters from Illinois" is in fact an answer to Fearon), and makes a point of visiting what was then the Illinois territory to see it for himself. Fearon takes this option seriously in behalf of the families whose interests he serves, but in April 1818, while still weighing the case for emigration there, he learns "that Mr. Birkbeck has published a book in London, 'Notes on a Journey to Illinois,' and that it has produced an extraordinary sensation" and then receives a letter from a member of his constituency informing him that they have decided, without the benefit of his final recommendation, to emigrate to the west bank of the Wabash River (p. 395). Birkbeck's enterprise helped constitute the decision faced by dissatisfied, reform-conscious Britons, and his writings were sometimes powerful enough to decide the question without further evidence—even when the evidence was in the process of being collected.

Henry Brougham reviewed Birkbeck's *Notes* for the influential *Edinburgh Review* and opened his remarks by testifying to his sense of the book's power: "We have no hesitation in pronouncing this one of the most interesting and instructive books that have appeared for many years."[28] These were not lean years for important books to be appearing from British publishers. They witnessed the publication of Byron's *Childe Harold's Pilgrimage,* Scott's first half-dozen *Waverley* novels, Mary Shelley's *Frankenstein,* Coleridge's *Biographia Literaria,* Wordsworth's *Excursion,* Shelley's and Keats's early volumes, translations of Goethe and Schiller, major works by Bentham and James Mill on utilitarianism, and Ricardo's *Political Economy*—most of which were reviewed in the *Edinburgh Review.* In his summary remarks Brougham took the trouble to describe some of the views that substantiated his claim for Birkbeck's book:

It is impossible to close this interesting volume, without casting our eyes upon the marvellous empire of which Mr. Birkbeck paints the growth in colours far more striking than any heretofore used in portraying it. Where is this prodigious increase of numbers, this vast extension of dominion to end? What bounds has Nature set to the progress of this mighty nation? Let our jealousy burn as it may; let our intolerance of America be as unreasonably violent as we please; still it is plain, that she is a power in spite of us, rapidly rising to supremacy. . . . If she goes on as rapidly for two or three more years, she must overtake and outstrip us.[29]

28. Henry Brougham, review of Morris Birkbeck's *Notes on a Journey in America,* in *Edinburgh Review* 30 (June 1818): 120.

29. Ibid., p.136.

Brougham's forecast may seem dire, but there were certainly English writers with a less foreshortened sense of the prospect. Hazlitt wrote, at about this same, time that "there are some persons of that reach of soul that they would like to live two hundred and fifty years hence, to see to what height of empire America will have grown up in that period, or whether the English constitution will last so long" (CWWH, 6:324). If Brougham's view seems wildly inaccurate, or at least grossly premature, this may be because he failed to take account of the importance to Britain of what still remained of its vast overseas empire after the loss of the American colonies. Brougham was by no means the only English writer who feared he saw in the emigration patterns an augury of immanent U.S. supremacy over Britain, however, and in this sense of general alarm lies perhaps the most powerful argument for seeing this historical moment as a new one for British representations of America.

Like Irving's comment that the animosity between the countries was increasing daily, Brougham's report locates itself in a context of a rapidly accelerating shift in Anglo–American relations—a sense of a change in the rate of change itself—that seemed to be increasing even as he wrote. Brougham, though, elaborates the point at which Irving only glances. When Brougham notes that "Birkbeck has offered one of the most tempting points of view in which emigration has ever yet been represented to men of moderate fortunes and industrious habits," he expresses worries about both the prospect of great gains for America, gains exponential in their slope, and the prospect of likewise exponential losses for the English. Such evidence may convey some sense of the extraordinary publicity that Birkbeck's project received, but it may also show why they have remained relatively invisible in the historiography of this period as pioneered by the great work of Thompson, E. D. H. Cole, and others: the emigrants in question in 1818 came from the English middle class (their domestic issue was taxes). Birkbeck represented a temptation to just this class, and this is what constituted its psychological threat to writers like Brougham. The example of Birkbeck's own emigration must have seemed portentous. When he left for America in 1817, he took with him more than £11,000, a shipload of prize English livestock, and his considerable talents in the fields of agriculture, politics, and literature. Birkbeck was at the wealthy end of this class of emigrants. Again, the case of George Keats, who emigrated with his inheritance of over a thousand pounds and education enough to move successfully in Louisville commercial circles, might be seen as more typical. Brougham's review was only one of many responses to Birkbeck that would appear in the coming year, much of it just as interesting as Brougham's in its combination of cultural analysis and national paranoia. Great as Birkbeck's impact was, however, it is important to stress that he merely crystallized an issue that had begun to occasion concern with the first jump in the levels of emigration from Britain to America soon after Waterloo.

3. Anxieties of Exodus

The concern over emigration intensified so rapidly partly on account of the work of William Cobbett. By the conclusion of the Napoleonic wars, Cobbett had undergone an extraordinary transformation from the conservative figure of Philadelphia's Peter Porcupine into the generally acknowledged spearhead of the English reform movement. To advance his campaign to rid English politics of "boroughmongers and placemen," he had also developed a powerful new literary organ, *Cobbett's Weekly Political Register,* a publication that enjoyed even more influence than *Porcupine's Gazette*—as much, perhaps, as any British journal has ever known. Afraid of prosecution for what he had been printing in the *Register,* Cobbett returned to America in 1817, where he would remain for a year and a half, this time a fugitive-in-exile and with a very different set of views. His writings on America—in the *Register,* both before and after his second visit, and in his book-length account of that visit in *Journal of a Year's Residence on Long Island* (1819)—differ in character from the Peter Porcupine publications in ways that indicate something of the larger shift in opinion. America has now displaced France as the great Other against which Cobbett defines English national identity, and the representation of this new great Other is at least as profoundly implicated in the politics of Cobbett's domestic reform movement as France had been (for other writers) in the reform campaign of the 1790s. Again, there can be no doubt that this shift had major consequences for both national identities, especially in view of the dependency, frequently mentioned in the surveys, of American readership on English publications.

Because of his deeply ingrained transatlantic orientation, Cobbett was quick to register and promote interest in the subject of emigration when it arose. The *Political Register* had always paid attention to America, but in January 1816 he contributed to the escalation of literary commerce between the two nations with the announcement of what he grandly billed as "Cobbett's American Project"—a project directed, as he explains "to Gentlemen, in England, who may wish to be supplied with American Publications; to Gentlemen, in America, who may wish to be supplied with English Publications; and to Readers in General." In subsequent months, he began to write at length and in earnest on the subject of "Emigration to America," articles apparently occasioned at least at first by requests from readers soliciting his advice on the subject.[30] An article in the June 22 issue registers the incipient sense of national crisis that has developed in just the year's time that has elapsed since Waterloo:

> The subject of Emigration is becoming, every day, more and more important. There is now really an alarm felt on this account. It is not the miserable only that are in motion. I hear of most respectable and most valuable men, who are selling off in order to go to America. Indeed, I *know* the fact. But lest your Cossacks should think, that I exaggerate, I will quote our London papers upon this subject.

Cobbett then quotes from the Morning *Chronicle* a passage of which the following provides a rhetorical sampling:

> *Never, in the memory of man, was there any thing known like the emigration now taking place.* The door of the French Minister, nay the street in which he lives, is crowded with persons applying for passports. Thousands have been issued—and those not to needy persons, but to families of large fortunes—to landed proprietors—to fund-holders—to manufacturers and artizans of eminence—and to men at the head of establishments, who are seriously contemplating the removal of their arts and their machines, to places less burdened by taxation. The extent of this evil will speedily be felt, in diminished consumption—in the number of persons thrown out of employ—and in the deficit of the Revenue. The river Thames presents a most dreary aspect.[31]

The reference to the door of the *French* Minister requires a word of clarification. Emigration to America by artisans of a certain rank remained illegal long after Waterloo and well past 1819. What changed with end of the Napoleonic wars was that emigration to *France* began to be permitted again. English men and women wishing to emigrate to America at this time had to travel first to another country, sometimes Canada but often France, and find passage from there.[32]

Cobbett is crafty enough to cite a newspaper whose picture of the emigration problem was rendered in starker colors even than his own, but the question of the evidentiary basis for what Cobbett calls the "alarm felt on this occasion" is a difficult one to resolve.[33] Actual Britain-to-America emigration statistics

---

30. There are briefer remarks, and somewhat dismissive, on this head in Cobbett's *Weekly Political Register* for September 30, 1815, also claiming to be prompted by requests for information (28:398–399).

31. *Weekly Political Register,* 30:769.

32. Helen I. Cowan explains other problems with the statistics, in *British Emigration to British North America: The First Hundred Years,* rev. and enl. ed. (Toronto: University of Toronto Press, 1961), p. 287.

33. For what it is worth, most modern historians of immigration would agree that the movement of people to America that begins with the year 1815 far surpassed any previous level of migration. The consensus among these historians is that there was a time before 1815 when emigration from Europe to America had dwindled to negligible numbers, though they are not precisely agreed as to how long a time that is: some say it begins with 1776, some with the Napoleonic Wars themselves, some with an even later date such as 1806. There is, in any case, strong unanimity among these historians that Waterloo marks a dramatic new phase. Maldwyn Jones's standard work on the subject, *American Immigration* (Chicago: University of Chicago

are unfortunately scarce for this period, and the ones we have are not altogether reliable, nor are they broken down to indicate proportions of English, Scottish, and Irish emigrants in the totals. The first year-by-year statistics begin in 1815:

1815	1,209
1816	9,022
1817	10,280
1818	12,429
1819	10,674[34]

The dramatic leap from 1815 to 1816 is perhaps enough to suggest a strong warrant for contemporary fears. On the other hand, the rise in the numbers between 1816 and 1818, while substantial, is not in accordance with the picture of geometrical progress that one gains from contemporary reports. And it is not even on the same level of magnitude with Cobbett's account of things in late

---

Press, 1960), with the benefit of research and hindsight, basically echoes the *Morning Chronicle*'s claim of 1816: "Though immigration had been a familiar aspect of American development throughout the colonial period, there was no precedent for a movement of such magnitude and persistence as that which began in 1815" (p. 93). It could be argued that Waterloo occasioned a kind of snapback effect after years of artificial restraint on both sides. This is what one recent historian describes as "a big spurt of immigration after the release of the dam erected by the Napoleonic wars"—see Franklin D. Scott, *The Peopling of America: Perspectives on Immigration* (Washington, D.C.: American Historical Association, 1984), p. 24. But, as this same historian goes on to suggest, this would have been more temporary in its consequences in the absence of farther reaching conditions: "the rapid growth of European populations in the early nineteenth century, the development of the factory system, developments in cross-Atlantic transportation for the timber trade, the reorientation of rural economies in the rise of new agricultural technologies, and political and religious discontent" (p. 24). And although such accounts aim to describe post-Waterloo American immigration from Europe in general, the conditions tend to hold a fortiori for the case of Britain: "During the agricultural depression which followed the Napoleonic wars," writes Marcus Lee Hansen:

> many of the more prosperous yeoman farmers of England gave up the struggle at home and transferred their households to a land where farming could be carried on with more profit and less anxiety. Until 1830 this class formed an important element of the immigrants settling in the Ohio Valley. They brought with them not only the capital that was so much needed, but also a skill in farming that was unknown to pioneer agriculture. (*The Immigrant in American History* [Cambridge, Mass.: Harvard University Press, 1940], pp. 20–21)

For a discussion of the Malthusian dimension of the post-Waterloo emigration crisis and its discourse, see W. A. Carrothers, *Emigration from the British Isles* (London: P. S. King & Son, 1929), pp. 32–89; and H. J. M. Johnston, *British Emigration Policy, 1815–1830* (Oxford: Clarendon Press, 1972), pp. 1–13, 129–139.

34. Taken from Cowan, *British Emigration to British North America*, p. 288. Also cited in Carrothers, *Emigration*, p. 305. The tailing off of these numbers in 1819 and 1820 is a function of the increase in numbers of British emigrating to British North America in this period, and this in turn is in part to be explained in terms of the government's deliberate attempt, by means of a program of subsidized emigration, to divert the flow of emigrants from the United States to Canada—see Johnston, *British Emigration Policy*, passim.

1818 when he spoke of the appeal to his compatriots of the Western Country (Illinois and Indiana): "that Newest of the New Worlds, to which so many thousands and hundreds of thousands are flocking, and towards which the writings of Mr. Birkbeck have, of late, drawn the pointed attention of all those Englishmen, who, having something left to be robbed of, and wishing to preserve it, are looking towards America as a place of refuge from the Boroughmongers and the Holy Alliance."[35]

One source of inaccuracy built into these statistics is that the legal restrictions I have described led many emigrants to indirect routes and covert exits. Were Cobbett's numbers exaggerated? Perhaps. Then again, these contemporary representations of waves of English departures for America were certainly in some degree self-fulfilling: the more powerful the opinion that England was being depleted of human resources and that America was developing colonies of English settlers, the greater the willingness to contemplate so momentous a move. Such are the exponential laws of a "tipping game" such as emigration.

It was precisely because the prospective émigrés could afford to *deliberate* such a move that the literature on America proliferated to the extent that it did in these years. In the very first wave of emigration after 1815 there seems to have been a snapback effect from the end of the war; many English subjects, on the brink of destitution, seem simply to have packed up and headed off when the first opportunities arose.[36] However, great numbers found themselves unable to move beyond the eastern cities in 1815 and 1816. Many appealed to the British consul in New York for aid, and nearly two thousand received help.[37] The second wave of emigration after Waterloo tended to involve those whom Cobbett described as having "something left to be robbed of." We can recall here Henry Fearon's claim that, within two years after Waterloo, "[e]migration had . . . assumed a totally new character: it was no longer merely the poor, the

35. William Cobbett, *Journal of a Year's Residence in the United States of America* (Gloucester, England: Alan Sutton, 1983), p. 243.

36. Johnston summarizes the conditions that led to the flight of the poor in 1815:
Several hundred thousand men discharged from the army, navy, and transport services sought employment in a country in which unemployment was already a large and permanent feature. Industries that had flourished in wartime now shrank and left thousands more out of work. In rural England peace meant a decline in the price of wheat, a tightening of the screw made all the more effective by a small harvest in 1816. Labourers in city and country alike were caught in the grip of falling wages while the price of bread and fuel remained high. It was estimated that almost 15 per cent of the population of England was indigent. Over 120,000 pauper children ran the streets of London. (*British Emigration Policy,* p. 5)

37. See Marcus Lee Hansen, *The Atlantic Migration 1607–1860* (Cambridge, Mass.: Harvard University Press, 1940), p. 85.

idle, the profligate, or the wildly speculative, who were proposing to quit their native country; but men also of capital, of industry, of sober habits and regular pursuits, men of reflection who apprehended approaching evils." For these new prospective emigrants, at the same time that the question of America gains a certain practical urgency by virtue of pending decisions about emigration, it also becomes a case, a subject on which to deliberate and decide.

4. Godwinian Theory in the Newest of New Worlds

Henry Fearon, as we have seen, was one of those surveyors sent to assemble evidence for deliberating this momentous decision for thirty-nine English families. Unfortunately, to which conclusion the evidence pointed never quite became clear for him. Writing from the Illinois Territory in December 1817, just weeks before its promotion to statehood, Fearon admits that he has not made sufficient progress in his explorations to answer the key questions, but he does attempt to set the terms in which they can be best contemplated:

> My mind continues undecided concerning our removal . . . . With the means of forming a judgment on this subject, I have endeavoured, as far as lies in my power, to supply you in the course of my preceding reports.
> Should your minds be favourable to a western country settlement, I should wish to press upon your deliberate re-consideration the following ideas.
> First,—Is it essential to your prosperity and happiness that you should leave England?
> Second,—Do the habits and character of the American people afford you rational grounds for desiring to become their fellow citizens?
> Third,—Have you all of the dispositions requisite in order to become cultivators of a wilderness?
> Fourth,—Assuming that you have those dispositions, are you fitted for such an entire change of pursuits, and can you endure the difficulties and dangers necessarily attendant on such a situation?
> If, after cool, deliberate, and rational consideration, with your minds as free from enthusiastic expectations connected with this continent, as they well can be under the existence of the present order of things in England, you can answer in the affirmative, then I have little doubt of the propriety of recommending to your attention the Illinois territory. (pp. 265–66)

The conception and rhetoric of Fearon's project shows the balance between urgency and deliberation in the postwar survey. But, while the last two of Fearon's criteria direct attention to his reader's personal qualifications, the first directs attention to the relationship of the English reader to England itself—to the "present order of things" there. (We can recall here Fearon's dark allusion in his introductory remarks to "motives and views" conducive to emigration that are "known and *felt* too generally to render description necessary.") And then the one criterion in Fearon's list that has to do primarily with America itself points not to its physical resources but to the issue of the "habits and character of the American people."

The linkage between this question of "national character" and the contemplated possibility of British emigration is subtle but strong among the "English Writers on America." In Fearon, we can trace its logic in a report filed the following April in which Fearon registers recent news that his friends, without having received all of his earlier reports, have come to a decision. The few sentences in which Fearon records his reaction to this news effect a most abrupt and revealing transition:

> Your commission to Mr. Flower, Mr. Birkbeck's associate, to purchase 9,000 acres in the Illinois, is certainly a bold measure; but as you desire my immediate return, I shall defer the discussion of its merits, until I am blessed with the pleasure of meeting you all face to face, and once more enjoying the indescribable delight of your society and an English fire-side. I shall, in all probability, embark by about the middle of next month. Captain H._____ sails in a few days, and I am sure will take particular care of this communication.
>
> The remark is now an old one, "That Americans have no national character." Half a century ago the observation was probably correct; but I think a personal acquaintance will show its utter want of foundation at the present period. (pp. 353–54)

This casual transition to the question of American character is clearly occasioned by the news of the decision to buy land in Illinois. It triggers an extended discussion that, together with his detailed critique of Birkbeck's *Notes,* dominates much of the remainder of book. The question of the character and manners of the Americans had arisen frequently Fearon's earlier reports, but in the final stages, when the decision on emigration is most immanent, and when attention is adverted to the Western Country, it suddenly crowds out all other considerations.

Both of these features typify much of the contemporary literature surveying America for prospective English emigrants, and neither makes intuitive sense. It seems odd on the face of it that the less-populated and most recently settled region should be taken as the site on which to investigate and negotiate the question of American character and manners.[38] To come to terms with the difficult cultural logic of this pattern it may help to think of Keats's Godwinian friend Charles Dilke, who, as we shall see, pleased himself with the idea that America would be the country to take up the human intellect where England leaves off. For the connection between emigration and national character lies in the perception that England was facing a crisis in its own destiny and that this crisis was formulated as a problem of national identity. The crisis took shape around troubling but not always explicit questions: What was the state of English society? Was English character shaped by a system of manners that was more or less advanced than that of the United States?

---

38. Thus, for example, when Mrs. Trollope came to America with her son Anthony in 1827, Cincinnati, Ohio, was the place in which she established the residence that would form the basis for *Domestic Manners of the Americans,* 2 vols. (London: Whittaker, Treacher, 1832).

Looking for answers to such questions in 1818 or so, at least within the terms of a roughly Godwinian framework, one might well have imagined the Western Country as the place in which to discover the outcome of the process of character formation in post-Constitution America. The Western Country, said Cobbett, was "that Newest of New Nations." If it took a generation after 1789 to see what the New Nation was, the site where that newness appeared was, according to some observers, the still newer nation that the New Nation was spawning.[39] It is as if the Midwest settlements, the America spawned within America, were the empirical laboratory in which to register what it meant, in those Godwinian terms, for a generation to be raised under the principles of a modern republican constitution.

In his critique of Birkbeck, Fearon himself implicitly highlights the Godwinian dimension of Birkbeck's discourse in his late section called "Causes for Leaving England." He quotes at length Birkbeck's rationale for thinking that the United States is a good place to raise children because it is a "society whose institutions are favourable to virtue" (p. 415). The quoted Birkbeck passage reads in part: "That institutions favourable to virtue, shall produce effects correspondent to their character upon the society blessed with them, is a conclusion so natural, that we should be inclined to suspect an error in the estimate of the institutions themselves, if we found a vicious people under a good government" (p. 415). Fearon then comments on it as follows:

> These are conclusions . . . exactly such as a man versed in theoretic speculations upon the nature of society would arrive at, when contemplating a country like this, previous to his leaving Great Britain. But I am sorry to say, that a very brief residence in America will most effectually dispel the charm. . . .
>
> Could we begin society anew—transported from our present abodes, could we be placed in another Eden, possessing there the aid of all the knowledge and virtue, and freed from all the error and vice of the present day, then we should have *rational* grounds to anticipate, that, under a good government, there would necessarily be found a virtuous people. But as this is not the case, we must, in forming our judgment on such a subject, look at man as he is, and speculate on society as we find it; and I think we shall discover, that the materials which go to the formation of individual and of national character, spring up from a thousand other sources besides that afforded by political institutions. (pp. 415–16)

Like others before him, in other words, Fearon challenges the entire Godwinian analysis as utopian, as taking place outside of what Burke had called the "dense medium" of "common life." And making this challenge, according to

---

39. Hansen, the historian of immigration, casually mentions what he calls "the growing belief that Morris Birkbeck was creating a new England in the Illinois prairies" (*The Atlantic Migration,* p. 99). But if the eastern states were a New England, political offspring of Great Britain, then it makes as much sense to call the "Western Country" a New America, political offspring of the United States.

Fearon, helps "in solving an otherwise difficult question, namely, why it is, that the people of England are so much in advance of their government; and why, on the other hand, the people of America remain so very far behind the principles upon which *their* political system is founded" (pp. 416–17).[40] Such is Fearon's anti-Godwinian answer to a problem that *Shelley's Philosophical View of Reform* had tried to resolve in terms more sympathetic to Godwin.

5. The "Mystery of Generation"

For another account in which the Western Country of post-Waterloo United States figures in the identification of national character, we can look again to Brougham's review of Birkbeck's *Notes* in the *Edinburgh Review,* where Brougham observes that the "new community of the United States [meaning the first "new nation"] is, in fact, already the source of an emigration beyond all comparison more extensive than ever was known in the most confined and overpeopled portions of the old world." Here is his elaboration of this point:

> [T]he extraordinary state of things in the Western part of the Union, developed by Mr. Birkbeck, shows us the process both of colonization and increase at one glance:—We see exposed to the naked eye, the whole mystery of the generation as well as the growth of nations; we at once behold in what manner the settled parts of America are increasing with unparalleled rapidity; and how new and extensive communities are daily created in the plains and the forests of the West, by the superfluous population of the Eastern settlements. Those settlements assume a novel and a striking aspect;—they no longer are to be regarded as new colonies, to which other communities send their overflowing numbers—they are already fully peopled States, which having reached maturity in a few years cannot stop in their growth; but become in their turn the *'officina gentium'* and send off their countless swarms to the hardly more recent but infinitely less peopled regions that surround them.[41]

Brougham's discussion is so extraordinary that one could well wish to dwell on certain aspects of it longer: on his anticipation of the Turner thesis about the frontier, for example, or on his adaptation of Scottish-Enlightenment ideas about what Marx would call "uneven developments" between societies to find in America the exposition of the "whole mystery" of national generation. Instead, I want to consider what Cobbett does with Brougham's idea about how empires reveal themselves in their colonies and then, after returning to the case of Keats, look at what Shelley does with some of Cobbett's views.[42]

40. Fearon had already reported to his friends that "*American theory is at least two centuries in advance of American practice*" (p. 366).

41. Brougham, review of Birkbeck, p. 122.

42. Is this the link between Turner and Brougham the Ricardian theory of rent (1817), with which Brougham was so familiar through his work on contemporary political economy for the *Edinburgh Review*? For contemporary references to the *officina gentium,* or "hive of nations," see Southey's "On the State of the Poor, the Principle of Mr. Malthus's Essay on Population and the Manufacturing System," *Quarterly Review* 8 (December 1812): 319–56. Thanks to Ernst

Cobbett's position on American manners—on the state of society and character of the people—was never quite perspicuous after his abandonment of the Peter Porcupine posture in favor of the role of Great Cobbett, champion of reform. To account for Cobbett's inconsistencies, Hazlitt remarked of him: "When he is in England, he does nothing but abuse the Boroughmongers, and laugh at the whole system: when he is in America, he grows impatient of freedom and a republic. If he had staid there a little longer, he would have become a loyal and a loving subject of his majesty King George IV" (CWWH, 8:55). Fearon visited Cobbett on Long Island soon after the former's arrival in America, and he wrote in an early report that Cobbett entertained a low opinion of Americans. When Cobbett published his *Journal of a Year's Residence on Long Island* the following year, he appended to his text a postscript, "Fearon's Falsehoods," denying the charges. Part of the confusion over Cobbett's positions stems from the conjunction of his genuinely positive accounts of American character and manners, on the one hand, and on the other, his insistence that he encourages no one to emigrate to America from Britain. The more genuine the emigratory option, the more qualified the account of America. The last of the three parts of the Long Island *Journal*, indeed, consists of a long report of his friend Thomas Hulme's visit to Birkbeck's settlement. The report is prefaced by Cobbett and followed by a long open letter from Cobbett to Birkbeck challenging Birkbeck's influential *Notes* and *Letters*. This indeed set off a polemical round-robin among several writers over the next five years. The point I wish to stress here is that Birkbeck's colony presented too real a temptation for British emigration to suit Cobbett's purposes. Cobbett needed the leverage of an *opportunity* for emigration, and the *idea* of an America to which Britons might properly be attracted, but he needed them to carry on his struggle for reform at home. Cobbett, in other words, had his own characteristically idiosyncratic and self-aggrandizing understanding of "the influence of America on the mind."[43]

One can see the Cobbettian dynamic at work in a chapter from part 2 of his *Journal of a Year's Residence:* "Manners, Customs, and Character of the People." It is a chapter that recasts earlier accounts by Charles Ingersoll and John Bristed and that indeed anticipates some of Tocqueville, but it represents America in terms that are quintessentially Cobbett's. After reviewing what he describes as a

---

Bernhardt for the reference. For an account of the continuing impact of Malthus in the post-Waterloo literary context, see Maureen McLane, "Literate Species: Populations, 'Humanities,' and *Frankenstein ELH* 63 (winter 1996): 959–88.

43. For an account of how Cobbett relates culture to agriculture, and of the place of the bizarre treatment of the growing of ruta begas in Cobbett's *Year's Residence,* see Elizabeth Helsinger, *Rural Scenes and National Representation: Britain, 1815–1850.* (Princeton, N.J.: Princeton University Press, 1996), pp. 109–12.

typical American household, Cobbett draws the inevitable comparison with England toward an idiosyncratic conclusion:

> When one sees this sort of living, with the houses *full of good beds,* ready for the guests as well as the family to sleep in, we cannot help perceiving, that this is that *"English Hospitality,"* of which we have *read* so much; but, which Boroughmongers' taxes and pawns have long since driven out of England. This American way of life puts one in mind of FORTESQUE'S fine description of the happy state of the English, produced by their *good laws,* which kept every man's property sacred, even from the grasp of the king. . . . [Here Cobbett cites Fortesque.]
>
> This passage . . . describes the state of England four hundred years ago; and this, with the *polish* of modern times added, is now the state of the Americans. Their forefathers brought the "English Hospitality" with them; for, when they left the country, the infernal *Boroughmonger Funding system* had not begun. The STUARTS were *religious* and *prerogative* tyrants; but they were not, like their successors, the Boroughmongers, taxing, plundering tyrants. . . . The Bishop-begotten and hell-born system of Funding has stripped England of every vestige of her ancient character. Her hospitality along with her freedom have crossed the Atlantic; and here they are to shame our ruffian tyrants, if they were sensible of shame, and to give shelter to those who may be disposed to deal them distant blows.[44]

The entire orientation of Cobbett's passage is toward England. It is not just that in his account American character and manners appear as a simple transplantation, with modern polish, of a seventeenth-century English society founded on good laws, an abundance of wealth, and a dissemination of literacy. It is also that America's role is primarily to remind England of what it once was and still can be (in addition, of course, to offering temporary shelter to those, such as Cobbett in 1819, who may be disposed to deal them distant blows.) According to the logic that Brougham sees operating between the east and west of America, Cobbett's eastern America stands as England's only living picture of its own essential character beneath the corruption that arrives with the advent of the system of public credit developed by the Whig commercial oligarchy in the 1690s. Here, then, we arrive at another explanation of Cobbett's resistance to the allure of the Western Country: as a site for the realization of the "future state" of America, it could function as an alternate history of the state of England after 1688—a new possibility for national afterlife.

A final indicator of the difference between the way in which America was still being viewed by the British in 1803 and how it would increasingly be viewed after Waterloo lies in Thomas Moore's term of reference for his object of satire in the preface to his *Poems Relating America.* When Moore mentions his disappointment with America he calls it "the western world [that] has long been looked to as a retreat from real or imaginary oppression."[45] The distinction between the "western world" and the "western country" means everything to the argument I am making. It is the difference between a vague and

44. Cobbett, *Journal of a Year's Residence,* pp. 193–94.
45. Moore, *Poetical Works,* p. 160.

generalized realm of political fantasy and abstraction, of utopian possibility, as against a specific stretch of land, already spawned by the American westward expansion, and figuring the generation of America from within its own newly constituted state. The boundary between the Western World and the Old World divides the modern from the ancient. The boundary between the Western Country and the Eastern Country of the United States divides two historical epochs in a sequence of stages.

As for Morris Birkbeck, I have presented him as an extreme example of a historical personage massively famous in his own time, and almost utterly unknown in ours. I have tried to revive him and the things he stood for in order to show how, in his exaggerated public figure, the colossus straddling the American West, he came to represent a number of crucial and related issues in Anglo-American literary culture of 1819. I have also tried to show how the gigantism that attends representation of his person in the British press and the paranoiac catastrophism that attends representation of his settlement both suggest just what an object of cultural cathexis he became in a few short months. The claim, however, that he was utterly unknown in our time, requires some qualification. For Birkbeck's name, at least, is known to two relatively small groups of antiquarian specialists. One is the group, largely amateur, of midwestern local historians. The other is the group of biographical scholars of Keats. And, though I myself was led to Birkbeck by pursuing leads provided in Keats's letters, I have tried to suppress Keats's name from the account so far in order to show how much can be said about the importance of Birkbeck to English literary culture in 1819 before his connection with the famous poet is even broached. But now it is time to reckon—time in this discussion and time in the history of Keats criticism—with the fact that all the sputter and sparkle of the running commentary Keats kept up with George and Georgiana in late 1818 and in 1819 was written in the time frame defined by the development of Birkbeck's "western settlement" and its overblown discursive representation in the British and American press.

6. Keats and "the Humanity of the United States"

Although Keats had a complicated and contingent relation to Birkbeck, one implication of the foregoing account is that, as an alert and politically aware reader in England in 1819 who was well connected in journalistic and printing circles, Keats was likely to have known of Birkbeck and his writings in any event. So many roads, literal and figurative, led to Birkbeck that, when William Faux reached Birkbeck's settlement in late 1819, he was scarcely surprised to encounter the son of Henry Hunt—Hunt himself was in prison awaiting trial for his role in the assembly at Peterloo and in the aftermath of the massacre. If young Hunt, Flower, Hulme, Faux, and John Woods could all find their way to Illinois, many others could as well, though their paths might be different. The road that led Keats's brother George to Birkbeck's doorstep indirectly involved Keats himself, for the fortunate London publisher of Birkbeck's successful *Letters from Illinois* was Taylor and Hessey, Keats's publisher. In a letter dated June 18, 1818, George thanks Taylor for the use of Birkbeck's book (a loan probably negotiated through the offices of the poet, who used his publisher as a library for his brothers). In this same letter, George tells Taylor that reading Birkbeck has heightened his enthusiasm for the prospects of emigrating even above the high level that he had attained beforehand—on the strength, presumably, of the *Notes,* to which the *Letters* comprised a sequel.[46] In the late spring, young George made up his mind to go west. He withdrew about a thousand pounds from his share of the meager family inheritance, married young Georgiana Wylie, and set off with her in early summer, accompanied by John and by Charles Brown, for the transatlantic port of departure in Liverpool.

While the George Keatses sailed to Philadelphia and made their way in the footsteps of Birkbeck's *Notes* and *Letters* to the far bank of the Wabash River, John Keats himself extended his walking tour through the Lake Country and on into Scotland.[47] In this way, the crucial analogy between the cases of Scotland and America vis à vis the British subject of this period, an analogy recently explored in convincing detail in Robert Crawford's *Devolving English Literature,* was in effect established by happenstance in the Keatsian psyche.[48] Happen-

46. George's exact words to Taylor were that Birkbeck's *Letters* had "raised my spirits (if it were possible for them to be higher), they certainly make my sanguine hopes appear somewhat more reasonable," *Letters,* 1:294. A month earlier Keats had already written to Benjamin Bailey explaining George's "resolution to emigrate to the back settlements of America, become farmer and work with his own hands after purchasing 1400 Acres of the American Government"; Keats adds that he approves of George's decision for many reasons "and the chief one is this—he is of too independent and liberal a Mind to get on in trade in this Country—in which a generous Ma[n] with a scanty recourse must be ruined. I would sooner that he should till the ground than bow to a Customer" (p. 287).

47. For a composite narrative and pictorial history of this tour, see Carol Kyros Walker, *Walking North With Keats* (New Haven: Yale University Press, 1992).

48. See Crawford, *Devolving English Literature* (New York: Oxford University Press, 1992), especially pp. 176–215. In a review essay of Crawford's book, I have tried to contextualize it in relation to recent work on the relation of Scotland and America. See "Devolutionary Criticism: Scotland, America, and Literary Modernity," *Modern Philology* 92 (November 1994): 211–19. The details of Keats's movements and correspondence in mid-to-late 1818 are significant in this context. While he was on the walking tour itself, the journal letters Keats composed were written to and for his brother Tom back in Hampstead. Once back home in Hampstead himself, however, or rather as soon as he received the awaited cue from George and Georgiana, he begins the series of journal letters to George and Georgiana in America that extended over the coming months with such impressive candor and speculative intelligence.

stance or otherwise, this much is important to recognize: Keats's movement into the phase of poetic composition for which he became so esteemed by subsequent generations of readers largely coincided with his movement, characteristically sympathetic, into the imaginary cultural space newly occupied by his brother toward the end of 1818.

Nothing is more characteristic of Keats's posture in these writings than his new combined sense of cultural alienation and curiosity. From the first of these long journal letters, in late October of 1818 (October 14 through 31 [his birthday]), we see Keats's reporting to the George Keatses dispassionately on the state of things in England (LJK, 1:391–405). From the second (December 16, 1818–January 2, 1819) on through the coming months, we find him not only continuing to report on the state of things in England but also, increasingly, wondering and wandering on the page about the question of what it would be like to be where George Keats is—or, in Adam Smith's language, what it would be like to be in George's "case." We have already seen one example of this strong impulse in Keats's questions to George in December: "What are you doing this morning? Have you a clear hard frost as we have? How do you come on with the gun? Have you shot a Buffalo? Have you met with any Pheasants?" (2:5). But questions about the weather and the local game soon grow into more complex inquiries about the particular state of society, the historical specificity of the case, in which George Keats now finds himself. We can detect the beginnings of this kind of double consciousness just the day before the buffalo-and-pheasant passage was recorded, in the very first entry of the long December-January epistle. Part way into a self-absorbed train of thought, Keats seems to pick his head up to ask:

> How are you going on now? The going[s] on of the world make me dizzy—there you are with Birkbeck—here I am with [B]rown—sometimes I fancy an immense separation, and sometimes, as at present, a direct communication of spirit with you. (p. 5)

Keats is very clear that this special communication has to do with his prior intimacy with his brother, and offers a thought experiment to clarify what he fears is an obscure point: "Suppose Brown or Haslam or any one whom I understand in the n[e]ther degree to what I do you, were in America, they would be so much the farth[er] from me in proportion as their identity was less impressed upon me" (p. 5). The meaning of this counter-factual supposition is in turn explained in relation to the question, precisely, of manners:

> Now the reason why I do not feel at the present moment so far from you is that I rememb[er] your Ways and Manners and actions; I know your manner of thinking, your manner of feeling: I know what shape your joy or your sorrow w[ou]ld take, I know the manner of you[r] walking, standing, sauntering, sitting down, laugh[ing] punning, and eve[r]y action so truly that you seem near to me. You will rem[em]ber me in the same manner. (p. 5)

The phrase—"in the same manner"—is involuted in this context, because Keats is talking about a manner of remembering manners. Moreover, this manner of remembering manners is something that Keats will immediately reinforce by proposing a weekly ritual for purposes of mutually commemorating their respective manners: "You will remember me in the same manner—and the more when I tell you that I shall read a passage of Shakespeare every Sunday at ten o Clock—you read one [at] the same time and we shall be as near each other as blind bodies can be in the same room" (p. 5).

It seems not even to have occurred to Keats that, if George is reading Shakespeare at 10 p.m. Sunday in Kentucky and he at the same time of day on Sunday in Hampstead, they will not actually be reading Shakespeare at the same time—another version of necessary anachronism, we might say.[49] But we must not fail to appreciate the impulse driving this primitive contrivance for calibrating different experiences of the same object—Shakespeare, the pole star—at the same time. Keats is trying to keep his and his brother's respective "manners" intelligible to each other. What is unclear in this experiment, and interestingly so, is whether Keats more fears George's fading from his memory or his cultural transformation in another environment. Evidence that it is not merely or necessarily the former becomes stronger in the coming weeks and months as Keats plays variations on his early thought experiments with George:

> I want to hear very much whether Poetry and literature in general has gained or lost interest with you—and what sort of writing is of the highest gust with you now. With what sensation do you read Fielding?—and do not Hogarth's pictures seem an old thing to you? Yet you are very little more removed from general association than I am—recollect that no Man can live but in one society at a time—his enjoyment in the different states of human society must depend upon the Powers of his Mind—that is, you can imagine a roman triumph, or an olympic game as well as I can. We with our bodily eyes see by the fashion and Manners of one country for one age—and then we die—Now to me manners and customs long since passed whether among the Babylonians or the Bactrians are as real, or even more real than those among which I now live—My thoughts have turned lately this way. (2:18)

In triangulating the cultural perspectives of mid-eighteenth century England and 1819 America with that of 1819 England, Keats betrays and generates a self-consciousness about the location of his present moment in a history of manners and states of society. It is this self-consciousness, developed in con-

49. A further irony of the situation is that, as Keats only later found out, George was not "with Birkbeck" for any length of time, having been so appalled by the squalor at Birkbeck's settlement that he and Georgiana quickly descended the Wabash, crossed the Ohio, and settled in Kentucky. It was there, alas, that they fell into the clutches of James Audubon, who Keats later concluded had swindled them. Keats would not learn of this change of plans until July, presumably because so little traffic was returning from the vicinity of the farther reaches of the Ohio in the western country.

junction with an awareness of even older and stranger systems of manners and customs that puts Keats in company with Scott and the other writers working in historical forms. It is just two days later, after all, that Keats embarks on that discussion for George's sake, of whether Godwin could have written the Waverley novels (2:24–26). And this at least in part explains the particularly marked way in which we can plot the epochs of his own moral and aesthetic—his "psychic"—development *as* the developing spirit of the age. Keats's imaginative exploration of, simultaneously, historical and geographical forms of cultural difference recalls the analogy in terms of which we have seen the concept of culture itself take shape in this period of Romantic historicism. Keats is rapidly assimilating this conceptual framework and modifying it to his own circumstances. The occasion of this acquisition and adaptation seems in large part to be the influence of America on his mind.

There is, however, a yet stronger claim to be pressed for the way in which the case of U.S. culture affects Keats in 1819. In a valuable corrective to a strong tendency in Keats criticism, Robert Ryan has shown that in those passages from (especially) the early letters, where commentators have seized on the chestnut about Keats's developing view of poetry and aesthetics—e.g., "poetry is like Adam's dream, he awoke and found it truth"—the frame of reference, when examined carefully, often turns out to be religion.[50] One can make an analogous corrective for certain key passages from the letters of the annus mirabilis in that *they* tend to have America as their implicit frame of reference. A good example is the letter of April 1819 about the vale of soul-making that I considered at some length in the last chapter. It is a letter that would certainly seem to count as evidence for Ryan's claim about the aesthetic chestnut passages taking religion as their frame of reference, and Ryan himself uses it that way.[51] "Soul-making," Keats insisted, is a system of salvation that does not offend our reason and humanity. Following the steps by which Keats enters into the soul-making passage, however, we discover that its context and thematics are social and historical. For Keats begins with a comparison of the culture of primitive America during the earlier European conquests and the culture of seventeenth-century France: "I have been reading lately two very different books Robertson's America and Voltaire's Siecle De Louis xiv It is like walking arm and arm between Pizarro and the great-little Monarch" (2:100). As between Pizarro's America and Louis XIV's France, Keats goes on to argue, there is not much to choose. In seventeenth-century France, there were the plagues of

50. Robert Ryan, *Keats: The Religious Sense* (Princeton, N.J.: Princeton University Press, 1976). See especially the discussion of Keats and Benjamin Bailey, pp. 114–57.
51. Ibid., pp. 198–201.

"Baliffs, Debts and Poverties." In savage America, he says, "where Men might seem to inherit quiet of Mind from unsophisticated senses; from the uncontamination of civilisation; and especially from their being as it were estranged from the mutual helps of Society and its mutual injuries—and thereby more immediately under the Protection of Providence—even there they had mortal pains to bear as bad; or even worse than those Baliffs, Debts and Poverties" (2:101). The case of the "great body of the people" is "lamentable" in both instances.

Remembering that this particular letter moves toward the analysis of "soul-making," and "soul-making" toward the poetic history of Psyche in the *Ode,* we can here resume the terms of the previous chapter's discussion of Keats's epochal sense of historical psychology in the context of the crucial American question. "The whole," as Keats sums it up in Lear's famous remark on humanity in the state of nature, "appears to resolve into this":

> —that Man is originally 'a poor forked creature' subject to the same mischances as the beasts of the forest, destined to hardships and disquietude of some other kind or other. If he improves by degrees his bodily accomodations and comforts—at each stage, at each accent there are waiting for him a fresh set of annoyances—he is mortal and there is still a heaven with its Stars abov[e] his head. The most interesting question that can come before us is, How far by the persevering endeavours of a seldom appearing Socrates Mankind may be made happy—I can imagine such happiness carried to an extreme—but what must it end in?—Death—and who could in such a case bear with death—the whole troubles of life which are now frittered away in a series of years, would the[n] be accumulated for the last days of a being who instead of hailing its approach, would leave this world as Eve left Paradise—But in truth I do not at all believe in this sort of perfectibility—the nature of the world will not admit of it—the inhabitants of the world will correspond to itself—Let the fish philosophise the ice away from the Rivers in winter time and they shall be at continual play in the tepid delight of summer. Look at the Poles and at the sands of Africa, Whirlpools and volcanoes—Let men exterminate them and I will say that they may arrive at earthly Happiness—The point at which Man may arrive is as far as the paralel state in inanimate nature and no further—For instance suppose a rose to have sensation, it blooms on a beautiful morning it enjoys itself—but there comes a cold wind, a hot sun—it cannot escape it, it cannot destroy its annoyances—they are as native to the world as itself: no more can man be happy in spite, the world[l]y elements will prey upon his nature—(2:101)

This might seem to suggest that history reduces to a zero-sum game—for every gain a corresponding and equal loss. In the terms of the vale of soul-making analysis, into which this passage immediately leads, this might be translated into the claim that every intelligence starts from the same state in the world and passes through the same stages. The changes in each individual soul in the course of its individuation would then become all the real change there was in the history of society. There would be no history. There would be no society.

To take this reading at face value, however, is to see Keats as committed to what might be called an undialectical materialism, a view that "the world" reduces to nature *tout court*. Whether this interpretation can be accepted will depend at least in part on how one reads his playful summary of the entire discussion of these issues at the end:

> If what I have said should not be plain enough, as I fear it may not be, I will [put] you in the place where I began in this series of thoughts—I mean, I began by seeing how man was formed by circumstances—and what are circumstances?—but touchstones of the heart? and what are touchstones but proovings of his heart? and what are provings of the heart but fortifiers or alterers of his nature? and what is his altered nature but his soul?—and what was his soul before it came into the world and had These proovings and alterations and *perfectionings?*—An intelligence—without Identity—and how is this Identity to be made? Through the medium of the Heart? And how is the heart to become this Medium but in a world of Circumstances?—There now I think what with Poetry and Theology you may thank your Stars that my pen is not very long winded. (2:103–104) (emphasis added)

The question, as before, has to do with the extent to which other souls form part of our "circumstances," or whether circumstances should be understood simply in terms of inanimate nature. Or to put it another way, it is whether and how society is involved in "circumstance."

It seems from the references to the Baliffs and Debts that affected popular life under Louis XIV that society must be so involved, and vice versa. Keats did imply that this society amounted to nothing better than the state of nature in savage America. On the other hand, he also chose the regime of one of Europe's most notorious despots as his civilized example to compare with the state of American savagery. Was there something in the nature of that particular comparison that led him too quickly to yield the idea of progressive stages of society and to commit himself prematurely to the notion of merely natural circumstance as formative of a soul? After all, if circumstances ultimately reduce to an idea of nature that is a zero sum game, then there is not much point in emphasizing the role of circumstances in individuation.

Viewing altered souls as part of the circumstances of the formation of other souls, however, can be a way of seeing that circumstances can alter. If this is so, then we must note the possibility of diverse ways of soul making in Keats. We can return in this connection to Keats's comment on a vision of "man" in which he "improves by degrees his bodily accomodations and comforts"—he did not, he wrote, "believe in this sort of perfectibility." This remark seems to leave the door open for another kind of perfectibility, and the playful summary suggests that it did, by virtue of its apposition between seeing the soul as the effect of an altering of one's nature and as the effect of a "perfectioning" of it. If it turns out that altered souls alter circumstances, and that altering implies perfecting, then Keats, after expelling one sort of perfectibilism through the front of his mansion of many apartments, would be allowing another sort to arrive through a side door.

I think it is fair to say that "the kind of perfectibility" that Keats was disavowing to George was William Godwin's kind. Keats apparently had many debates with his friend Charles Dilke about Godwin. He discusses both Godwin's thought and his fiction at some length in several letters to the George Keatses, including that curious one (January 2, 1819), in which he weighs the merits of the hypothesis, entertained by many of his contemporaries, that Godwin wrote the Waverley novels (2:24–26). Since much seems to come of Keats's involvement in that contagious game of America watching, so widespread though England in 1819, we should not close without considering the comment to George and Georgiana of 1818 in which Godwin is linked quite closely with a hilarious comment on the American character. Editorializing on a conversation among his London circle of friends, Keats comments:

> [Charles] Dilke, whom you know to be a Godwin perfectibil[it]y Man, pleases himself with the idea that America will be the country to take up the human intellect where england leaves off—I differ there with him greatly—A country like the united states whose greatest Men are Franklins and Washingtons will never do that.—They are great Men doubtless but how are they to be compared to those our country men Milton and the two Sidneys—The one is a philosophical Quaker full of mean and thrifty maxims the other sold the very Charger who had taken him through all his Battles—Those American's are great but not sublime Man—the humanity of the United States can never reach the sublime—Birkbeck's mind is too much in the American Style—you must endeavour to infuse a little Spirit of another sort into the Settlement, always with great caution, for thereby you may do your descendents more good than you may imagine. If I had a prayer to make for any great good, next to [their brother] Tom's recovery, it should be that one of your Children should be the first American Poet. (1:397–98)[52]

It is clear from the context that for Keats the reason American humanity could not reach the sublime lay not in nature but in their culture (the obverse, in effect, of the controversial argument that American *virtue* lay not in its resources but in its institutions). Thus, while Keats is rejecting a kind of historical perfectibility that is too narrowly utilitarian in character, he is clearly advocating another: improvement through what Shelley described in *The Philosophical View of Reform* and later in *A Defence of Poetry* as the refinement of the passions through poetry.

Since, like the vast majority of his British contemporaries, Keats had not visited the United States—had not indeed traveled beyond Scotland—he may be called one of those minds "poisoned" on America, as Irving says, by the British press. How one might construe this sublime "spirit" Keats wishes to see infused into American culture is a question that I wish to address indirectly in my clos-

---

52. Keats illustrates the American character with pre-Constitutional heroes, but we must recall that they are held heroes in "the United States"—i.e., in post-Constitutional America.

ing remarks on Shelley. Certainly, though, we can easily find ourselves tracing a circle if we try to imagine how Keats's nephew or niece—niece as it turned out—is supposed to do good for a culture that has so little good in it to begin with. We have seen versions of this circle before, in Bentham and Godwin, and it will come up again in Shelley, who does his best to make it virtuous.

The point I want to stress is that, however jaunty and idiosyncratic his rhetoric, Keats's remarks about the American "style" of mind epitomise much post-Waterloo discourse on the United States in their impulse to compare the production of character in the American cultural system with what happens in England. His own associative "style," furthermore, discloses his sense of the close connection between this notion of comparative national development and what we noted in the previous chapter about his replotting of his psychic development onto the scheme of stages of society: that long passage about what it means to be reading Fielding in different states of society is the passage that leads directly into Keats's declaration about the smokeability of Mary Tighe. Certainly, Keats's engagement with the case of U.S. culture in the context of the historicization of the culture of England in 1819 puts him in a position to become, as it were, an anthropologist to both cultures. And this in turn, as I have already argued, greatly enabled him to achieve the breakthrough into the perspective from which to see his way toward *The Eve of St. Agnes* and the *Great Odes*. He had learned to smoke a society whole, as he tells us, just at the end of that extraordinary run from January through September:

> When once a person has smok'd the vapidness of the routine of S[o]ciety he must have either self interest or the love of some sort of distinction to keep him in good humour with it. All I can say is that standing at Charing cross and looking east west north and south I can see nothing but dullness. (2:244)

In the following chapter, we come to a more markedly Popean judgment on the ubiquity of "dullness" in England in 1819, though a more involuted judgment, in Shelley's *Peter Bell the Third,* which was written just weeks later.

7. America in 1819: Poetry, Utility, Representation

Shelley was, of course, another "Godwin perfectibility man" in the Keats Circle, and he offers an even more explicit and more general account of the case of U.S. culture than Keats's in *A Philosophical View of Reform,* that tract begun toward the end of 1819 in the wake of the Peterloo massacre. On his way to making an argument about the condition and prospects of English society, for whose sake, he says flatly, he has produced his analysis, Shelley offers a long account of the U.S. republic as he saw it in 1819. As compared with the old governments of Europe and Asia, he concludes, the United States holds forth the example "of a free, happy, and strong people" and of "an immensely populous, and as far as the external arts of life are concerned, a highly civilized, community administered according to republican forms" (WPBS, 7:11). To head off the objection, as Irving does, that Americans "owe their superiority rather to their situation [i.e., to their geography] than to their government," Shelley reproduces the catalogue of European institutions that he had earlier praised the United States for being well rid of and, in doing so, makes a rhetorical suggestion for a social experiment: "Give them a king. . . . Give them an aristocracy. . . . Give them a priesthood. . . . Give them, as you must if you give them these things, a great standing army to cut down the people if they murmur . . . [and] the prosperity and happiness of the United States [would] be no more" (WPBS, 7:11). Shelley sees the United States as the full realization of the eighteenth-century ideal of utility. The surprising and decisive turn in this argument, however, is Shelley's suggestion that in spite of his acknowledgment of America's perfection within a utilitarian framework, England's *resistance* to utilitarianism affords it ultimately brighter social prospects. Shelley argues for these prospects in the celebrated passage about poets as unacknowledged legislators that is assimilated two years later into a better-known text, *A Defence of Poetry,* where it forms the conclusion to his cultural theory.[53]

In Shelley, too, the British ethnography of America can be seen to cut both ways, but with perhaps more immediate and explicit consequences for understanding *literary* history. Shelley shares many of Cobbett's views about this tyranny by fraud rather than by force. The entire middle section of his *Philosophical View of Reform,* a history of the English economy from 1641 to 1819, develops from Cobbett's widely known writings on this question, but the way in which Shelley's description of America implies a corresponding picture of England is a clear departure from Cobbett. Shelley's America is not an image of English antiquity modernized along a different axis from the one pursued in England, but rather an incarnation of the doctrine of utility as developed in eighteenth-century social theory.[54] Its representative system is perfect in its

53. Ibid., pp. 12–13. Henry Fearon employs a similar trope of subtraction and addition to relate England and America.

54. In this, Shelley may well have been following one of America's apologists, Charles Ingersoll, later author of "The Influence of America on the Mind," who had already conceded in his earlier defense of American manners, that the national strength lay mainly along the lines of the useful and mechanic arts and who had admitted that "there are not wanting native Americans who consider the fine arts and republicanism incompatible"—see *Inchiquin's Letters* (New York: I. Riley, 1810), p. 129. Since "Inchiquin" is a Jesuit, we may call his defense "casuistical" in the strict sense.

way, but its way is limited as the English way is not. What is the English way of representation? For Shelley, it is poetry. His account of American identity enables him to identify an England that is defined primarily by poetic activity. "The literature of England," wrote Shelley in the passage carried from the *Philosophical View of Reform* to the *Defence of Poetry,* "an energetic development of which has ever preceded or accompanied a great and free development of the national will, has arisen as it were from a new birth" (SPP, p. 508). The makings of this argument can be found in many late-eighteenth-century English polemics, including works of writers such as Burke and Wordsworth with whom Shelley would have disagreed on much else.[55] This point suggests the strange way in which opposition to the theory of political economy, as it was gaining ground in English social writings of this period, met a simultaneous challenge from, as it were, the right and the left. The invidious distinction made here between England and America is thus replayed on to the invidious distinction that is emerging here between imaginative or creative and other kinds of literature, a distinction against which the conciliatory argument—and indeed the very miscellaneous form—of Irving's *Sketch Book of Geoffrey Crayon* tries to militate.

Shelley would therefore have undoubtedly endorsed Keats's suggestion to George and Georgiana that it was by raising its first poet that they could best help the new world to learn a spirit different from that which admired Washington and Franklin. Shelley's discussion of the poet-legislator only amplifies what Keats's notion of such a spirit might entail. Many Americans themselves came to accept this recommendation. In the modern American academy, the prestige of Romantic literature, and of literature romantically defined, seems to bear continuing witness to the influence of Shelley's and Keats's account. And then there is the conspiracy of coincidence. John Keats's niece, born to George and Georgiana in early 1819, did not, alas, prove to be the first great American poet. The shadows of futurity in literary America fall elsewhere in 1819. Back east in this same year were born babies named Herman and Walt who would give American readers reason to think that Keats's hope for their character and manners, however misconceived one might judge it, was worth holding on to. In England, meanwhile, Shelley was working on a complex series of poetic negotiations focused on just these questions. The year's work that

---

55. For an elaboration of this point, see my "Poetical Liberties: Burke's France and the Adequate Representation of the English," in *The French Revolution and the Transformation Modern Political Culture,* ed. François Furet and Mona Ozouf. Vol. 3 in *The French Revolution and Modern Political Culture* (Oxford: Pergamon Press, 1989).

ended with Shelley's composition of "England in 1819" and the launching of *A Philosophical View of Reform* included an extraordinary array of work, in diverse genres, on the relation of pleasure to utility, history to casuistry, the past to "futurity," and the present moment in English literature to whatever else the world had to offer.

Section Two

Sublime Casuistry

Chapter Nine

THE CASE OF "THE CASE OF SHELLEY"

As a means of linking my case studies for England in 1819, I have made much use of Thomas Moore's ubiquity in that literary culture. He not only seems to have been everywhere, he also, as we have seen, often played key roles in major literary projects. The case of Shelley is no exception. Moore's relation to Shelley goes back to 1817, when Shelley had just completed what was by far his most ambitious and risky poem to date, *Laon and Cythna*.[1] In the course of its rocky prepublication history, as difficult as *Don Juan's* (and for similar reasons), Shelley wrote to his would-be publisher, advising that a sample of the manuscript be sent to Moore for a judgment—this was a little over two years before Moore was called in on the case of *Don Juan*.[2] Shelley soon opened a respectful correspondence with Moore and later sent him an inscribed copy of the published version, *The Revolt of Islam*. This all took place while Shelley was still living on the Thames at Marlow, but he certainly did not lose sight of Moore after leaving England for Italy in 1818. Moore is, after all, one of the handful of writers whom Shelley places at the bier of the dead poet in *Adonais,* his elegy for Keats: "[F]rom her wilds Ierne sent / The sweetist lyrist of her saddest wrong, / And love taught grief to fall like music from his tongue" (SPP, p. 399, ll. 269–71). In September 1819 Moore was on the short list of eight authors—

---

1. In the preface to the published version of this poem, *The Revolt of Islam,* Shelley announced it as "an experiment on the temper of the public mind, as to how far a thirst for a happier condition of moral and political society survives, among the enlightened and refined, the tempests which have shaken the age in which we live," *Poetical Works,* ed. Thomas Hutchinson, cor. G. M. Matthews (Oxford: Oxford University Press, 1970), p. 32.
2. Shelley urged this publisher, probably Longman, who had just published Moore's own oriental fable, *Lalla Rookh,* that to find a reader able to assess a long poem on the basis of just four sheets, they might "submit it to Mr. Moore's judgement, [for] he will make due allowance for these circumstances" (LPBS, 1:563). The follow-up letter to Moore himself is dated December 17, 1817 (LPBS, 1:582–83).

along with Byron, Keats, Leigh Hunt, Godwin, and Peacock—to whom Shelley directed his new publisher, Ollier, to send copies of his forthcoming works (LPBS, 2:118). Weeks later Shelley made Moore the dedicatee of one of his major compositions of 1819, *Peter Bell the Third*.

This remarkable work, a witty and recondite verse satire in a balladic stanza form, appears in seven sections totaling nearly eight hundred lines. Its curious title derives from a remarkable publishing event of March 1819, noted by Keats in his correspondence that month: Keats's friend John Hamilton Reynolds had composed a sight-unseen satirical parody of an advertised poem by Wordsworth, *Peter Bell,* and managed to get it into print before its target itself was published. The event raised a question of literary-historical causality— how could a satire predate its object? Although he did not engage the matter until the autumn of 1819, Shelley was not one to miss an opportunity for speculation on such questions of poetry and temporality. To the (literally) preposterous episode of the Reynolds parody, Shelley linked Wordsworth's own prefatory declaration that he had been working on *Peter Bell* since 1798. Wittily interpreting this comment in light of Wordsworth's use of the Platonic myth of preexistence in the Immortality Ode, Shelley addressed the "awful mystery" of the relationship between Wordsworth's new creation and Reynolds's "antenatal Peter" who Platonically heralded its arrival—"Like the soul before it is / Born from *that* world in to this" (ll. 29–30). In the event, *Peter Bell the Third* extends rather than solves this mystery, however, and does so by detailing the "after life" of Wordsworth's *Peter Bell* in the British press (just as, in an elegiac mode, Shelley's *Adonais* would later describe the afterlife of Keats among the writers who cared for him). The Wordsworthian creature thus becomes the *second* "Peter Bell"—whom Shelley calls "the Apostate"—and Reynolds and Shelley figure in the comic allegory as his prenatal and postmortal passages. Since *Peter Bell the Third* concerns an "after life," its seven section-titles identify the stages of the reception history of "Peter Bell" (character, text, and author) accordingly as (1) *Death,* (2) *The Devil,* (3) *Hell,* (4) *Sin,* (5) *Grace,* (6) *Damnation,* and (7) *Double Damnation.* And since Shelley enforces the conflation of character, text, and author as he does, the poem's staged sequence is able to merge the redemption plot of Wordsworth's homely ballad with a mock Christian allegory of the postpublication state of Peter Bell's soul *and* of the postpublication fate of his author's "poetical character."[3] In short, the poem is a tour de force and a marvelous variation on one of English writing's most-recurring themes in 1819: the question of the "future state."

3. In eighteenth-century critical idiom, the "moral character" of an author was routinely distinguished from that author's "physical character" or "poetical character."

In the formal act of "Dedication," *To Thomas Brown, Esq., The Younger, H.F.* (Historian of the Fudges), it is plain enough to see that Shelley is parodying the dedication Wordsworth had written for Southey in *Peter Bell* itself: "Robert Southey, Esq. P.L." (Poet Laureate). What is less obvious is why Shelley would dedicate the poem to Moore in the first place, and this question is worth a moment's speculation. We may hazard, first, that, because Moore was an enlightened but nonradical Whig and a man known to be close to the leaders of the Whig faction in Parliament, he would have certainly counted for Shelley as a representative of that special audience, the "select few," to whom Shelley often referred in his writings of this period.[4] Like Bentham, Shelley regarded this particular group of public figures in Britain as absolutely critical to the shaping of public sentiment and of mass action at this critical historical juncture. But if Moore's position in English literary culture helps explain why Shelley would dedicate a poem to him in 1819, it does not do much to explain why Shelley chose *Peter Bell the Third* in particular from among the range of significant writings he composed in this, his most productive period as a writer. To go further, then, we might note that, as a satiric poem in a comic or non-Juvenalian vein, *Peter Bell the Third* clearly mimics Moore's own late satiric mode in such works as *The Twopenny Post-Bag* and *The Fudge Family in Paris*. Critical commentary on the poem normally takes it to be working in the satirical mode of Byron, and this is by no means an unreasonable view: as Byron's close friend and fellow exile in Italy, Shelley would have had privileged access to the early anti–Lake School cantos of *Don Juan* in 1819. But Moore's extreme invisibility to modern readers, even to modern literary historians of the Romantic period, has made his role in the poem—as indeed in Byron's own satiric work—difficult to recognize.

There is, undoubtedly, much Moore both in *Don Juan* and in *Peter Bell the Third,* but there may be still a better way of explaining Shelley's choice of his dedicatee for his poem. It requires that we recognize *Peter Bell the Third,* more elaborately topical than anything else Shelley ever wrote, as a poem about the general literary culture of England in 1819. *Peter Bell the Third* ponders the extraordinary literary production in that most archaic of modes, lyric poetry, in the midst of the most advanced commercial metropolis in the world.[5] It surveys

---

4. See chap. 4 above, for Shelley's comments on the "select few." See also the characteristic reference to the "enlightened and refined" in the preface to *The Revolt of Islam,* n. 1 above.

5. See Ian Duncan's compelling discussion of a parallel archaism in the novel Britain's commercial economy, an "'archaic' mantel," as he says, which is not "a pupil shell the creature has failed to outgrow, but . . . the distinctive garment of its modernity": *Modern Romance and the Transformation of the Novel: The Gothic, Scott, Dickens* (Cambridge: Cambridge University Press, 1992), p. 5.

the effects on literary composition of the massive critical reviewing institution that was steadily strengthening its hold at this time. It explores what it means for a single writer, such as Wordsworth, to proclaim himself the privileged and pristine representative of the spirit of the age—the claim that Hazlitt, as I read him, poked fun at in *The Spirit of the Age* and that M. H. Abrams, as I read him, naively accepted at face value (and then mistakenly invoked Hazlitt's authority for doing so).[6]

On the reading I am proposing here, *Peter Bell the Third* becomes Shelley's poetic representation of this modern literary establishment, with its inimical reviewers, victimized poets, grandiose literary ambitions, and growing but unsophisticated reading public. It was this same establishment that Coleridge had defensively criticized in his *Biographia Literaria* (1817), when he devoted several early chapters to an exposé of its corruption. It was again this same establishment that had been the object of Wordsworth's even more defensive critique in his Essay Supplementary of 1815.[7] In fact, *Peter Bell the Third* alludes quite pointedly to Wordsworth's self-serving distinction between "the public" and "the people" from that same 1815 essay.[8] This occurs when the narrator of Shelley's dedicatory epistle, "Miching Mallecho," makes a Wordsworthian concession to Moore (or rather "Thomas Brown, Esq., The Younger, H. F."): "Your works, indeed, dear Tom, Sell better; but mine are far superior. The public is no judge; posterity sets all to rights" (SPP, p. 325). Like both Wordsworth's and Coleridge's discussions, furthermore, Shelley's poem seems to depend on a strong sense that the new birth of literature in his time goes hand-in-hand with the conascent monstrosity of Modern Criticism.

Perhaps the best explanation of Shelley's choice of dedicatee, therefore, is that Shelley settled on Moore because, as one who circulated so widely through the literary system of England in 1819, Moore had a claim stand for it. Hazlitt, too, seems to have intuited that Moore figured the interest of literature in this period as few others could. Building on this conclusion, however, one might speculate further that the new literary system Moore betokens in *Peter Bell the Third* is one that persisted for decades to come and that in a number of key respects still survives in our own contemporary literary institutions. If such

6. See above, chapter 3.

7. J. H. Reynolds also has a parody of the Essay Supplementary in his *Peter Bell,* an indication of the notoriety of that Wordsworthian text. See *Peter Bell* (London: Taylor and Hessey, 1819), pp. 27–29.

8. See Wordsworth, *Prose Works,* 3 vols. Edited by W. J. B. Owen and Jane Worthington Smyser (Oxford: Clarendon Press, 1974), 3:83–84.

a step seems to take us outside or beyond the "poem itself," I would insist that the poem offers some evidence of venturing just such a forecast, albeit in a playful mode—a mode reminiscent of nothing so much as Scott's witty prefaces to the "Tales of My Landlord" of 1816–1819. Shelley not only gives us to understand that the new literary system would survive but that it would come to strengthen its hold and heighten its contradictions in literary and critical institutions of the future that he locates in North America.

The evidence for such a view comes at the end of the dedicatory epistle to "Tom Brown" when "Miching Mallecho" rounds his comments to a close in a two-paragraph conclusion. Shelley sets up his punch line with a mock apologia-for-the-present-work, in the manner and idiom of Wordsworth:

> Allow me to observe that so much has been written of Peter Bell, that the present history can be considered only, like the *Iliad,* as a continuation of that series of cyclic poems which have already been candidates for bestowing immortality upon, at the same time that they receive it from, his character and adventures. In this point of view, I have violated no rule of syntax in beginning my composition with a conjunction; the full stop which closes the poem continued by me being, like the full stops at the end of the *Iliad* and the *Odyssey,* a full stop of very qualified import. (SPP, p. 325)

Shelley here satirizes the pretensions of contemporary apologists for poetry by making a parodic application of the exalted language of recent developments in higher criticism and philology to the practice of modern verse writing.[9] The ironies are especially complicated, however, in that, while Shelley here displays a shift from classical to contemporary literary analysis in apparently ludicrous terms, he would himself pursue a closely related line of argument in *A Defence of Poetry* less than two years later. Here, too, as in the *Defence* furthermore, the argument moves between retrodiction and prediction.

Thus, if the penultimate paragraph of the dedication satirically represents the relation of the classical (or premodern) literary past to the modern literary present of England in 1819, the final paragraph asks Tom Brown to consider the prospects for the (postmodern?) future:

> Hoping that the immortality which you have given to the Fudges, you will receive from them; and in the firm expectation that when London shall be an habitation of bitterns, when St. Paul's and Westminster Abbey shall stand, shapeless and nameless ruins in the midst of an unpeopled marsh; when the piers of Waterloo bridge shall become the nuclei of islets of reeds and osiers and cast the jagged shadows of their broken arches on the solitary stream,—some

---

9. For recent work on the way in which new forms of Biblical and classical criticism affected the understanding of the poetry-criticism relationship in this period, see Elinor Shaffer, *"Kubla Khan" and the Fall of Jerusalem* (Cambridge: Cambridge University Press, 1975), pp. 17–61; and Jerome McGann, "The Idea of the Indeterminate Text: Blake and Dr. Alexander Geddes," in *Social Values and Poetic Acts* (Cambridge, Mass.: Harvard University Press, 1988), pp. 152–72.

transatlantic commentator will be weighing in the scales of some new and now unimagined
system of criticism, the respective merits of the Bells and the Fudges, and of their historians;
I remain, Dear Tom, Yours sincerely,
Miching Mallecho.
December 1, 1819.
P.S. Pray excuse the date of place; so soon as the profits of this publication come in, I mean to
hire lodgings in a more respectable street. (SPP, p. 325)

As I noted in passing earlier (in chapter 2), Shelley's starting point in this passage
is Anna Barbauld's brilliant sketch of contemporary culture in *Eighteen Hundred
and Eleven,* a fact that may help explain the self-conscious dating and indeed the
mock excuse for its lack of an indication of place. "Place" does not matter in the
poem, except insofar as it indicates a cultural place. That is, *Peter Bell the Third*
depends on a sense of *topicality,* like all satire, but it is interested in topicality as a
cultural system: the location of culture itself. Likewise, its sense of the "contemporary" is not merely that of the present tense typically presupposed in the
referentiality of certain traditions of satire. Rather, it is a self-consciously *historicist* present tense. Like the present-tense moment produced at the end of
Keats's *Eve of St. Agnes,* the present-tense moment in *Peter Bell the Third* can be
seen, at least from one perspective, as datable on a historical time line, and thus
specifiable in terms of what Lévi-Strauss calls the chronological code. In *Peter
Bell the Third,* what the implicit time line codes is the cultural history of poetry
in its relation to criticism. This history extends in both directions from the
present of 1819: it reaches back to the past of Homeric reception, a reception
perpetually deferred by the failure of the *Iliad* and *Odyssey* to come to true "full
stops," and it reaches forward to the future in which the merits of Shelley's work
can be assessed in relation to the paradoxically unforeseeable prospect of a new
"system of criticism" of some "transatlantic commentator."[10]

10. I want to return here to Steven Goldsmith's *Unbuilding Jerusalem: Apocalypse and Romantic
Representation* (Ithaca, N.Y.: Cornell University Press, 1993), which carefully studies discursive
representation in Romantic politics with emphases that often differ from mine. Readers familiar
with Goldsmith's interpretation of Shelley, and of this passage in particular, will recognize the
moment of divergence. I tend to see what apocalyptic allusions Shelley offers in terms of a dialogue with historicism, and to believe that commentators on Shelley are inclined to underestimate the force of the latter. Thus, where Goldsmith calls the description of London in ruin an
"apocalyptic vision," stressing its "instant depopulation of the early nineteenth-century landscape" (pp. 214–15), I read it as a projected moment in a gradual and material historical transformation. Thus, too, when Goldsmith points out, quite rightly, that the "fourth act of *Prometheus
Unbound* is haunted by the force of history it claims to have overcome" (p. 217), I want to agree
but at the same time to insist that the recognition of this historical recalcitrance is very much the
point of Act IV, and another point of crucial overlap between this play and *The Cenci,* and indeed
with the works of later in the year. This recognition is actually already implicit in the initial "disappointment" suffered by the character aptly named "Spirit of the Hour" when, in surveying the
regenerated world at the end of act III, he/she does not see as dramatic an outward change as

Now, what if, in the same playful spirit of Miching Mallecho's Scott-like prefatory remarks, we were to identify a "transatlantic commentator" with an unimaginable system of criticism—or at least imaginable only as unimaginable—a system that might be capable of doing new and convincing justice to the case, so understood, of Shelley? Might we not well think of the very earnest and very American criticism of Harold Bloom at Yale in the 1950s? After all, Bloom's strongly revisionist first book, *Shelley's Mythmaking* (1959), is widely recognized as one of the pioneering efforts in the American revival of Romanticism after the debilitating critiques of humanist ideologues like Irving Babbitt and new critics like T. S. Eliot.[11] To take this step is to be carried into another, however, for Bloom's work on Shelley did not spring full blown from his own critical imagination. To think of Bloom and Shelley at Yale in the 1950s is necessarily, if one is aware of such things, to recall Bloom's teacher, Frederick Pottle. Pottle's 1950 essay, "The Case of Shelley," almost in spite of itself, made a major contribution—partly in its own right, partly through Bloom's work—to the American revival of Shelley in particular and more generally of Romanticism in a Shelleyan mode.

In what follows directly here, then, by way of laying the ground for a discussion of the case of Shelley, I would like to turn first to Pottle's important essay. I risk the sense of redundancy—the case of "The Case of Shelley"—in order to illuminate a fascinating but apparently blind repetition, for Pottle reiterates a discourse of casuistry, sensibility, and historicism already at work in Shelley without seeming to recognize that he is doing so. Pottle's repetition without acknowledgment, one might say, is the other side of that mirror of futurity about which Shelley began to write so eloquently in 1819, the obverse face of the paradox of Shelley's imagination of an unimaginable future system.

Shelley's is perhaps the most difficult of the cases of Romantic historicism that we must consider for England in 1819. His historicism is the most self-conscious and the most "unwilling," and it is precisely in his awareness of its unwillingness that he most recognizes it as the product of a historicist epoch. It is

---

he/she had "felt within" (III.4.126–30). Finally, while I agree with Goldsmith's claim that "Apocalyptic language asserts . . . its authority *over* social situations by claiming to be *free* of social situation" (p. 236), I would insist on the evidence, which I try to lay out in what follows, that Shelley is always engaged both with the social situation, what I am calling the "historical case," and indeed, quite directly, with its *concept* as well. For a recent reading of Shelley strongly emphasizing his materialist sense of "culture" in 1819, see Timothy Morton, *Shelley and the Revolution in Taste: The Body in the Natural World* (Cambridge: Cambridge University Press, 1994), especially pp. 187–91.

11. Only two other books of that era, I think, could rival the claim of Bloom's in this respect: Northrop Frye's *Fearful Symmetry* (Princeton, N.J.: Princeton University Press, 1947) and M. H. Abrams's *The Mirror and the Lamp* (New York: Oxford University Press, 1953).

not his own spirit, as he might have put it, but the spirit of the age-of-the-spirit-of-the-age. Shelley's work of 1819 provokes historical awareness of the condition of being historically aware. Shelley's mode of historicist representation and his concept of the historically representative are thus alike "mysterious," in a strict sense that becomes explicit when he describes the trinitarian structure of the multiply representative protagonist of *Peter Bell the Third:* "There is this particular advantage in an acquaintance with any one of the Peter Bells; that if you know one Peter Bell, you know three Peter Bells; they are not one but three, not three but one. An awful mystery after having caused torrents of blood, and having been hymned by groans enough to deafen the music of the spheres is at length illustrated to the satisfaction of all parties in the theological world, by the nature of Mr. Peter Bell" (SPP, p. 324). If Shelley's religious metaphors suggest that we are in the presence of an updated "mystery," his legalistic language—"to the satisfaction of all the parties"—suggests that we are in the presence of an updated "case," a point for which I shall argue when I return to the poem below. But as Shelley's case of Peter Bell seems to involve some sense of the mystery of the three-in-one, so my case of Shelley will involve another three-in-one, for I mean to address the problem of historical casuistry, briefly, in three different Shelley texts of 1819: *The Cenci, Peter Bell the Third* itself, and the *Ode to the West Wind*. I will take them up in that order, according to the decreasing explicitness of their address to this topic. In *The Cenci* "casuistry," named as such, is both the historical subject of the story and the explicit modality of the dramatic representation. In *Peter Bell the Third,* the language of the case is in play, as I suggested in chapter 3, but less conspicuously so, in spite of its crucial importance to both the pedagogy and performance of "judgment" in that text. In the *Ode to the West Wind,* the central questions of the objectivity and subjectivity—causality and agency—in the poem's understanding of historical determination are played out at the level of the grammatical case—a level that proves crucial in a poem where, as many commentators have stressed, grammatical resources are so intensively mobilized.

1. A Defense of Shelley

One of the standard critical anthologies of the 1960s was an enormous festschrift for Frederick Pottle, *From Sensibility to Romanticism,* edited by Harold Bloom and Frederick Hilles, which included essays by many of the most influential Romanticists then writing: Abrams, Bloom, Kathleen Coburn, David Erdman, Geoffrey Hartman, E. D. Hirsch, Earl Wasserman, and W. K. Wimsatt. In the brief introduction, the editors explain that the essays they have collected to honor Pottle's forty-year career at Yale address "a problem he has studied in

The Idiom of Poetry, and elsewhere, that of a 'shift in sensibility' between two broadly defined literary periods."[12] Arguably, though, Pottle's most influential comments about these matters appear not in *The Idiom of Poetry* but in the mid-century essay called "The Case of Shelley," an argument that participates in—perhaps even helps to precipitate—a "shift" rather like the one it seeks to describe.[13] The essay was produced so early in that postwar period of literary studies when Romantic paradigms began to dominate criticism that it conveys no acknowledgment of such a trend. Indeed, Pottle's explicit twofold agenda was to reflect on the low state of Shelley's critical reputation in 1950 and to explain it by reference to the decline in the kind of Romantic sensibility that he claimed Shelley exemplified.

As a piece of Shelley criticism, Pottle's essay is, as William Keach reminds us, the "classic advocacy" in our time.[14] Moreover, although Pottle's practical commentary on Shelley occupies only part of his essay, that commentary is cited vitually *passim* in Harold Bloom's 1959 appreciation, *Shelley's Mythmaking* (a revised 1955 dissertation with Pottle at Yale), the book that soon changed the face of Shelley studies and much else besides.[15] Bloom's book took Shelley's part, of course, as Pottle had done. More to the point, it did so precisely in terms of Pottle's account of the larger critical stakes in Shelley's reception, especially with regard to literary modernism, to the New Criticism, and to the general fate of Romanticism in what Pottle called the "sensibility" taking shape at the midpoint of the twentieth century. Pottle's able discussion deserved the amplification Bloom gave it, but, together with other cultural factors, its acquiring such a champion put Pottle in an awkward position when "The Case of Shelley" was solicited for critical anthologies about the poet. Such anthologies, and the interest they bespoke, had seemed unimaginable in the critical prospect held out by the essay itself. While Pottle's argument had predicted only continued gloom for Shelley's future reputation, it helped to usher in those better days for Shelley and for Romanticism that lay ahead.

12. Frederick W. Hilles and Harold Bloom, eds., *From Sensibility to Romanticism: Essays Presented to Frederick A. Pottle* (New York: Oxford University Press, 1965), p. 1. The two periods addressed in the festschrift are the two to which Pottle himself devoted most attention. Nothing is made in this introduction of the fact that the editors identify one of them as itself the "Age of Sensibility," which betrays a revealingly low level of *historical* recognition of the way in which categories of literary history can derive from the object studied. "Shifts of Sensibility" is the title of the very first chapter of *The Idiom of Poetry* (Ithaca, N.Y.: Cornell University Press, 1946), pp. 1–22.

13. Frederick A. Pottle, "The Case of Shelley," *PMLA* 67 (September 1952): 589–608.

14. William Keach, *Shelley's Style* (London: Methuen, 1984), p. i.

15. Harold Bloom, *Shelley's Mythmaking* (New Haven: Yale University Press, 1959). Bloom's index lists fifteen different citations to Pottle's commentary on Shelley. Subsequent references to Pottle's essay cited by page reference in the text.

There is surely an interesting story to tell about the American Shelley in the 1950s, a figure epitomized, perhaps, in the Promethean roles played by James Dean in a career as brief and (in its way) as brilliant as Shelley's. This story would consider Dean's portrayal of the Cain figure in the Steinbeckian-Miltonic *East of Eden* but also, more particularly, the protagonist in Nicholas Ray's *Rebel without a Cause*. In the latter, where the connection with the exploration of the universe is explicit, George Lucas found conjoined the themes of his two apparently disparate projects on Promethean adolescence: *American Graffiti,* on the one hand, and the ultra-Shelleyan *Star Wars* saga, on the other.[16] In view of my present aims, however, I turn away from these attractions and toward a much drier question about Pottle's methodology, especially his use of the case idiom in framing his practical comments about Shelley. Pottle's own commentators have paid little heed to the methodological dimension of his essay and have made that common noun in Pottle's title—"case"—expendable, as if the essay had better been called just "Shelley" or "Shelley's Reputation." And yet Pottle himself, from his very opening sentence, directs special attention to it: "Although this paper is entitled 'The Case of Shelley' an essay of this length can of course present only the brief of a case—hardly more than a dogmatic statement of the heads of an argument which, given room enough, I would undertake to make plausible through the presentation of evidence" (p. 589).

Pottle uses the term "case" several other times in the essay (pp. 596 [twice], 597, 599, 604, and 606), with varying shades of meaning and degrees of apparent self-consciousness. Moreover, he leads into the theoretical reflections which he offers as the point of the essay precisely by way of an observation about how the case in question is presented and handled. In other words, by attending to the caseness of the case, its "casuistry," Pottle proceeds to construct what Shelley's Miching Mallecho called a "system of criticism": "The statement of the case is methodical: that is, it proceeds according to a general theory of literary history which Shelley's reputation illustrates, but which was not derived from study of that reputation alone. The method is inductive or experiential; and since the implications of the experiential method as applied to the writing of literary history are by no means generally understood, I think I shall get farther in the end if I invest a considerable portion of my space in definition" (p. 589). In calling this a "system of criticism," I should clarify that I am re-

---

16. Marguerite Waller has written a shrewd and explicitly Bloomian essay about the linkages of Ray's and Lucas's romantic rebels, with the scene of failed Promethean knowledge at the Griffith Observatory in *Rebel without a Cause* as the key juncture supplying the common origin for both *American Graffiti* and *Star Wars*—strangely, though, Shelley is left out of the account: "Poetic Influence in Hollywood: *Rebel without a Cause* and *Star Wars,*" *Diacritics* 10 (September 1980): 57–66.

ferring to an *esprit systématique* (to invoke an appropriately "enlightenment" distinction) rather than to an *esprit de système*—that is, more to a principled procedure for inquiry than to an achieved organization of knowledge.[17] Pottle's procedure, as he explains it, cuts two ways. On the one hand, the case cannot properly be stated until the method in virtue of which it is constituted as a case is understood. On the other hand, the method is designed precisely to handle cases—rather than to achieve absolute self-commensurability.[18]

Pottle's "experientialist," the inquirer whom he takes pains to distinguish from both the positivist and the rationalist, has only pragmatic aims. The experientialist seeks "general principles" but only for the sake of explaining "certain facts" and making predictions on the basis of them. The "intent," finally, "is not general and abstract but specific and practical; not to devise a complete aesthetic but to indicate a workable basis for solving problems of literary criticism and literary history" (p. 592). Pottle's model of experientialist inquiry derives from his work in the physical sciences—this was the time not only before the so-called "theory boom" in criticism, but also before the widening of the "two cultures" divide began to make it seem unbridgeable.[19] Such a mode of inquiry, says Pottle, proceeds by the familiar "method of hypothesis and verification":

> After having pondered a "fair sample" of the facts concerned, the inquirer "gets a hunch" as to a principle by which those facts can be significantly ordered. . . . He then "verifies" his hypothesis by applying it to a great deal more of the material. If it continues to "make sense" of the material without any special adjustments, he finally stops verifying it, formulates it in a manner that best fits all the observations, and advances it for general consideration. He does not believe that this is necessarily and finally true. It is, and will always remain, tentative and provisional: a plausible explanation, a probable belief. (pp. 589–90)

There is much more to say about what might be called Pottle's "relativism of disciplined intuition," especially to situate it with respect to that great Enlightenment debate on the relationship of moral and natural philosophy as we have seen it registered in De Quincey, Byron, and Keats. Pottle's "method," however, is amply illustrated in its application to the case of Shelley.[20]

17. "The experiential method is a *method* and not a system," Pottle emphasizes (p. 590). For more on this kind of distinction in Condillac's *Treatise on Systems* and in D'Alembert's *Encyclopedia,* see Ernst Cassirer, *The Philosophy of the Enlightenment,* trans. Fritz C. A. Koelln and James P. Pettegrove (Princeton, N.J.: Princeton University Press, 1951), p. 8.

18. The practical critic's "intent is not general and abstract but specific and practical; not to devise a complete aesthetic but to indicate a workable basis for solving problems of literary criticism and history" (p. 592).

19. See C. P. Snow, *The Two Cultures and the Scientific Revolution* (Cambridge: Cambridge University Press, 1959).

20. The science-criticism question is far more fully developed in *The Idiom of Poetry,* where Pottle argues, for instance, that the "difference between the theories of physics and the theory of poetry need not be in the kind of mental operations involved" (p. 26).

The feature of the case that most interests Pottle is not the early controversy over Shelley's religious beliefs, in which, pro and con, most critics, like T. S. Eliot, conceded Shelley's talent and poetic accomplishment. Pottle is concerned instead with the point where Shelley's work is no longer perceived to have shown "poetic gifts of the first order" (p. 597). Pottle observes that, in the decades just prior to his own youthful discovery of Shelley in 1917, Shelley's reputation had reached its high-water mark. Major writers such as Swinburne, Hardy, Yeats, and Shaw were all passionate devotees; major critics such as A. C. Bradley and Oliver Elton wrote appreciative commentaries. The tide turned decisively around 1920 with the publication of Irving Babbitt's notorious New-Humanist manifesto, *Rousseau and Romanticism* (1919)—although it is not the academic critique of the New Humanist so much as the more broadly literary critique of the New Critics (most of them poets) that Pottle sees as the crucial assault. In order to account for this "revolt from Shelley" (p. 598) by the poet-critics of the period 1920–50, Pottle invokes the notion of "historic sensibility," which he had begun to elaborate in *The Idiom of Poetry* and which was later made the keynote of the Bloom-Hilles anthology.

The notion of a period-specific sensibility serves Pottle's analysis both as the expressive source of poetic idiom for any given moment and as the immediate framework for the critical judgment of works of the past. The *modern* sensibility is associated with the current "shipwrecked generations" and is described by Pottle as survivalist, "tight-lipped," and "tough-minded"; positivist in perception but nonpositivist in values; suspicious of pronounced rhythms in verse; interested in the single developed image; unattracted by reflexivity; determined to see poetry "operate through Irony, Paradox, and Understatement" (p. 600). (We now recognize in this trinity the normative core of the New Criticism.) Such a sensibility, says Pottle, is right to see Shelley as "the great central exemplar of the idiom and practice from which it must disengage itself" (p. 602)— just as Pope had been the exemplar of the pre-Romantic sensibility, the "pivot" (as Shelley himself once wrote) of the Romantic dispute in taste.

The judgment of modern criticism on Shelley, like that of the Romantics and Victorians on Pope, is itself judged by Pottle as "valid within its own frame of reference," "permanently valid . . . [but] not exclusively valid." Here is where the "reasoned relativism" of the so-called experiential method reemerges with added emphasis: "It is a necessary and laudable task to show the limitations of Shelley's poetry by measuring it against modern sensibility," but it is equally important "to expose the limitations of modern sensibility by measuring it against Shelley's poetry" (p. 604). What becomes in Pottle's analysis both a perpetuation and an expression of this modern sensibility's own limitations is the failure of Leavis and the New Critics to respect Shelley enough—and to respect former judgments of Shelley enough—to give a fair accounting of the poems they condemn. Pottle eventually offers three instances of recent "misreadings" of Shelley, which he attempts to "correct" by citing textual evidence. Conceding that he may not finally have *proven* a lyric such as *When the Lamp Is Shattered* to be a good poem and that he could not *compel* a reader to like it, Pottle nonetheless contends that by proper application of his method he *would* be able to "make any patient and candid modern reader agree that it is a respectable poem" (p. 608).

So ends Pottle's case for Shelley. There are all sorts of oddities about this important critical essay. One, as I have already suggested, involves the issue of prediction, an integral part of literary scholarship as Pottle understands it. Eschewing dialectical formulations in favor of "inductive" ones, however, Pottle's essay does not seem to have had any way of taking its own potential into account. Toward the conclusion of the essay, he predicts that "within fifty years" the "disesteem of Shelley is going to become general" in that "everybody will be saying about Shelley what the New Critics are saying now," and thus, with respect to his own argument, he foretells that, when "the significant Shelley criticism of this age is collected, it will be Leavis's essay or some essay like Leavis's that will be chosen, not anything I might write. My evaluation of Shelley (which is very different from Leavis's) is already old-fashioned. The sort of thing I can do was done as well as it could be done almost forty years ago by Bradley, Clutton-Brock, and Elton" (p. 602). In the end, however, and ironically, Pottle's essay has been the anthology piece of choice. Standing back from Pottle to set his own picture of things next to Shelley's, one could say that at one level, therefore, this approach to Shelley runs very much against the grain of the cultural dynamic I have tried to outline in my account of the sonnet *England in 1819*. Where in Shelley's poem the "reading" of England in 1819 is supposed to make possible a transforming illumination, in Pottle's essay the reading of the situation of English in 1950 counts for nothing, when taken on its own terms. It is as if Pottle's case *for* Shelley, even within the narrowed sphere of an academic literary community, had no means of anticipating its effect on the case *of* Shelley.

The ambiguity about the word "case" in Pottle's essay actually provides a ready index to some of its contradictions. On the one hand, as we have seen, Pottle insists that "the statement of the case is methodical," while, on the other, "The Case of Shelley" is clearly a case *for Shelley*, as Pottle also seems to acknowledge in admitting that he presents "only the brief of a case—hardly more than a dogmatic statement." Pottle holds a brief for Shelley, and does not hide that. He has not regretted the conversion experience that he narrates as evidence for Shelley's power. What further complicates matters is yet another suggestion by Pottle about how it "must be clear to any fair-minded observer that modern criticism of Shelley is not completely candid," by which he means that inimical modern critics of Shelley are, as he puts it, "still making a case" (p. 604).[21] Pottle's paronomasia with "case" is at once serious and playful, scientific and poetic, and draws on a richness of ambiguity in our usage. The case is the object of reasoned inquiry, but it is also the form of argument in which that inquiry is to be represented. Again, these senses of case are not clearly separable, in that the way in which a case is *taken,* for a given discourse, is mutually involved with the way a case is *made* in that discourse. Making a case involves a certain form of argumentation and thus implies a certain mode of explanation—a sense of connection captured in intimacy of the case and the cause. Conversely, it will be in terms of all cases that a given discourse regards as relevant to its domain that its case-making procedures will be worked out. This, we saw, was Kenneth Burke's point in *The Grammar of Motives.* We might also recall here what Pottle says about the "experientialist" critical project: its intent is "not general and abstract but specific and practical"; it aims only to "indicate a workable basis for solving problems of literary criticism and literary history." It, to that extent, is precisely what Burke calls a casuistry.

The unresolved equivocations in Pottle's essay—between the case that is "made" and the case that is methodically stated, or alternatively between the case that is made and the case that is taken (i.e., Shelley as "the great central exemplar of his period's sensibility")—might be said to contaminate various other areas of his discussion where he seems to have some stake in maintaining firm boundaries and distinctions. Three examples of distinctions that crucially serve his discussion are (1) the distinction that I have already cited between permanent and historical factors in the fate of a reputation; (2) the distinction between the materials of literary history (which he defines as one's own reading experiences and the reports of such experiences in other critics) and the ordering operations performed on those materials; and (3) the distinction between judgment and description of aesthetic objects (i.e., "Though our judgments of the value of Shelley's poems are bound to vary widely and unpredictably, all critics of all periods ought ideally to be able to *describe* his poems in the same way" [p. 604]).[22] All of these distinctions are *pragmatic* distinctions, in that none can be pressed with metaphysical rigor—and none is strictly observed even in the conduct of Pottle's own argument. Rather they are distinctions made to ad-

21. That is, they "are suppressing much that could be said for his poetry on their own grounds" (p. 604).

22. "So much for the historical materials. The principle which I offer for ordering it is that of aesthetic relativism" (p. 599).

dress the kind of problem that Pottle wishes to address. Then again, it seems fair to say that the kind of problem that Pottle wishes to address is constituted precisely in respect to distinctions such as these. To speak of the "problem of belief" in the case of Shelley implies the "experiential" ability to infer belief from literary texts, as Pottle bravely and blithely does, and then to think of those inferred beliefs as part of the "material" or data pool one works on. To speak of the "problem of declining reputation" in the case of Shelley is to be able to posit a describable object—"Shelley"—that can be represented apart from the vicissitudes of shifting literary taste, i.e., apart from what Pottle calls "sensibility."

It is perhaps an easy exercise to expose contradictions in Pottle's worthy attempt to formulate critical procedures of what he calls "evidence" and "respect," especially since the criticism of recent years has developed the capacity to gain insight into such discrepancies (no doubt at the expense of other blindnesses). If brief analysis can suggest how Pottle's vacillations between the scientific and rhetorical paradigms motivate his paronomasia with "case," such difficulties nonetheless persist in contemporary criticism, where contradictions of the case—or the "anecdote," "the detail," "the representatiive instance," and "the canon"—continue to vex our practice. I have tried to suggest how Kenneth Burke's dramatism, roughly contemporary with Pottle's account, anticipates some of these developments. But while a strong problematizing of the case was available to Pottle in the work of the maverick Burke, Shelley's own work not only thematizes casuistry and the case but does so precisely in regard to an emergent historicism. The final irony of Pottle's argument, then, is that his attention to the case *of* Shelley blinds him to the case *in* Shelley—to the extension of what Pottle admiringly calls Shelley's fondness for "figures within figures" to the figure of the case itself (p. 601).

We need actually look no further than Shelley's dedicatory epistle for *Peter Bell the Third* to gain some sense of this dimension of Shelley's writing. That metaphor of the future commentator "weighing" Shelley's work in the scales of a new critical system clearly bespeaks the metaphorics that we have consistently seen associated with the case form as André Jolles defines it—the case as at once the occasion and the form of "deliberation." A more nuanced, and perhaps more telling, indicator that Shelley was operating from within the discourse of casuistry, however, lies in the name with which he signs the poem's dedicatory epistle: "Miching Mallecho." Shelley takes care to remind his readers of the allusion he makes in the name of his signatory in the second of his two epigraphs for *Peter Bell the Third* (the first is a stanza from Wordsworth's own *Peter Bell*):

> *Ophelia:* What means this, my lord?
> *Hamlet:* Marry, this is miching mallecho; it means `mischief. (SPP, p. 323)

The lines appear in act 3, scene 2, of *Hamlet,* and they are the very first lines spoken after the performance of the dumb show that Hamlet has staged for an audience that pointedly includes Claudius. The pronouns "this" and "it" are thus deictic references to the staging of the murder scene. Ophelia's question, like most of the myriad questions posed in *Hamlet,* is a question about interpretation. Hamlet's answer, characteristically, is twofold: "miching mallecho" gives a name to the deictic reference; "mischief" is the answer to the question about its meaning.[23] Without getting into what has been called the "heavy weather" that Shakespeareans have made of Hamlet's curious phrase, we can therefore say that, in the context of the play itself, the phrase simply names the performance that Hamlet himself directs.[24]

But what about its "meaning"? The "mischief" that the work of Miching Mallecho does, of course, is to become "the thing / Wherein [to] catch the conscience of the king."[25] What is more, it does such mischief precisely by outlining a situation that the king can recognize as his own, thus allowing Hamlet to recognize his guilty reaction. Hamlet spells out his tactic to Horatio before the play begins: "There is a play tonight before the king. / One scene of it comes near the circumstance / Which I have told thee, of my father's death" (act 3, scene 2, ll. 73–75). In *Peter Bell the Third,* as in other work he produced in 1819, Shelley conceives his own role, as well, in terms of a kind of conscience catching. Only in Shelley it is not the individual conscience of the king but the general conscience of the nation that needs catching. This notion of the general conscience, catchable by a mass-mediated event such as a London theatrical production or a widely circulated poetic composition, is a necessary supplement to that new "casuistry of the general will," as I described it above in chapter 4. The possibility that a "thing" such as a play—or that any kind of literary production—could indeed catch the conscience of the English nation meant the world to Shelley in 1819. It held out a hope, to reinvoke the sonnet he sent to Leigh Hunt just weeks later, that the case of England in 1819 itself could be "illumined" and (thus) transformed.

2. The Play's the Thing: Casuistry in *The Cenci*

Although it was not accepted for the stage at Convent Garden as Shelley hoped, many modern commentators regard *The Cenci* as the most important dramatic work, its protagonist as the most compelling dramatic character, in all of En-

23. See the "longer notes" to the Arden edition of *Hamlet,* ed. Harold Jenkins (New York, Methuen, 1982), pp. 505–506.
24. Ibid., p. 505.
25. *Hamlet,* act 2, scene 2, ll. 591–92.

glish Romantic theater.[26] Shelley composed the play in the late spring and summer of 1819, while he was literally between the acts of his even more ambitious, though even less stageable, drama of that year, *Prometheus Unbound*. Shelley's preface to *The Cenci* opens with a useful account of his source and its contents:

> A Manuscript was communicated to me during my travels in Italy which was copied from the archives of the Cenci Palace at Rome, and contains a detailed account of the horrors which ended in the extinction of one of the noblest and richest families of that city during the Pontificate of Clement VIII, in the year 1599. The story is, that an old man having spent his life in debauchery and wickedness, conceived at length an implacable hatred towards his children; which shewed itself towards one daughter under the form of an incestuous passion. . . . This daughter, after long and vain attempts to escape from what she considered a perpetual contamination both of body and mind, at length plotted with her mother-in-law and brother to murder their common tyrant. The young maiden . . . was evidently a most gentle and amiable being, a creature formed to adorn and be admired, and thus violently thwarted from her nature by the necessity of circumstance and opinion. (SPP, p. 238)

I mean to argue here that Shelley's account of the circumstances of Beatrice Cenci's "story" and his account of the circumstances of his discovery of it are not casually, but deliberately, related. Indeed, I will be returning to a number of the terms of this brief account—*necessity, circumstance, opinion,* and *story itself*—to indicate the particular freight they bear in Shelley's Godwinian idiom. Before I do so, however, it will be helpful to fill in this sketchy account of Shelley's approach to this play and offer some preliminary analysis of how he frames it.

The preface's brief narrative of the historical events is anticipated by two documents written by Shelley, both of which are extant and thought to predate the play itself. The first is a translation in Shelley's hand of the Italian manuscript that was his source for the facts; the second a composition that appears as an entry in his notebook under the title, "Memorandum About the Cenci Case." This second text is of special interest because it mediates between the story told in the translated narrative and the plot of the play Shelley went on to compose.[27] It provides a step-by-step summary, with slight changes in emphasis, of

---

26. For such judgments, see for example, Jeffery N. Cox, *In the Shadows of Romance: Romantic Tragic Drama in Germany, England, and France* (Athens: Ohio University Press, 1987), who calls the play the only one in the period to "command anything like universal critical respect" (p. 139); and Joseph W. Donahue, Jr., *Dramatic Character in the English Romantic Age* (Princeton, N.J.: Princeton University Press, 1970), who calls Beatrice "a theatrical character whose statue towers over that of any other in the period" (p. 181). Jerrold Hogle concedes both points, in *Shelley's Process: Radical Transference and the Development of His Major Works* (New York: Oxford University Press, 1988), but offers a psychoanalytic explanation of them: "only because the play and its main characters show all the regressive modes of radical transference becoming simultaneously possible and oppressively interlocking" (p. 161).

27. As Paul Smith described in detail in "Restless Casuistry: Shelley's Composition of *The Cenci,*" *Keats-Shelley Journal* 13 (1964): 77–85.

the basic facts of the legal case that came before the Corte Savella, where (as Shelley reports) Beatrice's cause was tried twice, first with an acquittal and then with a conviction.

Shelley's way of formulating his narrative material in the so-called Memorandum on the Cenci Case—his emphasis on both cultural motivation and social institution—suggests that, like Scott, he was using the case form to think through a historicist problematic. That is, he was using the legal record to represent, for contemporary readers and audiences, the historically peculiar character of an episode from the past. Scott's novels were themselves, as I have noted, being taken up for theatrical adaptation almost as fast as he could compose them. Shelley, however, for reasons to be explained below, engaged with the historicization of the case directly in the dramatic mode. Further, according to a logic that we have already traced, this kind of engagement leads him to confront the issue of cultural anachronism quite sharply. Hence the declaration that comes midway along in the preface to *The Cenci:* "I have endeavoured as nearly as possible to represent the characters as they probably were, and have sought to avoid the error of making them actuated by my own conceptions of right or wrong, false or true, thus under a thin veil converting names and actions of the sixteenth century into cold impersonations of my own mind" (SPP, p. 240). Although *The Cenci* was not available in Britain until 1820, this striking comment uncannily anticipates by several months Scott's treatment of the problem of anachronism in the 1819 dedicatory epistle to *Ivanhoe,* the text that Lukács used to explicate the key notion of "necessary anachronism" as he applied the term from Hegel's new theory to Scott's new practice.[28] Thus, having briefly questioned the applicability of Hegel's concept to Scott's historicism earlier, I would now like to examine its relation to Shelley's in somewhat greater detail. While Shelley's work in this vein, like Scott's, may be illuminated by the Hegelian paradigm, it also differs from it with respect to the historical detemination and aesthetic representation of human agency.

The concept of "necessary anachronism" figures climactically in Hegel's analysis of "The External Determinacy of the Ideal [Work of Art]" in the lecture series (1818–31) published under the title *Aesthetics.*[29] It concludes a dis-

28. As far as I know, this is the first such prefatory remark of its kind in an English play. In the next decades, with the advent of Kemble's new techniques for historicizing the staging of Shakespeare, the attention to anachronism in the drama becomes more commonplace. In the 1840s, for example, Wordsworth could look back on his composition of *The Borderers* in the late 1790s and lament that he had not attended more carefully to the "manners" of the thirteenth-century society in which the action is ostensibly set.

29. G. W. F. Hegel, *Aesthetics: Lectures on Fine Arts,* trans. T. M. Knox, 2 vols. (Oxford: Clarendon Press, 1975). Hereafter cited by page number only in the text.

cussion that suggests that poets tend to select their subject matter from past epochs because such a choice makes it possible for the relationship of the internal and the external components of a culture to be itself externalized, brought into view. On Hegel's account, in other words, the aesthetic representation of a scene set in the past enables one to regard the crucial relationship, as Hegel puts it, between the inner subjectivity of character and the external objectivity of culture as making up a single world—what Hegel calls a "concrete reality." Hegel's concept of cultural intelligibility is grounded in a posited system of correspondences by which we know, for any individual, that his or her culture is his or hers. (The Hegelian premise about such a system of correspondences no doubt underlay Lukács's observation, to which I have referred more than once, about historicism's derivation of individual personality from the peculiarity of historical circumstances.) In Hegel's *Aesthetics,* this notion of the fit between character and culture, of how the internal and external elements of a given state of culture compose a single totality, becomes a problem when we ask how this totality can itself be integrated into a trans- or supraepochal conception of things. If this totality is defined in its historicity, how can it be opened toward the future subjects for whom it is represented in literary art?[30]

Hegel's argument elaborates the problem by way of an aesthetic—or, more precisely, a *theatrical*—metaphor. His analogy for the coherence of a historical culture—perhaps unsurprisingly, in light of the role assigned to conversation in Moore, Hazlitt, and Scott—is that of the mutual intelligibility of speakers in dramatic dialogue. The external element of culture has the coherence of a two speakers in a play who must not only speak intelligibly as individuals but constitute an intelligible relationship. The fit of internal character with an external culture so understood can then be metaphorized in terms of the fit between the participants in a staged dramatic dialogue and the audience that must find that dialogue intelligible: "The actors, for example, in the performance of a drama do not speak merely to one another but to us, and they should be intelligible in

---

30. The problem of historical representation for a set of relations configured in this way is as follows: if the historical culture understood as the formative condition of past character must have a coherence like that of the mutual intelligibility of characters speaking to one another in a play, how can this concrete totality be made likewise comprehensible to participants in a later, different cultural moment. Or, as Hegel himself puts it:

> [T]he question arises of how a work of art has to be framed in respect of the external aspects of locality, customs, usages, religious, political, social, moral conditions: namely whether the artist should forget his own time and keep his eye only on the past and its actual existence, so that his work is a true picture of what has gone; or whether he is not only entitled but in duty bound to take account solely of his own nation and contemporaries, and fashion his work according to ideas which coincide with the particular circumstances of his own time. (p. 265)

both these respects. And so every work of art is a dialogue with everyone who confronts it" (1:265). "Necessary anachronism" figures as the "solution" to this problem at the point when Hegel argues that the second-order "dialogue" between the speaking characters and the audience (understood as character and culture) can in turn, and by the same token, be offered in an aesthetic representation of the past itself as a dramatic scene for a modern audience to observe. The relation of past character to past culture in a historical representation can, and must, be as intelligible in its pathos as a scene played between two actors in one's own culture. The composition of the scene *as historical* thus involves a culture defined as the scene of dialogical exchange *and* of a relationship between any given character and that cultural scene *and* that character-culture relationship as a second-order scene in relation to the audience of the later moment in which it is represented.

As it happens, Hegel gives the problem of anachronism and its solution a nationalist inflection. The Germans, he charges, err on the "objectivizing" or antiquarian side of the historicist dilemma, paying all respect to the integrity of the cultural past at the expense of the culture of the present. The French err on the "subjectivizing" or modernist side of the dilemma, subordinating the difference of the past to the forms and desires of present culture. The English are said to get the balance right, to understand that the subjectivity of the present must penetrate the objectivity of the representation of the ancient "fit" between character and culture. The greatest English dramatists have remodeled the past world as they represent it in order to emphasize those correspondences with the present that allow us to find that world intelligible and thus "ours." The English grasp the paradoxical essence of the principle of necessary anachronism, which says, in the face of a pseudo-"naturalism" of fidelity to circumstance (past *or* present), that one can and must transgress nature in defense of nature's own laws. The first natural law of art, for Hegel, is that the true work of art must be intelligible to everyone in the "interests and passions of its gods and men" (1:264).

Like Hegel, but not after him, the Englishman Shelley configures the problem of anachronism and the pastness of past culture in *The Cenci* by way of two sets of parallel relations: past character to past culture, on the one hand, and present audience to that past character-culture relationship, on the other. Like Hegel, too, Shelley represents these relations with metaphors taken from theater itself. In the first place, he insists that the story of the Cenci family, told and retold with interest for two centuries, is itself, before it comes to him,

> a tragedy which has already received, from its capacity of awakening and sustaining the sympathy of men, approbation and success. Nothing remained as I imagined, but to clothe it to

the apprehensions of my countrymen in such language and action as would bring it home to their hearts. (SPP, p. 239)

The force of the parallelism implicit in cultural anachronism becomes clear in Shelley's later remark about Beatrice: "the crimes and miseries in which she was an actor and a sufferer are as the mask and the mantle in which circumstances clothed her for her impersonation on the scene of the world" (SPP, p. 242). Reading Shelley's metaphors in Hegel's terms, one would conclude that Beatrice, in her pure nature, steps into the world as into a tragedy, with its parts and its costumery. Her world is external to her, but it becomes hers, Hegel would say, by virtue of the fit, the pattern of correspondence, that develops between her and it.[31]

In the *Defence of Poetry*, perhaps reflecting on his recent dramatic efforts in *The Cenci*, Shelley produced a short account of the kind of fit he saw in different cultural moments, a kind of historical anthropology of such "correspondences": "Every epoch under names more or less specious has deified its peculiar errors; Revenge is the naked Idol of the worship of a semi-barbarous age; and Self-deceit is the veiled Image of unknown evil before which luxury and satiety lie prostrate" (pp. 486–87). The promise held out by the age of casuistical self-deceit, presumably, lies in the implicit recognition that revenge is unacceptable—that it must be covered up. But, so long as casuistry itself goes unexposed, the cycle of revenge will continue. The double triumph, of revenge over forbearance, and of self-deceit over honesty, is what constitutes the tragedy of *The Cenci* as it comes to Shelley's hands, already made and played, as he suggests, before he touches it. How then are we to understand his own work of "clothing" this action for the contemporary audience? What does it mean for him to put into costume this already "encostumed" (or accustomed) tragic action?

On the logic of Hegel's necessary anachronism, in which past culture is to past character as the past culture–character relationship is to present readers or audiences, we would assume that the clothes Shelley supplies for the tragedy of Beatrice's-being-clothed-tragically-by-her-circumstances would ultimately

---

31. For other accounts of the problem of embodiment in *The Cenci*, see Jerrold Hogle, *Shelley's Process*, pp. 148–150; and Andrea Henderson, *Romantic Identities: Varieties of Subjectivity 1774–1830* (Cambridge: Cambridge University Press, 1996), pp. 96–129. Both readings of the play helpfully link the issue of embodiment to the play's implicit theory of characterization, even though neither takes the analysis as far toward the problem of the "historical situation" as I think is called for by the play's interest in anachronism and casuistry. For an excellent account of the gender implications of embodiment and character in *The Cenci*, see Julie Carlson, *In the Theatre of Romanticism: Coleridge, Nationalism, and Women* (Cambridge: Cambridge University Press, 1994), pp. 188–204.

have to be put on by the audience itself. This would mean that we become the children of both Beatrice and Cenci, the offspring of their act of incest. This would mean not putting on Beatrice's knowledge with her power but putting on her self-deception with her weakness, even as she had done in the parricidal response to being raped by her own father. But just as we saw earlier that Shelley's spirit-of-the-age historicism was not capturable by the Hegelian paradigm of *Zeitgeist* and representative figure, so we must now realize that the Hegelian notion of anachronism is not the one that informs Shelley's conceptualization of that problem in *The Cenci*.

To see how Shelley is working out of the historicist framework of the Scottish Enlightenment rather than that of German Idealism, it may help to recognize the thematic overlap between *The Cenci* and *The Heart of Mid-Lothian*. Like Scott's post-Smithian subordination of casuistry to "sensibility" (what I earlier called the "case of the heart"), Shelley's stated project in *The Cenci* is to represent the story in such a way as to "touch the hearts of my countrymen." Like Scott, he seeks to catch the conscience of the nation by aesthetic means. Like Scott, as well, Shelley has markedly juxtaposed a historic legal case with significant attention to the form of the ethical case that obtained in that past culture. Although Shelley makes no mention of ethical casuistry in his "Memorandum" about the "case" that was brought before the Corte Savella, that discourse is conspicuously in evidence in both the play and its preface. Rome in 1599, the setting of Shelley's play, was a heyday for "jesuitical casuistry," and it is precisely the jesuitical mentality that Shelley describes when he stresses in his preface that, for the Roman Catholic of 1599, "[r]eligion pervades intensely the whole frame of society, and is according to the temper of the mind which it inhabits, a passion, a persuasion, an excuse, a refuge; never a check" (SPP, p. 241).[32] This passion, persuasion, or excuse shows crucially in the casuistical tendencies of the play's key characters, especially in those whom Shelley invented or most lavishly elaborated from the historical record.

One of his dramatic inventions, for example, is the priest Orsino, the treacherous counselor and would-be lover to Beatrice, who exemplifies the Rome of 1599 as a casuistical culture. Orsino's "self-anatomizing" soliloquies repeatedly display a mind bred to the ways of casuistry, as for example when, in a soliloquy that acknowledges his having become "a poor figure to [his] own esteem," he must assure himself: "I'll do / As little mischief as I can; that thought / Shall fee

---

32. See the historical trajectory for casuistry mapped by Albert R. Jonsen and Stephen Toulmin, *The Abuse of Casuistry* (Berkeley: University of California Press, 1988), where 1550–1650 is seen as the period of peak activity.

the accuser conscience."[33] Of course, Beatrice's is the centrally tragic conscience in the play, and, to see the casuistical mind at work, one could turn to any of the several speeches in act IV, where she talks herself into the murder of her father in spite of the scruples of her collaborators:

> . . . our act
> Will but dislodge a spirit of deep hell
> Out of a human form. (IV. ii. 6–8)

> Believe that heaven is merciful and just,
> And will not add our dread necessity
> To the amount of his offences. (IV. ii. 13–15)

> . . . his death will be
> But as a change of sin-chastising dreams,
> A dark continuance of the Hell within him,
> Which God extinguish! (IV. ii. 31–34)

> We do but that which 'twere a deadly crime
> To leave undone. (IV. iii. 37–38)

Earlier, Beatrice had recognized in Orsino the presence of "a sly equivocating vein" that "suits [her] not"; her very first words to him are "Pervert not truth, / Orsino" (I. ii. 147–48). By the end of the play, Beatrice has "teed" her conscience handsomely in Orsino's sort of currency. Indeed, she can even deny her role in the murder of her father at enormous expense to her accomplice, the servant Marzio, who undergoes the rack for her sake in the final trial scene as she persists in asserting her own innocence. Since Beatrice's acquired capacity for self-justification is what makes her homicidal scheme both possible and "necessary," one could say that the gradual immersion of her conscience in the murky medium of casuistry amounts to nothing less than the play's primary line of development.

A strong link thus binds the conceptualization of "action" in the play and its dependency on the form of the case. In fact, the link between the dramatic and

---

33. Orsino's self-anatomy involves a projection onto Beatrice of his own bad conscience, as we learn in his very first soliloquy: "I fear," he says,

> Her subtle mind, her awe-inspiring gaze,
> Whose beams anatomize me nerve by nerve
> And lay me bare, and make me blush to see
> My hidden thoughts. (I.ii.83–87)

the casuistical becomes virtually as explicit in Shelley's preface as it would in Kenneth Burke's writings of a century and a half later. The dramatic and the casuistical modes, Shelley suggests, have a similar relation to issues of principle, precept, or dogma. Just as casuistry is self-anatomizing and circumstantial, so too with the drama:

> There must . . . be nothing attempted to make the exhibition subservient to what is vulgarly termed a moral purpose. The highest moral purpose aimed at in the highest species of the drama, is the teaching the human heart, through its sympathies and antipathies, the knowledge of itself; in proportion to the possession of which knowledge, every human being is wise, just, sincere, tolerant and kind. If dogmas can do more, it is well; but a drama is no fit place for the enforcement of them. (SPP, p. 240)

Casuistry, like the drama, is not an inert body of rules—nor, for that matter, a repertoire of examples—but rather a form of practice, an activity, a strategy of application. It is always on the move—"restless" is Shelley's later word for it.[34] To explicate his point, Shelley cites two moral dogmas: one from Socrates and one from Christ. The first maxim is that "no person can be truly dishonored by the act of another," and the second is that "the fit return to make to the most enormous injuries is kindness and forbearance, and a resolution to convert the injurer from his dark passions" (i.e., "Revenge, retaliation, atonement are pernicious mistakes") (SPP, p. 240). While Shelley concedes that, "if Beatrice had thought in this manner she would have been better and wiser," he insists that in that event she would nonetheless have failed to interest a theatrical audience. She would not have been a character. She would not have been a case.[35]

But how, for any such audience, can the historical spectacle of casuistical self-deceit become the occasion of self-knowledge? Or, to return to the question about the play's relation to Hegelian "necessary anachronism," we may ask: how does *The Cenci* manage to avoid the sense that the mutual fit between Beatrice and her culture must be matched by the fit between the audience and that mutually fitting relationship? It is certainly true, as P. M. S. Dawson has written, that "*The Cenci* poses the story of Beatrice as a problem, and impels the audience to an examination of their own reactions in order to work out its solution, rather

34. On the relation of ethical and theatrical practice in *The Cenci*, see Julie Carlson, *In the Theatre of Romanticism*, pp. 194–95.

35. The interinvolvement of the categories of casuistry and dramatic circumstance extends even to the question of the case of persons in the theatrical audience (i.e., how they are situated). Qualifying his claim about how the spectacle of a morally perfect Beatrice could not interest theater-goers, Shelley argues that the "few" whom such a spectacle *might* have interested "could never have been sufficiently interested for a dramatic purpose, from the want of finding sympathy in their interest among the mass who surround them" (SPP, p. 240).

than imposing authorial dogma."[36] It is also reasonable to speculate with Stuart Sperry on the typical pattern that such "reactions" might follow:

> Let us consider the conflicting and alternative judgments we are invited to make. Beatrice's own crime is murder, parricide; the most heinous of offenses; the betrayal of one's begetter to whom honor and obedience are naturally due. Yet weigh against this our revulsion at incestuous rape, a violation, moreover, that is the deliberate and culminating cruelty against an innocent child who merits love and not dishonor. Caught up in the emotional dialectics of the predicament, the imagination of the reader is propelled back and forth between two sets of ethical imperatives in the effort to establish some preponderance between them, in the attempt, that is, to justify the one enormity by the other, only to find the task impossible.[37]

Sperry's reader-response narrative reads uncannily like an account of the process that we have been treating as constitutive of the case form—the irresolution of judgment, the vacillation of the mind, what Jolles called the *Schwanken und Schwingen* of the scales in the act of casuistical deliberation. But as with Scott's novels, and indeed with the other cases we have considered under the rubric of "England in 1819," *The Cenci* presents more than just a case. It presents a case of a case, a case made and taken as if with full understanding (as it were) of Jolles' account of the case as a cognitive form. Part of the "theater" in this drama, in other words, is the moral spectacle of deliberation itself. Where Hegel sees the English approach as resting on the perfect point of balance between the French subjective subordination of the past to the present and the German objective subordination of the present to the past, the Englishman Shelley seems more interested, like Scott, in the historical spectacle of balancing *acts* (as such)—and the institutional means by which they are conducted. The maxim is that circumstances alter cases, but Shelley's interest lies, in part, in the circumstances of casuistry itself. On this account, the casuistical resort to circumstantial justification proves to comprise, at once, the dramatic character of the action and suffering, the action and suffering of the dramatic character, and the means of interpreting both.

3. Requisites of Historical Judgment

In chapter 3, discussing the general revival of interest in casuistry in the post-Waterloo period, I cited Shelley's claim in the preface to *The Cenci* that

---

36. P. M. S. Dawson, *The Unacknowledged Legislator: Shelley and Politics* (Oxford and New York: Oxford University Press, 1980), p. 216. See also Lawrence Lockridge, "Justice in *The Cenci*," *The Wordsworth Circle*, 19 (spring 1988): 95–98. See Marlon Ross on Shelley's relation to didacticism in "Shelley's Wayward Dream-Poem: The Apprehending Reader in *Prometheus Unbound*," *The Keats-Shelley Journal* 36 (1987): 110–33.

37. Sperry, *Shelley's Major Verse: The Narrative and Dramatic Poetry* (Cambridge, Mass.: Harvard University Press, 1988), pp. 137–38. Sperry is in part working from Earl Wasserman's long and complex reading of the role of skepticism in *The Cenci* in *Shelley: A Critical Reading* (Baltimore: Johns Hopkins University Press, 1971), pp. 84–128.

Beatrice's dramatic character is actually *constituted* in the casuistical response her case elicits: "It is in the restless and anatomizing casuistry with which men seek the justification of Beatrice, yet feel that she has done what needs justification . . . that the dramatic character of what she did and suffered, consists" (p. 240). Now, in the context of the preface's account of the drama of historical circumstantiality, the force of this remarkable declaration can be allowed full resonance. It is not just that the duality of the audience response, the active "seeking" of the justification and passive "feeling" of the need for justification, corresponds to the duality of Beatrice's dramatic character—what she "did and suffered." Shelley's explicit and startling claim here is that the latter actually "consists" in the former: the play's action and suffering take place in the active and passive ("seeking" and "feeling") casuistical responses of its spectators. Moreover, the narrator of the preface illustratively performs the very point described here in the ekphrastic passage on the face of Beatrice in the Colonna-Palace portrait (then attributed to Guido) in which we are told that the "crimes and miseries in which she was an actor and a sufferer are as the mask and the mantle in which circumstances clothed her for her impersonation on the scene of the world" (p. 242). In this passage, it is clear that the Shelleyan narrator of the preface indulges precisely the sort of restless and anatomizing casuistry that constitutes Beatrice's dramatic character.[38]

We are now closer to understanding how the Shelleyan narrator's own dramatization of his point about the casuistical response to Beatrice helps answer the question about how one can imagine casuistry as producing self-revelation. But to do so we need to go back to those key terms in Shelley's initial description of Beatrice Cenci as "a young maiden" who was "evidently a most gentle and amiable being, a creature formed to adorn and be admired, and thus violently thwarted from her nature by the necessity of circumstance and opinion." The language that Shelley uses here belongs to a philosophical idiom strongly associated with the name of Shelley's father-in-law, William Godwin. It was Godwin who was identified in the 1790s with what was then called the doctrine of necessity. After his own conversion experience, Wordsworth is supposed to have told a young friend in the 1790s to throw away his books of

---

38. And indeed throughout the play, as Stuart Curran has noted in *Shelley's Cenci: Scorpions Ringed with Fire* (Princeton, N.J.: Princeton University Press, 1970), Shelley has "lavished on Beatrice 'the restless and anatomizing casuistry' that he asserts her history provokes among all classes of men (exercising it with such skill that he justifies her action by creating an ethical system necessitating it" (p. 140). See also Michael O'Neill's related comment apropos of *The Cenci* that "Shelley is made uneasy by and tries to offer a justification for the aesthetic pleasure given by "tragic fiction" in *The Human Mind's Imaginings: Conflict and Achievement in Shelley's Poetry* (Oxford: Clarendon Press, 1989), p. 74.

chemistry and read Godwin on necessity.[39] And it was Godwin, explaining the doctrine of necessity, who argued that our actions follow from our opinions and our opinions are governed by our institutionally determined circumstances. In crafting his characterization of Beatrice as he has done, Shelley is making a Godwinian account of her fate, and of her case.

Perhaps Shelley's most insightful comment on Godwin appears in a review he wrote in 1817 of one of Godwin's late novels, *Mandeville* (1817), which included an extended comparison of *Mandeville* and Godwin's first novel, *Caleb Williams,* which quickly followed the initial publication of the *Enquiry Concerning Political Justice* in the 1790s. One passage from this review has long been understood as particularly germane to *The Cenci.* It contrasts the title character of *Mandeville* with Falkland in *Caleb Williams,* the character often associated with Edmund Burke. Falkland is a benevolent aristocrat who covertly murders a tyrannical local landholder after the latter has insulted him in a public setting. It is because young Caleb Williams discovers Falkland's secret that he is hunted relentlessly by Falkland until Williams finally informs the authorities of Falkland's secret. This is Shelley's 1817 comparative commentary on the cases of Falkland and Mandeville:

> The interest of this novel is undoubtedly equal, in some respects superior, to that of *Caleb Williams.* Yet there is no character like Falkland, whom the author, *with that sublime casuistry which is the parent of toleration and forbearance,* persuades us personally to love, whilst his actions must for ever remain the theme of our astonishment and abhorrence. Mandeville challenges our compassion, and no more. His errors arise from an immutable necessity of internal nature, and from much of a constitutional antipathy and suspicion, which soon sprang up into a hatred and contempt and barren misanthropy, which, as it had no root in genius or in virtue, produces no fruit uncongenial with the soil wherein it grew. Those of Falkland arose from a high, though perverted conception of the majesty of human nature, from a powerful sympathy with his species, and from a temper which led him to believe that the very reputation of excellence should walk among mankind, unquestioned and undefiled. [my italics][40]

Applying these terms to *The Cenci,* one might say that, in their anatomizing casuistry, the spectators of the play sympathize with the case of Beatrice. But this is not in itself the sublime casuistry that Shelley has in view when he is speaking

39. For good recent accounts of Godwin on the "doctrine of necessity," see Peter H. Marshall, *William Godwin* (New Haven: Yale University Press, 1984), pp. 118–43; and Mark Philp, *Godwin's Political Justice* (Ithaca, N.Y.: Cornell University Press), pp. 89–96.

40. Shelley, *Prose Works,* 1:277. More than one commentator has invoked the notion of "sublime casuistry" here to make sense of what Shelley is doing in his conceptual framing of the action of *The Cenci.* See, for example, Wasserman, *Shelley,* pp. 115–26. My larger argument about the transformation of casuistry, the invention of the historical situation, and the transformations of the case provides, I hope, a more far-reaching frame of reference in both coming to terms with Shelley's project and seeing its broader implications. On the impact of *Mandeville* more generally in Shelley's work see Burton R. Pollin, "Godwin's Mandeville in Poems of Shelley," *Keats-Shelley Memorial Bulletin* 19 (1968): 33–40.

of Godwin. Nor is it exactly his task, as it would become Brecht's, to break out of this kind of theater of sympathy by way of an estrangement effect. Shelley's aim is to show that the sympathy of the spectator with Beatrice has its basis in a two-fold recognition: the first phase is the spectator's recognition of himself or herself in Beatrice.[41] This is the sort of recognition that Shelley describes in *A Defence of Poetry* when he argues that Athenian tragedies "are as mirrors in which the spectator beholds himself, under a thin disguise of circumstance, stript of all but that ideal perfection and energy which every one feels to be the internal type of all that he loves, admires and would become" (SPP, p. 490). The second phase of this recognition is that the spectator and the tragic subject (Beatrice, in this case) are alike in being agents largely determined by the particular historical situation in which each appears.

The possibility of such a recognition is itself a relatively recent historical phenomenon, in the sense that it is part and parcel with the age of the spirit of the age. Such a possibility is indeed the material basis for the "hope" that Shelley thinks it is reasonable for the English people to have in 1819, even in the face of the dire conditions that he lists in his end-of-year sonnet. Beatrice herself could have had no reasonable hope of this sort. Her historical situation is much like Tasso's, as Shelley described it in a letter of late 1818, after he visited the great library in Ferrara and consulted Tasso's manuscripts there. Shelley seems at first to have been offended by the obsequiousness of the poems he found in Tasso's papers, but the very fact of the *manuscript* state of these writings eventually led him to an act of historical casuistry in *defense of Tasso:*

> Some of those Mss of Tasso were sonnets to his persecutor which contain a great deal of what is called flattery. If Alfonso's ghost were asked how he felt these praises now I wonder what he would say. But to me there is much more to pity than to condemn in these entreaties and praises of Tasso. It is as a Christian prays to [and] praises his God whom he knows to [be] the most remorseless capricious & inflexible of tyrants, but whom he knows also to be omnipotent. Tasso's situation was widely different from that of any persecuted being of the present day, for from the depth of dungeons public opinion might now at length be awakened to an echo that would startle the oppressor. But then there was no hope. There is something irresistibly pathetic to me in the sight of Tasso's own hand writing moulding expressions of

---

41. From the point of view of audience psychology, the structure of action in *The Cenci* is strikingly like that of *Caleb Williams:* in both cases we confront a character (Beatrice, Caleb) patient beyond what we can imagine with repeated acts of abuse and persecution who finally takes the measures that have long been open to them to remedy their situations, only to dramatize a response that makes the reader regret the act that had seemed so necessary in the moment. The measure in the case of Falkland (informing the authorities) is different from that of Beatrice's, but then her case is more severe and her enemy more monstrous. The literature on Shelley's complex personal and intellectual relations with Godwin is too large to list here, but an excellent introduction is provided in William St. Clair, *The Godwins and the Shelleys* (Baltimore: Johns Hopkins University Press, 1989), especially pp. 315–43.

adulation & entreaty to a deaf & stupid tyrant in an age when the most heroic virtue would have exposed its possessor to hopeless persecution, and—such is the alliance between virtue & genius—which unoffending genius could not escape. (LPBS, 2:46–47)

Beatrice, obviously, inhabited the same kind of culture as Tasso, as far as Shelley was concerned, and this connection constitutes an important link between their cases.

It becomes crucial to recognize at this juncture that the "story" that Shelley made the basis for his dramatic composition in *The Cenci* was itself something he found in manuscript state. Indeed, in a politically explosive passage that appears in the first draft of the preface to *The Cenci* but was struck before publication, Shelley commented directly on the implications of the medium in which he discovered the narrative for the *events* of which it tells: "The papal Government has taken the most extraordinary precautions against the publicity of facts which offer so tragical a commentary on its own wickedness & weakness, so that the communication of the Mss had become a matter of some difficulty. This has produced a number of variations in the story all corresponding however in all points of importance."[42] Shelley's representation of the culture of Torquato Tasso and Beatrice Cenci makes clear, by contrast, that his hope for his own time depends on the possibility of the exchange of views in public forms, on the technologies that allow writing to be circulated in wider and wider readerships, and on the capacity of particular individuals to reach and shape public opinion.

It was just this set of conditions to which Hazlitt referred a few years later in his overview of the age of revolution (for the *Life of Napoleon*) when he wrote that "the French Revolution might be described as the remote but inevitable result of the invention of the art of printing." The press diffuses knowledge and inquiry, and as soon as "the world (that dread jury) are impannelled, and called to look on and be umpires in the scene, so that nothing is done by connivance or in a corner, then reason mounts the judgment-seat in lieu of passion or interest, and [public] opinion becomes law, instead of arbitrary will" (CWWH, 13:39). And it was this condition that Adam Smith had already begun to anticipate and to theorize in his account of human beings' sympathetically responding to the imagination of each other's cases. But while Shelley's sublime casuistry seems to depend on the possibility of the sort of "commerce" of public recognition that is implicit in the accounts of Smith and Hazlitt, it does not simply *reduce* to either Hazitt's widening of the public court of opinion or the exercise of commercial sympathy of the sort described in Smith's moral

42. Shelley, *Notebooks,* 3 vols., ed. H. Burton Forman (St. Louis: William K. Bisby, 1911), 2:90–91.

theory.[43] That is, Shelleyan "sympathy" is not conceived primarily as a form of Smithian exchange among contemporaries, members of a cohort in a world of commerce, but is instead a bridge between different historical situations. The three figures of casuistical sympathy we are considering—Tasso in the letter, Beatrice in *The Cenci,* and even Godwin's Falkland in *Caleb Williams*—all belong to a distinctly precommercial order. Like Scott's case-based historical fiction, Shelley's sublime casuistry crosses the premodern/modern divide, such that not only this or that character becomes an object of empathy or judgment but also whole cultures of judgment as well. The ethical capacities Shelley esteems most highly—those which distinguish his "select few" (a Falkland over a Mandeville)—involve acts of sympathy and judgment with noncontemporaries.

In relation to the question of exemplarity and history, Shelley is nonetheless not assuming a return to the kind of "teaching by example" that Koselleck sees as routine in historiographical practice for the age before historicism. He is not attempting to reestablish the fungibility of moral examples from different periods in respect to a set of moral precepts. As we have seen, the relationship of the precept and example is subjected to serious critique in Shelley's work of this period, culminating in *A Defence of Poetry.* Nor is Shelley *merely* interested in what Koselleck calls history as a teacher of direction or tendency, though he clearly sees the new possibilities of "movement" in history. To appreciate Shelley's project in all its subtlety, we need to discriminate between several senses of "case" or "situation" in play in his challenging casuistical work.

First, there is the sense of a scene of action, a set of circumstances confronted in the moment of judgment, that must be "typed" in some way—identified by kind—in order to understand how a normative framework should be brought to bear on one's will: roughly, the sense of the case in the various religiously oriented ethical casuistries of the sixteenth and seventeenth centuries, as shown in Beatrice Cenci's speeches in defense of her act of parricide. A second sense of the case or situation is that of a scene not of action but of suffering, a set of circumstances in which one is, according to the laws of probability, likely to feel this or that sort of impulse. This is the notion of the case, as we have seen, that governs Adam Smith's effort to go beyond the project of the earlier religious casuistry as he understood it in favor of a reliance on "sensibility" and a theoriza-

---

43. For an account of the relation between the discourse of the sublime and eighteenth-century political economy, see Peter de Bolla, *The Discourse of the Sublime: History, Aesthetics & the Subject* (Oxford: Blackwell, 1989), pp. 59–140. For a discussion of Shelley's relation to the sublime more generally, see Angela Leighton, *Shelley and the Sublime: An Interpretation of the Major Poems* (Cambridge: Cambridge University Press, 1984), especially pp. 1–47.

tion of the "sentimental." A third sense of the case, however, is the one that we have seen worked out theoretically in the arguments of Bentham in the post-Waterloo period. Here the case is to be understood as a scene of motivation, where the distinction between "action" and "feeling" is elided in favor of an understanding of character as formed in or derived from specifically historical conditions. This is the understanding of the case that I have described as the invention of the historical situation and linked with a doctrine that I have called, for convenience, a casuistry of the general will. Shelley, I have suggested, not only knew this argument in Bentham but also understood its relation to the Godwinian doctrines of the 1790s.

Shelley seems to have grasped that as a framework for action, his kind of casuistry required the general transformation of society from top to bottom, with all (as he put it) "its superstructure of maxims and forms." In the concept of a "sublime casuistry," though, Shelley hints at a stage beyond this historical casuistry, or at least suggests a way of describing the same phenomenon from another perspective, as if the casuistry of the general will—the discipline for altering the case of the state—had to be accompanied by a sensibility that is itself involved in relations between historical states. This is because, in the kind of casuistry with which a spectator can see the historical situation of a Tasso or a Beatrice as hopeless and see their efforts at self-exculpation as a function of their helplessness, one is able to achieve a sympathy defined not by the relations of getting and spending in Smith's commercial world but by what Edmund Burke (the prototype of Godwin's Falkland) called the "partnership not only between those who are living, but between those who are living, those who are dead, and those who are to be born."[44] Only in this kind of casuistry, in other words, is the historically conditioned dimension of epoch-making action fully acknowledged. Only in such a framework can we imagine the outlines of a progressive-regressive method and understand that when we make history we do so under conditions that are not, at least in the first instance, of our own making.

Shelley's work of this period registers the force of the new historicist concept even, or especially, when he seems bent on overcoming it in some way. Such an explanation accounts, I think, for that strange echo of his comment about anachronism in the preface to *The Cenci* ("I have . . . sought to avoid the error of making them actuated by my own conceptions of right or wrong . . . , thus under a thin veil converting the names and actions of the sixteenth century into cold impersonations of my own mind" [SPP, p. 240]) when he comes to

---

44. Burke, *Reflections,* p. 110. On Falkland and Burke, see Marilyn Butler, "Godwin, Burke, and *Caleb Williams*" *Essays in Criticism* 32 (July 1982): 237–57.

write *A Defence of Poetry:* "A Poet . . . would do ill to embody his own conceptions of right and wrong, which are usually those of his time and place, in his poetical creations, which participate in neither" (SPP, p. 488). In the preface, the poet avoids his own conceptions of right and wrong out of respect for historical relativity; in the *Defence,* the poet does so out of respect for historical transcendence. We might understand this apparent discrepancy as a function of Shelley's change in views over the year and a half between the two compositions. But we might also understand that Shelley grasps the strong interdependency of these concepts. It is *within* the argument of the *Defence* itself, after all, that we can find Shelley's distinction between a story and poem:

> A poem is the very image of life expressed in its eternal truth. There is this difference between a story and a poem, that a story is a catalogue of detached facts, which have no other bond of connexion than time, place, circumstance, cause and effect; the other is the creation of actions according to the unchangeable forms of human nature, as existing in the mind of the creator, which is itself the image of all other minds. The one is partial, and applies only to a definite period of time, and a certain combination of events which can never again recur; the other is universal, and contains within itself the germ of a relation to whatever motives or actions have place in the possible varieties of human nature. . . . The story of particular facts is as a mirror which obscures and distorts that which should be beautiful: Poetry is a mirror which makes beautiful that which is distorted. (SPP, p. 485)

This sort of passage is susceptible, on quick reading, to an interpretation that would reduce all that I have been arguing about Shelley's historicism to a flattened universalist posture. But while it is certainly true that the poem/story distinction looks invidious, it is also true that the relation of these two forms of mirroring is itself structured by a mirroring or chiastic trope. The poem and story are mirrors of one another's mirroring activities, and if the poem has beauty on its side, the story has reality to claim for itself. While the story distorts what "should be" beautiful, the poem beautifies what "is" distorted.

As a "poem," *The Cenci* beautifies that which has been distorted by story, *historia,* history as "what hurts," as Jameson memorably puts it. History's disfigurement of Beatrice, her grotesque mask and mantle of historical circumstance, appears as a disfigurement from the point of view of her prehistorical character, whose beauty is an "idealization" of her historical distortion. Shelley comes close to anticipating such a scheme in the 1819 preface to *The Cenci* when, describing the "story of the Cenci [as] indeed eminently fearful and monstrous," he argues the need to "increase the ideal, and diminish the actual horror of the events, so that the pleasure which arises from the poetry which exists in these tempestuous sufferings and crimes may mitigate the pain of the contemplation of the moral deformity from which they spring" (pp. 239–40). Before the end of the year Shelley would turn from tempestuous Rome in 1599 to confront the contemporary situation more directly in the sonnet, *England in 1819*. There he would in effect radicalize the claim of the Preface to *The Cenci*, suggesting now that the "poetry" which exists in the sufferings and crimes of "our tempestuous day," as he composes them for the sonnet, would not only provide pleasure to mitigate pain but would indeed become the constituted medium of a necessary and transformative illumination.

4. A Second Look at *Peter Bell the Third*

For Shelley, dramatic tragedy stages the history of the case in which the maxim that "circumstances alter cases" proves illusory. It is the mode in which the will to suspend disbelief relaxes into an identification with the historical actor who has to play his or her historical part but not with the part itself. It is the refusal of the notion that historical actors can, in either sense of the word, *become* their parts. But an issue that remains unclear after this analysis of *The Cenci* is whether, for the Shelley of 1819, the normative domain in virtue of which the world of "stories" is constituted as fallen, as cases, is to be located in the future state of a transcendent sphere or in the "future state" of a historical order. On this point, Shelley's historicism seems to differ almost as much from the late political economy of the Scottish Enlightenment through Bentham (in which universal history is without direction but not without directability) as from the rational system of Hegel (for whom universal history's direction and its directability amount to the same thing). For Millar, as for Bentham, the successive states of society follow a structured progression, but the states of the world that set the conditions for these unevenly developing societies do *not* follow such a progression. For Hegel, the states of the world do follow progressively to the moment of Hegel's own monumental articulation of the rational necessity of that very fact. Shelley, however, writes not from a *logic* of necessity but a from a *sentiment* of it. The "sentiment of the necessity" of change is thus a hope. It is a hope in a future state of aesthetically regulated social fulfillment born of specific conditions (a specific state of the society and of the world) but with universalist aspirations.

This emphasis is clear enough in *A Philosophical View of Reform*. Writing just at the end of 1819 or the beginning of 1820, Shelley led into his reflections "On the Sentiment of the Necessity of Change" by distinguishing two "circumstances" in the general contemporary sense of historical movement: "Two circumstances arrest the attention of those who turn their regard to the present political condition of the English nation—first that there is an almost universal sentiment of the approach of some change to be wrought in the institutions of the government, and secondly the necessity and desirableness of such a change." Shelley goes on to state that the first of these "propositions" could brook no public dissent, since it was a "matter of fact," and that the second, though a "matter of opinion," was nonetheless "clearly established" to the "mind of all," except those with vested interests to the contrary (WPBS, 7:20).

The assumed primacy of "fact" and "opinion" in his analysis should remind us that Shelley is self-consciously working in the Benthamite mode, arguing from the circumscribed horizon of the utilitarian maxim of the "greatest good for the greatest number." The "desire for change" in Shelley's account, presumably as both "fact" and "opinion," arises from what he calls "the profound sentiment of the exceeding inefficiency of the existing institutions to provide for the physical and intellectual happiness of the people." The criterion of "efficiency," however, suggests a first-order utilitarianism that, in keeping with the *View*'s critique of practical "application," betrays an insufficiently "philosophical" view of reform. It involves mechanical or nonreflexive models of political efficacy. In terms of Shelley's argument about the long-term shortcomings of American representational politics, in other words, such Benthamite "radicalism" fails to register that the goal of efficiency itself can never finally achieve a normative status. To represent an existing political will with fidelity or efficiency, rather than to improve as one represents it, is to fail to honor the second-order representational project of human perfectibility. To recall Shelley's paradoxical assumption, if one accepts that it is in the nature of the will to improve itself, then only a self-representation in which the will improves on itself can truly represent it.

Shelley's discussion of the limits of manuscript culture in the Italy of Tasso and Beatrice Cenci is carried on very much in this first-order utilitarian frame of reference. Shelley compares that culture invidiously with the public sphere of print culture in the late eighteenth and early nineteenth centuries in England, suggesting that in retrospect the situations of Beatrice and Tasso indeed appear to have been hopeless because of both the absence of a literary public and the means to reach it. Conversely, the print culture of Shelley's own moment and the technologies that enable its operations appear to be *necessary* conditions for hopefulness.[45] Print culture made it possible, as Shelley clearly implies in his

---

45. Two studies of the late 1980s have helped to redress what had been a relatively critical neglect of the question of Shelley's relation to audiences, publics, and publication: Ronald Tetreault, *The Poetry of Life: Shelley and Literary Form* (Toronto: University of Toronto Press, 1987), especially pp. 18–36; and Stephen C. Behrendt, *Shelley and his Audiences* (Lincoln: University of Nebraska Press, 1989), passim.

comments on the historical conditions that constrained Tasso and Beatrice Cenci, to achieve both a publicity of facts and of opinions. There is little reason to think, however, that Shelley considered that these new conditions amounted to *sufficient* grounds for radical social transformation. The problem turns out to be that, under a criterion of efficiency, the public sphere of letters, the literary system, inclines too much to the representation, precisely, of "fact" and "opinion." The conflicts played out in the new literary public sphere will be waged over what Shelley despairingly calls sad realities and enforceable dogmas.

Not surprisingly, it is in the poem in which he addresses this new literary system most directly, *Peter Bell the Third,* that Shelley most aggressively attempts to work through the issue of its own limitations. In its jocular balladic mode and allusive density, this poem not only manages a telling commentary on the new forms of secular typology—representative men and spirits of the age—as well as an anticipation of the "progressive-regressive method" (in its attention to the shaping of character in historical circumstance). It also, taking up its subject as a "case," very much concerns the failure of a literary culture conceived as a utilitarian sphere of fact and opinion to achieve true justice in its measures. And such a conception of the literary culture of this period was, as a matter of fact, generally enforced by the likes of the *Edinburgh Review.*

It was Francis Jeffrey, editor of that publication, who christened and then repeatedly chastised the Lake School of poetry in a series of reviews. The first of these attacks comes as early as 1802 in Jeffrey's notorious review of Southey's *Thalaba the Destroyer.*[46] Jeffrey's politics were explicitly Whiggish, his taste avowedly Augustan, a conjunction that defines the ideological framework of the Lake School's other great nemesis in this period, Lord Byron. Byron borrowed many of the arguments that he used against the Lakers, and in defense of Pope, quite directly from Jeffrey's writings, and, *Don Juan,* of course, provides ample illustration of Byron's Popean satire on the Lake School in the period of 1819.[47] At first glance, Shelley's treatment of the composite Lake Poet in *Peter Bell the Third* seems to take over wholesale the explicitly neo-Popean mode of *Don Juan,* which had been published between the time of the first two Peter Bells in early spring and the time when Shelley composed *Peter Bell the Third* itself. For example:

46. See Marilyn Butler on Southey's early preeminence in the school of poetry to which Wordsworth and Coleridge were also assigned in the early part of the Romantic period in "Plotting the Revolution: The Political Narratives of Romantic Poetry and Criticism," *Romantic Revolutions,* ed. Kenneth Johnston, et al. (Bloomington: Indiana University Press, 1990), pp. 133–57.

47. See Byron's portrait of Jeffrey in *Don Juan,* canto v, st. 11–16.

> Furious he rode, where late he ran,
>   Lashing and spurring his tame hobby;
> Turned to a formal Puritan,
> A solemn and unsexual man,—
>   He half believed *White Obi!* (ll. 548–52)

If Shelley's conspicuous mimicry of the style of *Don Juan* were not sufficient to identify it with the Byronic mode of satire, then certainly the poem's final vision would be. Shelley concludes with a condemnation of Wordsworth in unmistakably Popean terms, a mock apocalypse lifted directly out of *The Dunciad,* with Wordsworth, the counterpart of Pope's Colley Cibber, as the mighty dragon of dull wit:

> Seven miles above—below—around—
>   This pest of dulness holds its sway:
> A ghastly life without a sound;
> To Peter's soul the spell is bound—
>   How should it ever pass away? (ll. 768–72)

The silence here is reminiscent of the silence at the end of "Alastor," where the Wordsworthian poet acquiesces to the imagined comforts of a self-projected nature. But whereas in "Alastor" the critique is notoriously labile on account of the deep sympathy of the narrating poet with the Lake Poet whose solipsistic apostasy he relates, there initially appears to be no such sense of identification here in *Peter Bell the Third.*[48]

This view of the matter fails to grasp the complexity of the case in *Peter Bell the Third.* Indeed, it fails to recognize that the language of casuistry that punctu-

48. The claim that Shelley's poem does, in the first place, participate vigorously in the cultural movement we have been considering becomes clear when one compares Shelley's 1815 and 1819 poetic representations of Wordsworth. In lamenting Wordsworth's premature "death," Shelley seems deeply empathetic with his subject, especially in his fuller treatment of the matter in "Alastor." Such an interpretation need not rest on the poem's controversial preface, where what happens to the Wordsworthian poet is made to seem almost a direct function of his genius and goodness. One can see the evidence for it in the texture and rhetoric of the poem proper. The mode of "Alastor" is itself Wordsworthian; it seems to expose Wordsworth from within. By echoing Wordsworth even in the narrator's introductory verses, the poem seems to acknowledge a complicity in the Romantic ego it derides. The mode of *Peter Bell the Third,* on the other hand, seems to employ Augustan satiric distance to expose Wordsworth from without. This is, after all, one of the features that has led readers to see it as Byronic. See my "'Wordsworth' after Waterloo," in Johnson and Ruoff, eds., *William Wordsworth and the Age of English Romanticism,* pp. 84–111. Shelley's relation to Wordsworth is as poetically and psychologically complex as that of any two poets in the language. For a more detailed account of the Wordsworth-Shelley connection, see Kim Blank, *Wordsworth's Influence on Shelley: A Study of Poetic Authority* (London: Macmillan, 1988).

ates its preface (the allusions to conscience catching in *Hamlet,* the new system for "weighing" the merits of the Bells and the Fudges) is at least gesturally reactivated in the first section of the poem with the account of what might be called the allegory's triggering moment—the "death" of Peter Bell:

> And yellow death lay on his face;
>   And a fixed smile that was not human
> Told, as I understand the case,
> That he was gone to the wrong place:—
>   I heard all this from the old woman. (ll. 51–55)

For the Lake School ballad-narrator, the "case" of Peter Bell turns on the question of a judgment about his postmortal fate. The question is "up" or "down," and it is framed, to recall both the Preface to *The Cenci* and the *Defence of Poetry,* in terms of this narrator's "own conceptions of right or wrong." Peter's smile betrays that he has gone to the "wrong place." Understood as the initial moment in the reception history of the Lake School poets' writings of the 1790s—their first "death" into print—the presumption of adverse judgment on the "life" of Peter Bell would have to do with the inimical taste and reactionary politics Southey, Coleridge, and Wordsworth all had to confront in the first stages of their literary (after-) lives.

But far from siding with the enemies of the Lake poets, early or late, *Peter Bell the Third* is constantly staging their case as a *problem* for critical judgment. The great genius of this witty poem, in other words, is its capacity for the kind of second-order (i.e., historical) casuistry that, in addition to attacking the figure of the composite Lake Poet, takes account of the whole history of attacks within its own representation of the Lake Poets' checkered critical reception from the early 1790s through 1819. In part 5, Shelley depicts the Lake Poet in his *Lyrical Ballads* phase (1798–1800) with a powerful tribute. Despite the limitations of his earthly character, the Lake Poet's poetic genius is said to have triumphed in these poems:

> But Peter's verse was clear, and came
>   Announcing from the frozen hearth
> Of a cold age, that none might tame
> The soul of that diviner flame
>   It augured to the Earth. (ll. 433–37)

The Devil, however, whose stake in the matter runs high, is enraged at Peter's poetic triumph:

> When Peter's next new book found vent,
> The Devil to all the first Reviews
> A copy of it slyly sent,
> With five-pound note as compliment,
> And this short notice—"Pray abuse." (ll. 463–67)

Becoming progressively explicit in its topical references to the fate of the Lake Poets, the poem here seems to allegorize the next phase—that of Southey's *Thalaba the Destroyer* (1802) and Wordsworth's 1807 *Poems*—volumes that were decidedly "abused" by the likes of Jeffrey and the young Byron.

The later stages of this Romantic case-history can by summarized in brief detail. The Devil gathers up these reviews in a parcel and has them "Safely to Peter's house conveyed. / For carriage, ten-pence Peter paid—/ Untied them—read them—went half mad" (ll. 490–92). Peter then takes refuge in long excursions on his hobby horse and:

> After these ghastly rides, he came
> Home to his heart, and found from thence
> Much stolen of its accustomed flame,
> His thoughts grew weak, drowsy, and lame
> Of their intelligence.
>
> To Peter's view, all seemed one hue;
> He was no Whig, he was no Tory;
> No Deist and no Christian he;—
> He got so subtle, that to be
> Nothing, was all his glory. (ll. 559–68)

He is now in a position to be had for a farthing: "in his Country's dying face / He looked" and "coolly to his own soul said;—/ 'Do you not think that we might make / A poem on her when she's dead'" (ll. 589–96). These stanzas certainly convey a sense of deep disappointment in the failure of the Lake Poets to keep political faith.

This is not to say, however, that the stanzas are finally Byronic in attitude. In light of the way in which Peter's reception history is represented within the narrative of his poetic and political development, one simply cannot take the poem's own Popean attack on Wordsworth at face value. The perversion of Peter's genius, the self-aggrandizement and self-absorption of his later work, is on Shelley's account ultimately linked to the reviewers' first assault on him, and this assault is in turn linked to Byron's and Jeffrey's commitment to Popean satire. Such an interpretation of *Peter Bell the Third* gains resonance from a poetic fragment that Shelley composed perhaps as early as the first months of 1820. This poem constructs an elaborate analogy between the assumptions of a degraded Christian eschatology and those of the modern satirist. The argument is elaborated through two parallel series of conditional clauses and conclusions. The hypothetical case for Christianity is put this way: if the instruments of torture in Hell and the pains they inflict, as "seen through the caverns of the shadowy grave . . . / Are the true secrets of the commonweal, / To make men wise and just,"

> Then send the priest to every hearth and home
> To preach of burning wrath which is to come,
> In words like flakes of sulphur, such as thaw
> The frozen tears. . . . (ll. 1–16) (WPBS, 4:65–66)

Not only does Shelley try the case for satire framed in precisely parallel terms, but he also makes explicit its relation to the operation of conscience in a public setting:

> If Satire could awake the slumbering hounds
> Of conscience, or erase with deeper wounds,
> The leprous scars of Callous infamy'
> If it could make the present not to be,
> Or charm the dark past never to have been,
> Or turn regret to hope; who that has seen
> What Southey is and was, would not exclaim,
> "Lash on!" and be the keen verse dipped in flame;
> Follow his flight on winged words, and urge
> The strokes of the inexorable scourge
> Till it be broken on his flinty soul. . . . (ll. 16–28)

But Shelley goes on to deny each of these conditional premises, suggesting that they are just a function of a failure of realism, or what he calls in the Preface to *The Cenci,* the blindness of a "superstitious horror" (p. 240):

> This cannot be, it ought not . . . evil still—
> Suffering makes suffering—ill must follow ill.
> Harsh words beget hard thoughts, . . . , and beside
> Men take a sullen and a stupid pride
> In being all they hate in others' shame,
> By a perverse antipathy of fame. (ll. 35–40)

The Shelleyan solution, as we learn, is that it would be far better to take Southey on a country walk and tell him privately, "Softening harsh truths with friendship's gentle tone," what is wrong with his conduct—"Far better than to make innocent ink / With the stagnant truisms of trite Satire stink" (ll. 49–50). This is Shelley's very *un*-Byronic embrace of Godwinian "sincerity," his commitment to the momentous power of the heart-to-heart revelation.

The framing of Byronic satire, the way the poem brings that mode into view, becomes clearest at the point in the allegory when one of the early reviewers' complaints about Peter are couched in an idiom that alludes to the contemporary controversy over Pope: "What does the rascal mean or hope, / Not longer imitating Pope, / In that barbarian Shakespeare poking?" (ll. 475–77). The irony of the Shakespeare reference already belittles the perspective of the critic here, but neither is there independent reason to believe that Shelley would invoke Popean sanction in a quarrel about poetry. In 1821, Shelley wrote to Byron that Pope was "the pivot of a dispute in taste" in their time and then explained that he stood "neuter," if not on the other side of that dispute from Byron, presumably on account of an objection like the one stated in the *Satire on Satire* fragment (LPBS, 2:290). Nor is it likely that Shelley changed his mind in the months that elapsed between the composition of *Peter Bell the Third* in late 1819 and these later announcements. One of the most striking features of the argument of the *Satire on Satire* is that the enlightened satirist and the superstitious Christian have more in common than either suspects. Both participate in the degenerating cycle of retaliation and revenge, a scheme of accusation perpetuated by "stagnant truisms." This cycle was fully described in the ethical discussions of Shelley's "Essay on Christianity" and his essay "On Devils and the Devil," both of which probably predate *Peter Bell the Third*. In the former, for instance, Shelley puts these words in the mouth of his typical Christian: "Pain has been inflicted; therefore pain should be inflicted in return. Retaliation is the only remedy which can be applied to violence, because it teaches the injurer the true nature of his own conduct, and operates as a warning against its repetition."[49] In the *Satire on Satire* fragment, this is precisely the logic—a self-deceived logic, Shelley insists—according to which the satirist justifies the exercise of a vindictive wit.[50]

49. Shelley, *Prose Works,* 1:257.
50. I think we can see the centrality of these categories for *Peter Bell the Third* if we consider the way the poem uses the notion of damnation, for, just as the Christian pronounces himself saved in the act of damning others to the dark tortures of eternity, so the satirist pronounces himself saved in the act of damning others to the dark tortures of posterity. And this idea of "damnation" is played on in just these two senses in *Peter Bell the Third,* since the subtitles—Death, The Devil, Hell, Sin, Grace, Damnation, Double Damnation—belong to the system of repressive

The peculiar virulence of Shelley's critique of virulence may owe some-thing to his sense of his being generally allied with those whom he charges with polluting the "innocent ink" of contemporary literary culture with the stag-nant truisms of trite satire. Byron, of course, was one such tainted ally, and Moore was another. Certain other writers, closer to Shelley in their radicalism, though not in their social class, defended their satirical practice in even more unabashed terms. Perhaps the clearest articulation of the reformist mode of satire is a post-Waterloo essay by William Hazlitt that appeared in *The Examiner* in December 1815, "On the Doctrine of Philosophical Necessity." In this essay, Hazlitt invoked the doctrine widely associated with Godwin's *Political Justice,* to offer an apologia for political satire in the modern mode. The essence of this doctrine, as we saw in considering the moral mechanics of *Don Juan,* is the no-tion that the methods of analyzing causality in the moral and natural sciences are the same—that only their subjects differ. In Hazlitt's rephrasing it goes thus: "Man acts from a cause; and so far he resembles a stone; but he does not act from the same cause, and herein he differs from it" (CWWH, 20:61) Likewise, for Hazlitt, the machinery of the moral world also differs from that of the natural, even as the mechanics remains explicable in the same methodological frame-work: "The lever, the screw, and the wedge, are the great instruments of the me-chanical world: opinion, sympathy, praise, and blame, reward and punishment, are the lever, the screw, and the wedge of the moral world. A house is built of stone; human character depends on motives" (CWWH, 20:63). Shelley's "Satire on Satire" fragment clearly rejects this kind of behaviorism as too much caught up in a cycle of vindictiveness, but *Peter Bell the Third* makes clear that the analysis also extends to another level.

The reforming satirist responded to the Lake Poets as if theirs were simply a failure of character—the typical charge centers on vanity and egotism—and as if a poet's character were simply his or her own affair. Shelley's quasi-Benthamite critique of this position develops the notion of the second-order case—the national case, made visible through the media for representing public opinion, as the scene that all but determines the conduct of those who act in it. Shelley goes further, though, to dramatize a reflexive critique of the Benthamite position itself. Shelley's mentor Godwin had argued that actions are determined by opinions, which are in turn determined by circumstances,

---

Christianity into which Shelley suggests Wordsworth has relapsed. The satirical and reformist critic (Reynolds, Jeffrey, Hazlitt, Wooler, Byron, Moore) thus hoists Wordsworth on his own petard, damns him critically for his language of Damnation. For his pride in seeking for *Peter Bell* what he calls "a permanent station in the literature of his country," Wordsworth is given a perma-nent place in a dunciad.

which are in turn determined by institutions. But Godwin also seemed to hold out the hope that the expression of opinion, if (somehow) left unconstrained, could lead to a change of institutionally driven circumstance. Bentham shares this hope, and so, in part, does Shelley. In Shelley's conception of things, however, neither Bentham nor Godwin can imagine what it is *beyond* opinion that makes such an improvement possible. For Shelley, this "beyond" is the domain of poetry, whose relevance to political life, of course, Bentham took some pains to deny. Shelley's *Peter Bell the Third* suggests that those who traffic only in the utilities of public opinion misunderstand the causes of the moral world and therefore tackle the politics of political culture on the wrong level even or, especially, at the moment when they think they have gotten it right. It is not just a matter of addressing the case of the nation but of recognizing its historical-poetic unconscious as the source of its normative order. Taking a position that uncannily repeats elements of Southey's self-defense in 1817, Shelley suggests that writers who traffic only in the utilities of public opinion misunderstand the causes of the moral world. In the case of Wordsworth, or that of Southey himself, according to Shelley, those who traffic in public opinion help turn one of the nation's poetic legislators into an agent for her actual legislators—into a "government poet" much as Gifford had become, in Hazlitt's words, a "government critic."

Chapter Ten

HISTORY'S LYRE: THE "WEST WIND" AND THE POET'S WORK

*A*lthough the poem Shelley dedicated to Thomas Moore in 1819, like *A Defence of Poetry,* was not published for two decades after its composition, Tennyson's friend, Arthur Henry Hallam seemed to grasp the literary views and principles that informed Shelley's writings of 1819 when he invoked them (along with Keats's writings of the same period) to explain the revolution in "modern poetry" in which he saw his friend Tennyson taking part. Indeed, the domain of public opinion is precisely what Wordsworth began to turn against so vehemently in the 1815 Essay Supplementary, as Hallam also recognized in his 1831 explication of the young Tennyson. Hallam understood as well that Shelley actually radicalized the Wordsworthian suspicion of a "poetry of opinion" in favor of a poetry of sensation.[1] Shelley's *Peter Bell the Third* thus proves to be at once a satire of Wordsworth's attack on the domain of public opinion as expressed in the periodical reviews, *and* a sympathetic engagement with the very terms of that Wordsworthian attack. Shelley, in other words, seems at once to challenge Wordsworth's pompous claim to rise above public opinion and to valorize that Wordsworthian claim against his enemies, who were becoming legion by 1819.

I have tried to show that, as in the case of *The Cenci,* merely to situate *Peter Bell the Third* in a social-historical movement is to take only one step in coming to terms with it. The second step is to recognize how it situates *itself* in that movement by means of a keen Shelleyan self-consciousness about the trend that set the conditions for its production. Just as Shelley, along with Mary Shelley, anticipated the satirical attacks on Southey's and Wordsworth's renegadism as early as 1814 and 1815, in other words, so he also seems to have been

---

1. See my "Hallam, Tennyson, and the Poetry of Sensation: Aestheticist Allegories of a Counter-Public Sphere," *Studies in Romanticism* 33, no. 4 (winter 1994), especially pp. 533–34.

most astute about the effect of these attacks in 1819. And just as the poem is influenced by Byron as an individual writer, so it also makes its Byronism a subject of its own self-critique. Like the *Satire on Satire, Peter Bell the Third* (the case of a case) implicitly locates itself in a dialectical reception history, in effect looking forward, as its preface implicitly promises, to the sort of second-order analysis we have been exploring here.

Peter Bell the Third thus multiplies its critical object in order to complicate its critical subject. Indeed, because "Peter Bell" names both person and thing, it also complicates the object-subject distinction itself, personifying the text in a way that anticipates critical practice in our own time, as when we speak of what a text knows or wants. Peter Bell figures as a case, insofar as he challenges the norms by which he or it would be weighed. He raises a question *for* the conscience of the nation and *about* the critical establishment that presumes to condemn him. Seen in this way, *Peter Bell the Third* stages in the public sphere of literature and print journalism a kind of spectacle of the nation's historical situation. It dramatizes a supraindividual case of the sort implied in *The Cenci*. As we have seen, Shelley strongly invites a reading of *Peter Bell the Third* as a kind of public theater in his framing allusions to the conscience-catching play-within-the-play in Hamlet.

Several of the great texts of Shelley's so-called annus mirabilis in 1819 address the problematics of the collective case so understood—in varying degrees of directness, to be sure, but some very directly indeed. We saw a good example in the passage from the preface to *Prometheus Unbound,* where the allegorically collective figure of Prometheus is distinguished from Milton's Satan on the grounds that the "character of Satan engenders in the mind a pernicious casuistry which leads us to weigh his faults with his wrongs and to excuse the former because the latter exceed all measure" (SPP, p. 133). It is true that, in the preface to *Prometheus Unbound,* casuistry seems to carry an unmistakably pejorative connotation. The conceptual framework of casuistry is nonetheless crucial to the construction of the action and situation of Shelley's lyric drama. Prometheus the character and *Prometheus Unbound* the play are both indeed constituted precisely as an overcoming of the sort of casuistry that defines the character of Satan—that is, the sort of casuistry in terms of which Prometheus's self-excusing condemnation of Jupiter is cast. This condemnation, readers familiar with the play recall, defines the frozen stasis of the play's initial situation, the impasse that will be surmounted only by Prometheus's "recalling"—remembering, recanting, repeating—of his, as it were, Satanic curse on the head of Jupiter. This moment of acknowledgment is played out in the form of a conjuring of the "Phantasm of Jupiter" to speak Prometheus's own curse to and on himself as spectator.[2] Playing out the benign or comic version of the play-within-the-play in *Hamlet,* Shelley's Prometheus manages at this crucial moment to "put himself in the case of the other" (in Adam Smith's terms), specifically the case of Jupiter, who had been the object of the curse in the first instance.

In *Prometheus Unbound,* then, casuistry serves as the dramatic medium in which the sublime action of the play unfolds, even as it seems to be disdained as a discursive form. Prometheus surpasses Satan by emulation—an act of imitation that seeks to surpass its object—rather than by eradication. He moves through the case of Satan, and the casuistry of Satanic ethics, to achieve the moral stature that makes him a candidate for apocalyptic union with Asia in act 3.[3] It is in keeping with *both* of his great dramatic works of 1819 that Shelley praised Boccacio in a letter to Leigh Hunt of September 1819: "How much do I admire Bocaccio. . . . He is a moral casuist. . . . The opposite of the Christian, Stoical, ready made world systems of morals" (LPBS, 2:122). Arguing, as I have, that Shelley's interest in casuistry anticipates Pottle's, I mean that Shelley's work is involved in a historicization of the case very much of the sort that is implied in Pottle's use of "the case of Shelley" as a way of identifying his role as "the central exemplar of the idiom and practice" of Romanticism. That is, Shelley's understanding of cases and casuistries can be shown to address the problem of what Pottle calls a historical "shift in sensibility," a notion of a normative scheme as period specific.

As I have been arguing all along, the reinvention of casuistry in this period must be understood as part of a more general altering of the case—an altering of the very *conception* of the case, in which the new notion of the "historical situation" becomes operative. In respect to issues of personal ethics, this alteration is not—or not merely—a shift in scale. The "historical situation" is not just an ethical or juridical situation writ large. For part of what it means to alter the concept of the case in this way is to alter the concept of the cause. That is to say,

---

2. That is,

> Heap on thy soul by virtue of this Curse
>   Ill deeds, then be thou damned, beholding good,
>   Both infinite as is the Universe,
>   And thou, and thy self-torturing solitude. (Act I, 292–95).

For a deconstructive account of "the complex problematic of the recall," see Carol Jacobs, *Uncontainable Romanticism: Shelley, Brontë, Kleist* (Baltimore: Johns Hopkins University Press, 1989), pp. 27–29.

3. One might argue a similar point about the parallel formation/reformation of the character of Asia in act II of *Prometheus Unbound,* only Asia's course lies through the institution of the catechism rather than that of casuistry.

altering the concept of the case means forming a new understanding of human motivation, of "what is involved" (as Kenneth Burke wrote of his own project on motivation) "when we say what people are doing and why they are doing it" (GM, p. xvii). The alteration of the case—the invention of what I have been calling a historicist casuistry—clarifies a crucial point about the relatively recent discourse on the general or collective will, as initially proposed by Rousseau. The notion of a collective or general will does not merely involve an aggregate or higher-order category of taxonomy above the "individual will." The notion involves a new understanding of the relation of the will to the situations in which it may be understood to operate. To think of the case as an "object" of the individual will is both to imagine a transcendent scheme of norms and to understand the field of experience in which these norms can be applied as a field of generic possibilities, *kinds* of situations. To think of the case as an object of general or collective will, however, is at the same time to understand that same case as deeply conditioning the will in its individual operations. The "historical situation" of one's experience—one's contemporary "culture and society" understood as a political and development "state"—is, in respect to the individual, no more a determined object of an ethical encounter than it is a determining factor in the constitution of the encountering subject in its "individual" modality. The elementary grammatical distinction of case itself, erect or oblique, nominative or objective, is precisely what gets complicated in the shift in casuistical scale.

We have seen these issues in play in the post-Waterloo theories of Jeremy Bentham, in the novels of Scott, in the ethical epic of Byron, in the writings of Keats and others about the history of "Psyche," and in the numerous post-Waterloo literary surveys of American manners. We have considered some of the material conditions of the emergence of this conceptual configuration, and we have acknowledged some of the theoretical issues that haunt it—for example, the question of how to locate freedom of agency in the collective will while denying, or all but denying, it in the individual. Nowhere can we find the conceptual framework more sensitively acknowledged, and its problems more strenuously wrestled with, than in Shelley's major work of 1819. Nowhere in this work, however, are the problems more challengingly addressed than in his attempt to confront them in the lyric form. It helps to keep in mind that, while the allusion to Hamlet's "miching mallecho" in *Peter Bell the Third* invokes a sense of that work's theatricality, it nonetheless remains a work in ballad stanzas about a certain Romantic type, the lyric poet. Peter's verse, we recall, "was clear, and came / Announcing from the frozen hearth / Of a cold age, that none might tame / The soul of that diviner flame / It augured to the Earth." As a kind of coda to this larger argument, then, I propose to address the implications of the foregoing analysis of Shelley's historical casuistry for Shelley's achievement—and his influence and reception—in the lyric mode.

1. Lyricism and Historicism

There are two ways of approaching this question of the historicity of Shelley's lyric achievement that cannot be pursued in appropriate detail here, though both are valuable for following certain topics further into the literary culture of the nineteenth century. The first is to consider Shelley's lyric production for the "little volume of *popular songs* wholly political" that he told Hunt he was working on at this time (LPBS, 2:191). The presumed centerpiece of this volume, *The Mask of Anarchy*, is Shelley's most direct engagement with the Peterloo massacre and the public furor that followed it. The poem's impressive lyricism—the "Voice of Liberty" that dominates the latter part of the poem—is almost perfectly describable in the terms Shelley used of Peter Bell's verse. It was generated almost exclusively out of an engagement with newspaper reports of the events of August, and it was intended to recirculate in that same periodical audience. The "voice" that the speaker of the poem claims to hear from across the sea, while "asleep in Italy," must in one sense be simply the voice of Hunt's *Examiner*, in whose pages Shelley was following the news. To close the circle, Shelley sent the poem back to Hunt for publication there. In its poetic work on the *Examiner's* journalistic representations, the *Mask* not only recodes the identifications of public characters into an allegorical scheme—"I met Murder on the way—/ He had a mask like Castlereagh"—it also displaces the everyday time of the periodicals into a quasi-apocalyptic framework, anticipating the displacement of "empty homogenous time" by "messianic time" in Benjamin's twentieth-century analysis.[4] In the process, one might say, the poem establishes new possibilities for seeing the historicity of the lyric form in relation to the public media of post-Waterloo British culture, and, indeed, when the poem was eventually published, in 1830, it was taken up by the Chartists who sought to realize just those possibilities.[5]

4. On Shelley's appropriations from Christian eschatology in the poem, see Morton Paley, "Apocapolitics: Allusion and Structure in Shelley's *Mask of Anarchy*," *HLQ* 54 (1991): 91–109. For a fresh new reading of Shelley by way of the Frankfurt School, see Rob Kaufman, "Legislators of the Post-Everything World: Shelley's *Defense* of Adorno," *ELH* 63 (fall 1996): 707–33. Adorno's 1957 lecture, "Lyric Poetry and Society," remains the single most valuable brief treatment of that topic, and I have implicitly relied on its arguments in what follows: collected in Stephen Eric Bronner and Douglas MacKay Kenner, *Critical Theory and Society* (New York: Routledge, 1989), pp. 155–71.

5. See Anne Janowitz, "'A Voice from across the Sea': Communitarianism at the Limits of Romanticism," in *At the Limits of Romanticism*, ed. X. Favret and X. Watson, pp. 83–100.

The second approach would involve a revisiting of the once-controversial, now neglected, question of the genealogy of the dramatic monologue, perhaps the most important lyric form to emerge in the Victorian period. In spite of a number of good books in the 1980s, studies of Browning and of the dramatic monologue more generally have been recently inactive.[6] It has long been recognized that Browning's primary literary debt was to Shelley and that the monologue form he developed was characterized by two key elements: (1) a complex dialectic of sympathy and judgment and (2) an implied historicity of context. In the terms I have been developing for Shelley, it would not be hard to rewrite the standard histories of the development of the dramatic monologue form as a lyric instantiation of the historicist case.[7] Two lines of inquiry, both involving Byron, would have to be pursued to carry out this analysis properly. First, one would have to conduct a careful comparison of the relation of *The Cenci* to the theatrical case history Byron wrote in explicit opposition to it, *Marino Faliero*.[8] Second, and in part to explicate the relation of these plays to each other and to the historicization of the case, one would have to look at Shelley's remarkable 1818 poem in heroic couplets, *Julian and Maddalo,* for, in that poem, a philosophical dispute between two characters normally read as "Shelley" and "Byron" is resolved by resort to dramatized case, a visit to a madman in an asylum. The virtually uninterrupted lyric ravings of this character, called "the Maniac," constitute much of the second half of the poem, run nearly to its conclusion, and leave the philosophical debate unresolved. In critical glosses on this poem, the Maniac has long been associated with Tasso (and with Byron's *Lament of Tasso*), a point that reminds us of Shelley's comment (cited above) on Tasso's "situation" as " widely different from that of any persecuted being of the present day." Extract *Shelley's* "Lament of Tasso" from the context of *Julian and Maddalo* and you have as close a Romantic prototype for the dramatic monologue as you are likely to find.[9]

6. For example, Herbert F. Tucker, *Browning's Beginnings: The Art of Disclosure* (Minneapolis: University of Minnesota Press, 1980); Mary Ellis Gibson, *History and the Prism of Art: Browning's Poetic Experiments* (Columbus: Ohio State University Press, 1987); and Loy D. Martin, *Browning's Dramatic Monologue and the Post-Romantic Subject* (Baltimore: Johns Hopkins University Press, 1985).

7. The classic among these histories remains Robert Langbaum's *The Poetry of Experience: The Dramatic Monologue in the Modern Literary Tradition* (New York: Random House, 1957).

8. In special need of attention for the comparison of these plays is the question of the "rarity" of Beatrice in relation to Shelley's notion of the "select few," as against the "singularity" of Faliero in relation to Byron's nominalism. We will have no full account of the casuistry of *either* play until we can explain this terms of this difference.

9. For relevant commentaries on *Julian and Maddalo,* see, for example, Charles Robinson, *Shelley and Byron: The Serpent and the Eagle Wreathed in Flight* (Baltimore: Johns Hopkins Univer-

In deciding against such attractive options in favor of a discussion of Shelley's *Ode to the West Wind,* I am swayed in part by a sense of the importance of this lyric in the tradition of Shelley commentary, not least in the influential commentaries of Pottle and Bloom. When Bloom announces that he is "following a recent article by Pottle in this approach to Shelley as a prophetic poet," he is not only setting up his own reading of the *Ode* but is also referring to a comment of Pottle's that bears directly on that poem:

> Shelley is a passionately religious poet. His theory of poetry . . . identifies poetry and prophecy. . . . When he invoked the breath of Autumn's being, he was not indulging in an empty figure. The breath ("spiritus") that he involked was to him as real and as awful as the Holy Ghost was to Milton. . . . This is the faith of the prophet, the faith held by the authors of Isaiah and of the Revelation, though of course their theologies differed widely and fundamentally from Shelley's. Shelley's main passion as a poet was not, in an ordinary sense, to reform the world; it was to create an apocalypse of the world formed and realized by Intellectual Beauty or Love. (p. 594)

Pottle's concern to divorce political reform from religious transformation is troubling here and his commentary verges from respect for a notion of an "historic sensibility" into something more mystical: Bloom, however, makes bold to take that step and thus, in the act of "following" Pottle, he outstrips him. Identifying Blake and Shelley as poets "of the rank and kind of Ezekiel" and calling them "prophets as he was a prophet," Bloom declares: "They 'speak unasked' into their historical situation as he spoke unasked into his, and we ought to be very wary before we condemn their prophetic aspirations."[10] It is the boldness of Bloom's admonition, his own "speaking unasked" to 1950s America that seems to me to go beyond, or swerve away from, the position of his teacher. And it does so precisely by evacuating the "history" from the concept of the "historical situation" as he deploys it. I do not deny that the *Ode* is in some sense about "the nature and function of the nabi in relation to his own prophecies." Like Abrams, however, Bloom treats Shelley as if "the future state" were too simply a name for an immaterial afterlife. By contrast I wish to show that Shelley's conception of the prophetic "spirit" is a good deal more Spinozist, and a good deal less, well, "literal," than Bloom's account would suggest. There is something about this spirit, as Jerrold Hogle suggests, that "allows it to be . . .

---

sity Press, 1976), pp. 81–112; Kelvin Everest, "Shelley's Doubles: An Approach to 'Julian and Maddalo,'" in *Shelley Revalued: Essays from the Gregynog Conference,* ed. Kelvin Everest (Leicester: 1983), pp. 63–88; Timothy Clark, *Embodying Revolution: The Figure of the Poet in Shelley* (Oxford: Clarendon Press, 1989), pp. 184–212; and O'Neill, *The Human Mind's Imaginings,* pp. 52–72. For the relation of *The Cenci* and *Marino Faliero,* see Charles Robinson, *Shelley and Byron,* pp. 144–60; and Julie Carlson, *In the Theatre of Romanticism,* pp. 176–212.

    10. Bloom, *Shelley's Mythmaking,* p. 66.

so 'inside' the poet's thoughts and words and so 'outside' them . . . at the same time."[11] This something has to do with its relation to the new conception of the "historical situation" implicit in the "spirit of the age," the poem's dramatization of the very kind of historical determination that Shelley claims a poet must not be able to recognize.

The place accorded the *Ode to the West Wind* in Shelley criticism is thus central indeed, but my primary reason for taking up the *Ode* has less to do with its elaborate and relevant reception history than with what Adorno might call its linguistic craft—the lyric poet's commitment to "linguistic *form*," the act of self-abandonment "to language as if devoting himself completely to an object."[12] I wish to focus on its compressed and highly formal handling of some of the large issues we have been considering in Shelley's work and in England in 1819 more generally. These issues might be rephrased in terms of the great Sartrean questions of 1948—"What is writing?" "Why write?" "For whom does one write?"[13]—especially if we add the great Audenesque question of 1939 about whether poetry can make anything happen, whether and under what conditions "history" can be counted among the makings of poetry.[14] The period in British history that saw the major transformation in modern historiography was not itself a historiographical age. It was an era better known for other forms, by no means excluding the lyric. The transformation in the understanding of literature and of history occur correlatively, as I have argued throughout, and in the intense literary-historical dynamic of the formal linguistic patterning of the *Ode* one can see this proposition powerfully dramatized. In the closing pages, then, I will in effect be prosecuting a reading of the *Ode*—in terms of its turns or tropes, its allusive character, its repetitions, and its formal structure. I offer it as a final case for my account of Romantic historicism in this book.

2. A Revolution in the Turns of Season

The problems posed by the *Ode,* as commentators have long recognized, begin with the opening lines. Before we have any reason to associate the "West Wind" with, let us say, the "Spirit of the Age," with which we are now familiar from Shelley's other writings of the period, we run into a grammatical problem

11. Hogle, *Shelley's Process,* p. 6.

12. Adorno, "Lyric Poetry and Society," p. 161. For exemplary criticism of poems as political in their formal dimension, see John Barrell, *Poetry, Language, and Politics* (Manchester: Manchester University Press, 1988).

13. These questions form the primary chapter headings of Sartre's *What Is Literature?*

14. On Shelley's relation to what I am calling Auden's question, see Thomas Edwards, *Imagination and Power: A Study of Poetry on Public Themes* (New York: Oxford University Press, 1971), pp. 159–68.

traceable to the alignment of the initial metaphors in which the West Wind is represented:

> O wild West Wind, thou breath of Autumn's being,
> Thou, from whose unseen presence the leaves dead
> Are driven, like ghosts from an enchanter fleeing,
>
> Yellow, and black, and pale, and hectic red,
> Pestilence-stricken multitudes. (ll. 1–5)

After "breath of Autumn's being," one is disposed to see in the ensuing figure a picture of Autumn sitting like Aeolus in his cave and driving the leaves away with his mighty exhalations. It is the unseen presence of the wind itself, however, from which the leaves are said to be driven, and precisely by *what* the leaves are driven is left, as it were, up in the air. The ensuing simile of the ghosts and the enchanter ought to settle this question, but in fact it only complicates matters further. The ghosts that are likened to the leaves are not depicted as being driven from the enchanter (the counterpart of the unseen presence) by anything in particular. Moreover, they are not depicted as being *driven* from him at all; they are depicted as *fleeing* him. Further still, insofar as some force is involved in the metaphor, it seems to work in the other direction, for the enchanter's power would presumably tend to hold the ghosts against their will.[15]

Metaphorical mismatching is by no means rare in Shelley. It is surely not unusual for him to compose a catalogue of figures that do not neatly add up, and commentators have developed various ways of generalizing about the significance of the practice, whether as a sign of Shelley's incompetence, as in the Leavisite tradition, or of his protodeconstructive half-insight, in poststructuralist criticism. But even the contradictions of the opening lines might not demand special attention if it were not for what Shelley does with the metaphors in the ensuing lines, which comprise the stanza's second movement:

> O Thou,
> Who chariotest to their dark wintry bed
>
> The winged seeds, where they lie cold and low,
> Each like a corpse within its grave, until
> Thine azure sister of the Spring shall blow

---

15. Paul Fry calls this last contradiction "the crux of the simile, and of the ode," in *The Poet's Calling in the English Ode* (New Haven: Yale University Press, 1980), p. 210. The figure is also jarring in respect to its predecessor, as Fry points out, because it implies that the ghosts are visible and the enchanter unseen.

> Her clarion o'er the dreaming earth, and fill
> (Driving sweet buds like flocks to feed in air)
> With living hues and odours plain and hill. . . . (ll. 5–12)

Having left behind the apparently destructive effects of the Autumn wind, its scattering of the pestilence-stricken multitudes, this passage focuses on the wind's function in delivering the seeds to their place of implantation. The presence of similar words and tropes in this movement signals that it reunites the first movement, but the differences show strongly conventionalizing tendencies. Indeed, the passage amounts to a miniature nature poem rendered in the familiar Christianized pastoral framework of the redemption of the soul after the death of the body. Eschatologically, it is the apocalypse of the beautiful rather than the sublime.

If we focus on the operation of the figures, the tropes or tunes of these lines, we see that the metaphors cooperate, corroborate, and cohere. By contrast with what we noted in the opening movement, for example, we find nothing especially complicated about "driving" in this context, and metaphorical elaboration of the term now runs not against the grain but very much with it: "like flocks to feed in air." This is the wind of Autumn comprehended in its azure sister-wind of the Spring. (Their "sisterhood" itself will prove to be a function of the passage's vernal perspective.)

The clarity that results from the alignment of the metaphors in this movement is perhaps explicitly marked in the reference to the clarion (l. 10), a horn noted for, and indeed named for, its clear tone: *Clarion,* from *clario,* from *clarus* (clear), as the polyglot Shelley would certainly have known. The poem's second movement is as clear as the first is obscure, and the juxtaposition of the two movements suggests that both the obscurity and the clarity are tellingly motivated.[16] The two movements comprise an introduction to the *Ode* only, therefore, when they are read together.[17]

To gain a better idea of what is at stake in the *Ode's* opening juxtaposition of two diverse manners or modes, we must consult the lines that have long been recognized as a prototype for the theme's topoi of the *Ode,* one of the climac-

16. Paul de Man's analysis of figuration in "The Triumph of Life" is a precedent for what follows in that it too discriminates second-order considerations of coherence/incoherence in the play of Shelley's tropes. I refer especially to De Man's analysis of how, unlike most images in the poem, "light" tends to be figured coherently: "Shelley Disfigured," in *Deconstruction & Criticism* (New York: Seabury Press, 1979), p. 57.

17. Two of the most suggestive recent interpretations of the *Ode* focus only on one or the other of the these related movements, in effect not seeing them as movements, or related, in the relevant respects. Fry's deconstructionist account sees the poem as a coming to terms with what I have been calling the initial, destructive movement: "There is enough mystery in the first tercet

tic passages in Shelley's *The Revolt of Islam*.[18] The passage in question is the speech that Cythna makes to Laon in canto 9 at a time when the two of them, having been the intellectual leaders of the revolution in the Golden City, are weathering a counterrevolution much like the one that Shelley and other reformers saw themselves confronting in the years after Waterloo. Here, as in Lukács's account of this same period, the experience of counter revolution lends motive and perspective to an attempt to make sense of the entire Revolutionary epoch. Cythna represents the epoch through a sustained conceit. It is a seasonal topos that develops in two distinct cycles, although its cycles are themselves rhetorical rather than meteorological. The first is completed in a single stanza:

> 'The blasts of autumn drive the winged seeds
> 　　Over the Earth,—next come the snows, and rain,
> And frosts, and storms, which dreary winter leads
> 　　Out of his Scythian cave, a savage train;
> 　　Behold! Spring sweeps over the world again,
> Shedding soft dews from her aetherial wings;
> 　　Flowers on the mountains, fruits over the plain,
> And music on the waves and woods she flings,
> And love on all that lives, and calm on lifeless things. (st. 21)

This account of the seasonal cycle obviously employs certain figures, chiefly prosopopeia (personification), but, like the opening stanza of the "West Wind" *Ode,* it offers no explicit allegorization of its terms. That sort of gloss must await the second movement of Cythna's speech beginning two stanzas later. But it is already clear from this stanza why the speech should prompt Stuart Curran to call it the long first draft of the *Ode.* In recognizing the features that allow us to see the passage that way, however, we must not fail to notice the crucial ways in which the *Ode* revises in rewriting. One crucial revision in this first stanza, for example, is that the wind of autumn is represented only in its capacity as charioteer of the seeds. The destructive powers are all given to the winter. This fact suggests that Cythna's speech may be called a "first draft" for the *second movement* of the "West Wind" *Ode,* but not for the *Ode* itself. It is also one reason why,

---

to supply a whole poem ," he begins (*Poet's Calling*, pp. 208–210). Edward Duffy's Christianizing and Eliotic reading finds the poem's seminal beginning the second, preservative movement, in which the "verbal seeds" of the poem's traditionalizing renaming of Golgotha as part of a broader "resurrection *logos*" are "already embedded." See "Where Shelley Wrote and What He Wrote For: The Example of 'The Ode to the West Wind,'" *Studies in Romanticism* 23 (fall 1984): 365–67.

18. Stuart Curran, for example, calls it the "long first draft" of the *Ode.* See Stuart Curran, *Shelley's Annus Mirabilis* (San Marino, Calif.: Huntington Library, 1975).

when Cythna begins explicitly to emblematize her terms in the ensuing stanza, she represents autumn and spring as akin to one another:

> O Spring, of hope, and love, and youth, and gladness
>   Wind-winged emblem! brightest, best and fairest!
> Whence comest thou, when, with, dark Winter's sadness
>   The tears that fade in sunny smiles thou sharest?
>   Sister of joy, thou art the child who wearest
> Thy mother's dying smile, tender and sweet;
>   Thy mother Autumn, for whose grave thou bearest
> Fresh flowers, and beams like flowers, with gentle feet,
> Disturbing not the leaves which are her winding-sheet. (st. 22)

That the two seasons are mother and daughter here, but sisters in 1819, raises a question about Shelley's employment of the family romance of natural history, a question that remains in play for the *Ode*. For the moment, however, I only mean to emphasize the connection between Cythna's model and, narrowly, the *second* movement of the *Ode*.

The second movement of her own speech is quite consonant, in respect to the seasonal arrangement, with the first. The primary difference is that, after the intervening emblematization of the figures, the entire seasonal cycle becomes the vehicle of a historical allegory in which Laon and Cythna, as the intellectual leaders of their revolution, are the central agents. By examining this allegory, we gain a sense of how it is recoded in *Ode to the West Wind* two years later:

> Virtue, and Hope, and Love, like light and Heaven,
>   Surround the world.—We are their chosen slaves.
> Has not the whirlwind of our spirit driven
>   Truth's deathless germs to thought's remotest caves?
>   Lo, Winter comes!—the grief of many graves,
> The frost of death, the tempest of the sword,
>   The flood of tyranny, whose sanguine waves
> Stagnate like ice at Faith, the inchanter's word,
> And bind all human hearts in its repose abhorred.
>
> The seeds are sleeping in the soil: meanwhile
>   The tyrant peoples dungeons with his prey,
> Pale victims on the guarded scaffold smile
>   Because they cannot speak; and, day by day,
>   The moon of wasting Science wanes away

Among her stars, and in that darkness vast
  The sons of Earth to their foul idols pray,
And gray priests triumph, and like blight or blast
A shade of selfish care o'er human looks is cast.

This is the winter of the world;—and here
  We die, even as the winds of Autumn fade,
Expiring in the frore and foggy air.—
  Behold! Spring comes, though we must pass, who made
  The promise of its birth,—even as the shade
Which from our death, as from a mountain, flings
  The future, a broad sunrise; thus arrayed
As with the plumes of overshadowing wings,
From its dark gulphs of chains, Earth like an eagle springs. (st. 23–25)

This is consonant with stanza 22 in that, in both passages, the forces and stages of this regenerative process appear in the same sequence. First comes Autumn's dispersal of the seeds, explicitly metaphorized as the driving of "truth"'s deathless germs by the spirit of the revolution's intellectual leaders. Next comes "the savage train" of winter's meteorological hardships, explicitly metaphorized as a bloody terror followed by the spirit-chilling Restoration of tyranny and superstition. On the other side of this winter of the world (so like what England suffered in 1817, the year of Oliver's counterespionage, the Pentridge rebellion, and the prosecution of William Hone for blasphemy), Cythna envisions the spring in which the seeds of science and liberty, after dispersal and underground development, issue forth in a regenerated world. Again, as in the first movement of her speech and the second (or "clarion") movement of the *Ode,* the autumn wind is identified only with its positive function in the stage of the enlightened dissemination of ideas.

The similarity of Cythna's seasonal allegory to the representation of the seasonal cycle in the second movement of *Ode to the West Wind* is sufficiently strong to suggest that Cythna's historical allegory has been reinscribed within the later poem. But the fact that its terms are confined to the second movement of the poem suggests that such a representation is, at best, only part of the story. The competition we noted between the representations of the West Wind in the first and second movements of the *Ode* suggests that Cythna's account may actually be subject to serious challenge within the *Ode:* in the first two movements of the *Ode* taken together, the autumn wind is ascribed both the destructive and preservative functions that, in Cythna's speech, are relegated to separate seasons. It is not a matter of dead ideological leaves that must be cleared so that new ideological seeds might grow. Rather, what happens to the leaves themselves in the *Ode* must in some sense be construed as the whole story. Even more tellingly, the metaphors in Cythna's speech, like those in the second movement of the *Ode* (but unlike those in the first), all point in the same direction. Her figures align analogically with one another and are mutually corroborative. They are not threatened by an alternative configuration of mutually disconfirming metaphors, and neither the rest of the poem nor Shelley's preface offers any reason to doubt that Cythna's speech articulates his representation of England in 1817.[19]

Since it is now evident that the natural history encoded within the *Ode* involves some overcoming of Cythna's political allegory not only in matter but also in manner, we need to attend more closely to how that allegory works. Looking first at Cythna's commitment to analogical correspondences, for example, we can say not only that her metaphors cohere but also that the entire passage is founded on the premise that history is like nature, revolution like the natural cycle. In his *Reflections on the Revolution In France,* Edmund Burke argued that English history had been a success story because the English had worked in the spirit of philosophic analogy and patterned their government after the method of nature. He was talking about a system of inheritance that emulated the process by which traits are passed from one generation to the next in natural cycles. Cythna's account implies an understanding of cultural transmission, and perhaps even a view of history, surprisingly similar to what Burke outlined. Hence Cythna's representation of the winds of autumn and spring not only as kindred spirits, so to speak, but also as mother and daughter. We recall that spring is first addressed as "the child who wearest / Thy mother's dying smile, tender and sweet." This metaphor assumes even more central importance in Cythna's subsequent explication of her allegory, where she foretells how, though they will not live to see the ultimate regeneration of the Golden City, Laon and she will have affected the outcome:

> The good and mighty of departed ages
>   Are in their graves, the innocent and free
> Heroes, and Poets, and prevailing Sages,
>   Who leave the vesture of their majesty
>   To adorn and clothe this naked world;—and we
> Are like to them—such perish, but they leave
>   All hope, or love, or truth, or liberty,

19. See especially the account of the French Revolutionary epoch, "the age in which we live," in Shelley's preface, *Poetical Works,* ed. Hutchison, pp. 33–34.

Whose forms their mighty spirits could conceive,
To be a rule and law to ages that survive. (st. 28)

Since the relation of the intellectual to posterity is represented in terms of a legacy, this account may be seen as unfolding what was implicit in Cythna's representation of the filial relationship of the Autumn and Spring. Indeed, the more closely one reads, the more this formulation seems to participate in the myth of second nature: ideas are organic and they are transmitted along the lines of a natural inheritance. They constitute the legacy of a woven moral fabric in which the naked infant of the future can be adorned and clothed.[20] What Cythna offers is perhaps less a model of the role of the intellectual in the culture than a cultural model of the intellectual's role in history.[21]

The analogizing coherence of Cythna's metaphors with one another, to pursue this hypothesis a bit further, might itself be called the *rhetorical* analogy of the doctrine of "philosophic analogy" which they promulgate. As the meta-

20. For some helpful remarks on what he calls the "family structure of Shelleyan revolution" in this poem, see Ronald Paulson, *Representation of Revolution (1789–1820)* (New Haven, Conn.: Yale University Press, 1983), pp. 280–81. For a fuller account of the ideology of second nature in the period see my *Wordsworth's Second Nature*, pp. 64–81, 126–27, 233–34.

21. What makes this system of terms especially relevant here is that they were probably suggested to the young Shelley by Godwin in their 1812 series of exchanges about history. Shelley had initially sent to Godwin a polemic urging concerted intellectual effort to abolish immediately everything tainted by superstition and falsehood in contemporary society. On March 4, Godwin responded that:

[E]very institution and form of society is good in its place and in the period of time to which it belongs. How many beautiful and admirable effects *grew out* of Popery and the monastic institutions in the period when they were in their genuine *health and vigour.* To them we owe almost all our logic and literature. What excellent effects do we *reap,* even at this day, from the feudal system and from chivalry! In this point of view nothing perhaps can be more worthy of our applause than the English Constitution. (italics mine; C. Kegan Paul, *William Godwin: His Friends and Contemporaries* 2 vols. (London, 1876), 2:206)

In responding to Shelley's reply, which was meant to be conciliatory, Godwin expressed continuing dissatisfaction:

You say, "I will look to events in which it will be impossible I can share, and make myself the cause of an effect which will take place ages after I shall have moulded into dust." In saying this you run from one extreme to another. I have often had occasion to apply a principle on the subject of education, which is especially applicable here—"Be not easily discouraged; sow the seed, and after a sesson, and when you least look for it, it will germinate and produce a crop." [He here goes on to cite examples of his experience with "children with whom I have been concerned."]

These instances of surprise are owing solely to the bluntness of our senses. You find little difference between the men of these islands of Europe now and twenty years ago. If you looked more into these things you would find that the alteration is immense. The human race has made larger strides to escape from the state of childhood in these twenty years than perhaps in the hundred years preceding. (Ibid., p. 208 [March 30, 1812])

phors conspire to preserve their sense in this passage, so the passage represents the seasonal process, and through it the historical process, as a conspiracy of preservation. Returning to the second movement of the *Ode,* we find that, under such a dispensation, sense is actually preserved in more than one sense: the outcome of the process is to fill the plain and hill with "living hues and odours." In both Cythna's speech and the second movement of the *Ode,* this conspiracy is filial in structure and succeeds inevitably in overcoming the recalcitrant wintry forces of tyranny and superstition which seem to interrupt its mission.

In the second movement of the *Ode,* the Wind's preserving function, to chariot the seeds to their wintry bed, stands side by side with the clearing of the leaves of the previous year's growth, as represented in the first movement: this is all summarized pointedly in the exclamation that closes the first part, "Destroyer and Preserver; hear, oh hear!" Because of the movement structure of the first stanza—in which the wind is treated first as the driver of the leaves and then as the charioteer of the seeds—one may be inclined at this point to see the destructive and preservative functions of the wind as quite separable. It scatters the leaves, and it also happens to implant the seeds. But by ascribing to the autumnal power two functions conventionally (as in *The Revolt of Islam*) relegated to different seasons—autumn and winter—the *Ode* forces one to see destruction and preservation as unified at some level of abstraction, despite their apparent autonomy. By the end of the *Ode*'s last stanza, we are also invited to recognize a similar unity in the functions that were, even in the first stanza of this ode, relegated to autumn and *spring.* In the first stanza, the autumn's sister spirit of the spring fulfills the process of regeneration. She blows her clarion over the dreaming earth. In the final stanza, however, it is the autumn wind itself that is to be, through the poet's lips, the trumpet of an awakening prophecy to the earth. Since in the *Ode* "Autumn" subsumes the opposed functions of destruction and preservation, as well as the functions of the two rival sisterwinds, we are forced as readers to a second-order thematic synthesis in an attempt to comprehend the topos of the wind. The play of themes or topii, in other words, confronts us with a question: How are we to conceive of the power in which the thematic distinctions conventionally made between both autumn and winter, on the one hand, and autumn and spring, on the other, are overcome?

The play of tropes leads us by different means to roughly the same place. The corroborative or analogous organization of the figures in the destruction movement and the disanalogous organization of the figures in the preservation movement can themselves be regarded as second-order tropes, tropes of tropes. The wind then becomes that trope which constitutes the conjunction of these two, apparently incompatible, second-order tropes. This move likewise forces a question: If the wind is neither the power of analogy nor the power of disanalogy, how are we to represent the relationship of these tropes-of-tropes with each other? I will be suggesting below that the answers to both of these questions, and others like them, are not "understood" but only *imagined* by the *Ode,* in Shelley's late and somewhat technical sense of that term. For now it is perhaps enough to suggest that the dialectic of the tropes in the *Ode* elevates it to meet the criterion of true poetry set forth in the *Defence.* The language of the poem is "vitally metaphorical" in that it marks the before unapprehended relations of things.

3. The Elementary Case

The most controversial issue in the criticism of Shelley's *Ode* is probably the question of its structure, particularly in respect to the five-stanza organization of the poem. Some of the conclusions we have reached in the analysis of topoi and tropes can be corroborated in the analysis of structure. The progression of the first three stanzas through the zones of the land, the atmosphere, and the sea would have been obvious to most readers even if Shelley had not recapitulated it at the start of stanza 4: "If I were a leaf, . . . a cloud, . . . a wave." But like so many of the individual simplicities of this poem—the line about falling on the thorns of life, for example—this one resists ready analysis. One key question is whether this triadic formation is "structural" in the sense of constituting a principle of the poem's making, one that can be understood as generating it? Many commentators have linked this triangulation of terms to the poem's reliance on tercets and to the sonnetlike stanzaic form in which rhymes occur in threes. But what then is the structural relation of stanzas 4 and 5 to the first three?

No progress can be made with the poem, I think, without first challenging the exclusively tripartite model of the poem's structure—as Eben Bass did many years ago, when he noticed the poem's implicit invocation of the ancient quartet of the natural elements.[22] To see in the initial trio of stanzas a passage from earth to air to water is inevitably to expect a stanza on fire. Fire in fact dominates the closing movement of the poem, in stanza 5, and it is present *in potentia* as the threat of lightning in the middle of the initial three-part movement. But where one would *expect* to see fire, at the opening of four, one is confronted instead with the figure of the poet, in the appearance of the first-person pronoun that had hitherto been withheld. Harold Bloom once urged that the poem be read as "a poem about Shelley's relationship to 'Prometheus

---

22. Eben Bass, "The Fourth Element in 'Ode to the West Wind,'" *Papers on Language and Literature* 3 (1967): 327–38.

Unbound.'"[23] We could certainly read the poem in worse ways, and the suggestion is useful to keep in mind in stanza 4 especially. Like the mythic character who gives his name to Shelley's most important poetic work to this date, and indeed to the volume in which the *West Wind* initially appeared, the poet is evidently introduced to bring fire into the poem and thus to complete its four-part elemental structure.[24] But why does it require two parts for the poem to complete this act of fire bringing? This is the question that Bass could not answer. Drawing on Pythagorean and Oriental cosmologies, respectively, James Rieger and Stuart Curran have suggested that Shelley builds his poem on five elements, including a master element that subsumes the other four: ether, for Rieger, and the wind itself, for Curran.[25] But this does not answer the question of why fire comes last. Nor does it do full justice to the evidence on the basis of which so many readers before Bass read the *Ode* as a poem of triads.[26]

Since fire is what is looked for to complete the quartet, the question of why there are two stanzas beyond the first triad is perhaps better approached through the recognition that the Promethean poet of the *Ode* is identified with fire in the poem under two antithetical aspects. He (his fire) is both the subject and object of the wind's operation. As object, the poet would be understood to participate in the world of the elements on which the wind acts; as subject, he would act on it—with, or as, or like the wind. In rhetorical terms, this duality of aspect appears as a problem about whether the poet's relation to the wind will be metonymic or metaphoric; the play of metonymy against metaphor is, indeed, one of the poem's most conspicuous rhetorical features from the start. In grammatical terms, the duality of aspect appears in the play of objective and subjective cases in the last two parts of the poem, as for example in the famous lines—"O lift me as a wave, a leaf, a cloud! / I fall upon the thorns of life! I bleed!"—a fortunate fall into the subjective case. It also appears in the grammar of the poet's climactic imperative—"Be thou me, impetuous one!"—a solecism with respect to case that at once enacts the speaker's windlike impetuosity and casts a shade of doubt on the hoped-for resolution.

The structure of the *Ode*'s five sections, then, must be understood as complex in the precise sense of involving two substructures that interlock, and this

23. Bloom, *Shelley's Mythmaking,* p. 67.

24. Neil Fraistat argues for a complex interrelation of the poems in this volume in *The Poem and the Book: Interpreting Collections of Poetry* (Chapel Hill: University of North Carolina Press, 1985), pp. 141–87.

25. Curran, *Shelley's Annus Mirabilis,* p. 162; James Rieger, *The Mutiny Within* (New York: G. Brazillier, 1967), pp. 169–71.

26. Rieger's Pythagorean reading of the poem does, however, acknowledge the importance of competing three-to-five, four-to-five, and four-to-one ratios in the poem: ibid., pp. 170–71.

interlocking must be understood to occur in the figure of the firebringing Promethean poet.[27] The ambiguous status of fire perfectly suits it to help play the role of the zeugma that holds the two substructures in relation to each other *and* to function as the dialectical wild card among the quartet of elements. On the one hand, fire is clearly one of the four elements, and its implication in their interaction is suggested in the complex metaphor in stanza 2, where "Black rain, and fire, and hail, will burst" from the solid atmosphere of "the dome of a vast sepulchre"—metaphorical of the closing night of the "dying" year of Peterloo. At the same time, however, fire is also the element that has the capacity to transform the other three. This is true in the ancient conception of the elemental quartet, as Shelley would have had it from Socrates; it is true in the later alchemical treatments of the conception; and it is true in the Christian apocalyptic tradition to which so much of the *Ode* alludes: "The day of the Lord," writes Peter, will come like a thief in the night "and the elements shall melt with fervent heat, the earth also and all the works therein shall be burned up" (2 Peter 3:10—King James Bible). More simply put, the point is that, in the *Ode,* as in *Prometheus Unbound,* "fire" involves two ranges of connotation—not only light, heat, and electricity but also the ability to control these things: intelligence. It stands both *as* an element and *for* the power to control the elements.

The double binding or bonding of this poetic element, in the context of the *Ode's* interlocking substructures, thus leads us back to the sort of conclusion we reached in looking closely at the first stanza: that the poem is the site of conceptual contest, a negotiation of competing claims about fire as a case and a cause. Is the operation of fire to be understood *among* the play of the objective elements of nature or as over *against* the other three elements? Is it an instrument of divine change in an ultimately fixed order of things or of human change in a world where destinies are forged as time moves on? In the terms of the myth, was Prometheus, in man's behalf, the thief of fire or the agent by which it was restored to its rightful place? The central question for the *Ode* might therefore be posed: Is the poet's fire like the other elements in the lawlike way it is subject to that force for change that is represented by the wind? If so, then how is any real change possible, how do we escape the persistent regularity which governs the interaction of the elements? Or is the poet like the wind in giving the law to change? Is he legislator or legislated?[28]

---

27. For an analysis of the rhyme scheme of the poem that I think tends to support this view, see J. J. Oversteegen, "Shelley's Ode to the West Wind, A Case of Whig History" in *Comparative Poetics,* ed. D. W. Fokkema, Elrud Kune-Ibsch, and A. J. A. van Zoest (Amsterdam: Editions Rodolpi, 1975), p. 115.

28. The relevance of this contest to Shelley's contemporary intellectual history can, I think, be established. The first conception pertains to the line of naturalistic necessitarianism that

We know that just (perhaps even days) after composing the *Ode,* Shelley set to work on *A Philosophical View of Reform*. The first chapter of the *View* culminates in the famous paragraph, reused in the *Defence,* in which Shelley pronounced that poets were "the unacknowledged legislators of the world." As I noted earlier, this celebrated pronouncement is consistently read out of its problematizing context. Insofar as the previous claims in this paragraph are about a failure of acknowledgment, they suggest that this failure is on the poets' side. The celebrated writers of England in 1819, Shelley argues, and by extension the inspired writers of any age, fail to acknowledge the power that operates in and through them to enable them to imagine what they imagine. It is precisely at the moment in the text when writers seem to be reduced to the status of objective instrumentality in the service of higher laws and powers that they are suddenly given the status of subjects, agents, and lawmakers.

A similarly problematic instance of chiasmas occurs when some of the same language appears in the concluding section of the *Ode to the West Wind*. In that stanza, the metaphor of instrumentality (in the fullest sense) first occurs in the poet's opening imperative "Make me thy lyre, even as the forest is." Everyone recognizes that this invokes the sense of instrumentality implicit in the Romantic topos of the Aeollan harp. Less widely acknowledged is the fate met by this sense of instrumentality before the section is completed, for the final imperative in this section is the one that involves the trumpet: "Be through my lips to unawakened Earth / The trumpet of a prophecy!" In one of the best commentaries on the poem we have, Earl Wasserman takes the common view that the sense of instrumentality in this metaphor points in the same direction as was implicit in the lyre metaphor.[29] Insofar as "trumpet" might be understood as the sound of the prophecy, its trumpet*ing,* this reading can be defended. The breath that winds the trumpet is that of the West Wind, just as in *A Philosophical View of Reform* (earlier in that paragraph used to conclude the *Defence*), the spirit of the age is understood to animate the poet's work. Read in another way, however, the lines from the *Ode* reverse the directionality implicit in the earlier command. In the context of the initial imperative about the lyre, it is difficult

---

Shelley inherited from Godwin and Hume—for both of whom the issue of historical change is an intellectual crux, but especially for Godwin, who attempted to adapt Hume's conservative necessitarianism to radical purposes in the 1790s. What became political justice, we recall, was first planned as a treatise in natural philosophy. The other has to do with the sort of change that is implicit in the Prometheus legend itself, the change in the mode of change that is made possible by Prometheus's appropriation of fire to the uses of man.

29. In Wasserman, *Shelley: A Critical Reading* (Baltimore: Johns Hopkins University Press, 1971), p. 250.

not to read the "trumpet" of the penultimate line as an instrument, and, read this way, the metaphor turns itself inside out. This is so because, not only does the wind become in two senses the poet's instrument, it is the work of the poet that is "making" the wind that instrument. The wind will be the trumpet of a prophecy through the poet's lips: "through," in the sense now not of passive access but of active agency. The phrase is here roughly analogous with "By the incantation of this verse." Both prepositions convey the sense of "by virtue of" or "by the power of."

This representation of mutual making may be said to elaborate the paradox of Shelley's suggestion in the preface to *The Revolt of Islam* that writers are in some sense the authors of the influence (authors, that is, of the spirit of the age) by which their being is unwillingly pervaded. Perhaps some such idea of the mutuality of causation also lurks in Shelley's endorsement of Tasso's comment that there are only two creators in the world, God and the poet (LPBS, 2:530), the unstated conclusion being that God and the poet are the creators, or authors, of one another. God makes the poet to make God, and vice versa. The Wind makes Shelley make the Wind make Shelley make the Wind and so on.

4. The Absent Cause

I do not mean to suggest that the models of historical change implicit in the *Ode*'s complex structure are precisely the same as those whose competition is enacted in the movements of stanza one. It seems telling that the organic model of regeneration taken over from Cythna's speech in the second movement is a system of change involving the three elements besides fire, but it is difficult to know what to conclude from this. My purpose in pressing the analysis of structure is mainly to show, first, that careful attention to the *Ode* leads one to see it as a strife between conceptual models and, second, that it makes some sense to see these as models of historical change. On the other hand, I also wish to show that the structural tensions are left unresolved, just as the thematic and figurative tensions are. Or rather, as I suggested earlier, they are left to the imagination. Since I am here invoking Shelley's late, quasi-technical sense of the word, and since no form of the word "imagine" appears in the *Ode,* this claim needs some elaborating.

Shelley's mature idea of imagination is not fully articulated until early 1821, with *A Defence of Poetry,* but it is already being developed in 1819 with *Prometheus Unbound* and related writings. I believe it derives in some measure from Spinoza's discussion of the imagination in prophecy in the *Theologico-Political Treatise.* Although Shelley translated at least a sizeable portion of this work, some fragments of which translation survive, it has been very little dis-

cussed in Shelley commentary. At least some of this translation seems to have
been carried out in 1819, and Spinoza's categories, as I hope to show, are most
germane to the *Ode*.[30] Spinoza's tract, if I may risk a tendentious reduction,
aims ultimately to investigate the possibility of a faith appropriate to the people
of a free society, a faith not based in superstition and (what amounts to the same
thing for Spinoza) not dictated by fear. With such a goal in view, it is appropriate that he turn first to the question of prophecy, since, as he says, "a prophet is
one who interprets the revelations of God to those who are unable to attain to
sure knowledge of the matters revealed, and therefore can only apprehend
them by simple faith" (p. 13). Perhaps this interest in the question of faith, despite the mistrust of superstition, is what has turned Shelleyans away from this
text as a would-be source for the *Ode*. We recall that, in Cythna's speech, faith is
called "the inchanter's word," and Cythna herself seems to have very little to do
with it. When the figure of the enchanter reappears in the problematic opening
lines of the *Ode,* it likewise seems to fall under a similar shadow of suspicion. In
the powerful conclusion of the *Ode,* however, the poet not only calls his poem
a prophecy but also suggests that its promise can be fulfilled only by the "incantation" of the verse, a term etymologically related to enchantment. And in that
same early 1820 letter to Hunt about Ollier's shortcomings and the necessity of
overthrowing the system of society from its ideological foundations, Shelley
went on to write: "This remedy does not seem to be one of the easiest. But the
generous few are not the less held to tend with all their efforts towards it. If faith
is a virtue in any case it is so in politics rather than religion; as having the power
of producing that belief in which is at once a prophesy [sic] and a cause" (LPBS:
2:563).

In the opening chapter of the *Treatise,* Spinoza specifically investigates what
is meant in scripture by "the spirit of God breathed into the prophets, or by the
prophets speaking with the Spirit of God."[31] To that end, he says, one must "determine the exact signification of the Hebrew word *ruagh,* commonly translated spirit." The word, he explains, "literally means wind, e.g., the south wind,
but it is frequently employed in other derivative significations" (p. 19). He goes
on to discriminate no fewer than nine such meanings, and he then lists six
meanings of the phrase "of God." This philological exercise puts him, he says,

30. See Kenneth Neill Cameron, *Shelley: The Golden Years* (Cambridge, Mass.: Harvard University Press, 1974), p. 302; Ingpen and Peck give various dates for the translation in *Works,*
7:36–40.

31. Spinoza, *"A Theologico-Political Treatise" and "A Political Treatise,"* trans. R. H. M. Elwes
(New York: Dover, 1951), p. 19. Hereafter cited by page reference in the text.

in a position to explain those passages of Scripture which speak of "the Spirit of God":

> In some places the expression merely means a very strong dry, and deadly wind, as in Isaiah xi. 7, "The grass withereth, the flower fadeth, because the Spirit of the Lord bloweth upon it." Similarly in Gen. i. 2: "The Spirit of the Lord moved over the face of the waters." At other times it is used as equivalent to a high courage, thus the spirit of Gideon and of Samson is called the Spirit of the Lord, as being very bold, and prepared for any emergency. (p. 22)

More specifically, Spinoza claims that this sort of information enables him to explain such phrases as "The Spirit of the Lord was upon a prophet":

> [They] are quite clear to us, and mean that the prophets were endowed with a peculiar and extraordinary power, and devoted themselves to piety with especial constancy; that thus they perceived the mind or the thought of God, for we have shown that God's Spirit signifies in Hebrew God's mind or thought, and that the law which shows His mind and thought is called His Spirit; hence that the imagination of the prophets, inasmuch as through it were revealed the decrees of God, may equally be called the mind of God, and the prophets be said to have possessed the mind of God. (p. 24)

Conceding to prophets their extraordinary power, which he specifically calls "imagination," Spinoza is careful to define it narrowly. In a key passage, Shelley's translation of which survives, Spinoza argues that with the exception of Christ no one "ever apprehended the revelations of God without the assistance of the imagination, that is of words or forms imaged forth in the mind" (WPBS, 7:274). The qualification to prophecy, Shelley's translation goes on, is therefore "rather a more vivid imagination than a profounder understanding than other men" (WPBS, 7:274). This indeed explains the prophetic ability to perceive much that is beyond the boundary of the intellect, for "many more ideas can be constructed from words and figures than from the principles and notions on which the whole fabric of reasoned knowledge is reared" (Spinoza, p. 25).[32]

One does not need to know the rest of Spinoza's work, its commitment to rearing a whole fabric of reasoned knowledge from certain principles, to see that his comparisons between imagination and understanding are invidious. Several of his elaborations in the *Treatise* plainly show the bias of the argument: "Men of great imaginative power are less fitted for abstract reasoning, whereas those who excel in intellect and its use keep their imagination more restrained and controlled, holding it in subjection, so to speak, lest it should usurp the place of reason" (p. 27). He also explains that "prophets were said to possess the Spirit of God because men knew not the cause of prophetic knowledge, and in

---

32. One problem in this account, to which I shall return below, is that Spinoza is himself constructing an idea of prophetic authority on the basis of the words and figures in such phrases as "the spirit of God."

their wonder referred it with other marvels directly to the Deity, styling it Divine knowledge" (p. 27). As it turns out, prophetic knowledge is no knowledge at all, "prophecy never rendered the prophet wiser than he was before," and "to suppose that knowledge of natural and spiritual phenomena can be gained from the prophetic books, is an utter mistake" (p. 27).

From late 1819 onward, Shelley's thinking seems increasingly to engage Spinoza's discussion of imagination and prophecy, but, as he comes to accept Spinoza's terms of description for the imagination, he also rejects the invidious comparison with systematic reason. Indeed, in the *Defence of Poetry,* where Shelley developed the distinction between reason and imagination most fully, the invidiousness clearly favors imagination. Spinoza relates reason and imagination inversely, strength in one coming at the expense of the other, and defines imagination specifically in terms of a reliance on "words and figures." This representation anticipates the passage in the *Defence* where Shelley argues that poetry is the expression of the imagination and that the language of poetry is vitally metaphorical. It also seems consistent with the account in the *Defence* of how ideas are constructed from such language by the readers of various eras to follow. For Spinoza, the use of this vitally metaphorical language is what leaves the prophet in the dark about such ideas as may be constructed from his work. In both *A Philosophical View of Reform* and the *Defence,* all great writers participate in the condition of Spinoza's prophets. All are hierophants of an unapprehended inspiration, influences that move without being moved, words that express what they conceive not. Finally, in both of Shelley's discussions, the power of prophetic writing can stand at odds with intellectual systems, a central point in Spinoza's argument: it carries out its work, says Shelley, in spite of "whatever systems" the writers in question have "professed to support" (*Works,* 7:21).

Suppose a poem were to dramatize the paradoxical encounter between a power theorized in this way, the Spinozist spirit of God, and a poet-philosopher who aims to represent in words and figures the power that moves him, but who understands, by virtue of the theory itself, that he cannot finally understand the power he represents. What would such a poem look like? My claim here is that it would look rather like the *Ode to the West Wind*. Of course, one might object that this sort of thing is nothing new for Shelley by 1819, that he had dramatized a similar encounter in *Mont Blanc* four years earlier. The meditation on the white peak may well be taken as the imagining of a Spinozist immanent deity: "Everything takes place by the power of God. Nature herself is the power of God under another name" (Spinoza, p. 25). But by contrast with Mont Blanc, the West Wind is consistently represented as a power of change. In both the *View* and the *Defence,* moreover, the power that moves the writer irrespective of his will or system is directly identified as "the spirit of the age" (*Works,* 7:20; SPP 508). If it makes sense to think of the West Wind in connection with the spirit of the age—as it does not make much sense to think of Mont Blanc in that connection—then we might see the *Ode to the West Wind* as the imagining of the spirit of Spinoza's deity under a historical aspect.[33] Indeed, it is arguable that Shelley's special emphasis on *imagining* the mind of the immanent deity has everything to do with its acquisition of a historical dimension, and that *both* developments go hand in hand with Shelley's late self-consciousness about textuality, his sense of the productive uncertainty of words and figures as a medium of thought.[34]

5. Fallen Leaves

The *Ode's* special self-consciousness about its words and figures has been implicit in much that we have already noted about it. It remains only to consider, in the light of "imagination," one doubly pertinent word/figure: the "leaves" of the *Ode.* The fullest anticipation of the *West Wind's* seasonal topoi, Cythna's speech in the *Revolt,* gives the leaves very little play. They do not appear in either of the elaborations of the cyclical pattern, and what mention they receive in the intervening stanza about Spring's filial relation to Autumn is casual: spring is said to bear fresh flowers for her mother, "with gentle feet, / Disturbing not the leaves which are her winding-sheet." We know that, in *Queen Mab,* the leaves

33. Hegel says somewhere that "to be a philosopher one must first be a Spinozist," and it is plausible that some of the resemblances between Shelley's late thought and Hegel's, since no direct influence has ever been established, may owe in part to their common source in Spinoza.

34. Tillottama Rajan has explored Shelley's complex sense of textuality in works of his late period, in "Deconstruction or Reconstruction: Reading Shelley's *Prometheus Unbound,*" *Studies in Romanticism* 23 (fall 1984): 317–338. Having persuasively established the "ungrammaticalities" of "the play's dramatic syntax," Rajan comments:

> Described this way the play almost seems to invite deconstruction. But the question of whether to deconstruct the text cannot be considered apart from critical reflection occurring at the time the text was written or from its own reflection on its relationship to the reader. The idea that romantic criticism is committed to a Coleridgean notion of the organic unity of the work can no longer go unchallenged. Deconstructive criticism has traced the notion of the text as self-contesting to Nietzsche's *The Birth of Tragedy* . . . , and one could trace the concept even further back to De Quincey's use of the figure of the palimpsest to describe the trace structure characteristic of consciousness and its products. (pp. 320–21)

This represents only half of Rajan's concern, for she is interested in the dialectic of "protodeconstructive theories" and proto-hermeneutic theories in Shelley. But some of her interest in making Shelley's "post-structuralism" historically plausible might be better served by looking back to Spinoza rather than forward to De Quincey or Nietzsche. Poststructuralist poetics concerned with the Althusserian concepts of the "absent cause" were derived directly from Spinoza's writings, as Althusser himself often acknowledges. See, for example, *Reading Capital,* trans. Ben Brewster (London: Verso, 1970), p. 187.

play a far more prominent role, as they would again in the *Ode,* and they are seen as problematic in the cycle of things.[35] The leaves in this passage, scattered by the Autumn wind, as in the *Ode,* are seen first as choking the seeds and deforming the earth on which they lie and only on second thought as fertilizing the soil to make regeneration possible.[36] None of this is accommodated in Cythna's account. The *Ode* addresses the issue of decay in its very first lines, but the leaves on which pestilence makes its mark take on a very different coloration. They become the poet's leaves—"what if my leaves are falling like its [the forest's] own?" These may be considered the leaves of laurel, the sibylline leaves recently recalled by Coleridge's volume, and, perhaps, too, the leaves of the Biblical topos of the tree of man. But we must not fail to see them as the fallen pages of Shelley's text, lapses from the initial inspiration that is the encounter with the *West Wind*'s power. "When composition begins," Shelley said in the *Defence,* "inspiration is already on the decline" (SPP, p. 504). Taking the "declension" seriously, we may say that composition establishes the *case* of inspiration.

The topos of the leaf as the page of text is, of course, not a novel one with Shelley. Rousseau and Dante, to take only two authors Shelley knew well, both pun in this way. But two developments within the Shelley circle between the completion of *The Revolt of Islam* and the composition of the *Ode* deserve particular notice. On September 30, 1817, just ten days after finishing *The Revolt,* and just weeks after composing Cythna's moving and climactic speech to Laon, Shelley's friend Hogg wrote him to express his doubt about a matter of pedagogy: "I do not hold that the turning over of dry brown mouldering leaves can teach the antient languages, for if that were so the autumnal wind would before

35. See I. J. Kapstein, "The Symbolism of the Wind and the Leaves in Shelley's 'Ode to the West Wind,'" *PMLA* 51 (1936): 1069–79.
36. The passage runs as follows:

> Thus do the generations of the earth
> Go to the grave, and issue from the womb,
> Surviving still the imperishable change
> That renovates the world even as the leaves
> Which the keen frost-wind of the waning year
> Has scattered on the forest soil, and heaped
> For many sessons there, though long they choke,
> Loading with loathsome rottenness the land,
> All germs of promise. Yet when the tall trees
> From which they fell, shorn of their lovely shapes,
> Lie level with the earth to moulder there,
> They fertilize the land they long deformed,
> Till from the breathing lawn a forest springs
> Of youth, integrity, and loveliness,
> Like that which gave it life, to spring and die. (*Queen Mab* sect 5, ll. 1–15)

the 8th of Nov. have become an admirable linguist."[37] The observation is not memorable but the terms in which it is couched may have been. Soon, Leigh Hunt, one of Shelley's other closest friends, published a volume of verse, *Foliage,* that elevated this same topos to the status of an organizational principle. The original poems in the volume were gathered under the rubric "Greenwoods," the translations (which Shelley specifically discouraged Hunt from pursuing further) under "Evergreens."[38]

It would be like Shelley, and perhaps also an enactment of the point at issue, to have developed his new sense of textuality out of a pun, rather than the other way around. In any case, this new dimension of the autumn leaves as pages of text is responsive to the development in Shelley's self-consciousness about textuality that culminates in the *Defence,* and Shelley's sense of the relationship between textuality and Prometheanism is best approached through the *Defence*'s central discussion of Dante, the poet with whom Shelley increasingly identifies as he moves toward *The Triumph of Life.* The *Defence* represents Dante in persistently Promethean terms; he becomes indeed, for Shelley, nothing less than the great prototype of the promethean poet. He is "the first religious reformer," "the first awakener of entranced Europe," and, most explicitly, the "Lucifer [or 'Light-bearer'] of that starry flock which in the thirteenth century shone forth from republican Italy, as from a heaven, into the darkness of the benighted world" (SPP, 499–500). Most relevant to the *Ode,* though, is the account of how this light was generated out of the poetry: "His very words are instinct with spirit; each is as a spark, a burning atom of inextinguishable thought; and many yet lie covered in the ashes of their birth, and pregnant with a lightning which has yet found no conductor."[39] "Spirit," "spark," "inextinguishable," "ashes,"

---

37. Michael Ferber comments sensitively on the "leaves" in *The Poetry of Shelley* (Harmondsworth: Penguin, 1993), pp. 106–107.

38. Shelley wrote to Hunt: "You ought to exercise your fancy in the perpetual creation of new forms of gentleness and beauty. You are formed to be a living fountain and not a canal however clear." Presumably the living fountain is more in touch with the spirit of the age that works through the great writers of the day. Later in the same letter he talked of politics: "I fear that in England things will be carried violently by the rulers, and that they will not have learned to yield in time to the spirit of the age." See LPBS, 2:530–31.

39. Cf. the use of this last term in connection with the spirit of the age in the letter of November 6, 1819, less than two weeks after the composition of the *Ode:* "[T]he people are nearly in a state of insurrection, & the least unpopular noblemen perceive the necessity of conducting a spirit which it is no longer possible to oppose" (LPBS, 2:149). There are important mesmeric overtones in Shelley, as Nigel Leask has persuasively demonstrated in "Shelley's Magnetic Ladies": Romantic Mesmerism and the Politics of the Body," in *Beyond Romanticism,* ed. Stephen Copley and John Whale (London: Routledge, 1992), pp. 53–78. See also Alison Winter's broader study of British mesmeric practice in the nineteenth century, which promises to radically transform our historical understanding of issues such as "influence" (forthcoming from University of Chicago Press).

"lightning," "conductor"—these are the sorts of terms that figure prominently in the *Ode*'s development of an alternative to the organic or "cultural" model of social regeneration.

In the *Ode,* the paronomasia of the leaves works subterraneously from the start but emerges at the end in the third and final use of the key verb "drive," which is associated with "conductor," just as other terms are associated with the terms from the discussion of Dante's Prometheanism:

> Be thou, Spirit fierce,
> My spirit! Be thou me, impetuous one!
> Drive my dead thoughts over the universe
> Like withered leaves to quicken a new birth! (ll. 61–64)

If we take the account in the *Defence* as understood in this passage, then the simile "like withered leaves" is problematic in the extreme. For if thought decays as composition begins, then the pages of text, "withered leaves," are not so much a metaphor for the dead thoughts as the form that thought takes when it dies. The dead thoughts are driven not *like* withered leaves, but *as* withered leaves; they ride the boundary between metaphor and metonymy. Such paronomasia is a function of the textuality to which it playfully alludes. It marks yet another revision of the trope in Cythna's speech in which the blasts of autumn drive the winged seeds over the earth, and in which this work is explicitly identified with the driving of truth's deathless germs to thought's remotest caves by the whirlwind of the intellectuals' spirit. Although this may at first seem to augur a return to the mode of *Queen Mab,* where the leaves are understood to fertilize the seeds, seeds have fact disappeared from the scene of the *Ode*'s final stanza.

In *Poet's Grammar,* Francis Berry sees the problem, but not the point, when he says of this passage: "Leaves, dead or living, do not bear seeds." "Shelley's mistake," he says, "is not deeply relevant."[40] But Shelley's mistake could scarcely be more deeply relevant in that it challenges the very metaphor of cultural seminality in social regeneration. The presence of fire creates the possibility of writing the leaves into a very differently conceived model of change:

> And, by the incantation of this verse,
> Scatter, as from an unextinguished hearth
> Ashes and sparks, my words among mankind! (ll. 65–67)

---

40. In Francis Berry, *Poets' Grammar: Person, Time, and Mood in Poetry* (London: Routledge and Paul, 1958), p. 152.

The withered leaves of text have not disappeared. Instead, they constitute the substance slowly being consumed on the unextinguished hearth. Their figurative status in the poem is being transformed by the figure of fire. The seeds of thought that had independent status and a very different relationship to the wind in the earlier treatments of the question, now give way to the sparks that lie next to the ashes. Under this new dispensation, the scattering of the leaves and the production of the new thoughts would both be accomplished by the inspiring wind. Fire is the element that is itself preserved only at the expense of destroying something else, and wind is the power that sustains this twofold process at the same time, in the same breath.[41] Many more ideas can be constructed from words and figures than from the principles and notions on which the whole fabric of reasoned knowledge is reared, as Spinoza argued, but every construction (including mine here) will involve some destruction.

After discussing the production and reception of Dante's poetry, Shelley generalized his remarks to suggest that all genuine poetry is Promethean in mission and at the same time entered an important qualification about the role of will in carrying out that mission:

> What were Virtue, Love, Patriotism, Friendship &c.—what were the scenery of this beautiful Universe which we inhabit—what were our consolations on this side of the grave—and what were our aspirations beyond it—if Poetry did not ascend to bring light and fire from those eternal regions where the owl-winged faculty of calculation dare not ever soar? Poetry is not like reason, a power to be exerted according to the determination of the will. A man cannot say, "I will compose poetry." The greatest poet even cannot say it: for the mind in creation is as a fading coal which some invisible influence, like an inconstant wind, awakens to transitory brightness. (SPP, pp. 503–504)

Early on, a skeptical Shelley may have been unwillingly drawn into a reckoning with the movement of history in his calculations, poetic and prosaic, for improving the social order. Later, in the period he saw as critical for English society, his hopes for improvement seemed to rest on an act of political faith that he hoped would be self-fulfilling. It had to do with defining poetry against the rational will, and aligning it with the spirit of the age, precisely because this alignment lifted it clear of the calculating faculty, and indeed of the entire utilitarian calculus in which he had once invested his energy. God makes the poet to make God, and vice versa. The Wind makes Shelley make the Wind make Shelley

---

41. That same breath, furthermore, is shared not only between the poet and the wind but between the poet and his reader as well; the breath of the reader's incantation makes this change possible. There is a strong sense in which the West Wind's inspiration has been interchangeable with the readerly audience from the start. How else can we explain the poem's repeated exhortation to a "breath" that it "hear" the poet's words?

make the Wind. But perhaps better: Shelley is led by the events of post-Revolution history to construct an account whereby he and post-Revolution history make each other. It is as if Shelley had glimpsed that profound lesson later articulated by Marx at mid-century, still in force with Sartre and Lévi-Strauss a century later, and then reworked into the "historicism" Jameson fashioned from Althusser's Spinozist principle of structural causality: that human beings make their own history, but not just as they please.

Having come so far in this account of the *Ode,* we are also now returned to that point in my opening analysis of the end-of-year sonnet, *England in 1819,* where I raised a question about how to read the moment of pivot and predication that follows the catalogue of conditions that define the state of the nation. These conditions, we saw in line 13, the break point of the Elizabethan sonnet form, "Are graves from which a glorious phantom may / Burst to illumine our tempestous day." Whether or not we accept the idea that these "graves" relate to the engraved letters that print the text, we can see that they correspond fairly closely to the falling or fallen "leaves" of Shelley's text in the *Ode to the West Wind.* They amount to so many cases in which the English people must collectively recognize the phantasmal character of their own historical situation, and in recognizing it, must change it. In Hamlet, this phantom corresponds to the ghost of Hamlet's father. It is the marker of that play's temporal unevenness, its time out of joint. In *Prometheus Unbound,* the phantom corresponds to the Phantasm of Jupiter, where the figures of conscience, fatherhood, and judgment all converge. We properly associate Shelley's phantasms and phantoms of history with the related figures we have been considering among the cases of "England in 1819": figures of the sensible heart, the psyche, soul, spirit of the age, future state, national character, and the winds of historical change. In none of these instances, however, does the figure in question stand for an identification of that which is merely an affair of "consciousness," the immaterial internality of a material externality. Each of these figures cuts athwart the distinction we use to contain it. Each matters in the making of history, then and now.

Index

Abrams, M. H.: Becker anticipating, 235n.52; *The Mirror and the Lamp,* 489n.11; *Natural Supernaturalism,* 73, 78, 177–78, 178n.50, 185; on Wordsworth, 41, 177–78, 486

Achinstein, Sharon, 77n

action: agency and the historical situation, 37, 195; Godwin's account of, 213, 452, 509, 523–24; Hazlitt on, 523; Hume on causality of, 242; in *Old Mortality,* 213; Wordsworth on suffering and, 372. *See also* motivation

Address to the People on the Death of Princess Charlotte, An (Shelley), 25–26, 31

"Adonais" (Shelley), 430, 431n.74, 483, 484

Adorno, Theodor, 54, 56, 254, 529n.4, 532

Advice for Young Ladies (Barbauld), 115, 150n.120

agency. *See* action

ages. *See* epochs

Alastor (Shelley), 409, 518, 518n

Alexander, J. H., 280n

Alkon, Paul K., 161n.14

Almon, John, 166n

Althusser, Louis: on absent cause, 549n.34; on contradictions, 183; on Hegelian contradiction, 192; on historicism, 60n.25; on historicism of Lévi-Strauss, 97n.6; on Marx as influenced by Scottish Enlightenment, 258; on overdetermination, 183; and return to history, 4n; on Romantic change in concept of time, 101; taxonomy of causes, 80n.70

Altick, Richard D., 14n, 44n.89

America, 441–80; anachronism in, 277–78; British representations of, 447; British writing about political system, 7; as a case, 279; Cobbett on, 449, 454, 459, 467–68; Fearon's *Narrative,* 278, 279, 441, 456; Godwin as influenced by Constitution, 453; Keats and, 469–77; as lacking poetic genius, 191; literary backwardness of, 447; manners in, 278, 444, 445–48, 464; Moore's 1803 visit to, 270, 270n.7, 442–45, 450; newspapers linking Britain and, 273; and Romantic literature, 447, 479; Shelley on, 29, 189–91, 477–80; special relationship with Britain, 447; uneven development in, 466. *See also* emigration to America; Western Country

Americanization, 453

anachronism: America a site of, 277–78; in Barbauld's "The Backwardness of the Spring 1771," 118; in *The Cenci,* 109–10, 298, 502–4, 513; in creating interest in the antiquarian, 140; emergence of new conception of, 107–8; Hegel on necessary, 500–502; in Keats's plan to read Shakespeare with his brother, 472; Kemble attending to in Shakespeare, 500n.28; necessary anachronisms in Waverley novels, 96, 109, 133, 140, 500; and Sartre, 107n.43; specifying cultures in relation to, 109

anatopism, 108

Anderson, Benedict, 101, 102–4, 173, 174, 281

Anderson, J. E., 175n.42

555